SPORTS ECONOMICS

Sports Economics, the most comprehensive textbook in the field by celebrated economist Roger D. Blair, focuses primarily on the business and economics aspects of major professional sports and the National Collegiate Athletic Association. It employs the basic principles of economics to address issues such as the organization of leagues, pricing, advertising, and broadcasting as well as the labor market in sports. Among its novel features is the candid coverage of the image and integrity of players, teams, managers, and the leagues themselves, including cases of gambling, cheating, misconduct, and performance-enhancing drugs. The text also discusses other controversial subjects such as disciplining participants, discrimination, the financing of facilities, and how salaries are determined. Blair explains how economic decisions are made under conditions of uncertainty using the well-known expected utility model and makes extensive use of present value concepts to analyze investment decisions. Numerous examples are drawn from the daily press. The text offers ample boxes to illustrate sports themes, as well as extensive use of diagrams, tables, problem sets, and research questions.

Roger D. Blair is Walter J. Matherly Professor and Chair of the Department of Economics at the University of Florida, where he has taught since 1970. He received his Ph.D. from Michigan State University. Professor Blair is the author or coauthor of numerous books, including *Antitrust Economics* (with David Kaserman), *Law and Economics of Vertical Integration and Control* (with David Kaserman), *Monopsony: Antitrust Law and Economics* (with Jeffrey Harrison), *Monopsony in Law and Economics* (with Jeffrey Harrison, Cambridge University Press, 2010), *Intellectual Property: Economic and Legal Dimensions of Rights and Remedies* (with Thomas Cotter, Cambridge University Press, 2005), *The Economics of Franchising* (with Francine Lafontaine, Cambridge University Press, 2005), and Volume II of *Antitrust Law* (with Herbert Hovenkamp, Christine Durrance, and Philip Areeda). He is also the editor or coeditor of many volumes, including *Proving Antitrust Damages*. Professor Blair has written more than 170 articles or chapters in professional economics journals, law reviews, and books.

Sports Economics

Roger D. Blair

University of Florida

CAMBRIDGE UNIVERSITY PRESS
Cambridge, New York, Melbourne, Madrid, Cape Town,
Singapore, São Paulo, Delhi, Tokyo, Mexico City

Cambridge University Press
32 Avenue of the Americas, New York, NY 10013-2473, USA

www.cambridge.org
Information on this title: www.cambridge.org/9780521876612

First published 2012

Printed in the United States of America

A catalog record for this publication is available from the British Library.

Library of Congress Cataloging in Publication data

Blair, Roger D.
Sports economics / Roger D. Blair.
p. cm.
Includes bibliographical references and index.
ISBN 978-0-521-87661-2 (hardback)
1. Sports – Economic aspects. 2. Professional sports – Economic aspects. I. Title.
GV716.B53 2011
796.06'91–dc23 2011025092

ISBN 978-0-521-87661-2 Hardback

Cover photo: Sarah Goldberger

For the real sports in my life – Alec, Devon, Riley, and Brett Blair.

– Papa

Contents

Preface . . . . *page* xxi

Commonly Used Abbreviations xxiii

I INTRODUCTION

1 Introduction to Sports Economics 3

1 **Introduction** 3

2 **Tools of Analysis** 4

2.1 Present Value Calculations 4

2.2 Economics of Uncertainty 4

3 **The Sports Business** 5

3.1 Sports Leagues and Organizations 5

3.2 Competitive Balance 6

3.3 Pricing Decisions 7

3.4 Advertising and Promotion 7

3.5 Broadcast Rights 8

3.6 Insuring Player Talent 8

3.7 Sports Leagues and Antitrust Policy 9

4 **Image and Integrity** 9

4.1 Gambling in Sports 9

4.2 Cheating in Sports 9

4.3 Misconduct by Participants 10

4.4 Performance-Enhancing Drugs 10

5 **Facilities, Franchises, and Public Policy** 11

5.1 Demand for Sports Franchises and Events 11

5.2 Economic Impact Studies 11

5.3 Financing Sports Facilities 11

6 **The Sports Labor Market** 11

6.1 Competition and Monopsony 11

6.2 Monopsony in the NCAA 12

6.3 Bidding and Bargaining in the Sports Labor Market 12

6.4 Economic Value of Multiyear Contracts 13
6.5 Final Offer Arbitration 13
6.6 Players' Unions and Collective Bargaining 13
6.7 Sports Agents 13
6.8 The Role of Sports Agents 14
6.9 Turning Pro Early 14
6.10 Discrimination in the Sports Labor Market 14
7 Concluding Remarks 14
References and Further Reading 15

2 The Business of Sports 16
1 Introduction 16
2 Profit and Profit Maximization 17
2.1 A Numerical Example 18
3 Revenue and Costs 19
3.1 Revenue Sources 19
3.2 Costs of Generating Revenues 24
3.3 Club Profit 24
4 Profit and Team Quality 25
4.1 Selecting Team Quality 25
4.2 Quality and Attendance in the NFL 26
5 Value of a Professional Club 26
5.1 Stand-Alone Investments 32
5.2 Franchise Value Growth in the NFL 32
5.3 Capital Appreciation in MLB 33
5.4 Other Benefits 35
6 Concluding Remarks 35
Problems and Questions 35
Research Questions 38
Appendix 38
References and Further Reading 44

3 Sports Leagues and Organizations 46
1 Introduction 46
2 League Formation 47
2.1 Cooperation off the Field 47
2.2 Leagues as Joint Ventures 47
2.3 Leagues as Cartels 48
3 Sports Leagues and Profit Maximization 48
4 Rules and Procedures of Sports Leagues 50
4.1 League Membership 50
4.2 League Governance 52
4.3 Production of Athletic Competition 52
4.4 Marketing the League's Products 53
4.5 Players' Market 53

4.6 Other Inputs 54
4.7 Consensus 54
5 **Revenue Sharing** 54
5.1 Transfer to Weaker Teams 54
5.2 Revenue Sharing in MLB 55
6 **Sports Leagues, Monopoly Power, and Consumer Welfare** 56
7 **League Expansion** 58
7.1 American League 59
7.2 National League 60
8 **Concluding Remarks** 62
Problems and Questions 62
Research Questions 63
References and Further Reading 63

4 Competitive Balance 65
1 **Introduction** 65
2 **Definition of Competitive Balance** 65
3 **Measures of Competitive Balance** 67
3.1 Noll-Scully Measure 67
3.2 Herfindahl-Hirschman Index 69
3.3 A Caveat on Statistical Measures 70
4 **Economic Analysis of Competitive Balance** 70
4.1 Free Agency 70
5 **Dealing with Competitive Imbalance** 73
5.1 Reserve Clause 73
5.2 Revenue Sharing 75
5.3 Economic Implications of Revenue Sharing 76
5.4 Salary Caps 77
5.5 Reverse-Order Player Drafts 79
5.6 Luxury Taxes 79
5.7 Economic Implications of Luxury Taxes 80
6 **Concluding Remarks** 82
Problems and Questions 82
Research Questions 83
References and Further Reading 84

II THE SPORTS BUSINESS

5 Pricing Decisions 89
1 **Introduction** 89
2 **Competitive Pricing** 89
3 **Simple Monopoly Pricing** 90
3.1 Empty Seats and Ticket Pricing 93
3.2 Ticket Pricing and Demand Elasticity 93

4 **Price Discrimination** 95
4.1 Conditions Necessary for Successful Price Discrimination 96
4.2 Profit Maximization and Price Discrimination 97
4.3 Ticket Pricing 97
5 **Peak Load Pricing** 99
6 **Season Tickets and Other Bundling** 102
7 **Two-Part Pricing** 104
7.1 Two-Part Pricing: Identical Demands 104
7.2 Two-Part Pricing: Nonidentical Demands 105
8 **Pricing Complements** 107
9 **Ticket Scalping: A Pricing Failure** 110
9.1 Student Tickets: A Scalping Opportunity 111
9.2 Tickets to the Final Four 111
9.3 Demand Shifts and Scalping 111
9.4 Example: The Masters 111
9.5 Antiscalping Laws 112
10 **Concluding Remarks** 113
Problems and Questions 113
Research Questions 115
References and Further Reading 115

6 Advertising in the Sports Industry 117
1 **Introduction** 117
2 **Optimal Advertising by a Firm** 118
2.1 Numerical Example 118
3 **Sports Advertising by Firms** 120
3.1 Sports Publications 124
3.2 Naming Rights 124
3.3 Sponsorships 128
3.4 Endorsements 129
4 **Strategic Behavior in Advertising** 130
5 **League-Wide Advertising** 131
5.1 Economic Theory 132
5.2 Problems in Practice 133
5.3 A Numerical Example 134
6 **Concluding Remarks** 135
Problems and Questions 135
Research Questions 136
References and Further Reading 136

7 The Market for Sports Broadcasting Rights 137
1 **Introduction** 137
2 **Market Structure** 138
2.1 Sports Broadcasting Act 139

3 **Bidding for Broadcast Rights** 141
3.1 A Numerical Example 143
3.2 The Winner's Curse 145
3.3 Bidding and Uncertainty 146
3.4 Other Benefits to Broadcasters 147
3.5 *Monday Night Football* 148
3.6 Bottom Line 149
4 **Vertical Integration in Sports** 149
4.1 Transaction Costs 152
4.2 Strategic Behavior 152
5 **Sports Networks** 152
5.1 College Conferences 153
6 **Concluding Remarks** 153
Problems and Questions 154
Research Questions 156
References and Further Reading 156

8 Insuring Player Talent 158
1 **Talent: A Risky Asset** 158
2 **Risk Aversion and Insurance** 159
2.1 Expected Utility Model 159
2.2 Risk Aversion and Risk Neutrality 160
2.3 Risk Aversion 161
2.4 Risk Neutrality 163
2.5 Measuring Expected Utility 163
2.6 Certainty Equivalent 164
3 **Shifting Risk through Insurance** 164
4 **The NCAA Insurance Program** 166
4.1 Premiums 167
5 **Team Insurance Purchases** 168
5.1 The Jeff Bagwell Example 169
5.2 Insurance Decisions 170
6 **Concluding Remarks** 171
Problems and Questions 171
Research Questions 173
Appendix 173
References and Further Reading 174

9 Sports Leagues and Antitrust Policy 175
1 **Introduction** 175
2 **The Economic Rationale for Antitrust** 175
3 **The Antitrust Laws** 178
3.1 Section 1 of the Sherman Act 178
3.2 Section 2 of the Sherman Act 179

4 **Economic Analysis in Antitrust Enforcement** 179
4.1 Market Definition 180
4.2 Analysis of the Relevant Product Market 180
4.3 Analysis of the Relevant Geographic Market 181
4.4 Monopoly Power 181
5 **League Rules and Antitrust Policy** 182
5.1 Legal Rules and Agreements 183
6 **Antitrust Challenges by League Members** 184
6.1 NCAA Restraints on Broadcasting 184
6.2 NFL Ban on Public Ownership 185
6.3 Relocation Restrictions 186
7 **Antitrust Challenges by Outsiders** 187
7.1 *American Football League v. National Football League* 187
7.2 Restrictions on Entry 189
7.3 *United States Football League v. NFL* 189
7.4 Restrictions on Schedules by Organization 190
7.5 Restrictions on Equipment 191
8 **Concluding Remarks** 194
Problems and Questions 194
Research Questions 196
References and Further Reading 196

III IMAGE AND INTEGRITY

10 Sports Gambling 201
1 **Introduction** 201
2 **The Economics of Gambling** 201
2.1 Expected Utility of Gambling 203
3 **The Business of Sports Books** 204
3.1 Point-Spread Wagers 204
4 **Gambling by Professional Athletes** 205
4.1 The Added Risks of Betting on Baseball 208
5 **NCAA and Gambling on College Sports** 209
5.1 NCAA Policy on Gambling 209
5.2 NCAA Sanctions for Gambling 210
6 **An NBA Nightmare** 214
7 **Concluding Remarks** 215
Problems and Questions 215
Research Questions 217
References and Further Reading 217

11 Cheating in Sports 218
1 **Introduction** 218
2 **Deterring Cheating** 219
2.1 A General Model of Deterrence 219
2.2 Control Variables 220

2.3 Changing the Probability of Detection 221
2.4 Changing the Penalty for Cheating 221
3 Cheating to Win 223
3.1 Violating the Rules of Play 224
3.2 Jane Blalock and the Ladies PGA Tour 224
3.3 Rosie Ruiz and the Boston Marathon 224
3.4 Deliberate Rules Violations 226
3.5 Using Illegal Equipment 227
3.6 Cheating at the Daytona 500 229
3.7 NCAA Violations 230
3.8 The NFL's Spygate Episode 231
4 Cheating to Lose 233
4.1 Point Shaving in Basketball 234
4.2 Corruption in Sumo Wrestling 235
4.3 Fixing Matches in Tennis 236
5 Concluding Remarks 238
Problems and Questions 238
Research Questions 239
References and Further Reading 240

12 Misconduct and Discipline 241
1 Introduction 241
2 Disciplining Players for Misconduct 241
2.1 Personal Conduct Policy of the NFL 242
2.2 General Policy of the NFL 243
2.3 Prohibited Conduct 243
2.4 Persons Charged with Criminal Activity 243
2.5 Persons Convicted of Criminal Activity 243
2.6 Persons Engaged in Violent Activity in the Workplace 244
2.7 Duty to Report Prohibited Conduct 244
2.8 Appeal Rights 244
3 Deterring Misconduct 244
3.1 Deterring Risk Averters 245
3.2 Deterring the Risk Seeker 246
3.3 Suspensions and Implicit Fines 248
4 Fighting 249
5 Violence in Sports 250
5.1 Intentionally Hurting an Opponent 251
6 Problems with the Law 253
6.1 Drunk Driving 253
6.2 Repeat Offenders 253
6.3 Weapons Charges 254
6.4 Dog Fighting 255
7 Other Forms of Misconduct 256
7.1 Criticizing Game Officials 256

7.2 Offensive Language and Gestures 257
7.3 On-Field Dress Code Violations 258
7.4 Some Safety Concerns 258
8 Concluding Remarks 259
Problems and Questions 260
Research Questions 261
References and Further Reading 262

13 Steroids and Other Performance-Enhancing Drugs 263
1 Introduction 263
2 Prevalence of Abuse 263
3 Banned Substances: Benefits and Risks 265
3.1 Anabolic Androgenic Steroids 265
3.2 Beta-2 Agonists 266
3.3 Stimulants 266
3.4 Diuretics 266
3.5 Hormones 266
3.6 EPO 267
3.7 Blood Doping 267
3.8 Austrians Get Tough on Blood Doping 267
4 Steroid Policies in Sports 267
4.1 NCAA Policy 267
4.2 Major League Baseball 268
4.3 National Football League 269
4.4 National Basketball Association 270
4.5 National Hockey League 270
4.6 U.S. Track and Field 271
4.7 Men's and Women's Professional Tennis 272
4.8 Men's and Women's Golf 272
5 Sanctions and Deterrence 274
5.1 Deterrent Function 275
5.2 The Trade-Off between p and F 279
5.3 Olympian Efforts at Deterrence 280
6 Additional Sanctions 281
6.1 Financial Consequences 281
6.2 Lost Reputation 281
7 Concluding Remarks 283
Problems and Questions 284
Research Questions 285
References and Further Reading 286

IV FACILITIES, FRANCHISES, AND PUBLIC POLICY

14 Competing for Sports Franchises and Events 289
1 Introduction 289
2 The Economic Incentives to Be a Host 289

2.1 Job Creation 290
2.2 Greater Tax Revenue 290
2.3 Prestige/Exposure 291
2.4 Consumption Value 292
3 The Competition for Franchises and Events 292
3.1 Stadiums, Ballparks, and Arenas 293
3.2 Stadium Leases 293
4 The Dark Side of City Competition 294
4.1 The "Need" for New Facilities 295
4.2 Revenue Guarantees 295
4.3 Stadium Revenues 295
5 The Winner's Curse 295
6 Should a Sports Franchise Be Subsidized? 296
7 Competition, Subsidies, and Team Location 297
8 The Use of Eminent Domain 300
9 Concluding Remarks 301
Problems and Questions 301
Research Questions 303
References and Further Reading 303

15 Economic Impact of Sports Events 305
1 Introduction 305
2 Economic Impact Analysis: Fundamentals 305
3 Multipliers: Simple Economic Theory 306
3.1 Simple Multipliers 307
3.2 Two Caveats 307
3.3 More General Multipliers 308
3.4 Estimating Local Multipliers 310
4 Measuring Incremental Spending 310
4.1 Substitution 311
4.2 Attribution 311
5 Professional Surfing Contests: An Example from Hawaii 312
6 Estimation and Verification 313
6.1 Economic Impact of the Super Bowl 313
6.2 MLB's All-Star Game 314
6.3 Impact of College Football 316
7 Concluding Remarks 317
Problems and Questions 317
Appendix 318
References and Further Reading 319

16 Financing Sports Facilities 320
1 Introduction 320
2 Investing in a Sports Facility 321
2.1 A Numerical Example 321
2.2 Some Further Considerations 321

2.3 Scrap Value 322
2.4 The Giants–Jets Stadium 323
3 **Private and Public Financing** 323
3.1 Nationals Park 325
3.2 Stadium Financing in the National Football League 326
4 **Funding and Subsidies for Other Facilities** 327
4.1 Subsidizing Community Facilities 328
4.2 Political Realities and Municipal Commitments 329
5 **Public Financing of Sports Facilities** 331
5.1 Taxing the Tourists in Orlando 331
5.2 Alternative Sources of Tax Revenue 332
5.3 Debt Financing and Equity 334
6 **Concluding Remarks** 334
Problems and Questions 335
Research Questions 336
References and Further Reading 336

17 Salary Determination: Competition and Monopsony 338
1 **Introduction** 338
2 **Demand for Athletic Talent** 340
2.1 Market Demand for Labor 342
2.2 Equilibrium Wage 342
2.3 Numerical Example 343
3 **Monopsony in the Labor Market** 343
3.1 Social Welfare Loss of Monopsony 345
3.2 Numerical Example 346
4 **Sources of Monopsony Power** 347
4.1 Reserve Clause 347
4.2 Player Drafts 347
4.3 Collusion among the Clubs 348
5 **Collusion in MLB's Free-Agent Market** 348
6 **Measuring Monopsony Power** 350
6.1 Lerner Index of Monopsony Power 350
7 **Monopsonistic Exploitation: Theory and Empirical Evidence** 351
7.1 Empirical Evidence 351
7.2 A Broader Look at Market Value 353
8 **Concluding Remarks** 354
Problems and Questions 354
Research Questions 356
References and Further Reading 356

V SPORTS LABOR MARKET

18 The National Collegiate Athletic Association as a Collusive Monopsony 361
1 **Introduction** 361

2 The Incentive to Collude 362
3 Effect of Collusive Monopsony on Costs 364
3.1 Marginal Cost 364
3.2 Average Cost 365
4 NCAA: A Collusive Monopsony 366
4.1 Limits on Prices and Quantities 366
4.2 Revenue Sharing 370
4.3 Sanctions for Cheating 370
4.4 The Evolution of Sanctions 370
4.5 Consequences of the Death Penalty: SMU 371
5 Antitrust Challenges by Coaches 372
5.1 *Hennessey v. NCAA* 372
5.2 *Law v. NCAA* 373
6 Antitrust Challenges by Student-Athletes 376
6.1 *In re: NCAA 1-A Walk-on Football Players Litigation* 376
6.2 *White v. NCAA* 377
6.3 *O'Bannon v. NCAA* 377
7 Concluding Remarks 378
Problems and Questions 378
Research Questions 379
Appendix 380
References and Further Reading 381

19 Salary Determination: Bidding and Bargaining 383
1 Introduction 383
2 Auctioning Player Talent 384
2.1 Economic Results of an English Auction 384
2.2 Barry Zito Moves across the Bay 386
2.3 Bidding for Coaches 387
2.4 Nick Saban's Comings and Goings 388
2.5 Billy Gillispie Hits the Big Time 389
2.6 Head Coach Salaries 390
3 Bargaining 391
3.1 Greg Maddux: An Example 392
3.2 Carlos Zambrano Negotiates an Extension 393
3.3 Larry Johnson's Holdout 393
3.4 Brady Quinn's Holdout 394
3.5 Darrelle Revis's Holdout 394
3.6 Coaches' Contracts 395
3.7 Incentives and Bonuses 396
4 The Posting System in MLB 397
4.1 Akimori Iwamura – Tampa Bay (Devil) Rays 398
4.2 Kei Igawa – New York Yankees 398
4.3 Daisuke Matsuzaka – Boston Red Sox 399
4.4 Tsuyoshi Niskioka – Minnesota Twins 401

4.5 Gaming the Posting System 401
5 Concluding Remarks 402
Problems and Questions 402
Research Questions 403
References and Further Reading 404

20 Economic Value of Multiyear Contracts 405
1 Multiyear Contracts 405
2 Fundamentals of Contract Valuation 406
3 Contracts with Uncertain Terms 408
4 Value of Multiyear Contracts without Guarantees 410
5 Contracts with Option Years 411
6 Contracts with Signing Bonuses 412
7 Guarantees 412
8 Contracts with Incentive Provisions 413
9 Concluding Remarks 413
Problems and Questions 414
Research Questions 417
References and Further Reading 417

21 Final Offer Arbitration in Major League Baseball 418
1 Introduction 418
2 Are "Final" Offers Really Final? 418
3 The Economics of Settlements in Final Offer Arbitration 419
3.1 The Economic Condition for Settlements 421
3.2 Condition for Settlements 422
3.3 Problems in Reaching Settlements 423
3.4 Some Summary Remarks 424
3.5 Costs of Reaching Settlements 424
4 Some Empirical Evidence on Arbitration Results 426
5 The Threat of Final Offer Arbitration Protects Players 428
6 Concluding Remarks 429
Problems and Questions 429
References and Further Reading 430

22 Players' Unions and Collective Bargaining 432
1 Introduction 432
2 Organizing the Players' Unions in the Major Leagues 432
2.1 Major League Baseball Players Association 433
2.2 National Football League Players Association 433
2.3 National Basketball Players Association 434
2.4 National Hockey League Players Association 435
2.5 Executive Directors 435
3 Unions and Antitrust Policy 435
4 Unions and Collective Bargaining 436

4.1 Unions: Goals and Economic Consequences 436
4.2 Two Approaches to Excess Supply 438
5 **Bilateral Monopoly in Sports** 438
5.1 A Simple Model of Bilateral Monopoly 439
5.2 Bargaining in the Major Leagues 441
6 **Free Agency** 442
6.1 Major League Baseball 442
6.2 National Football League 442
6.3 National Basketball Association 443
6.4 National Hockey League 443
7 **Salary Caps and Luxury Taxes** 443
7.1 Hard Salary Caps 443
7.2 Soft Salary Caps 445
7.3 Luxury Taxes 445
8 **Minimum Salaries** 446
9 **Revenue Sharing** 447
10 **Concluding Remarks** 448
Problems and Questions 448
Research Questions 449
References and Further Reading 450

23 The Role of Sports Agents 451
1 **Introduction** 451
2 **Roles of Sports Agents** 451
2.1 On-Field Performance 452
2.2 Negotiating Salaries 452
2.3 Negotiating among Several Clubs 452
2.4 Endorsements and Other Opportunities 454
3 **Financial Management** 456
3.1 The Tank Black Story 457
4 **The Principal–Agent Problem** 457
4.1 Principal–Agent Contracts 458
5 **Corrective and Preventive Measures** 461
5.1 Reputation 462
5.2 Players' Union Supervision 462
5.3 Contract Law 463
6 **Concluding Remarks** 463
Problems and Questions 464
Research Questions 465
References and Further Reading 466

24 Should an Athlete Turn Pro "Early"? 467
1 **Introduction** 467
2 **To Stay or Not to Stay?** 468
2.1 Potential Costs of Leaving School 468

2.2 Potential Benefits of Leaving School 470
2.3 In Principle, the Choice Is Simple 471
3 **How Early Entrants Have Fared in the NFL Draft** 471
4 **A Simple Economic Model** 473
4.1 Decision Rules 475
4.2 Uncertainty 476
5 **Age Limits in Professional Sports** 477
5.1 Age Limits Vary by Sport 477
6 **Leaving High School Early** 480
7 **Concluding Remarks** 481
Problems and Questions 481
Research Questions 483
References and Further Reading 484

25 Discrimination in Sports 485
1 **Introduction** 485
2 **Discrimination: Concept and Identification** 485
2.1 Identifying Discrimination 486
3 **Economics of Discrimination** 486
3.1 Impact of Discrimination 487
3.2 Competition and Discrimination 489
3.3 Fan Discrimination 490
3.4 Role Discrimination 491
4 **Racial Discrimination** 492
4.1 Racial Discrimination: Players 492
4.2 Racial Discrimination: Coaches 493
5 **Gender Discrimination** 494
5.1 Men and Women in Professional Golf 494
5.2 Men and Women in Professional Tennis 497
6 **Title IX and Gender Discrimination** 498
6.1 Compliance with Title IX 499
6.2 Congressional Compliance Guidelines 500
6.3 Impact on Coaching Opportunities 502
6.4 Support for Title IX and Women's Sports 503
7 **Concluding Remarks** 504
Problems and Questions 504
Research Questions 506
References and Further Reading 507

Subject Index 509

Author Index 527

Preface

This textbook grew out of my dissatisfaction with other textbooks on sports economics that were available. As my own course evolved over time, these books became increasingly unsuitable for my class in part because of coverage and in part because of level and organization. This book reflects my interests and those of my students at the University of Florida. Unlike other books on this subject, this one includes extensive use of present values, choice under uncertainty, pricing models, and numerical examples. The content includes multiyear contracts, insurance, sports gambling, misconduct (and its discipline), the steroid scandal, and many other topics that are not standard fare in the existing sports economics textbooks.

An important pedagogical feature of this book is the involvement of students in the learning process through problem solving. At the end of each chapter, there are *Problems and Questions* that are intended to help students learn the concepts in the text. There are also some *Research Questions* that will help students learn how to find information and present it.

This text is almost self-contained. Most economic concepts are presented and explained so that a student with no economics background can master the material. Nonetheless, those students who have taken an introductory course at the level of Michael Parkin's *Economics* will find the going much easier. The mathematics in the text does not exceed that in any introductory text: arithmetic, simple algebra, and geometry.

This book can be used in a variety of ways. There is probably too much material for a one-semester course. The core material that should be covered is found in Chapters 2–8, 14–16, 17, 19, and 22. The interests of the instructor and those of his or her students should dictate the selection of other chapters.

In writing this book, I have accumulated many debts. Several friends and colleagues have offered useful advice. Jim Fesmire, Jim Mak, and Jason Winfree read the manuscript and offered numerous suggestions for improvement. I hope that they will not be disappointed in the end result. Numerous people read smaller chunks of the earlier drafts: Jeff Rudnicki, Mark Rush, and Jim West were particularly helpful. Three anonymous reviewers pointed out some weaknesses that I hope have been corrected. Others who provided valuable assistance include Derek Drayer, Ross Elliott, Bryan Lynch, and Morgan Miller. The manuscript preparation was handled in part by Corinne Turcotte and Sarah Goldberger. Sarah helped complete the manuscript, organized the various pieces of the puzzle, and kept the whole project moving through some trying times. I will always be grateful for her help and good cheer. She deserves much of the credit and none of the blame for the finished product.

My editor at Cambridge, Scott Parris, was a continuing source of enthusiasm and encouragement during a process that took longer than I expected. Thanks to Scott for his remarkable patience.

I owe the largest debt of all to Christina DePasquale, who knows more about sports than anyone I know. She helped with the research, wrote some useful summaries, typed most of the manuscript, and kept my spirits up with her own enthusiasm for sports. Without her help, there is no way that this project would have been completed.

Finally, I thank Chau, Don and Gretchen, Dave and Christy, Alec, Devon, Riley, and Brett for always being there and for making life worthwhile.

Commonly Used Abbreviations

ACC	Atlantic Coast Conference
AFL	Arena Football League
ATP	Association of Tennis Professionals
CBA	Collective Bargaining Agreement
HGH	Human Growth Hormone
IAAF	International Association of Athletics Federations
IOC	International Olympic Committee
LPGA	Ladies Professional Golf Association
MLB	Major League Baseball
MLBPA	Major League Baseball Players Association
MLS	Major League Soccer
NASCAR	National Association for Stock Car Auto Racing
NBA	National Basketball Association
NBPA	National Basketball Players Association
NCAA	National Collegiate Athletic Association
NFL	National Football League
NFLPA	National Football League Players Association
NHL	National Hockey League
NHLPA	National Hockey League Players Association
PBA	Professional Bowlers Association
PGA	Professional Golf Association
SEC	Southeastern Conference
USADA	United States Anti-Doping Association
USGA	United States Golf Association
USOC	United States Olympic Committee
USTA	United States Tennis Association
WADA	World Anti-Doping Association
WTA	Women's Tennis Association

I

INTRODUCTION

1

Introduction to Sports Economics

1 INTRODUCTION

The term *sports* has many meanings encompassing a wide array of human activity that is neither work nor rest. Sports includes athletic competition, of course, but also recreational hunting and fishing, auto racing, exercise activities, and even poker. For the most part, in this book we focus on the activities covered in the sports section of local newspapers. Even this is fairly broad because that includes both amateur and professional sports, as well as recreational activities of all sorts: cycling, sailing, surfing, hiking, and many others. The coverage extends to both team and individual sports that are played in the United States and around the world. In our study, we touch on many of these, but our attention is largely on the major league professional team and individual sports that are most popular in the United States: football, baseball, basketball, hockey, golf, and tennis. Some additional attention is paid to intercollegiate sports under the auspices of the National Collegiate Athletic Association (NCAA).[1]

Studying the economics of sports does not involve much discussion of batting averages, field goal percentages, or rushing yardage. From an economic perspective, these performance statistics are important because they affect the outcomes of the games. To the extent that winning leads to more fans and greater attendance, athletic performance improves economic performance – that is, profit – of the team. This, of course, is important for the team and for the athlete because salaries and bonuses reward performance. Unlike many avid sports fans, however, we will not dwell on performance statistics for their own sake. The point is that we are interested in the business and economics of professional and amateur sports.

In the next section, we briefly explore the analytical tools that are useful in studying sports economics. The balance of this chapter provides a tour of the book and its coverage.

[1] The appendix to this chapter provides a list of commonly used acronyms.

2 TOOLS OF ANALYSIS

In studying sports economics, we rely in this book primarily on the fundamental principles of microeconomics, which are probably familiar to most students. Reading this book will be much easier if you have already studied microeconomics, but the book is largely self-contained. In other words, these fundamental principles are presented here so that the reader can learn the economics necessary to analyze sports economics. Instead of having a survey chapter at the beginning, the book develops the economic tools as they are used in studying the economics of sports. I have found this approach to be effective in my own teaching because it allows us to get into sports at the outset.

The economic analysis uses numerous graphs. Consequently, some basic understanding of plane geometry is necessary. In addition, many numerical examples are presented. These require some elementary algebra. The text proceeds on the assumption that the reader is familiar with the basics of algebra and geometry, which do not extend beyond those used in standard principles of economics texts. Finally, our focus on the business side of sports leads to an examination of profit and profit maximization. To a large extent, the principles are illustrated graphically, but solving some numerical examples requires a smattering of basic calculus. The book avoids the use of calculus by providing all the algebraic information necessary to solve the numerical examples.

2.1 Present Value Calculations

There are many instances when either the costs or the benefits of a decision extend into the future. In such cases, it is useful to express these streams of costs and benefits in common values to avoid mistakes by comparing apples to oranges. In the appendix to Chapter 2, we develop the arithmetic of present value calculations. In Chapter 2, such calculations are used to understand the value of cash flows. This tool is used in many other places in the book to understand the values of multiyear employment contracts, naming rights, franchises, and other issues.

There are times when the value of a future stream of income is not stated correctly from an economic perspective. For example, when Barclays bought the naming rights to the new home of the New Jersey Nets, it committed \$20 million per year for 20 years. This may appear to be a \$400 million deal, but the present value of that stream of payments is "only" a bit more than \$170 million if the relevant interest rate is 10 percent.

This methodology for calculating the present value of a stream of future payments is used throughout the book to measure rates of return on investments in sports franchises and sports facilities. The values of other multiyear contracts involving stadium naming rights and broadcast licenses are also sensibly calculated as present values.

2.2 Economics of Uncertainty

We live in an uncertain world and therefore must sometimes make decisions before having full information. We buy tickets to a game before knowing whether the star quarterback will sit out with an injury or whether it will be postponed to a later date because of rain. Teams sign players to multiyear contracts before knowing how the athlete will perform, whether he will be injured, and whether he will maintain his competitive zeal. All investments in franchises, facilities, coaches, endorsements, and naming rights involve uncertain returns, but commitments must be made before the realization of the benefits.

The expected utility model developed in Chapter 8 provides a framework for analyzing decisions in the presence of uncertainty. The model is then used to analyze the demand for insurance policies to cover the risk of injury. The expected utility model proves useful in analyzing sports gambling and the deterrence of cheating, misconduct, and the use of performance-enhancing drugs.

3 THE SPORTS BUSINESS

The sports industry is a big business. Billions of dollars are spent on tickets to professional and college athletic events. Billions of dollars are spent on player salaries and tournament purses. Billions of dollars are spent to secure broadcast rights, and still more is spent on advertising. Sports facilities, such as the new Yankee Stadium, the Cowboys Stadium, and the Giants-Jets Stadium, each cost more than a billion dollars to construct. As fans, we are concerned with the competition on the field, but as students of sports economics, we focus our attention on various business issues in the sports industry.

In Chapter 2, we recognize that sports franchises, which we will often refer to as *clubs* or *teams*, are businesses. The image of a sports franchise owner as the head of a small family business run largely as a hobby is quaint but seriously misleading. Economically successful franchises may be closely held businesses that are not publicly traded, but this does not mean that they are not operated as businesses with an eye on the bottom line.

In Table 1.1, a sample of estimated franchise values in the four major leagues are displayed. As one can see, these franchises are extremely valuable assets that demand careful managerial attention. Indulging the whims of wealthy owners is an expensive proposition and is not apt to occur very often. This is not to say that all franchises are well managed, but it is to say that profit is important.

In Chapter 2, we examine team profit and the principles of profit maximization. For a sports franchise, like any other business, profit is the difference between total revenue and total cost. We identify the most important revenue sources for sports franchises and the peculiar nature of the costs incurred in earning those revenues.

3.1 Sports Leagues and Organizations

Professional sports teams are organized into leagues such as the National Football League (NFL), the National Basketball Association (NBA), and the National Hockey League (NHL). NCAA teams are organized into conferences such as the Big Ten, Pac 10, and the Southeastern Conference (SEC). Individual sports

Table 1.1. A Sample of Estimated Franchise Values, 2009–2010

Team and League	Value ($millions)
National Football League	
Dallas Cowboys	1,650
Washington Redskins	1,550
New England Patriots	1,361
Major League Baseball	
New York Yankees	1,600
New York Mets	870
Boston Red Sox	858
National Basketball Association	
New York Knicks	607
Los Angeles Lakers	586
Chicago Bulls	511
National Hockey League	
Toronto Maple Leafs	470
New York Rangers	416
Montreal Canadiens	339

Source: http://www.forbes.com/business/sportsmoney.

organizations are also formed. Examples include the PGA Tour for men's golf and the Women's Tennis Association (WTA) for women's tennis. Leagues and organizations form to provide a more desirable product for the fan – championships, reliable schedules, traditional rivalries, meaningful statistics, and consistent rules of play. All improve the quality of the competitive contests for the fans' enjoyment. The improvement over ad hoc games or matches translates into greater profits that are split in some fashion between the club owner and the athletes.

In Chapter 3, we take a closer look at leagues and organizations from an economic perspective as a kind of joint venture or as a cartel. We also survey the rules and procedures of leagues to appreciate further the scope of business integration that a league entails. Finally, we examine the impact of leagues on consumer welfare.

3.2 Competitive Balance

The term *competitive balance* refers to the extent to which teams are evenly matched. This is important to a league because the quality of the product, which is competition on the field, is higher when teams are evenly matched. With higher quality comes greater fan interest, a greater willingness to pay for tickets, higher TV ratings, more sales of logoed items, and higher naming rights fees. These are obviously important for team profits. As we will see, a satisfactory measure of competitive balance is elusive. Moreover, various efforts to reduce competitive *imbalance*, which include reverse-order player drafts,

Table 1.2. Payrolls in Major League Baseball, 2011

Team and League	Payroll
American League	
New York Yankees	$202,689,028
Texas Rangers	$92,299,264
Seattle Mariners	$86,524,600
Kansas City Royals	$36,126,000
National League	
Philadelphia Phillies	$172,976,379
Atlanta Braves	$87,002,692
Milwaukee Brewers	$85,497,333
Pittsburgh Pirates	$45,047,000

Source: http://content.usatoday.com/sportsdata/baseball/mlb/salaries/team.

revenue sharing, and salary caps, have resulted in limited success. The problem can easily be seen in Major League Baseball (MLB).

Competitive balance in MLB is difficult to achieve because there is substantial imbalance in the team payrolls. In Table 1.2, we show the highest payrolls in each league, along with the lowest and the two middle values. It is plain to see that teams can hardly be evenly matched in the American League when the Yankees spent nearly six times as much as the Kansas City Royals on players, and the Yankees spent more than twice as much as the two middle teams. Similar imbalance can be seen in the National League.

3.3 Pricing Decisions

It is obvious that pricing decisions are crucial to financial success. If prices are too high, profitable ticket sales are lost. If prices are too low, money is being left on the table. In Chapter 5, we begin with simple competitive and simple monopoly pricing, which are already familiar. We then examine a variety of more complicated pricing options that allow the club to extract more consumer surplus from the fan.

3.4 Advertising and Promotion

Advertising and other forms of promotion are designed to increase the fans' willingness to pay. To the extent that the resulting increase exceeds the cost of advertising and promotion, these efforts will be profitable. In Chapter 6, we analyze the incentives to advertise by teams and by the league as a whole. Here, we highlight the public-good aspect of league-wide advertising. We also examine some interesting forms of sports advertising such as Citi Group's commitment of $20 million per year for 20 years to name the new Citi Field where the Mets play. Endorsement deals, event sponsorships, and TV advertising are also discussed.

Table 1.3. Top Media Rights Deals – Public Universities, 2010

Rank	School	Average Annual Value ($millions)
1	Georgia	11.6
2	Ohio State	11
3	Florida	10
4	Alabama	9.4
	Texas	9.4
6	Nebraska	8.6
7	Tennessee	8.3
8	Connecticut	8
	Kentucky	8
10	North Carolina	7.5
	Oklahoma	7.5
12	LSU	7.4
13	Michigan	7.2
14	Arizona	6.7
15	Wisconsin	6.3

Source: Sports Business Resource Guide and Fact Book 2011.

3.5 Broadcast Rights

For some leagues, broadcast rights can be sold for extremely large sums. NBC's deal with the International Olympic Committee is worth billions. The NFL also has billion-dollar deals with ESPN, CBS, Fox, and NBC. In Chapter 7, we turn our attention to the demand for broadcast rights and the important role that such fees play in the success of the major sports leagues.

Although media rights deals are more modest for NCAA members, they still involve substantial sums. Table 1.3 reveals that some major athletic programs receive considerable sums for their media rights. The names are familiar: Texas, Ohio State, Florida, Georgia, among others.

3.6 Insuring Player Talent

The talent required to play major league sports is extremely valuable and is put at risk every day. Injuries – on and off the field – as well as illness can destroy, or at least seriously impair, that talent. Insurance provides a way to shift that risk to someone else. In Chapter 8, we develop the analysis of decisions under uncertainty. We use this to explain the demand for insurance, which we apply to sports. Professional clubs insure player contracts, and the NCAA has an insurance program that permits top draft prospects to buy insurance covering career-ending injuries. This program allows student-athletes to borrow the insurance premiums for policies providing up to $1.0 to 3.0 million of coverage.

3.7 Sports Leagues and Antitrust Policy

The major sports leagues have considerable market power and are not bashful about exploiting it. This has aroused some antitrust scrutiny and resulted in many antitrust challenges. The now-defunct United States Football League (USFL) filed suit against the NFL and won $1 in damages. In Chapter 9, we see that antitrust challenges have not been very successful in the past. The antitrust laws, however, pose a continuing threat to anticompetitive behavior by sports leagues and their members.

4 IMAGE AND INTEGRITY

Professional athletes are entertainers and larger than life. They perform their athletic feats at an extremely high level for our benefit as fans. Because we enjoy the performance, we pay for admission, we watch on television, we buy logoed merchandise, we use equipment endorsed by our favorite athletes, and we even eat the fast food recommended by the stars. All of this economic activity results in many dollars ending up in the pockets of owners and athletes. It all depends on the preferences of the fans. Consequently, it is important for each sport to maintain its image and protect the integrity of the game. In this regard, we examine four areas of concern: gambling, cheating, misconduct, and performance-enhancing drugs. These issues are examined in Chapters 10 through 13.

4.1 Gambling in Sports

We begin in Chapter 10 with an economic analysis of gambling based on the expected utility model presented in Chapter 8. This provides an explanation for the gambler's behavior. We also provide a brief look at the operation of sports books. All professional leagues and tours as well as the NCAA have strict prohibitions on gambling. The details of these policies vary from sport to sport, but they are all intended to protect the integrity of the athletic contests and therefore the image in the minds of the fans.

4.2 Cheating in Sports

Competitors have a burning desire to win, and that creates the temptation to cheat. Although we generally disapprove of cheating to win, we understand it. Chapter 11 discusses why someone might cheat. Defensive holding in football, hand checking in basketball, scuffing baseballs, and making bad line calls in tennis are a few of the ways that athletes sometimes cheat in an effort to win. To preserve the integrity of the competition, there are punishments for such cheating. The aim of these punishments is to deter cheating by making it "unprofitable." We use the expected utility model to show how, when, and why penalties deter cheating to win.

A more serious problem arises with cheating to lose. From time to time, there are scandals that involve point shaving in basketball, performance breakdowns in baseball and football, and rogue game officials. Typically, these episodes are induced by gambling interests who want to influence the outcome of games for their own financial gain. The punishment for this kind of behavior is harsh – usually lifetime bans from the sport and possibly criminal prosecution by state or federal authorities.

4.3 Misconduct by Participants

When a fan is arrested on a DUI or for domestic violence, it is deplorable but not big news. When a prominent athlete does the same thing, it may be in the headlines. The image of the game and the league is tarnished when those we hope will be role models engage in misconduct. We discuss this in Chapter 12. Bad behavior extends in many directions. In recent years, there have been allegations of sexual assault, bar brawls, shootings, weapons possession, drugs of all kinds, and dog fighting, to name just a few.

The commissioner's office deals with these episodes in different ways depending on the athlete's past history and the specific circumstances. All disciplinary efforts are designed to punish the bad actor so others will be deterred from engaging in similar conduct. Once again, we use the expected utility model to illustrate the deterrent effect of league punishments. This model is also used to analyze the sanctions imposed on players for engaging in dangerous on-field behavior such as helmet-to-helmet hits in football, throwing at batters in baseball, and stick-wielding assaults in hockey.

4.4 Performance-Enhancing Drugs

The use of performance-enhancing drugs is addressed in Chapter 13. It poses an integrity problem because those athletes who take the drugs have an advantage over those who do not. Consequently, competition may be impaired. In addition, records set by athletes who trained without the benefits of steroids, human growth hormone (HGH), excessive caffeine, and the like have been broken by athletes who are juiced up on such drugs. Many fans find this disappointing. It is one thing for Roger Maris to break Babe Ruth's home run record by virtue of his skill, conditioning, and discipline and quite another for those who have broken Maris's record to do so with the help of performance-enhancing drugs.

The use of such drugs to accomplish certain feats that were out of reach without them strikes many as dishonest. Moreover, it sets a bad example for young athletes. As a result, the image of these athletes and the sport in general is impaired. If that results in a loss of fan interest, everyone ultimately suffers.

The major sports leagues and organizations all have rules against the use of steroids, HGH, and other performance-enhancing drugs. Each has its own system of testing, and each has its own set of sanctions. In the NFL, for example, first-time offenders receive a four-game suspension, which amounts to an implicit fine equal to one-fourth of the player's salary. In MLB, the punishment is a 50-game suspension, which amounts to a fine of nearly one-third of a year's salary. Testing increases the probability of getting caught, and the heavy penalties reduce the expected net benefits. Both of these effects are intended to be a deterrent to use of steroids and other performance-enhancing drugs.

5 FACILITIES, FRANCHISES, AND PUBLIC POLICY

In this part of the book, we are concerned with the desire of cities to play host to a sports franchise or an event, such as the Olympics, the Super Bowl, or MLB's All-Star Game. At least in part, this desire is based on a belief that there will be a significant economic benefit to the community. This, in turn, leads to the provision of facilities by the city. These issues are examined in Chapters 14 through 16.

5.1 Demand for Sports Franchises and Events

In Chapter 14, we examine the demand for sports franchises and events. First, we look at the economic incentives to be a host. Some of these are tangible, such as jobs and tax revenues, and others are intangible, such as prestige and the consumption value of having a home team. We then turn our attention to the ways in which cities compete with one another to become the host and how sports franchises exploit this competition.

5.2 Economic Impact Studies

There is a belief that sports franchises bring enhanced economic activity that ripples through the local economy and thereby increases income. The same has been claimed for major events such as the Super Bowl. The NFL claims that the economic impact of a Super Bowl is more than a quarter of a billion dollars.

In Chapter 15, we outline the methodology of economic impact analysis. We explore the right way and the wrong way of doing these analyses. The sources of exorbitant claims become clear through this discussion.

5.3 Financing Sports Facilities

Sports facilities are often financed by the host city. For example, when a city is selected to host the Summer Olympics, it must provide satisfactory venues for a wide array of events. Some existing facilities can be used, but many new ones must be built – and paid for by the city's residents, with some help from taxpayers in the state. Stadiums for football, arenas for basketball and hockey, and ballparks for baseball are often supplied wholly or in part by the host city. In financial terms, these are seldom good investments. In Chapter 16, we examine why this is the case.

6 THE SPORTS LABOR MARKET

In the final section of the book, our focus is on the sports labor market. This leads to the consideration of monopsony, bidding wars, bargaining, unions, sports agents, and discrimination.

6.1 Competition and Monopsony

Chapter 17 begins by presenting the principles of salary determination in a competitive labor market. We then introduce buying power and the model of monopsony. The sources of monopsony power in professional sports include

Table 1.4. Revenues of Top 10 NCAA Programs, 2008–2009

University	Revenue (in $millions)
Texas	138.5
Ohio State	119.9
Florida	108.3
Alabama	103.9
LSU	100.1
Penn State	95.6
Michigan	95.2
Tennessee	92.5
Wisconsin	89.8
Auburn	87.0

Source: Sports Business Resource Guide and Fact Book 2011.

the reserve system that bind a player to one club, the player drafts, and collusion among the clubs in dealing with free agents. A particular episode of collusion in MLB's free-agent market illustrates the economics of monopsony in action.

In this chapter, we also present a measure of monopsony power and monopsonistic exploitation. Some empirical results regarding the extent of exploitation in MLB illustrate the benefit of monopsony to the MLB owners.

6.2 Monopsony in the NCAA

The NCAA has more than a thousand colleges and universities as its members. These institutions are dedicated to higher education, but they also have athletic programs that are businesses. A sample of the revenues earned by the most lucrative college programs is shown in Table 1.4. Although many programs are not profitable, there can be no doubt that these are big businesses. Despite their nonprofit status, they all have an eye on the bottom line because surpluses in the revenue-generating sports are needed to support the non-revenue-generating sports, such as golf, lacrosse, and tennis. Individually, they have little buying power, but collectively they have plenty.

In Chapter 18, we introduce the model of collusive monopsony. We show how the NCAA has used its organization to behave like a collusive monopsony. We also illustrate its monopsonistic behavior in the markets for coaches and athletes. We then review the NCAA's successes and failures in antitrust cases challenging the collusive conduct of its members.

6.3 Bidding and Bargaining in the Sports Labor Market

After a century of bondage under the despised reserve system, professional baseball players were set free by a labor arbitrator. This decision signaled the end of the reserve system, which had been adopted by the other major leagues.

Now some form of free agency exists in every league. A free agent can strike a deal with any team interested in his services. For the top players, clubs engage in competitive bidding. It is a kind of auction, and the club offering the most attractive deal wins the player's commitment for the time specified in the resulting contract.

Chapter 19 also introduces the economics of bargaining that goes on in the sports labor market. This extends to coaches as well as players. Finally, we review the curious combination of bidding and bargaining incorporated in the posting system for signing some star players from Japan.

6.4 Economic Value of Multiyear Contracts

Following the demise of the reserve system, a club could not rely on retaining a player's services following the current season. As a result, clubs began signing players to multiyear contracts. Some are for only 2 years, but others extend to 10 years. In all of these deals, one thing is always true: a dollar received in the future is worth less than a dollar received today. Derek Jeter, the Yankees' shortstop, signed a three-year deal for the 2011–2013 seasons. Those dollars received in 2013 are not worth as much as they would be if they were received in 2011.

In this chapter, we analyze the economic value of multiyear contracts by using the present value methodology developed in Chapter 2. This analysis includes signing bonuses, option years, performance incentives, and other terms of the contracts.

6.5 Final Offer Arbitration

Under the Collective Bargaining Agreement in MLB, veterans with at least three years of service but fewer than six years are eligible for final offer arbitration. After bargaining in good faith, some players and their clubs reach an impasse. At that point, the player may file for final offer arbitration. Each side submits its final offer to the arbitration panel. The panel reviews the evidence submitted and picks one of the two offers – no compromise is permitted. In Chapter 21, we examine the process and review the results. We also provide an economic explanation for the settlements that predominate the process.

6.6 Players' Unions and Collective Bargaining

In Chapter 22, we focus on the players' unions that have emerged in the major sports leagues. By organizing the players and bargaining collectively on their behalf, the union has market power that offsets the monopsony power of the owners. The result has been a dramatic rise in players' salaries and benefits. This chapter also introduces the bilateral monopoly model, which provides an explanation for the division of the surplus that results from the bargaining process.

6.7 Sports Agents

In the professional sports leagues, the union does not bargain with management for a specific player's salary. In the NFL, the NBA, and the NHL, there are salary caps, which limit the size of the total payroll. Thus, there is a pool of money that each club must spend on salaries. It is then every player for himself. Some players bargain for less than their market value because they want the club to have money to pay other good players. Other stars do not seem to care and get as big a share of the total salary as they can.

6.8 The Role of Sports Agents

Players have found that it is in their interest to employ a sports agent to represent them in the negotiations over new contracts. In Chapter 23, we introduce the sports agent and examine his or her role in the sports labor market. We also introduce the principal–agent problem and the contractual efforts to resolve the conflict of interest between a player and his or her agent.

6.9 Turning Pro Early

For most of us, there are critical dates for entering the labor market: high school graduation, college graduation, completion of advanced degrees. We know when it is time to stop studying and start working. For aspiring professional athletes, the choice is not as clear-cut. Aside from some age restrictions imposed by the leagues and organizations, an athlete can turn pro whenever he or she can compete. Turning pro "early" simply means that athletes begin their careers with all or some remaining NCAA eligibility. This, however, does not mean that the decision is premature. There are plenty of examples of very successful players who turned pro right out of high school – Lebron James, Kobe Bryant, and Kevin Garnett, to name just a few NBA stars. There are also plenty of examples of players who left college before using all of their eligibility.

In Chapter 24, we examine the costs and benefits of remaining in school for an additional year of education, training, and emotional development. There are pros and cons to delaying the start of a professional career, and we develop a simple model to analyze them. We also examine the age restrictions imposed by the major sports leagues as organizations.

6.10 Discrimination in the Sports Labor Market

In Chapter 25, we analyze a controversial issue: discrimination in the sports labor market. After a review of what we mean by discrimination, we examine some empirical evidence of discrimination. We also point out that economists do not try to change preferences but instead alter incentives so that people are less apt to act on those preferences. We focus on some steps that have been taken to deal with discrimination. Finally, we turn our attention to the controversial Title IX program, which is designed to provide equal opportunities to boys and girls in high school and to men and women in college. The program has been enormously successful in increasing female athletic participation. Given limited budgets, however, these gains have come at the expense of men's programs. This has resulted in an interesting controversy.

7 CONCLUDING REMARKS

This concludes our tour of the book. As you have seen, a wide array of topics are covered. These topics require the use of many principles of microeconomics.

We do not cover every aspect of sports because that would be too broad, but studying the material here will enable you to understand many aspects of the sports industry that we do not analyze explicitly.

REFERENCES AND FURTHER READING

Bradbury, J. C. (2007). *The Baseball Economist: The Real Game Exposed.* New York: Penguin Group.

Noll, Roger G. (1974). *Government and the Sports Business.* Washington, DC: The Brookings Institution.

Parkin, Michael. (2010). *Microeconomics*, 9th ed. Boston: Addison Wesley.

Quirk, James, and Rodney Fort. (1997). *Pay Dirt: The Business of Professional Team Sports.* Princeton, NJ: Princeton University Press.

Quirk, James, and Rodney Fort. (1999). *Hard Ball: The Abuse of Power in Pro Team Sports.* Princeton, NJ: Princeton University Press.

Szymanski, Stefan. (2009). *Playbooks and Checkbooks: An Introduction to the Economics of Modern Sports.* Princeton, NJ: Princeton University Press.

Zimbalist, Andrew. (1999). *Unpaid Professionals: Commercialism and Conflict in Big-Time College Sports.* Princeton, NJ: Princeton University Press.

Zimbalist, Andrew. (2003). *May the Best Team Win: Baseball Economics and Public Policy.* Washington, DC: The Brookings Institution.

Zirin, Dave. (2010). *Bad Sports: How Owners Are Ruining the Games We Love.* New York: Scribner.

2

The Business of Sports

1 INTRODUCTION

As fans, we are most interested in the action on the field or in the arena because that is where the excitement takes place. We crave "the thrill of victory and the agony of defeat," as ABC's *Wide World of Sports* television program put it. But sports is a big business that has some interesting economic characteristics. Sports businesses take many forms depending on the segment of the industry. Sports franchises in the professional leagues are athletic teams on the field, but they are businesses off the field, selling tickets, food and drinks, logoed apparel, parking, souvenirs, and broadcast rights. In individual sports, such as bowling, golf, tennis, and track, the athletes have their own businesses in a very real sense; they are sole proprietors with profits and losses based on earnings or winning, and expenses of many kinds. Athletes need facilities – bowling alleys, tennis courts, golf courses, arenas, ballparks, and tracks – and these are also businesses in their own right. Similarly, athletes need equipment – balls, bats, helmets, shoes, uniforms – and equipment manufacturers are obviously businesses. Advertisers, broadcasters, concessionaires, sports agents, and apparel manufacturers are all involved in some aspect of the business of sports.

Amateur sports are also big businesses. The National Collegiate Athletic Association (NCAA) members manage substantial athletic budgets and must make business decisions on a daily basis. These decisions include hiring and firing coaches, picking corporate sponsors, investing in new or expanded training facilities, adding or deleting a sport, and pricing tickets, among many other things. On a smaller scale, high school athletic directors, recreational league directors, local Little League organizers, and the like are in the same boat.

The goal of nearly every sports business is profit.[1] These businesses require investments, some of which are substantial, and investors expect to enjoy a return on these investments. This requires operating profit. It is useful to keep

[1] Even in not-for-profit businesses such as the NCAA members are interested in generating surpluses (close kin of profit) so that they can fund further expenditures on nonrevenue sports, facilities, equipment, and the like.

this in mind because much of what we see off the field is driven by the pursuit of profit.[2] ESPN's decision to spend more than $1 billion per year for *Monday Night Football* broadcast rights, Citigroup's decision to pay $20 million per year for the naming rights to the Mets' new ballpark, and Nike's pervasive sponsorship of top athletes and athletic programs are all driven by the pursuit of profit. The Boston Red Sox spent more than $50 million for the right to negotiate with Daisuke Matsuzaka, a star pitcher from Japan. This investment was aimed at success on the field, but also success on their books.

In this chapter, we develop the principles of profit maximization as they apply to the business of sports. We examine the unique nature of some costs and revenues in these businesses. Finally, we take a look at the value of sports franchises. In many cases, costs are incurred in the current period while the revenues are received in net future periods. Comparisons of costs and revenues then require the calculation of present values. The appendix to this chapter reviews the fundamentals of present value calculations, which will prove useful here and elsewhere in the book.

2 PROFIT AND PROFIT MAXIMIZATION

Because we are going to proceed on the assumption that sports businesses make decisions in an effort to maximize their profit, it is a good idea to have a solid understanding of what we mean by *profit*.[3] At the most basic level, profit (π) is simply the difference between total revenue (TR) and total costs (TC):

$$\Pi = TR - TC.$$

Total revenue is simply the price charged times the quantity sold, and total cost is the cost of producing and distributing the product. Consequently, profit is a function of the quantity produced and sold:

$$\Pi(Q) = TR(Q) - TC(Q).$$

Now, total revenue is fairly easy to understand because economists, accountants, and managers all use the term in the same way. It merely means sales receipts, which have few subtleties. Of course, we must make sure that we are measuring net sales revenues, which account for all discounts, rebates, and allowances. Aside from this caution, however, "everyone" is on the same page when discussing total revenue. Total cost, however, is an entirely different matter. The concept of cost is a source of confusion because economists and noneconomists use the term somewhat differently. As an economic matter, we include all of a firm's opportunity costs as part of total cost. This means that total cost must include the market value of all the inputs employed.

[2] Some sports economists have suggested that profit maximization may not be the appropriate objective. There are, however, few examples of business decisions that cannot be explained as an effort to improve profits.

[3] For an interview with an owner who makes it clear that baseball is a business, see "Astros' Owner Discusses Business of Baseball," *Sports Business Journal*, August 13, 2007.

For example, when owners such as the late George Steinbrenner (New York Yankees), Mark Cuban (Dallas Mavericks), and Jerry Jones (Dallas Cowboys) expend managerial effort on their clubs, the market value of their time and effort is a cost to the team, which must be included in a sensible calculation of profit. When the Los Angeles Dodgers used their former spring training facility in Vero Beach, Florida, the true cost included forgone opportunities to use it for something else. We are not talking about the operating cost of Dodgertown while the Dodgers were there, which obviously must be included in the cost calculation. Instead, we are talking about the market value of alternative uses for the facility. For example, the Dodgers may have been able to rent it to other teams. If so, that forgone rent is an opportunity cost that must be included in the profit calculation. Similarly, when the University of Michigan plays football in Michigan Stadium, it incurs an opportunity cost that must be included if we want to measure its profits accurately. After we have calculated all of the costs that are incurred in producing, promoting, and distributing the product, we can then think about maximizing profit – that is, maximizing the difference between total revenue and total cost.

The seller will maximize profits by producing that quantity where *marginal* revenue equals *marginal* cost. To maximize profit, the quantity should be expanded until the increment in profit is zero. This is to say, output should be increased until no further increase in output will increase profit. Thus, profits are maximized when the change in profit due to a small increase in output is zero.

$$\frac{\Delta \Pi}{\Delta Q} = \frac{\Delta TR}{\Delta Q} - \frac{\Delta TC}{\Delta Q} = 0,$$

where Δ denotes a small change.

Marginal revenue is defined to be the change in total revenue resulting from a small change in quantity, and $\Delta TR/\Delta Q$ is marginal revenue. Analogously, marginal cost is defined to be the change in total cost resulting from a small change in output; therefore, $\Delta TC/\Delta Q$ is marginal cost. Profit maximization thus requires the equality of marginal revenue and marginal cost. This, of course, is the familiar condition for profit maximization that you have encountered before in your study of economics.[4]

2.1 A Numerical Example

Suppose that the demand for Brett's Best baseball gloves is

$$P = 180 - 5Q,$$

where P is measured in dollars per glove and Q is measured in millions of gloves. For all linear demand curves, the associated marginal revenue curve has the

[4] Michael Parkin (2010), *Microeconomics*, 9th ed., Boston: Addison-Wesley, pp. 274–275.

same intercept on the price axis and is twice as steep (that is, the absolute value of the slope of marginal revenue is twice the absolute value of the slope of the demand). In this case, MR is

$$MR = 180 - 10Q.$$

Suppose that total cost is

$$TC = 25Q^2$$

and marginal cost is then

$$MC = 50Q.$$

Profit (π) can then be written as:

$$\pi = (180 - 5Q)Q - 25Q^2.$$

Profit maximization requires producing where

$$MR = MC = 180 - 10 = 50Q.$$

Thus, the optimal quantity for Brett's Best is 3 million gloves. The price is found by substituting the optimal quantity into the demand function:

$$P = 180 - 5(3) = 165.$$

The maximum profits for Brett's Best are found by substituting the optimal quantity into the profit function:

$$\begin{aligned}\pi &= 180(3) - 5(3)^2 - 25(3)^2 \\ &= \$270\ \textit{million}.\end{aligned}$$

3 REVENUE AND COSTS

The basic principles of profit maximization can be employed in analyzing decisions in the sports industry. In doing so, however, there are some peculiarities that we should recognize. First, there are several sources of revenue. The data in Box 2.1 provide a rare look at revenue sources for a National Basketball Association (NBA) team.

3.1 Revenue Sources

A sports franchise derives revenue from several sources. Traditionally, clubs relied on gate receipts and associated stadium revenues. These remain extremely important, but other sources are growing in importance. The sales of broadcast rights, venue naming rights, trademark licensing deals, advertising revenues, and luxury suites have all grown in importance in recent years. Interestingly, the variable costs of generating these revenues are not large once a club is committed to putting on a full schedule of games.

Box 2.1 *Local Revenues of New Orleans Hornets**

Hurricane Katrina forced the Hornets to relocate to Oklahoma City. The Hornets were obligated to share all revenues above $40 million with the city and, as a result, filed a report regarding local revenues for the 2006–2007 season. The report, which provides a rare look at local revenues, revealed the following breakdown for the 35 regular season games played in Oklahoma City:

Source	Revenue
Ticket sales	$24,842,147
Sponsorship and advertising	$9,353,513
Suite sales	$3,027,047
Club seats	$874,000
Concessions	$591,712
Merchandise	$125,143
Parking	$96,067
Other	$5,860
TOTAL	$38,915,489

The club generated another $5.5 million in local revenues in New Orleans as well.

* John Lambardo, "Rare Look into NBA Team Biz," *Sports Business Journal*, June 11, 2007.

Gate Receipts. This refers to ticket sales. Typically, ticket prices vary according to the location of the seat. Better seats usually cost more than less desirable seats, but this is not always the case. Gate receipts are limited by the number of home games played and the number of seats in the facility. In this regard, ticket pricing will be an important managerial decision.[5] If ticket prices are too high or too low, considerable profits may be lost. For example, Neyland Stadium at the University of Tennessee holds 104,079 fans. If its seven home games are sold out, which they usually are, the university will sell 728,553 tickets for the season. If the games would have sold out even if ticket prices had been $1 or $2 more, underpricing would have resulted in leaving $728,553 to $1,457,106 on the table. This added revenue could help pay the head football coach's salary!

Attendance is extremely important for financial success because of the impact on gate receipts and overall stadium revenues. In the major professional leagues, attendance is usually quite good. For the 2009–2010 seasons, attendance figures are displayed in Table 2.1. In the National Football League (NFL), attendance for the league as a whole was exceptionally high. More than 98 percent of seats were filled. A closer look at the individual clubs reveals that

[5] We examine pricing decisions in Chapter 5.

Table 2.1. Total and Average Attendance, 2009–2010

League	Games	Total	Average
National Football League	256	17,007,172	66,434
National Hockey League	1,230	20,898,997	16,991
Major League Baseball	2,430	73,053,807	30,063
National Basketball Association	1,230	21,087,015	17,144

Source: *Sports Business Journal*, various issues.
http://en.wikipedia.org/wiki/List_of_sports_attendance_figures.

most teams were essentially sold out. There were, however, a few teams with poor win–loss records and relatively poor attendance. For the National Hockey League (NHL), overall attendance was more than 91 percent of capacity. Given the large number of home games (41) and the fact that some of them are in midweek, this is quite respectable.

Stadium Revenues. Fans show up at a game with a ticket, but their spending does not stop there. Fans also pay for parking and usually buy an assortment of things from concessionaires: food, drinks, programs, and souvenirs. These items are usually priced at an extremely healthy markup over their cost. As a result, these extras are also an important revenue source for the club. Such goods and services and game tickets are clearly complements in consumption.[6] No one goes to a stadium to buy an overpriced hot dog. Instead, one goes to the stadium to watch a game *and* buys an overpriced hot dog. The two products – stadium hot dogs and sports entertainment – are consumed together. By definition, these are complements. As a result, if the club wants to maximize profits, these goods and services cannot be priced without regard to their interrelated demands. In Chapter 7, we briefly examine how a club should price complementary goods to maximize profits. To a great extent, the clubs can subcontract the provision of these goods and services to concessionaires. To apply these principles, the club would then have to monitor the quality and pricing of the goods and services supplied by the concessionaires, but the club need not actually perform the supply function itself. The club still profits from concession sales through the license fee that it charges the concessionaires for the privilege of being the concessionaire. In other words, if the concession business generates, say, $1 million, then the privilege of being the concessionaire is worth $1 million. Competitive bidding by equally efficient concessionaires should result in a license fee of $1 million. The winning concessionaire is then left with a competitive return on his or her investment.

Broadcast Revenues.[7] Recent NFL contracts have generated substantial revenues for each football club. The six-year, $3.6 billion *Sunday Night Football*

[6] Pricing complements are examined in Chapter 5. See also, Krautmann, Anthony, and David J. Berri (2007), "Can We Find It at the Concessions? Understanding Price Elasticity in Professional Sports," *Journal of Sports Economics*, 8, 183–191.

[7] We examine the market for sports broadcast rights in more detail in Chapter 7.

Table 2.2. Local Broadcast Revenues and Payrolls, 2001 Major League Baseball American League

Team	Media Revenue[1]	Payroll[2]	Percent
New York Yankees	$56,750,000	$109,791,893	51.7
Seattle Mariners	37,860,000	75,652,500	50.0
Boston Red Sox	33,353,000	109,558,908	30.4
Chicago White Sox	30,092,000	62,363,000	48.3
Texas Rangers	25,284,000	88,504,421	28.6
Cleveland Indians	21,076,000	91,974,979	22.9
Baltimore Orioles	20,994,000	72,426,328	29.0
Detroit Tigers	19,073,000	49,831,167	38.3
Tampa Bay Devil Rays	15,511,000	54,951,602	28.2
Toronto Blue Jays	14,450,000	75,798,500	19.1
Anaheim Angels	10,927,000	46,568,180	23.5
Oakland Athletics	9,458,000	33,810,750	28.0
Minnesota Twins	7,273,000	24,350,000	30.0
Kansas City Royals	6,505,000	35,643,000	18.3

[1] *Sports Business Journal*, p. 42, December 31, 2001.
[2] Associated Press, 2003. http://sportsillustrated.cnn.com/baseball/mlb/news/2001/04/09/team_payrolls.

deal with NBC was worth an average of $112.5 million per NFL team. This amounts to $18.75 million per year. The eight-year, $8.8 billion *Monday Night Football* contract with ESPN was worth another $275 million per team, which is another $34,375,000 per year. The regular Sunday games were under contract with CBS and Fox. Together, they provided still another $41.7 million per team, per year. Altogether, the TV revenues amounted to $94,825,000 per team. To appreciate the relative significance of these revenues, we can compare them to team payrolls. In 2006, the salary cap was only about $95 million per year, so the TV contracts with NBC, CBS, Fox, and ESPN alone covered almost 100 percent of the salary cap. For the NFL, at least, it is obvious that broadcast revenue is crucially important to the clubs and, of course, to the players.

In Major League Baseball (MLB), broadcast revenues are similarly important. There is, however, an additional twist that leads to uneven revenues across teams: *local* broadcast rights. The local broadcast revenues by team are shown in Tables 2.2 and 2.3 for the American and National Leagues, respectively. These data are fairly old given that they are for the 2001 season. Unfortunately, similar data do not seem to be available for more recent seasons. The tables also show opening day payroll for each team and how much of that payroll was covered with the local broadcast revenue alone.

The magnitude of the local broadcast revenues varies considerably across clubs. The Yankees topped the American League with nearly $57 million, whereas the Kansas City Royals had only $6.5 million in local broadcast revenues. Kansas City only covered 18.3 percent of its $35,663,000 payroll with

Table 2.3. Local Broadcast Revenues and Payrolls, 2001 Major League Baseball National League

Team	Revenue[1]	Payroll[2]	Percent
New York Mets	$45,251,000	$93,174,428	48.6
Los Angeles Dodgers	27,342,000	108,980,952	25.1
Chicago Cubs	23,559,000	64,015,833	36.8
Atlanta Braves	19,988,000	91,851,687	21.8
Philadelphia Phillies	18,940,000	41,664,167	45.5
Colorado Rockies	18,200,000	64,015,833	28.3
San Francisco Giants	17,197,000	63,332,667	27.2
Florida Marlins	15,353,000	35,504,167	43.2
Arizona Diamondbacks	14,174,000	81,206,513	17.5
Houston Astros	13,722,000	60,382,667	22.7
San Diego Padres	12,436,000	38,333,117	32.4
St. Louis Cardinals	11,905,000	77,270,855	15.4
Pittsburgh Pirates	9,097,000	52,698,333	17.3
Cincinnati Reds	7,861,000	45,227,882	17.4
Milwaukee Brewers	5,918,000	43,089,333	13.7
Montreal Expos	536,000	34,774,500	1.5

[1] *Sports Business Journal*, p. 42, December 31, 2001.
[2] Associated Press, 2003. http://sportsillustrated.cnn.com/baseball/mlb/news/2001/04/09/team_payrolls.

local broadcast revenues, whereas the Yankees covered 51.7 percent of its $109,791,893 payroll. Similar disparities in the National League can be seen in Table 2.3. The other New York team, the Mets, topped the National League with more than $45 million in local broadcast revenues. Only two other teams had as much as half of that in local broadcast revenues.[8]

Broadcast revenues are similarly important for the NBA and the NHL. In individual sports – golf, tennis, bowling, and auto racing – broadcast revenues are also significant revenue sources.

Trademark Licensing Fees. All professional and college teams have logos that can increase the value of ordinary items. In most cases, neither the team nor the college actually produces the items, but at least some of the added value can be extracted through trademark licensing fees. All logoed merchandise – jerseys, jackets, hats, shirts, posters, coffee mugs – generates trademark licensing fees. This intellectual property (that is, the trademark) is protected under the Lanham Act and is jealously guarded by the leagues and colleges. Trademark licensing is an attractive revenue source because the clubs incur almost no cost in generating that revenue. There are legal expenses associated with negotiating contracts and challenging infringers who produce counterfeit merchandise, but not much else.

[8] These disparities contribute to competitive balance problems, which we examine in Chapter 4.

Naming Rights. There are some peculiar venue names – Comerica Park, the Staples Center, and FedEx Field, to name just a few. These names provide no hint of who plays what sport in the venues. There are a few venues that have no corporate logo attached – Yankee Stadium, Dodger Stadium, and Michigan Stadium come to mind. However, the vast majority of sports venues carry a commercial message from a corporate sponsor. Deals for naming rights have been rising substantially over time. The contracts for the Barclays Center (new home of the NBA's New Jersey Nets) and Citi Field (home of MLB's New York Mets) each came in at $20 million per year for 20 years. As we know, although the nominal value of the Barclays deal may be $400 million, the economic value is the present value of $20 million a year for 20 years.[9] At an 8.0 percent discount rate, this is:

$$PV = \sum_{t=1}^{20} \$20\ million/(1.08)^t,$$

which is "only" $196,362,000. Although it is not $400 million, this is a tidy sum nonetheless.

3.2 Costs of Generating Revenues

In the short run, nearly all of a club's costs are fixed. Salaries of all players and other club personnel are essentially fixed by contract. Costs associated with the venue and office space can be adjusted slightly but are nearly fixed. Travel costs, meals, and the like can also be adjusted slightly, but there is limited flexibility. More important, none of these costs are influenced by attendance. Thus, ticket pricing will be unaffected by variations in these costs.

In the long run, more costs are variable. For clubs that want to continue participating in a league, however, there is a schedule of games that must be met. There are so many home games and so many away games that must be played. There are preseason and postseason commitments as well. This, of course, limits a club's flexibility with regard to costs even in the long run. Nonetheless, there are some important changes that can be made: location, venue, team personnel, salary structure, and team quality. Changes in these variables will lead to cost changes that may or may not be consistent with profit maximization.

3.3 Club Profit

Profit is the difference between the sum of all the club's revenues and the sum of all the costs incurred in generating those revenues. We have identified various sources of revenue: gate receipts, stadium revenues, broadcast revenues, trademark licensing fees, and naming rights fees. For the most part, there are no operating costs associated with generating these revenues, with the obvious exception of gate receipts. There are, of course, transaction costs in negotiating the contracts associated with the sale of naming rights, broadcast rights, and trademark licenses. To the extent that stadium parking and concessions are contracted out, these contracts must also be negotiated and monitored.

[9] For those readers who are unfamiliar with present value calculations, the fundamentals are contained in the appendix to this chapter.

Profit can be written as:

$$\Pi = \sum_{i=1}^{5} TR_i - \sum_{i=1}^{5} TC_i,$$

where TR_i is the total revenue from source i, and TC_i is the total cost of generating revenue from source i. Management's job is to make the right choices to maximize the difference between the sum of the revenues and the sum of the costs. As one would expect, some managers are better at this than others.

4 PROFIT AND TEAM QUALITY

In principle, there is an intuitively plausible relationship between profit and team quality. Fans like to watch exciting games where the outcome is uncertain. This is a result of competitive balance between the opponents.[10] Tight, hard-fought games are more fun to watch than lopsided games in which the outcome is never in doubt. However, fans also prefer to see their team win. As a result, attendance should increase with improvement in the team's performance. Presumably, better teams win more than weaker teams. Thus, improved team quality should translate into more wins and therefore increased attendance.[11] With a given set of prices, increased attendance turns into increased revenue from gate receipts, parking, and concessions. This increased revenue should lead to higher profit, but it costs more to field a higher-quality team than a lower-quality team. Consequently, there is a trade-off and therefore an optimal level of team quality that will vary from team to team depending on variation in the fan base.

4.1 Selecting Team Quality

The club's general manager should select team quality to maximize profit. To put the most profitable team on the field, the general manager should acquire better players until the expected increment in revenue is equal to the increment in cost. In other words, improve quality until the expected marginal benefit of doing so is just equal to the marginal cost of doing so.

Suppose that S represents the number of stars on the roster. We assume that the more stars a team has, the more games it wins and the more popular the team is with the fans. This increased popularity is reflected in a greater willingness to pay for tickets. As an example, suppose that the price of a ticket is a function of quantity (Q) and team quality. Team quality is determined by the number of stars (S) on the team. We can then write profit (π) as follows:

$$\pi = P(Q, S)\,Q - C(Q) - C(S).$$

Here, $C(Q)$ is the cost of having fans in attendance and $C(S)$ is the cost of having stars on the team. Profit is maximized by adding stars until the marginal

[10] We examine competitive balance in more detail in Chapter 4.

[11] For some empirical evidence, see Roger D. Blair, Christina DePasquale, and Christine Piette Durrance (2010), "Does Quality Still Matter? Evidence on Wins and Attendance in the National Football League," unpublished manuscript. Department of Economics, University of Florida.

benefit of another star is just equal to the marginal cost of another star. In this simple model, the marginal benefit is the change in price that can be charged due to the added star ($\Delta P/\Delta S$) times the number of teams (Q) or ($\Delta P/\Delta S)Q$. The marginal cost of adding stars ($\Delta C/\Delta S$) is the increase in team payroll necessary to bid another star away from a rival team. Profit maximization requires adding stars until the marginal benefit equals the marginal cost. This equality will determine the optimal number of stars on the team. This will also determine the resulting price of a ticket. Holding everything else constant, this will maximize the club's profit.

4.2 Quality and Attendance in the NFL

Attendance in the NFL does not appear to be very sensitive to team quality. Contrary to popular belief, not all NFL games are sold out, but team quality does not seem to have much to do with it. In Table 2.4, total attendance, percentage of capacity, and the win–loss record for each NFL team are shown for the 2010 season. It is true that some teams with poor records also had poor attendance. The Oakland Raiders with an 8–8 record had attendance that amounted to only 73.7 percent of capacity. Similarly, the 7–9 St. Louis Rams filled only 81 percent of their seats. At the same time, however, some poor teams had surprisingly good attendance. For example, the Carolina Panthers were only 2–14, but its attendance was 98.4 percent of capacity. Some mediocre teams did quite well. The Seattle Seahawks had a dismal 7–9 record, but attendance was 100 percent of capacity. At the other end of the spectrum, the 11–5 New York Jets filled only 95.3 percent of its seats, and the Atlanta Falcons with a 13–3 record filled only 95.2 percent of its seats.

This casual look at the relationship between wins and attendance suggests that wins may not matter, but a more careful statistical analysis of the data reveals that attendance increases with increases in the number of wins.[12] The effect, however, is small. One additional win appears to increase attendance for the year by about 3,000 fans. Over an eight-game season, this is only 375 fans per game. Thus, quality matters, but not much. Apparently, the NFL is so popular that the demand is quality inelastic.

5 VALUE OF A PROFESSIONAL CLUB

Ultimately, the value of a professional team is determined by its profitability. After all, a professional team is an income-generating asset. The value of such an asset is the present value of the stream of expected future profits:

$$PV(\Pi) = \sum_{t=1}^{T} \Pi_t/(1+i)^t + v/(1+i)^T,$$

where Π_t is the (expected) profit in year t, i is the discount (or interest) rate, and T is the owner's time horizon. The time horizon (T) may be indefinite, but it may be a finite number depending on the circumstances. The final term,

[12] See Blair, DePasquale, and Durrance, *ibid.*

Table 2.4. Attendance and Performance in the National Football League, 2010

Team	Attendance	% Capacity	W–L
Dallas Cowboys	696,377	108.8	6–10
Washington Redskins	665,380	90.7	6–10
NY Giants	632,156	95.8	6–10
NY Jets	628,768	95.3	11–5
Denver Broncos	599,264	98.4	4–12
Carolina Panthers	580,965	98.4	2–14
Baltimore Ravens	569,817	100.3	12–4
Houston Texans	568,643	100 •	6–10
Green Bay Packers	566,362	91.1	10–6
New Orleans Saints	560,304	96	11–5
San Francisco 49ers	488,124	99.3	6–10
Philadelphia Eagles	553,152	102.3	10–6
Tennessee Titans	553,144	100	6–10
New England Patriots	550,048	100	14–2
Atlanta Falcons	542,800	95.2	13–3
Miami Dolphins	541,959	90.1	7–9
Kansas City Chiefs	541,380	88.2	10–6
Seattle Seahawks	535,942	100	7–9
Indianapolis Colts	535,802	106.3	10–6
Cleveland Browns	528,933	90.3	5–11
San Diego Chargers	524,241	91.9	9–7
Buffalo Bills	442,366	86.5	4–12
Pittsburgh Steelers	504,669	97.1	12–4
Jacksonville Jaguars	504,262	93.8	8–8
Arizona Cardinals	502,197	99	5–11
Chicago Bears	497,561	101.1	11–5
Cincinnati Bengals	482,917	92.1	4–12
Minnesota Vikings	470,009	94.1	6–10
Detroit Lions	450,286	87.3	6–10
St. Louis Rams	423,383	81	7–9
Tampa Bay Buccaneers	394,513	75.1	10–6
Oakland Raiders	371,448	73.7	8–8

W–L = win–lose record.

$v/(1+i)^T$, is the market value of the franchise at time T discounted to the present.

The actual profitability of major league clubs is unclear. The owners are reluctant to admit that they earn any profit because the players' unions are always pressing for a larger share of the total revenues. If the owners can persuade the union that they are not making any profit, presumably the union will understand that they cannot ask for more of the revenue. Claims of no profit are difficult to prove or disprove because the owners' books and financial

Table 2.5. National Football League Franchise Values, 2010

Team	Current Value ($mil)	Revenue ($mil)	Operating Income ($mil)
Dallas Cowboys	$1805	$420	$143.3
Washington Redskins	1550	353	103.7
New England Patriots	1367	318	66.5
New York Giants	1182	241	2.1
Houston Texans	1171	272	36.5
New York Jets	1144	238	7.6
Philadelphia Eagles	1119	2660	34.7
Baltimore Ravens	1073	255	44.9
Chicago Bears	1067	254	37.3
Denver Broncos	1049	250	22.0
Indianapolis Colts	1040	248	43.2
Carolina Panthers	1037	247	15.0
Tampa Bay Buccaneers	1032	246	56.1
Green Bay Packers	1018	242	9.8
Cleveland Browns	1015	242	36.1
Miami Dolphins	1011	247	−7.7
Pittsburgh Steelers	996	243	17.9
Tennessee Titans	994	242	23.3
Seattle Seahawks	989	241	34.0
Kansas City Chiefs	965	235	47.8
New Orleans Saints	955	245	36.7
San Francisco 49ers	925	226	21.0
Arizona Cardinals	919	236	28.1
San Diego Chargers	907	233	24.7
Cincinnati Bengals	905	232	49.4
Atlanta Falcons	831	231	34.5
Detroit Lions	817	210	−2.9
Buffalo Bills	799	228	28.2
St. Louis Rams	779	223	29.0
Minnesota Vikings	774	221	17.9
Oakland Raiders	758	217	2.2
Jacksonville Jaguars	725	220	25.9
Average	1,265	320	84.6

Source: Forbes.

records are not generally available to the public.[13] Many clubs are privately held, and therefore, their financial records are not available through Securities and Exchange Commission (SEC) filings. Those clubs that are publicly held are

[13] All of the clubs are incorporated, but nearly all of them are "closely held," that is, they are not publicly traded on any stock exchange. As a result, their financial records do not have to be disclosed. Mandatory disclosure is designed to protect the investing public, but no such protection is necessary when the general public cannot invest in a closely held corporation.

Table 2.6. National Basketball Association Franchise Values, 2010

Team	Current Value ($mil)	Revenue ($mil)	Operating Income ($mil)
Los Angeles Lakers	$607	$209	$51.5
New York Knicks	586	202	21.0
Chicago Bulls	511	168	51.0
Detroit Pistons	479	171	46.9
Cleveland Cavaliers	476	159	5.0
Houston Rockers	470	160	30.3
Dallas Mavericks	446	154	−17.4
Boston Celtics	433	144	12.9
Phoenix Suns	429	148	20.7
San Antonio Spurs	398	133	19.1
Toronto Raptors	386	133	18.0
Miami Heat	364	126	8.0
Orlando Magic	361	107	−2.2
Philadelphia 76ers	344	115	7.6
Utah Jazz	343	118	7.9
Portland Trail Blazers	338	121	−20.3
Denver Nuggets	321	115	4.6
Golden State Warriors	315	113	11.9
Washington Wizards	313	110	4.9
Oklahoma City Thunder	310	111	12.7
Atlanta Hawks	306	103	−2.0
Sacramento Kings	305	109	−2.8
Los Angeles Clippers	295	102	10.0
Indiana Pacers	281	97	−15.7
Charlotte Bobcats	278	96	−15.1
New Jersey Nets	269	92	−13.9
Minnesota Timberwolves	268	96	−6.8
New Orleans Hornets	267	95	−0.1
Memphis Grizzlies	257	88	−7.1
Milwaukee Bucks	254	91	−7.4
Average	430.5	150	22.05

Source: Forbes.

often part of a much larger business entity. For example, the Tribune Company owned the Chicago Cubs, but the company also owns various news media. In consolidated financial disclosures to the SEC, however, one cannot reconstruct the profits and losses of the Cubs operation. There is nonetheless one indicator that there must be some profits available for investors: there is no apparent shortage of would-be owners.

The franchise values are substantial – to say the least. In Tables 2.5 through 2.8, I present the *Forbes* estimates of franchise values in the NFL, MLB, the NBA, and the NHL. There is an obvious pattern: the more popular the sport, the

Table 2.7. Major League Baseball Franchise Values, 2010

	Current Value ($mil)	Revenues ($mil)	Operating Income ($mil)
American League Team			
New York Yankees	1600	441	24.9
Boston Red Sox	870	266	40.0
Los Angeles Angels of Anaheim	521	217	12.0
Chicago White Sox	466	194	26.4
Texas Rangers	451	180	4.7
Seattle Mariners	439	191	10.5
Minnesota Twins	405	162	25.0
Cleveland Indians	391	170	10.1
Baltimore Orioles	376	171	19.4
Detroit Tigers	375	188	−29.5
Kansas City Royals	341	155	8.9
Toronto Blue Jays	326	163	13.1
Tampa Bay Rays	316	156	15.7
Oakland Athletics	295	155	22.1
Average	947.5	298	23.5
National League Team			
New York Mets	858	268	26.2
Los Angeles Dodgers	727	247	33.1
Chicago Cubs	726	246	25.5
Philadelphia Phillies	537	233	14.5
St. Louis Cardinals	488	195	12.8
San Francisco Giants	483	201	23.5
Houston Astros	453	189	7.1
Atlanta Braves	450	188	1.5
San Diego Padres	408	157	32.1
Washington Nationals	387	184	33.5
Colorado Rockies	384	183	20.1
Arizona Diamondbacks	379	172	−0.6
Milwaukee Brewers	351	171	10.2
Cincinnati Reds	331	166	17.8
Florida Marlins	317	144	46.1
Pittsburgh Pirates	289	145	15.6
Average	573.5	206.5	20.9

Source: Forbes.

higher the franchise value. There is another pattern that may not be so obvious. Within a sport, franchise values are systematically higher the greater the population in the area. The positive relationship is most pronounced in the NBA and the NHL and least pronounced in the NFL.

There are both costs and benefits of owning a sports franchise. Because there seems to be no shortage of willing owners, the perceived benefits must

Table 2.8. National Hockey League Franchise Values, 2010

Team	Current Value ($mil)	Revenue ($mil)	Operating Income ($mil)
Toronto Maple Leafs	505	187	82.5
New York Rangers	461	154	41.4
Montreal Canadiens	408	163	53.1
Detroit Red Wings	315	119	15.3
Boston Bruins	302	110	2.6
Philadelphia Flyers	301	121	13.3
Chicago Blackhawks	300	120	17.6
Vancouver Canucks	262	119	17.6
Pittsburgh Penguins	235	91	−1.6
Dallas Stars	227	95	6.4
New Jersey Devils	218	104	6.9
Los Angeles Kings	215	98	0.7
Calgary Flames	206	98	4.6
Minnesota Wild	202	92	−2.3
Colorado Avalanche	198	82	2.3
Washington Capitals	197	82	−9.1
Ottawa Senators	196	96	−3.8
San Jose Sharks	194	88	−6.2
Anaheim Ducks	188	85	−5.2
Edmonton Oilers	183	87	8.2
Buffalo Sabres	169	81	−7.9
Florida Panthers	168	76	−9.6
St. Louis Blues	165	79	−6.2
Carolina Hurricanes	162	75	−7.3
Columbus Blue Jackets	153	76	−7.3
New York Islanders	151	63	−4.5
Nashville Predators	148	74	−5.5
Tampa Bay Lightning	145	76	−7.9
Atlanta Thrashers	135	71	−8.0
Phoenix Coyotes	134	67	−20.1
Average	228.1	97.63	31.2

Source: Forbes.

outweigh the perceived costs. Otherwise, we would have to conclude that the present and prospective owners were economically irrational. The economic analysis of these costs and benefits is complicated, but some familiar economic principles will aid our understanding. First, we examine a sports franchise as a stand-alone investment that is closely held by an individual or a small group of investors. Following that analysis, we examine the sports franchise as part of a diversified firm. As such, there may be substantial synergies that result from owning the club.

5.1 Stand-Alone Investments

Considered as a stand-alone investment, the anticipated benefits are the operating profits and capital appreciation, which is the difference between the market value of the franchise at some future date and the original purchase price. At the point of purchase, the anticipated value to the new owner is the present value of the operating profits plus the present value of the franchise's fair market value at the end of the owner's time horizon. Thus, the expected benefits, $E[B]$, can be expressed as:

$$E[B] = \sum_{t=1}^{T} \frac{E[\Pi_t]}{(1+i)^t} + \frac{V_T}{(1+i)^T},$$

where T is the owner's investment horizon, $E[\Pi_t]$ is the expected operating profit in year t, and V is the fair market value of the franchise at time T. These expected benefits must exceed the original purchase price if the purchase is going to be economically sensible. Accordingly, a purchase will occur only if:

$$E[B] - P > 0$$

where P is the purchase price.[14]

It is difficult to get good information on actual profits of professional clubs because the financial data are usually confidential. We can, however, discover information on franchise values that are illuminating.

5.2 Franchise Value Growth in the NFL

The average NFL franchise value grew substantially during Paul Tagliabue's reign as commissioner. Table 2.9 presents the average franchise values during the 1995–2005 period. As one can see, the average value increased in every year from 1995 through 2005. The percentage increase varied considerably from one year to the next during that period from a high of 40.49 percent in 1998 to a low of 8.75 percent in 1996. Because owning an NFL franchise is not a short-term investment, annual rates of return are not too important. As we will see, the compound annual growth rate in franchise values over a 10-year period was substantial.

The question is what compound growth rate will increase the average franchise value from \$160 million to \$819 million over 10 years. We can calculate the interest rate necessary to grow the average franchise value of \$160 million in 1995 to \$819 million in 2005 by using what we know about present and future values. From the appendix to this chapter, we know that

$$PV(1+i)^t = FV.$$

By substitution, we have:

$$(\$160)(1+i)^{10} = \$819.$$

[14] This is the net present value rule that we have seen earlier: $NPV = E[B] - P$ because $E[B]$ $(PV(E[\pi_t]))$.

Table 2.9. National Football League Franchise Values during Tagliabue Tenure

Year	Average Value (in millions)	Rate of Return from Year to Year[1]
1995	$160	
1996	$174	8.75%
1997	$205	17.82%
1998	$288	40.49%
1999	$385	33.68%
2000	$423	9.87%
2001	$466	10.17%
2002	$531	13.95%
2003	$628	18.27%
2004	$733	16.72%
2005	$819	11.73%
Rate of Return from 1995–2005: 17.7%		

[1] Rates of return were calculated from data in the table.
Source: Sports Business Journal.

This can be solved for the interest rate i as follows:

$$(1+i)^{10} = \frac{819}{160}$$

$$1+i = \left(\frac{819}{160}\right)^{1/10},$$

which yields:

$$i = \left(\frac{819}{160}\right)^{1/10} - 1 = 0.177.$$

Thus, the average franchise value in the NFL rose by a compound annual growth rate of 17.7 percent. This rate of return compares favorably with investments generally.

From Table 2.5, we can calculate the average NFL franchise value in 2010. The same process can be used to see how well the owners have fared under Roger Goodell's leadership. Because the average value in 2010 was $1.265 billion and the average in 2005 was $819 million, the average value rose by $446 million over five years. Thus, the average annual compound growth rate was 9 percent.

5.3 Capital Appreciation in MLB

In Table 2.10, we present the most recent purchase price for various MLB clubs. These purchase prices were then adjusted for inflation and expressed in 2005 dollars. Based on the 2005 valuation of each club, Table 2.10 shows the compound annual rate of return for each investment. These rates of return appear to vary quite a bit across clubs, but comparisons are difficult to make because

Table 2.10. Appreciation of Major League Baseball Franchises

Team	Price	Year	Adjusted Price	2005 Team Values	Rate of Return
Arizona Diamondbacks	$160	2002	$173.60	$286	18.11%
Atlanta Braves	$12	1976	$41.19	$405	8.2%
Baltimore Orioles	$173	1993	$233.80	$359	3.6%
Boston Red Sox	$700	2002	$759.90	$617	−6.7%
Chicago Cubs	$20.5	1981	$44.04	$448	10.1%
Chicago White Sox	$20	1981	$42.97	$315	8.7%
Cincinnati Reds	$270	2006			
Cleveland Indians	$323	2000	$366.30	$352	−0.8%
Colorado Rockies	$120	1991	$172.10	$298	4.0%
Detroit Tigers	$82	1992	$114.15	$292	7.5%
Florida Marlins	$158.5	2002	$172.07	$226	9.5%
Houston Astros	$115	1992	$160.08	$416	7.6%
Kansas City Royals	$96	2000	$108.88	$239	17.0%
Los Angeles Angels of Anaheim	$183.5	2003	$194.77	$368	37.5%
Los Angeles Dodgers	$430	2004	$444.57	$482	8.4%
Milwaukee Brewers	$220	2005			
Minnesota Twins	$36	1984	$67.67	$216	5.7%
New York Mets	$80.75	1986	$143.89	$604	7.8%
New York Yankees	$10	1972	$46.72	$1,026	9.8%
Oakland Athletics	$180	2005			
Philadelphia Phillies	$30.18	1981	$64.84	$424	8.1%
Pittsburgh Pirates	$90	1996	$112.03	$250	9.3%
San Diego Padres	$80	1994	$131.78	$354	9.4%
San Francisco Giants	$100	1992	$139.20	$410	8.7%
Seattle Mariners	$106	1992	$147.55	$428	8.5%
St. Louis Cardinals	$150	1996	$186.71	$429	9.7%
Tampa Bay Devil Rays	$65	2004	$67.20	$209	211.0%
Texas Rangers	$250	1998	$299.94	$353	2.4%
Toronto Blue Jays	$112	2000	$127.02	$214	11.0%
Washington Nationals	$450	2006			

Note: There are missing data because there is no need to adjust prices of franchises that sold after 2005.

of substantial changes within MLB that affect the calculations for one club and not another. For example, some sales occurred in the early 1980s before the advent of luxury seating, the modern ballpark design, and lucrative broadcast deals. The return on these purchases incorporates the benefits of these developments. Other purchases were made after 2000 when some of these changes were already incorporated in the purchase price. We can get a sense of this by looking at the purchase prices expressed in 2005 dollars. The more distant purchase prices were much lower than the more recent prices even after adjusting for inflation. For example, the 1972 purchase of the New York Yankees was $46.72 million, the 1981 purchase of the Chicago Cubs was $44.04 million, and the 1976 purchase of the Atlanta Braves was $41.19 million. In contrast, the 2002 purchase of the Boston Red Sox was at a price of $759.9 million, the 2004 purchase of the Los Angeles Dodgers was at a price of $444.57 million, and the 2006 purchase of the Washington Nationals was at a price of $450 million. Table 4.6 shows that appreciation in MLB values has not always been positive. For the most part, negative growth rates occurred on recent purchases. In most cases, the returns have been positive and in many instances substantial. With a few exceptions, these rates of return have been below 10.0 percent. Although these rates may not appear very high, we must remember that they have been adjusted for inflation. In addition, each club may be generating operating profits.

5.4 Other Benefits

There are other benefits to supplement the profits and capital appreciation of owning a franchise. For one thing, owners become celebrities to some extent. How many more people know who Jerry Jones, Robert Kraft, Jerry Buss, and George Steinbrenner are because they own or owned sports teams than would know them otherwise? Their ownership gives them a visibility that they would not have otherwise. For some owners, this is really important. As a result, they may be willing to pay something for that celebrity status.

6 CONCLUDING REMARKS

The focus of this chapter has been on sports as a business. There is a wide array of business ventures in the sports industry. Our primary concern has been on professional team sports, but the basic principles of profit maximization also apply to those participating in individual sports as well as equipment manufacturers and venue owners.

PROBLEMS AND QUESTIONS

1. Assuming that the Chicago Cubs are committed to participating in MLB next season, which of the following costs are variable?
   a. Player payroll
   b. Travel expenses for away games
   c. Disability insurance on players' contracts
   d. Advertising of home games
   e. Postgame cleanup and repair
2. In 2007, the Oakland Raiders traded Randy Moss, a superb but troublesome wide receiver, for a fourth-round draft pick. Provide an economic explanation for this move.
3. Provide an economic explanation for Citigroup's decision to commit $20 million per year for 20 years to name the New York Mets' new ballpark "Citi Field."

4. Centerplate had been the New York Yankees' concessionaire for more than 40 years, but there were rumblings that the Yankees would switch to a new provider when their new ballpark opened. Why would they make such a change?
5. The coach of the University of Minnesota's Golden Gophers, Glen Mason, was fired after his team blew a 31-point lead in the 2006 Insight Bowl. The firing came one year after Mason received a four-year contract extension. Although he was scheduled to earn $1.65 million per year, the buyout cost for Minnesota was "only" $4.0 million. Provide an economic analysis of Minnesota's decision to fire Mason.
6. Ace Andrews plays professional tennis for a living but is not too successful despite his big first serve. In 2008, Ace could have earned $75,000 as a teaching pro at the Atlanta Tennis Club. He won $100,000 in prize money in various tournaments around the country. In doing so, he spent $20,000 on transportation and lodging. He also spent $7,000 on meals. His coach/trainer charged him $5,000 for the year. His condo rent in Atlanta was $800 per month, and his car payment was $300 per month.
   a. What was Ace's net income in 2008?
   b. What was Ace's net profit as a professional tennis player?
7. Before the 2007 season, the Chicago Cubs spent a lot of money on free agents. For example, they spent $136 million for an eight-year deal with left-fielder Alfonso Soriano, $21 million for a three-year deal with starting pitcher Jason Marquis, and $40 million for a four-year deal with another pitcher, Ted Lilly. As a result, the annual payroll went up by $20 to $30 million. Because player salaries are a fixed cost, ticket prices should not have risen as a result of the increased payroll, yet ticket prices did rise. What happened here?
8. The New York Yankees own Yankee Stadium free and clear, but the club decided to build a new ballpark right next door. Explain the economic decision to build a new ballpark.
9. Following the Florida Gators repeat in 2007 as NCAA champions in men's basketball, the demand for souvenir T-shirts was

$$P = 100 - 0.0002Q$$

and the corresponding marginal revenue was

$$MR = 100 - 0.0004Q,$$

whereas the constant marginal (and average) cost was $4.00.
   a. Find the optimal price and quantity.
   b. How much profit would the Gators realize on these sales?
10. After the Indianapolis Colts won Super Bowl XLI in 2007, the demand for a Peyton Manning jersey was:

$$P = 210 - 0.0002Q$$

with a corresponding marginal revenue of:

$$MR = 210 - 0.0004Q.$$

If the marginal cost of producing a jersey is $10, how much are the trademark licensing rights worth?

11. Henry Hacker is a professional golfer who was having some trouble with his driver. He decided to skip the next two tournaments on the PGA tour to work with his swing coach. He paid his coach $1,000 and used $100 worth of golf balls. As a result, his driving improved considerably, and he now hits his tee shots longer and straighter. What costs did Henry incur over this time?
12. Pete Kendall, an offensive lineman with the New York Jets, was extremely cooperative. At the club's request, he switched positions, helped two promising rookies, and restructured his contract. The following year, he was disappointed that the Jets did not reciprocate and adjust his contract. He said that "you never can expect a team to do the right thing out of the goodness of their hearts."
    - **a.** Explain why Kendall should not have been surprised.
    - **b.** What will make teams do the "right thing"?
13. Table 2.10 indicates that the Chicago Cubs were worth $___ million in 2010, whereas the Chicago White Sox were worth only $___ million. What factors might explain the difference?
14. Michael Illitch bought the Detroit Tigers in 1992 for $82 million, which amounted to $114.15 million in 2005 dollars. By 2005, the Tigers were worth $292 million. Calculate the real compound annual rate of return on that investment.
15. Many club owners claim that they are not making any profit and, in fact, are losing money. At the same time, franchise values continue to appreciate. Does this make sense?
16. In 1965, Rankin Smith bought the Atlanta Falcons for $8.5 million. Some 36 years later, his family sold the team for $545 million. Ignoring any operating profits or losses, what was the *nominal* rate of return on the investment? In contrast, what was the *real* rate of return on the investment?
17. What is the value of the naming rights to Citi Field if the appropriate discount rate is 10 percent?
18. The average NFL franchise value was $160 million in 1995 and $___ million in 2010. Ignoring inflation, what was the average annual compound growth rate in the NFL franchise value?
19. Some high schools have copied college logos for their teams. Although imitation may be the highest form of flattery, some colleges are not flattered. The *New York Times* reported that "Colleges Tell High Schools Logos Off Limits." Why would colleges do this?
20. In 2010, the owners of the Boston Red Sox paid $480 million to purchase the Liverpool FC soccer team. Why would they do this?

21. In late 2010, negotiations over the sale of the Detroit Pistons bogged down. The owner wanted \$400 million, but the most probable buyer was only willing to pay \$370 million. One complicating fact was that the New Orleans Hornets had sold for only \$300 million. How would you use that sales price in evaluating the worth of the Pistons?

RESEARCH QUESTIONS

1. Consult the MLB franchise valuations for 2009 provided by *Forbes*. Compute the compound annual rate of appreciation for each MLB team using the data in Table 2.10 for 2005 as the base.
2. Use the NFL franchise values provided by *Forbes* to determine whether these values are correlated with the population in their hometowns.

APPENDIX: THE FUNDAMENTALS OF PRESENT VALUE CALCULATIONS

In many business contexts, costs and revenues extend into the future. In some instances, costs are incurred now, and operating profits are received in the future. For example, if we invest in a sports facility, the construction costs are incurred in the present and the operating profits are earned over the future life of the facility. To analyze the costs and benefits, we have to master the fundamentals of compound interest and present value calculations. To determine the value of future sums, we must look at the present value of the future payments. Although present value calculations can be complex in practice, the basic concept is straightforward and the fundamentals are easily mastered.

A.1 Calculating Future Values

Consider a lender who can earn 10 percent interest annually on her loans. If she lends \$1.00, she will have \$1.10 at the end of the first year:

$$(\$1.00)(1.10) = \$1.10.$$

At the end of two years, the lender would have \$1.21 because her interest would compound, that is, she would earn 10 percent interest on her loan plus 10 percent interest on the interest earned in the first year:

$$\begin{aligned}(\$1.00)(1.10)(1.10) &= (\$1.00)(1.10)^2 \\ &= \$1.21.\end{aligned}$$

It is important to note that the lender does not receive just an additional \$0.10 in interest in the second year. Instead, she receives \$0.11. The extra penny results from earning 10 percent interest on the \$0.10 interest earned in the first year.

As a general proposition, the future value (FV) of \$1.00 at an annual interest rate of i percent in n years can be written as

$$FV = \$1.00(1 + i)^n.$$

Table A2.1. Future Value of $1 at End of *n* Periods: $FV = \$1(1+i)^n$

Years	5%	6%	7%	8%	9%	10%
1	1.050	1.060	1.070	1.080	1.090	1.100
2	1.103	1.124	1.145	1.166	1.188	1.210
3	1.158	1.191	1.225	1.260	1.295	1.331
4	1.216	1.262	1.311	1.360	1.412	1.464
5	1.276	1.338	1.403	1.469	1.539	1.611
6	1.340	1.419	1.501	1.587	1.677	1.772
7	1.407	1.504	1.606	1.714	1.828	1.949
8	1.477	1.594	1.718	1.851	1.993	2.144
9	1.551	1.689	1.838	1.999	2.172	2.358
10	1.629	1.791	1.967	2.159	2.367	2.594
11	1.710	1.898	2.105	2.332	2.580	2.853
12	1.796	2.012	2.252	2.518	2.813	3.138
13	1.886	2.133	2.410	2.720	3.066	3.452
14	1.980	2.261	2.579	2.937	3.342	3.797
15	2.079	2.397	2.759	3.172	3.642	4.177
16	2.183	2.540	2.952	3.426	3.970	4.595
17	2.292	2.693	3.159	3.700	4.328	5.054
18	2.407	2.854	3.380	3.996	4.717	5.560
19	2.527	3.026	3.617	4.316	5.142	6.116
20	2.653	3.207	3.870	4.661	5.604	6.727
30	4.322	5.744	7.612	10.062	13.257	17.449
40	7.040	10.285	14.974	21.724	31.408	45.259
50	11.467	18.420	29.457	46.901	74.357	117.39
60	18.679	32.987	57.946	101.25	176.03	304.46

The values of one dollar to be received in n years at various interest rates can be computed on most simple calculators. In Table A2.1, future values of one dollar for various interest rates and for various years are shown. These table values can be used when a calculator is not handy.

After this future value of a dollar is computed, the future value of any specific sum in *n* years can be found by multiplying the future value of $1.00 by that sum. For example, suppose that the interest rate is eight percent, and we want to know the value of $930,000 in 12 years. We know that the value of $1.00 in 12 years at an interest rate of eight percent is $(\$1.00)(1.08)^{12} = \$2.518$. Consequently, the value of $930,000 at the end of 12 years will be $(\$930{,}000)(2.518) = \$2{,}351{,}740$.

A.2 Present Value Calculations

The converse of this proposition is that $1.00 to be received at some point in the future is worth less than $1.00 today because $1.00 today can be invested and over time will earn compound interest until that point in the future. To determine how much less, we must answer the question, "What sum earning a 10 percent return will be worth $1.00 in a year?" The answer is found by solving a simple equation:

$$\$X(1.10) = \$1.00$$
$$\$X = \frac{\$1.00}{1.10}$$
$$\$X = 0.91.$$

Accordingly, \$1.00 to be received a year from now is worth only \$0.91 today if the interest rate is 10 percent.

If the dollar is received at the end of two years, the calculation is a bit more complicated, but the principle is the same:

$$\$X(1.10)(1.10) = \$1.00$$
$$\$X = \frac{\$1.00}{(1.10)^2}$$
$$\$X = \$0.83.$$

That is, the present value of a dollar to be received two years from now is only 83 cents if the interest rate is 10 percent. This procedure generalizes quite nicely. The present value (PV) of \$1.00 to be received in n years discounted at i percent per year is

$$PV = \frac{\$1.00}{(1+i)^n}.$$

Again, these values can be computed on a simple calculator. Alternatively, one can consult the entries in Table A2.2 for the years and interest rates shown.

A.3 Present and Future Values

Now, we can see the relationship between present and future values:

$$PV = \frac{FV}{(1+i)^n}.$$

The present value equals the future value divided by the discount factor. This relationship allows us to calculate the present value of any sum to be received in the future at any interest rate. For example, suppose one were to receive a deferred payment of \$843,000 in seven years and the interest rate is 12.5 percent. The present value of that future sum would be

$$PV = \frac{\$843{,}000}{(1.125)^7},$$

which is \$369,624. In other words, if one started with \$369,624 and invested it at 12.5 percent per year for seven years, the original investment would be worth \$843,000 at the end of the seven-year period. In this case, we could not use Table A2.2 because it does not have the information for an interest rate of 12.5 percent, so a calculator is necessary. See Question 3 for a case in which the table is useful.

Table A2.2. Present Value of $1 to be Received in *n* Years: $PV = 1/(1+i)^t$

Years	5%	6%	7%	8%	9%	10%
1	0.952	0.943	0.935	0.926	0.917	0.909
2	0.907	0.890	0.873	0.857	0.842	0.826
3	0.864	0.840	0.816	0.794	0.772	0.751
4	0.823	0.792	0.763	0.735	0.708	0.683
5	0.784	0.747	0.713	0.681	0.650	0.621
6	0.746	0.705	0.666	0.630	0.596	0.564
7	0.711	0.665	0.623	0.583	0.547	0.513
8	0.677	0.627	0.582	0.540	0.502	0.467
9	0.645	0.592	0.544	0.500	0.460	0.424
10	0.614	0.558	0.508	0.463	0.422	0.386
11	0.585	0.527	0.475	0.429	0.388	0.350
12	0.557	0.497	0.444	0.397	0.356	0.319
13	0.530	0.469	0.415	0.368	0.326	0.290
14	0.505	0.442	0.388	0.340	0.299	0.263
15	0.481	0.417	0.362	0.315	0.275	0.239
16	0.458	0.394	0.339	0.292	0.252	0.218
17	0.436	0.371	0.317	0.270	0.231	0.198
18	0.416	0.350	0.296	0.250	0.212	0.180
19	0.396	0.331	0.277	0.232	0.194	0.164
20	0.377	0.312	0.258	0.215	0.178	0.149
30	0.231	0.174	0.131	0.099	0.075	0.067
40	0.142	0.097	0.067	0.046	0.032	0.022
50	0.087	0.054	0.034	0.021	0.013	0.009
60	0.054	0.030	0.017	0.010	0.006	0.003

A.4. Valuing a Stream of Future Payments

A stream of future payments can be discounted to present value by using these basic principles. The present value of a stream of future payments ($w_1, w_2, \ldots, w_n$) is given by

$$PV(w) = \frac{w_1}{1+i} + \frac{w_2}{(1+i)^2} + \cdots + \frac{w_n}{(1+i)^n}.$$

Assume, for example, that the future payments are as follows:

Year	Payment
1	$200,000
2	$600,000
3	$300,000
4	$800,000
5	$1,200,000

Table A2.3. Present Value of an Annuity for n Years: $PV = \sum_{t=1}^{n} 1/(1+i)^t$

Years	5%	6%	7%	8%	9%	10%
1	0.952	0.943	0.935	0.926	0.917	0.909
2	1.859	1.833	1.808	1.783	1.759	1.736
3	2.723	2.673	2.624	2.577	2.531	2.487
4	3.546	3.465	3.387	3.312	3.240	3.170
5	4.329	4.212	4.100	3.993	3.890	3.791
6	5.076	4.917	4.767	4.623	4.486	4.355
7	5.786	5.582	5.389	5.206	5.033	4.868
8	6.463	6.210	5.971	5.747	5.535	5.335
9	7.108	6.802	6.515	6.247	5.995	5.759
10	7.722	7.360	7.024	6.710	6.418	6.145
11	8.306	7.887	7.499	7.139	6.805	6.495
12	8.863	8.384	7.943	7.536	7.161	6.814
13	9.394	8.853	8.358	7.904	7.487	7.103
14	9.899	9.295	8.745	8.244	7.786	7.367
15	10.380	9.712	9.108	8.559	8.061	7.606
16	10.838	10.106	9.447	8.851	8.313	7.824
17	11.274	10.477	9.763	9.122	8.544	8.022
18	11.690	10.828	10.059	9.372	8.756	8.201
19	12.085	11.158	10.336	9.604	8.950	8.365
20	12.462	11.470	10.594	9.818	9.129	8.514
30	15.3725	13.7048	12.4000	11.2578	10.2737	9.4269
40	17.1591	15.0453	13.3317	11.9248	10.7574	9.7791
50	18.2550	15.7619	13.8007	12.2335	10.9617	9.9148
60	18.9283	16.1614	14.0392	12.3766	11.0480	9.9672

If the interest rate is 15 percent, then the present value of this stream of future payments is calculated as follows:

$$PV(w) = \frac{\$200{,}000}{1.15} + \frac{\$600{,}000}{(1.15)^2} + \frac{\$300{,}000}{(1.15)^3} + \frac{\$800{,}000}{(1.15)^4} + \frac{\$1{,}200{,}000}{(1.15)^5}.$$

This amounts to $1,878,869.

Query: What have we assumed about the timing of the payments?

A.5 Present Value of a Stream of Equal Amounts

There is an easy way to determine the present value of a stream of future payments when they are equal. For example, suppose that the winner of a lottery will receive $200,000 per year for 20 years. If the appropriate discount rate is 5.0 percent, then

$$PV = \$200{,}000 \sum_{t=1}^{20} \frac{1}{(1.05)^t}$$

where the sigma denotes summation. Table A2.3 shows the sum of the present values of future payments for various years and various interest rates. In this case, the present value of one dollar per year for 20 years at a discount rate of

5.0 percent is $12.462. As a result, the present value of the lottery payments is as follows:

$$PV = (\$200{,}000)(12.462) = \$2{,}492{,}400.$$

A.6 Importance of Discount Rates

Because the present value of a future sum is equal to that future value divided by the discount factor,

$$PV = \frac{FV}{(1+i)^t},$$

it is clear that the discount (or interest) rate will influence the present value. It is instructive, however, to examine some numerical examples to see just how much of an impact a change in the discount rate can have on the present value. Consider a future value of $100,000 and alternative discount rates of 10 percent, 12.5 percent, and 15 percent. At a 10 percent discount rate, the present value of $100,000 to be received in five years is

$$PV = \frac{\$100{,}000}{(1.10)^5} = \$62{,}092.$$

At a discount rate of 12.5 percent, the present value falls to

$$PV = \frac{\$100{,}000}{(1.125)^5} = \$55{,}493,$$

which is a decrease of 10.6 percent below the present value at a 10 percent discount rate. If we increase the discount rate to 15 percent, the present value falls further:

$$PV = \frac{\$100{,}000}{(1.15)^5} = \$49{,}718.$$

Thus, the present value of $100,000 to be received in five years is reduced by another $5,775 because of the increase in the discount rate from 12.5 percent to 15 percent.

A.7 Selecting a Discount Rate

Because the present value calculations are so sensitive to the numerical value of the discount rate, serious attention must be paid to selecting the discount rate. It is useful to think about the purpose of discounting to understand what constitutes an appropriate discount rate. To this point, we have proceeded as though the discount rate represents the time value of money, but there is more to it than that. In addition, there are considerations of inflation. To the extent that prices rise over time, a future dollar will buy fewer goods and services. Ask your grandparents how much gasoline one could buy for $3 in 1960. The rate of inflation acts in the same way as the time value of money. Finally, to the extent that there is some risk of nonpayment, a risk factor should also be included. Thus, the discount rate should reflect three factors: (1) the time value of money, (2) expected inflation, and (3) payment risk. These factors must be captured if one is to select the proper discount rate for valuing alternative payment schemes.

PROBLEMS AND QUESTIONS

1. Paul was injured in an accident. In addition to considerable discomfort, the best estimate is that his medical expenses in 2009 will be $100,000. In the future, those expenses will increase at 10% per year. Paul had been earning $50,000 per year, but will only earn 80% of that in the future. Labor economists expect those in Paul's occupation to experience a 3% annual increase in earnings. Assume Paul has a 10-year work life and a 20-year expected natural life remaining. Also assume that the appropriate discount rate is 5.0%. How much should Paul be awarded? (Ignore tax considerations.)
2. If we assume no default risk and use an inflation-free discount rate, can we ignore future raises for an impaired worker?
3. What is the present value of $500,000 to be received in 20 years if the discount rate is 6.0 percent?
4. What is the present value of $80,000 per year for 10 years at a discount rate of 9.0 percent?
5. Because of an antitrust violation, a business was destroyed. Its owner wants to collect for the value of his business.
   a. What is the value of the business?
   b. What is the appropriate horizon?
   c. How would one decide on a discount rate?
6. There is a lamentable delay in cases getting to court. Suppose Bill's past and future losses are as follows:

2008	$50,000
2009	$60,000
2010	$85,000
2011	$95,000
2012	$110,000
2013	$120,000
2014	$150,000

   How would you calculate his damages if the trial occurred at the end of 2010?

REFERENCES AND FURTHER READING

Alexander, Donald L., and William Kern. (2004). "The Economic Determinants of Professional Sports Franchise Values." *Journal of Sports Economics*, 5, 51–67.

Blair, Roger D., Christina DePasquale, and Christine Piette Durrance. (2010). "Does Quality Still Matter? Evidence on Wins and Attendance in the National Football League," unpublished manuscript. Department of Economics, University of Florida.

DeGennaro, Ramon P. (2003). "The Utility of Sport and the Returns to Ownership." *Journal of Sports Economics*, 4, 145–153.

Depken, Craig A., II, and Dennis P. Wilson. (2010). "The Uncertainty of Outcome Hypothesis in Division IA College Football," unpublished manuscript. Belk College of Business, UNC – Charlotte.

Fleischer, Arthur A., Brian L. Goff, and Robert D. Tollison. *National Collegiate Athletic Association: A Study in Cartel Behavior.* Chicago: University of Chicago Press, 1992.

Kesenne, Stefan. (2007). "Revenue Sharing and Owner Profits in Professional Team Sports." *Journal of Sports Economics*, 8, 519–529.

Knowles, Glenn, Keith Sherony, and Mike Haupert. (1992). "The Demand for Major League Baseball: A Test of the Uncertainty of Outcome Hypothesis." *American Economist*, 36, 72–80.

Krautmann, Anthony, and David J. Berri. (2007). "Can We Find It at the Concessions? Understanding Price Elasticity in Professional Sports." *Journal of Sports Economics*, 8, 183–91.

Meehan Jr., James W., Randy A. Nelson, and Thomas V. Richardson. (2007). "Competitive Balance and Game Attendance in Major League Baseball." *Journal of Sports Economics*, 8, 563–580.

Miller, Phillip. (2007). "Private Financing and Sports Franchise Values: The Case of Major League Baseball." *Journal of Sports Economics*, 8, 449–467.

Neale, W. C. (1964, February). "The Peculiar Economics of Professional Sports." *Quarterly Journal of Economics*, 78, 1–14.

Parkin, Michael. (2010). *Microeconomics*, 9th ed. Boston: Addison-Wesley.

Peel, D. A., and D. A. Thomas. (1992). "The Demand for Football: Some Evidence on Outcome Uncertainty." *Empirical Economics*, 17, 323–331.

Quirk, James, and Rodney Fort. (1992). *Pay Dirt: The Business of Professional Team Sports.* Princeton, NJ: Princeton University Press, 240–293.

Quirk, James, and Rodney Fort. (1999). *Hard Ball: The Abuse of Power in Pro Team Sports* (chapter 5). Princeton, NJ: Princeton University Press.

Rottenberg, S. (1956, June). "The Baseball Players' Labor Market." *Journal of Political Economy*, 64, 242–258.

Schmidt, Martin B., and David J. Berri. (2006). "What Takes Them Out to the Ball Game?" *Journal of Sports Economics*, 7, 222–233.

Scully, Gerald W. (1994). *The Market Structure of Sports* (chapter 6). Chicago: University of Chicago Press.

Soebbing, Brian P. (2008). "Competitive Balance and Attendance in Major League Baseball: An Empirical Test of the Uncertainty of Outcome Hypothesis." *International Journal of Sport Finance*, 3, 119–126.

Szymanski, Stefan. (2009). *Playbooks and Checkbooks: An Introduction to the Economics of Modern Sports* (chapter 1). Princeton, NJ: Princeton University Press.

Tainsky, Scott, and Jason A. Winfree. (2008). "Financial Incentives and League Policy: The Example of Major League Baseball's Steroid Policy," *European Sport Management Quarterly*, 8, 67–81.

Zimbalist, Andrew. (2003). *May the Best Team Win* (chapter 4). Washington DC: Brookings Institution.

3

Sports Leagues and Organizations

1 INTRODUCTION

We are all familiar with the fact that athletic competition is often organized in sports leagues. The major professional leagues immediately spring to mind: the National Football League (NFL), National Hockey League (NHL), National Basketball Association (NBA), and Major League Baseball (MLB). There are leagues everywhere, however: recreational bowling, golf, softball, and tennis leagues are local fixtures for many adults. For children, there are Little League Baseball, Pop Warner Youth Football, high school leagues, and many others. At the college level, we call them *conferences* rather than leagues, but the Pacific-10 (PAC-10), Big Ten, Southeastern Conference (SEC), and Atlantic Coast Conference (ACC) are the same as other sports leagues in many respects. They have schedules, rules for postseason play, championships, rules for revenue sharing, and so on.

There are also organizations that put on athletic competition for individual athletes: the PGA Tour and Ladies PGA (LPGA) in professional golf, the Association of Tennis Professionals (ATP) and Women's Tennis Association (WTA) in professional tennis, the Professional Bowlers Association (PBA) in professional bowling, and various others for boxing, equestrian events, figure skating, speed skating, and track and field. For individual sports, tournaments or specific events rather than a season-long schedule of systematic competition are organized to determine a champion.

The economic question is why sports leagues and organizations exist. There is a sound economic reason for organizing athletic competition in leagues: it is simply a more profitable way of supplying athletic competition to the fans.

In this chapter, we focus primarily on the major professional leagues and, to a more limited extent, on organizations. We develop the economic rationale for the emergence of leagues and cover a bit of their history. Leagues require adherence to a set of rules, policies, and procedures. We examine the scope of those rules and the partial integration that emerges in the form of a joint venture when league members agree on those rules. Next, we turn to the issue of whether a sports league should be characterized as a single entity or as a cartel. Finally, we provide an assessment of the significance of leagues for social welfare.

2 LEAGUE FORMATION

Sports fans want to watch athletic competition and are willing to pay for the privilege. Although there were professional sports before there were leagues and organizations, economic success was limited by the erratic schedules, lack of championships, and the absence of systematic rivalries. In the early days, leagues began to evolve because they were a more efficient way to produce what fans want to consume. A league provides a reliable schedule so that sports fans can plan to attend a game and keep track of how their favorite teams are doing. Leagues also provide championships so fans will know which team is the best. Championships also heighten fan interest in the outcome of each game. Traditional rivalries – Yankees and Red Sox, Dodgers and Giants, Cowboys and Redskins – develop and are perpetuated through league schedules and the pursuit of championships. The end result is greater fan interest and therefore a greater demand for the product – competition on the field.

2.1 Cooperation off the Field

A sports league is a *cooperative* venture among on-field competitors. Cooperation off the field is necessary – and socially beneficial – because of the nature of the product being produced, which is athletic competition on the field. However, cooperation may go too far and consequently be socially harmful. Members of the sports league may refrain from competing off the field where competition would reduce their profits but be beneficial to the fans or to the athletes. The ideal (or socially optimal) level of cooperation off the field is not entirely clear.[1]

2.2 Leagues as Joint Ventures

Perhaps the best way to characterize a sports league is as a joint venture. The term *joint venture* does not have a single, unambiguous meaning, but the idea is pretty clear. The essence of a joint venture is a business enterprise in which two or more independent entities collaborate to achieve some commercial objective. A joint venture allows businesses to pool their complementary assets and capabilities for some specific purpose without the need for complete integration. That is, the efficiencies of integration can be achieved without the disappearance of the individual joint venture partners.[2] In MLB, for example, the individual clubs are separately owned and operated. Each club files its own tax return and finds its own investors. At the same time, the clubs cooperate on many dimensions to make their output attractive to the fans, to pool their

[1] We turn our attention to this issue in Chapter 10.

[2] For an example from the petroleum industry, Shell and Texaco remained separate companies but joined forces in a refinery on the West Coast. The joint venture, which was owned 50–50 by Shell and Texaco, operated under the name Equilon Enterprises.

broadcast rights, and to negotiate with the players union – among many other things.[3]

A joint venture blends various elements of competition and cooperation. The members of a sports league cooperate to produce and market athletic competition. Nonetheless, the cooperation off the field is somewhat limited, and the clubs continue to compete in other ways. For example, the clubs compete among themselves for coaches, free agents, and management personnel. At the same time, they participate in player drafts, share broadcast revenues, and agree on location restrictions.

The members of a joint venture partially integrate their resources in pursuing a common goal: maximizing their profits. Sports leagues partially integrate the resources of the members (1) to produce the athletic competition and (2) to market it to the public to maximize the profits of the clubs. The owners are required to surrender a good deal of their autonomy to ensure the efficient management of the sport. More cooperation extends to scheduling, membership in the league, player eligibility, and rules governing play.

2.3 Leagues as Cartels

A *cartel* is a group of independent firms that agree not to compete with one another to earn supra-competitive profits. Cartels may fix prices, restrict production, reduce quality, rig bids, divide markets, or refuse to deal with others.[4] Some observers have characterized sports leagues as cartels. This characterization is not entirely inappropriate. In a very real sense, sports leagues divide markets on a geographic basis. Usually, there is a considerable distance between any club and its nearest rival. This provides a measure of local monopoly power to each club. There are, of course, some cities that can support two teams (New York, for example), but most cities have only one. The leagues try to restrict team mobility to maintain the league stability. The leagues also pool their broadcast rights to prevent the clubs from competing with one another in that market. Finally, there is extensive revenue sharing within leagues, which rewards less fortunate teams for their cooperation. Thus, the behavior of the league members has much in common with a cartel.

3 SPORTS LEAGUES AND PROFIT MAXIMIZATION

Sports leagues comprise separately owned businesses – the clubs. Their economic fortunes are interdependent because they must cooperate among themselves to put the most profitable product in front of their fans. Nonetheless, each club has its own profit to maximize, which causes some conflict among league members. From an economic perspective, we should expect each club to be concerned primarily with its own profit rather than the profits of the

[3] Much the same is true of organizations. For example, the PGA Tour is comprised of on-course competitors who cooperate in many ways to promote interest in Tour events.

[4] For an examination of cartels, see Roger D. Blair and David L. Kaserman, *Antitrust Economics* (2nd ed.), New York: Oxford University Press (2009), chapters 9 and 10.

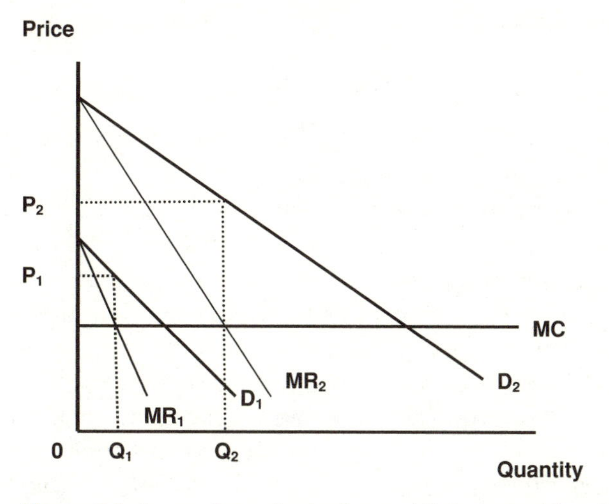

Figure 3.1. League formation leads to a shift in demand from D_1 to D_2 and an increase in profits.

other members. To the extent that the success of the other clubs contributes to its own success, each club will care about the financial well-being of the others. However, the motivation is selfish. In this context, *selfish* is not a pejorative term. It simply means that each club is concerned with its own profit. For example, the New Orleans Saints want other NFL clubs to do well because this improves the Saints' profits – not because the Saints particularly care about the welfare of the other clubs in the NFL.

Leagues form primarily because it is in the financial interest of their members to do so. By this, we mean that the production and distribution of the output are more profitable when the teams are organized into a league than when they are not. Club profits are improved because costs are lower and demand is higher. Although the cost-effectiveness may be significant, the main reason for enhanced profit comes on the demand side. Because leagues can provide predictable schedules, the formation of traditional rivalries, championships, and performance records, fans value the game more. As the games become more popular with fans, their willingness to pay for tickets, concessions, parking, and licensed merchandise rises. Sponsors pay more for naming rights as the sponsor's visibility improves with greater fan interest. Network and cable television providers pay more for the broadcast rights. All of this contributes to the bottom line of each league member. In short, league formation leads to higher demand for athletic competition and related products.[5] In Figure 3.1, D_1 represents the demand for watching professional baseball games without a league, and D_2 is the demand when the teams are organized into a league. If MC represents the marginal cost of fan attendance, it is plain to see that profits will be higher with a league than without a league. Profit without a league is

$$\pi_1 = (P_1 - MC)\,Q_1,$$

[5] This does not necessarily mean that demand will be high enough to support a league; see Problem 8 at the end of the chapter.

whereas profit with a league is

$$\pi_2 = (P_2 - MC)\,Q_2.$$

Because P_2 exceeds P_1 and Q_2 exceeds Q_1, π_2 is clearly larger than π_1. Thus, there is a powerful profit motive for league formation.

League formation can improve profits simply by making the athletic competition more attractive to the fans.[6] To be successful, however, the clubs must cooperate with one another off the field in many ways. In doing so, a good deal of autonomy and independence must be sacrificed. Each club must resist the temptation to "cheat" by taking steps to improve its own profits at the expense of league stability. A baseball club, for example, could cheat by spending very few payroll dollars, profiting from shared broadcast revenues and the fans' willingness to pay to see high-quality visitors. It might not matter much if one team did this, but if several teams did, team quality would suffer throughout the league, which would reduce fan interest. Rampant uncooperative conduct ultimately could lead to the collapse of the league. If the league collapses, demand will fall, and all league members will be worse off.

Much the same can be said for conferences in the National Collegiate Athletic Association. Florida State University joined the ACC and Penn State joined the Big Ten for economic reasons: easier access to bowls, enhanced broadcast revenues, and better schedules, among other things. Increased profit potential has resulted in every major football program belonging to a conference with the exception of Notre Dame. This is not to say that athletic conferences are precisely the same as professional leagues. It nonetheless remains true that conference formation provides some of the same profit-enhancing potential.

4 RULES AND PROCEDURES OF SPORTS LEAGUES

To produce a commercially attractive product – athletic competition – professional sports leagues find it efficient to operate under a set of rules and procedures to structure their business conduct. These are necessary for efficient production, marketing, and distribution of the clubs' product. In this section, we examine the scope of these league rules.

4.1 League Membership

First and foremost, the league's founders must resolve who will be in and who will not. The league must decide on the number of franchises and their locations. This is obviously important to maximize the profits of those who are included in the league. If the league is successful, there will be potential members who want to be admitted to the league but will be denied entry to preserve the profits of the incumbent members.[7] The league will develop a set of

[6] Leagues typically go beyond simply making the product more attractive. The pursuit of profit also leads to restrictions on entry, limits on output, control of quality, and the use of various pricing strategies.

[7] As we shall see in Chapter 9, denying admission to a league can result in antitrust suits, but the leagues are apt to win those suits.

prerequisites for ownership of a franchise. These prerequisites will include the owners' wealth because an important league concern is financial stability. As much as one team may want to see its rivals fail on the field, no league member wants to see its rivals fail financially. That would not be good for the league because fan support, broadcast contracts, and merchandise licensing depend on continuity. As a result of this concern, any transfer of ownership must be approved by the league. For example, in May 2007, MLB approved the sale of the Atlanta Braves, which could not have been consummated otherwise.[8] In the case of the Pittsburgh Steelers, the sale of ownership interests held by some family members to Dan Rooney required approval by the NFL. Similar approval was necessary for billionaire real estate developer Stephen Ross to acquire the Miami Dolphins.[9]

The league is also concerned with its image as it affects its popularity and fan support. MLB, for instance, will not permit the owner of a gambling casino to be an owner or operator of an MLB club. There are, however, loopholes in this regulation. Michael Ilitch owns the Detroit Tigers, and his wife owns the Motor City Casino.[10] This may seem to be a cute trick, but the two partners insist that the baseball operations are wholly separate from the casino operations. MLB may not like it, but they do not have a spouse rule to prevent such arrangements. The NFL similarly prohibits franchise ownership by those with ownership interests in gambling ventures. This is why two of the Rooney brothers who owned casino gambling interests in dog and horse tracks had to sell their interests in the Steelers.

Franchise locations must be determined if league members are going to maximize their profits. Naturally, the club owners will want to locate in metropolitan areas that are large enough to provide a fan base that will support a team. Each franchise wants to enjoy local monopoly power, and therefore, franchise locations cannot be too close together. At the same time, there are locations that can support more than one club – New York, Chicago, Los Angeles, and the San Francisco Bay Area, for example, all have two MLB teams. As we will see later, it is important to put multiple franchises in such locations to head off the formation of a rival league. Relocations are also important to league stability. If a franchise owner wants to move, it is because there are more profitable opportunities elsewhere, but moving may hurt another owner. For example, suppose that the Jacksonville Jaguars wanted to move to Chicago. Such a move might help the Jaguars, but it would hurt the owners of the Bears. To avoid league instability, relocations usually require approval of the owners as a group.[11]

[8] Associated Press, "Owners Approve Sale of Braves," May 17, 2007.

[9] Judy Battista, "Owners Agree to Steelers' Restructured Ownership," *New York Times*, December 18, 2008; Associated Press, "Developer Completes Deal to Take Control of Dolphins," *New York Times*, Jan. 21, 2009.

[10] Murray Chass, "A Marriage Is a Partnership, Except in Baseball," *The New York Times*, Dec. 26, 2006.

[11] Refusing to approve a relocation can result in an antitrust suit; see the discussion of the Raiders case in Chapter 10.

4.2 League Governance

The major sports leagues are essentially governed by the membership. As a group, the owners decide on a set of rules that are formalized in a document that may be characterized as a constitution. It will incorporate a set of bylaws, rules, policies, and procedures that govern the conduct of a league's business and that of its members. Individual members agree to abide by those rules because they are designed to maximize profits. The bylaws are not set in stone and may be changed by mutual agreement. There are periodic meetings of the league owners that provide opportunities to change the rules and procedures. Voting rights are also spelled out by the league, so everyone knows how things are done.

An extremely important aspect of league governance is the authority granted to the commissioner by the league members. The commissioner is an employee of the league, which is owned by the club owners. However, those owners grant authority to the commissioner to make decisions that may adversely affect one or more of the owners. For example, Roger Goodell, the NFL commissioner, announced a tougher policy regarding off-field behavior by players. He suspended Pacman Jones for an entire season, which hurt the Tennessee Titans defense. He also made it clear that he would impose sanctions on the clubs that did not control and discipline any off-field misconduct of their team members. In effect, the commissioner threatened to punish his bosses, which may seem strange, but such is the power granted to the commissioner. This power is exemplified in Goodell's handling of "spygate."[12] When the New England Patriots got caught spying on the New York Jets early in the 2007 season, Goodell fined the Patriots $25 million and took away their first-round choice in the 2008 NFL draft. Although Robert Kraft, the Patriots owner, was one of Goodell's bosses, he was subject to the authority of the commissioner's office.

There is no doubt that the commissioner of a major sports league must walk a fine line. He has to exercise the authority granted to him for the benefit of the league and its owners. At the same time, he is bound to render decisions that those owners will not like very much. Before feeling too sorry for them, however, we should note that they are extremely well paid. The commissioner of the NHL is the lowest paid at more than $7 million. The others receive at least $10 million per year (see Table 3.1). The equivalent positions in sports organizations pay a lot less, but the annual salaries are still impressive. The executive chairman and president of the ATP earns $1.4 million per year. His counterpart at the WTA is paid $866,000. Tim Finchem, the commissioner of the PGA Tour, earned $4.76 million in 2007, and his counterpart at the LPGA earned $500,000.

4.3 Production of Athletic Competition

The athletic competition on the field requires a set of uniform rules governing play. It is "three strikes and you're out" in every MLB ballpark. Field goals are always worth three points in every NFL stadium. The three-point line is the

[12] The impermissible spying by New England is examined in Chapter 12.

Table 3.1. Salaries of the Commissioners, 2010

Sport	Commissioner	Salary
Baseball	Bud Selig	$18.35 million
Football	Roger Goodell	$11.2 million
Basketball	David Stern	$10.0 million
Hockey	Gary Bettman	$7.1 million

same on every NBA court. More generally, the rules of play must be uniform if players and fans are going to understand what is happening during games.

League members must agree to the dates and locations of the games. We cannot have the Redskins prepared to play the Cowboys on Sunday at 1:00 P.M. in Dallas, while the Cowboys expect to play Monday night in New York against the Giants. This much is obvious, but there are less obvious scheduling issues. For example, some teams may face a series of away games against strong opponents early in the season. This could lead to a bad start and a tough uphill battle for the rest of the season, but the team must adhere to that schedule once it is set by the league.

League members also must agree to the procedure for determining the league champion. Eligibility for postseason play must be determined. Then the structure of the playoffs must be agreed on by league members. Will it be a three-game, five-game, or seven-game series? Will it be a single elimination tournament? Clearly, there must be agreement on this issue.

4.4 Marketing the League's Products

The basic product – athletic competition – is marketed to fans. This results in gate receipts and associated stadium revenues from parking and various concessions. It also generates substantial broadcast revenues from radio, network television, and cable television. New sources of Internet revenue are emerging as well. League members also generate trademark licensing revenues that flow from the popularity of the sport and its star players. These products are promoted by team and league-wide advertising.[13] Decisions on league-wide advertising and revenue sharing are clearly important.

4.5 Players' Market

Members of a league agree on various aspects of the market for players. Clubs agree on eligibility requirements. Usually, this involves age, but in the case of women's leagues, it involves gender as well. Clubs also agree on how and when player drafts will be conducted. The reverse-order draft is designed to help weaker teams improve, but draft positions can be traded according to league rules. Clubs also agree on mobility restrictions, limits on compensation, salary caps, standard contract terms, penalties for off-field behavior, and a host of

[13] We examine advertising in Chapter 6 and broadcasting in Chapter 7.

other player issues. All of this is subject to collective bargaining with the players' union.

4.6 Other Inputs

League members develop stadium standards regarding size, construction, and design. League members also have "tampering" rules that limit the competition for coaches and club executives.

4.7 Consensus

There must be some consensus on these league rules. Each club may feel somewhat constrained, but eventually a certain amount of independence must be sacrificed for the benefits of league success to materialize.

5 REVENUE SHARING

There is a considerable amount of revenue sharing in the major sports leagues. The national broadcast revenues are shared equally among the teams in each league. Trademark licenses generate shared revenue. Gate receipts are not shared in the NBA, but they are shared in the NFL and in MLB. In the NFL, there is a 60–40 split between the home team and the visiting team. In MLB, the split is less generous: the home team keeps 85 percent, and the visitor receives 15 percent.

One purpose of revenue sharing is to prop up financially weak teams. In the fast-food industry, one chain benefits from the financial struggles of another chain. McDonald's, for example, would benefit from the failure of Burger King. This is not the case in sports leagues. The bankruptcy of the Coyotes hurt the other clubs in the NHL because leagues benefit from stability.

5.1 Transfer to Weaker Teams

Suppose that a team in a strong market has payroll costs of $100 million and revenues of $160 million. As a result, it has $60 million to cover other costs and provide some profit for the owners. Another team is in a weak market and has revenues of only $80 million. Because of its much lower revenue, it spends only $80 million on its payroll. Its payroll is equal to its revenue, and the club has other costs; thus, its net profits are negative, and the franchise is financially troubled. This problem can occur even for efficiently managed clubs. Some franchise locations simply will not generate enough fan interest to be profitable.

Revenue sharing can help out the club in the weak market. Suppose that there is a 75–25 revenue split. This means the home team gets 75 percent of the gate revenue and gives 25% to the visiting team. The team in the strong market now has revenues of (.75)($160) + (.25)($80), which amounts to $140 million. Given its payroll costs of $100 million, its gross profits will be $40 million instead of $60 million. The team in the weak market now has revenues of (.25)($160) + (.75)($80), which is $100 million. Given its payroll costs of $80 million, this team will now have $20 million to cover other costs. The revenue sharing will obviously help to prop up the financially troubled team.

There is no doubt that revenue sharing can assist financially strapped clubs. This does not mean, however, that those clubs will improve their rosters by spending more on payroll. Just because a team can afford to do something is no reason for actually doing it. What drives business decisions is the pursuit of profit. Consequently, we should examine how revenue sharing affects profits and determines the impact on incentives.

Fans like to see good teams that are winners, so a team's total revenue is a function of the number of wins (W):

$$TR_1 = TR_1(W_1).$$

The more games a team wants to win, the more it will need to spend on good players. As a result, the total cost is a function of the number of wins:

$$TC_1 = TC_1(W_1).$$

Profit is then

$$\pi_1 = TR_1(W_1) - TC(W_1).$$

The club will maximize its profits by selecting the team quality that will win the optimal number of games. The optimal number of wins is found where $MR_1 = MC_1$. This is the familiar condition that the firm should "produce" the number of wins where $MR_1 = MC_1$.

The optimal number of wins changes when there is revenue sharing because the marginal value of a win is reduced while the marginal cost is unchanged. Assume that s is the share of total revenue that goes to the home team and $(1 - s)$ goes to the visitor. Clearly, $0 < s < 1$. Profit then becomes

$$\pi_1 = sTR_1(W_1) + (1 - s)TR_2(W_2) - TC(W_1).$$

Now the optimal number of wins is found where

$$sMR_1 - (1 - s)MR_2 - MC_1 = 0.$$

An additional win by team 1 increases its revenue by MR_1, and it gets to keep sMR_1 of that. When team 1 wins another game, team 2 loses a game, and its revenue falls by MR_2. Team 1 receives $(1 - s)$ of that reduced revenue, which is why $(1 - s)MR_2$ is subtracted from sMR_1. The net effect of another win is much lower with revenue sharing because part of MR_1 is shared with team 2 and part of team 2's revenue reduction is absorbed by team 1. The marginal cost, however, does not change. Consequently, the incentive to improve team quality to win more games is reduced for all teams.

5.2 Revenue Sharing in MLB

Revenue sharing in MLB takes two forms. First, each team sends 31 percent of its *local* revenue to the commissioner's office. These funds are pooled and divided equally among the 30 MLB clubs. Obviously, this plan will redistribute some revenue from clubs in stronger markets to clubs in weaker markets. A differential remains, however, and this provides some incentive for clubs in strong markets to conduct their business efficiently. The plan does, of course, dampen that incentive to some extent.

MLB's second revenue sharing program involves the distribution of money from the Central Fund, which collects revenue from various sources such as the national broadcast contract. These funds are distributed disproportionately based on a club's relative revenue position. This is also designed to help teams in weaker markets.

Box 3.1 *A Revenue Sharing Example*

As an example, suppose that the revenue sharing plan is a 10-team league requiring each team to contribute 25 percent of its revenue to the league, which returns .25 percent of the total collected to each team. The effect on net revenue after sharing is as follows:

Team	Revenue	Net Revenue
1	$50 million	51.5625
2	$40 million	44.0625
3	$30 million	36.5625
4	$20 million	29.0625
5	$20 million	29.0625
6	$20 million	29.0625
7	$15 million	25.3125
8	$15 million	25.3125
9	$10 million	21.5625
10	$5 million	17.8125

6 SPORTS LEAGUES, MONOPOLY POWER, AND CONSUMER WELFARE

Sports leagues have been characterized as monopolies, that is, the sole producer of a certain sport. For example, MLB is the only seller of major league baseball games and is therefore a monopolist. This is not to say that there are no substitutes for MLB games. In fact, there are many *imperfect* substitutes. There are minor league, college, and high school baseball games. There are other major league sports as well as a wide array of other ways for a fan to spend his or her discretionary income – movies, concerts, vacations, recreation, and dining out to name just a few. However, if a fan wants to see an MLB game in St. Louis, he or she will watch the Cardinals play the visiting team. The Cardinals have a local monopoly in supplying MLB action in St. Louis. Subject to the competition provided by imperfect substitutes, the Cardinals will exploit their local monopoly to maximize their profits.

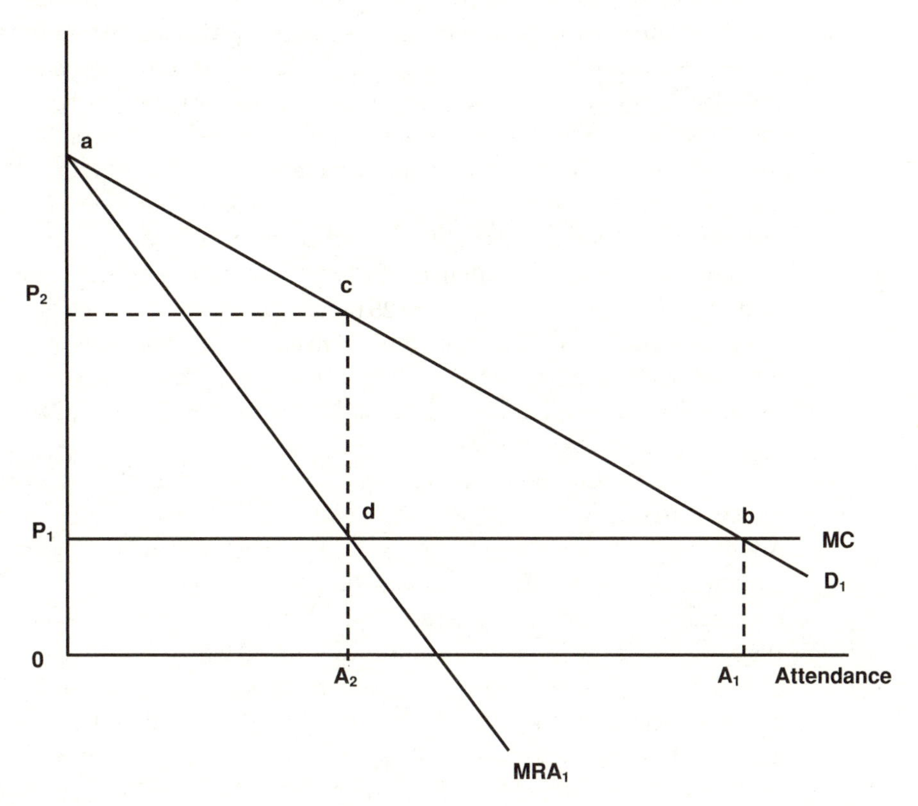

Figure 3.2. To maximize profits, the Cardinals will sell A_2 tickets at a price of P_2. This results in a social welfare loss equal to area *cdb*.

Monopoly power is the ability of a seller to raise prices above the competitive level without losing enough sales that the price increase is unprofitable.[14] Those higher prices are a symptom of what really concerns economists: social welfare losses. Economists object to monopoly because it leads to underproduction of the output and a consequent misallocation of scarce resources. In Figure 3.2, for example, let D_1 be the demand for tickets to a Cardinals game. If the marginal cost of fan attendance is *MC*, then the competitive price will be P_1, which equals MC_1 and A_1 fans will attend the game. Every fan who is willing to pay a price equal to or greater than the cost to society of his or her attendance will be able to attend.

Consumer surplus is the difference between the fan's willingness to pay and the price that is actually paid. In this competitive price case, consumer surplus is equal to the triangular area abP_1. This is as good as it can get – that is, consumer surplus cannot be any larger without imposing losses on the Cardinals. In St. Louis, however, the Cardinals have a local monopoly on MLB games.

[14] This, of course, requires that those substitutes that exist cannot be very close; otherwise consumers would simply buy the cheaper alternative.

Interested in maximizing profits, the Cardinals will not set ticket prices equal to P_1. Instead, they will set a price of P_2, and fan attendance will only be A_2. The Cardinals' profits will be equal to $(P_2 - MC)A_2$, which is equal to the rectangular area P_2cdP_1 in Figure 3.2. This area would be consumer surplus at competitive prices but becomes profit at the monopoly price. Consumer surplus with monopoly pricing is now the much reduced triangular area acP_2. The sum of the fans' consumer surplus and the Cardinals' profit falls short of the consumer surplus at a competitive ticket price. The difference is the deadweight social loss of monopoly, which is equal to the triangular area *cbd*.

This welfare loss is a measure of allocative inefficiency. At A_2, the resources necessary for one more fan to attend the game cost *MC*. The value of those resources as employed in providing a seat for one more fan is given by the fan's willingness to pay, which is P_2. From a social welfare perspective, too few resources are being devoted to providing seats for this game. This is what is meant by allocative inefficiency.

Because of monopoly pricing, attendance is A_2 rather than A_1. This reduces the costs to society by $(A_1 - A_2)MC$, but it reduces the value to fans by the area under the demand curve between A_1 and A_2. The difference is the welfare loss.

This analysis, however, assumes that we can get the benefits of the league organization without the emergence of monopoly power, but this may not be the case. As a result, consumers may be better off with monopoly sports leagues than without leagues at all. We can see this in Figure 3.3, which reproduces all of the information in Figure 3.2. Suppose, for example, that the demand would only be D_2 without the monopoly sports league. Competition would lead to a price of P_1, but the attendance would only be A_3 because demand is D_2 without the value-enhancing benefits of league organization. Consumer surplus in that event would only be equal to the triangular area efP_1, which is clearly smaller than area abP_2. In this example, consumers are better off with the league than without it, but that need not always be the case.[15]

7 LEAGUE EXPANSION

Leagues are usually not static – they expand over time by adding new franchises. Once in a great while, there are rumors of a league contraction, but this has not happened in the past 50 years.[16] Expansion occurs for two reasons. First, expansion may be necessary to take advantage of a profitable opportunity. Second, and more important, leagues expand to preempt the development of a rival league. As population grows and shifts, metropolitan areas that could not have supported a team in the past become financially viable locations. The expansion history of MLB provides a good example. For decades, MLB comprised two eight-team leagues. During that time, the league champions were determined

[15] See Problem 7 at the end of the chapter.

[16] MLB came pretty close to contracting in 2001. Bud Selig, the commissioner, announced that MLB would shrink by two teams. The prime candidates were the Minnesota Twins and the Montreal Expos.

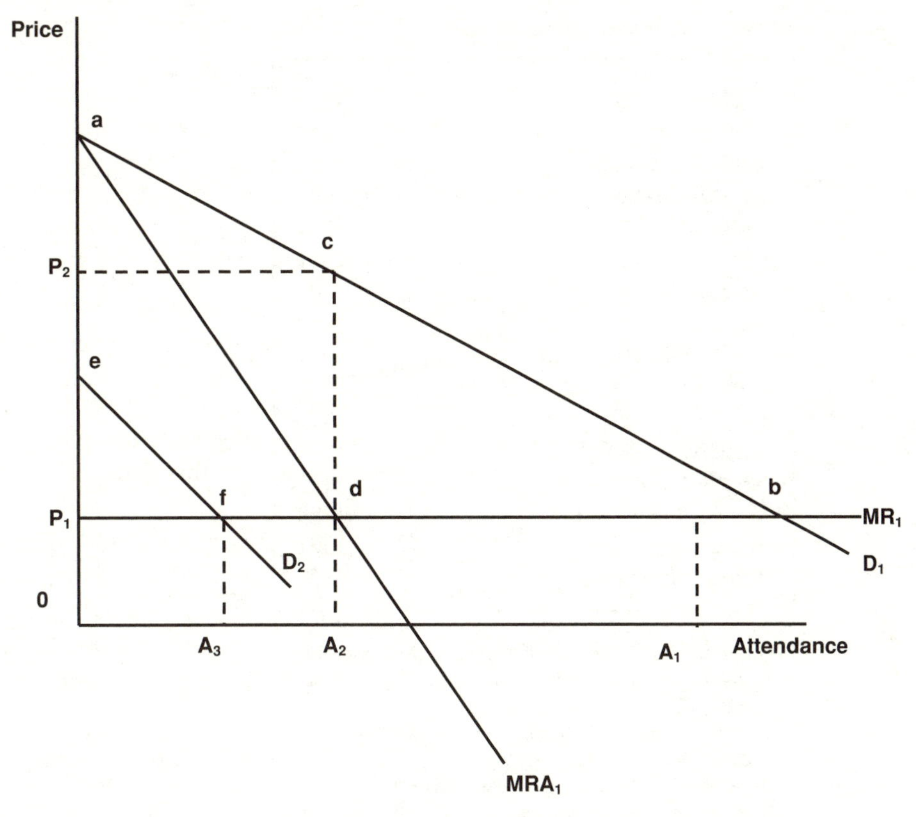

Figure 3.3. Consumers may be better off with a monopoly sports league than with no league at all.

by the final regular season win–loss records in each league. The only postseason play was the World Series, which pitted the National League Champion against the American League Champion.

The current members of the American and National Leagues are listed in Tables 3.2 and 3.3, respectively. Many of the teams have been around for more than 100 years, but there are quite a few young clubs as well. These young clubs are the product of expansion. The American League grew from 8 to 14 teams, and the National League doubled in size from 8 to 16 clubs.

7.1 American League

The American League was founded in 1901. For the next 60 years, it remained the same size: eight teams. There was some geographic relocation but no increase or decrease in size. In 1961, that began to change when the American League grew to 10 teams with the addition of the Anaheim (now Los Angeles) Angels and the new Washington Senators, which became the Texas Rangers in 1972 when the team moved to Arlington. In 1969, the Kansas City Royals entered the American League, which then had an uneven number of teams. In 1977, the American League grew to 13 with the addition of the Toronto Blue Jays and the Seattle Mariners. For the next two decades, the American League had 13 teams.

Table 3.2. American League Origins

Team	Year
Baltimore Orioles[1]	1901
Boston Red Sox	1901
Chicago White Sox	1901
Cleveland Indians	1901
Detroit Tigers	1901
Kansas City Royals	1969
Los Angeles Angels of Anaheim	1961
Minnesota Twins[2]	1901
New York Yankees	1901
Oakland Athletics[3]	1901
Seattle Mariners	1977
Tampa Bay Devil Rays	1998
Texas Rangers	1961
Toronto Blue Jays	1977

[1] Originally the Milwaukee Brewers but became the St. Louis Browns in 1902, and finally the Baltimore Orioles in 1954.

[2] The Washington Senators until 1961 and then became the Minnesota Twins.

[3] Began as the Philadelphia Athletics until 1955, then became Kansas City Athletics until 1968, and finally the Oakland Athletics.

Finally, in 1998, it grew to its present size by adding the Tampa Bay Devil Rays, which are now just the Rays.

7.2 National League

Before there was any expansion, a major dislocation occurred in 1958 when the Giants left New York for San Francisco and the Dodgers left Brooklyn for Los Angeles. This geographic expansion was soon followed by growth from 8 to 10 teams. In 1962, the Houston Astros and New York Mets joined the National League. Three more teams were added in 1969: the Milwaukee Brewers (then the Seattle Pilots until 1970), the San Diego Padres, and the Montreal Expos, which became the Washington Nationals in 2005. At this point, the National League had 13 teams. Some 14 years later, the National League added the Colorado Rockies and the Florida Marlins and thereby expanded to 15 teams. The Arizona Diamondbacks were added in 1998 to bring the National League to its present size of 16 clubs.

The importance of this expansion is plain to see. First, the number of MLB teams nearly doubled from 16 to 30. Second, we now have six teams on the West Coast, two in Texas, and one each in Denver and Kansas City. These areas were previously unserved by MLB. Third, there were some very attractive areas that a new league could have embraced. Just look at the desirable locations

Table 3.3. National League Origins

Team	Year
Arizona Diamondbacks	1998
Atlanta Braves[1]	1871
Chicago Cubs	1874
Cincinnati Reds	1882
Colorado Rockies	1993
Florida Marlins	1993
Houston Astros	1962
Los Angeles Dodgers[2]	1884
Milwaukee Brewers[3]	1969
New York Mets	1962
Philadelphia Phillies	1880
Pittsburgh Pirates	1882
San Diego Padres	1969
San Francisco Giants[4]	1879
St. Louis Cardinals	1882
Washington Nationals[5]	1969

[1] Began as Boston Braves, then became Milwaukee Braves in 1959, and then the Atlanta Braves in 1966.
[2] Started as the Brooklyn Dodgers and then moved to Los Angeles in 1958.
[3] Originally the Seattle Pilots in 1969 and then became the Milwaukee Brewers in 1970.
[4] Initially the New York Giants and then moved to San Francisco in 1958.
[5] Played as the Montreal Expos until 2005 when they became the Washington Nationals.

that might have supported a third major league – San Diego, Denver, Seattle, Houston, Miami, Washington, D.C., and New York. A new league would have posed a considerable threat to MLB's monopoly. First, because it would be an outsider, it would not have to abide by the rules of MLB with respect to location, scheduling, and even rules of play. More important, a new league would have increased competition for players and diluted the quality to some extent. It would also have provided competition for broadcast revenues, merchandise sales, and coaches. The gradual expansion of the incumbent leagues headed off the formation of a rival league and the disequilibrium that it may have brought with it.

A league will not expand into every financially viable location. It is necessary to leave some markets unserved because clubs can get more from their current home city by having a credible threat of moving. If all viable locations are being served, a threat to leave is not credible, and the team will not be able to obtain so many concessions.

8 CONCLUDING REMARKS

In this chapter, we have been concerned with the nature of sports leagues and organizations. We found that they exist because they improve profits for the clubs and incomes for the athletes. We examined some of the rules that leagues impose on their members and the economic rationale for those rules. We also examined the history of league expansion.

PROBLEMS AND QUESTIONS

1. If a league expands into every financially viable location, it will be impossible for a rival league to enter. We know, however, that cities such as Los Angeles, San Antonio (Texas), and Columbus (Ohio), do not have NFL franchises. Why not?
2. A league could own all of the franchises rather than have them owned independently. (Major League Soccer, for example, is owned by a syndicate.) In that way, franchise location could be optimized and resources could be directed to their most valuable use. What is wrong with this strategy?
3. Leagues have rules that members must abide by regarding (a) ownership identity and (b) location/relocation. Explain why each of these is important for the league and its members.
4. The NFL rule against public ownership of the franchises meant that the corporations had to be closely held. Why would the NFL care?
5. Some economists have argued that leagues expand strategically to prevent the formation of rival leagues, but expansion of any business enterprise occurs in response to new (profitable) opportunities. How can we tell the difference between strategic expansion to prevent entry and profit-maximizing expansion?
6. Sports leagues impose a variety of restrictions: (1) exclusive territories, (2) limitation on franchise relocation, and (3) limits on entry, to name a few. How are these restrictions related to the quality of the athletic contests on the field?
7. Return to Figure 3.2 and the surrounding discussion in the text. Construct an example where consumers (fans) are better off without a monopoly sports league.
8. Despite their best efforts, some leagues fold. We have witnessed the demise of football, soccer, and team tennis leagues. Assume that a league of professional badminton teams has formed. Show the conditions under which it might fail.
9. When Florida State joined the ACC and Penn State joined the Big Ten, they improved their profit potential. How did the incumbent members of the ACC and Big Ten benefit? In other words, why were the new members permitted to enter?
10. Suppose that the demand for tickets to a game is given by

$$P = 100 - 0.002A,$$

and the corresponding marginal revenue is

$$MR = 100 - 0.004A,$$

where A is the number of attendees. Assume that the constant marginal cost of fan attendance is 10.

a. What are the price and attendance with competition?

b. How much consumer surplus exists?

c. What are the monopoly price and attendance?

d. How much profit does the monopolist earn?

e. How much consumer surplus is left (if any)?

f. Calculate the social welfare loss.

11. During the negotiations between the NFL and the NFL Players Association in 2011, many commentators criticized both sides for not worrying about the fans. How should these parties have taken into account the fans' interests?

RESEARCH QUESTIONS

1. The NHL has experienced extremely rapid growth since 1970. Trace the evolution of the NHL from 1970 to the present. What has happened to the value of the preexpansion franchises? What were the motivations for expansion?
2. Return to the structure of MLB in 1960. How many teams were in each league, and where were they located? If MLB had not expanded, would you think that rival leagues could have emerged? Suggest the structure of a rival league that could have formed at the time.
3. The Arena Football League (AFL) is in its third decade. How did this league survive when the World Football League (WFL) and the United States Football League (USFL) could not?
4. How has Notre Dame managed to prosper with no conference affiliation?
5. How do college athletic conferences differ from professional sports leagues?
6. Read "No Pro Baseball in Montreal, and Little Hope of Any" by Alan Schwarz, *New York Times*, June 18, 2010. Why is there no hope of a new franchise for a city of 1.6 million people?

REFERENCES AND FURTHER READING

Bae, Sanghoo, and Jay Pil Choi. (2007). "The Optimal Number of Firms with an Application to Professional Sports Leagues." *Journal of Sports Economics*, 8, 99–108.

Blair, Roger D., and David L. Kaserman. (2009). *Antitrust Economics* (2d ed., chapters 9 and 10). New York: Oxford University Press.

Bradbury, J. C. (2007). *The Baseball Economist: The Real Game Exposed*, Chapter 16. New York: Penguin Group.

El-Hodiri, M., and J. Quirk. (1971). "An Economic Model of a Professional Sports League." *Journal of Political Economy*, 70, 1302–1319.

Fort, Rodney, and Young Hoon Lee. (2006). "Stationarity and Major League Baseball Attendance Analysis." *Journal of Sports Economics*, 7, 408–415.

Fort, Rodney, and Joel Maxcy. (2001). "The Demise of African American Baseball Leagues: A Rival League Explanation." *Journal of Sports Economics*, 2, 35–49.

Fort, R., and J. Quirk. (1995). "Cross-Subsidization, Incentives, and Outcomes in Professional Team Sports Leagues." *Journal of Economic Literature*, 23, 1265–1299.

Kahn, Lawrence M. (2007). "Sports League Expansion and Consumer Welfare." *Journal of Sports Economics*, 8, 115–138.

Kesenne, S. (2007). "The Peculiar International Economics of Professional Football in Europe." *Scottish Journal of Political Economy*, 54, 388–399.

Noll, Roger G. (1974). *Government and the Sports Business* (chapter 2). Washington, DC: The Brookings Institution.

Noll. R. G. (2003). "The Organization of Sports Leagues." *Oxford Review of Economic Policy*, 19, 530–551.

Quirk, James, and Mohamed El Hadiri. "The Economic Theory of a Professional Sports League" chapter 2 in Noll, Roger G., ed. (1974), *Government and the Sports Business*, Washington, DC: The Brookings Institution.

Quirk, James, and Rodney Fort. (1992). *Pay Dirt: The Business of Professional Team Sports* (chapters 8 and 9). Princeton, NJ: Princeton University Press.

Quirk, James, and Rodney Fort. (1999). *Hard Ball: The Abuse of Power in Pro Team Sports* (chapter 6). Princeton, NJ: Princeton University Press.

Scully, Gerald W. (1994). *The Market Structure of Sports* (chapter 1). Chicago: University of Chicago Press.

Szymanski, Stefan. (2003). "The Economic Design of Sporting Contests." *Journal of Economic Literature*, 41, 1137–1187.

Szymanski, Stefan. (2004). "Professional Team Sports Are Only a Game: The Walrasian Fixed-Supply Conjecture Model, Contest-Nash Equilibrium, and the Invariance Principle." *Journal of Sports Economics*, 5, 111–126.

Szymanski, Stefan. (2009). *Playbooks and Checkbooks: An Introduction to the Economics of Modern Sports* (chapter 2). Princeton, NJ: Princeton University Press.

Yost, Mark. (2006). *Tailgating, Sacks and Salary Caps.* Chicago: Kaplan Publishing.

4

Competitive Balance

1 INTRODUCTION

At least in team sports, demand by the fans is driven by the uncertainty of the game's outcome. Close games between evenly matched teams are more fun to watch (especially if your team wins) than lopsided games in which one team has no real chance of winning. If one is not a fan of either team, Ohio State versus Wisconsin is far more appealing entertainment than Ohio State versus Toledo. In addition to their being traditional rivalries, Oklahoma versus Texas, Oregon versus Oregon State, and Florida versus Tennessee are popular games because the teams are usually pretty good in an absolute sense and evenly matched. The outcome is uncertain, and therefore, the game has an element of suspense that adds to the fun of watching. As a result, it is important to achieve some semblance of equality of talent, which we may refer to as *competitive balance.*

All major sports leagues are concerned about competitive balance. This term refers to the ability of teams within a league or conference to hold their own on the field. The league recognizes that the demand for tickets would suffer if the Cowboys *always* beat the Redskins who *always* beat the Giants. In that event, the games would not be contests – they would be exhibitions. The need for competitive balance – or at least some semblance of competitive balance – leads to league rules that limit competition off the field to improve competition on the field. These rules include (1) revenue sharing, (2) salary caps and luxury taxes, and (3) reverse-order player drafts.

In this chapter, I provide a definition of competitive balance and examine some statistical measures of competitive balance. We will see that there is an economic explanation for competitive imbalance, and the measures taken to correct this imbalance also receive economic analysis. Finally, we consider some other reasons for the observed imbalance.

2 DEFINITION OF COMPETITIVE BALANCE

Concerned about competitive *imbalance* in Major League Baseball (MLB), Commissioner Bud Selig appointed a Blue Ribbon panel to investigate the perceived problem and offer some corrective actions. The panel's report set out a workable definition of competitive balance:

> In the context of baseball, proper competitive balance should be understood to exist when there are no clubs chronically weak because of MLB's financial structural features. Proper competitive balance will not exist until every well-run club has a regularly recurring hope of reaching post-season play.[1]

This definition would seem to work for any major sports league or conference. The idea, of course, is that teams in a league or conference are able to compete regularly on the field or in the arena on reasonably equal terms.

This definition does not require perfect equality across all teams in the league every year. Perfect equality might not even be desirable – there would never be an underdog to root for and never be an upset. If all teams were perfectly matched, the outcomes would be truly random depending on vagaries such as bad calls by the officials, small mental errors by the coaches and/or players, and "off" days by some of the players. There is some optimal degree of uncertainty in the outcomes that maximizes fan interest. Thus, the league wants a degree of competitive balance to create uncertainty regarding the outcomes but not necessarily perfect equality.

The Blue Ribbon panel's definition does not require that every team be in the thick of the pennant race every year. It does, however, require that every team have a shot on a regularly recurring basis. Thus, we should not see perennial cellar dwellers. There should not be teams that experience losing records year in and year out. If there are such teams and it is due to financial considerations, then *competitive imbalance* exists. In other words, if those perennial cellar dwellers cannot put a better team on the field because they cannot afford to do so, then corrective action will be necessary, or imbalance will persist indefinitely.

Another feature of this definition that is crucial is the "well-run" qualifier. If a club is not well run, it may not be competitive, but that is not the league's fault. Poor coaching, poor drafting of players, poor salary cap management, and a host of other managerial shortcomings can result in perennially weak teams. For example, the Detroit Lions in the National Football League (NFL) have floundered in recent years. Because of their poor record, they have had very favorable draft positions, which they have squandered on players who have been weak performers. This has nothing to do with the financial structure of the league. Instead, it is poor management.[2] The effect on the field will be *competitive imbalance*, but there is not much the league can do to smarten up the management. Each club in the NFL is an independent business entity. Its owners select the managerial personnel and acquire players through the draft trades and free-agent signing. It would be extremely difficult for the league to step in and demand that key managers be removed.

[1] Richard Levin et al. (July 2007), *The Report of the Independent Members of the Commissioner's Blue Ribbon Panel on Baseball Economics*, p. 7.

[2] In 2008, the owners of the Lions had had enough of Matt Millen's poor performance as general manager and fired him.

3 MEASURES OF COMPETITIVE BALANCE

Competitive balance is a vague term, but we know intuitively that it means the teams are roughly equal in ability. We may say that there is more competitive balance within a league when there is more parity and therefore greater uncertainty of outcome in league games, but this is not a measure of competitive balance. Unfortunately, an ideal measure of competitive balance is elusive, but such a measure would be useful for comparison purposes. Here, we examine two statistical measures of competitive balance and provide some illustrations of their use.

3.1 Noll-Scully Measure

One way to measure competitive balance is to use the performance that would occur if all the teams were equal in playing strength as a benchmark. Then we can compare the actual performance to the benchmark to see whether we have competitive balance. The smaller the deviation of the actual performance from the benchmark, the greater the degree of competitive balance.

One such measure, developed by Roger Noll and Gerald Scully, was popularized by James Quirk and Rodney Fort.[3] This measure relies on the standard deviation, which is a statistical measure of variability.[4] The benchmark is the standard deviation of team winning percentages in a league where all the teams are evenly matched. This idealized standard deviation is:

$$\sigma_I = 0.50/\sqrt{N},$$

where N is the number of games that a team plays during the season. This means that the numerical value of σ_I depends on the length of the season. In the NFL, there are 16 games in the regular season, and therefore, σ_I is equal to 0.125.[5] For MLB, however, there are 162 games in the regular season. This longer season leads to a much lower value for σ_I. In fact, for MLB, σ_I equals 0.039.[6] The National Basketball Association (NBA) and the National Hockey League (NHL) play 82 games in the regular season. Consequently, the idealized standard deviation will be approximately equal to 0.055.[7] Although the NFL's σ_I is greater

[3] James Quirk and Rodney Fort, *Pay Dirt: The Business of Professional Team Sports*, Princeton University Press, 1997, pp. 240–292. The measure was proposed by Roger Noll, "Professional Basketball," *Stanford University Studies in Industrial Economics*, 1988. The measure was used by Gerald Scully, *The Business of Major League Baseball*, Chicago: University of Chicago Press, 1989.

[4] The variance of a random variable x is defined to be:

$$\sigma^2 = E\left[(x - \bar{x})^2\right] \sigma^2 = \frac{i}{n} \sum_{i=1}^{n} (x_i - \bar{x})^2,$$

where $\bar{x}$ is the mean or expected value of x. The standard deviation of x is the positive square root of the variance:

$$\sigma = \sqrt{\sigma^2}.$$

[5] $\sigma_I = (0.50)/\sqrt{16} = (0.50)/4 = 0.125.$

[6] $\sigma_I = (0.50)/\sqrt{162} = (0.50)/12.7279 = 0.039.$

[7] $\sigma_I = (0.50)/\sqrt{82} = (0.50)/9.055 = 0.055.$

Table 4.1. Competitive Balance: Noll-Scully Measure, 2005–2010

League	2005	2006	2007	2008	2009	2010
NFL	1.6944	1.448	1.6607	1.6631	1.6115	1.4973
MLB (NL)	1.3876	1.2626	1.2503	1.7289	1.7434	1.6934
MLB (AL)	2.0538	1.8856	1.7105	1.7816	1.9111	1.8291
NHL	1.9789	1.8524	1.1929	1.5863	1.5433	n.a.
NBA	2.4583	2.395	3.0538	3.1165	2.9501	n.a.

AL = American League; n.a. = not available; NL = National League.

than σ_I for the NBA and the NHL, and σ_I for the NBA and NHL is higher than that for MLB, these numerical values are what would result from *perfect* competitive balance. Each team has an equal chance of winning each game. The differences in the numerical values are due solely to the length of the season in each league. The longer the season, the smaller the standard deviation with perfect competitive balance.

The Noll-Scully measure of competitive balance standardizes for varying schedule lengths. It is the ratio of the actual standard deviation to the idealized standard deviation: σ_A/σ_I. The farther this ratio deviates from 1.0, the less competitive balance there is. As an empirical matter, there has been a statistically significant departure from the ideal standard deviation in all of the major sports leagues throughout their history.

The actual standard deviation in a league is given by

$$\sigma_A = \left[1/n \sum_{i=1}^{n} (W_i - 0.5)^2 \right]^{1/2},$$

where n is the number of teams in the league and W_i is the winning percentage of team i.

Quirk and Fort summarized the data on competitive balance in the four major professional sports leagues.[8] Their summary provides the ratio of the actual standard deviation to the ideal (or benchmark) standard deviation on a decade-by-decade basis for each league from 1901 through 1990. The ratio exceeded 1.0 for each league for each decade. Moreover, the deviation was statistically significant in each case, which means that it is unlikely the difference was accidental. In other words, the chances that these results were all flukes are extremely low.

Table 4.1 displays the results for each league for each year during the 2005–2010 period. It is clear that there is still an absence of competitive balance. The NBA has been particularly imbalanced. In MLB, the National League appears to enjoy more balance than the American League. The NFL and NHL are in between.

[8] Quirk and Fort, note 3 above, at p. 247.

Table 4.2. Herfindahl-Hirschman Index – Major League Championships, 1980–2009

League	Herfindahl-Hirschman Index*
Major League Baseball	749
American League	1272
National League	1177
National Football League	884
National Basketball Association	1822
National Hockey League	1058

* $HHI = \sum_{i=1}^{n} s_i^2 (10{,}000)$.

3.2 Herfindahl-Hirschman Index

The Herfindahl-Hirschman Index (*HHI*) is a well-known measure of industrial concentration. It is used primarily to evaluate the competitiveness of industries for antitrust purposes.[9] The *HHI* is the sum of the squared market shares:

$$HHI = \sum_{i=1}^{n} s_i^2,$$

where s_i is the share of firm i and n is the number of firms. If there is pure monopoly, the *HHI* equals 1; if there is pure competition, the *HHI* will be close to zero. To avoid a lot of messy decimals, the antitrust authorities have modified the *HHI*. It is now customary to multiply the squared market shares by 10,000. For example, a share of 0.05 when squared is 0.0025, but when multiplied by 10,000, it becomes 25. In what follows, we will adopt this convention. Now, the *HHI* for a pure monopoly is 10,000 and again approaches zero for competitive industries.

When the *HHI* is applied to competitive balance, we usually look at the concentration of championships over time. Table 4.2 shows the *HHI* for each of the major professional sports leagues over the 1980–2009 period. For the 1980–2009 period, there were 30 championships. Consequently, s_i, which is team i's share of these championships, will be equal to the number of championships won by team *i* divided by 30. Each team's share was squared and multiplied by 10,000. To calculate the HHIs displayed in Table 4.2, these team figures were then summed. The *HHI* for the NBA was the highest among the four major sports leagues at 1822. The lowest *HHI* was for MLB's World Series at 749. The next highest was for the NFL's Super Bowl. The NHL's Stanley Cup concentration was next. To put these entries in perspective, the Department of Justice and the Federal Trade Commission consider an industry to be unconcentrated

[9] The index gained widespread attention because of its use by the antitrust agencies. See 2010 Department of Justice and Federal Trade Commission Merger Guidelines, available at www.doj.gov.

if the *HHI* is below 1,500. It generally considers such markets to be competitive. When the *HHI* exceeds 2,500, a market is deemed to be "highly concentrated." Values of the *HHI* between 1,500 and 2,500 signify "moderate" concentration.

Over the 1980–2009 period, MLB's World Series was unconcentrated with an *HHI* of only 749. Because there were 30 World Series, the lowest possible value of the *HHI* would be 333, which would require a different winner every year. If we had a different winner every year, each winner's share would be 1/30 or 0.033. Squaring this and multiplying by 10,000 yields 11.1 for team 1. Multiplying this by the number of winners (30) provides an *HHI* of 333. The American League and National League Championships were somewhat more concentrated with HHIs of 1,272 and 1,213, respectively.

For the NFL's Super Bowl, the *HHI* was 884, which put it in the unconcentrated category. The NHL's Stanley Cup was similarly unconcentrated with an *HHI* of 1,056. The highest *HHI* value went to the NBA. Its championships were in the moderately concentrated range with an *HHI* of 1,822.

None of the four major sports leagues had complete competitive balance because there were repeat winners. There were fewer in baseball than in any of the others. There were more repeats in basketball. The NFL and the NHL are in between MLB and the NBA. Precisely how we should interpret these results is not clear, but the *HHI* values do not suggest undue concentration in any of them except perhaps basketball.

3.3 A Caveat on Statistical Measures

We have described and illustrated two summary statistics that are meant to capture competitive balance. This concept, however, is complicated and not fully amenable to measurement by a single statistic.[10]

4 ECONOMIC ANALYSIS OF COMPETITIVE BALANCE

From an economic perspective, competitive *imbalance* is easy to understand: wins are worth more in some cities than in others.[11] In other words, the willingness of fans to pay for wins is higher in some cities than in others. Once we recognize that fact, we can appreciate the inevitability of competitive imbalance.[12] In this section, we will formalize this idea and explore some efforts at improving competitive balance.

4.1 Free Agency

Initially, we assume that there is complete, unfettered free agency for the players. In other words, every player is free to play for any club that will hire him or

[10] There are other proposed measures. For example, see Brad R. Humphreys, "Alternative Measures of Competitive Balance in Sports Leagues," *Journal of Sports Economics*, 3, 133–148.

[11] This section depends on the insights of Simon Rottenberg, (1956), "The Baseball Players Labor Market," *Journal of Political Economy*, 64, 242–258. Also, see Quirk and Fort, *supra* note 3, at pp. 240–294.

[12] This insight can be traced to the seminal insights of Simon Rottenberg (1956), "The Baseball Players' Labor Market," *Journal of Political Economy*, 64, 253–256.

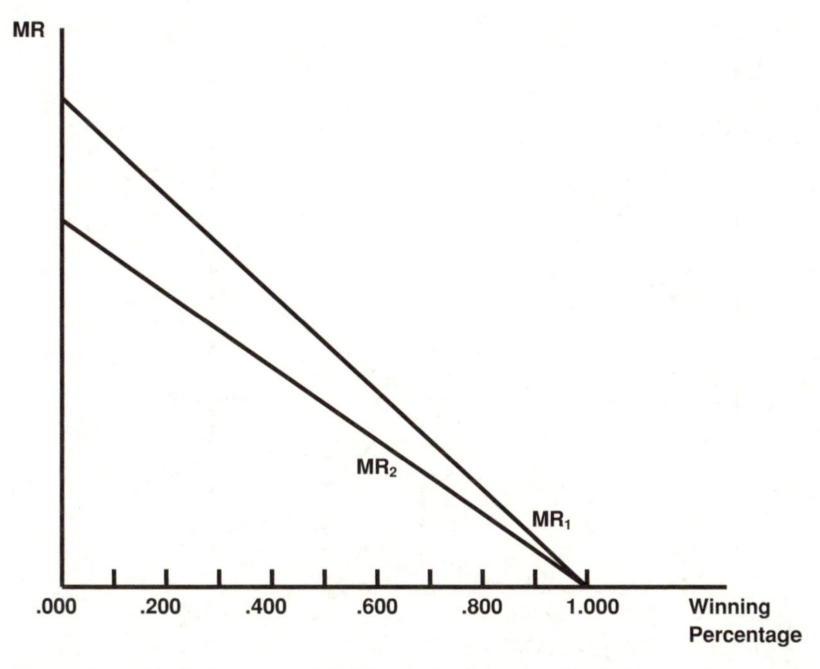

Figure 4.1. Marginal revenue of additional wins is positive but declining in both strong and weak markets.

her. To make the analysis simple, suppose that we have a two-team league. The host city for team 1 is a "strong" market. By "strong," we mean that the demand for wins is high. Demand for a high-quality (i.e., winning) team is a complicated function of population, income, wealth, and local preferences. In contrast, the host city for team 2 is a "weak" market. Its weakness again is a function of population, income, wealth, and local preferences.

A team's total revenue (TR) is a function of the team's winning percentage:

$$TR = TR(W),$$

where marginal revenue (dTR/dW) is positive, but negatively sloped. In Figure 4.1, two hypothetical marginal revenue functions are shown. Team 1's marginal revenue function is MR_1, whereas team 2's is MR_2. Now, the equilibrium requires that MR_1 equal MR_2. The reason for this can be seen by supposing that the equality does not hold. If MR_1 were less than MR_2, team 2 would value an additional win more than team 1 and would pay something to get an added win. It can do this by hiring away some of team 1's better players. Rather than pay these players to keep them, team 1 will let them go because the loss in revenue that results from fewer wins is less than the revenue gain to team 2 of added wins. Thus, team 2 rationally outbids team 1.[13]

In Figure 4.1, we must have $MR_1 = MR_2$, but we must also have the winning percentage add up to 1.000. We can solve this problem graphically by turning one of the marginal revenue functions around, which is what we have done in Figure 4.2. The horizontal axis measures the winning percentage for team 1

[13] This does not mean that mistakes are never made. The Yankees outbid everyone for Carl Pavano, who cost the Yankees nearly $40 million and produced next to nothing for them.

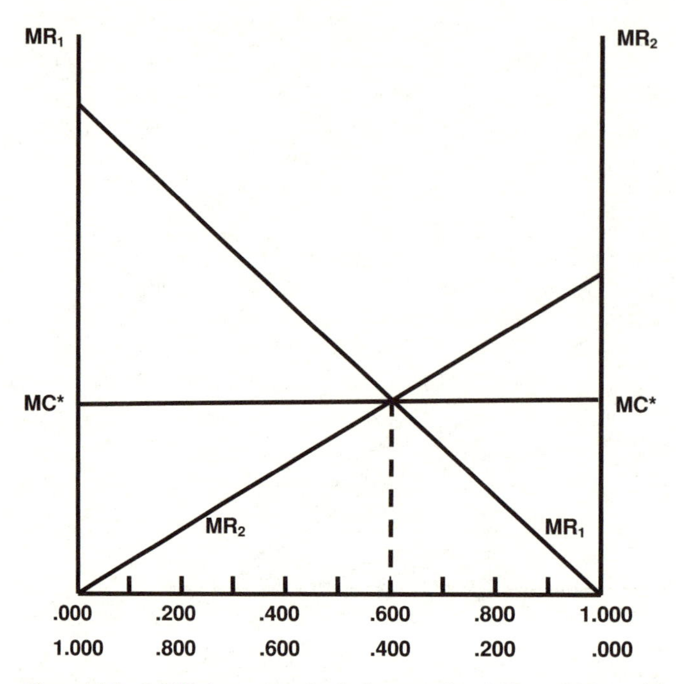

Figure 4.2. Equilibrium occurs in the league when $MR_1 = MR_2$ and the winning percentages add up to 1.000.

from left to right and the winning percentage for team 2 from right to left. The vertical axes measure the marginal revenues for teams 1 and 2 as indicated. At the intersection of MR_1 and MR_2, $MR_1 = MR_2$ *and* the winning percentages – 0.600 for team 1 and 0.400 for team 2 – add up to 1.000. It turns out that team 1 wins more games than team 2 because of market forces.

Consider what happens if some players on team 1 turn out to be better than expected and team 1 wins 70 percent of its games. Team 2 will then win only 30 percent. In Figure 4.2, we can see that MR_2 will exceed MR_1 with team records of .700 and .300. Note that this is not an equilibrium. Because a move from .300 to .400 is worth more to team 2 than it "costs" team 1 to move from .700 to .600, team 2 will bid away some of team 1's talent. This shift in talent will continue until $MR_1 = MR_2$. No further shift in player talent will occur because MR_1 exceeds MR_2 when team 1's record is below .600. As a result, it will be sensible for team 1 to pay its players enough to keep them.

Figure 4.2 also shows that marginal cost of wins (MC) is equal to marginal revenue. How does this happen? Suppose that marginal cost were below MC^* in Figure 4.2 at the point where $MR_1 = MR_2$. If so, MR_1 would be above MC^* at $w_1 = .600$ and MR_2 would also be above MC at $w_2 = .400$. Both teams would then want to increase their winning percentage because profits would rise. As a consequence, each team would try to hire more talent and the player salaries would rise, which causes marginal cost to move toward MC^* in Figure 4.2. The bidding war stops when marginal cost reaches MC^* because profits of each team are maximized at that point.

In contrast, if marginal cost were above MC^* at the point where $MR_1 = MR_2$, both teams would want to reduce their winning records because marginal cost would then exceed MR_1 and MR_2 at $w_1 = .600$ and $w_2 = .400$. To remain employed, player salaries would have to fall and marginal cost would sink back to MC^*.

5 DEALING WITH COMPETITIVE IMBALANCE

Various rules and procedures have been proposed for dealing with competitive imbalance. Most of them do not work because they cannot offset market forces. This is the invariance principle that Rottenberg explained: no matter what we try to do, profit maximization will result in players going to teams where they are highly valued. In this section, we consider the reserve clause, revenue sharing, salary caps, and luxury taxes as means of improving competitive balance.

5.1 Reserve Clause

The reserve clause was a contractual device that prevented players from moving to another team.[14] In the late 1800s, baseball's National League began to incorporate the reserve clause in its standard player contracts. This clause provided that

> It is further understood and agreed that the club shall have the right to "reserve" the said player for the season next ensuing provided that the player shall not be reserved at a salary less than that being paid in the current season.

At the end of one season, the player was bound to his present team for the following season. To play during that second season, the player had to sign a contract for that year. Because the new contract also contained a reserve clause, the player was tied to that team for a third season. This continued indefinitely until the team no longer wanted the player's services. At that time, the player's contract could be sold for cash or traded for the contract of another player. In the event that the player was washed up – that is, could no longer perform at the MLB level – he would simply be released. Gerald Scully has observed that the reserve clause conferred "essentially an indefinite property right in the player's service that was exclusive to the club holding the contract."[15] This bundle of property rights could be sold to another club. If the Dodgers sold a player's contract to the Phillies, then the player had two choices: he could move to Philadelphia, or he could retire. Once he was under contract to the Phillies, he would be bound to them until they no longer wanted his services.

Teams have long argued that the reserve clause was designed to help teams achieve financial stability, which would contribute to competitive balance. If a team in a weak market acquired the rights to a great player, it could keep him

[14] Quirk and Fort, *supra* note 3, at pp. 179–208, provide a good historical account of the rise and fall of the reserve clause.

[15] Gerald Scully (1995), *The Market Structure of Sports*, Chicago: University of Chicago Press, at p. 12.

without incurring much cost. In the first place, the player could not play for anyone else unless his contract was sold or traded. Moreover, the reserve clause prevented a competitive offer, and therefore, the team need not pay full market value to the player. However, just because teams could afford to keep premiere players did not mean that they would do so. After all, the teams are interested in having the team quality that maximizes profit.

If the teams are free to sell players for cash, the reserve system will result in the same distribution of talent and therefore the same records as with free agency. We can see this in Figure 4.2. Consider the case in which each team has a .500 record. At that point, MR_1 exceeds MR_2. It will be optimal for team 2 to sell players to team 1 and for team 1 to buy players from team 2. The quality of team 2 will fall and it will lose more games. The quality of team 1 will rise and it will win more games. The selling of players will stop when equilibrium is restored. Thus, w_1 will rise to .600 and w_2 will fall to .400. The normal forces of economics dictate that we will observe competitive imbalance because imbalance is more profitable than balance.

Each player is an asset to the team that has him under contract. If a player on team 2 is worth more to team 1 than to team 2, the player's contract will be sold to team 1. In a free market, assets flow to their highest valued use because it is economically rational for them to do so. Both teams are better off financially. Of course, the result on the field is quite different: one team improves at the expense of the other team. With respect to competitive balance, the simple reality is that a player reservation system has no effect on competitive balance in a league that permits cash sales of players' contracts.

There are several economic implications of the reserve clause. First, wealth is transferred from the players to the owners because the owners have the property rights. Suppose a player could earn $100,000 as a real estate salesman if he were not playing professional baseball. If this is his next best alternative, this establishes his minimum salary as a baseball player. Suppose that he is currently playing for the Braves where his talents are worth $1.5 million. If he were playing for the Cubs, his talent would be worth $1.9 million. Under the reserve system, the Braves would have to pay him at least $100,000 or he would quit playing baseball. If he were being paid $100,000, the Braves would earn a profit of $1.4 million by keeping him under contract. If the Cubs were to buy his contract for $1.7 million, the Braves would reap additional profits of $300,000. The Cubs must pay the player $100,000, but would still come out ahead by $100,000: $1.7 million to the Braves plus $100,000 to the player equals $1.8 million for a player worth $1.9 million to the Cubs. The teams split up the $1.8 million surplus generated by the player.

Compare this to free agency. With free agency, the player can sign with either the Braves or the Cubs. Because the Braves will pay up to $1.5 million, the Cubs must pay at least that amount. The Cubs will not pay more than $1.9 million. Ultimately, the player will sign with the Cubs for an amount between $1.5 and $1.9 million, say, $1.7 million. In this case, the player gets most of the surplus while the Cubs get a little and the Braves get nothing. Thus, the reserve system distributes wealth away from the player and to the clubs.

A second implication of the reserve system is that income is transferred from the strong-market teams to the weak-market teams, which will improve financial stability, but not competitive balance.

Box 4.1 *Can the Yankees Buy Success?*

The answer to this question is not as clear as one might suppose because it depends on what we mean by "success." In the 1998–2010 period, the Yankees won the most games during the regular season 7 out of 13 times while spending 1.7 to 3.2 times the American League average on their payroll.

During this period, the Yankees won six American League championships and four World Series Championships.

This may not seem like a sufficient return on the payroll expenditures (see Table 4.4), but *Forbes* found that the Yankees franchise was worth considerably more than any other MLB club.

5.2 Revenue Sharing

Teams in strong markets have more revenue than teams in weak markets. As a result, revenue sharing can help the teams in weak markets and enable them to be more competitive in the market for player talent. We would expect that, with better talent, the weak-market teams will improve, and competitive balance will likewise be improved. However, as we will see, this is a myth because teams will still choose the quality level that maximizes profits.

Let us consider sharing gate receipts. Suppose the home team gets a fraction α and the visiting team gets $(1-\alpha)$ of the gate receipts where $0.5 < \alpha < 1.0$. For example, in the NFL, gate receipts were split 60–40, so $\alpha = 0.6$ and $(1-\alpha) = 0.4$. When team 1 increases its winning percentage, it increases its revenue but only gets to keep α of the increase. At the same time, when it increases its winning percentage, team 2's winning percentage falls. This decreases team 2's revenue and team 1 absorbs $(1-\alpha)$ of that decrease in revenue. Thus, team 1's total revenue with revenue sharing (TR_1^*) is:

$$TR_1^* = \alpha TR_1 + (1-\alpha) TR_2,$$

where TR_1 and TR_2 are total revenues without revenue sharing for teams 1 and 2, respectively. Now, consider what happens when team 1 increases its winning percentage. The impact on TR_1^* has two components:

$$MR_2^* = \alpha MR_1 - (1-\alpha) MR_2.$$

As w_1 increases, TR_1 increases, and team 1 gets to keep α of that increase. This is the first term on the right-hand side, αMR_1. However, when w_1 rises, w_2 falls, which causes TR_2 to decrease. Because of revenue sharing, team 1 must absorb $(1-\alpha)$ of that decrease. This is the second term on the right-hand side, $-(1-\alpha) MR_2$. Because the change in w_2 is negative, $(1-\alpha) MR_2$ is deducted from αMR_1 to determine the net effect of increasing w_1.

A similar result holds for team 2:

$$MR_2^* = \alpha MR_2 + (1 - \alpha)MR_1.$$

Because teams 1 and 2 face the same talent market, they will operate where:

$$MR_1^* = MC^* = MR_2^*,$$

but this means that

$$\alpha MR_1 - (1 - \alpha)MR_2 = \alpha MR_2 - (1 - \alpha)MR_1.$$

After algebraic rearrangement, we can see that this requires that $MR_1 = MR_2$. However, when $MR_1 = MR_2$, w_1 is not equal to w_2. In fact, w_1 and w_2 do not change with revenue sharing; that is, revenue sharing does not improve competitive balance. Again, competitive *imbalance* results from the difference in the MR curves, which are completely unaffected by revenue sharing. Thus, weaker teams may be able to "afford" to buy better talent because of revenue sharing, but doing so is not consistent with profit maximization. This result is perfectly consistent with the invariance principle. Even under revenue sharing, player talent flows to the team where it is most valuable.[16]

5.3 Economic Implications of Revenue Sharing

There is no doubt that revenue sharing can help teams in weaker markets improve their financial stability. Suppose team 1 has total revenue of $150 million at the equilibrium while team 2 has $100 million. If the teams share revenues on a 75–25 basis, team 2's fortunes will improve. Total revenue for team 1 will now be:

$$\begin{aligned} TR_1^* &= .75TR_1 + .25TR_2 \\ &= .75(\$150) + .25(\$100) \\ &= \$137.5 \text{ million.} \end{aligned}$$

Total Revenue for team 2 will now be:

$$\begin{aligned} TR_2^* &= .75TR_2 + .25TR_1 \\ &= .75(\$100) + .25(\$150) \\ &= \$112.5 \text{ million.} \end{aligned}$$

Thus, the net effect of revenue sharing in this example is to transfer $12.5 million from team 1 to team 2, which obviously improves matters for team 2. This improvement may be desirable from the league's perspective.

A second implication of revenue sharing is that player salaries are depressed. This may seem a little surprising at first, but revenue sharing acts like a tax of sorts. Because $MR_1^* < MR_1$ at every value of w_1 and $MR_2^* < MR_2$, the amount that teams 1 and 2 are willing to spend on players falls with revenue

[16] The empirical research on the effects of revenue sharing on competitive balance generally supports the economic theory.

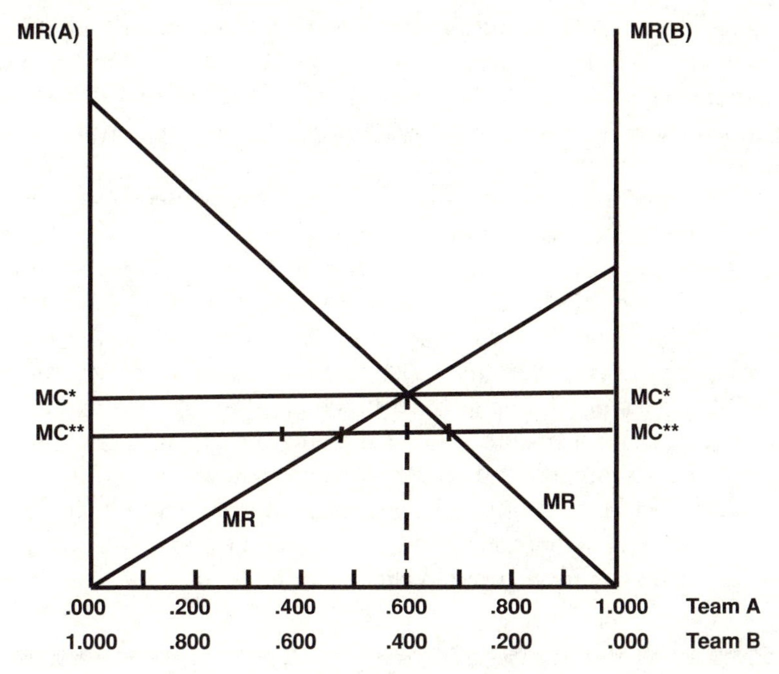

Figure 4.3. A salary cap may permit competitive balance but does not ensure it because competitive balance does not maximize team profits. Moreover, the salary cap may be set too high.

sharing. Thus, wealth is shifted from the players to the owners, which is great for the owners but not so great for the players.

5.4 Salary Caps

A salary cap limits each club's ability to spend money on talent. In the NFL, for example, there is a hard cap on the maximum total amount that a club is permitted to spend on its player's salaries. There is no upper bound on an individual player's salary as long as the total payroll does not exceed the specified maximum for the season in question. This prevents the wealthiest teams from spending any more than their poor cousins. In addition to the NFL, the NBA and the NHL also have salary caps. Among the four major sports leagues, only MLB has no cap.[17]

To analyze the effect of the salary cap, we start with equilibrium in the absence of a salary cap. In Figure 4.3, $MR_1 = MR_2 = MC^*$. Team 1 has a .600 record while team 2 has a .400 record. Concerned about competitive balance, the league imposes a salary cap. To be interesting, the cap must be a binding constraint; it must lie below the unrestricted expenditures. In Figure 4.3, let the average and marginal cost of acquiring the talent necessary to win games be $MC^{**} < MC$ under the salary cap.

[17] MLB tries to inhibit "excessive" spending by imposing a stiff luxury tax, which kicks in when the total payroll exceeds the designated level.

Each team has the same amount to spend. If the management is similarly competent, then the teams should be of equal quality, and their records will be the same: $w_1 = w_2 = .500$. Notice, however, that at $w_1 = w_2 = .500$, we are not in equilibrium. Because $MR_1 > MC^{**}$ at $w_1 = .500$, team 1 will want to spend more than the salary cap will allow. At the same time, $MR_2 = MC^{**}$ and team 2 will be maximizing its profits. The league must therefore police team 1 because it has an incentive to cheat by overspending on players.

If the salary cap were a bit higher so that MC were above MC^{**} but below MC^{*}, team 1 would still want to spend above the cap if $w_1 = .500$ because MR would still be above MC. Now, however, team 2 would not want to spend all of its allotted salary cap. At $w_2 = .500$, MR_2 would be below MC, and the team would be too good. If it could spend less than the cap, it would have a lower quality team, and its record would fall below .500. Team 1 would benefit, and we would have competitive imbalance even with a salary cap.

In contrast, if the salary cap were even lower, MC would fall below MC^{**}. Let $w_1 = w_2 = .500$, both MR_1 and MR_2 would be above MC. This, of course, would lead both teams to want to cheat in order to maximize profits.

Box 4.2 *Gaming the NHL Salary Cap**

The NHL salary cap is supposed to be a binding constraint on the amount that the clubs can spend on players. Some clubs try to game the system by finding creative ways to circumvent the rules. Some have been successful, but some have not.

The idea is simple: use a long-term contract that extends well beyond the player's expected career. In 2009, for example, forward Marian Hossa at age 30 signed a 12-year contract with the Chicago Blackhawks for a total of $62.8 million. The payments in the last four years will be only $1.0 million per year. The NHL was suspicious, but let it stand.

In 2010, the Devils went too far and the NHL rejected Ilya Kovalchuk's contract. He signed a 17-year contract worth a total of $102 million. He was to receive $95 million over the first 10 years and $550,000 per year for the remainder. Since Kovalchuk was 27, the contract envisioned him playing until age 44. The NHL decided that neither the Devils nor Kovalchuk really had such an expectation.

In 2010, the Chicago Blackhawks won their first Stanley Cup (NHL Championship) since 1961. Because the team was relatively young, there was the prospect of a dynasty with multiple Stanley Cups on the horizon. However, the NHL salary cap reared its ugly head. In the summer of 2010, the Blackhawks either traded or cut eight players. As young players develop, their market values increase, and keeping them together becomes impossible under the salary cap. Something has to give, and the result is a decrease in team quality.

* Dave Caldwell, "Arbitrator Rejects Kovalchuk's Deal," *New York Times*, Aug. 9, 2010.

5.5 Reverse-Order Player Drafts

The reverse-order player draft is designed to help less talented teams. Those teams with the worst record during the previous season get to choose first in the draft. For example, following a disastrous 1–15 record in 2007, the Miami Dolphins got the first pick in the 2008 NFL Draft. With this opportunity, they selected Jake Long from the University of Michigan to shore up their offensive line. If Jake Long turns out to be the player the Dolphins hope he will be, the team will improve, and competitive balance will tend to improve.

The problem, of course, is that early-round picks often turn out to be mediocre players. There are many – too many – college stars who cannot make the transition to the NFL. For some players, the NFL can see glaring weaknesses – too small, too slow, too short – and these players go undrafted. However, there are colossal failures that have fooled the NFL clubs. Peyton Manning and Ryan Leaf were the top draft picks in 1998. Manning is on his way to a Hall of Fame career, whereas Leaf flunked out of the NFL in 2002. Leaf played in 1998, but not well. Because of a shoulder injury, he did not play in 1999 at all. After floundering in 2000 and 2001 due to attitude and injury problems, Leaf retired at the start of the 2002 season.

Draft picks can be traded. It is possible to trade a high draft pick for two or more lower picks. It is also possible to trade a draft pick for a current player. For example, during the 2007 NFL Draft, the Oakland Raiders traded Randy Moss to the New England Patriots for a fourth-round draft pick. This trade worked out spectacularly for the Patriots because Moss had a fabulous year as Tom Brady's "go to guy" with 98 receptions and 23 touchdowns.

When teams lose free agents, the NFL commissioner can award extra draft picks to the team. The precise algorithm that determines the compensation is somewhat of a mystery, but some compensation is usually awarded in later rounds.

Even with the reverse-order draft, the invariance principle rears its head once again. Irrespective of how talent is distributed through the draft, players' contracts can be traded and talent will tend to flow to the club that can make the most profitable use of it.

5.6 Luxury Taxes

In MLB, there is no salary cap, but there is a luxury tax, which the Collective Bargaining Agreement refers to as a "competitive balance tax." A club is free to spend as much as it wants on player talent, but if a club's payroll exceeds the specified tax threshold, it will be taxed by MLB. The tax applies to the difference between the actual payroll and the threshold. For example, in 2010, the tax threshold was $170 million. If a club spent this amount or less, it paid no tax. The Yankees, however, spent $215,074,135, so they exceeded the threshold by $45,074,135. For them, the tax rate was 40 percent. As a result, they had to pay a luxury tax of $18,029,654. This, of course, means that the payroll costs in 2010 were actually $233,103,789.

Table 4.3 sets out the tax thresholds for the 2007–2011 seasons. It also provides the tax rates. For 2007, the tax on the Yankees and the Red Sox was

Table 4.3. Luxury Tax Thresholds and Rates

Season	Threshold	Rates* (%)
2007	$148 million	40, 22.5
2008	155	22.5, 30, 40
2009	162	22.5, 30, 40
2010	170	22.5, 30, 40
2011	178	22.5, 30, 40

* For 2007, any club that was over the 2006 threshold was subject to a 40% tax. All others were subject to a 22.5% tax. For 2008–2011, the rate charged depended on whether a club had exceeded the threshold in prior years.
Source: Collective Bargaining Agreement, Article XXIII – Competitive Balance Tax.

40 percent because they had been over the threshold in 2006. For everyone else, the tax rate was 22.5 percent. No other team had to pay any tax in 2007. Based on their past history, the luxury tax rates for New York and Boston were going to be at the 40 percent rate. If a club had gone over the threshold in 2007, it would have paid 22.5 percent in 2007 and would then have had to pay 30 percent in 2008. If it then went over the 2008 threshold, it would have faced the 40 percent rate in 2009.

The luxury tax went into effect in 2003. Between 2003 and 2010, the Los Angeles Angels had to pay a luxury tax of $927,059 in 2004. The Boston Red Sox paid a total of $13.86 million in taxes over the 2004–2007 seasons. The Yankees paid luxury taxes in every single year. Their total salary expenditures for 2003–2007 were $945 million, and they had luxury taxes on top of that of $121.6 million.

The only other club that has ever paid the luxury tax is the Detroit Tigers. The history of payments by year by club is shown in Table 4.4.

Has the luxury tax improved competitive balance? One would certainly think so because it raises the cost of talent at the margin. For example, when the Yankees had an opportunity to acquire Carlos Beltran, they elected not to do so because they would have had to pay about $40 million in luxury taxes over the life of a six-year contract. As one would expect, a 40 percent tax increases the price substantially and can lead even the wealthiest teams to pass.

In another sense, however, the luxury tax has hardly slowed down the Yankees' spending. Table 4.5 shows the Yankees payroll from 1998 through 2010, the ratio of the Yankee payroll to the American League average, and the Yankees' performance in terms of total wins. It is pretty clear that the Yankee payroll is considerably more than the average, and it is reflected in the team performance.

5.7 Economic Implications of Luxury Taxes

The luxury tax has two economic implications. At the margin, player talent costs more to teams that are over the tax threshold. This will lead them to

Table 4.4. History of Luxury Tax Payments, 2003–2010

Year	Team	Tax
2003	New York Yankees	$11,798,357
2004	New York Yankees	25,964,060
	Boston Red Sox	3,148,962
	L.A. Angels	927,057
2005	New York Yankees	33,978,702
	Boston Red Sox	4,148,981
2006	New York Yankees	26,009,039
	Boston Red Sox	497,849
2007	New York Yankees	23,881,386
	Boston Red Sox	6,064,287
2008	New York Yankees	26,862,702
	Detroit Tigers	1,305,220
2009	New York Yankees	25,689,173
2010	New York Yankees	18,029,654
	Boston Red Sox	1,487,149

forgo signing some players who would improve performance on the field. Consequently, competitive balance should improve. Second, the luxury tax will reduce player salaries to some extent. Suppose Lefty Gomez is worth $10 million to a team with no tax worries and $12 million to the Yankees or the Red Sox. Presumably, the player could get $12 million from the Yankees or the Red Sox, who usually have taxes to consider. However, the total cost including the luxury tax would be $16.8 million – the $12 million salary plus $4.8 million in luxury tax. The player is not worth that much to the Yankees or the Red Sox, so he will get $10 million from some other team.

Table 4.5. Yankees Payroll versus American League Average without Yankees, 1998–2010

Season	Yankees	AL Average	Ratio
1998	$73,963,968	42,698,218	1.73
1999	91,990,955	46,508,238	1.98
2000	113,365,877	53,437,796	2.12
2001	109,791,893	63,264,103	1.73
2002	125,928,538	65,044,797	1.94
2003	149,710,995	61,786,712	2.42
2004	182,835,513	61,657,997	2.96
2005	208,306,817	65,262,457	3.19
2006	194,663,079	74,923,614	2.60
2007	189,639,045	85,394,352	2.22
2008	209,081,577	88,291,223	2.37
2009	201,449,289	85,127,720	2.37
2010	206,333,389	88,572,108	2.33

6 CONCLUDING REMARKS

Competitive balance is a concern of all professional sports leagues. Imbalance can lead to reduced fan interest and a general decline in profitability. However, the problem stems from the fact that fans are not equally willing to support a winner. Put differently, winning is worth more to some teams than to others. The result is that market forces lead to competitive imbalance. Efforts to cope with this imbalance have included reserve clauses in player contracts, revenue sharing, salary caps, reverse-order player drafts, and luxury taxes. These have proved to be largely ineffective in dealing with competitive imbalance.

PROBLEMS AND QUESTIONS

1. In 2005–2007, Roger Federer and Rafael Nadal totally dominated men's professional tennis. Does this indicate an absence of competitive balance on the ATP tour?
2. Tiger Woods dominated the PGA Tour for a decade. Is there an absence of competitive balance? Since attendance and TV ratings are higher when Woods is participating in a tournament, can we conclude that competitive balance is unimportant?
3. The Duke, Rice, Stanford, and Vanderbilt football teams struggle in their respective conferences year in and year out. Can you explain why this occurs?
4. Assume that professional teams are profit maximizers. Consequently, each team will strive to achieve the profit maximizing win–loss record. How would a club select the optimal win–loss record?
5. Some people believe that free agency spells disaster for sports leagues:

   Free agency means that the wealthy teams in large markets will buy all of the star players, and there will be severe competitive imbalance.

   Carefully analyze this claim from an economic perspective.
6. Explain why the profit maximizing behavior of teams can lead to competitive *imbalance*. Under what conditions will competitive balance emerge from the profit maximizing behavior of teams in a sports league?
7. Most major sports leagues try to discourage the sale of player contracts for cash. Why?
8. Suppose that there is a reserve clause in the standard player contract. Hammerin' Hank is paid $200,000 by the Dodgers even though his value to the team is $800,000. For the Giants, Hank's value would be $1.2 million.
   a. Will the Dodgers sell Hank's contract to the Giants? Explain why or why not.
   b. If Hank's contract were sold, how much would he be paid to play for the Giants?
   c. If Hank's contract were sold, how much would the Dodgers get for him?

9. During the 2007 season, the Atlanta Braves were looking for some offensive punch to bolster their pennant chances. They acquired Mark Teixeira from the Texas Rangers for Jarrod Saltalamacchia and four minor-league players. Explain the economic logic of this trade.
10. In 2007, the Boston Red Sox had a payroll of $163.1 million. How much was their luxury tax bill?
11. Coming off a great senior year at the University of Nebraska, Tank Jones was drafted by the St. Louis Rams. Jones's three-year contract called for a $9.3 million signing bonus. His annual salary was $400,000 in year 1, $600,000 in year 2, and $900,000 in year 3.
    a. For salary cap purposes, what was his annual compensation?
    b. What was the economic value of the contract on signing day?
12. Do you see any economic reason why a league might want the large market teams to be in the playoffs with disproportionate frequency?
13. Writing about the Tamp Bay Rays' talented outfielder, Carl Crawford, Ben Shpigel proclaimed that "Crawford, with Talent Cultivated by Rays, May Be Too Good to Stay" (*New York Times*, September 12, 2010).
    a. What does this headline mean?
    b. Where is Carl Crawford now?
14. Suppose that revenues are shared as follows. Each club sends αTR to the league headquarters. These funds are pooled and divided evenly among all teams. Show that the invariance principle holds with this revenue-sharing scheme.

RESEARCH QUESTIONS

1. Examine the records of the Pac-10 teams over the past 10 years. Focus only on conference games and titles. Does it look like there is competitive balance using the Blue Ribbon panel definition?
2. Use the ratio of actual to ideal standard deviations of winning percentages as a measure of competitive balance. Looking only at conference games, do you find competitive balance in the SEC?
3. What is the *HHI* for championships in the Big Ten over the past 20 years?
4. Go to StubHub.com or one of the other ticket resellers and see whether there is a difference between the price of a Michigan–Ohio State game ticket and a Michigan–Indiana ticket.
5. Babe Ruth's contract was sold by the Boston Red Sox to the New York Yankees. Find five other examples of great players whose contracts were sold to clubs in larger cities.
6. When MLB collects luxury taxes from the Yankees and Red Sox, what does it do with them? Does it matter?

REFERENCES AND FURTHER READING

Balfour, A., and Porter, P. K. (1991). "The Reserve Clause in Professional Sports: Legality and Effect on Competitive Balance." *Labor Law Journal*, 42, 8–18.

Berri, D. J., S. L. Brook, B. Frick, A. J. Fenn, and R. Vicente-Mayoral. (2005). "The Short Supply of Tall People: Competitive Imbalance and the National Basketball Association." *Journal of Economic Issues*, XXIV, 1029–1041.

Bradbury, J. C. (2007). *The Baseball Economist: The Real Game Exposed* (chapter 6). New York: Penguin Group.

Cain, Louis P., and David D. Haddock. (2006). "Measuring Parity: Tying Into the Idealized Standard Deviation." *Journal of Sports Economics*, 7, 330–338.

Chang, Y-M., and S. Sanders. (2009). "Pool Revenue Sharing, Team Investments, and Competitive Balance in Professional Sports: A Theoretical Analysis." *Journal of Sports Economics*, 10, 409–420.

Crooker, John R., and Aju J. Fenn. (2007). "Sports Leagues and Parity: When League Parity Generates Fan Enthusiasm." *Journal of Sports Economics*, 8, 139–164.

Depken, Craig A. II. (2002). "Player Talent in Major League Baseball." *Journal of Sports Economics*, 3, 335–353.

Depken, C. A., II, and D. P. Wilson. (2006). "NCAA Enforcement and Competitive Balance in College Football." *Southern Economic Journal*, 72, 826–845.

Dobson, S., and Goddard, J. (2004). "Revenue Divergence and Competitive Balance in a Divisional Sports League." *Scottish Journal of Political Economy*, 51, 359–376.

Eckard, E.W. (1998). "The NCAA Cartel and Competitive Balance in College Football." *Review of Industrial Organization*, 13, 347–369.

Eckard, E. W. (2001). "Free Agency, Competitive Balance, and Diminishing Returns to Pennant Contention." *Economic Inquiry*, 39, 430–443.

Fort, Rodney, and James Quirk. (2004). "Owner Objectives and Competitive Balance." *Journal of Sports Economics*, 5, 20–32.

Fort, R. D. (2006). Competitive Balance in North American Professional Sports. In J. Fizel (Ed.), *Handbook of sports economics research* (pp. 190–208). Armonk, NY: M.E. Sharpe.

Fort, R. D., and Y. H. Lee. (2008). Attendance and the Uncertainty-of-Outcome Hypothesis in Baseball. *Review of Industrial Organization*, 33, 281–295.

Gustafson, E., and L. Hadley. (2007). "Revenue, Population, and Competitive Balance in Major League Baseball." *Contemporary Economic Policy*, 25, 250–261.

Hadley, Lawrence, James Ciecka, and Anthony C. Krautmann. (2005). "Competitive Balance in the Aftermath of the 194 Players' Strike." *Journal of Sports Economics*, 6, 359–378.

Horowitz, I. (1997a). "The Increasing Competitive Balance in Major League Baseball." *Review of Industrial Organization*, 12, 373–387.

Humphreys, Brad R. (2002). "Alternative Measures of Competitive Balance in Sports Leagues." *Journal of Sports Economics*, 3, 133–148.

Kahane, L. H. (2003). "Comments on 'Thinking About Competitive Balance'." *Journal of Sports Economics*, 4, 288–291.

Kesenne, Stefan. (2004). "Competitive Balance and Revenue Sharing: When Rick Clubs Have Poor Teams." *Journal of Sports Economics*, 5, 206–212.

Kesenne, Stefan. (2005). "Revenue Sharing and Competitive Balance: Does the Invariance Proposition Hold?" *Journal of Sports Economics*, 6, 98–106.

Koning, R. H. (1999). *Competitive Balance in Dutch Soccer* (SOM Research Report 99B04). Faculty of Economics, University of Groningen.

Krautmann, A. C., and Hadley, L. (2006). "Dynasties Versus Pennant Races: Competitive Balance in Major League Baseball." *Managerial & Decision Economics*, 27, 287–292.

Larsen, Andrew, Aju J. Fenn, and Erin Leanne Spenner. (2006). "The Impact of Free Agency and the Salary Cap on Competitive Balance in the National Football League." *Journal of Sports Economics*, 7, 374–390.

Lee, Y. H. (2009). The Impact of Postseason Restructuring on the Competitive Balance and Fan Demand in Major League Baseball. *Journal of Sports Economics*, 10, 219–235.

Lee, Y. H., and R. Fort. (2005). "Structural Change in Baseball's Competitive Balance: The Great Depression, Team Location, and Racial Integration." *Economic Inquiry*, 43, 158–169.

Maxcy, J., and M. Mondello. (2006). "The Impact of Free Agency on Competitive Balance in North American Professional Team Sports Leagues." *Journal of Sport Management*, 20, 345–365.

Meehan, Jr., James W., Randy A. Nelson, and Thomas V. Richardson. (2007). "Competitive Balance and Game Attendance in Major League Baseball." *Journal of Sports Economics*, 8, 563–580.

Miller, Philip A. (2007). "Revenue Sharing in Sports Leagues: The Effects on Talent Distribution and Competitive Balance." *Journal of Sports Economics*, 8, 62–82.

Quirk, James, and Rodney Fort. (1992). *Pay Dirt: The Business of Professional Team Sports* (chapter 7). Princeton, NJ: Princeton University Press.

Quirk, J. (2004). "College Football Conferences and Competitive Balance." *Managerial and Decision Economics*.

Rottenberg Simon. (1956). "The Baseball Players' Labor Market." *Journal of Political Economy*, 64, 253–256.

Sanders, Shane. (2008). "A Constructive Comment on 'Rematches in Boxing and Other Sporting Events'," *Journal of Sports Economics*, 9, 96–99.

Sanderson, Allen R. (2002). "The Many Dimensions of Competitive Balance." *Journal of Sports Economics*, 3, 204–228.

Schmidt, Martin B., and David J. Berri. (2001). "Competitive Balance and Attendance: The Case of Major League Baseball." *Journal of Sports Economics*, 2, 145–167.

Schmidt, Martin B., and D. J. Berri. (2003). "On the Evolution of Competitive Balance: The Impact of An Increasing Global Search." *Economic Inquiry*, 4, 692–704.

Schmidt, Martin B., and David J. Berri. (2005). "Concentration of Playing Talent: Evolution in Major League Baseball." *Journal of Sports Economics*, 6, 412–419.

Scully, Gerald. (1989). *The Business of Major League Baseball*. Chicago: University of Chicago Press.

Scully, Gerald. (1995). *The Market Structure of Sports*. Chicago: University of Chicago Press, p. 12.

Surdam, David G. (2002). "The American "Not-So-Socialist" League in the Postwar Era: The Limitations of Fate Sharing in Reducing Revenue Disparity in Baseball" *Journal of Sports Economics*, 3, 264–290.

Sutter, Daniel, and Stephen Winkler. (2003). "NCAA Scholarship Limits and Competitive Balance in College Football." *Journal of Sports Economics*, 4, 3–18.

Utt, Joshua, and Rodney Fort, (2002). "Pitfalls to Measuring Competitive Balance with Gini Coefficients." *Journal of Sports Economics*, 3, 367–373.

Whitney, J. D. (1988). Winning games versus winning championships: The economics of fan interest and team performance. *Economic Inquiry*, 26, 703–724.

Zimbalist, Andrew S. (2002). "Competitive Balance in Sports Leagues: An Introduction," *Journal of Sports Economics*, 3, 111–121.

Zimbalist, Andrew. (2003). *May the Best Team Win* (chapter 3). Washington, DC: Brookings Institution.

II

THE SPORTS BUSINESS

5

Pricing Decisions

1 INTRODUCTION

Professional teams, university athletic departments, event sponsors, and sports facility owners all provide something of value to sports fans and participants. Through their pricing decisions, they extract some of that value for themselves. The more that they extract, the more profit they earn at the expense of the fans and participants. As a result, pricing decisions are critical to their financial success. These pricing decisions also have important welfare consequences because they may result in allocative inefficiency. In this chapter, we examine various pricing models that have been used to extract value from the consumer. We begin with competitive pricing to provide a benchmark for comparison. We then examine various ways to exploit monopoly power: simple monopoly pricing, price discrimination, peak load pricing, bundling, two-part pricing, and pricing complements. Finally, we examine ticket scalping, which is the practice of reselling tickets at prices above the face value.

2 COMPETITIVE PRICING

We begin by examining the results of competitive pricing. Suppose that the demand for tickets to a basketball game is represented by D in Figure 5.1. The marginal cost of each additional spectator is low and we assume that it is constant.[1] When marginal cost is constant, average cost is also constant and equal to marginal cost. The constant marginal and average cost are shown as $MC = AC$ in Figure 5.1. Now, in competitive markets, price is driven to marginal cost by competing sellers. If the organizer of the basketball game were to price at the competitive level, price would be P_1, which is equal to MC, and the number of spectators would be Q_1.

Because price is equal to marginal (and average) cost, the organizer earns no excess (or economic) profit. That is, total revenue will just equal total cost.

[1] In many applications, it is convenient to assume constant marginal cost because it reduces clutter in the figures. Moreover, this assumption is at lease approximately accurate.

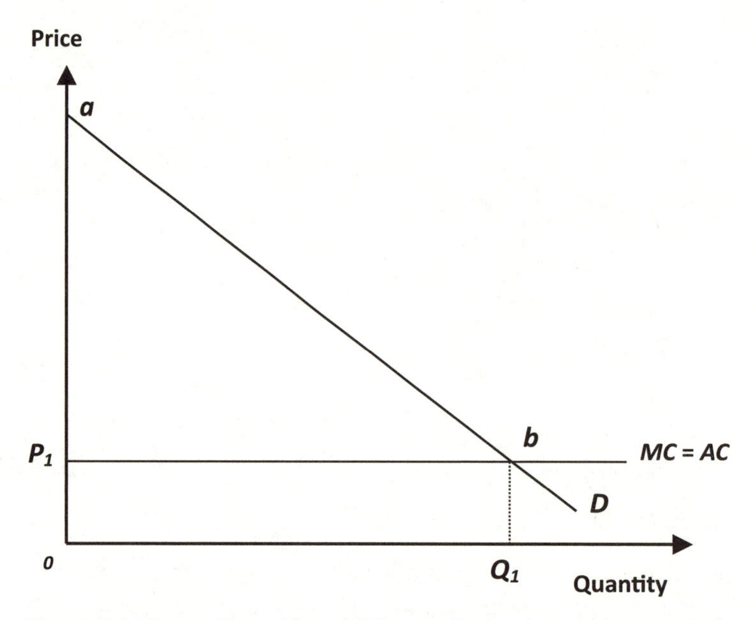

Figure 5.1. Competitive pricing of tickets results in price equal to marginal cost: $P_1 = MC$. With competitive pricing, consumer surplus is equal to area abP_1. Because $P_1 = AC$, the organizer earns no excess profit.

The spectators, however, enjoy substantial consumer surplus. The demand shows their willingness to pay for tickets while the price shows what they must pay in the market. The difference between the two is consumer surplus. As a general matter, *consumer surplus* is the difference between the maximum amount that consumers are willing to pay and the amount that the market forces them to pay. In Figure 5.1, consumer surplus is the area under the demand curve and above the marginal cost curve. In this case, consumer surplus equals the triangular area abP_1. Competition in this market leads to the maximum consumer surplus. Any smaller output will reduce consumer surplus. An output larger than Q_1 will not occur because price would then have to be below cost and firms will never want to sell at below-cost prices. As we will see, there are ways that an event organizer with market power can extract some of this consumer surplus and thereby turn it into profit for himself.

3 SIMPLE MONOPOLY PRICING

There is no doubt that Jerry Jones, the owner of the Dallas Cowboys, knows that he provides the only NFL game in Dallas. The USTA knows that it is the only supplier of the U.S. Open Tennis Championship in New York City every year. If you want to watch an NBA game in Chicago, you go to a Bulls game. These owners and organizers have market power (or monopoly power) because they can control the number of tickets available (up to the maximum seating capacity, of course). They can extract some consumer surplus through simple monopoly pricing.

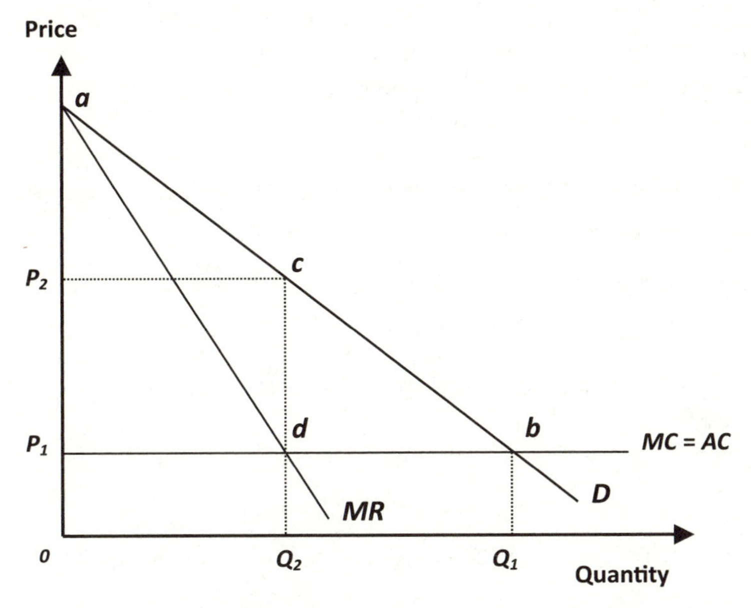

Figure 5.2. Simple monopoly pricing of tickets leads to profit of $(P_1 - P_2)\, Q_2$ and consumer surplus of area acP_2. Monopoly pricing leads to a social welfare loss equal to area *cbd*, which is due to allocative inefficiency.

For a monopolist, profit (π) generally is the difference between total revenue and total cost:

$$\pi = PQ - C(Q)$$

where price P is a function of quantity Q and $C(Q)$ is the cost function. Now, the monopolist maximizes its profit by selling that number of tickets where marginal revenue equals marginal cost. In Figure 5.2, this solution results in a price of P_2 and a quantity of Q_2. Comparing this outcome to the competitive outcome, we can see that the price has risen considerably from P_1 to P_2, whereas the output has declined considerably from Q_1 to Q_2.

With competitive pricing, consumers enjoyed consumer surplus equal to area abP_1. Because of monopoly pricing, consumer surplus shrunk to area acP_2. Here, the organizer earns profit equal to:

$$\pi = (P_2 - AC)\, Q_2,$$

which is area P_2cdP_1. As Figure 5.2 reveals, monopoly pricing has converted some consumer surplus into profit. The monopoly profit of P_2cdP_1 and consumer surplus of acP_2 fall short of the consumer surplus under competitive conditions. The difference is the triangular area *cbd*, which is referred to as the deadweight social welfare loss of monopoly. This social welfare loss is due to allocative inefficiency. The monopolist allocated too few resources to its endeavor. This can be seen in Figure 5.2 by comparing the fan's willingness to pay P_2 with the price and social cost MC. One more ticket would increase welfare by the difference $P_2 - MC$. Although an output of Q_2 is *privately* profitable, it is socially inefficient. Thus, simple monopoly pricing is inefficient because it causes some consumer surplus to disappear. Nonetheless, the monopoly profit shown in Figure 5.2 is the most profit that can be earned if the monopolist sets a single price for all tickets. As we will see, however, a monopolist can do even better by using other pricing strategies.

Box 5.1 ***Comparison of Competition and Monopoly***

Suppose that the demand for tickets is given by the linear demand

$$P = 90 - 0.004\,Q$$

and that the marginal (and average) cost of a fan attendance is constant and equal to $10.

Competitive Solution: Competition results in price equal to marginal cost:

$$90 - 0.004\,Q = 10$$

Solving for Q, we get $Q = 20{,}000$. Consumer surplus will be equal to

$$CS = \tfrac{1}{2}(90 - 10)(20{,}000),$$

which is $800,000.

Monopoly Solution: If a monopolist controlled the market, its marginal revenue would be

$$MR = 90 - 0.008\,Q.$$

Profit maximization requires producing where $MR = MC$:

$$90 - 0.008\,Q = 10$$

or where Q = 10,000. Price is found by substituting into the demand function.

$$\begin{aligned} P &= 90 - 0.004\,Q \\ &= 90 - 0.004(10{,}000) = 50. \end{aligned}$$

The monopolist's profit would be:

$$\begin{aligned} \pi &= (P - MC)\,Q \\ &= (50 - 10)(10{,}000) \\ &= \$400{,}000. \end{aligned}$$

Consumer surplus with monopoly is:

$$\begin{aligned} CS &= \tfrac{1}{2}(90 - 50)(10{,}000) \\ &= \$200{,}000. \end{aligned}$$

Comparison:

Price: $10 under competition and $50 under monopoly.
Attendance: 20,000 fans under competition and 10,000 under monopoly.
Profit: $0 under competition and $400,000 under monopoly.

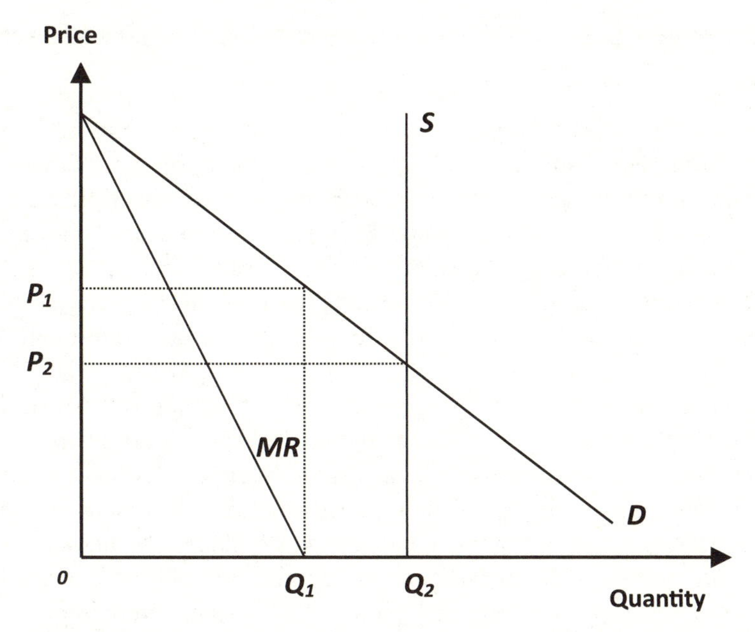

Figure 5.3. If a sports facility is too large, profit maximization requires selling Q_1 tickets at a price of P_1, which leaves $Q_2 - Q_1$ seats empty.

3.1 Empty Seats and Ticket Pricing

We have all seen instances when there are many empty seats at a ball game. How does that make any sense? Clearly, prices must be too high if there are empty seats. A mistake must have been made when choosing the price to charge, right? Not necessarily.

Actually, the problem may well be that there are too many seats for the demand. In other words, the facility is too big. For simplicity, suppose that the marginal cost of an additional spectator is zero. Tickets should be priced to maximize profit, which means maximizing total revenue because marginal cost is zero. In Figure 5.3, we can see that that occurs at a price of P_1 and a quantity of Q_1. (How do we know that?) If the stadium has a capacity of Q_2, there will be $Q_2 - Q_1$ empty seats – that is, there will be an excess supply of *seats* but not of *tickets.* There is sufficient demand to sell out, but only at a price of P_2. Reducing price to P_2, however, will reduce total revenue. (How do we know?) Consequently, the empty seats do not necessarily signify a pricing error. Instead, they signify a capacity error.

3.2 Ticket Pricing and Demand Elasticity

A profit-maximizing monopolist operates where marginal revenue equals marginal cost. We know that marginal revenue is the change in total revenue due to a small change in output:

$$MR = \Delta TR/\Delta Q + \Delta(PQ)/\Delta Q.$$

Box 5.2 ***Prices Rising, Prices Falling***

Prices of tickets may be adjusted because of changes in demand, changes in cost, or both.* For example, the Chicago Bears reached the Super Bowl following the 2006 season. In March 2007, the Bears raised their ticket prices. About 73 percent of all seats are "club" seats. The price of club seats increased by $5. Prices for the nonclub seats rose by $8 or $9. Ticket prices for Bears games at Soldier Field now range from $65 to $104. The most likely explanation for the increase in ticket prices is increased demand due to fan excitement over the Bears' success.

The Boston Red Sox increased the price of a box seat to $105 for the 2007 season. This increase can be traced to two main factors: improvements to Fenway Park and signing Daisuke Matsuzaka. The increased ticket prices, however, were not driven by these higher costs. Instead, they were driven by the increased demand resulting from the improved ballpark and team.

During the 2005–2006 season, the principal owner of the Charlotte Bobcats saw too many empty seats at home games. The average attendance at Bobcats games was about 1,000 below the NBA average. He recognized that ticket pricing could be a source of the problem. At the time, the Bobcats were in last place. For a last-place team, demand may have been too low to support the price structure.

Through several mediocre years, the New York Knicks continued to sell out every home game, but a horrible 2005–2006 team led to a 15 percent reduction in season ticket sales. Early in the 2006–2007 season, the Knicks failed to sell out for the first time in more than 400 consecutive games at Madison Square Garden. Poor team quality and no marketable star player resulted in a decrease in demand. Price was too high for the quality of the product.

* Sources for this box include the following: Editorial, "Hot Stove Economics," boston.com, Dec. 15, 2006; Michael Silverman, "A $105 Box Seat? It'll Be Fenway Reality in 2007," Herald.com, Nov. 16, 2006; Erik Spanberg, "Bobcats to Study Lowering the Prices," *Sports Business Journal*, Feb. 20, 2006; Richard Sandomir, "Good Seats and Plenty of Them for the Knicks," *New York Times*, Nov. 9, 2006.

Now this leads to the following relationship between marginal revenue and the elasticity of demand:

$$\begin{aligned} MR &= P + Q(\Delta R/\Delta Q) \\ &= P(1 + (Q/P)(\Delta P/\Delta Q) \\ &= P(1 + 1/\eta), \end{aligned}$$

where η is the elasticity of demand.

Because marginal cost is necessarily positive, marginal revenue must be positive if profits are maximized. This requires that demand be elastic – that is, the absolute value of η must be larger than 1.

Sports franchises are generally considered local monopolies, and therefore, demand should be elastic. This does not conform to empirical reality, however. Ticket prices appear to fall in the inelastic region of the demand curve. This, of course, is an interesting and perplexing characteristic of pricing in professional sports teams.

This phenomenon has been studied widely, and the results are remarkably consistent. Beginning with Roger Noll's seminal work, empirical studies have consistently found that demand is price inelastic.[2] In several studies, attention has centered on the National Football League (NFL) ticket pricing. For example, Welki and Zlatoper investigated individual game attendance over the 1991 NFL season and found that a $1 rise in the average ticket price resulted in a minor decrease in attendance.[3] In further work, Welki and Zlatoper analyzed a larger data set covering different years and found results that supported their earlier findings.[4] Most recently, Coates and Humphries looked at attendance over a 10-year period and found that the price variable was statistically significant.[5] This means that price may have had a discernible effect on demand. Again, demand appeared to be price inelastic. Krautmann and Berri have offered a possible explanation.[6] Fans do not simply buy the privilege of watching a game. They also buy an assortment of complements: stadium parking, programs, food, drinks, and souvenirs. The more fans in attendance, the higher the sales of these complements. In that event, it makes sense to reduce ticket prices somewhat to attract more fans and earn profits on the sale of complements.

4 PRICE DISCRIMINATION

Instead of selling each ticket at the same price, a team might find it more profitable to charge different prices to different customers. Economists call this practice *price discrimination* because different buyers are being charged different prices for the same thing. Not all differential pricing is price discrimination. For example, the price of box seats along the third base line is higher than the price of bleacher seats at Yankee Stadium. For a Redskins game, seats in the upper level cost $65, whereas lower-level seats cost $110. Tickets to the Final Four of the National Collegiate Athletic Association (NCAA) Men's Basketball Championship range from $140 in the nosebleed section to $220 for lower-level seats. In these examples, however, there is a quality difference – the more expensive seats are "better" than the cheaper seats and therefore command a

[2] Roger G. Noll (1974), "Attendance and Price Setting," chapter 4 in Noll, Roger G., ed., *Government and the Sports Business*, Washington, DC: The Brookings Institution.

[3] Andrew M. Welki and Thomas J. Zlatoper (1994), "US Professional Football: The Demand for Game-Day Attendance in 1991," *Managerial and Decision Economics*, 15, 489–495.

[4] Andrew M. Welki and Thomas J. Zlatoper (1999), "US Professional Football Game-Day Attendance in 1991," *Atlantic Economic Journal*, 27, 285–298.

[5] Dennis Coates and Brad R. Humphries (2007), "Ticket Prices, Concessions and Attendance at Professional Sporting Events," *International Journal of Sports Finance*, 2, 161–170.

[6] Anthony C. Krautmann and David J. Berri (2007), "Can We Find It at the Concessions? Understanding Price Elasticity in Professional Sports," *Journal of Sports Economics*, 8, 183–191.

Table 5.1. Price Discrimination on the Golf Course

Course	Pricing	
Olomana Golf Links	Nonresidents	$95.00
	Second visit	$80.00
	Kama'aina	
	Juniors	$20.00
	Seniors	$35.00
	All others	$40.00
Turtle Bay Resort	Nonresidents	$175.00
	Hotel guests	$140.00
	Kama'aina	$65.00
The Challenge at Manele	Nonresidents	$225.00
	Resort guests	$210.00
	Kama'aina	
	Juniors	$75.00
	Lanai residents	$80.00
	Others	$100.00
Makaha Valley	International guests	$80.00
	Nonresidents	$60.00
	Kama'aina	$34.00
	Juniors	
	Nonresident	$35.00
	Kama'aina	$20.00

Source: Honolulu Advertiser.

higher price. This is not price discrimination because two different things are being sold.

A really good example of price discrimination is provided by the greens fees charged at golf courses in Hawaii. Every course charges local residents *kama'aina* prices while charging nonresidents a higher price.[7] This pricing practice is very visible and not hidden from consumers. A few examples will show how significant the price differences can be. Table 5.1 reveals that some golf courses (Makaha Valley) even discriminate between nonresidents from the United States and foreign visitors. Some courses (Olomana Golf Links, Makaha Valley) discriminate on the basis of age: seniors, adults, and juniors all pay different prices. Others (The Challenge at Manele) discriminate between local residents from their island and all other *kama'aina*.

4.1 Conditions Necessary for Successful Price Discrimination

Two conditions are necessary for successful price discrimination. First, the seller – a pro team, an event organizer, a facility owner – must be able to identify two or more separate groups that have different demands. If everyone has the

[7] *Kama'aina* is a Hawaiian word that means "long-time local resident." This pricing practice pertains to hotels, rental cars, and admissions to all tourist attractions.

same demand, efforts at price discrimination will not result in different prices. In other words, the optimal prices will be the same for everyone. Even if there are different demands, the seller must still be able to identify them to exploit the difference. If the seller cannot identify the separate demands, he will not know how to set different prices. Second, the seller must be able to prevent or at least minimize arbitrage, which is the practice of buying in the low-price market and reselling in the higher-price market. If arbitrage cannot be prevented, price discrimination will fail because no one will buy in the high-price market. In Hawaii, the presumption is that visitors and local residents have different demands for playing golf. Arbitrage is prevented by requiring that anyone asking for the *kama'aina* rate show a Hawaii driver's license. Arbitrage is nearly impossible because the golfer is buying an intangible privilege to play golf. Consequently, a local resident cannot pay the greens fee and resell it to a visitor.

4.2 Profit Maximization and Price Discrimination

Assuming that the conditions for price discrimination have been met, the seller will want to set prices and outputs to maximize its profit, which is:

$$\pi = P_1 Q_1 + P_2 Q_2 - C(Q),$$

where P_1 and Q_1 are price and output in market 1, P_2 and Q_2 are found in market 2, and $Q_1 + Q_2 = Q$. Profit maximization requires operating where marginal revenue equals the marginal cost:

$$MR_1 = MR_2 = MC,$$

where MR_1 is marginal revenue in market 1, MR_2 is marginal revenue in market 2, and MC is marginal cost.

For the case of two linear demands and constant marginal (and average) cost, the results can be seen in Figure 5.4. The firm equates MR_1 to MC and MR_2 to MC. The heights of the MR_1 and MR_2 curves are equal to each other and equal to marginal cost. The equality of the marginal revenues across markets makes sense. Suppose that MR_1 was not equal to MR_2; for example, suppose that $MR_1 = 10$ and $MR_2 = 5$.

Removing a unit of output from market 2 reduces total revenue by 5, but selling that output in market 1 increases total revenue by 10. Thus, profit can be increased by such reallocations, and therefore, profit cannot be maximized until all such reallocations have been made.

4.3 Ticket Pricing

Consider the pricing decisions of a sports team. In Figure 5.5, the stadium has a fixed capacity at Q^*. There are two separate demands for seats: D_1 and D_2. For simplicity, assume that the marginal cost is approximately zero *once the decision has been made to put on a game.* This is approximately correct because nearly all of the costs incurred by the team are associated with having the facility, the coaches, and the players. When an extra fan attends the game, the

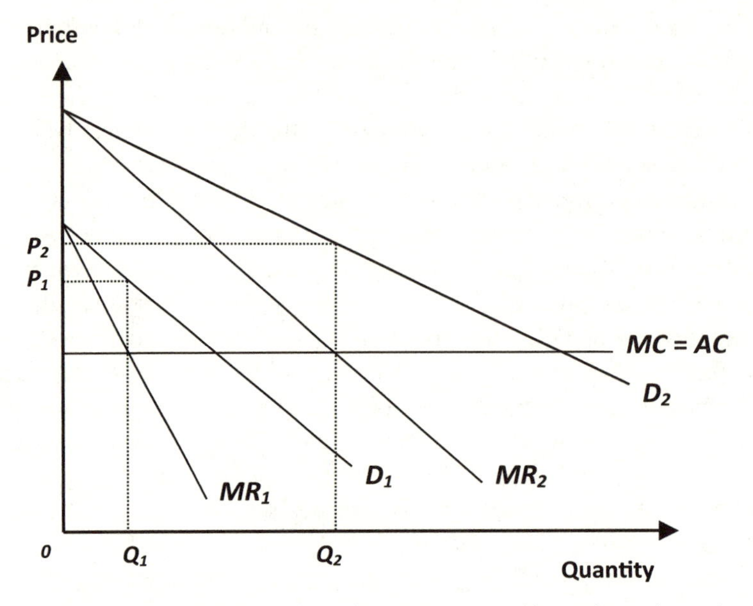

Figure 5.4. Price discrimination with constant cost and linear demands requires equating marginal revenue in each market to marginal cost. Prices are found on the demand curve.

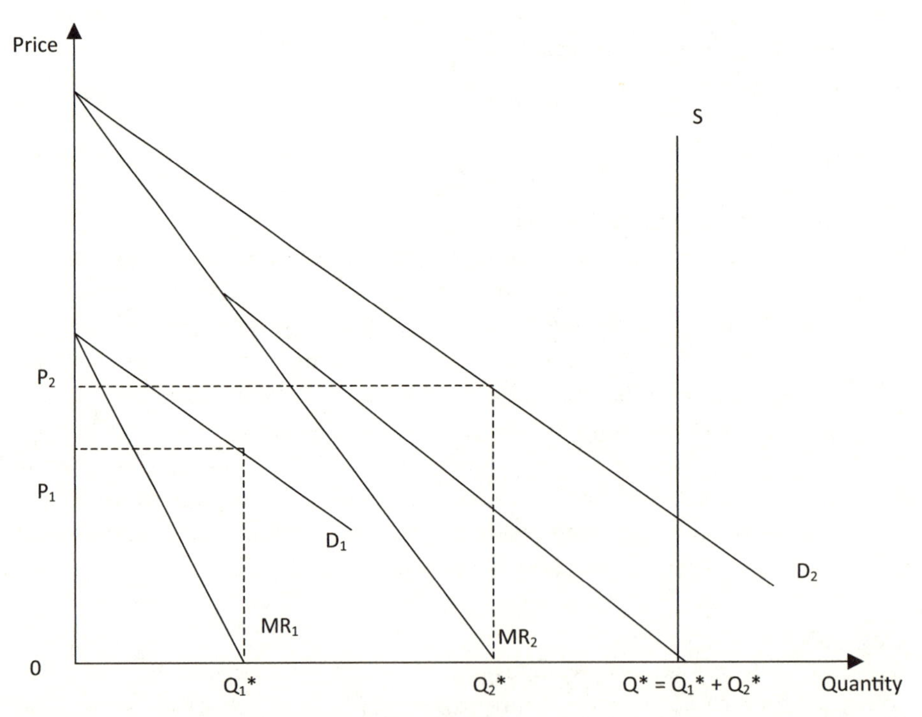

Figure 5.5. When stadium capacity is not a binding constraint, the optimal allocation of Q^* will be found where $MR_1 = MR_2$ such that $Q_1^* + Q_2^* = Q^*$.

added cost is trivial if not actually zero. Assuming for present purposes that the marginal cost is zero, profit is given by:

$$\pi = P_1 Q_1 + P_2 Q_2 - FC,$$

where FC is the fixed cost of putting on the game. Under these conditions, revenue maximization and profit maximization are equivalent because the costs are fixed. For the moment, we will ignore stadium capacity. The profit-maximizing ticket sales and prices are found where in Figure 5.5, this results in $MR_1 = MR_2 = 0$ in the sale of Q_1^* tickets at a price of P_1 in market 1 and Q_2^* tickets sold at a price of P_2 in market 2. In this case, $Q_1^* = Q_2^* = Q^*$. In other words, the stadium capacity is precisely correct to permit profit maximization without any excess capacity.

The foregoing results hold when $Q_1^* + Q_2^* = Q^*$. In other words, the stadium capacity does not prevent the club from selling the total quantity of tickets necessary to operate where $MR_1 = MR_2 = 0$. This is shown in Figure 5.5.

It is very convenient that the optimal number of tickets needed in the two markets adds up precisely to the stadium capacity. This raises two related questions: What happens if $Q_1^* + Q_2^* < Q^*$ and what happens if $Q_1^* + Q_2^* > Q^*$? The answer to the first question can be seen in Figure 5.5. If the size of the stadium is not a binding constraint, then $Q_1^* + Q_2^* < Q^*$. Revenue maximization then requires charging prices P_1^* and P_2^* and selling quantities Q_1^* and Q_2^* in the two markets. There will be unsold seats, but that is of no concern. As we saw in the preceding section, it is not necessary to sell every seat to maximize profit.

Things are more complicated when the stadium capacity is a binding constraint, that is, when $Q_1^* + Q_2^* > Q^*$. In that event, the club cannot operate where $MR_1 = MR_2 = 0$ because the stadium has too few seats. In Figure 5.6, the demand curves and the corresponding marginal revenue curves are the same as those in Figure 5.5. The marginal cost is zero until the capacity of Q^* is reached, and then it is vertical. Profit maximization requires that $MR_1 = MR_2 = MC$ and that the quantities add up. In other words, $Q_1 + Q_2 = Q^*$ *and* $MR_1 = MR_2 = MC$. To find this graphically, we construct the horizontal sum of the marginal revenue curves and label it ΣMR. At each height of MR_1 and MR_2, add the corresponding quantities and plot that height and quantity. Now, the ΣMR curve crosses the vertical portion of MC, which means that all the tickets will be sold. These tickets will be allocated to the two markets such that $MR_1 = MR_2$. In this case, we can see that this requires that $\hat{Q}_1$ and $\hat{Q}_2$ tickets go to fans in markets 1 and 2, respectively. The prices are found on the demand curves for the two markets: $\hat{P}_1$ and $\hat{P}_2$.

5 PEAK LOAD PRICING

When a sports team or a golf course practices price discrimination, it is dealing with *simultaneous* demands. For example, all fans want to watch the same game at the same time, and all the golfers want to play on the same day. *Peak load pricing* deals with *sequential* demands. Golf courses, for example, face

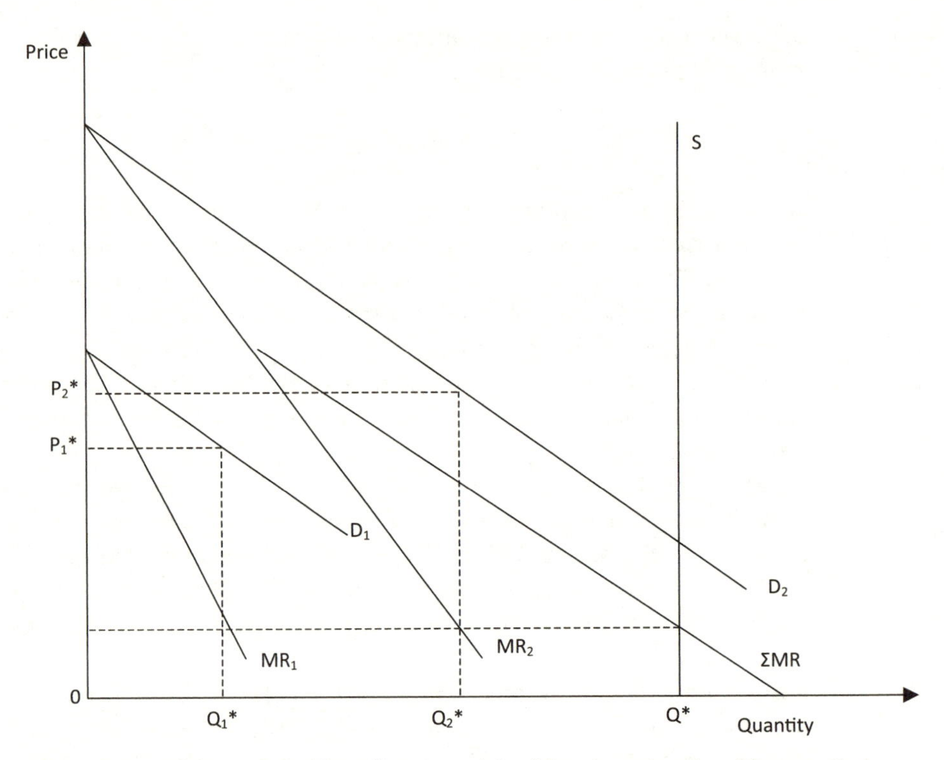

Figure 5.6. Profit is maximized by selling Q_1^* and Q_2^* tickets in markets 1 and 2, respectively.

one demand on weekdays and a different (higher) demand on weekends. Racquetball courts face a prime-time demand and a non-prime-time demand for court time each day. Indoor tennis facilities are packed in the winter but not in the summer. We refer to the demand that stretches a facility's capacity as the *peak demand* and the somewhat reduced demand at other times as the *off-peak demand.* Setting different prices for peak and off-peak customers can result from profit maximization, but these different prices are not discriminatory because a round of golf on Saturday morning is not the same thing as a round of golf on Thursday afternoon. In this case, timing matters.

The golf courses in Hawaii all do some peak load pricing. In fact, greens fees can vary on a single day because morning play is more popular than afternoon play. Table 5.2 contains a few examples of peak-load pricing in action. At every course, the greens fees on the weekends are higher than during the week. For example, at Coral Creek Golf Course, a Thursday morning round costs $50, whereas a Saturday morning round costs $60. In addition, most courses alter their rates on a single day because of peak load considerations. For example, on Saturday and Sunday at the Makaha Resort, the greens fee is $55 before 11:30, $40 from 11:30 until 1:00, and $35 after 1:00. On a Wednesday at the Coral Creek Golf Course, the greens fee is $48 before 1:00 and $35 after 1:00.

Finding the profit-maximizing peak and off-peak price is straightforward – at least in principle. This is illustrated in Figure 5.7 where peak demands and the associated marginal revenue are D_P and MR_P, respectively. Similarly, D_{OP} and

Table 5.2. Peak Load Pricing on the Golf Course

Course	Pricing	
Makaha Resort	Weekdays	$39 before 8:30
		$49 from 8:30 to 1:00
		$39 after 1:00
	Weekends	$59 before 11:30
		$49 from 11:30 to 1:30
		$39 after 1:30
Hawaii Kai Golf Course	Weekdays	$100 before 1:00
		$70 after 1:00
	Weekends	$110 before 1:00
		$70 after 1:00
Coral Creek Golf Course	Nonresident	$130 from 6:04 to 8:12 and 10:52 to 11:56
		$80 from 12:04 to 12:52
		Weekdays and weekends
	Kama'aina	Weekdays
		$50.00
		$40.00 before 7:00 and after 12:00
		$30.00 after 2:00
		Weekends
		$60.00 from 6:04 to 8:12 and 10:52 to 11:56
		$42.00 from 12:04–12:52

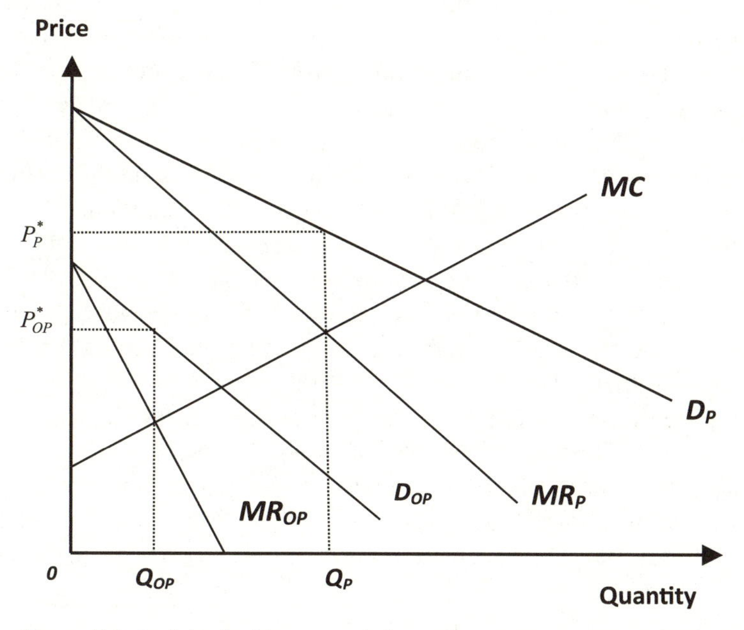

Figure 5.7. Peak load pricing to maximize profit requires operating where MR_P equals MC during peak periods and where MR_{OP} equals MC during off-peak periods.

MR_{OP} are off-peak demand and marginal revenue. Marginal cost is MC. In this model, marginal cost increases with increases in output. When demands are sequential, the facility can be operated at two different rates. Precisely the same principles of profit maximization apply if marginal cost is not constant. The optimal prices will be determined by operating where MR_P equals MC during the peak period and where MR_{OP} equals MC during the off-peak period. The optimal prices are P_P^* and P_{OP}^*.

6 SEASON TICKETS AND OTHER BUNDLING

We say that *commodity bundling* has occurred when a seller combines two or more separate products into one package (or bundle) for a single price. This practice is widespread in and out of the sports business. In the NFL, for example, a season ticket holder must pay for preseason games, which are pretty awful, to get the regular season game tickets. At the University of Florida (and most other major football schools), there are a few games that will not be competitive – they are almost "preseason" (or exhibition) games used to prepare the team for the real schedule (and generate revenue, of course). A season ticket holder must pay for these early games to get tickets to see the more interesting and important games. For many Major League Baseball (MLB) teams, the only way to get good seats for the 30 or so games one really wants to attend is to buy season tickets to all 81 home games.[8]

Bundling extends beyond season ticket pricing policies. At many golf courses, a golfer pays a single fee for a round of golf and the use of a golf cart. Thus, the course bundles permission to play with the use of a golf cart. For big events such as the Super Bowl, a fan can pay a single price for a package that includes airfare, hotel accommodations, ground transportation, parties, and a ticket to the game. As a final example, NFL Sunday was originally marketed as a bundle of satellite access to all NFL games for the entire season. This practice was challenged as an illegal tying arrangement that violated the antitrust laws. As part of the settlement, the NFL changed its marketing practice.[9]

Bundling tickets can improve a team's profits when two conditions are met. First, fans must have different valuations of the tickets being bundled. Second, price discrimination must not be possible. As we will see, when price discrimination is possible, pricing strategy will provide higher profits than bundling provides. A numerical example illustrates this point.

Suppose that Al is a real NFL fan. He loves the eight regular season home games and is willing to pay $1,200 for those tickets. He recognizes that the preseason games are largely meaningless practice sessions, but being a real fan, he is willing to pay $100 for those tickets. Bill, on the other hand, is only willing to pay $1,000 for the regular season tickets, but he is willing to

[8] As the U.S. economy slowed down in 2007–2008, full-season sales began to sag for the 2008 MLB season. The clubs responded by offering smaller packages of 41, 20, and 10 games.

[9] For an extensive analysis of tying arrangements, see Roger D. Blair and David L. Kaserman (2009), *Antitrust Economics* (chapter 18), New York: Oxford University Press.

Table 5.3. National Football League Regular Season Ticket Price Valuations

	Preseason	Regular
Al	$100	$1,200
Bill	$150	$1,000

pay $150 for the preseason games. For these two fans, the team faces the valuations in Table 5.3.

If the tickets were sold separately, the team would maximize its revenues on the preseason games by charging $100 for the two tickets. At $100, Al and Bill both buy the tickets, and revenue is $200. If the price were higher, only Bill would buy them and revenue would only be $150. For the eight regular season games, the revenue maximizing price is $1,000 because both Al and Bill buy them. As a result, selling the tickets separately generates a maximum total revenue of $2,200. Bundling the preseason and regular season tickets improves matters for the club. Notice that Al would pay $1,300 for a season ticket that included both preseason games and regular season games. Bill is willing to pay $1,150 for such a season ticket. Thus, the team can charge $1,150 for a season ticket, and both Al and Bill will buy the season tickets. Bundling, therefore, will increase total revenue to $2,300 – an increase of $100, which goes straight to the bottom line.

Box 5.3 *Importance of Preseason Games**

In the NFL, each team plays four "preseason" games, which do not count toward the regular season standings. These games used to be called "exhibition" games, but the name was changed to improve their image. Upgrading the image seemed useful because season ticket holders were paying for tickets to those meaningless games. Giants co-owner John Mara conceded that the "product" (the game) is often not very good. Due to the fear of injury, most – if not all – of the starters do not play or play no more than the first quarter. LaDanian Tomlinson, the San Diego Chargers' great running back, does not play in any preseason games. Starting quarterbacks often play only one series and then sit on the bench.

In late August 2007, the New York Giants met the New England Patriots in a preseason game. The game was sold out, but only half of the seats were filled. Tom Brady and the rest of the starters did not play. So why does the NFL retain these preseason games?

The answer is simple: money. The tickets to that meaningless Giants–Patriots games cost $90. The preseason games account for 20 percent of the regular season ticket revenue. For the league as a whole, the preseason games generate about $400 million in ticket revenue plus TV revenue plus parking plus concessions. The owners are not willing to give up that revenue, and so we will continue to have meaningless preseason games.

* John Branch, "Only the Prices of Tickets Are in Regular-Season Form," *New York Times*, Aug. 31, 2007.

Table 5.4. Two-Part Pricing at the Swamp, 2009

Booster Class	Contribution	Season Tickets
Orange and Blue	$100–1,799	2
Varsity Club	$1,800–2,299	2
Fightin' Gators	$2,300–2,799	2
Scholarship Partner	$2,800–4,499	2
Scholarship Club	$4,500–8,299	4
Grand Gator	$8,300–14,499	6
Bull Gator	$14,500 +	8

Source: http://gatorboosters.org/html/membership_football_donor_benefits.html.

7 TWO-PART PRICING

Another pricing strategy that can enhance profits by extracting additional consumer surplus is *two-part pricing*. This involves charging a lump-sum access fee and then a separate user fee. Tennis clubs and racquetball clubs often have an annual membership fee that gets you in the door. As the member uses the facility, he or she pays an hourly court fee. Some golf courses are semiprivate, which means that the golfer buys a membership and then pays lower greens fees (that is, user fees) than nonmembers would have to pay. Even private golf clubs may require cart fees that can serve as user fees in addition to annual membership dues.

At the University of Florida, season tickets to Gator football games (for non-UF students) are sold at relatively low prices. To have the privilege of buying season tickets, however, the fan must make a lump-sum "donation" to the University Athletic Association. Depending on the size of the "donation," a fan may purchase from two to eight season tickets. The contribution categories and the numbers of season tickets a fan may buy are shown in Table 5.4. As one can see, if a fan wants to buy eight season tickets at $32 per game for seven home games, the fan must donate at least $14,300. Renewing these season tickets for the next year requires another contribution of $14,300. As a result, the price per game is $2,075, which is a far cry from the face value of $45.

7.1 Two-Part Pricing: Identical Demands

Suppose that a golf club's members all have the same demand for playing golf. The club will maximize its profit on each member to maximize total profit. For purposes of illustration, assume that all members have the following demand curve:

$$P = 80 - Q,$$

with a corresponding marginal revenue of

$$MR = 80 - 2Q,$$

and assume that marginal cost is equal to 10. If the club maximizes profit (π) with a single price policy, the profit that can be earned on each member would be:

$$\pi = (80 - Q)Q - 10Q = 80Q - Q^2 - 10Q.$$

To maximize profits, the club will operate where $MR = MC$:

$$80 - 2Q = 10.$$

Consequently, the optimal number of rounds of golf per member is 35. By substituting 35 for Q in the demand function, we find the optimal greens fee to be

$$P^* = 80 - Q^*,$$

or

$$P^* = 45.$$

The maximum profit per member is then

$$\begin{aligned}\pi &= (P^* - MC)Q^* \\ &= (45 - 10)(35),\end{aligned}$$

or $1,225 per member.

At this solution, each member enjoys some consumer surplus equal to $\frac{1}{2}$ (80–45)(35), which equals $612.50. The club, of course, would like to extract that amount. With two-part pricing, the club can do just that. The club will charge a greens fee equal to marginal cost and charge annual dues equal to the consumer surplus that each member enjoys when price equals marginal cost. Let's see why this is correct.

The demand and marginal cost are displayed in Figure 5.8. If the golf club employs the traditional approach to profit maximization, it will produce that quantity where $MR = MC$, which is 35 in the example, and charge the price that is consistent with this quantity, which is $45 in this case. The profit is given by the rectangle *abcd.* (Why?) In this case, profit is $1,225.

If the golf club uses a two-part pricing strategy, however, profits will be much larger. The greens fees will be set at marginal cost: $P = MC$ or $P = \$10$ in the example. This fee will maximize consumer surplus, all of which the golf club can extract through the lump-sum annual dues. In addition to the profit *abcd,* the use of a two-part pricing strategy permits the club to earn areas *eba* and *bfc.* In other words, the annual dues will be *efd,* which is obviously much larger than *abcd.*

7.2 Two-Part Pricing: Nonidentical Demands

Things are a lot more complicated when the demands are not identical.[10] Primarily, this is because some consumers may not enjoy enough consumer

[10] This section relies on more advanced mathematical methods. The results, however, are worth noting. When demands are not identical, user fees exceed marginal cost, and the lump-sum fees are below the maximum.

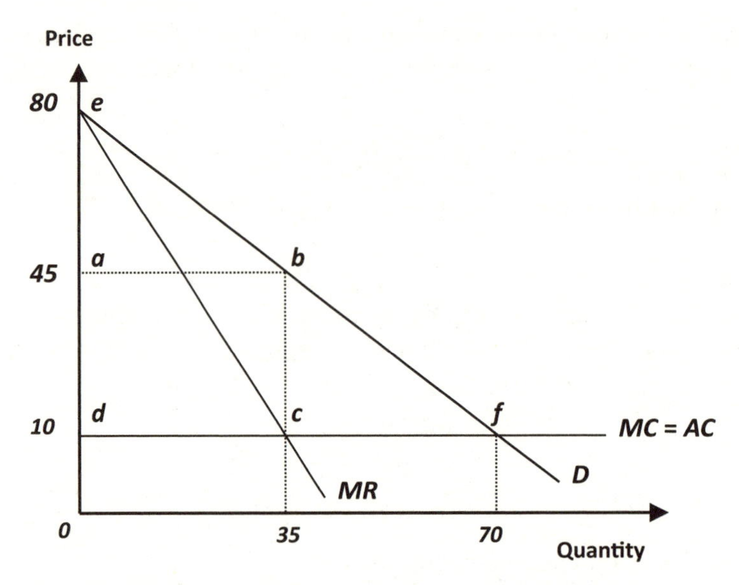

Figure 5.8. Two-part pricing with identical demands that extracts all of the consumer surplus involves a lump sum fee equal to the consumer surplus at competitive prices and user fees equal to the competitive price.

surplus to warrant paying a substantial lump-sum fee, but it may still be profitable to keep them in the market.

For example, suppose there are two members with the following demands:

$$P_1 = 80 - Q_1$$
$$P_2 = 100 - Q_2.$$

At a greens fee equal to marginal cost, consumer surplus for member 1 and consumer surplus for member 2 are

$$CS_1 = \tfrac{1}{2}(80 - P)Q = \$2{,}450$$
$$CS_2 = \tfrac{1}{2}(100 - P)Q = \$4{,}050.$$

Now there are several options available to the club. *First,* suppose that varying dues can be charged. Then the club will set $P = MC = \$10$ and levy annual dues of \$2,450 on member 1 and dues of \$4,050 on member 2. This is obviously price discrimination but not uncommon. For example, member 1 may be a junior member and member 2 is an adult. Because of differences in income, they have different demands.

Second, suppose the annual dues must be the same for all members. If the dues are \$4,050, the club will only sell to member 2, and profit will be \$4,050. Member 1 will be priced out of the market because annual dues of \$4,050 exceeds the consumer surplus of member 1 when the greens fee is set at *MC*, which is \$10.

To determine whether the club should have both members or just member 2, we have to calculate the profit that flows from having both members and compare it to the \$4,050 that would be earned by having only member 2.

Profit maximization is now more complicated. Profit with two-part pricing is

$$\pi = 2CS_1 + (P - MC)(Q_1 + Q_2).$$

The reason why $2CS_1$ is in the profit function is because the annual dues cannot exceed the consumer surplus of member 1, but it will be collected from both members.

Consumer surplus for member 1 is equal to ½(80 − P)Q. From the demand curve, we know that $Q = 80 - P$, so we can write consumer surplus as ½(80 − P)(80 − P). Because there are two consumers, the first term will be (80 − P)(80 − P). In addition, the sum of Q_1 and Q_2 is the sum of the two demand curves: 180 − 2P. Now the profit can be written as:

$$\begin{aligned}\Pi &= (80 - P)(80 - P) + (P - 10)(Q_1 + Q_2)\\ &= (80 - P)^2 + (P - 10)(180 - 2P).\end{aligned}$$

Now profit maximization requires operating where

$$\frac{d\Pi}{dP} = 2(80 - P)(-1) + (P - 10)(-2) + (180 - 2P) = 0.$$

As a result, the optimal price is

$$P^* = 20.$$

Substituting into the demand functions, we find the optimal quantities:

$$\begin{aligned}Q_1^* &= 60\\ Q_2^* &= 80.\end{aligned}$$

Given these greens fees and quantities, we can find consumer surplus for member 1:

$$CS_1 = \frac{1}{2}(80 - 20)(60) = \$1{,}800.$$

As a result, the club profit will be

$$\begin{aligned}\pi^* &= 2(\$1{,}800) + (20 - 10)(60) + (20 - 10)(80)\\ &= \$3{,}600 + 600 + 800 = \$5{,}000.\end{aligned}$$

We should also note that in this case, the greens fee ($20) exceeds marginal cost ($10). The annual dues that are charged to each member are necessarily somewhat smaller than they would be if the greens fees were equal to marginal cost. The club earns more profit by having both members than by having just member 2. This result is not general, however; there will be cases for which it will be profit maximizing to price some members out of the market.

8 PRICING COMPLEMENTS

A sports team sells a variety of complementary goods: a ticket, parking, food, drinks, programs, souvenirs, and so on. The demands for these products are interrelated, and therefore, prices and quantities have to be selected carefully if the team hopes to maximize profits. For example, if ticket prices are set too high, then attendance will fall and there will be an adverse effect on the revenues from parking, food and drink sales, and programs. For simplicity, consider the prices of tickets and food at the game. The number of tickets (T) is a function of their price (P_T) and the price of food (P_F):

$$T = T(P_T, P_F).$$

Similarly, the demand for food (F) at the ballpark is

$$F = F(P_T, P_F).$$

Because tickets and food are complements,

$$\frac{\partial T}{\partial P_F} < 0 \quad \text{and} \quad \frac{\partial F}{\partial P_T} < 0.$$

Thus, if the price of food rises, this will decrease the number of tickets sold. Similarly, if the price of tickets falls (and attendance increases as a result), the quantity of food sold will rise because the demand for food will rise – that is, shift to the right.

For this case, profits are earned on ticket sales and on food sales. These profits are interrelated because the two goods are complements. We can write profit as

$$\pi = P_T T + P_F F - C(T) - C(F).$$

To maximize profit, the team will have to operate where the increment in profit goes to zero:

$$\frac{\partial \pi}{\partial T} = P_T + \frac{\partial P_T T}{\partial T} + \frac{\partial P_F F}{\partial T} - MC_T = 0$$

$$\frac{\partial \pi}{\partial F} = P_F + \frac{\partial P_F F}{\partial F} + \frac{\partial P_T T}{\partial F} - MC_F = 0.$$

To maximize profits, these two equations must be solved simultaneously because the decision on tickets affects profits on food and the decision on food affects the profits on tickets.

The recession that began at the end of 2008 caused several MLB clubs to reconsider their pricing decisions. To prop up ticket sales, several clubs began to offer bargains at the concession stand. The San Diego Padres, for example, introduced a "Five for Five Dollars" special that included a hot dog, a large soft drink, a bag of popcorn, a bag of peanuts, and a cookie. Priced separately, these would cost $13 to $15. The Milwaukee Brewers took a page from the fast-food industry and began offering dollar items. The Pittsburgh Pirates introduced "Dollar Dog Nights." In Cincinnati, the dollar menu includes hot dogs, soft drinks, popcorn, cookies, and ice cream cones. Managerial consultants predict that the trend toward promotional pricing will continue.

The managerial problem associated with setting optimal prices for a wide array of complements can be quite complicated because of the marginal effects on all of these revenue sources.

Table 5.5. Pricing Complements in Major League Baseball, April 2010

Team	Avg. Ticket Price	Beer	Hot Dog	Parking	Program	Total
Boston	$52.32	$7.25	$4.50	$27.00	$5.00	$96.07
Chicago Cubs	$52.56	$6.25	$4.25	$25.00	$5.00	$93.06
San Francisco	$28.79	$5.75	$4.50	$20.00	$5.00	$64.04
NY Yankees	$51.83	$6.00	$3.00	$23.00	$5.00	$88.83
Chicago White Sox	$38.65	$6.50	$3.25	$23.00	$4.00	$75.40
Toronto	$23.84	$6.90	$5.00	$14.29	$4.76	$54.79
St. Louis	$30.14	$6.50	$4.00	$10.00	$2.50	$53.14
Seattle	$25.53	$5.50	$3.50	$17.00	$3.00	$54.53
NY Mets	$32.22	$5.50	$5.00	$19.00	$5.00	$66.72
Houston	$29.29	$5.00	$4.75	$15.00	$4.00	$58.04
Philadelphia	$32.99	$6.75	$3.75	$12.00	$5.00	$60.49
Oakland	$22.04	$5.00	$3.50	$17.00	$5.00	$52.54
LA Dodgers	$29.66	$6.00	$5.00	$15.00	$5.00	$60.66
Washington	$30.63	$6.00	$4.50	$5.00	$5.00	$51.13
Detroit	$23.48	$5.00	$3.00	$5.00	$5.00	$41.48
League Average	$26.74	$5.79	$3.79	$12.24	$3.48	$52.04
Cincinnati	$19.19	$5.25	$1.00	$12.00	$4.00	$41.44
Baltimore	$23.42	$6.25	$2.50	$8.00	$5.00	$45.17
Cleveland	$22.12	$5.50	$4.25	$12.00	$1.00	$44.87
Florida	$19.06	$7.00	$5.00	$8.00	$5.00	$44.06
Pittsburgh	$15.39	$5.00	$2.50	$10.00	$0.00	$32.89
Atlanta	$17.05	$6.75	$4.25	$12.00	$0.00	$40.05
San Diego	$15.15	$5.00	$4.00	$4.00	$0.00	$28.15
Arizona	$14.31	$4.00	$2.75	$10.00	$0.00	$31.06
LA Angels	$18.93	$4.50	$3.00	$8.00	$3.00	$37.43
Texas	$20.65	$5.00	$4.75	$8.00	$5.00	$43.40
Colorado	$19.50	$5.50	$3.25	$8.00	$5.00	$41.25
Minnesota	$31.47	$7.00	$3.75	$6.00	$3.00	$51.22
Milwaukee	$22.10	$5.50	$3.25	$8.00	$0.00	$38.85
Kansas City	$19.38	$6.00	$4.00	$6.00	$5.00	$40.38
Tampa Bay	$19.75	$5.00	$5.00	$0.00	$0.00	$29.75

Source: Team Marketing Report, available at teammarketing.com.

In Table 5.5, we can see the results of some pricing decisions by MLB clubs. For each club, we display the average ticket price, and the prices of an array of complements – beer, hot dogs, parking, and programs. As one can see, there is substantial variation in the prices of individual components across clubs. There are also substantial variations in the aggregate cost of the package of complements. The total was highest in Boston at $96.07. This sum was equal to the Chicago Cubs and $30 more than the San Francisco Giants. Compared with the least expensive (Tampa Bay), Boston was more than $50 higher.

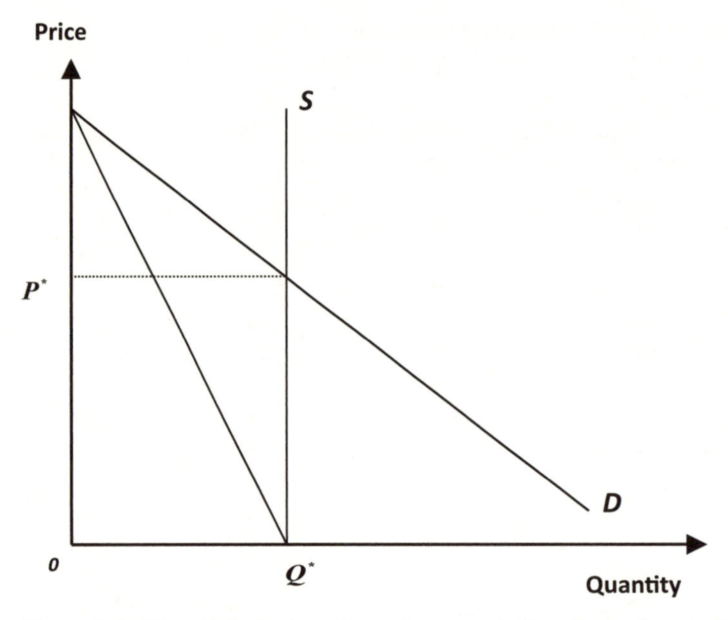

Figure 5.9. When S is inelastic at Q^*, stadium capacity is perfectly aligned with demand. At a price of P^*, all tickets will be sold.

9 TICKET SCALPING: A PRICING FAILURE

When someone sells a ticket with a face value of, say, $50 for more than $50, *ticket scalping* is said to occur. Why would anyone pay more than the face value of a ticket? Usually, it is because the face value is too low and the market fails to clear. Ticket scalping is usually a manifestation of *excess* demand. In other words, at the face price, the quantity demanded exceeds the quantity supplied.

Suppose that Penn State knows what the demand is for its football tickets. We have plotted the demand curve (D) in Figure 5.9 along with the corresponding marginal revenue (MR). Once Penn State commits to putting on a game, the marginal cost of additional spectators is (nearly) zero. Basically, all of the costs are fixed: coaches' salaries, player scholarships, referees, cost of clean up, and so on. Consequently, given that the game will be played, Penn State will maximize its profit by maximizing total revenue. Because profit is

$$\pi = TR - FC,$$

where TR denotes total revenue and FC denotes fixed costs, profit maximization requires that Penn State determine a price and attendance such that $MR = 0$. In Figure 5.9, that will be at P^* and Q^*. If the stadium holds precisely Q^* fans, then the supply of seats will be fixed at Q^* and supply will be perfectly inelastic. In Figure 5.9, the market clears if tickets are offered at P^* and are not transferable.[11] Everyone who wants to pay P^* will be able to attend the game, and there will be no ticket scalping.

[11] If tickets are transferable, some scalping may occur. Can you explain why?

9.1 Student Tickets: A Scalping Opportunity

Suppose that the Penn State students are entitled to buy a ticket at P^*, but do not value the ticket that highly. In other words, at a price of P^*, the students do not want to attend the game. It is in their economic interest, however, to buy the tickets (provided that they are transferable) and resell them at a profit to those who value them more highly than P^*. The students are on the portion of the demand curve to the right of Q^*. Given the inelastic supply of seats, some fans located on the demand curve to the left of Q^* would be unable to buy tickets because the students had priority and bought them. These fans will pay more than P^* and, therefore, the students can earn a profit.

9.2 Tickets to the Final Four

March Madness culminates in the Final Four of the NCAA Men's Basketball Championship. Tickets to the Final Four are in hot demand, and ticket scalpers can command substantial premiums. The face value of the tickets is quite reasonable for a major sports event. For the 2008 edition at the Alamodome in San Antonio, ticket prices ranged from $140 to $220 depending on the proximity to the court:

$220 for lower level
$190 for middle level
$170 for lower rows of upper level
$140 for upper level.

These tickets are hard to buy at the face value. In late March 2008, StubHub offered a lower-level sideline ticket for $4,706. On eBay, there was a pair of tickets offered on a "Buy It Now" basis for $899 – probably in the upper level.

9.3 Demand Shifts and Scalping

Return to the original equilibrium in Figure 5.9. At that point, Penn State has it just right as P^* and Q^* clear the market. Everyone who is wiling to pay P^* can buy a ticket and all tickets are sold. Suppose that Penn State is having a good year and is going to face Ohio State in a big game. As a result, demand for that game shifts to the right, but Penn State cannot (or does not) adjust the ticket price nor can it increase the number of seats. Now there will be excess demand at P^*. To clear the market, the price must rise to the point where the new demand intersects the inelastic supply curve. Some people will be willing to sell their tickets at a price above P^*, and we should expect to see some ticket scalping.

9.4 Example: The Masters

A ticket to the Masters Golf Tournament has a face value of $175. Each ticket entitles a golf fan to attend all four rounds of the golf tournament. Currently, there are literally thousands of people on the waiting list for tickets. It has been estimated that those at the end of the queue have a 10-year wait in front of them, and the waiting list is closed. In fact, except for a brief period in 2000, the waiting list has been closed since 1978.

In 2010, two people from Gainesville, Florida, paid $500 each for tickets. Because the face value was $175, they obviously were scalping "victims." At the tournament, a man in the parking lot offered to buy the tickets for $2,000 per ticket. Clearly, a further scalping opportunity was there. For some reason, the tournament organizers do not want to set prices at a level that will clear the market. By selling a fixed number of tickets at prices far below the market clearing level, the organizers create the excess demand necessary for scalping to occur. Because the tournament organizers are forgoing additional revenue and profit, it is not clear why they do this.

Box 5.4 *An Update on Tickets to the Masters*

By 2008, the face price of the four-day ticket to the Masters had risen to $175, but this price is still far below the market value of the tickets. Just before the 2008 tournament, StubHub, an online ticket reseller, had several options available:

Thursday at $1,086
Thursday and Friday at $2,348
Saturday at $925
Sunday at $1,000
Saturday and Sunday at $2,236
Thursday through Sunday at $3,695

The options available on eBay were fewer and more expensive. There were two four-day tickets at auction. The bidding was at $4,000 for the pair but had not yet closed. There was another pair offered on a "Buy It Now" basis for $7,499.99.*

* The prices quoted were found on StubHub and eBay on March 26, 2008.

9.5 Antiscalping Laws

Scalping is illegal in many states and cities. In Denver, for example, scalping is a misdemeanor that carries a maximum fine of $999 and up to a year in jail. In other places, scalping is limited to one degree or another. In Georgia, for example, scalping is legal provided that the transactions do not take place within 1,500 feet of the venue, but it is not entirely clear just why scalping should be illegal or restricted. After all, one can readily see that social welfare is improved when a willing buyer and a willing seller consummate a transaction. The good in question ends up in the hands of the person who values it most highly.

Suppose Dave owns a ticket to the Super Bowl, and it is worth $200 to him. To Christina, who is a real football fan, that ticket is worth $1,000. If Dave sells the ticket to Christina for $600, the transaction improves welfare: Dave gives up something worth \$200 to him and receives something (money) worth \$600. Thus, Dave is better off by \$400. Christina gave up \$600 for something worth \$1,000 to her, so she is also better off by \$400. This appears to be a win–win situation that obviously increases social welfare. Both parties are better off and no one is worse off as a result of the ticket sale.[12]

10 CONCLUDING REMARKS

It is pretty clear that sensible pricing decisions are necessary if a seller is going to maximize its profits. This is true for sports teams, event organizers, and facility owners. In this chapter, we started with simple competitive and monopoly pricing. We then moved on to more complicated pricing methods that yield greater profits than will the simple pricing mechanisms. These alternatives include price discrimination, peak load pricing, and two-part pricing. In some circumstances, pricing related goods is important. In the sports context, we explored the profit motive for bundling together goods such as preseason and regular season tickets into one season ticket. We also worked through the principles of pricing complements. Finally, we examined the causes and consequences of ticket scalping.

PROBLEMS AND QUESTIONS

1. Suppose that demand is given by

$$P = 100 - Q,$$

marginal revenue is

$$MR = 100 - 2Q,$$

and marginal cost is constant at 20.

   a. What single price will maximize a monopolist's profit?
   b. What will be the prices and quantity under two-part pricing?
   c. Calculate the profits for each option.

2. Does price *discrimination* have anything to do with *bias* or *prejudice*? What does it mean exactly?
3. Many universities charge a low price for student tickets and a much higher price for general admissions.
   a. What happens if the university cannot prevent arbitrage?
   b. What does your school do to prevent (or at least impede) arbitrage?
4. In a "Pepper and Salt" cartoon in the *Wall Street Journal*, a hacker is informed that he will be charged an "environmental impact fee" because

[12] There is a risk in dealing with a scalper – the ticket may be counterfeit. In that event, the purchaser will be a victim of fraud, which should be illegal because it usually decreases social welfare. The scalping is not the problem; it is the fraud.

he has a very high handicap. If poor golfers are charged more than good golfers, explain why that may not amount to price discrimination.

5. Explain why peak load pricing is not price discrimination.
6. Under some circumstances, bundling is a violation of the antitrust laws. Recently, the NFL settled an antitrust class action lawsuit involving "NFL Sunday," which is a package of all NFL Sunday games. The complaint involved the NFL's requirement that the customer buy the whole season. Class members wanted the option of buying some Sundays but not necessarily all Sundays.
   - a. Why should the NFL's requirement be objectionable?
   - b. How is competition harmed by the bundling?
7. In our model of price discrimination, we assumed that consumer demand is unaffected by price discrimination, but that is not always the case. In Hawaii, *kama'aina* pricing at the golf course could backfire. Insulted and/or irritated by this pricing strategy, some visitors may choose not to play golf.
   - a. How would this influence demand?
   - b. Could eliminating *kama'aina* pricing actually increase profit?
8. Assume that all consumers have identical demands:

$$P = a - bQ,$$

and that marginal cost is constant and equal to c. Using a two-part pricing strategy, show that the optimal price equals c and that the profit equals the maximum consumer surplus.

9. Suppose that Al Alum is desperate to see the Notre Dame–USC game but does not have a ticket and the game is sold out. Bill bought a ticket from the University ticket office for $50. Al is willing to pay $250 for a ticket, and Bill is willing to sell for $250.
   - a. If Bill sells the ticket, is he guilty of ticket scalping? Explain.
   - b. Is social welfare improved by Bill's selling to Al? Explain.
   - c. Should the transaction be prohibited? If so, why?
10. Suppose Bull Gator Ben has paid his $14,300 donation and purchased eight season tickets at $32 per game. He discovers that he only needs seven tickets for the Tennessee game and sells the eighth ticket for $150.
    - a. If there are six home games, how much did Ben pay for each ticket?
    - b. Although he sold a ticket for $150, did he make a profit on the sale?
    - c. Is he guilty of ticket scalping?
11. If ticket scalping exists, the face price of a ticket is below market value. Why does the university sell tickets at prices below the market clearing level?
12. Suppose that the demand for tickets is given by

$$P = 50 - 0.00025Q$$

and that marginal revenue is $MR = 50 - 0.0005Q$.

   a. If the marginal cost of an additional spectator is zero, what is the profit-maximizing price?
   b. If the stadium seating capacity is 80,000, what should the price be?

13. Suppose that the demand is given by

$$P = a - bQ,$$

marginal revenue is

$$MR = a - 2bQ,$$

and marginal cost is equal to zero.

   a. What are the competitive price and output?
   b. What is the consumer surplus?
   c. What are the monopoly price and output?
   d. What is the monopoly profit?
   e. What is the consumer surplus?

14. In section 4.3, *Ticket Pricing*, treat quantity as the decision variable and show that the results are precisely the same.
15. Return to section 6, and look at the valuations placed on the tickets by Al and Bill. If the team could engage in price discrimination, would it do so? If it would, what effect would that have on profits?
16. What could be done with the unsold tickets in Figure 5.3?
   a. Give them to youth groups?
   b. Sell at special game-day prices?

   What problems – if any – would these solutions create?

RESEARCH QUESTIONS

1. What arguments support the ban on ticket scalping?
2. Identify the groups that lobby for and against antiscalping laws. Explain their interest in the legislation.
3. There are 35 states that do not prohibit ticket scalping and 15 states do. Using the arguments against ticket scalping, can you see why some states have antiscalping statutes and others do not?

REFERENCES AND FURTHER READING

Alexander, Donald L. (2001). "Major League Baseball: Monopoly Pricing and Profit-Maximizing Behavior." *Journal of Sports Economics*, 2, 341–355.

Blair, Roger D., and David L. Kaserman. (2009). *Antitrust Economics*. New York: Oxford University Press.

Ferguson, D. G., K. G. Stewart, J. C. H. Jones, and A. Le Dressay. (1991). "The Pricing of Sports Events: Do Teams Maximize Profit?" *Journal of Industrial Economics*, 39, 297–310.

Fort, R. (2004). "Inelastic Sports Pricing." *Managerial and Decision Economics*, 25, 87–94.

Kesenne, S., and W. Pauwels. (2006). "Club Objectives and Ticket Pricing in Professional Team Sports." *Eastern Economic Journal*, 32, 549–560.

Krautmann, A. C., and D. J. Berri. (2007). "Can We Find It at the Concessions? Understanding Price Elasticity in Professional Sports." *Journal of Sports Economics*, 8, 183–191.

Mulligan, J. G. (2001). "The Pricing of a Round of Golf: The Inefficiency of Membership Fees Revisited." *Journal of Sports Economics*, 2, 328–340.

Noll, Roger G. (1974). *Government and the Sports Business* (chapter 4). Washington, DC: The Brookings Institution.

Porter, P. K. (2007). "The Paradox of Inelastic Sports Pricing." *Managerial & Decision Economics*, 28, 157–158.

Shmanske, S. (1998). "Price Discrimination at the Links." *Contemporary Economic Policy*, XVI, 368–378.

6

Advertising in the Sports Industry

1 INTRODUCTION

Advertising is part of the landscape in both professional and amateur sports. It comes in all shapes and sizes. In 2006, Anheuser-Busch spent more than a quarter of a billion dollars on sports advertising. American Express was a corporate sponsor of the 2006 National Basketball Association (NBA) draft. Sony sponsored the Hawaiian Open golf tournament on the Professional Golf Association (PGA) Tour. The Pittsburgh Steelers play their home games at Heinz Field. We now have "Bears football presented by Bank One," and the White Sox start their home games at 7:11pm because of 7-Eleven's support. Phil Mickelson and Annika Sorenstam tout Callaway Golf, and Tiger Woods is a Nike man. Gatorade is the "official" sports drink of the National Football League (NFL). All of these are examples of advertising in sports, which is a multibillion dollar business.

The reason for all this activity is simple: profit. Advertising (and other forms of promotion) is designed to increase demand for the advertiser's product. Some advertising does this by being informative, whereas other forms do this by being persuasive. In either event, the idea is to increase the quantity demanded at the same price or, viewed differently, to increase the price at the same quantity. Teams advertise their games to increase attendance, whereas leagues and organizations advertise the athletic competition that their members produce. Of course, producers of a wide array of goods and services advertise to sports fans on television and radio as well as at the venue. All of the billions of dollars that are spent on advertising are geared toward improving the advertiser's profit. To be successful, the ads must increase the advertiser's total revenue by more than they increase its total cost.

In this chapter, we begin with a simple economic theory of firm advertising. Next, we take a look at who is doing the advertising. This includes a look at naming rights and sponsorships as well as other forms of advertising. In addition, we examine strategic behavior when it comes to the advertising decision. Finally, we examine league-wide advertising by the NFL and others.

2 OPTIMAL ADVERTISING BY A FIRM

Business firms, which include professional teams, sports facilities such as golf courses, and equipment manufacturers, invest in advertising to improve sales and profits. The amount spent on advertising varies across firms according to the marginal impact that each firm believes that ad spending will have on the bottom line. As we will see, a profit-maximizing firm will increase ad spending until the marginal benefit of an additional unit of advertising equals the added cost, which is the price of an ad slot.

Demand for the firm's product is a function of price and advertising expenditures. Accordingly, we may write the demand function as

$$P = P(Q, A),$$

where P is price, Q is output, and A is total advertising. We assume the usual inverse relationship between price and quantity. In other words, price must be reduced to sell more output. Advertising is supposed to increase the price that can be charged for any given quantity. This, of course, will depend on whether the ads themselves are effective. In principle, an ad campaign could be so offensive to consumers that sales actually suffer, but that campaign would be short-lived, and the ad agency would be replaced. For what follows, we assume that advertising works as intended – that is, it increases demand.

With advertising in the analysis, profit is the difference between total revenue and the costs of production and advertising:

$$\Pi = P(Q, A)Q - C(Q) - wA,$$

where $C(Q)$ is the cost of producing the output and w is the price of an ad slot. To maximize profits, the firm will have to select the optimal output and the optimal amount of advertising. As a result, the firm will produce where marginal revenue equals the marginal cost of production and buy ad slots up to the point where the marginal benefit of another ad slot ($Q\Delta P/\Delta A$) equals the price (w).

The effect of advertising can be seen in Figure 6.1. Price and quantity are measured on the two axes. Along $D(A_1)$, the amount spent on advertising is held constant at wA_1 dollars. When advertising increases from wA_1 to wA_2, the demand shifts to $D(A_2)$. Thus, at a quantity of Q, consumers are willing to pay a price of P_1 when wA_1 is spent on advertising. When more is spent on advertising, consumers are willing to pay P_2 for the same quantity. In this case, the advertising was effective because it increased the value of the good to consumers. As long as the increase in total revenue, $(P_2 - P_1)Q$, exceeds the increase in advertising expenditures, $w(A_2 - A_1)$, the added expenditure is profitable. Further expenditures will be made until that is no longer the case.

2.1 Numerical Example

Suppose that the demand function is:

$$P = 100 - 3Q + 4A^{1/2}.$$

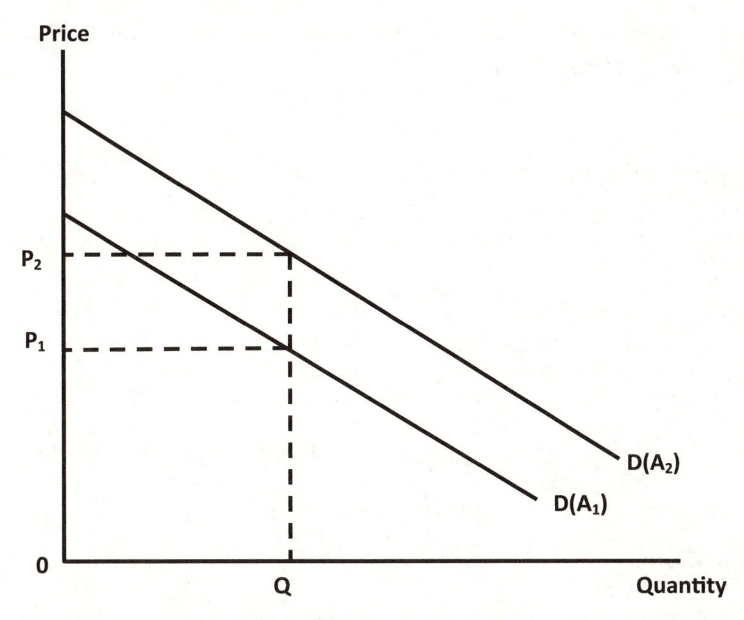

Figure 6.1. The effect of advertising is to shift demand upward so a higher price can be charged for any given quantity.

For this demand, the marginal revenue associated with an increase in output is

$$MR = 100 - 6Q + 4A^{1/2},$$

and the marginal benefit to additional advertising is

$$MB = Q(2A^{-1/2}),$$

and the production cost is:

$$C = 4Q^2 + 10Q.$$

and, therefore, the marginal cost of production is

$$MC = 8Q + 10.$$

For simplicity, assume that the cost of a unit of advertising is \$1, that is, $w =$ \$1. Then, A is the expenditure on advertising, and we can write the firm's profit as:

$$\Pi = PQ - C(Q) - A.$$

By substitution, we have:

$$\Pi = 100Q - 3Q^2 + 4A^{1/2}Q - 4Q^2 - 10Q - A.$$

To maximize profit, the firm must produce where marginal cost equals marginal revenue,

$$100 - 6Q + 4A^{1/2} = 8Q + 10, \quad (1)$$

and at the same time, it must advertise to the point where the marginal benefit equals the cost of advertising,

$$2QA^{-1/2} = 1. \quad (2)$$

These two conditions must hold simultaneously.

First, solve equation (2) for $A^{1/2}$: $A^{1/2} = 2Q$.

Then, substitute for $A^{1/2}$ in (1) and solve for the optimal value of Q:

$$100 - 6Q + 8Q - 8Q - 10 = 0,$$

which yields the optimal output:

$$Q^{*} = 15.$$

Now substitute $Q = 15$ into equation (2) to find the optimal value for A:

$$A^{1/2} = 2Q = 30,$$

and, therefore,

$$A^{*} = 900.$$

Thus, given the demand and cost conditions specified, the firm should produce 15 units of output and spend $900 on advertising to maximize its profits.

3 SPORTS ADVERTISING BY FIRMS

In 2009, the top 100 sports advertisers spent about $6.7 billion on sports advertising. Because their total ad spending was about $23 billion, these firms allocated more than 29 percent of their total ad spending to sports. These expenditures include ads on radio and television sports programming, signage at venues, and print ads in sports publications. Of course, some advertisers devote much more of their ad spending to sports than others do. Among the top 100, some allocated nearly all of their ad dollars to sports, whereas others allocated as little as 3.6 percent.[1]

The top 10 sports advertisers are aggregated by product group, and the results are displayed in Table 6.1. As this table reveals, the top product groups were *cars and trucks* with more than $1.4 billion in sports advertising, *communications* with $951 million, and *beer* with $617 million. These results are intuitively appealing because sports programming attracts an audience that these firms want to target with their advertising.

Table 6.2 shows the PGA tournaments and their sponsors for 2011. These data show that the main sponsors were car companies financial institutions, insurance companies, high-end consumer electronics, and luxury vacation companies. Sponsoring a PGA tournament is a good way for a company to advertise, and thus it makes sense that these companies have the type of clientele who pay attention to professional golf.

[1] The entire list of the top 100 sports advertisers in 2009 can be found in Street and Smith's *Sports Business Resource Guide & Fact Book* 2011.

Table 6.1. Sports Advertising by Product Group, 2009

Product	Advertising Dollars
Beer	$617,170,237
Cars and Trucks	1,366,271,511
Communications	951,731,122
Electronics	393,763,820
Entertainment	249,600,688
Financials	322,548,046
Food and Drink	976,407,156
Insurance	425,237,653
Pharmaceuticals	402,953,841
Retail	347,737,215
Sports	309,972,383
Other	382,845,382

Source: Sports Business Resource Guide & Fact Book 2011.

Producers of goods and services know their customers. For each firm, there is a target audience for its advertising messages: the present and prospective customers. In allocating advertising dollars, the firm wants to reach this target audience in the most effective way. It wants the biggest bang for the buck. Consequently, potential advertisers on sports programming are interested in the economic and demographic characteristics of each sport's fan base. If gender is an important customer characteristic, a potential advertiser would take into consideration that 53 percent of Major League Baseball (MLB) fans are male, whereas 59 percent of National Hockey League (NHL) fans are male. If ethnicity is important, then the fan-base breakdown along ethnic lines – white, African American, Hispanic, Asian – will be of interest. In addition to gender and ethnicity, fan bases are analyzed by household income. Even more refined analyses are done by age groups. In this way, if a producer wants to reach African American males in the 18 to 35 age range with household income above $50,000, the best sports programming can be selected.

There are research firms that compile economic and demographic information that is useful to potential advertisers. Scarborough Research, for example, surveyed more than 220,000 people in 79 U.S. markets to isolate the interest in NBA basketball.[2] They also gathered information on age distribution, gender, and income. As a result, a potential advertiser would know that 8.0 percent of the adults in San Antonio are 18 to 34 years old and are loyal NBA fans. In addition, 28.3 percent of the adults in San Antonio are men and are loyal NBA fans, whereas only 25.1 percent are women. With respect to income, 14.4 percent of the adults in San Antonio are loyal fans and earn more than $75,000. Similar information is available on other cities.

[2] Demographics of NBA Fans," *Sports Business Journal*, October 22, 2007.

Table 6.2. Professional Golf Association Tournaments and Their Sponsors, 2011

Tournament	Sponsor
Hyundai Tournament of Champions	Hyundai
Sony Open	Sony
Bob Hope Classic	Chrysler
Farmers Insurance Open	Farmers Insurance
Waste Management Phoenix Open	Waste Management
AT&T Pebble Beach National Pro-Am	AT&T
Northern Trust Open	Northern Trust
WGC–Accenture Match Play Championship	Accenture
Mayakoba Golf Classic	Mayakoba, OHL
Honda Classic	Honda
WGC–Cadillac Championship	Cadillac
Puerto Rico Open	Seepuertorico.com
Transitions Championship	Transitions Optical
Arnold Palmer Invitational	MasterCard
Shell Houston Open	Shell
The Masters	
Valero Texas Open	Valero Energy Corporation
The Heritage	
Zurich Classic of New Orleans	Zurich Financial Services
Wells Fargo Championship	Wells Fargo
The Players Championship	
Crowne Plaza Invitational at Colonial	Crowne Plaza Hotels
HP Byron Nelson Championship	HP
Memorial Tournament	Nationwide Insurance
FedEx St. Jude Classic	Smith & Nephew
U.S. Open	
Travelers Championship	Travelers
AT&T National	AT&T
John Deere Classic	John Deere
The British Open	
Viking Classic	Viking Range
RBC Canadian Open	RBC Bank
Greenbrier Classic	Eaton Corporation, Franklin American Mortgage Company
WGC-Bridgestone Invitational	Bridgestone
Reno-Tahoe Open	Eldorado Hotel Reno, NV Energy, The Legends at Sparks Marina, EMPLOYERS, Montreux Golf and Country Club
PGA Championship	
Wyndham Championship	Wyndham Worldwide
The Barclays	The Barclays
Deutsche Bank Championship	Deutsche Bank
BMW Championship	BMW
The Tour Championship	Coca-Cola

(*continued*)

(*ctd.*)

Tournament	Sponsor
Justin Timberlake Shriners Hospitals for Children Open	
Frys.com Open	Frys Electronics
McGladrey Classic	McGladrey
Children's Miracle Network Classic	Children's Miracle Network Hospitals
CIMB Asia Pacific Classic	CIMB Group
WGC-HSBC Champions	HSBC Group
Presidents Cup	
Omega Mission Hills World Cup	Omega Watches

Box 6.1 ***Not All Sports Are Equal****

An advertiser has an array of sports programming available, but all sports are not equally good at delivering the target audience. Scarborough Research has used surveys to identify those sports most popular with various ethnic groups. For example, the percentages of African American men who are avid fans of various sports are as follows:

Football	
NFL	41.6%
College	28.3%
AFL	4.3%
Basketball	
NBA	28.1%
WNBA	5.5%
College	20.6%
Auto Racing	
NASCAR	10.0%
NHRA	4.5%
Indy Car	3.3%
Champ Car	2.2%
Golf	
PGA Tour	8.9%
Ladies PGA	1.8%
Baseball	
MLB	18.4%
Minor League	4.2%

AFL = Arena Football League; NASCAR = National Association for Stock Car Auto Racing; NHRA = National Hot Rod Association.

* Bill King, "Tightening up Your Message," *Sports Business Journal*, April 30, 2007.

Table 6.3. Advertising in Sports Publications, 2010

Publication	Advertising Dollars 2010
Sports Illustrated	$138.4 million
ESPN The Magazine	$82.3 million
Golf Magazine	$44.8 million
Golf Digest	$42.3 million
Runner's World	$20.8 million
Golf World	$15.1 million
Bicycling	$11.3 million
Cycle World	$8.8 million
Tennis	$5.6 million
Sporting News	$5.0 million
Transworld Skateboarding	$4.9 million
Transworld Motocross	$2.6 million
Transworld Surf	$2.4 million
SI for Kids	$1.3 million
Transworld Snowboarding	$0.9 million

Source: Sports Business Resource Guide & Fact Book 2011.

3.1 Sports Publications

Advertising can be directed at sports fans by placing ads in magazines that are read by those people (see Table 6.3). The most widely read sports magazine is *Sports Illustrated*, which earned $138.4 million in ad revenue in 2010. *ESPN The Magazine* received $82.3 million in ad revenues. The other sports magazines are aimed more at those who participate in the sport. Golfers, for example, read *Golf*, *Gold Digest*, and *Golf World*, which collectively earned $78.2 million.

3.2 Naming Rights

The New York Yankees play baseball in Yankee Stadium, and the Dallas Cowboys played football in Texas Stadium for many years and now play in the new Cowboys Stadium. These stadium names seem fairly logical given the tenants. However, these teams are rare exceptions because their homes do not bear the name of a corporate sponsor.[3] Nearly everyone in MLB, the NFL, the NBA, and the NHL plays in a ballpark, stadium, or arena that has a corporate name attached. Typically, the team sells the naming rights for a facility that it does not even own. This, of course, provides a source of revenue without any accompanying cost.[4] In Table 6.4, the NFL teams are listed along with the name of their home field. As we can see, many stadiums have been named – for a fee, of course.

Ever alert for a new revenue source, some NFL teams are selling the naming rights to their practice facilities. Because these facilities receive no TV or

[3] There is a high opportunity cost of maintaining tradition. The Yankees have turned down offers of $50 million per year for the naming rights to their new stadium.

[4] See Chapter 2 for further discussion of naming rights and their value to the clubs.

Table 6.4. National Football League Stadiums, 2010

Team	Stadium Name
Arizona Cardinals	University of Phoenix Stadium
Atlanta Falcons	Georgia Dome
Baltimore Ravens	M&T Bank Stadium
Buffalo Bills	Ralph Wilson Stadium
Carolina Panthers	Bank of America Stadium
Chicago Bears	Soldier Field
Cincinnati Bengals	Paul Brown Stadium
Cleveland Browns	Cleveland Browns Stadium
Dallas Cowboys	Cowboys Stadium
Denver Broncos	Invesco Field
Detroit Lions	Ford Field
Green Bay Packers	Lambeau Field
Houston Texans	Reliant Stadium
Indianapolis Colts	Lucas Oil Stadium
Jacksonville Jaguars	Altel Stadium
Kansas City Chiefs	Arrowhead Stadium
Oakland Raiders	McAffe Stadium
Miami Dolphins	Dolphins Stadium
Minnesota Vikings	Mall of America Field
New England Patriots	Gillette Stadium
New Orleans Saints	Louisiana Superdome
New York Giants	New Meadowlands Stadium
New York Jets	New Meadowlands Stadium
Philadelphia Eagles	Lincoln financial Field
Pittsburgh Steelers	Heinz Field
San Diego Chargers	Qualcomm Stadium
San Francisco 49ers	Monster Park
Seattle Seahawks	Qwest Field
St. Louis Rams	Edward Jones Dome
Tampa Bay Buccaneers	Raymond James Stadium
Tennessee Titans	LP Field
Washington Redskins	FedEx Field

radio exposure, the fees are not too high. The New York Jets now practice at the Atlantic Health Jets Training Center and receive about $2.0 million per year. For $2.0 million per year, the Houston Texans practice at the Methodist Training Center, and the Philadelphia Eagles receive $2.4 million for practicing at the NovaCare Complex. Several other teams – Seattle Seahawks, Pittsburgh Steelers, and Tennessee Titans – have also collected naming rights fees for their practice facilities.

Naming practice facilities is not limited to football. In the NHL, the Phoenix Coyotes practice in the Alltel Ice Den, and the Columbus Blue Jackets are in the Dispatch Ice Haus. The Philadelphia Flyers are in the Sovereign Bank Flyers Skate Zone. In the NBA, the Boston Celtics practice in the Sports Authority

Training Center at Healthpoint, and the Los Angeles Lakers are in the Toyota Sports Center. From the corporate sponsor's perspective, this is another form of advertising. The corporate name is prominently attached to the ballpark, stadium, or arena for all the world to see.

Major corporations – Reliant Energy, Federal Express, Royal Phillips Electronics, Nationwide Insurance, American Airlines, among many others – have put their names on athletic facilities. Naming rights deals are multiyear contracts that are often in the 15- to 30-year range. For example, the Staples Center contract calls for annual payments of \$5.8 million for 20 years. The Reliant Stadium deal obligates Reliant Energy to pay \$10 million per year for 30 years. In 2007, two deals set new records for naming rights contracts. Citi Group agreed to \$20 million per year for 20 years to name the new home of the Mets Citi Field. Barclays also committed \$20 million per year for 20 years to put its name on the new home of the New Jersey Nets. As with any other multiyear contract, we must look at present values:[5] the cost to the advertiser is the present value of the annual payments. In general, the cost of the commitment at the beginning is

$$PV\left[Payments\right] = \sum_{t=1}^{T} P_t/(1+i)^t,$$

where P_t is the annual payment, T is the length of the contract, and i is the discount rate. For the Staples contract, the cost at the beginning of the contract would have been

$$PV\left[Payments\right] = \sum_{t=1}^{20} \$5.8/(1.10)^t,$$

assuming a 10 percent discount rate. This amounts to roughly \$49,379,000. The deal was erroneously reported to be worth \$116 million. (Why "erroneously"?)

Some naming rights contracts do not survive for the entire period. Enron, for example, fell on hard times because of a corporate accounting scandal. No team would want to play its home games at Enron Field because the name surely conjures up a decidedly negative image. Some corporate names may disappear through merger with another firm. First Union, for example, was acquired by Wachovia, and therefore, First Union disappeared. When Ameriquest Mortgage Company began struggling financially, its deal with the Texas Rangers ended, and Ameriquest Field became Rangers Ballpark in Arlington. As these examples illustrate, the value of the future payments is far from certain. Consequently, we should replace the annual contract amount with the expected amount. Accordingly, we should look to the present value of the expected payments:

$$PV\left[E\left(payments\right)\right] = \sum_{t=1}^{T} E\left[P_t\right]/(1+i)^t.$$

[5] You will recall that we developed the present value calculations in the appendix to Chapter 2.

Box 6.2 *Barclays Breaks the Bank*

Barclays is a London-based investment bank that is well known internationally but does not have much visibility in the United States. The massive Atlantic Yards project planned for Brooklyn provided an opportunity for Barclays to enter in a highly visible way. If things go as planned, the New Jersey Nets will relocate to Brooklyn for the 2011–2012 season. Their new arena (along with a few other buildings) is known as the Barclays Center.

Barclays should get the visibility that it craves. The Barclays Center will be the centerpiece of Atlantic Yards, which was designed by Frank Gehry and will have apartment towers and commercial space. It will be located on 22 acres in Brooklyn and cost $4 billion. This visibility does not come cheap – Barclays will pay the Nets $20 million a year for 20 years. This is more than twice the commitment Phillips Electronics made to name the Phillips Arena in Atlanta.

There are risks on both sides. There is always a risk that Barclays will be sold. In fact, there were rumors around the time of signing that Bank of America was interested in acquiring Barclays. There was some risk that Atlantic Yards would not go forward because of lawsuits and some public opposition. Moreover, there is always some chance that Atlantic Yards will be built but be unsuccessful. Although this does not seem too likely, it could happen.

Accounting for the uncertainty of future payments reduces the economic value of the contract.

The wisdom of spending large sums on naming rights has been called into question by Eva Marikova Leeds, Michael Leeds, and Irina Pistolet in "A Stadium by Any Other Name: The Value of Naming Rights."[6] The authors found no statistical evidence that a naming rights deal improves the profits as reflected in the stock of the sponsoring firm. This raises an obvious question: why do sponsors continue to spend increasing sums to buy these rights? Blair and Haynes provide an answer grounded in economics.[7]

[6] Eva Marikova Leeds, Michael Leeds, and Irina Pistolet (2007), "A Stadium by Any Other Name: The Value of Naming Rights," *Journal of Sports Economics*, 8, 581–595.

[7] The explanation is fairly straightforward. Naming a sports venue is a form of advertising, but only one form. To the extent that rivals employ equally effective advertising, the impact of naming a venue will be neutralized, and the sponsor will not gain at the expense of its rivals. This apparently is what investors expect to happen because the observed impact of a naming rights deal in the stock market occurs well before consumers are reminded of Heinz catsup or Fed Ex shipping services while watching NFL games. In other words, even at the first mention of naming rights deal, investors expect equally effective advertising by rivals to follow. As a result of these expectations, the data will not reveal a statistically significant announcement effect. The absence of a boost in profits does not mean that the purchase of naming rights was a mistake. If the purchaser had not spent the money on some form of advertising, the results would have been worse because rivals would have gained an advantage. The empirical results do mean, however, that naming an arena is better than any other form of promotion at the margin.

3.3 Sponsorships

Sponsorships of sporting events provide another form of advertising. Most postseason bowl games are sponsored, but not all of them. For example, the Hawaii Bowl and the Hula Bowl have had some trouble finding a title sponsor. Among the major bowls, only the Rose Bowl and Grand Slam golf tournaments have resisted selling their tradition and prestige to a corporate sponsor. Some of the traditional bowls with long histories now have odd-sounding names. The 2011 Orange Bowl, for example, was the Discover Orange Bowl. Similarly, the 2011 Sugar Bowl was the Allstate Sugar Bowl, and the Cotton Bowl was the AT&T Cotton Bowl. The old Citrus Bowl is now the Capital One Bowl. Some of the less prestigious bowls also have strange names: the Chick-fil-A Peach Bowl, the Brut Sun Bowl, the AutoZone Liberty Bowl, and the Meineke Car Care Bowl, to name just a few.

Box 6.3 ***The NFL Protects Its Sponsors***

Companies pay a lot to be an NFL sponsor. In return, their products are the "official" shoe, drink, fast food, or whatever of the NFL. To protect these official products from conflicting messages by nonsponsor producers, the NFL has rules forbidding players from wearing the logo of a nonsponsor. Violating the rule can be costly, as Brian Urlacher, a star linebacker for the Chicago Bears, found out. At the 2007 Super Bowl media day, Urlacher wore a cap sporting the vitaminwater logo. Because Gatorade was the official NFL drink, Urlacher was guilty of wearing gear that advertised a product not approved by the NFL. He was fined $100,000 for the violation.

The $100,000 was the standard fine for a Super Bowl violation. At the Pro Bowl, the fine would have been $50,000 for the same offense. During the regular season, the fine would have been only $10,000.

Question: Why is there a difference in the size of the fine?

Golf tournaments on the PGA Tour and the LPGA Tour have corporate sponsors, too. However, the most prestigious golf tournaments on the PGA Tour, that is, the so-called Grand Slam or *major* tournaments, do not have corporate names in their titles. They are still the Masters, U.S. Open, British Open, and the PGA Championship. There are, however, many traditional tournaments

As Leeds, Leeds, and Pistolet point out, some marketers have claimed that naming rights provide a particularly cost-effective form of advertising. The fact that the data do not support such claims is not surprising because equilibrium demands that any advantage disappear. If naming rights provided a bigger bang for the buck – that is, if the marginal benefit of a dollar spent on naming rights were larger than a dollar spent on other advertising vehicles – one would expect the price of naming rights to rise and thereby eliminate the differentials. Essentially, competition among would-be sponsors would bid up the naming rights price tag (Blair and Haynes, "Comment on 'A Stadium by Any Other Name: The Value of Naming Rights'," *Journal of Sports Economics*, 10, 204–206.)

that have corporate sponsors: the AT&T Pebble Beach National Pro-Am, the Shell Houston Open, the EDS Byron Nelson Championship, and the Crowne Plaza Invitational at Colonial, to name a few. A larger sample is contained in Table 6.3.

Being able to put a corporate name on a golf tournament increases the advertising value to a sponsor and therefore increases the amount that the sponsor is willing to pay. This increases the size of the purse available for the golfers competing in the tournament. As a result, tradition may suffer, but the participants benefit. To the extent that increased purses result in better fields and therefore better-quality golf, fans also benefit because the show is better. These sponsorships are made to promote the sponsor's product. If the promotion is effective, the demand increases. Consumers therefore ultimately pay for the sponsorship in the form of higher prices for goods and services, but that effect is diffused throughout the market.

The Los Angeles Open was a venerable stop on the PGA Tour. It was held at the demanding Riviera Country Club. In 1989, it went corporate when Nissan became the title sponsor. Following the 2007 season, Nissan pulled out of a contract that was to run through 2010. Fortunately, Northern Trust, a Chicago-area bank with a substantial presence in California, stepped in to replace Nissan. Now we have the Northern Trust Open. For that, Northern Trust paid about $8 million per year. As a result, the total purse for the golfers rose to $6.2 million in 2008. This larger purse did not induce Tiger Woods to play, but there was plenty of star power for the fans.

Some tradition-rich events have decided not to sell their titles. We have mentioned the Rose Bowl and the Grand Slam golf tournaments. The same is true of the four major tennis championships – the Australian Open, French Open, Wimbledon, and the U.S. Open. This is not to say that they do not have sponsors, which they do, but the title is not for sale. Precisely the same thing is true of NASCAR's most prestigious event – the Daytona 500. From 1991 until 1993, the event was the "Daytona 500 by STP" – it was never the "STP Daytona 500." When STP decided to drop its sponsorship, it was not replaced. Now, the owners of the Daytona International Speedway cannot imagine a set of circumstances under which they would sell the title sponsorship. The usual title sells for an annual fee in the low seven figures. For the Daytona 500, however, some have estimated that the title would command twice that amount because of the fame of that event.

3.4 Endorsements

For highly visible athletes, endorsement income can be substantial,[8] but from the sponsor's perspective, player endorsements provide another advertising vehicle.[9] There are many examples of substantial deals. Roger Federer, a

[8] We examine endorsement income in more detail in Chapter 23.

[9] It is not just athletes and coaches who have endorsements. Several ESPN broadcasters have shoe deals. Erin Andrews has a deal with Reebok, and Chris Fowler, Kirk Herbstreit, and Lee Corso have deals with Nike.

professional tennis player, got an endorsement deal with Nike that was an extremely good deal for the company. Federer negotiated it himself before he began his amazing Grand Slam run. It paid him only $1 million per year. His 10-year extension in 2008 was reportedly worth $13 million per year.[10] In the United States, tennis is a secondary sport, and therefore, Federer's endorsement promotes the Nike brand generally. In Europe and Asia, however, tennis is more important. In these markets, Federer's endorsement is expected to improve sales of tennis shoes and apparel.

Nike is a major figure in the market for baseball gear. In an effort to maintain that position, it secures endorsements from highly visible baseball players. Albert Pujols agreed to a three-year deal with Nike to endorse its baseball shoes, batting gloves, and apparel. The deal was worth some $3 million.

Advertisers have to be careful about who endorses their products. If an athlete disgraces himself, he also disgraces the brand that he endorses. Usually, advertisers respond quickly to any sort of negative news. For example, Nike wasted no time distancing itself from Michael Vick when he agreed to plead guilty to dog-fighting charges. Ads stopped running, and signature merchandise disappeared. As the revelations regarding the use of steroids and human growth hormone spread, more endorsees will be abandoned because sponsors will not want the negative association with their products.

4 STRATEGIC BEHAVIOR IN ADVERTISING

Although there is some advertising when products are relatively homogeneous, advertising is more prominent in markets with differentiated goods, such as automobiles, fast food, soft drinks, and athletic apparel. When there are a relatively small number of firms selling differentiated products, we have an oligopoly with all the complications that accompany that market structure. If there are many firms, we have monopolistic competition. An investment in advertising is most effective when the advertiser's rivals do not also advertise. However, rivals know that and will engage in rivalrous advertising. This non-price battle may lead to no net benefit because one firm's ad neutralizes the rival's ad.

From Table 6.1, we can see that three beer producers spent substantial sums on sports advertising in 2004: Anheuser-Busch spent $293,400,122, Miller Brewing spent $131,815,521, and Coors Brewing spent $82,244,902. In soft drinks, there was less spending on sports advertising than in the beer industry, but the big three still spent sizable amounts: Coca-Cola spent $142,761,624, Pepsi Cola spent $68,392,812, and Dr. Pepper/7-Up spent $32,335,927. In markets with a small number of competitors, much advertising is cancelled out. To some extent, Coca-Cola's advertising is offset by Pepsi ads, and neither gains at the expense of the other. However, if one firm failed to advertise, it would give the

[10] The actual payments may depend on performance in the Grand Slams and Federer's ranking.

rival a chance to take away a good deal of the other's business. This is captured in the following hypothetical example.

If neither firm advertises, they split the market, and each earns $15 million in profit. If they both advertise, the ads neutralize one another, and the firms still split the market, but the advertising cost drops firm profit to $10 million. Clearly, the firms are better off if they do not advertise because each would earn $15 million rather than $10 million. A binding agreement – an enforceable contract – not to advertise is unavailable because such agreements are illegal under the antitrust laws.[11] Courts will not enforce illegal contracts, and therefore, no binding agreements are possible.

Despite the fact that the best solution for the two firms is not to advertise because each would then have $15 million in profits, they will both advertise. If Firm 2 does not advertise, and Firm 1 does advertise, Firm 1 will gain a larger share of the market at Firm 2's expense. As a result, it will earn $20 million by advertising rather than $15 million if it also does not advertise. If Firm 2 advertises, and Firm 1 does not, it will earn $10 million by advertising but only $8.5 million if it does not advertise. Thus, advertising yields more profit for Firm 1 than not advertising no matter what Firm 2 does, and therefore, Firm 1 will advertise. Firm 2's reasoning is precisely the same. As a result, both firms will advertise and each firm's profit will be $10 million instead of $15 million. If the firms could collude successfully, they would agree not to advertise and would have higher profits as a result. However, they cannot collude successfully because of the absence of binding contracts. This is an interesting economic result. In the absence of binding agreements, the two firms behave in a way that fails to maximize their joint profits. If the firms were to agree not to advertise, there is a real danger that the rivals will cheat on one another. As we have just seen, it is in each firm's interest to cheat by advertising when neither firm can be absolutely sure what the other will do. As a result, both advertise to their mutual detriment.

5 LEAGUE-WIDE ADVERTISING

An examination of Table 6.1 reveals that some leagues and organizations also advertise. Among the top 100 advertisers were the NFL ($55.8 million), the NCAA ($38.4 million), the PGA Tour ($31.0 million), and NASCAR ($30.0 million). Although not in the top 100, MLB, the NBA, and the LPGA also advertise on television. The obvious question that this poses is why a league or organization would advertise on behalf of its members. The answer, of course, is that it is profitable to do so. Now, let's see why that is the case.

When the NFL advertises (promotes) NFL football, it hopes to increase the overall demand for NFL football games. All teams benefit from the league-wide advertising to one degree or another. Note, however, that the benefit that the Dallas Cowboys enjoy does *not* reduce the benefits obtained by the Tampa Bay Bucs and the Minnesota Vikings. Thus, we call this league-wide advertising a

[11] The application of the antitrust laws in the sports industry is examined in Chapter 9.

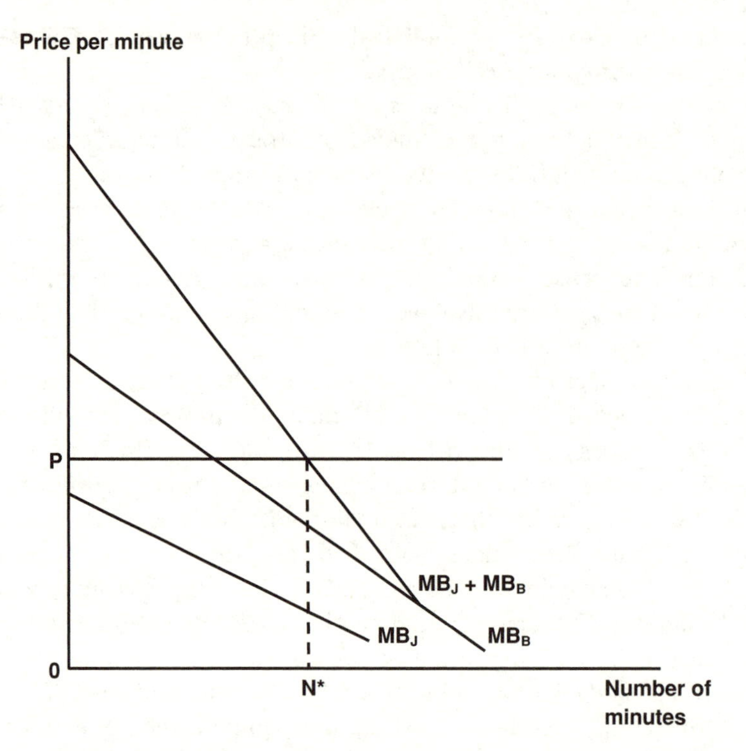

Figure 6.2. Optimal league-wide advertising is found where $MB_B + MB_J = P$.

public good.[12] It is marked by "nonrivalry" in consumption. If Christina and Sarah share a pizza, each slice that Christina eats is a slice that Sarah cannot eat. The pizza is a private good. However, no matter how much of the music being played is consumed by Christina, the amount left for Sarah is not diminished. Thus, the music is a public good. League-wide advertising has the same characteristic. The problem for the NFL is deciding how much to spend on advertising when advertising is a public good. At a theoretical level, the problem is not difficult to solve, but the solution may be difficult to implement and administer in practice.

5.1 Economic Theory

To simplify the graphical analysis while explaining the essence of the decision problem posed by public goods, we will suppose that there are only two teams in the league – the Bucs and the Jaguars. Because the benefits to the Bucs and to the Jaguars are not rivalrous – that is, the benefit enjoyed by the Bucs does not reduce the benefits flowing to the Jaguars – the marginal benefit schedules of the two teams should be added *vertically* – not horizontally. In Figure 6.2, the marginal benefit curves for the Bucs and for the Jaguars are shown as MB_B and MB_J, respectively. You will recall that the marginal benefit of an additional ad is the increase in price that results from the ad times the quantity sold. In this

[12] For a good discussion of public goods, see Jeffrey M. Perloff (2007), *Microeconomics*, 4th ed., Boston: Addison-Wesley, pp. 623–630.

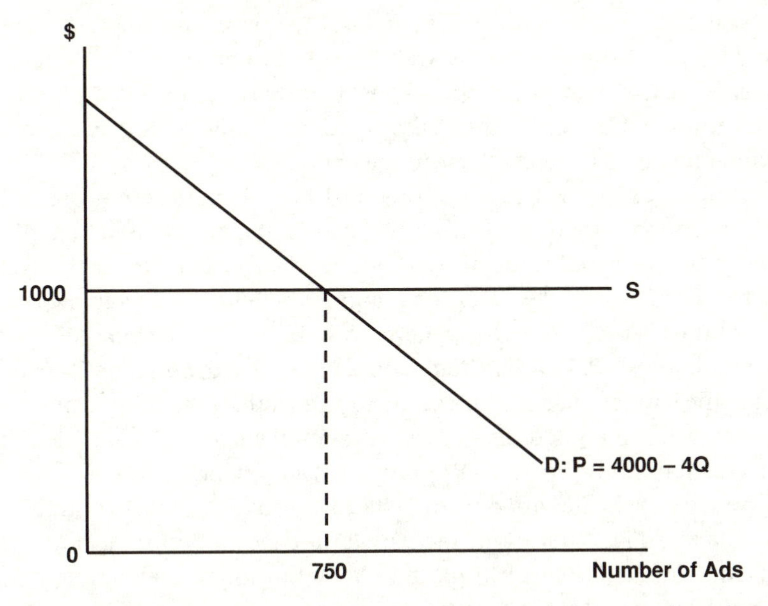

Figure 6.3. A league will buy the number of ads at which the price of an ad equals the vertical sum of the demands of league members.

case, each team benefits from the same ad, so the marginal benefit curve for the Bucs and the marginal benefit for the Jaguars should be added vertically to get the total marginal benefit of advertising. The vertical sum of these curves is shown as $MB_J + MB_B$. The price per minute of TV advertising is shown as the horizontal line at P. The reason the price of ad slots is constant is because that price is determined by demand and supply in the market for advertising time. Because neither the NFL nor any individual team is a particularly large buyer with buying power, they take the price as given.

At a price of P per minute of national advertising time, the optimal number of minutes for the Bucs and Jaguars combined is N^*. This is where supply is equal to demand:

$$P = MB_B + MB_J,$$

at $N = N^*$. This is the number of minutes that maximizes joint profits.

5.2 Problems in Practice

The theory of public goods as applied to league-wide advertising is fairly simple. There are, however, several practical difficulties in implementing the theory. First, each team is in a market that has somewhat different characteristics. Consequently, each team will have a different marginal benefit schedule. For the league to know how much advertising to buy, it would need information on the individual marginal benefit schedules of each league member. This information will not be easy to obtain. Second, each team will suspect that it may not have to pay for the advertising if it opts out. However, if a team opts out, it will still get plenty of benefit from whatever advertising is done. In essence, the opt-out firm wants to be a *free rider.* All teams in the league have the same incentive, and the result may well be suboptimal. In other words, too little advertising will be done by the league. One solution to this problem is to give the commissioner's office the authority to make advertising decisions and then compel the teams to contribute to the cost.

Third, prescribing a fair and practical way of sharing the cost will be challenging and may be impossible. In Figure 6.2, the height of MB_B at $N = N^*$ represents the marginal value of N^* minutes of advertising to the Bucs. Similarly, the height of MB_J at $N = N^*$ is the marginal benefit to the Jaguars. If each team contributes in proportion to its marginal benefit, then the allocation of the total advertising cost, PN^*, will be fair. It does not look fair, however. One team would be paying a much bigger share of the total cost than the other would be paying. This may cause a good deal of resentment even though that allocation leads each team to want precisely N^* minutes of advertising.

An allocation that appears to be fair is to split the cost evenly. If each team pays half of PN^*, then both teams will find N^* suboptimal but for different reasons. The Jaguars will think that N^* is too much advertising because $\frac{1}{2}P$ exceeds MB_J at N^*. In contrast, the Bucs will think that N^* is too little advertising because $\frac{1}{2}P$ is less than MB_B at N^*. Thus, each team will be disgruntled and dissatisfied with the commissioner's decision.

5.3 A Numerical Example

We can construct a simple numerical example by assuming that each team has precisely the same marginal benefit schedule. Suppose that the individual demand for advertising by each team in the NFL is:

$$Q = 2{,}000 - 4P.$$

For convenience, write this demand in inverse form:

$$P = 500 - 0.25Q.$$

Because all of the demands are the same, we can obtain the *league* demand by multiplying the slope and the intercept of a *team* demand by 32, which is the number of teams in the NFL. Thus, the demand for advertising by the league as a whole is

$$P = 16{,}000 - 8Q.$$

If the price of an ad is \$2,000, the league will buy where supply equals demand:

$$2{,}000 = 16{,}000 - 8Q,$$

which implies that the optimal number of ad minutes is:

$$Q^* = 1{,}750.$$

One could argue that each team should contribute proportionally. In this case, each team would pay \$62.50 per ad. At $P = 62.50$, each team would want exactly

1,750 ads, which we can see by substituting $62.50 into the team's demand function.

6 CONCLUDING REMARKS

Firms use advertising to inform and persuade consumers to buy their goods and services. Advertising expenditures are intended to shift the demand so that consumers will buy more at any given price or, alternatively, pay more for any given quality. For advertising to be effective, it must reach the right audience in sufficient numbers.

Sports advertising – that is, advertising at sporting events, on sports programming, and in sports publications – is a good way to reach a larger number of people with identifiable economic and demographic characteristics. Consequently, sports advertising is a multibillion dollar business.

PROBLEMS AND QUESTIONS

1. A 30-second ad slot on the Super Bowl broadcast cost $2.6 million. What explains this high price?
2. The Chicago Bears are being sponsored by Bank One. The contract pays $2.5 million a year for 12 years. It was reportedly worth $30 million. At an 8% discount rate, how much is it really worth?
3. American Express was a corporate sponsor of the NBA draft in 2006. In theory, how could one tell what the net value of that sponsorship was worth to American Express?
4. In the numerical example in section 2.1, find the maximum profit by substituting Q^* and A^* into the profit function. Show that profit falls when the firm deviates from either Q^* or A^*.
5. One year, the Hawaii Bowl was played in Maui in front of 12,000 fans. ESPN's telecast hit some 800,000 homes. Being a title sponsor would have cost $500,000. How would you decide whether to be a title sponsor?
6. In Figure 6.2, how many minutes of advertising would each team buy on its own? Show that this is suboptimal for the group.
7. In 2001, American Airlines entered into a 30-year contract worth $195 million for the naming rights to the home of the Dallas Mavericks, Dallas Stars, and Dallas Desperados. The contract calls for annual payments of $6.5 million. Explain carefully how you would calculate the economic value of the contract.
8. If the appropriate discount rate is 10 percent, what was the economic value of Barclays' commitment in 2007? Clearly state any assumptions you need to make.
9. In December 2009, the *New York Times* reported that "Naming Rights Finds New Life in China." Why would naming rights be important now when they were not so important earlier?

10. In December 2009, the *New York Times* reported that "Gillette to Limit Role of Tiger Woods in Marketing." Use the optimal advertising model to explain this decision.
11. From time to time, we see ads on TV for milk, orange juice, beef, and eggs without any reference to a brand. Why?
12. The *New York Times* announced in 2009 that "Toyota [is] Pulling out of Formula One to Cut Costs." Could Toyota's decision be "penny wise and pound foolish"?

RESEARCH QUESTIONS

1. Look at the naming rights fees in the NFL.
   a. How have these fees changed over time?
   b. Is there any correlation between the fee paid and the size of the local market in which the team is located?
2. Some teams in different sports share the same facility. For example, the NBA's Los Angeles Lakers and Los Angeles Clippers share the Staples Center with the NHL's Los Angeles Kings. In that event, who gets the naming rights revenue?
3. Construct a table of naming rights for MLB. Identify the sponsor (if any) and the current naming rights deal that is in place.
4. What happened to Tiger Wood's endorsement deals following the revelations concerning his marital infidelity?

REFERENCES AND FURTHER READING

DeSchriver, T. D., and P. E. Jensen. (2003). "What's in a Name? Price Variation in Sports Facility Naming Rights." *Eastern Economic Journal,* 29, 359–376.

Gerrard, B., M. M. Parent, and T. Slack. (2007). "What Drives the Value of Stadium Naming Rights? A Hedonic-Pricing Approach to the Valuation of Sporting Intangible Assets." *International Journal of Sport Finance,* 2, 10–24.

Leeds, E. M., M. A. Leeds, and I. Pistolet. (2007). "A Stadium by any Other Name: The Value of Naming Rights." *Journal of Sports Economics,* 8, 581–595.

Smith, D. R. (2008). "Big-Time College Basketball and the Advertising Effect: Does Success Really Matter?" *Journal of Sports Economics,* 9, 387–406.

7

The Market for Sports Broadcasting Rights

1 INTRODUCTION

The major sports leagues and organizations own the broadcast rights to their athletic contests. Given the enormous popularity of sports in the United States, these broadcast rights can be worth considerable sums of money. The National Football League's (NFL's) broadcast rights provide an excellent (although admittedly extreme) example. In 2010, the NFL's broadcast rights brought in more than $3.8 billion. Such numbers are driven by other numbers – the Nielsen ratings and the audience demographics. The hugely popular NFL can command billions of dollars for its broadcast rights because of its high Nielsen ratings. Broadcasters want sports programming largely for one reason: to sell advertising slots. The price of those ad slots is determined by the number and demographic characteristics of the viewers that the programming delivers. As a result, the broadcast license fees for less popular sports are more modest than those for the NFL. In 2010, for example, the United States Tennis Association received some $43.3 to 48.3 million for broadcast, cable, and international TV rights to the U.S. Open.[1] Similarly in 2007, Major League Soccer (MLS) signed its first TV contracts with ESPN, Univision, Fox Soccer Channel, and HDNet for only $20 million.[2] This may seem like a meager beginning, but until MLS gains popularity in the United States, it will not command a high price for its broadcast rights.

Broadcast license fees are an important source of revenue to large and small alike. The billions of dollars generated by the NFL are just about enough to cover the player payroll. For the U.S. Figure Skating Association, its contract with ABC/ESPN provided only $12 million per year. For the association, however, this was significant because the rights fees accounted for more than 65 percent of its budget.

In this chapter, we examine the market for broadcast rights. Along the way, we discuss the importance of broadcast revenues to the clubs, the importance

[1] Because of lower than expected ratings, the contract was restructured for 2007. John Ourand and Daniel Kaplan, "Open TV Deal Altered," *Sports Business Journal*, May 7, 2007.

[2] Tripp Mickle, "A Year of Firsts in TV Deals," *Sports Business Journal*, April 9, 2007.

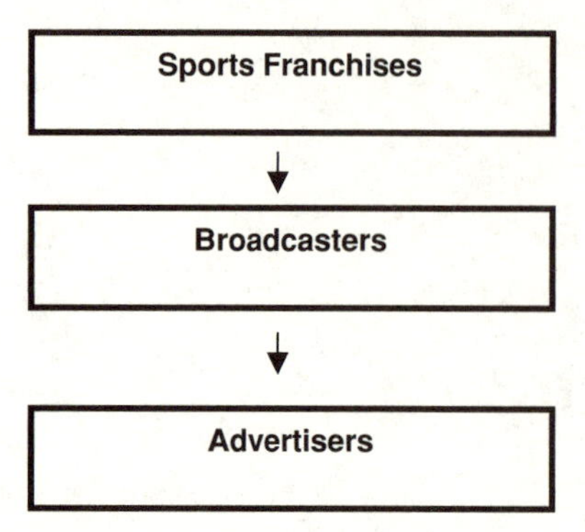

Figure 7.1. Broadcast rights are purchased from a sports franchise so ad slots can be sold to advertisers.

of league-wide contracts, some antitrust issues that have been legislated away, and the so-called winner's curse. An extremely interesting shift toward vertical integration is analyzed as well. Although it is a bit counterintuitive at first, we will see that vertical integration may well make sports fans better off.

2 MARKET STRUCTURE

The market structure for sports broadcasting rights can be illustrated by looking at a single sport, say, professional football. Each professional football club owns the broadcast rights for its home games. In principle, it can sell these rights or not as it wishes. If it elects to sell them, it can sell them to any network broadcaster or cable operator. Broadcasters are interested in acquiring these rights because they can then provide sports programming for fans to watch. The resulting audience is attractive to some advertisers because their ad messages will reach a fairly large audience with identifiable economic and demographic characteristics. This flow is shown in Figure 7.1 in which the broadcast rights are sold to broadcasters by the sports franchises, and the resulting ad slots are sold by the broadcasters to the advertisers.

In Figure 7.1, there appears to be competition everywhere. In the NFL, there would seem to be 32 teams competing with one another to sell their broadcast rights. There are four networks and a host of cable operators that compete with one another to acquire broadcast rights and to sell the resulting ad slots. There are, of course, hundreds of advertisers competing to buy ad slots on the sports programming. This appearance of competition, however, is deceiving. First, the football clubs do not compete with one another in selling their broadcast rights. Instead, they pool these rights and sell them as a package. Second, once a broadcaster has purchased the exclusive rights to broadcast NFL games on, say, Monday night, it then has a monopoly on the corresponding ad slots. As a result, the market is not nearly as competitive as it first appears.

When NFL clubs pool their broadcast rights and sell them as a package, they are agreeing among themselves not to compete with one another in that market. This is analogous to Coke and Pepsi agreeing to put three Cokes and three

Pepsis in every six-pack. In both agreements, the parties refrain from competing with one another. In most cases, such agreements run afoul of the antitrust laws. In particular, Section 1 of the Sherman Act prohibits collusive agreements that restrain trade:

> Every contract, combination . . . or conspiracy in restraint of trade or commerce . . . is hereby declared to be illegal.[3]

Although the broad language would appear to condemn literally all contracts, the Supreme Court has made it clear that only *unreasonable* restraints are illegal. To be deemed unreasonable, a restraint should lead to higher prices, lower quantity, or reduced quality. The NFL's plan to pool its broadcast rights and sell them as a package was designed to eliminate competition and to raise the price of those rights. Consequently, the NFL had a problem.

In 1961, the NFL and its members asked a federal district court judge to rule that a contract between the NFL and a TV network granting exclusive broadcast rights did not violate the Sherman Act. In effect, the NFL wanted a judgment that pooling the broadcast rights of its members and selling them as a package to a network were permissible under the antitrust laws. Much to the NFL's disappointment, the court held just the opposite: that the pooling eliminated competition among the football clubs in the sale of their broadcast rights. The court found that this elimination of competition was a violation of the Sherman Act and therefore would be impermissible.[4] Undaunted by this judicial rebuff, the NFL turned to Congress for relief and got it in the form of the Sports Broadcasting Act of 1961 (SBA).

2.1 Sports Broadcasting Act

The NFL pooled the broadcast rights of its members and sold them as a package to CBS in 1961. When the district court held that this "pooling" impermissibly eliminated competition among the teams and therefore was anticompetitive, the NFL appealed to Congress. At the NFL's urging, Congress passed the SBA. The SBA allowed professional sports leagues in football, baseball, basketball, and hockey to pool their TV broadcast rights for sale to a network. By doing so, it removed the threat of antitrust prosecution under §1 of the Sherman Act. The major professional sports leagues were not granted blanket antitrust immunity by the SBA; there were several limitations. First, the broadcast agreements could not impose territorial limitations on the purchasers of the broadcast rights. The only exception applied to blackouts to protect a team that had not sold out a home game. If, for example, the Detroit Lions home game with the Green Bay Packers were not sold out, the television broadcast of that game could be blacked out in the Detroit area. Second, agreements were not exempt if they permitted broadcasts on days traditionally reserved for high school and college football games – Friday nights and Saturdays, respectively. Finally, the

[3] The Sherman Act, 15 U.S.C. §§1–8, was passed in 1890. It condemns restraints on competition that result in higher prices and lower output. Violations of the Sherman Act are felonies and carry heavy penalties. We look at this in more detail in Chapter 10.

[4] See *United States v. NFL*, 196 F. Supp. 445, 447 (E.D.Pa. 1961).

Table 7.1. Nielsen's Top-Rated Network Sports Programs, January–October 2010

Rank	Network	Program
1	CBS	Super Bowl XLIV: Colts–Saints
2	Fox	NFC Championship: Saints–Vikings
3	CBS	AFC Championship: Colts–Jets
4	Fox	NFC Divisional Playoff: Viking–Cowboys
5	CBS	AFC Divisional Playoff: Jets–Chargers
6	Fox	NFC Wildcard: Packers–Cardinals
7	NBC	NFC Wildcard: Eagles–Cowboys
8	NBC	Vancouver Winter Olympics: Opening Ceremony
9	ABC	NCAA BCS Championship Game: Alabama–Texas
10	CBS	AFC Divisional Playoff: Colts–Ravens
11	CBS	AFC Wildcard: Ravens–Patriots
12	NBC	Vancouver Winter Olympics: Wednesday Night (Day 6)
13	Fox	*NFL on Fox*: Packers–Eagles
14	CBS	*NFL on CBS*: Patriots–Jets
15	Fox	NFC Divisional Playoff: Saints–Cardinals
16	Fox	*NFL on Fox*: Cowboys–Vikings
17	ABC	NBA Finals: Lakers–Celtics (Game 7)
18	NBC	Sunday Night Football: Vikings–Packers
19	Fox	*NFL on Fox*: Eagles–Cowboys
20	Fox	*NFL on Fox*: Vikings–Patriots

Source: Street & Smith's *Business Resource Guide and Fact Book 2011*. See this reference for a more complete list.

SBA specifically provided that it applied only to the specified agreements. It did not have anything to do with the applicability or nonapplicability of the antitrust laws to any other aspect of the sports business.

As a result of the SBA, the NFL's members could jointly market their broadcast rights without fear of antitrust prosecution. The same was true for the NBA, the National Hockey League (NHL), and Major League Baseball (MLB). This, of course, gave each league substantial market power in dealing with the networks and cable operators. The structure of the market was no longer competitive. The economic results were predictable: the sports league became the sole seller and therefore could maximize its profits on the sale of broadcast rights just as any monopolist would. The revenues would be shared by all members of the league. By making the networks and cable operators bid against one another, the league can extract a good deal of the profit that is generated by selling ad slots to advertisers.

The value of competitive bidding can be illustrated by MLB's experience in Europe. Before the entry of two new bidders for MLB's cable rights in Europe, the price was about $10 million over five years. When the North American Sports Network (NASN) entered the bidding, the rights fee jumped. Then along came ESPN. To avoid losing the MLB deal, NASN increased its offer by several million dollars. MLB finally got nearly $20 million over five years for its European cable rights. All of that increase flows directly to MLB's bottom line.

It is clear why the NFL can command billions of dollars for its broadcast licenses. According to the A.C. Nielsen ratings, professional football accounted for the top seven sports programs on network television between January and October 2010. Among the top 20 sports programs, the NFL accounted for 16 of them. Only the Opening Ceremony of the Vancouver Winter Olympics at 8, the Bowl Championship Series championship game at 9, the Winter Olympics again at 12, and the NBA Finals at 17 cracked the top 20. Notably absent from the top 20 are several blockbuster events: the National Collegiate Athletic Association (NCAA) Men's Basketball Championship game, the World Series, the Kentucky Derby, the Masters Gold Championship, and many others.

As for sports programming on cable, ESPN's *Monday Night Football*, the NFL Pro Bowl, and NCAA football dominated the top 20. TBS and TNT accounted for the remaining sports in the top 20 with MLB and NBA action.

Box 7.1 *Limits on Ownership of Broadcast Rights*

With one game remaining on the 2007 NFL schedule, the New England Patriots were undefeated. No team since the 1972 Miami Dolphins had gone through the regular season undefeated. The Patriots' final game against the New York Giants was scheduled for TV coverage on the NFL network, which was available only on cable. Next systems carried it as part of a premium tier. Of some 115 million TV households, only 40 million subscribed to the NFL network. Thus, only about 35 percent of all TV households could watch the Patriots' effort at a historic win. With war raging in Iraq, the housing market in a deep slump, a financial crisis in the mortgage market, and assorted other problems, Senator John Kerry found time to intervene by sending a letter to NFL Commissioner Roger Goodell urging him to settle any disputes that would deprive firms of free access to the game. His appeal was heard. At the last minute, the NFL permitted the game to be simulcast on NBC and CBS.

3 BIDDING FOR BROADCAST RIGHTS

Packages of broadcast rights are sold by the major sports leagues, NCAA conferences, and organizations such as the United States Tennis Association and the Professional Golf Association Tour. These are not sold like loaves of bread for which there are huge quantities and many buyers. Instead, each package is sold by a monopolist in a kind of auction with only a few buyers. The highest bidder for a particular package is the winner. ESPN, for example, won the bidding for *Monday Night Football*, and NBC won the rights to *Sunday Night Football*. Neither ESPN nor NBC bought individual weeks; they bought the whole season for one (very large) lump sum. Now, let's see what determines the size of this lump sum.

Table 7.2. Nielsen's Top-Rated Cable Sports Programs, January–October 2010

Rank	Network	Program
1	ESPN	*Monday Night Football:* Giants–Cowboys
2	ESPN	*Monday Night Football:* Packers–Bears
3	ESPN	*Monday Night Football:* Vikings–Jets
4	ESPN	*Monday Night Football:* Saints–49ers
5	ESPN	*Monday Night Football:* Ravens–Jets
6	ESPN	*Monday Night Football:* Patriots–Dolphins
7	ESPN	*Monday Night Football:* Chargers–Chiefs
8	TBS	ALCS: Rangers–Yankees (Game 6)
9	ESPN	NFL Pro Bowl
10	ESPN	NCAA Football: Boise St.–Virginia Tech
11	TBS	ALCS: Rangers–Yankees (Game 4)
12	ESPN	*Monday Night Football:* Titans–Jaguars
13	ESPN	Lebron James: *The Decision*
14	ESPN	NBA Eastern Conference Semifinals: Celtics–Cavaliers (Game 6)
15	TNT	NBA Western Conference Finals: Lakers–Suns (Game 5)
16	TBS	ALCS: Rangers–Yankees (Game 3)
17	TNT	NBA Western Conference Finals: Lakers–Suns (Game 3)
18	TBS	ALCS: Rangers–Yankees (Game 1)
19	ESPN	NBA Eastern Conference Finals: Celtics–Magic (Game 4)
20	TNT	NBA Western Conference Finals: Lakers–Suns (Game 4)

Source: Street & Smith's *Business Resource Guide and Fact Book 2011.* See this reference for a more complete list.

Suppose we are looking at *Sunday Night Football.* NBC wants to broadcast NFL games on Sunday evenings so it can sell ad slots to advertisers. The marginal cost of producing ad slots, which is shown in Figure 7.2, is assumed to be constant until the maximum number is reached at Q_2. The marginal cost then becomes vertical because further ad slots cannot be produced. The demand for the ad slots is determined by the audience that the programming delivers. It is not only the number of viewers but also their economic and demographic characteristics that will determine their value to advertisers. For *Sunday Night Football,* the demand for ad slots is given by D in Figure 7.2. Given this demand, the maximum profit that can be earned in this market is found by selling Q_1 ad slots at P_1 per ad slot. (Why?) Profit will then be equal to $(P_1 - c)Q_1$. This profit is shown as area P_1abc in Figure 7.2. The network can then use the remaining unsold ad slots to promote other programming on NBC and any affiliates. To earn these profits, however, it must purchase the broadcast rights from the NFL. These rights are worth $(P_1 - c)Q_1$ to NBC, and therefore, NBC should be willing to bid up to that amount for those rights. The other networks – CBS, ABC, Fox, and ESPN – also value those broadcast rights for the same reason. There may be reasons why one network is better able to use that programming than another, but they can all use NFL games on Sunday night.

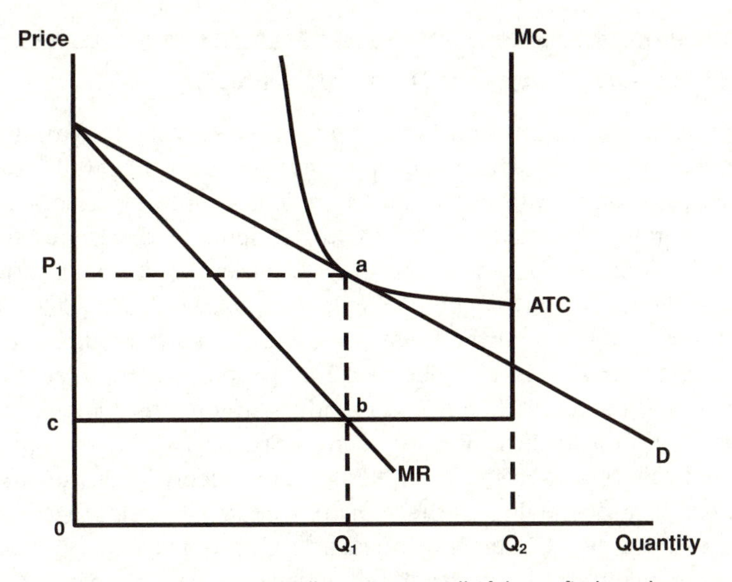

Figure 7.2. A sports league will try to extract all of the profit through competitive bidding.

As a result, the bidding will be competitive.[5] At the limit, NBC will pay $(P_1 - c)Q_1$ for those broadcast rights. The NFL will then have extracted all of the monopoly profit through this auction. The effect of this is to make NBC's average total cost curve (ATC) tangent to the demand in Figure 7.2 at Q_1. The ATC curve includes the marginal (and average) operating cost, which is shown as *MC*, and the average license fee, which will be equal to $(P_1 - c)Q_1/Q$. NBC then earns a competitive return on the ad slots that it sells even though the price it charges is well above the marginal cost of producing the ad slots. In other words, all of the operating profit is used to pay the broadcast rights fee to the NFL. The NFL, however, does not get to keep all of this profit. The players receive a big piece of that pie and therefore benefit greatly from the television contracts.

3.1 A Numerical Example

Suppose that the demand for ad slots on a sports program is given by

$$P = 1{,}010 - 2Q.$$

And the corresponding marginal revenue is

$$MR = 1{,}010 - 4Q.$$

The marginal (and average) cost of producing broadcast rights by the NFL clubs is zero. For the broadcaster, the marginal cost of the ad slots is constant and equal to 10. For the moment, assume that there is no license fee. The broadcaster's profit function is then:

$$\pi_B = (1{,}010 - 2Q)Q - 10Q.$$

[5] This assumes that the networks do no collude. In other words, we assume that the networks do not agree to refrain from competitive bidding.

Box 7.2 *The Pan Am Games: An Undervalued Property*[*]

The Pan American Games are held every four years in the year preceding the Summer Olympics. The games are managed – but not well – by a non-profit corporation that the Brazilian Olympic Committee oversees. Although ESPN Deportes has purchased the exclusive rights in the United States for the Spanish-language broadcast, no one has picked up the English-language broadcast rights. No one bought the English-language rights in 2003 either. Part of the reason may be that the price is too high given the anticipated advertising revenue that such a broadcast would generate. A more serious problem, however, involves timing. The broadcast rights are granted about two months before the Pan Am Games begin. Sixty days is not enough time for ESPN and others to develop a marketing plan, incorporate the games into the schedule, and actually sell the ad slots. The result is that these broadcast rights are undervalued. Managing broadcast rights more efficiently would obviously generate potentially large additional revenues with almost no additional cost.

Question: Does the fact that a nonprofit company manages these broadcast rights explain the inefficiency?

* John Ourand, "ESPN Deportes Gets Rights to Pan Am Games," *Sports Business Journal*, May 7, 2007.

Profits are maximized by selling ad slots such that marginal revenue is equal to marginal cost:

$$1{,}010 - 4Q = 10$$

The optimal number of ad slots to sell is then 250 and the price is $510. (Why?) The profit would then be found by substituting into the profit function:

$$\pi_B = [1{,}010 - 2(250)](250) - 10(250) = \$125{,}000.$$

This means that owning the broadcast rights will enable a broadcaster to earn $125,000 in operating profits. These would be economic profits because a competitive return is already incorporated in the cost function. The owner of the broadcast rights can then auction the rights to the highest bidder. Assuming that all broadcasters are equally efficient, until the bidding reaches $125,000, it will be profitable to raise the bid in order to acquire the broadcast rights. Consequently, competitive bidding by equally efficient broadcasters will lead to a bid of $125,000 for the broadcast rights. As a result, the NFL ultimately gets all of the profit inherent in the broadcast rights.

Box 7.3 *March Madness 2007*[*]

CBS bought the broadcast rights to March Madness – the NCAA Men's Basketball Championship. Two weeks before the tournament began, CBS had sold nearly all of its ad inventory for the live broadcasts, and it was completely sold out for its online offering of March Madness on Demand (MMOD).

CBS's March Madness broadcasts commanded pretty hefty ad rates:

Early Rounds

Day games	$85,000
Prime-time games	$350,000
Final Four	$1.3 million

These rates are for 30-second ad slots. In addition to these revenues, CBS expects another $21 to $25 million for MMOD.

* John Ourand, "CBS's NCAA Ad Rates Hit High," *Sports Business Journal*, March 10, 2008.

3.2 The Winner's Curse

The so-called winner's curse arises in all competitive bidding situations. In the present case, we are talking about broadcast rights being sold at auction. Suppose that ABC, CBS, Fox, NBC, and ESPN are all bidding for the same package of broadcast rights. As the offers increase, some of the bidders drop out of the bidding. Ultimately, one bidder prevails and wins the bid. Now the winner may wonder why no one else believed that those rights were worth what the winner just agreed to pay for them. Presumably, the other bidders could produce the same games and offer ad slots to the same advertisers. Why were those broadcasters unwilling to pay the same licensing fee? Are they too risk averse? Do they know something that the winner does not know? If the winner paid too much, money will be lost and the winner will indeed suffer the "winner's curse."

There is a real possibility of a winner's curse when it comes to bidding on broadcast rights. It is not that the costs are hard to predict. After all, the bidders are experienced in broadcasting sports programming. This is not to say that costs can be predicted precisely, but there is a tolerable amount of imprecision. Instead, it is the demand for advertising slots that may be far more unpredictable. The ad slots cannot be sold before bidding on and being awarded the broadcast rights. As an example, consider the commitment made by NBC for the broadcast rights for the Olympic Games in 2010 and 2012.

NBC had already negotiated a deal with the International Olympic Committee (IOC) to broadcast the Olympic Games from 2000 to 2008. Subsequently, the IOC decided to entertain bids for the broadcast rights to the 2010 and 2012 Olympics. Although it was not announced publicly, the word on the street was that if the IOC did not get a $2.0 billion offer, it would defer the bidding to a later date. It is hard to say whether the rumor had any substance. In any event, NBC

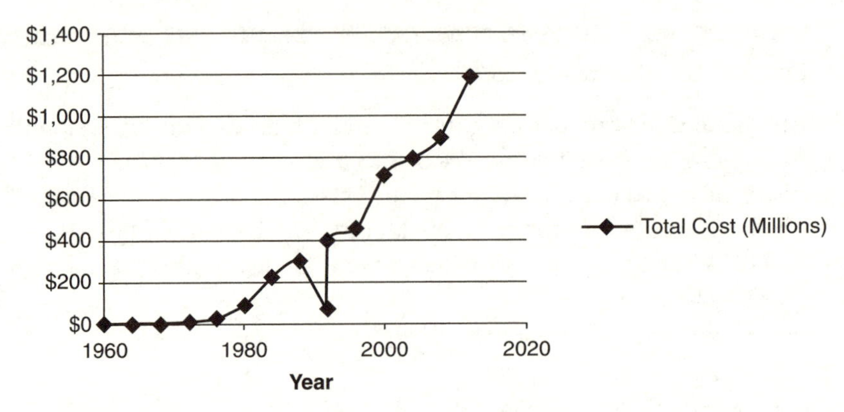

Figure 7.3. Media rights for Summer Olympics, 1960–2012. *Source: Sports Business Resource Guide and Fact Book 2011.*

bought the rights for $2.2 billion, which included some $160 to $200 million from General Electric, to become a worldwide Olympic sponsor.

Neither Fox nor ABC-ESPN thought that the broadcast rights were worth $2.0 billion. Fox offered only $1.3 billion based on its analysis of growth and uncertainty about how the world will look in seven to nine years. ABC-ESPN offered to share revenues with the IOC but would provide no cash. This revenue-sharing option was not acceptable for the IOC because it wanted cash.

Given the IOC's alternatives, several questions come to mind. First, could NBC have won with a lower bid? Obviously, if the IOC were committed to selling the rights for 2010 and 2012 at that time, NBC paid way more than was necessary because the next best offer was $900 million lower. However, there was some market intelligence that the IOC was not so anxious to sell that it would have accepted less than its reservation price of $2 billion. In any event, NBC wanted to preserve its role as the Olympic broadcaster and was willing to commit $2 billion well in advance. Second, did competitive bidding lead NBC into a winner's curse? It is not at all obvious that NBC will suffer the winner's curse. Even if NBC paid more than it had to pay to get the broadcast rights, it might still sell enough ad slots at prices that will make the whole thing profitable. Only time will tell whether the acquisition was profitable.

The broadcast rights to the Summer and Winter Olympics have climbed steadily and dramatically over the years. This is because of their growing popularity but also improved technology in broadcasting. Better use can now be made of those broadcast rights. Figures 7.3 and 7.4 show the tremendous increase in the rights fees for the Summer and Winter Olympics, respectively.

3.3 Bidding and Uncertainty

Figuring out how much to bid for broadcast rights is complicated by uncertainty. First, bidding takes place before the broadcaster or cable operator knows

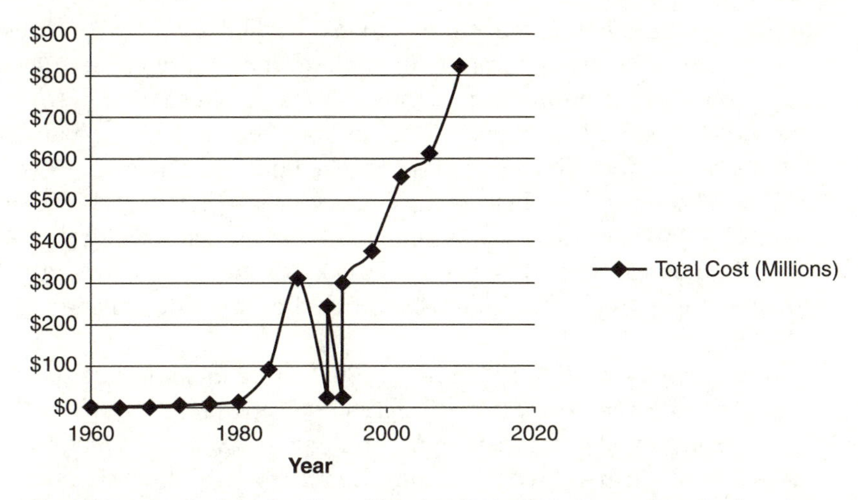

Figure 7.4. Media rights for Winter Olympics, 1960–2010. *Source: Sports Business Resource Guide and Fact Book 2011.*

either its costs or its revenues. This makes it difficult to forecast the profits that can be earned. Second, every bidder wants to pay as little as possible, but the best bid depends on what other bidders are likely to do. These latter concerns can be illustrated by the bidding for the cable rights to the U.S. Open Tennis Championship.[6] The bidders for the cable rights to the 2009 tournament included USA Network, ESPN, Versus, and Tennis Channel. For any one of these competitors, predicting what the others would bid was not easy.

USA Network appeared to be moving away from sports programming. As a result, one might suppose that its bid would be rather low. ESPN was clearly interested, but the U.S. Open comes at an awkward time for ESPN because of its obligations to MLB and to college football. Tennis Channel, which is partially owned by the USTA, would have an obvious interest, but the value of that programming to Tennis Channel might be less than to ESPN or USA because fewer people receive Tennis Channel. Finally, Versus would benefit from broadening its sports programming, but the value of the U.S. Open coverage to Versus was cloudy. The pros and cons for each cable network seem hard to sort out. This, of course, makes for tough decisions on how much to bid. No one wants to pay more than necessary, but how much is necessary depends on the competition.

3.4 Other Benefits to Broadcasters

Obviously, the main source of benefits to broadcasters is the sale of ad slots, but there are other benefits that flow from sports broadcasting.

Promoting Other Programming. A broadcaster may benefit by using sports programming to promote its other programming. For example, NBC was last

[6] Daniel Kaplan and John Ourand, "Four Bidding for the U.S. Open Cable Rights," *Sports Business Journal,* November 12, 2007.

in overall ratings before it acquired *Sunday Night Football* (*SNF*). It used *SNF* to promote and thereby pump up the ratings of its entire prime-time lineup.[7] NBC's plan was to promote three new shows – *Heroes, Friday Night Lights,* and *Kidnapped.* The strategy appears to have been at least partially successful. *Kidnapped* was a bust and was cancelled quickly. The critics loved *Friday Night Lights* but the audience was less enthusiastic. *Heroes,* however, was a smash hit. By midseason, it was among the top five shows with the 18- to 49-year-old demographic, which is the group that advertisers like best. At least some of this success can be attributed to the promotion made possible by *SNF.*

Improving Credibility. For some reason, being a major league sports broadcaster improves a network's overall credibility. Apparently, the power of the NFL is quite substantial in this regard. According to the *Sports Business Journal,* "in 1987, the [NFL] catapulted ESPN into America's most influential sports brand. In 1994, it made Fox a legitimate fourth broadcast network."[8] Presumably, the enhanced credibility makes it easier to sell ad slots and thereby increases profits, but this should not be overstated. The fact remains that the programming must deliver audiences with the right demographics or advertisers will abandon even the most credible network.

3.5 *Monday Night Football*[9]

ESPN began broadcasting *Monday Night Football* in 2006. The rights fee in 2006 was $1.1 billion. This fee works out to about $130 million per game or $40 million per hour.[10] These fees are 83 percent more than ESPN paid in 2005 for the rights to Sunday night broadcasts. Did ESPN pay too much for these *Monday Night Football* rights?

This question is tough to answer without a great deal of additional information. ESPN's president, George Bodenheimer, appeared confident that ESPN could make good use of *Monday Night Football*: "Our company is positioned to use a product like the NFL in ways that stretch 24/7, around the world, 365 days across 11 businesses." ESPN has television, radio, print, video game, fantasy, and web businesses. As a result, it is unlike the sports division of the major networks. ESPN sells advertising space just like the networks do, but it also collects subscriber fees from the cable operators. ESPN's monthly subscriber fee is $2.86. Its ability to charge such a high fee is due in no small part to its NFL programming.

The NFL was aware of its unique value to ESPN, and it was able to take a large piece of that value due to competition. ESPN knew that Comcast and Rupert Murdoch posed a competitive threat. In the end, ESPN agreed to an eight-year deal for a total of $8.8 billion.

[7] Andrew Marchand, "'SNF' Perks up the Peacock," *Sports Business Journal,* Jan. 22, 2007.

[8] *Ibid.*

[9] Richard Sandomir, "NFL Learns Its Worth and Makes ESPN Pay," *New York Times,* Sept. 8, 2006; and Gregg Easterbrook, "Follow the Monday Money," ESPN.com, Sept. 11, 2006.

[10] This is about 20 times as much as the average prime-time programming costs.

Box 7.4 *The ESPN Model*

ESPN's business model is somewhat different from other networks. It buys the rights to produce sports programming. For example, it paid the NFL for the rights to produce *Monday Night Football*, which delivers a large audience with desirable demographics. It also provides ad slots. ESPN sells the programming along with the ad slots to cable operators on a subscription basis. The cable operator pays ESPN a specified amount per cable subscription. Each subscriber's monthly cable bill reflects the ESPN fee. The cable operator then sells the ad slots to local and national advertisers.

ESPN's model works. It accounted for 9 of the top 10 highest rated sports programming on cable in 2010.

3.6 Bottom Line

It is extremely difficult to say whether any winner has suffered the winner's curse. Hindsight is always 20–20, but business decisions must be made *ex ante*. All sorts of contingencies may materialize that upset the most carefully laid plans. To determine whether a network has paid too much for a package of broadcast rights requires a careful analysis of (1) the ad revenues for the sports covered by the license, (2) increased ad revenues of programs surrounding the game, (3) the value of the advertising on other network shows, and (4) enhanced credibility that results in higher fees and lower promotional costs.

4 VERTICAL INTEGRATION IN SPORTS

When a firm supplies some of the inputs that it needs to produce the output that it sells, we say that the firm is vertically integrated. Because the vertical integration is further away from the ultimate consumer, we call this "upstream" or "backward" integration. Similarly, if a producer also performs the distribution function by acting as a wholesaler, that firm is also vertically integrated. In this case, we refer to this as "downstream" or "forward" integration because the firm is moving toward the consumer. In Figure 7.1, a broadcaster could become vertically integrated if it acquired a sports franchise. We have seen some examples of that: CBS used to own the New York Yankees; Ted Turner owned TBS and the Atlanta Braves.[11] The Tribune Company owned both WGN and the Chicago Cubs.[12] There are other examples as well. This raises an interesting question: Why are broadcasters vertically integrating backward into the sports franchise business?

[11] Now, Time Warner owns TBS and the Braves, which it is selling.

[12] In 2009, the Cubs were sold.

There are a host of reasons for vertical integration.[13] One of the most prominent reasons deals with *successive monopoly*, which refers to a market structure in which the sports franchise has monopoly power in the sale of broadcast rights and the broadcaster has monopoly power in the sale of advertising slots on the sports broadcast.[14] This explanation would not seem to apply in the case of professional sports franchises, however.

A brief analysis of the successive monopoly model will reveal why it is not applicable here. In the usual successive monopoly model, the upstream monopolist produces an input that it sells to the downstream monopolist. The pricing of the input takes into account the profit-maximizing behavior of the downstream monopolist. A simple example will illustrate this. Suppose that the upstream firm produces broadcast rights at zero marginal cost. The broadcaster produces the ad slots at a constant marginal cost of MC. Now, the profit functions of the sports franchise (π_F) and the broadcaster (π_B) are as follows:

$$\pi_F = wQ,$$

and,

$$\pi_B = PQ - (w + MC)Q,$$

where w is the price charged by the club and P is the price of the ad slots. In order to maximize its profits, the broadcaster would sell that quantity of ad slots where its marginal revenue (MR) is equal to marginal cost ($w + MC$):

$$MR = w + MC.$$

If we rearrange this condition, we get the derived demand faced by the club:

$$w = MR - MC.$$

The club will then set w such that its profits are maximized. This involves an output where its marginal revenue equals zero because marginal cost is zero. In Figure 7.5, we have the demand by advertisers shown as D in the left-hand panel along with the corresponding marginal revenue (MR). The derived demand by the broadcasters for broadcast rights is shown in the right-hand panel as $d = MR - MC$ and the corresponding marginal revenue is mr. Now, the franchise would sell Q_1 to maximize its profits and charge w_1. The broadcaster would then maximize its profits by selling Q_1 to advertisers at a price of P_1.

In this model, we have successive monopolies, which lead to double marginalization. The upstream firm marks up its product above cost, and the downstream firm does the same. The downstream firm's markup applies to the marked-up price that it pays to the upstream firm. Vertical integration will lead

[13] For a survey, see Roger D. Blair and David L. Kaserman, *Law and Economics of Vertical Integration and Control*, New York: Academic Press (1983).

[14] See, e.g., Michael Leeds and Peter von Allmen, *The Economics of Sports* (2nd ed.), Boston: Pearson Addison Wesley (2005), pp. 89–92.

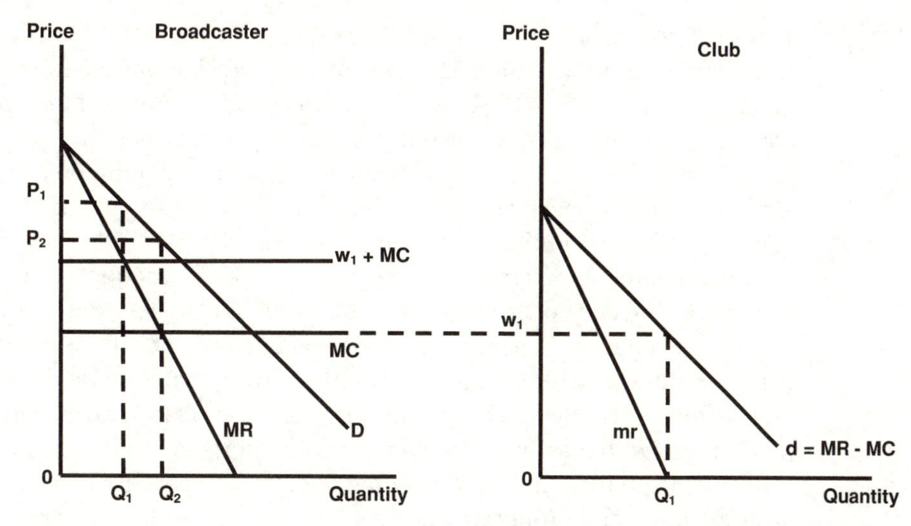

Figure 7.5. In the presence of successive monopoly, vertical integration expands output and decreases price.

to an expansion of output because it eliminates one of the two markups. This improves overall profit *and* lowers the final price. These results are summarized in Figure 7.5. If the broadcaster were vertically integrated, it would recognize that the marginal cost of generating the broadcast rights is zero. It would then operate where its marginal revenue is equal to its marginal cost: $MR = MC$. This results in an output of Q_2 and a price of P_2 for the ad slots.

This model, however, does not describe the way that this market works. First, return to Figure 7.5 and observe that we may have a case of successive monopoly, but only because the sports franchise created it. The Atlanta Braves, for example, have a monopoly over their broadcast rights. They create a successive monopoly by selling all of them exclusively to a single network. There are, however, other networks and cable operators, and therefore the Atlanta Braves can extract all of the monopoly profit through the competitive bidding process. If the broadcaster bought the sports franchise, the purchase price would reflect those monopoly profits. If the present value of the profits from selling ad slots on broadcasts of Braves games were, say, $200 million, then acquiring the Braves would cost $200 million plus the profits on other aspects of that baseball franchise. If the broadcaster is going to gain on the acquisition, something else must be going on. Second, note that in a sports league the franchise is putting on a schedule of games. It does not sell varying quantities as this model requires. The broadcast rights automatically determine the total number of ad slots available for sale. The franchise requires that the whole package be purchased for a lump sum as described earlier. Consequently, the successive monopoly explanation for vertical integration would not seem appropriate, at least not without some modification. This, of course, raises the question of why, then, do we observe vertical integration.

4.1 Transaction Costs

In our simple economic models, we usually assume that transactions take place at no cost to the seller or the buyer. In the real world, of course, transaction costs can be significant.[15] Think of the protracted contract negotiations between some free agents and the various teams interested in signing them. Additionally, contracts for new facilities can take many months to negotiate. The same can be said for the contracts involving broadcast rights.

Vertical integration greatly reduces the costs of contracting. In other words, the transaction will not be subject to the contracting process, and therefore, the costs of negotiating, executing, and enforcing contracts will be avoided. The firm's resources are directed administratively by managers within the firm. Of course, this alternative involves some costs. If costs are lower with vertical integration than with market transactions, we should expect to see vertical integration emerge. In that case, vertical integration is simply more efficient because costs are lower and profits are higher.

4.2 Strategic Behavior

Vertical integration can make sense if it pays to shift revenues or profits upstream or downstream. In the case of broadcast revenues, sharing may be avoided by moving them from the club to the broadcaster. This, of course, only makes sense if the two are vertically integrated.

A vertically integrated firm can report revenues and profits upstream or downstream as it wishes. Return to Figure 7.5. If a broadcaster owned the club, it could transfer the broadcast rights at a price of zero to the broadcast division. The club division would have neither profits nor revenues from the sale of broadcast rights to share with other teams or the players. In leagues with extensive revenue sharing, this could amount to a substantial change in the bottom line.

5 SPORTS NETWORKS

An interesting (and potentially important) development is the recent emergence of sports networks created by leagues and conferences. These include the Big Ten Network, the NFL Network, the MLB Channel, and the Comcast SportsNet. The Southeastern Conference (SEC) and the NHL may not be far behind. This is an example of forward (or downstream) integration as the league or conference produces the athletic competition and also broadcasts it to the television audience. The league or conference does not just license the broadcast rights. Instead, it puts together a network and then sells the distribution rights to cable operators and networks. On the basis of our analysis in the

[15] Recognition of transaction costs can be traced to Ronald H. Coase, "The Nature of the Firm," *Economica*, 4, 386–405. Coase's insights have been extended in many ways. See Oliver Williamson, "Transaction Cost Economics," in Richard Schmalensee and Robert Willig, eds., *Handbook of Industrial Organization*, New York: Elsevier, 1989. See also Roger D. Blair and David L. Kaserman, *Law and Economics of Vertical Integration and Control*, New York: Academic Press, 1983, at pp. 11–27.

Table 7.3. Broadcast Revenue of Six Major National Collegiate Athletic Association Conferences, 2010

Conference	Revenue (per year)
Big 10	$242 million
Southeastern Conference	$205 million
Big 12	$78 million
Atlantic Coast Conference	$67 million
Pac 10	$58 million
Big East	$33 million

Source: http://www.walletgenius.com/2010/06/15/the-value-of-the-tv-contracts-of-the-6-major-ncaa-conferences.

preceding section, it is not entirely clear just why these networks are necessary. The NFL, for example, can license its broadcast rights to others. In principle, it should be able to extract all of the profit through competitive bidding. If the independent broadcasters are not equally efficient, the highest bid need only be a bit above the maximum bid of the second most efficient broadcaster. Thus, the winning bidder will retain some profit. This profit would have to be quite large for vertical integration to make sense; otherwise it would not be worth the risk and the bother. At this time, several leagues and conferences seem to believe that there are added profits to be earned through vertical integration. Only time will tell whether they are right.

5.1 College Conferences

Most of the major conferences have their own networks, but the majority owner and operator is ESPN Regional Television. The Big Ten is the only conference that is the majority owner of its own network. The Fox Entertainment Group is a minority interest in the Big Ten network. The sports networks for the SEC, the Big 12, and the Big East are owned and operated by ESPN Regional Television. The Atlantic Coast Conference's sports network was owned by Raycom Sports, but that was taken over by ESPN Regional Television with the 2011–2012 season.

The broadcast revenues earned by the major college conferences are considerable. Table 7.1 summarizes these revenues. As we can see, the Big Ten is the leader with $242 million followed by the SEC with $205 million. Revenues for the others are substantially lower, falling in the $33 to $78 million range. As with professional teams, these revenues have an attractive property: they are almost pure profit.

6 CONCLUDING REMARKS

Leagues, conferences, and event organizers sell broadcast rights to networks and cable operators. This revenue source is particularly attractive because it involves little additional cost. Consequently, these revenues flow to the bottom line on the income statement. For their part, the broadcasters demand that sports programming because advertisers want to gain access to the audience that sports programming attracts. We have found that vertical integration appears unnecessary because the leagues can earn all of the profit through competitive bidding. Nonetheless, there is some movement toward vertical integration. This will require further reflection and analysis.

PROBLEMS AND QUESTIONS

1. A prominent sports economist points out that some firms that paid a lot for Super Bowl ads did not experience much of a boost in product sales. However, he suggests that "a winner's curse explanation goes wanting."
   - **a.** What is the winner's curse?
   - **b.** Why might he doubt its relevance here?
   - **c.** What do you think?
2. Suppose the University of Florida decided to auction the naming rights for its basketball facility. After a vigorous bidding war, the new name will be Blair Burgers Arena. The company's CEO is concerned that his $50 million investment may have been excessive. How can one tell whether Blair Burgers has suffered the winner's curse?
3. Rodney Fort examined a possible trend in media provider ownership of sports franchises that could boost the price of franchises. This makes current owners wealthier, but they would have to sell out to realize the gain. As a result, "while resources move to a higher valued use, not all will be happy with the outcome."
   - **a.** Who would be unhappy?
   - **b.** Can an existing owner be worse off as a result?
4. Is it true that a nonprofit organization has no incentive to behave efficiently?
5. The Sports Broadcasting Act does not apply to agreements that limit the geographic scope of broadcasts (except for blackouts). Why would Congress impose this limitation on the exemption?
6. Congress permitted an exception to the SBA when a home team was not sold out. Why would it do that?
7. Why did Congress protect high school and college games from NFL competition in the Sports Broadcasting Act?
8. Brett and Devon live next door to each other in a Boston suburb. They decide to go to a Boston Red Sox game. Describe the transaction costs that they will incur in attending the game.
9. Suppose the demand for ad slots on a sports program is:

$$P = 1{,}010 - 5Q,$$

Which means that marginal revenue is

$$MR = 1{,}010 - 10Q,$$

while the marginal and average cost of providing the ad slots is 10.

a. How much are the broadcast rights worth? Explain.

b. Explain how the event organizer can extract all of this value.

c. Would vertical integration generate additional value?

10. In the spring of 2009, the U.S. economy was in the doldrums. As a result, the IOC delayed indefinitely the bidding for the U.S. broadcast rights. Explain why delaying may make sense.

11. The NCAA had an 11-year broadcast deal with CBS to carry the March Madness Men's Basketball Championship. Instead of sticking with CBS after 2010, the NCAA can opt out of the $6 billion deal. If it does so, it will give up the guarantee for 2011–2013. How should the NCAA decide? (Use the expected utility model here.)

12. Return to the numerical example in Section 7.3. Suppose one network is more efficient than the others in using the broadcast rights and the demand for its ad slots is

$$P = 1{,}050 - 2Q,$$

And its marginal revenue is

$$MR = 1{,}050 - 4Q.$$

Assume that the costs are the same.

a. How much profit can this network generate?

b. How much will it have to bid to obtain the broadcast rights?

13. The men's final of the U.S. Open Tennis Championship is always scheduled for a Sunday. However, the final was postponed because of weather in 2008, 2009, and 2010. This has had an impact on the price of ad slots and therefore on the broadcast license fees. Explain why.

14. Tiger Woods played a full season in 2007 and the PGA Tour's Nielsen ratings averaged 2.1. In 2008, he was out for most of the year with a knee injury and ratings sagged to 1.7. They bounced back to 2.0 in 2009 when he returned to full-time play. Based on this evidence, how would you calculate Tiger Wood's value to the PGA Tour?

15. Did Congress make a mistake when it passed the Sports Broadcasting Act?

a. Who benefits?

b. Is anyone harmed? If so, who?

16. A Moody's analyst predicted in 2011 that the NFL's media rights would double from $4 billion to $8 billion by 2020. If it does so, what would have been the annual compound growth rate?

RESEARCH QUESTIONS

1. Compare the broadcast revenues in MLB, the NBA, and the NHL with the team payrolls. Are these rights as significant for these leagues as for the NFL?
2. Contact one of the major leagues and see whether you can get an explanation for the decision to develop a network. How does the league gain through vertical integration?
3. Analyze the dispute between the NFL and Comcast over the NFL Network. This dispute went to court and to the Federal Communications Commission but was settled before decisions were reached in either forum.
4. IMG College pays Ohio State $11 million per year, Florida $10 million, and Texas $9.4 million for their "marketing and media rights." What precisely does this cover? How does IMG College profit from the deal?
5. The Big Ten started its own sports channel in 2007.
   a. How has it fared financially?
   b. Which conferences have followed suit? How have they done?
6. Look at the Nielsen ratings for the World Series for 2000 to the present. Does it seem to matter which teams are playing in the series? How do you think that this influences the value of the broadcast rights?

REFERENCES AND FURTHER READING

Baimbridge, M., S. Cameron, and P. Dawson. (1996). "Satellite Television and the Demand for Football: A Whole New Ball Game?" *Scottish Journal of Political Economy*, 43, 317–333.

Blair, R. D., and D. L. Kaserman. (1983). *Law and Economics of Vertical Integration and Control*. New York: Academic Press.

Coase, R. H. (1937). "The Nature of the Firm." *Economica*, 4, 386–405.

Falconieri, S., J. Sakovics, and F. Palomino. (2004). "Collective versus Individual Sale of Television Rights in League Sports." *Journal of the European Economic Association*, 2, 833–862.

Forrest, D., R. Simmons, and S. Szymanski. (2004). "Broadcasting, Attendance and the Inefficiency of Cartels." *Review of Industrial Organization*, 24, 243–265.

Horowitz, Ira (1974). "Sports Broadcasting," chapter 8 in Noll, Roger G., ed., *Government and the Sports Business*. Washington, DC: Brookings Institution.

Leeds, M., and P. von Allmen. (2005). "*The Economics of Sports*, 2nd ed. Boston: Pearson Addison Wesley, 89–92.

Noll, Roger G. (1974). *Government and the Sports Business* (chapter 8). Washington, DC: The Brookings Institution.

Noll, R. G. (2007). "Broadcasting and Team Sports." *Scottish Journal of Political Economy*, 54, 400–421.

Surdam, D. G. (2005). "Television and Minor League Baseball: Changing Patterns of Leisure in Postwar America." *Journal of Sports Economics*, 6, 61–77.

Szymanski, Stefan. (2009). *Playbooks and Checkbooks: An Introduction to the Economics of Modern Sports* (chapter 5). Princeton, NJ: Princeton University Press.

Siegfried, J. J., and Hinshaw, C. E. (1979). "The Effect of Lifting Television Blackouts on Professional Football No-Shows." *Journal of Economics and Business,* 32, 1–13.

Williamson, O. (1989). "Transaction Cost Economics," in Richard Schmalensee and Robert Willig, eds., *Handbook of Industrial Organization.* New York: Elsevier.

Zuber, R. A., and Gandar, J. M. (1988). "Lifting the Television Blackout on No-Shows at Football Games." *Atlantic Economic Journal,* 16, 63–73.

Zimbalist, Andrew, (2003). *May the Best Team Win* (chapter 2). Washington, DC: The Brookings Institution.

8

Insuring Player Talent

1 TALENT: A RISKY ASSET

Player talent is a valuable asset that is put at risk every time athletes play or practice. Some injuries – even if relatively severe – can be overcome. There are numerous examples of football players who have overcome serious knee and shoulder injuries. Willis McGahee, for example, suffered a devastating knee injury during the 2003 Fiesta Bowl game while playing for the University of Miami. The Buffalo Bills took a huge chance by drafting him in the first round of that year's National Football League (NFL) draft. McGahee sat out his entire rookie year rehabbing his knee, while earning $1.8 million. He recovered from the injury and rushed for 1,128 yards and 13 touchdowns in 2004. Dan Marino, the great Miami Dolphins quarterback, played for years after having torn his Achilles tendon. Tommy John was an ace of the Los Angeles Dodgers pitching staff for years after elbow surgery.[1] Sometimes, however, injuries can end a career. In some sports – golf, tennis, cycling, track, and professional football – the athlete is out of luck if he or she suffers a career-ending injury because incomes are not guaranteed. In other sports, notably baseball and basketball, professional contracts are guaranteed, which means that the athlete gets paid even if he or she cannot perform. A career-ending injury does not void the contract or lead to a financial disaster for the player, but the financial loss does fall on the team, which must pay both the athlete who can no longer play and his replacement.

The value of athletic talent is a risky asset. Who bears that risk depends on the contract. For example, Carl Pavano signed a four-year contract with the New York Yankees in 2005. The contract was reported to be worth $39.95 million. Pavano developed shoulder problems in his first year (2005) and could not pitch after June 27. Pavano worked to rehab his shoulder but developed back, buttocks, and elbow problems. To make matters worse, he was in a car accident and cracked some ribs. He did not pitch at all for the Yankees in 2006

[1] That surgical procedure, which involved transplanting a tendon from the forearm to the elbow, is now known as "Tommy John surgery."

but remained optimistic about his health in 2007. In 2007, Pavano developed further problems. After just two starts, he went on the disabled list and was scheduled for Tommy John surgery. This ended 2007 for him as well as most of 2008 because of the prolonged rehab that such surgery requires. Before his injury in 2005, Pavano won four games while pitching 100 innings. The Yankees paid him some $17 million for the 2005 and 2006 seasons, which works out to $4.3 million per win or $170,000 per inning. If Pavano had not regained his physical abilities, the Yankees would still have had to pay for the remaining two years on his contract.[2] That is, the risk of a career-ending injury falls squarely on the team in Major League Baseball (MLB). When contracts are not guaranteed, as is generally the case in the NFL, the risk of a career-ending injury falls on the player's shoulders. This, of course, is true for all amateur athletes as well. If a college player is injured, the expected value of his future professional compensation is lost.

For teams and players, insurance is a way of shifting the risk to someone else. In this chapter, we examine the demand for insurance – that is, the demand for shifting risk to someone else. Along the way, we develop a simple model of decision making in the face of uncertainty. This economic model will prove useful in Chapters 10 through 13 as well. We also examine the insurance program authorized by the National Collegiate Athletic Association (NCAA) as well as the insurance coverage available to professional teams.

2 RISK AVERSION AND INSURANCE

If a person is risk averse, he or she does not like risk and is willing to pay someone else to bear it. How much one is willing to pay depends on how risk averse the person is. A simple model of decision making under uncertainty will clarify this concept.

2.1 Expected Utility Model

A model that describes optimal decisions in the presence of uncertainty must account for various attitudes toward risk. For example, suppose an individual is faced with a choice between two risky prospects. Prospect 1 involves a payment of $100 with probability 0.5 or a payment of $300 with probability 0.5. Prospect 2 involves a payment of $50 or $350 with equal probabilities. The expected value of each prospect is $200:

$$\text{Prospect 1:}(.5)(100) + (.5)(300) = 50 + 150 = 200$$

$$\text{Prospect 2:}(.5)(50) + (.5)(350) = 25 + 175 = 200$$

Some individuals will be indifferent between prospects 1 and 2, whereas others would prefer one or the other. We need a decision model that can

[2] As it turned out, Pavano returned in late August 2008. Thus, the Yankees got almost one full season out of Pavano for nearly $40 million. Following 2008, Pavano became a free agent and signed with the Cleveland Indians for a modest (by Major League Baseball standards) amount.

accommodate these preferences. The expected utility model, which was developed by John von Neumann and Oskar Morgenstern, is based on the premise that consumers will make choices to maximize expected utility.[3] In other words, the desirability of risky prospects will be determined according to the expected value of the decision maker's utility function. More specifically, the consumer will value a risky prospect involving outcome A with probability p and outcome B with probability $(1 - p)$ as

$$U((A, B; p)) = pU(A) + (1 - p)U(B),$$

which is expected utility, and we will abbreviate that as $E[U(\cdot)]$. If the expected utility of risky prospect X is larger than the expected utility of risky prospect Y, then X will be chosen over Y. In the foregoing numerical example, the decision maker would compare

$$U(100{,}300; 0.5) = (.5)U(100) + (.5)U(300)$$

with

$$U(50{,}350; 0.5) = (.5)U(50) + (.5)U(350)$$

and select the one with the higher value.

2.2 Risk Aversion and Risk Neutrality

Much of the early interest in decisions under uncertainty centered around games of chance. For a time, it was thought that a decision maker would focus on the expected value of a gamble. If the expected value exceeded the cost of playing, then the decision maker would play. However, this view was called into question nearly 250 years ago by Nicholas Bernoulli, who contrived the St. Petersburg Paradox. In an updated form, suppose that a Las Vegas casino offered you the following gamble. You flip a coin. If it comes up heads on the first toss, you would win \$2. If a head first appears on the second toss, you would win \$4. You would get \$8 if the first head appeared on the third toss, \$16 if the first head appeared on the fourth toss, and so on. Whenever the first head appears, the game is over and you receive $(\$2)^n$ where n is the number of tosses it took to get the first head. What is the expected value of the game? Surprisingly, the expected value is infinite. As the number of tosses it takes to obtain the first head rises, the payoff rises, but the probability of these outcomes falls proportionately. For any value of n, the payoff is $(\$2)^n$, but the probability of getting the first head on toss n is $1/(2)^n$. As a result, the expected payoff for each outcome is \$1. Some sample calculations are shown in Table 8.1. Because the possible outcomes extend to infinity, the expected value of the game is infinite. Not surprisingly, no one would be willing to pay an infinite amount to play such a game. This lack of enthusiasm for paying an infinite amount to play the game was thought to be paradoxical – after all, that would be an actuarially fair price to pay for the privilege of playing. However, this merely suggests that

[3] John von Neumann and Oskar Morgenstern (1945), *The Theory of Games and Economic Behavior*, Princeton, NJ: Princeton University Press.

Table 8.1. Expected Value of the St. Petersburg Game

Outcome	Probability	Payoff	Expected Payoff
H	1/2	$2	$1
TH	1/4	4	1
TTH	1/8	8	1
TTTH	1/16	16	1
TTTTH	1/32	32	1
TTTTTH	1/64	64	1

decision makers do not focus exclusively on expected values. In fact, consumers may actually value gains and losses differently, which will cause them to behave quite differently from those who look only at expected values.

We can describe a consumer's attitude toward risk in terms of his or her attitude toward actuarially fair gambles. By way of definition, an actuarially fair gamble is one in which the expected value of the gamble (i.e., the expected payoff) is just equal to the price that one must pay to play. For example, suppose a consumer was afforded the opportunity to engage in the following gamble: a fair coin is tossed in the air, and if it lands on heads, he or she receives $10; if it lands on tails, he or she must pay $10. Because a fair coin will land on heads half of the time and on tails the other half, this is an actuarially fair gamble. We can easily calculate the expected value of the gamble as:

$$E[V] = \tfrac{1}{2}(\$10) + \tfrac{1}{2}(-\$10) = 0.$$

Because zero is the price of playing, the gamble is actuarially fair. In contrast, consider a Boy Scout raffle in which the prize is a 10-speed bicycle. Suppose that 500 tickets are sold for $1 a piece and that the value of the bike is $150. Because there are 500 tickets, the probability that any one ticket will be selected is 1/500 or 0.002. Accordingly, the expected value of a ticket can be computed as:

$$E[V] = 0.002(\$150) + .998(\$0) = \$.30,$$

which is less than the price paid for the ticket. We describe the raffle as being actuarially unfair because the expected value of the gamble is less than the price of playing.

2.3 Risk Aversion

A consumer is said to be *risk averse* if he or she refuses to accept any actuarially fair gambles. This person abhors risk and will not assume risk without some sort of compensation. Another way of saying this is that a risk averter will pay a positive price to shift risk to someone else. A risk averter will sacrifice something to obtain a reduction in risk. This attitude toward risk is captured in the shape of the consumer's von Neumann-Morgenstern utility function. In Figure 8.1, we measure wealth on the horizontal axis and utility on the vertical axis. The risk averter's utility function is positively sloped because more

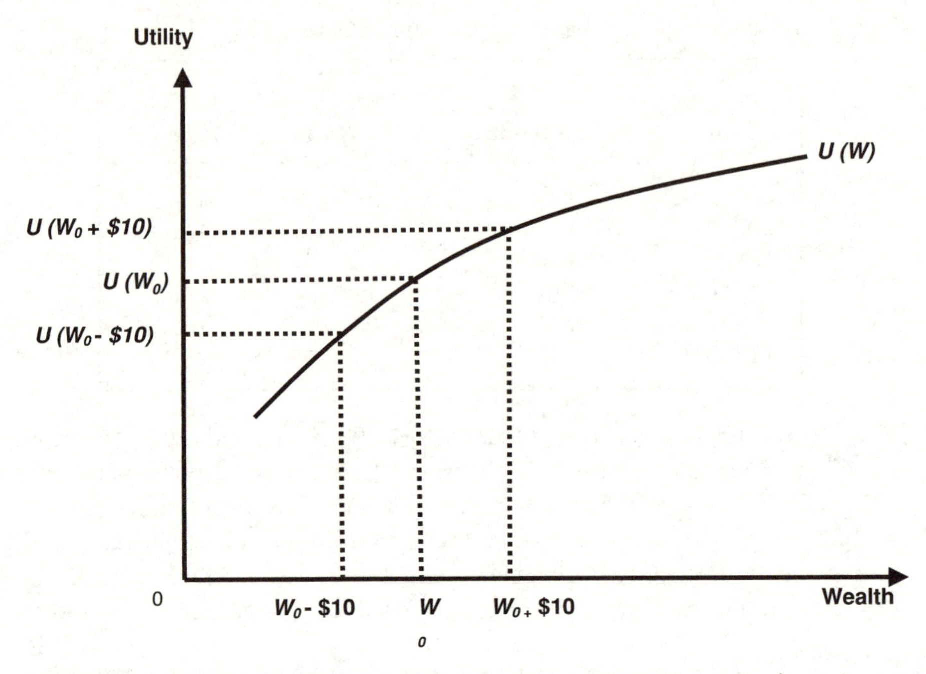

Figure 8.1. A risk averter's utility function is strictly concave; utility increases at a decreasing rate.

wealth is always preferred to less wealth. Note, however, that the utility function increases at a decreasing rate – that is, it is *concave.* One can appreciate the implications of this in the following example.

Consider how Cautious Carl responds to the coin flipping gamble. If Carl does not gamble, he enjoys wealth of W_0 and the corresponding utility of that wealth, $U(W_0)$, which is the height of the utility function directly above W_0. The gamble involves betting \$10 on the toss of a fair coin. If Carl wins, his wealth will be $W_0 + \$10$. If he loses, however, his wealth will be $W_0 - \$10$. However, Cautious Carl is not motivated by changes in wealth per se. Instead, he is concerned with changes in utility. If Carl gambles and wins, we can see that his utility increases from $U(W_0)$ to $U(W_0 + \$10)$. If Carl gambles and loses, his utility falls from $U(W_0)$ to $U(W_0 - \$10)$. In Figure 8.1, we can see that the loss in *utility* when Carl loses exceeds the gain in *utility* when Carl wins. If the gamble is actuarially fair, Carl will win \$10 half of the time and lose \$10 the other half. For Cautious Carl, this is not actuarially fair in terms of utility because half of the time he will lose $U(W_0) - U(W_{0-}10)$, and he will win only $U(W_0 + \$10) - U(W_0)$ the other half. The expected value of the gamble is zero in dollar terms. In terms of utility, he will come out behind on average. Consequently, a risk averter will reject an actuarially fair gamble. Naturally, we are not saying that a risk averter will never engage in a situation in which the outcome is uncertain. This would be impossible because the world is a risky place. Everyday, we risk our lives in many ways: driving to school or work, crossing the street, jogging, flying in an airplane, and so on. So we are not saying that a risk averter will never bear risk. We are saying, however, that a risk averter will try to avoid or reduce

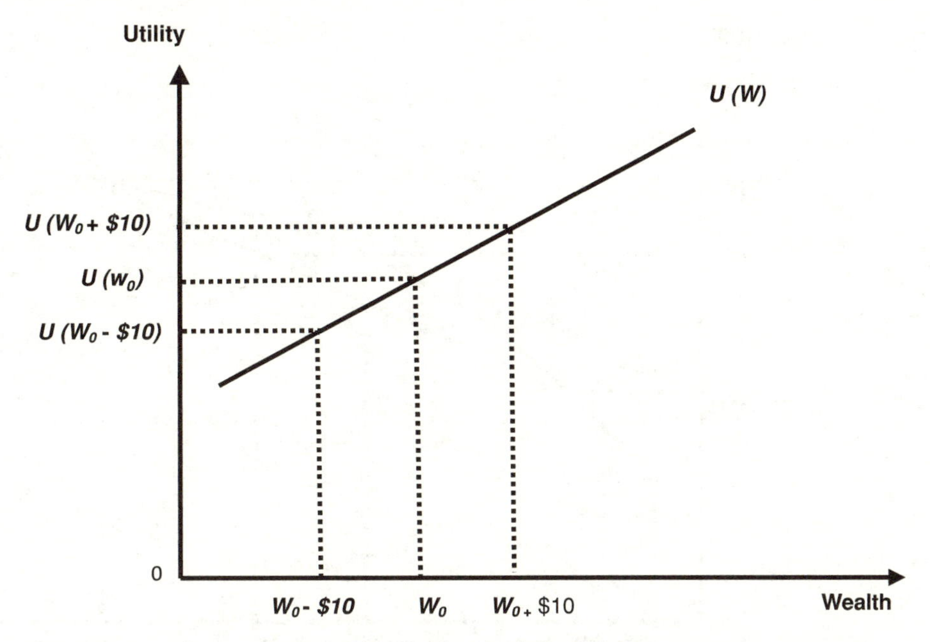

Figure 8.2. A risk-neutral consumer's utility function is linear; it increases at a constant rate.

risk. If Cautious Carl were to gamble, he would require favorable odds. Precisely how favorable the odds would have to be depends on the precise shape of his utility function.[4]

2.4 Risk Neutrality

Consumers who are indifferent to risk are called *risk neutral.* These consumers will not have a preference for or against actuarially fair gambles. The reason for this attitude can be seen in the shape of the utility function represented by the straight line in Figure 8.2. Because of the linearity of the utility function, the gains and losses in a coin flipping gamble are equal in monetary terms *and* are equal in utility terms. Specifically, in Figure 8.2, we see that the increase in utility from gambling and winning is $U(W_0 + \$10) - U(W_0)$. The loss in utility from gambling and losing is $U(W_0) - U(W_0 - \$10)$. It is apparent that these differences are equal because of the linearity of the utility function. Consequently, if the gamble is actuarially fair, on average the risk-neutral consumer neither gains nor loses in utility terms. As a result, he or she will be indifferent about accepting or rejecting actuarially fair gambles.

2.5 Measuring Expected Utility

There is a simple graphical way of measuring expected utility, which is illustrated in Figure 8.3. Suppose the possible outcomes are W_1 and W_2. The height of the utility function above W_1 is the $U(W_1)$, and the height of the utility function above W_2 is the $U(W_2)$. Construct a chord (that is, a straight line)

[4] The results that we found in Figure 8.1 hold for all strictly concave utility functions.

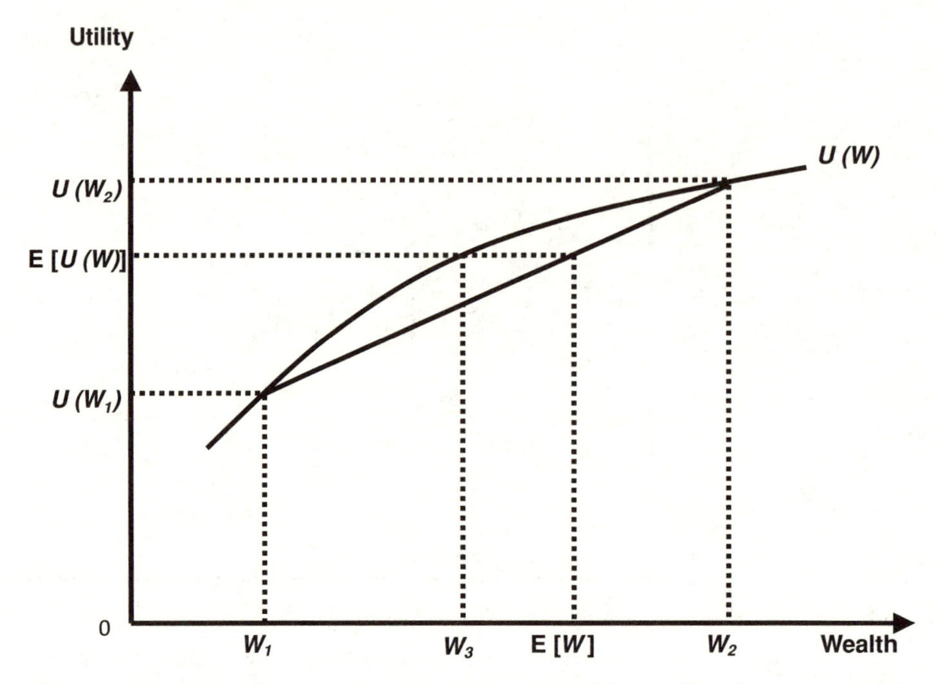

Figure 8.3. Expected utility is given by the height of the chord directly above the expected wealth.

connecting these two points on the utility function. Now use the probabilities of W_1 and W_2 to calculate the expected wealth:

$$E[W] = pW_1 + (1 - p)W_2.$$

Plot $E[W]$ on the wealth axis. The expected utility of wealth in this risky situation is given by the height of the chord above the $E[W]$. These results hold for all values of W_1, W_2, and p. In other words, this method is general. In the Appendix to this chapter, there is graphical proof that this procedure works as a general proposition.

2.6 Certainty Equivalent

The certainty equivalent of a risky prospect $(W_1, W_2; p)$ is a certain (i.e., non-stochastic), value of wealth that is worth as much as the risky prospect to the decision maker. In other words, the certainty equivalent (W_3) is a value of wealth such that

$$U(W_3) = E[U(W)].$$

In Figure 8.3, W_3 is the certainty equivalent of the risky prospect that has an expected value of $E[W]$.

3 SHIFTING RISK THROUGH INSURANCE

When the New York Mets signed John Franco, a 40-year-old relief pitcher, to a three-year contract reported to be worth $10 million, they faced a risk. If Franco

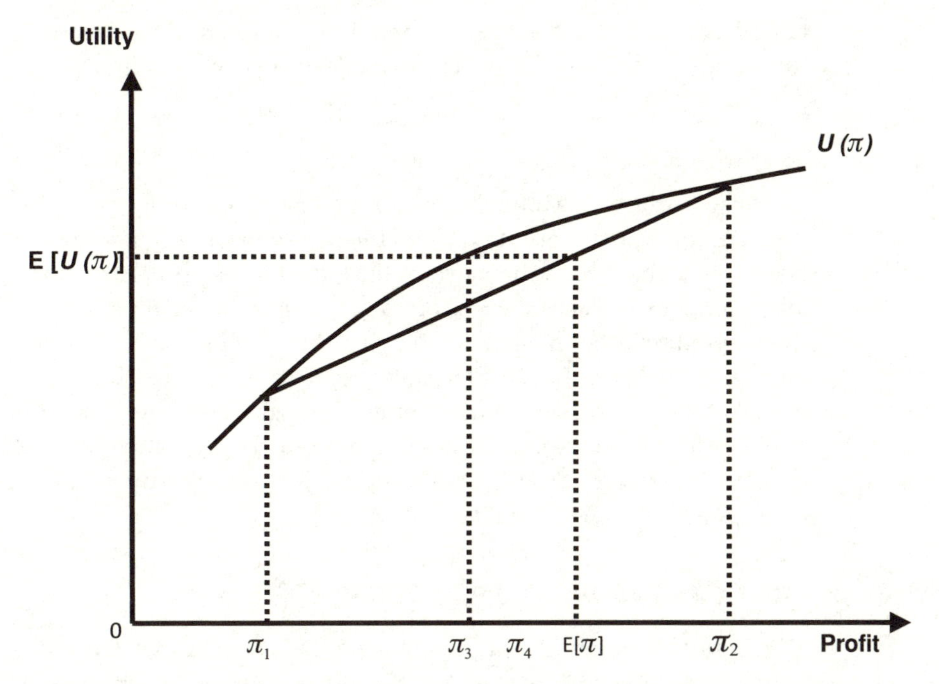

Figure 8.4. A risk averter will buy insurance if the premium results in $U(\pi) > E[U(\pi)]$.

suffered a career-ending injury, the contract would still have to be honored, that is, Franco would have to be paid. The probability of such an injury may be fairly high for a 40-year-old player, but that is an empirical issue. In any event, the Mets bought disability insurance to shift the risk of financial loss to the insurance company in the event of an injury. The premium on the Franco policy was $700,000. Our expected utility model explains why the Mets would pay so much for the insurance.

In Figure 8.4, $U(\pi)$ represents the Mets' utility of profit. Because $U(\pi)$ is concave, we may infer that the Mets are risk averse. Team profit is π_2 if the player is not hurt, and π_1 is the team profit if he is hurt. If the probability of a career-ending injury is p, then the probability of no career-ending injury is $(1 - p)$ because the probabilities have to add up to one. The team's expected profit is

$$E[\pi] = p\pi_1 + (1 - p)\pi_2,$$

which is between π_1 and π_2, as shown in Figure 8.4. The value to the team of this risky situation is given by the expected utility of π, which is measured as the height of the chord connecting $U(\pi_1)$ and $U(\pi_2)$ directly above $E[\pi]$.

We can see that the team would be indifferent between having π_3 with certainty and facing the risk because π_3 is the certainty equivalent:

$$U(\pi_3) = E[U(\pi)].$$

The team would prefer any profit greater than π_3 with certainty than having the risky profit with an expected value of $E[\pi]$. For example, if an insurance company would bear the risk for a premium of $\pi_2 - \pi_4$, the team would buy the insurance because the utility of π_4 exceeds the expected utility:

$$U(\pi_4) > E[U(\pi)],$$

as can be seen in Figure 8.4.

Buying insurance shifts the risk to the insurance company. If the player is not injured, the team profit is π_2 less the insurance premium of $\pi_2 - \pi_4$, which leaves the team at π_4. If the player is hurt, the team's profit is π_1, but the insurance company replaces the loss of $\pi_2 - \pi_1$ to put the team back at π_2. Because the team purchased insurance, however, the net position is π_2 less the insurance premium of $\pi_2 - \pi_4$, which leaves the team at π_4. Thus, the team winds up at π_4 whether the player gets hurt or does not get hurt. Therefore, π_4 is certain and the value to the team of that certain profit is the height of the utility function at π_4, which is greater than the $E[U(\pi)]$. As a result, the team is better off with insurance than without it.

4 THE NCAA INSURANCE PROGRAM

NCAA athletes with bright professional potential can be injured while still amateurs. Early in the 2006 season, Michael Bush, a running back at Louisville, was considered to be the number one or two running back prospect in college football. Early in the season, he broke his leg in a game and was finished for the season. Fortunately, he has recovered and will have a solid NFL career, but if he had been disabled, he had some protection. Bush had purchased a $2 million disability insurance policy. He was not alone in this regard. Many NCAA athletes buy disability insurance to provide some financial security in the event of a career-ending injury.[5] Usually, there are about 100 athletes covered by the NCAA's disability insurance program each year. As one might expect, most of them – 75 or so – are football players.

Private disability insurance has been available to elite athletes for decades. The NCAA insurance program – Exceptional Student Athlete Disability Insurance – was introduced in 1990. The idea was not to compete with private insurers. Instead, the aim was to thwart unscrupulous agents who promised to buy disability insurance for star players if they promised to be clients when they turned pro. The NCAA insurance program does not provide coverage for athletes in individual sports, so golf, tennis, and track athletes are on their own. Nor does it cover athletes in "minor" team sports: soccer, lacrosse, field hockey, and swimming. The coverage is available only for athletes with significant professional potential in baseball, basketball, football, and ice hockey – that is, for those headed to the major leagues: MLB, the NBA or Women's NBA, the NFL, and the National Hockey League (NHL). To be eligible, an athlete must be projected to be drafted in the first three rounds of the NFL or NHL draft or in the first round of the MLB, NBA, or WNBA draft. Thus, the program is only for the

[5] Michael Bush presumably would have been the second running back selected in the 2007 NFL draft. Instead he was picked 100 overall in the fourth round. He signed a four-year contract that contained a $500,000 signing bonus. No doubt, he suffered a major financial loss, but this loss was not covered because he was not disabled.

most highly regarded NCAA athletes. Players such as Tom Brady, the New England Patriots' great quarterback who was drafted in the sixth round, would have been ineligible for the current NCAA insurance program. Tom Brady is not the only notable example. Kurt Warner, who won a Super Bowl with St. Louis, and Ian Scott, who started the 2007 Super Bowl for the Bears, are others who would have been ineligible for the NCAA insurance program.

The disability insurance provides 24/7 coverage for any injury or sickness that results in disability. In most cases, an athlete is given a year to recover from the injury or sickness. At the end of that time, the athlete's condition will be evaluated by a qualified physician. If he or she determines that the athlete has suffered continuous total disability, the insurance benefit will be paid. As an example, Ed Chester was a highly rated defensive tackle at the University of Florida. In the 1998 game against Louisiana State University, Chester suffered a terrible knee injury that ended any hope of an NFL career. At the end of a year, a physician determined that he could not play football. He collected $1 million on his insurance policy and moved on with his life.[6]

Box 8.1 ***Suing for a Failure to Insure***

Decory Bryant was a football star at the University of Georgia in 2003. Under the NCAA disability insurance program, a player must be projected as a first, second, or third round pick in the NFL draft to be eligible for coverage. When Bryant was deemed eligible for coverage in October 2003, he requested a $500,000 policy. Apparently, Georgia athletic department officials mailed incomplete paperwork, which the insurance company received too late to provide desired coverage. Sadly, Bryant suffered a neck injury that ended his NFL prospects. Because of Georgia's failure to file the insurance forms correctly, Bryant had no financial protection. He sued the University of Georgia athletic association and one of its administrators.*

* Associated Press, "Injured Player Sues for Insurance Problem," *Gainesville Sun*, December 9, 2004.

4.1 Premiums

Each athlete's insurance application is considered on an individual basis. The program administrator decides how much coverage is available to the athlete. Policies are usually written for $1 or $2 million, although some go as low as $500,000 and the maximum is $3 million. The insurance premiums are in the $8,500 to $9,500 per million dollars of coverage range. The precise amount depends on market conditions at the time the athlete applies for coverage. Because most student-athletes do not have much extra money, they usually finance the premiums. Loans for these purposes are fairly safe. If the athlete is not hurt, the loan can be repaid from the signing bonus. If the athlete is hurt,

[6] Ed Chester works at a Boys' and Girls' Club and acknowledges that his insurance payout allows him to work at a job he loves.

the loan can be repaid from the insurance proceeds. Either way, the lender gets his money plus interest. There is, however, the possibility of an unfortunate circumstance. If an athlete qualifies for insurance but is not drafted for some reason other than an injury, then he or she will be stuck with the insurance bill. In that event, the lender faces some default risk.

For those players who are apt to be selected at the top of the NFL draft, the NCAA program is too restrictive. These athletes are in line for signing bonuses in the $10 to $30 million range. The NCAA's limit of $3 million is simply too low. To get the coverage that they need, they turn to private insurance, which is often underwritten by Lloyd's of London. These policies cost somewhat more per million dollars of coverage. Nonetheless, those players who want $5 to $10 million of disability insurance can turn to them. When the athletes go outside the NCAA for coverage, they must still abide by the NCAA rules regarding loans to cover the premiums.

5 TEAM INSURANCE PURCHASES

In MLB and the NBA, player contracts are guaranteed.[7] If a player is injured and cannot play out his contract, the team must pay him anyway. To guard against off-the-field misadventures, the contracts typically prohibit a host of activities: snowboarding, skiing, and riding motorcycles, among other things. If an athlete is injured while participating in a prohibited activity, the team's obligation to pay him disappears, but injuries can occur while playing, practicing, or training. For example, in February 2007, an MRI revealed a partial tear in the rotator cuff of Kris Benson's throwing shoulder. In this case, the Orioles were still on the hook for Benson's 2007 salary of $7.5 million. The Orioles signed Steve Trachsel, a free agent, for $3.1 million to fill the gap in their starting rotation left by Benson's injury. Injuries can also occur because the world is an uncertain place. For example, Carl Pavano suffered several broken ribs when he got into an automobile accident. As a result of these risks and the size of player contracts, teams face substantial financial risk. Often, they buy insurance coverage to shift the risk.

At times, insurance coverage seems to be inadequate. For example, Mark Cuban, owner of the Dallas Mavericks, complained that the insurance coverage for players participating in the 2002 World Championship was inadequate to cover potential losses to the Mavericks. There were five Maverick players who could have been called on to play: Michael Finley and Raef La Frentz for the United States, Steve Nash for Canada, and Shawn Brown and Dirk Nowitzki for Germany. The combined value of their contracts was $240 million. Had they all been injured, Dallas would have had to pay their salaries and then have to pay their replacements. Although the probability that all five players would get severely injured in one tournament is small, Cuban's point was that the insurance would not cover his loss in the event of serious injuries.

[7] There are some exceptions. For example, J. D. Drew's contract with the Red Sox allowed the team to get out of the contract if Drew's past injuries did not permit him to perform at a high level. The San Francisco Giants put a clause in Barry Bonds's 2007 contract that would have voided their obligation if he had been indicted for perjury. These are exceptions, however.

Table 8.2. Jeff Bagwell's Statistics, 2000–2005

Year	Games	Home Runs	Average
2000	159	47	.310
2001	161	39	.288
2002	158	31	.291
2003	160	39	.278
2004	156	27	.266
2005	39	3	.250

Statistics were drawn from http://www.mlb.com.

5.1 The Jeff Bagwell Example

The Houston Astros bought a disability insurance policy on Jeff Bagwell, their slugging first baseman.[8] It was not easy to find an insurer because there had recently been some large insurance recoveries. For example, the Baltimore Orioles bought insurance to cover Albert Belle's five-year, $65 million contract in 1999.[9] Belle played in 1999 and 2000, but a degenerative hip condition made him unable to play in 2001. The Orioles were able to recover $27.3 to $35.0 million from the insurance policy. These sorts of large payouts have made many insurers reluctant to write insurance policies on hefty contracts. Insurers have raised the premiums and imposed substantial deductibles to reduce their exposure. No doubt, the policy on Jeff Bagwell was not cheap, but it did prove to be a bargain. As it turned out, that decision was a good move for the Astros because Bagwell was totally disabled by the end of the 2005 season.

For the 2000–2005 seasons, Jeff Bagwell was an outstanding performer for the Astros. His statistics were most impressive (see Table 8.2).[10]

In 2005, however, Bagwell's arthritic right shoulder became a serious problem, and he missed 115 games after going on the disabled list in May. He came off the list in September and was added to the Astros' postseason roster. Shoulder pain limited him to serving as the designated hitter in the World Series against the White Sox.

On January 12, 2006, Bagwell's shoulder was examined by James Andrew, a world-renowned orthopedic surgeon. Dr. Andrews informed Bagwell that he was disabled, but Bagwell refused to believe that his playing days were over. He was determined to go to spring training to prepare for the 2006 season. Under the terms of the policy with Connecticut General Life Insurance, if Bagwell had participated in spring practice and played at all in 2006, the contract would have been void. The Astros therefore sent Bagwell a letter informing him that he was attending spring training for the purposes of rehabilitation only. Bagwell

[8] This anecdote is based on information drawn from the following newspaper accounts: Jose DeJesus Ortiz, "Bagwell Policy a Rarity," *Houston Chronicle*, Feb. 2, 2006; Jose DeJesus Ortiz, "Bagwell Insurance Claim Denied," *Houston Chronicle*, March 28, 2006; and Brian McTaggart, "Insurance Settlement Reached," *Houston Chronicle*, Dec. 16, 2006.

[9] Jose DeJesus Ortiz, "Bagwell Policy a Rarity," *Houston Chronicle*, Feb. 2, 2006.

[10] Statistics provided by ESPN.com.

found that he could not throw at all without a "tremendous amount of pain" that he could no longer handle.

The Astros filed a claim to recover $15.6 million of Bagwell's 2006 salary of $17 million. At first, Connecticut General denied the claim on the basis that Bagwell's condition had not changed between the end of the 2005 season and January 2006. The Astros argued that Dr. Andrews's assessment that Bagwell was disabled was the first time his disability had been determined. After some legal wrangling, the Astros' claim was settled in mid-December 2006. The terms of the settlement were not disclosed.

5.2 Insurance Decisions

When the New York Yankees persuaded Roger Clemens to rejoin them for part of the 2007 season, the prorated salary came to $18 million. At 44 years old, Clemens could easily suffer a season-ending injury. The Yankees began to look around for insurance to cover the financial risk of such an injury. The problems were not uncommon in the insurance industry: availability and affordability. Given Clemens's age and his history of groin and hamstring problems, the probability of injury was substantial. This made it tougher to find a willing insurer. Estimates of the premium for such a policy were $2 million. It is not certain that the Yankees ever insured the Clemens contract.

Box 8.2 *No Cooperation, No Insurance**

Participants on various professional tours are *independent contractors* rather than employees. As an independent contractor, each athlete is responsible for his or her own expenses for training, equipment, travel, lodging and food, and insurance. If the athletes can cooperate and form a cohesive association, they can often get the benefits of group insurance, which tends to be substantially less expensive than individual policies. Absent cooperation, however, group policies may be unavailable.

The financial consequences of serious injury and no insurance coverage are highlighted by the accident suffered by Stephen Murray. While participating in a Dew Action Sports Tour event, Murray flipped off his bike and landed on his head. The accident left him paralyzed below the shoulders. Before Murray's injury, no one had suffered such a severe injury in BMX freestyle, skateboarding, or motocross freestyle.

NBC, which owns the Dew Tour, is willing to work with an athletes association to provide group insurance, but NBC insists that the initiative must start with the athletes. This has been a problem because the athletes cannot seem to cooperate in organizing one.

Because of the absence of insurance, Stephen Murray must rely on fund raisers to pay his medical bills and living expenses.

* Matt Higgins, "Severe Injury Brings Concern and a Call for Insurance," *New York Times*, July 23, 2007.

Barry Bonds signed a one-year contract with the San Francisco Giants for the 2007 season. The salary was $15.8 million. Because Bonds was going to turn 43 at midseason and given his fragile knees, the Giants must have considered insurance coverage but ultimately decided to forego it. After assessing the risk and the cost of coverage, the Giants decided to bear the risk themselves rather than shift it to an insurance company. Part of the reasoning may have been that knee injuries would be excluded from the coverage as preexisting conditions. In that event, the Giants might reasonably have assumed that the probability of any other season-ending injury was low.

6 CONCLUDING REMARKS

In this chapter, we have examined the economics of uncertainty. In that connection, we introduced the expected utility model and used it to explain why risk-averse decision makers would want to buy insurance. Given the substantial value of athletic talent, it is not surprising that many athletes and their clubs are interested in disability insurance. The NCAA's insurance program for highly regarded athletes with significant professional potential was examined. In addition, several examples from MLB were also discussed.

As we will see in subsequent chapters, the expected utility model can be used to analyze gambling, the deterrence of misconduct, and various business decisions.

PROBLEMS AND QUESTIONS

1. Find the expected utility of the gamble offered to Cautious Carl in Figure 8.1. Do you see why Carl refuses to gamble? Explain. Find the certainty equivalent in Figure 8.1.
2. Cautious Carl hates risk and usually avoids gambles. Could his chances of winning be so good that he would accept a gamble? Explain why or why not and illustrate on a graph.
3. Could an insurance company sell insurance at an actuarially fair premium? Explain why or why not.
4. Return to Figure 8.4 and answer the following questions:
   a. Is the team risk averse? Explain.
   b. Suppose that the insurance premium was greater than $\pi_2 - \pi_3$. Would the team buy insurance anyway because it is risk averse? Explain your reasoning.
   c. If the team were risk neutral, would it buy insurance?
   d. What is the actuarial value of the risk – that is, what is the expected loss?
5. On an installment of *Who Wants to Be a Millionaire*, a contestant had reached the $125,000 level. Confronted with a difficult question, he eliminated two of the wrong answers but still had no clue as to the correct answer. Guessing correctly would have increased his winnings by $125,000

and would have kept him in the game. Guessing incorrectly would have reduced his winnings to $32,000 and, therefore, would have resulted in a loss of $93,000. He elected to quit and thereby keep the $125,000 he had already won. Is this contestant risk averse? Explain your answer.

6. During the spring, the University of Southern California's star wide receiver, Dallas Catchings, decided to play for the Trojans during the 2009 season and then head for the fame and fortune of the NFL. If he does not suffer a serious injury, his wealth will be $15 million, but if he does suffer a serious injury, his wealth will be zero. If the probability of a serious injury is 0.10,
   a. what is his expected wealth?
   b. if he is risk neutral, will he buy insurance? Explain your reasoning.
   c. if he is risk averse, will he buy insurance? Explain your reasoning.
7. Use the expected utility model to analyze a potential first-round draft pick's financial exposure due to injury. How much insurance would he want to buy? How much is usually available? Is he underinsured?
8. Cautious Carl owns the Hogtown Hens, a professional baseball team. He just signed Homerin' Hank to a multiyear contract worth $100 million. The payments are guaranteed even in the event of a career-ending injury. The probability of a career-ending injury in the first year is 0.2. If Hank suffers no injury, the Hens' wealth will be W; if Hank is injured, wealth falls to $W - 100$. See the figure below.
   a. What is the Hens' expected wealth?
   b. What is the expected utility of wealth?
   c. What is the actuarial value of the risk that the Hens face?
   d. Would Cautious Carl be interested in buying insurance on Hank's contract?
   e. If Carl would be interested in buying insurance, what is the maximum insurance premium he would pay?

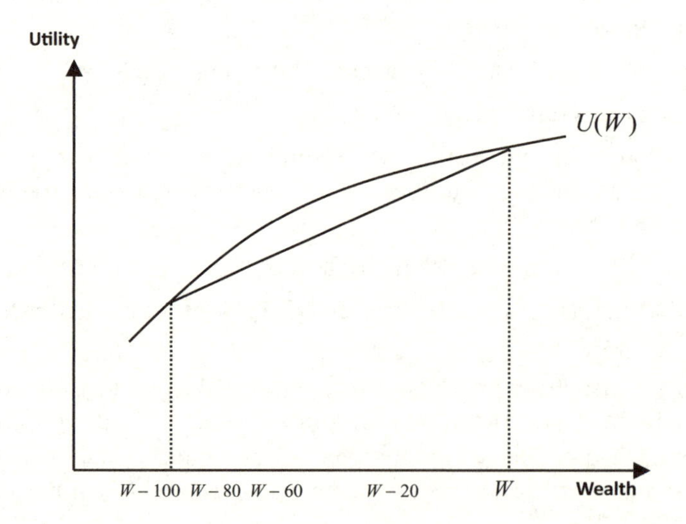

9. Even though the owner of the Hogtown Hens is risk averse, she refused to buy insurance to cover Sammy Slugger's $18 million contract. How can that make sense from an economic perspective?
10. The probability of a career-ending injury for an elite NCAA football player is about one in a hundred. The premium for a $1.0 million policy is $15,000.
    a. What is the actuarially fair premium?
    b. Are the athletes being overcharged?
    c. If so, why do they pay it?

RESEARCH QUESTIONS

1. Identify 10 players who were not drafted in the first three rounds of the NFL draft but who are starters today.
2. What is the current premium for a $1 million insurance policy by position? Does the variation make sense to you?
3. Under the NCAA disability insurance program, an athlete may recover for "continuous total disability." This raises several questions:
    a. What does this mean with respect to everyday life?
    b. Suppose a knee injury slows a wide receiver from 4.3 speed to 5.3 speed. Can he recover given that he is now too slow to play in the NFL?
    c. If a series of concussions results in a recommendation that the athlete stop playing football, can he recover benefits?
4. Why does the NCAA program fail to cover athletes in other sports, say, golf and tennis?

APPENDIX: GRAPHICAL MEASUREMENT OF EXPECTED UTILITY

Consider a risky situation where the possible outcomes are W_1 and W_2 as shown in Figure 8A.[11] Suppose that the probability of receiving W_1 is $1/n$ and the probability of receiving W_2 is $(n-1)/n$. Now, the expected utility of wealth is:

$$E[U(W)] = pU(W_1) + (1-p)U(W_2).$$

After substituting for the probabilities, we can write this as:

$$\begin{aligned} E[U(W)] &= (1/n)U(W_1) + (n-1)/nU(W_2) \\ &= (1/n)U(W_1) + (n-1)/n[U(W_1) + (U(W_2) - U(W_1))] \\ &= U(W_1) + (n-1)/n[(U(W_2) - U(W_1))] \end{aligned}$$

In Figure 8A, we want to show that the expected utility of wealth is given by the height of the chord connecting *a* and *b* directly above the expected

[11] I am indebted to Adolfo Marzol for useful suggestions on this appendix.

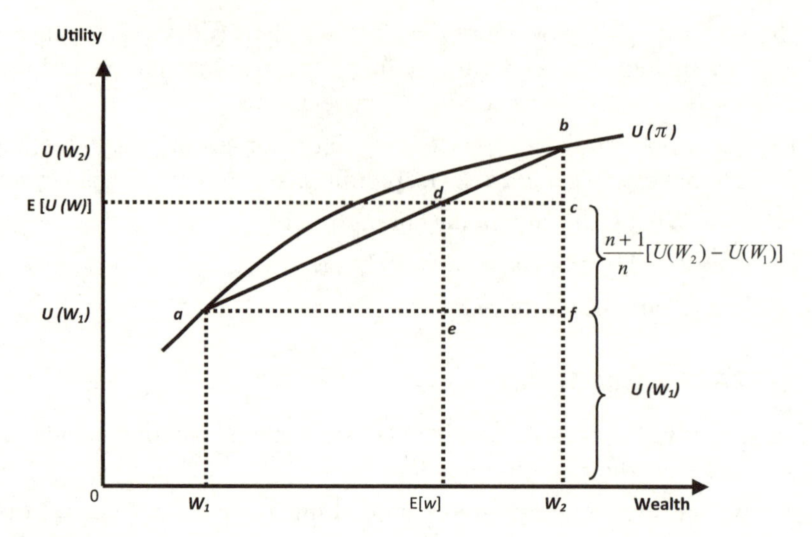

Figure 8A.

wealth. First, note that triangles *ade* and *dbc* are similar because the corresponding angles are identical. Next, note that the line segment *bc* has length $(1/n)[U(W_2) - U(W_1)]$ and, therefore, that the ratio of *bc* to *cf* is $1/(n-1)$. This means that *ae* has length $(n-1)/n(W_2 - W_1)$ while *de* has length $1/n(W_2 - W_1)$. Finally, notice that:

$$\begin{aligned} E[W] &= \frac{1}{n}W_1 + \frac{n-1}{n}W_2 \\ &= \frac{1}{n}W_1 + \frac{n-1}{n}[W_1 + (W_2 - W_1)] \\ &= W_1 + \frac{n-1}{n}[W_2 - W_1]. \end{aligned}$$

Thus, point *d* lies on the chord connecting *a* and *b* directly above $E[W]$. The height of *d* is the $E[U(W)]$, which is what we set out to demonstrate.

REFERENCES AND FURTHER READING

Bollinger, C. R., and J. L. Hotchkiss. (2003). "The Upside Potential of Hiring Risky Workers: Evidence from the Basketball Industry." *Journal of Labor Economics*, 21, 923–944.

Lehn, K. 1982. "Property Rights, Risk Sharing, and Player Disability in Major League Baseball." *Journal of Law and Economics*, 25, 343–366.

von Neumann, John, and Oskar Morgenstern. (1945). *The Theory of Games and Economic Behavior.* Princeton, NJ: Princeton University Press.

9

Sports Leagues and Antitrust Policy

1 INTRODUCTION

As we have all seen, teams compete vigorously on the field, but off the field, there is a lot more cooperation than competition. This cooperation provides some benefits to the fans because the athletic competition that we love to watch could not be provided without substantial cooperation. There is no doubt, however, that cooperation benefits the teams and results in higher profits. These higher profits, of course, must come from somewhere: the fans, the sponsors, the broadcasters, the coaches, the athletes. In most sectors of the economy, the antitrust laws do not permit competing firms to collaborate in ways that injure the public. However, sports leagues and organizations have some unique characteristics that may lead to a different application of the antitrust law. In this chapter, we examine the role that the antitrust laws have played in shaping the conduct of sports leagues and organizations. We begin this chapter with a brief review of the economic rationale for antitrust, our central antitrust statutes, and their interpretation.[1] Along the way, we develop the crucial concepts of market definition and monopoly power. We then turn to the application of antitrust policy to sports leagues and organizations. After a brief look at the general approach to evaluating league rules, we turn our attention to antitrust challenges by league members and by outsiders.

2 THE ECONOMIC RATIONALE FOR ANTITRUST

The economic argument for competition and against monopoly centers on the social welfare losses that flow from the profit-maximizing behavior of a monopolist. We can see the nature of such welfare losses in Figure 9.1. Demand is

[1] For more on antitrust generally, see Keith N. Hylton, *Antitrust Law: Economic Theory and Common Law Evolution*, New York: Cambridge University Press, 2003; Herbert Hovenkamp, *The Antitrust Enterprise: Principle and Execution*, Cambridge, MA: Harvard University Press, 2005; and Roger D. Blair and David L. Kaserman, *Antitrust Economics*, New York: Oxford University Press, 2009.

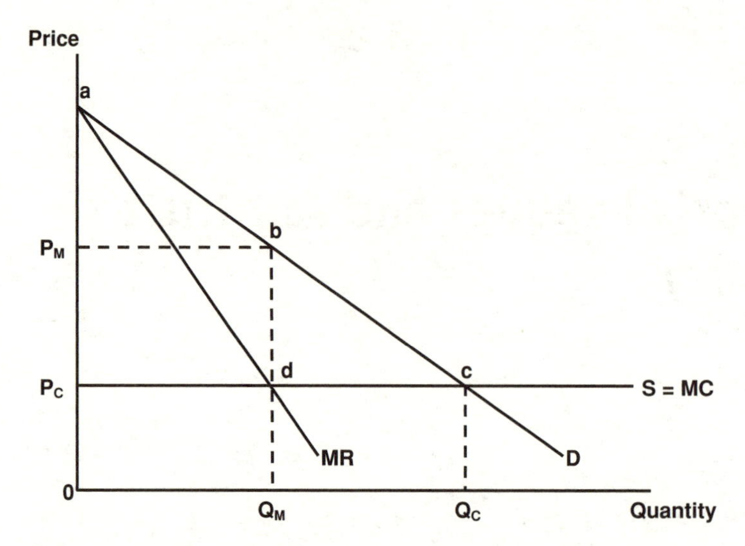

Figure 9.1. The monopolist produces where marginal revenue and marginal cost are equal. The result is a social welfare loss equal to area *bcd.*

labeled *D*, and long-run industry supply is labeled *S*.[2] The competitive output is found where demand and supply are equal. This is shown as Q_C in Figure 9.1. The competitive price that corresponds to Q_C is P_C, which is equal to marginal and average cost. At the competitive price and output, the competitive firms earn just enough profit to keep their resources in this particular industry. Furthermore, price is such that any consumer who is willing to pay the cost to society of an additional unit of output can buy that extra output.

Social welfare is the sum of consumer surplus and producer surplus. Consumer surplus is the difference between what consumers are willing to pay (i.e., the value of the good to consumers) and the amount that they have to pay due to market forces. It can be measured as the area under the demand curve above the price. In Figure 9.1, consumer surplus is equal to the triangular area acP_C. Producer surplus is the difference between the lowest price that suppliers are willing to accept and the price they actually receive in the market. In general, it is the area above the supply curve and below the market price. In this case, there is no producer surplus because the supply curve is flat, and therefore, the market price is equal to the minimum price that suppliers will accept. As a result, social welfare is equal to consumer surplus, in this case: area acP_C. Given the demand and cost conditions depicted in Figure 9.1, this is as good as it gets – no change in price or quantity will improve social welfare. Competition in the market maximizes social welfare, which is the economic argument in favor of competition.

Now suppose that the market becomes monopolized. If this market were under the control of a single firm, the long-run supply curve in Figure 9.1 would be the marginal and average cost curve for the monopolist. Instead of having

[2] The long-run supply is flat because we have assumed that input prices do not rise with increases in industry output, that is, this is a constant cost industry.

many separate, independently owned firms, we would have a single firm with many separate plants or production facilities. In this case, however, the decision on the quantity of output would be substantially different from the competitive output, as would the equilibrium price. To maximize its profits, the monopolist will restrict its output until marginal revenue (MR) equals marginal cost (MC).[3] At this point, the profit-maximizing output is Q_M, and the corresponding price is P_M.

The privately optimal (i.e., profit maximizing) output shrinks from the competitive optimum of Q_C to the monopoly output of Q_M. Excess profit for the monopolist amounts to $(P_M - P_C)Q_M$, which is area $P_M bdP_c$ in Figure 9.1. This sum had been consumer surplus when the market was competitive but has now been transformed into profit for the monopolist. It is a transfer from consumers to the producer, which is paid by those consumers who continue to buy this product at the higher price P_M. Considered as a transfer within society, economists usually have little to say about such a transfer on social welfare grounds because both producers and consumers are members of society, and everyone counts in the evaluation of social welfare.[4] The economist's main concern is with those former consumers who are priced out of the market by the monopolist. The economic objection to monopoly flows from the resulting misallocation of resources, which can be seen by considering output Q_M. At this quantity, the marginal social value placed on the output, as measured by price, is P_M. The marginal social value of the resources used to produce Q_M, as measured by the marginal cost, is P_C. Thus, the profit-maximizing monopolist will refuse to produce an extra unit of output even though consumers are willing to pay more than the social cost of the increase in output. This restraint on output causes a loss to society.

Again, social welfare is the sum of consumer surplus and producer surplus. With competition, consumer surplus is area acP_C, and producer surplus is zero. Thus, social welfare is area acP_C. With monopoly, however, consumer surplus falls to area abP_M, and producer surplus (or profit) rises to area $P_M bdP_C$. As is plain to see in Figure 9.1, the sum of consumer surplus and producer surplus under monopoly falls short of that sum under competition by the area of the triangle bcd. This area is referred to as the *deadweight social welfare loss of monopoly.*

[3] For the monopolist, profit (π) is:

$$\pi = R(Q) - C(Q),$$

where $R(Q)$ is the total revenue function and $C(Q)$ is the cost function. Profit maximization requires producing that quantity of output where:

$$\frac{d\Pi}{dQ} = \frac{dR(Q)}{dQ} - \frac{dC(Q)}{dQ} = 0.$$

Thus, profit maximization requires the equality of marginal revenue $(dR(Q)/dQ)$ and marginal cost $(dC(Q)/dQ)$. See Chapter 5 for this and other pricing strategies.

[4] There is a problem, however, when the pursuit of monopoly profits results in socially unproductive use of scarce resources. There is a substantial literature on "rent-seeking" behavior that examines these problems.

This deadweight social welfare loss of monopoly (the welfare triangle) is the fundamental *economic* objection to monopoly.[5] The primary damage caused by monopoly flows from the fact that too little output is produced, and therefore, too few resources are employed in this industry. Notice that neither the monopoly profit nor the monopoly price is the economic problem. Instead, these are symptoms of the real problem, which is the misallocation of resources.

3 THE ANTITRUST LAWS

Largely because of the perceived problem of monopoly, the Sherman Act was passed in 1890. This Act is the cornerstone of antitrust policy in the United States. The fundamental purpose of the Sherman Act is the protection of competition as a market structure and as a process for allocating resources. As a result, the two main provisions deal with monopolizing conduct and collaborative (or conspiratorial) efforts to behave like a monopoly. An antitrust violation is a felony, and conviction can result in substantial criminal penalties. Corporations can be fined as much as $100 million. Individuals may be fined as much as $1 million, be imprisoned for up to 10 years, or both. On top of these penalties, victims of antitrust violations may sue for injuries that result from antitrust violations. Private plaintiffs recover three dollars for every dollar of damages when they are successful in court.

3.1 Section 1 of the Sherman Act

Section 1 deals with collusive efforts to emulate monopoly:

> Every contract, combination . . . , or conspiracy, in restraint of trade or commerce . . . , is hereby declared to be illegal. Every person who shall make any such contract or engage in any such combination or conspiracy shall be deemed guilty of a felony.

Because the statute does not define precisely what constitutes an impermissible *restraint of trade* and because every contract necessarily imposes restraints, it took some judicial interpretation to identify the scope of illegal conduct. That scope is pretty broad. Nearly any agreement that may raise, depress, fix, peg, or stabilize price is illegal under the Supreme Court's interpretation of Section 1.[6] In fact, this broad prohibition has condemned bid rigging by both buyers and sellers; agreements not to submit competitive bids; and agreements among competitors on prices to be charged, credit to be extended, and quantities to be produced. It has also condemned market-sharing schemes and collusive refusals to deal. Thus, the essence of a Section 1 violation is an agreement not to compete in the market on some dimension.

[5] The emphasis on *economic* is deliberate. There may be many objections to monopoly on political and social grounds. Our focus, however, is on economics.

[6] This sweeping prohibition was set out in *United States v. Socony-Vacuum Oil Co.*, 310 U.S. 150 (1940). This decision provides the precedent for deeming many agreements illegal *per se*. The *per se* label means that the conduct is presumed to be harmful and therefore illegal.

3.2 Section 2 of the Sherman Act

Despite the economist's objection to monopoly, the Sherman Act does not forbid the structural condition of monopoly. Instead, it tries to prevent the emergence of monopoly by prohibiting some behavior that could lead to a structural monopoly. Specifically, Section 2 of the Sherman Act holds that

> Every person who shall monopolize,... any part of the trade or commerce among the several States, or with foreign nations, shall be deemed guilty of a felony.

As with Section 1, we needed some judicial interpretation of Section 2 to know just what kinds of monopolizing conduct are impermissible. Some behavior is not objectionable even though it may result in a structural monopoly. In its *Grinnell* opinion, the Supreme Court set out a two-prong test for illegal monopolization:

> The offense of monopoly under §2 of the Sherman Act has two elements: (1) the possession of monopoly power in the relevant market and (2) the willful acquisition or maintenance of that power as distinguished from growth or development as a consequence of a superior product, business acumen, or historic accident.[7]

Thus, a firm will only be guilty of illegal monopolization if it has acquired or maintained monopoly power in an exclusionary or predatory way rather than through competitive, honestly industrial efforts. This is a sensible policy because we do not want to punish a firm for winning the competitive battle so convincingly that all other firms fall by the wayside. Indeed, it may be socially beneficial for a monopolist to charge as much as possible. This means a greater reward for superior skill and better signals to the market to attract new entry.

4 ECONOMIC ANALYSIS IN ANTITRUST ENFORCEMENT

When it comes to evaluating the conduct of sports leagues and organizations, the *rule of reason* is employed. This means that the market structure is examined, the purpose and effect of the conduct are determined, and the economic consequences are identified. Both the procompetitive and anticompetitive aspects of the conduct are analyzed. Under the rule of reason, conduct is impermissible only when the anticompetitive consequences of the conduct outweigh the procompetitive consequences. In other words, there must be some net harm to society before business conduct will be condemned by the antitrust laws. Traditionally, courts engage a rule of reason analysis by first defining the relevant market and then assessing the defendant's market power in that market. After all, as Judge Richard Posner has noted, firms that lack power are unlikely to abuse consumers, and if they do, the market will quickly discipline them. Courts are not interested in spending a lot of time answering the other difficult questions raised by the rule of reason if they are confident that the marketplace will correct any anticonsumer decisions made by the

[7] *United States v. Grinnell Corporation*, 384 U.S. 563, 570–571 (1966).

defendants. If market power is established, courts proceed to evaluate any evidence of harm to consumers, workers, or suppliers, as well as justifications or explanations by the defendants about how allegedly harmful conduct actually reduces costs, promotes efficiency, or otherwise is beneficial to society. Finally, courts examine whether any challenged conduct is more restrictive than necessary to achieve legitimate goals. All of this creates many tricky issues for the courts as they involve economic principles that can be somewhat elusive for those untrained in economics.

4.1 Market Definition

In an antitrust inquiry, it is nearly impossible to overstate the importance of market definition. Often, the definition of the market determines the outcome of the antitrust inquiry. For example, if the relevant market is Major League Baseball (MLB) games in San Francisco, then the Giants have a monopoly because they are the only source of those games in that location. However, if the market is major league baseball games in the Bay Area, then the Giants face competition from the Oakland A's, and the Giants do not have a monopoly. If the market is major league sports in San Francisco, then the Giants face competition from the 49ers (National Football League; NFL) and the Warriors (National Basketball Association; NBA). If the geographic scope extended to all of California, then the Giants face substantial competition from several MLB teams, NFL teams, NBA teams, and National Hockey League (NHL) teams. There is even more competition if the market is the entire West Coast. If the product market includes college sports, minor league teams, golf and tennis tournaments, or other forms of entertainment, competition expands even further. These considerations of market definition clearly matter for determining the actual market structure.

As this example suggests, there are two dimensions to a relevant antitrust market: (1) a product dimension and (2) a geographic dimension. For either component, we are interested in reasonable substitutability.

4.2 Analysis of the Relevant Product Market

The definition of the relevant *product* market should encompass all products that are reasonable substitutes for one another. In theory, we rely on the cross-elasticity of demand to identify substitutes. The cross-elasticity of demand (θ_{AB}) is defined as the percentage change in the quantity demanded of product $A(Q_A)$ divided by the percentage change in the price of product $B(P_B)$:

$$\theta_{AB} = \frac{\%\Delta Q_A}{\%\Delta P_B},$$

where Δ denotes a small change. If the cross-elasticity of demand is positive, products A and B are substitutes. In other words, when the price of B rises, consumers turn to product A – that is, they substitute A for B when B becomes relatively more expensive. This definition of substitutes includes both close and remote substitutes. For antitrust purposes, however, we are concerned with *reasonably close substitutes.* Economic theory does not provide a critical value for θ_{AB} that separates "close" substitutes from more remote substitutes. Consequently, some practical approach for defining product markets is necessary.

The approach to product market definition embodied in the Department of Justice/Federal Trade Commission (DOJ/FTC) Merger Guidelines offers a pragmatic way of identifying the relevant product market. The DOJ/FTC approach is to ask whether a hypothetical monopolist of the proposed group of products could *profitably* raise price by 5 to 10 percent and maintain that price for at least a year. If so, that group constitutes a relevant product market because other substitutes are not close enough to undermine the increase in price. If such a price increase cannot be maintained, the next closest substitutes must be included in the proposed relevant product market, and the process is then repeated to determine whether even more products should be included.[8]

From the buyer's perspective, we want to identify the goods and services that are reasonably interchangeable for each another in consumption. If a seller of product A were to raise its price, what other goods and services could be substituted for the higher-priced product A? For example, if the price of San Francisco Giants tickets were to rise, could buyers reasonably substitute a ticket to an A's game, a 49ers game, or a concert ticket? If so, they are all in the same product market. If not, they are in separate product markets.

4.3 Analysis of the Relevant Geographic Market

In analyzing the relevant *geographic* market, the inquiry is largely the same: identifying reasonable substitutes. The relevant geographic market includes all locations that are reasonably substitutable sources of a product from the customer's perspective. If price were to rise in a particular location, the question is where else could the buyer go for the product in question. If buyers have no reasonable alternatives, the original location is the relevant geographic market. If there are reasonable alternatives in a location nearby, then these must be included in the relevant geographic market.

4.4 Monopoly Power

Monopoly power is the power of a seller to influence price by adjusting output. In Figure 9.1, the monopolist was able to raise the market clearing price to P_M by reducing output from Q_C to Q_M. From an economic perspective, the concept of *market* power is the same thing as monopoly power – control over price through adjustments in output.[9] The monopolist deviates from the competitive price and output because it is profitable to do so. A measure of monopoly power should capture this deviation. The Lerner Index of monopoly does just that.

[8] *Department of Justice and Federal Trade Commission Horizontal Merger Guidelines*, April 2, 2010, at §1.1, as revised.

[9] Thomas G. Krattenmaker, Robert H. Lande, and Steven C. Salop (1987), "Monopoly Power and Market Power in Antitrust Cases," *Georgetown Law Journal*, 76, 241.

A monopolist operates where marginal revenue equals marginal cost. Now, marginal revenue is equal to $P + Q\Delta P/\Delta Q$, and therefore, we have

$$P + Q\Delta P/\Delta Q - MC = 0,$$

or

$$P - MC = -Q\Delta P/\Delta Q.$$

Dividing both sides by P yields:

$$(P - MC)/P = -(Q/P)(\Delta P/\Delta Q) = -1/\eta.$$

The Lerner Index is then $\lambda = -1/\eta$, where η is the elasticity of demand.

The elasticity of demand (η) is defined as the percentage change in the quantity demanded (Q_D) divided by the percentage change in price (P):[10]

$$\eta = \frac{\%\Delta Q_D}{\%\Delta P}$$

The elasticity of demand measures the relative responsiveness of the quantity demanded by consumers to changes in price. One of the major determinants of the elasticity of demand for a specific good or service is the availability of substitutes. The easier it is for the consumer to substitute for the good or service in question, the more elastic the demand will be. The greater the elasticity of demand, the lower the monopoly power. This results from the buyer's ability to substitute other goods and services for the good in question in response to any price rise.

5 LEAGUE RULES AND ANTITRUST POLICY

The conduct that violates Section 1 of the Sherman Act has two defining characteristics: (1) it flows from an *agreement* among ostensible competitors and (2) it is anticompetitive, which is to say that it tends to increase price, decrease output, or decrease quality. The susceptibility of a sports league or organization to Section 1 prosecution depends on whether the league is a single entity or a joint venture. If a sports league is deemed to be a *single entity*, then agreements among its members cannot violate Section 1 of the Sherman Act. The members of the league would not be viewed as independent actors capable of conspiracy. Instead, they would be seen as parts of a single business entity. A single entity cannot conspire with itself, because conspiracy requires two or more parties.

In contrast, if a sports league is merely a *joint venture*, then it is subject to Section 1 scrutiny, but under the rule of reason. Agreements among members of the league may violate Section 1 because the members are capable of

[10] More precisely, $\eta = \frac{\partial Q}{\partial P} \cdot \frac{P}{Q}$.

conspiracy; they are independent actors. However, the courts have recognized that members of a sports league must agree on many things to produce athletic contests.

This issue was resolved by the Supreme Court in its *American Needle* decision.[11] For decades, the National Football League pooled the trademarks of its members and granted nonexclusive licenses for their commercial use. In other words, the clubs agreed to license their trademark rights as a package. Although the clubs did not compete, no one complained. However, when the NFL decided to award an exclusive, 10-year license to Reebok, the other producers of logoed merchandise – jerseys, hats, jackets, and the like – were shut out of the market. One of the foreclosed firms, American Needle, sued the NFL, alleging that its licensing practices violated Section 1 of the Sherman Act. The issue before the Supreme Court was whether the NFL is a single entity or an association of independent firms.

In a surprisingly unanimous decision, the Supreme Court held that the NFL is not a single entity for antitrust purposes. This is a potentially significant decision because it means that the 32 NFL clubs are legally capable of conspiring among themselves in violation of Section 1 of the Sherman Act. This does not mean that all agreements are unlawful; only competitively unreasonable agreements are unlawful. Consequently, any agreement that restrains competition will have to be evaluated under the rule of reason, which requires a weighing of the procompetitive and anticompetitive consequences of the restraint in question.

5.1 Legal Rules and Agreements

Members of a sports league clearly agree to abide by a laundry list of rules. There is no dispute about the existence of the agreement. Many of these rules are clearly confining and thereby impose restraints on each member's freedom to compete in the market. However, league rules are not automatically condemned by the antitrust laws. These league rules are designed to regulate the conduct of the league and its members. Because a sports league and its members market athletic competition, they must have rules that define and regulate that competition. No one could market competition in the arena or on the playing field if there were no rules to create and define the athletic competition to be sold to the fans. For example, all members must agree on the rules of play, schedules, the playoff structure, determination of championships, roster sizes, and many other things.

Under Section 1 of the Sherman Act, it is only agreements that *unreasonably* restrain trade that are illegal. When a rule is challenged, the court will examine the economic effects and weigh the procompetitive consequences against the anticompetitive harm – if any. Those rules that on balance are procompetitive are permissible under the antitrust laws, and those that are anticompetitive are not.

[11] *American Needle, Inc. v. National Football League,* 130 S. Ct. 2201 (2010).

Box 9.1 ***Baseball's Curious Antitrust Exemption***

Alone among major leagues, MLB enjoys an antitrust exemption that seems to be based on historical accident and congressional inaction. The problem began in the late 1800s when the club owners developed a widespread network of exclusionary, anticompetitive agreements. When these agreements were challenged in 1922, the Supreme Court dropped the ball.

In *Federal Baseball Club of Baltimore, Inc. v. National League of Professional Baseball Clubs*, the plaintiff objected to several of the exclusionary practices. The Supreme Court never reached the substantive antitrust questions. Instead, the Court disposed of the matter on jurisdictional grounds. No matter how anticompetitive an agreement among ostensible competitors may actually be, if the agreement does not restrain *interstate* commerce, it cannot violate the Sherman Act.

The business of baseball, according to Justice Oliver Wendell Holmes, was providing exhibitions of professional baseball, which were necessarily local affairs. The Court held that professional baseball did not involve *interstate* commerce and therefore did not fall within the scope of the federal antitrust laws. Holmes, of course, knew full well that the teams necessarily traveled across state lines, but he characterized the travel as "incidental." This decision, which was a clear blunder on Holmes's part, provided shelter from antitrust prosecution.

When precisely the same issues came before the Court some 30 years later, it did not justify the illogic of *Federal Baseball* but reaffirmed because Congress had not acted to specifically bring MLB within the scope of the Sherman Act. In 1972, the Supreme Court had another chance to correct its error but pointed to the fact that MLB had enjoyed an antitrust exemption for 50 years without congressional action.

6 ANTITRUST CHALLENGES BY LEAGUE MEMBERS

Many league rules have been challenged by league members, and many of those challenges have failed. Here we briefly deal with a challenge to an National Collegiate Athletic Association (NCAA) restriction on television broadcasts, an NFL ban on public ownership, and an NFL restraint on franchise relocation.

6.1 NCAA Restraints on Broadcasting

In *NCAA v. Board of Regents of the University of Oklahoma and University of Georgia Athletic Association*,[12] the NCAA's restrictive television policy came under fire. This important decision made it clear that NCAA rules, which all

[12] 468 U.S. 85 (1984). The NCAA has rules that affect athletes and coaches that we examine in Chapter 19. Here, we focus on rules that restrain the NCAA members.

member institutions must abide by, would be evaluated under the rule of reason for their legality. The NCAA is subject to antitrust scrutiny, but agreements among its members are not automatically illegal.

At issue in this case was the NCAA's television plan for the 1982–1985 seasons. The plan restricted the freedom of individual members to negotiate television contracts, it limited the total number of games that could be telecast, and it restricted the number of times that any one school could appear on television. The Supreme Court noted that because the NCAA members compete with one another for television revenues, fans, and athletes, the NCAA television plan limited competition among its members. Thus, it was a horizontal restraint. However, because some restraints are necessary to produce athletic competition on the field, the Court analyzed the plan under the rule of reason.

The Court identified the product being marketed as *college football* games. It acknowledged that a wide array of rules had to be imposed to preserve the character of that product: amateurism, academic pursuit, rules of play, recruiting rules, and so on. Because these rules make a product available that might not exist otherwise, they are procompetitive and therefore beneficial to consumers.

The NCAA television plan, however, restrained price and output competition among member institutions. It therefore had the potential to harm consumers. As a result, the NCAA needed some powerful justification for its plan and the restraints that it embodied, but the NCAA was unable to demonstrate any procompetitive efficiencies that increased the competitiveness of college football broadcast rights. The NCAA also failed to show that its plan enabled it to penetrate the market by offering an attractive package of games. On the contrary, the evidence was that fewer television rights were sold as a result of the plan.

The NCAA argued that televised games would reduce live attendance at games that were not being televised. For example, if the Michigan–Notre Dame game were on television, live attendance at Purdue, Indiana, and Michigan State games might suffer. Under the NCAA plan, some games such as Michigan–Notre Dame would not be televised, and live attendance at other games would increase. Notice, however, that live attendance increases because of a reduction in competition. Fans who would prefer to watch a major match up on television would be denied that opportunity and therefore substitute a less desirable alternative. This is protectionist – not procompetitive. As a result, the NCAA failed the rule of reason test.

6.2 NFL Ban on Public Ownership

The NFL had a policy against public ownership of NFL franchises.[13] Of course, all franchises are incorporated to get the benefits of limited liability, but they are closely held, and the shares are privately traded. When an owner wants to sell his or her franchise, 75 percent of the NFL clubs must agree on the new owner.

[13] The NFL made an exception for the Green Bay Packers, which was a not-for-profit corporation owned by Green Bay residents.

This became a problem for Billy Sullivan, who owned the New England Patriots, when he experienced some financial distress for reasons unrelated to football. He wanted to sell 49 percent of his stock in a public offering. This would provide some much needed cash but still leave him in control of the Patriots. When Sullivan could not sell this stock publicly, he decided to sell the whole franchise for $84 million in 1988. Just four years later, the new owner sold the franchise for $110 million. Because of this quick profit, Sullivan realized that he had missed out on the opportunity for a large capital gain. He sued the NFL for the lost profit that he could have made had he been able to keep the franchise.[14]

Sullivan alleged, and the jury found, that the relevant market was national in scope and involved ownership interests in NFL franchises generally and in the New England Patriots specifically. The court found that the NFL policy reduced the output of ownership interests in NFL franchises. In fact, the policy completely wiped out a type of ownership – public ownership of stock. By doing so, "the NFL is literally restricting the output of a product – a share in an NFL team."

The NFL policy against public ownership is likely to depress the resale price of a franchise. This is probably true because there may not be too many people who want a whole franchise, but many who would like a small piece. Does that mean, however, that the present owners were harmed? Presumably, the one who bought the Patriots at a depressed price in 1988 sold the Patriots at a depressed price in 1992. How would one know whether there was a net injury?

The NFL argued that the ban on public ownership was important to the success of the league. It pointed out that the interests of the league could be in conflict with the short-run interests of common shareholders. Although the court did not find this persuasive, it did find that it should be considered in a rule of reason analysis. In the end, however, the court ruled in Sullivan's favor. The NFL ban was simply too restrictive.

6.3 Relocation Restrictions

To maximize profits overall, leagues often dictate the location of new franchises and limit the relocation of existing franchises. In this way, each franchise will have a local monopoly, which it can exploit. Each franchise is separately owned, however, and that may lead to some conflict. The owner of a franchise that is not enjoying adequate local support may want to move to greener pastures. If the league tries to prohibit such a move, the owner of the franchise may sue. This is precisely what happened when Al Davis wanted to relocate the Oakland Raiders to Los Angeles and the NFL denied permission to do so.[15]

[14] *Sullivan v. NFL* 34 F.3d 1091 (1st Cir. 1994). For an analysis, see John Lopatka and Jill Herndon (1997), "Antitrust and Sports Franchise Ownership Restrictions: A Sad Tale of Two Cases," *Antitrust Bulletin*, 42, pp. 749–791. For a contrary view, see Genevieve F. E. Birren (2004), "NFL vs. Sherman Act: How the NFL's Ban on Public Ownership Violates Federal Antitrust Laws," *Sports Law Journal*, 11, 121–139.

[15] *Los Angeles Memorial Coliseum Commission v. NFL* 736 F.2d 1381 (9th Cir. 1984).

A central issue in the *Raiders* case was whether the NFL was a single entity or simply a collection of individual firms. As a single entity, the NFL would have been immune from Section 1 attack because a firm cannot conspire with itself. As a collection of independent firms, however, collaboration among those firms could be challenged as an unreasonable restraint of trade. In the *Raiders* case, the court found that the NFL was not a single entity, and therefore its league rules would be judged under the rule of reason.

The NFL's rules required that three-fourths of the clubs had to approve the relocation of a franchise into the natural home market of an existing franchise. It attempted to justify the rule by claiming that it was necessary to preserve fan loyalty. It was also allegedly necessary for the orderly establishment of new teams. Under the rule of reason, the court held that there were less restrictive ways of achieving these ends. As a result, the NFL failed the test of reasonableness. More specifically, the court found that the jury had a reasonable basis for concluding that the league had prevented the Raiders' move without any objective justification to shelter the Los Angeles Rams from competition. The reason the NFL would do this, the court suggested, is that each owner was acting contrary to the best interests of the league as a whole. Instead, they acted to protect their own club's interest in avoiding competition. This is precisely why the NFL did not behave as a single entity in this particular case. If the Raiders relocation was subject to approval of a Board of Directors interested solely in joint profit maximization, the court implies that the move would have been approved.

7 ANTITRUST CHALLENGES BY OUTSIDERS

There have been numerous antitrust suits filed by outsiders involving the conduct of sports leagues, professional tours, and the NCAA. Interestingly, nearly all have been private suits – some successful, some not. Neither the Department of Justice nor the Federal Trade Commission has been particularly interested in the conduct of sports leagues. In this section, we examine a sample of antitrust challenges to the conduct of a league by an outsider.[16]

7.1 *American Football League v. National Football League*

By the late 1950s, the NFL had a dozen teams in 11 cities: New York, Philadelphia, Pittsburgh, Washington, Baltimore, Cleveland, Detroit, Los Angeles, San Francisco, Green Bay, and Chicago (which had two teams). The NFL had conflicting incentives with respect to league expansion. On the one hand, the NFL's members can extract more concessions from host cities when the threat of moving to another city is credible. This, of course, requires that there be desirable locations without an existing NFL team. On the other hand, if there were too many desirable cities without NFL franchises, there would be room for a rival league to enter and compete with the NFL. By 1956, the NFL considered

[16] For a compact economic analysis of leagues, see Robert D. Tollison (2000), "Understanding the Antitrust Economics of Sports Leagues," *Antitrust*, 14, 21–24.

many expansion plans and ultimately decided to award four new franchises. The first two went to Dallas and Minneapolis–St. Paul in 1960. Additionally, one of the Chicago teams (the Cardinals) moved to St. Louis in 1961. Later, two more expansion franchises were slated for Atlanta and New Orleans. While this was going on in the NFL, the fledgling American Football League (AFL) was taking shape.

When Lamar Hunt founded the AFL in 1959, it began with franchises in several cities already hosting NFL teams: New York, Los Angeles, and Dallas. It also placed a team in Oakland in close proximity to San Francisco. In addition, the AFL had franchises in Boston, Buffalo, Houston, and Denver. Thus, the AFL had eight teams in eight cities. At that time, there were still quite a few cities with no professional football: Atlanta, Miami, New Orleans, Tampa–St. Petersburg, Seattle, Cincinnati, Kansas City, and Milwaukee, among others.

In its suit, the AFL complained that the NFL had monopoly power when it came to locating franchises.[17] As a result, it could prevent the AFL from succeeding by preempting the most desirable cities. It pointed to the undeniable fact that the NFL was present in all of the major metropolitan locations (with the exception of Boston). The AFL also pointed out that the owners of the Vikings had paid a franchise fee to the AFL but withdrew and went with the NFL when that opportunity arose. On this basis, the AFL contended that the NFL could do the same thing in other cities. That is, had the NFL chosen to do so, it could have exercised its monopoly power and taken away several other cities from the AFL. This allegation seems a little odd. What market is being monopolized here? If an entrepreneur decides to join an established league rather than a new, untested league, is that evidence of monopoly? How are consumers hurt?

There were some facts that undermined the AFL's claims. Foremost among these facts was the AFL's obvious success. The AFL was founded in 1959 and had a full schedule of games by 1960. The AFL competed successfully for outstanding players and obtained a television contract with ABC. As a result, the court found that the NFL did not have monopoly power, and therefore the first element of illegal monopolization was not present. Consequently, the AFL's antitrust challenge failed.

Following a period of intense competition between the NFL and the AFL, which led to escalating player salaries, the NFL and the AFL decided to merge. Because this would have resulted in a monopoly, there was some concern that a merger would not be permitted. To avoid that problem, the leagues persuaded Congress to amend the Sports Broadcasting Act to permit the merger.[18] More specifically, the SBA was amended so that agreements by "the member clubs of two or more professional football leagues ... [to] combine their operations in [an] expanded single league ... if such agreement increases rather than decreases the number of professional football clubs so operating" were not illegal. This provision was strictly limited to the NFL–AFL merger. It provided no protection for the merger of any other sports leagues.

[17] 323 F. 2d 124 (4th Cir. 1963).

[18] We encountered the Sports Broadcasting Act in Chapter 7.

Subsequently, another new league formed – the World Football League (WFL). This league was not successful and folded after a year and a half. One WFL survivor tried to enter the NFL but was turned down. That team also sued the NFL as we will see next.

7.2 Restrictions on Entry

In most instances, the exercise of monopoly power leads to excess profits, which naturally attracts entry. When a sports league appears to be profitable, new teams will want to enter the league and garner a share of the monopoly profit enjoyed by the current members. League expansion, however, could result in lower average profits for league members. When that is the case, the league will reject the potential entrant's application. This raises an antitrust question: Can league members deny access to league membership? In short, the answer is "yes."

The WFL tried to compete with the NFL but, as noted earlier, failed after a season and a half. One of the teams, the Memphis Southmen, had been successful in the WFL. Following the demise of the WFL, it decided to change its name to the Grizzlies and apply for membership in the NFL. The NFL rejected the Grizzlies' application for several reasons: (1) it had recently expanded into Seattle and Tampa, (2) scheduling required an even number of teams, and (3) there was some unsettled labor litigation. The Grizzlies sued.[19]

For antitrust purposes, the relevant market was defined as major league professional football in the United States. The NFL had a monopoly in that market. Thus, the first prong of the *Grinnell* test was satisfied. The question then was whether the NFL had acquired and maintained that monopoly through exclusionary or predatory practices. The court observed that Congress permitted the merger of the NFL and the AFL well before the WFL was formed. As a result, the original formation was not objectionable on antitrust grounds. As for maintaining its monopoly, the court found that excluding the Grizzlies was actually procompetitive because the Grizzlies and the Memphis area provided an organization and a site that could be part of a rival league. Merely joining the NFL and sharing its pot of gold are not the same as providing legitimate competition with a rival league. The Grizzlies were unable to convince the court that their exclusion from the NFL reduced competition in any relevant market.

7.3 *United States Football League v. NFL*

The USFL was another new league, but with a twist. It began as a spring league. No doubt, the organizers were convinced that the demand for football was insatiable. As usual, by spring, the NFL season was over, there was no college football, and not even any high school football. The USFL wanted to fill that gap and make some money along the way. The concept seemed sound enough, and the USFL obtained television contracts with ABC and ESPN. Despite the television revenue, however, the USFL lost some $200 million during the 1983–1985 seasons. It decided that the spring scheduling strategy was not working. As a result,

[19] *Mid-South Grizzlies v. NFL*, 720 F. 2d 772 (3d Cir. 1983).

it decided to move to a fall schedule and go head to head with the NFL. When it could not land a network television contract, the USFL could not proceed profitably and went out of business. In an effort to recoup some of its losses, the USFL sued the NFL for alleged antitrust violations.[20]

The USFL contended that the NFL had monopolized professional football in the United States. A jury actually agreed with the USFL and found the NFL guilty. When it came to damages, however, the jury awarded nominal damages of only $1,[21] which is not what the USFL had in mind.

The jury verdict is a mystery for several reasons. An important issue in the case involved the television contracts that the NFL had and the USFL wanted at least a piece of. At trial, the jury did not find that the NFL's television contracts with the three networks denied the USFL access to an essential ingredient for success. In other words, the existence of the contracts did not prevent the USFL from offering a product that one or more of the networks might find attractive. For the USFL's claim to be persuasive, at a minimum, it would have had to show that it was precluded from competing with the NFL for television contracts. If it could compete but failed to win because the networks preferred the NFL, then the NFL would have done nothing exclusionary in an antitrust sense. Instead, it would have competed successfully on its merits. As a matter of antitrust policy, we do not condemn those who win the competitive battle by supplying a superior product.

The NFL's television contracts with ABC, CBS, and NBC precluded the NFL from entering into a contract with any cable company. Thus, cable opportunities were available to the USFL. As for the network contracts, each one allowed the network to decide whether it wanted to continue for another year. Thus, competition could take place on renewal dates, which were not infrequent. Moreover, the contracts were not exclusive, which means that a network could have signed a separate deal with the USFL and broadcast both NFL and USFL games during the same season. The network could have broadcasted USFL games when it was not broadcasting NFL games. The USFL's economic problems were apparent. It failed to get any network contracts for a fall schedule because each network preferred the NFL and other programming. The network preference was driven by its pursuit of profits. It could sell the ad slots on NFL games for more than it could sell ad slots on USFL games. The USFL could not win in the market so it chose to try the courts. That did not work out either; the jury awarded only nominal damages of $1.

7.4 Restrictions on Schedules by Organization

Organizations put together scheduled events to fill their season calendars. For example, the PGA)Tour starts in early January and runs through the final Tour Championship event in the fall. Every week has a PGA Tour–sanctioned golf

[20] 842 F. 2nd 1335 (2d Cir. 1988). For a more extensive account, see Lori J. Brown (1987), "The Battle: From the Playing Field to the Courtroom – *United States Football League v. National Football League*," *University of Toledo Law Review*, 18, 871–888.

[21] This sum was trebled to $3 as the Clayton Act dictates. The attorneys for the USFL were awarded reasonable attorneys fees of $25 million.

tournament in a different location. If a tournament organizer wants a spot on the PGA Tour schedule, he or she must apply and satisfy the PGA Tour that the course is suitable, the purse is adequate, and the tournament will be well organized. It is then up to the PGA Tour to decide whether to include that tournament. If it does so, it must drop a tournament because it limits the sanctioned tournaments to one per week. The PGA Tour's decision is going to leave one tournament organizer unhappy. Similar considerations apply to the Ladies PGA, the tennis tours (Association of Tennis Professionals [ATP] and Women's Tennis Association), bowling (Professional Bowlers Association), track, and others. From time to time, these decisions can lead to antitrust challenges.

The ATP was originally formed to promote the interests of the top male tennis players from around the world. Through this representation, the ATP could schedule events, pursue greater prize money for the players, and insist on better facilities. It is in the interest of the ATP players to provide the best-quality sports entertainment possible because this will increase the popularity of tennis and thereby increase the economic well-being of the players.

Because of a perceived drop in the popularity of tennis as sports entertainment, the ATP decided to improve the quality of tennis as a spectator sport by improving the quality of its schedule. Tennis professionals are independent contractors rather than employees, and thus the ATP had to create incentives for the top players to appear at certain tournaments. In doing this, the ATP designated certain events as *ATP World Tour 1000* tournaments. One tournament that had previously enjoyed top designation was demoted to the second tier, the *ATP World Tour 500.* The ATP replaced the Hamburg (German) tournament with one in Shanghai. The German Tennis Federation filed an antitrust suit against the ATP and its Board of Directors.[22]

The claim was that by creating incentives for the best players to play elsewhere, Hamburg was put at a competitive disadvantage. The ATP's position was that its purpose was to improve product quality and thereby compete more effectively with other sports as a form of entertainment. The jury found in favor of the ATP.

7.5 Restrictions on Equipment

Usually, sports leagues and organizations can impose rules on the equipment that can be used.[23] This, of course, does not prevent an aggrieved party from filing a lawsuit. This is precisely what happened when the United State Tennis Association (USTA) adopted an International Tennis Federation rule prohibiting the use of the "spaghetti racquet."[24] The racquet design made it possible for average professionals to put an astonishing amount of spin on the ball. This ban was justified because the racquet design altered the character of the game. The manufacturer of the spaghetti racquets, Gunter Harz, sued the

[22] *Deutscher Tennis Bund v. ATP Tour Inc.*, 610 F. 3d. (3d Cir. 2010).

[23] An extremely well-reasoned analysis of this issue is provided by John E. Lopatka, (2009). "Antitrust and Sports Equipment Standards: Winners and Whiners." *The Antitrust Bulletin*, 54, 751–800.

[24] *Gunter Harz Sports v. USTA*, 511 F. Supp. 1103 (D. Neb. 1981).

USTA for unreasonably restraining trade by forbidding the use of its racquet. In this case, the court found that the USTA did not conspire with the manufacturers of traditional racquets to exclude Gunter Harz. Rather, the USTA had exercised its rule-making authority in an effort to preserve the character of tennis as we know it. The court held that the purpose of the ban furthered the USTA's "legitimate goals of preserving the essential character and integrity of the game of tennis." Moreover, the court found no evidence that the USTA had any intention to injure Gunter Harz or any other manufacturer. The USTA's concern was that spaghetti racquets would alter the game and artificially enhance the skill and ability of players. As a result, the court found this restraint to be reasonable.

Some 10 years later, a similar suit was filed when the United States Golf Association (USGA) and the PGA Tour limited the use of the Ping Eye 2 Irons manufactured by the Karsten Manufacturing Company.[25] In the mid-1980s, Karsten developed its Ping Eye 2 Irons, which had square-bottomed grooves in the face. These came to be known as U-grooves as opposed to the V-grooves on the irons manufactured by Karsten's rivals. For a variety of reasons, including the U-grooves, the Ping Eye 2 became immensely popular among professional golfers and especially among amateurs. Karsten, of course, was an economic success as its market share skyrocketed. However, some major figures on the PGA Tour began complaining that the Ping Eye 2 Irons provided too much spin control of the golf ball, especially from bad lies in the rough. This added spin reduced the premium for driving the ball in the fairway where the grass is closely mowed and the lies are good. Thus, the Ping Eye 2 made it easier for golfers with less skill to achieve better scores than they could without the U-grooves.

Some – if not all – of those who complained had conflicts of interest. First, those golfers using Ping Eye 2 Irons may have been winning money in tournaments that those complaining would have earned. Second, all professional golfers of any stature had endorsement deals with club manufacturers that competed with Karsten. This is not to say that their motives were impure, but it does cast a cloud over their complaints.

In any event, the USGA did not ultimately rule that golf clubs with U-grooves were "nonconforming," which would have banned their use. The USGA did, however, rule that the space between grooves had to meet a certain dimension. Since the Ping Eye 2 Irons failed this specification, the clubs were nonconforming. Karsten sued and the USGA changed its groove specifications so Karsten was apparently back in business.

The PGA Tour, however, prohibited the U-grooves and would not budge. This was serious because many amateurs want to use the same equipment that the pros use. Karsten feared that its sales to amateurs would suffer greatly if the Ping Eye 2 clubs were not permitted on the tour. It feared that its

[25] An excellent description of the dispute is provided in *Gilder v. PGA Tour, Inc.*, 936 F. 2d 417 (9th Cir. 1991).

reputation would be tarnished as well because it would be producing an "illegal" club. Karsten sued the PGA Tour on the grounds that its rule was an unreasonable restraint. It denied that the U-grooves provided any extra spin, and therefore there was no danger of diminishing skill requirements. There was no jury verdict in this case. After four years of legal wrangling and millions of dollars in legal fees and expenses, the case settled one week before it was scheduled to go to trial. It was a total loss for the PGA Tour as the PGA Tour agreed to pay $50 million in legal fees and to allow the Ping Eye 2 Irons to be used on tour.

As a final example, the NCAA was accused of violating the Sherman Act by altering the rule regarding the design of lacrosse stick heads. For some 30 years, the design requirements had been unchanged. Concerned about player safety, the NCAA altered the design requirement so that the ball would be dislodged more easily. The NCAA set specifications that unwittingly favored Warrior Sports, Inc., which had patents covering the NCAA proposed design. Before the change was implemented, the NCAA changed the rule in 2008.

Before the latest change, Warrior would have had a monopoly on conforming lacrosse stick heads. The 2008 rule would take away Warrior's monopoly and allow several competitors to produce conforming designs. The court reasoned that the 2008 rule did not harm competition in the lacrosse stick head market and therefore did not violate the Sherman Act.[26]

Box 9.2 ***Did Minnesota Hockey Unlawfully Exclude a Rival?****

Minnesota Hockey Inc. is the governing body for amateur hockey in Minnesota. Minnesota Hockey organizes youth hockey leagues in District 6, which covers the South and West metro area of the Twin Cities. It promulgated a rule forbidding its players from participating in outside leagues. The alleged rationale for this rule was that hockey is "physically taxing" and that the rule would protect young players from injury. A for-profit rival league operator, Minnesota Made Hockey (MMH), complained that the rule violated Section 2 of the Sherman Act because it had the effect of excluding MMH from the market for youth hockey services in the relevant area.

Assuming that there is good reason to protect young hockey players from injury, the rule had obvious social benefits. Assuming that the rule prevents competition from MMH, the rule has obvious detrimental effects. How can these conflicting effects be weighed in deciding whether the rule is an *unreasonable* restraint and, therefore, unlawful?

* *Minnesota Made Hockey v. Minnesota Hockey Inc. d. Minn,* No. 0:10-cv-03884-JRT-JJK, 1/4/11.

[26] *Warrior Sports, Inc. v. NCAA,* 588 F. 3d 908 (6th Cir, 2010).

Box 9.3 *For Some Equipment, Nonconforming Is Good**

In most cases, equipment manufacturers dread the "nonconforming" label because that means the equipment cannot be used in official competition. Golf clubs with U-grooves, spaghetti-string tennis racquets, aluminum baseball bats, and other products depend on official acceptance for their economic survival. But then there are basketball shoes.

Athletic Propulsion Labs makes a $300 basketball shoe that has a spring in the sole. The company brags that the shoe allows players to jump higher and thereby gives the player an edge that he or she did not earn. The NBA informed the company that their shoe was nonconforming because it gave a player a competitive advantage. The company was elated rather than dismayed. Now the company really had something to brag about. Its press release blared *N.B.A. Bans Basketball Shoes by Athletic Propulsion Labs Based on League Rules Against "Undue Competitive Advantage" That Increases a Player's Vertical Leap.* When the sports news media picked up the story, the company enjoyed plenty of free advertising, and sales soared. Apparently, many a school-yard player is looking for a competitive edge.

* John Branch, "Rejection by N.B.A. Gives New Shoes Even Greater Bounce," *New York Times*, October 20, 2010.

8 CONCLUDING REMARKS

In this chapter, we examined the applicability of the antitrust laws to sports leagues and organizations. We began with a review of the Sherman Act's prohibition of collusion and monopolizing conduct. The economic rationale for those prohibitions is the social welfare loss of monopoly. Following this, we examined a sample of antitrust cases filed by members of sports leagues and by outsiders. The results of those efforts were mixed. In general, the judicial outcomes seem sound.

PROBLEMS AND QUESTIONS

1. A monopolist faces the following demand:

$$P = 100 - 0.1Q$$

and associated marginal revenue

$$MR = 100 - 0.2Q.$$

The monopolist has a constant marginal cost equal to 40. Find the following: (a) the profit-maximizing price and output, (b) its profit, (c) consumer surplus, and (d) the deadweight social welfare loss.

2. If the NFL has a monopoly, what exactly is it monopolizing? Can you think of a substitute for NFL football?
3. Every fall, we can watch baseball, college football, pro football, golf, NASCAR, and basketball, among other entertainment options on TV. Are these in separate markets or the same market? Explain.
4. Investor groups in Los Angeles, California; San Antonio, Texas; and Columbus, Ohio, want to enter the NFL with new teams but are denied entry by the league. Is this an illegal restraint of trade? Explain.
5. Suppose the NFL decided that each team would charge precisely the same price for tickets to home games. Would this be price fixing? Would it be anticompetitive? Should it be illegal? Explain.
6. For more than 50 years, there has been no attempt by a rival baseball league to compete with MLB. Monopoly profits ordinarily attract entry unless there are formidable entry barriers. In baseball, which is it: entry barriers or no excess profit? Explain.
7. In *Sullivan*, what was the product market? If you had a million dollars to invest, can you think of any investment alternative to shares in the Patriots? Could Sullivan have won without the market that he alleged? Explain.
8. Would it be desirable to avoid having criminals – drug dealers or gamblers – own sports franchises? How could this be prevented if the stock of sports franchises were traded publicly?
9. In the *Ping* case, the manufacturer insisted that the U-grooves did not affect the performance of the golf club. If this were so, why did Karsten not simply switch to a V-groove configuration?
10. How much would the PGA Tour benefit economically from banning Ping's U-groove clubs? Can you find an anticompetitive motive for (a) the PGA Tour or (b) the PGA Tour members?
11. How is a sports league different from a cartel?
12. From an antitrust perspective, how can we permit the cooperation that sports leagues really need and forbid the cooperation that reduces social welfare?
13. When NASCAR organized its Sprint Cup series, it necessarily had to limit the number of events. As a result, the Kentucky Speedway was left off the schedule. When the track owner sued, its antitrust suit was dismissed. Can you think of sound economic reasons for this outcome?
14. Spira Footwear puts its patented WaveSpring in its running shoes. Because the International Association of Athletics Federations and USA Track and Field both have rules forbidding "assisted devices," Spira filed an antitrust suit alleging that it was improperly excluded. What do you think?
15. In *Minnesota Made Hockey v. Minnesota Hockey Inc.*, the plaintiff alleged that the defendant had monopoly power in the market for "youth hockey services in the South and West metro area of the Twin Cities." What evidence would be needed to prove that this was the relevant market?

RESEARCH QUESTIONS

1. Read the entire *Sullivan* opinion. Does the court's economic reasoning make sense? Explain.
2. Read the *Raiders* opinion. Evaluate the court's reasoning. Make an *economic* argument for the NFL's point of view.
3. In the five years following the *NCAA* ruling, was there an increase in the availability of televised college football games?
4. In the *Ping* case, the PGA Tour alleged a concern for the integrity of the game because of the use of irons with U-grooves. Trace changes in equipment since 1990 that arguably reduce skill requirements.
5. The Oakland Raiders sued the NFL so that the team could move to Los Angeles. What happened after the court ruled in their favor?

REFERENCES AND FURTHER READING

Adams, W., and J. W. Brock. (1997). "Monopoly, Monopsony, and Vertical Collusion: Antitrust Policy and Professional Sports." *Antitrust Bulletin*, 42, 721–747.

Birren, Genevieve F. E. (2004). "NFL vs. Sherman Act: How the NFL's Ban on Public Ownership Violates Federal Antitrust Laws," *Sports Law Journal*, 11, 121–139.

Blair, R., and D. Kaserman. (2008). *Antitrust Economics*, 2nd ed. New York: Oxford University Press.

Blair, Roger D., and David L. Kaserman. (2009). *Antitrust Economics.* New York: Oxford University Press.

Bradbury, J. C. (2007). *The Baseball Economist: The Real Game Exposed* (chapter 14). New York: Penguin Group.

Freitas, Robert E. (2000). "Overview: Looking Ahead at Sports and Antitrust Law." *Antitrust*, 14, 15–20.

Fehr, Steven A. (2000). "The Curt Flood Act and Its Effect of the Future of the Baseball Antitrust Exemption." *Antitrust*, 14, 25–30.

Goldfein, Shepard. (2000). "Relocation of Professional Sports Teams: Protecting the Championship Season." *Antitrust*, 14, 63–67.

Hovenkamp, Herbert. (2005). *The Antitrust Enterprise: Principle and Execution.* Cambridge, MA: Harvard University Press.

Hylton, Keith N. (2003). *Antitrust Law: Economic Theory and Common Law Evolution.* New York: Cambridge University Press.

Krattenmaker, Thomas G., Robert H. Lande, and Steven C. Salop. (1987). "Monopoly Power and Market Power in Antitrust Cases." *Georgetown Law Journal*, 76, 241.

Lehn, K., and M. Sykuta. (1997). "Antitrust and Franchise Relocation in Professional Sports: An Economic Analysis of the *Raiders* Case." *Antitrust Bulletin*, 42, 541–563.

Lopatka, John E. (2009). "Antitrust and Sports Equipment Standards: Winners and Whiners." *The Antitrust Bulletin*, 54, 751–800.

Lopatka, John, and Jill Herndon. (1997). "Antitrust and Sports Franchise Ownership Restrictions: A Sad Tale of Two Cases." *Antitrust Bulletin*, 42, 749–791.

Noll, Roger G. (1974). *Government and the Sports Business* (chapter 11). Washington, DC: The Brookings Institution.

Quirk, James, and Rodney Fort. (1992). *Pay Dirt: The Business of Professional Team Sports* (chapter 5). Princeton, NJ: Princeton University Press.

Roberts, G. R. (1997). "*Brown v. Pro Football, Inc.*: The Supreme Court Gets It Right for the Wrong Reasons." *Antitrust Bulletin*, 42, 595–639.

Roberts, G. R. (2003). "The Case for Baseball's Special Antitrust Immunity." *Journal of Sports Economics*, 4, 302–317.

Ross, Steven F. (2000) "Myths, Realities, and Creative Approaches to Antitrust and Franchise Relocation Issues." *Antitrust*, 14, 57–62.

Ross, Steven F. (2003). "Antitrust, Professional Sports, and the Public Interest." *Journal of Sports Economics*, 4, 318–331.

Szymanski, Stefan. (2009). *Playbooks and Checkbooks: An Introduction to the Economics of Modern Sports* (chapter 3). Princeton, NJ: Princeton University Press.

Tollison, Robert D. (2000). "Understanding the Antitrust Economics of Sports Leagues." *Antitrust*, 14, 21–24.

Winfree, Jason A. (2009). "Owners Incentives During the 2004–05 National Hockey League Lockout." *Applied Economics*, 41, 3275–3285.

Winfree, Jason A. (2009). "Fan Substitution and Market Definition in Sports Leagues." *Antitrust Bulletin*, 54, 801–822.

Zimbalist, Andrew. (2003). *May the Best Team Win* (chapter 2). Washington, DC: The Brookings Institution.

Zimbalist, Andrew. (2009). "The BCS, Antitrust and Public Policy." *The Antitrust Bulletin*, 54, 823–856.

IMAGE AND INTEGRITY

10

Sports Gambling

1 INTRODUCTION

John Daly, a flawed hero on the PGA Tour, revealed that he may have lost as much as $60 million gambling.[1] Charles Barkley chimed in with his own admission that he had lost over $10 million gambling.[2] These accounts are sensational because of the magnitude of the losses, but it comes as no surprise that some athletes gamble. Gambling is a fact of life in sports. Fans, athletes, coaches, officials, and owners gamble on something – athletic events, lottery tickets, card games, casinos, horse races, and the like. Some of the gambling is legal, but much of it is not. All of the major sports leagues and organizations find gambling troublesome. As a result, all of them prohibit gambling to one extent or another through rules, bylaws, codes of conduct, and contractual provisions. Violations of these prohibitions may carry heavy penalties. The major concern is protecting the image of the sport and the integrity of the competition. Unfortunately, both image and integrity have been undermined from time to time by gambling-related scandals.

In this chapter, we examine why people gamble.[3] We also analyze the gambling business and how the major professional sports leagues, organizations, and the National Collegiate Athletic Association (NCAA) have reacted to the prevalence of gambling.

2 THE ECONOMICS OF GAMBLING

To gamble, a person must accept some risk. Unlike risk averters, who try to shift risk to others, risk seekers embrace risk. By way of definition, a consumer who accepts all actuarially fair gambles is called a *risk seeker* or *risk lover.*

[1] John Daly (2006), *My Life In & Out of the Rough*, New York: Harper Collins.

[2] Hoffer, Richard, "Goodbye, Mr. Chips," *Sports Illustrated*, May 15, 2006.

[3] There is substantial literature on the efficiency of gambling markets. For an excellent survey of the literature on gambling markets, see Raymond D. Sauer (1998), "The Economics of Wagering Markets," *Journal of Economic Literature*, 36, 2021–2064. Our focus in this chapter is quite different; we are concerned with gambling as it pertains to image and integrity.

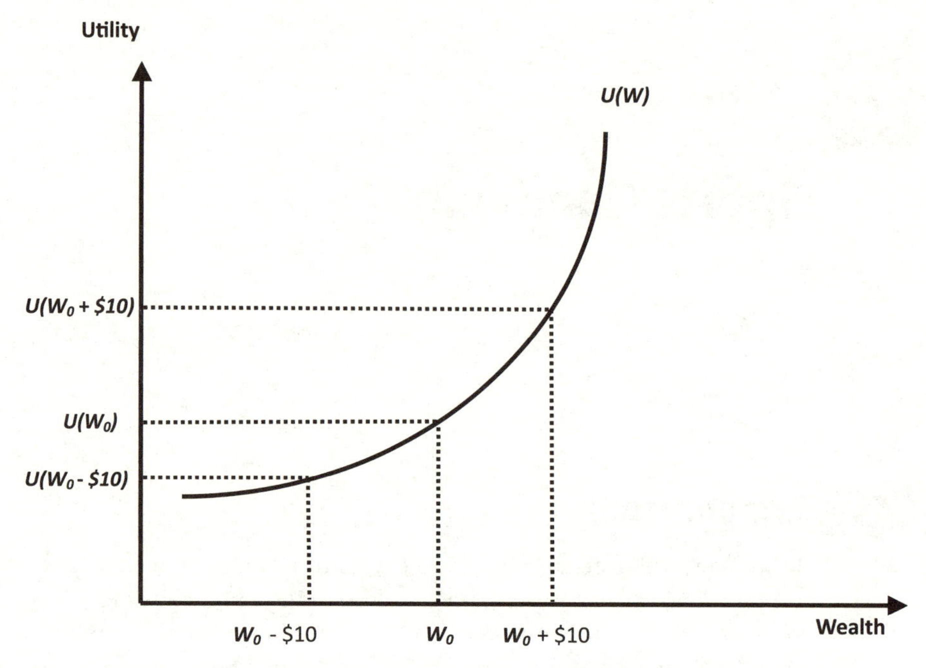

Figure 10.1. A risk lover has a convex utility function; utility increases at an increasing rate.

In contrast to the risk averter, a risk seeker actually would pay something for the privilege of engaging in actuarially fair gambles. If a Las Vegas casino offered a variety of actuarially fair gambles, risk seekers would be willing to pay for admission. In contrast to a risk averter, a risk seeker will not pay anything to shift an actuarially fair risk to someone else. The risk seeker's attitude toward risk is captured in the shape of his or her utility function. Once again measuring wealth on the horizontal axis and utility on the vertical axis, we depict a risk seeker's utility function in Figure 10.1 Because increases in wealth are always welcome, the utility function is positively sloped. The individual preference for risk is expressed by the *convexity* of the utility function. As we can see, a convex utility function increases at an increasing rate, which explains gambling behavior.

Suppose that Gamblin' Gary is offered the same coin flipping gamble that Cautious Carl rejected in Chapter 3. A fair coin is tossed in the air. If it comes up heads, Gary wins \$10, if it comes up tails, Gary loses \$10. If Gary does not gamble, he has a wealth level of W_0 and enjoys a utility level of $U(W_0)$. If he gambles and wins, he experiences a utility level of $U(W_0 + \$10)$. If he gambles and loses, his utility falls to $U(W_0 - \$10)$. Consequently, when the gamble is fair, he will win half of the time and lose the other half. His expected wealth, therefore, is calculated as

$$E[W] = \tfrac{1}{2}(W_0 - 10) + \tfrac{1}{2}(W_0 + 10) = W_0.$$

On average, Gary neither wins nor loses in monetary terms. In utility terms, however, we have a different story. On average, he will come out ahead in utility

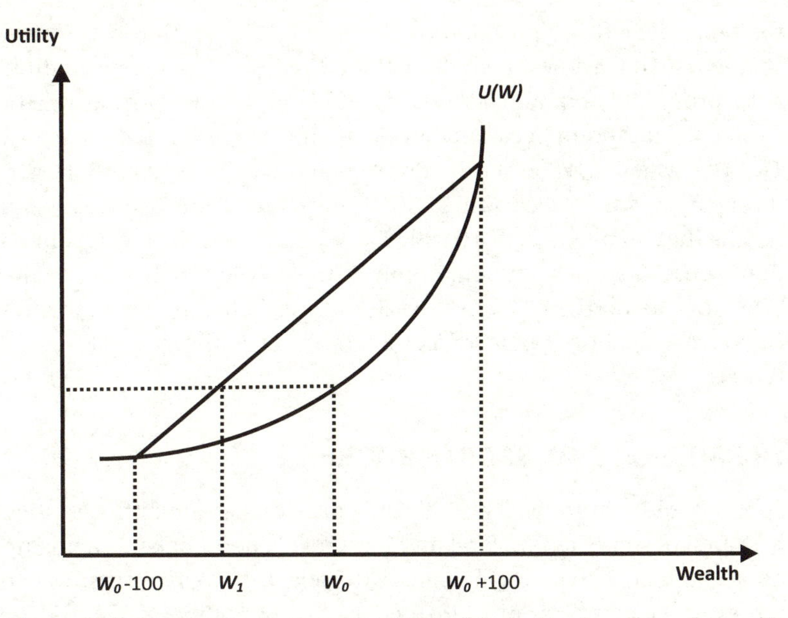

Figure 10.2. A risk lover will accept actuarially unfair gambles; he will "pay" something to gamble.

terms because the increase in utility when he gambles and wins is larger than the decrease in utility when he gambles and loses:

$$U(W_0 + 10) - U(W_0) > U(W_0) - U(W_0 - 10).$$

Thus, Gary will come out even in monetary terms, but he will come out ahead in utility terms by accepting this actuarially fair gamble. Consequently, Gamblin' Gary will be better off if he accepts all actuarially fair gambles. In fact, Gary will accept some gambles that are actuarially *unfair*. In other words, he will pay for the privilege of gambling. Precisely how unfair the gamble can be before Gary will reject it depends on the precise shape of his utility function.

2.1 Expected Utility of Gambling

We can examine the risk seeker's decisions in the expected utility model that we developed in Chapter 3. Suppose that Gamblin' Gary is a loyal fan of the Los Angeles Dodgers. The Dodgers are about to play an important game against their arch rival, the San Francisco Giants. On the basis of recent performances, injury reports, and basic talent, Gary knows that the probability that the Dodgers will win is less than half. One of Gary's buddies offers to bet $100 on the Giants. Will Gary take the bet? The answer, of course, is "it depends." Now, let's see on what it depends.

In Figure 10.2, we see Gary's convex utility function $U(W)$, which increases at an increasing rate. His current wealth is W_0. If he takes the bet and wins, he will have wealth $W_0 + \$100$; if he loses, he will have wealth of $W_0 - \$100$. Recall that the expected utility of this risky prospect is given by the height of the chord connecting the two possible outcomes directly above the expected wealth. In Figure 10.2, the risky equivalent of his certain wealth, which is W_0 if he refuses the bet, is W_1. If the probability of winning is such that his expected wealth is at least W_1, Gary will take the bet. At $E[W] = W_1$, the expected utility of the risky prospect is equal to the utility of his certain wealth. At this point, Gary would be indifferent between betting on the Dodgers and not because $U(W_0) = E[U(W)]$ when $E[W] = W_1$. If the expected wealth is slightly larger than W_1, the $E[U(W)]$ will exceed the $U(W_0)$. We can see that W_1 is less than W_0. This means that on average, Gary will lose $W_0 - W_1$. In other words, in an expectations sense, Gary will pay something for the privilege of betting on the Dodgers. Why does he do this? The answer lies in the utility associated with gambling. On average, he does not lose in utility terms even though he loses in monetary terms.

3 THE BUSINESS OF SPORTS BOOKS

Sports books – both legal and illegal – provide betting opportunities for those in search of some action. First and foremost, a bookmaker is a businessperson, not a gambler. As with any business, the goal is to earn profits. To earn a profit, however, the gamblers must lose on average. In other words, in the aggregate, the return on gambling must be negative for the sports book to earn profits.

A bookie is something like a broker who earns a commission for his efforts. The bookie brings together those who want to bet on the Bears and those who want to bet on the Colts. This is why we say that a gambler *places* a bet with a bookie; the bookie does not want to bet with his customers. Instead, the bookie hopes to find someone else to bet on the other team. From the bookie's perspective, he or she wants to have equal sums bet on each team. When that happens, there is no risk for the bookie as the losers pay the winners.[4] The bookie earns his profit on a kind of commission basis.

3.1 Point-Spread Wagers

Bets on football and basketball games involve almost even-money bets on the basis of point spreads. When the Florida Gators played the Ohio State Buckeyes for the Bowl Championship Series National Championship in 2007, the Buckeyes were favored by 7.5 points. Bookies were taking bets on the basis of the point spread. If you were foolish enough to bet on Ohio State, they would have had to win by at least 8 points for you to have won. If you had bet on the Gators, you would have won the bet if the Gators won the game or if they had lost by less than 8 points. The point spread adjusts over time as the game approaches to induce gamblers to bet equal sums on each team. For a given point spread, there may be more bets on Ohio State than on Florida. In that event, the spread widens, thereby encouraging more people to bet on Florida. If this results in too many bets on Florida, the spread will narrow. The bookie is trying to adjust the spread so that there will be one dollar bet on Florida for every dollar bet on Ohio State. When the bookie achieves this balance, he is completely indifferent as to who wins the game.

[4] For illegal sports books, there is, of course, the risk of getting caught and being prosecuted.

The bookie earns a profit on this business by offering odds of 11 to 10. That is, whether you bet on the favorite to cover the point spread or the underdog to beat the spread, you bet $11 to win $10. If you lose, you pay $11, but if you win, you receive only $10. Suppose there is one bet on the University of Southern California (the favorite) to beat Notre Dame (the underdog) and one bet on Notre Dame to beat the spread. The bookie collects $11 from each gambler. After the game, the winner gets her $11 back plus $10, and the loser loses $11. On a total handle of $22, the bookie earns $1. For the bookie, this is a commission of about 4.5 percent ($1/$22). Thus, the profitability of a sports book depends on the volume of business and the elimination of risk by balancing the amounts bet on each team.

Bookies can lose money in a number of ways. Clearly, the most troublesome problem is balancing the sums wagered. If the betting gets out of balance, the bookie will have some risk because he must pay the winners. Suppose, for example, that $2,200 is wagered on the Steelers–Bengals game, but it is not balanced: $550 is bet on the Steelers and $1,650 is bet on the Bengals. If the Bengals win the game, those who bet on the Bengals get their $1,650 back, plus $1,500 because they win $10 for each $11 bet. The bookie has only $550 from those who bet on the Steelers, and therefore, the bookie must pay $950 out of his own pocket. In contrast, if the Steelers win, the bookie returns $550 to the winners plus $500. He has $1,650 from the losers to cover this sum and, therefore, earns a profit of $1,150. Bookies can minimize this sort of variance in returns by refusing to accept any more bets on one of the teams when the action gets too far out of balance.

Sports bookies may cancel all bets on a contest if the betting suddenly and suspiciously gets out of balance. When large sums are bet at the last moment, the sports bookie may suspect that the game has been fixed. For example, Betfair, an online sports book, voided all bets on a tennis match between Nikolay Davydenko and Martin Vasallo Arguello. Although Davydenko was ranked number 4 in the world and Arguello was ranked 87th, large amounts were bet on Arguello to win. A good deal was bet on Arguello even after Davydenko had won the first set. The total wagered was $7 million, which was 10 times the usual amount wagered. This was enough for Betfair to cancel all bets on the match.

4 GAMBLING BY PROFESSIONAL ATHLETES

The major professional leagues and organizations do not permit gambling by its members on their sports. For example, when Jim Furyk and Tiger Woods were locked in a playoff in the NEC Invitational, Furyk found himself in a bunker and in danger of losing. Watching the playoff in the clubhouse, Phil Mickelson offered to bet $20 at 25–1 odds that Furyk would put the ball in the hole for a par.[5] Mike Weir took that bet and lost $500 to Mickelson when Furyk

[5] "Mickelson Breaks Gambling Regulations," *Golf Today.* http://www.golftoday.co.uk/news/yeartodate/news01/mickelson4.html.

made the shot. This constituted a technical violation of Section VI-B of the PGA Tour Player Handbook:

> A player shall not have any financial interest, either direct or indirect, in the performance or in winnings of another player . . . whether through purse-splitting, prize money "insurance," financial assistance, bets, or otherwise.

The PGA Tour's gambling regulations are intended to preserve the integrity of the competition. Although Mickelson's bet could hardly impair the integrity of a playoff worth hundreds of thousands of dollars to the winner, it did violate the PGA Tour regulations and thereby attracted the attention of Tour Commissioner Tim Finchem.

The National Football League (NFL) has frowned on gambling for many years. Its policy on gambling is part of its general concern for the "integrity of the game." As part of the standard player contract, the player must acknowledge his responsibilities to preserve the image of the NFL:

> Player recognizes the detriment to the League and professional football that would result from impairment of public confidence in the honest and orderly conduct of NFL games or the integrity and good character of NFL players. Player therefore acknowledges his awareness that if he accepts a bribe or agrees to throw or fix an NFL game; fails to promptly report a bribe offer or an attempt to throw or fix an NFL game; bets on an NFL game; knowingly associates with gamblers or gambling activity; uses or provides other players with stimulants or other drugs for the purpose of attempting to enhance on-field performance; or is guilty of any other form of conduct reasonably judged by the League Commissioner to be detrimental to the League or professional football, the Commissioner will have the right, but only after giving Player the opportunity for a hearing at which he may be represented by counsel of his choice, to fine Player in a reasonable amount; to suspend Player for a period certain or indefinitely; and/or to terminate this contract.

Thus, NFL players are not permitted to bet on NFL games nor are they permitted to associate with gamblers or gambling activities in a way that will discredit the NFL. The sanctions may include a fine or a suspension. In the past, Paul Hornung (Green Bay Packers) and Alex Karras (Detroit Lions) were suspended for an entire year for gambling. It could have been worse – the commissioner could have imposed a lifetime suspension.

A lifetime suspension from the National Basketball Association (NBA) is precisely what Jack Molinas got for gambling on his team's games. In 1953, Jack Molinas was drafted by the Fort Wayne (now Detroit) Pistons. He signed a contract that prohibited gambling on NBA games. Like the NFL, the NBA also has a rule that prohibited such gambling. When Molinas admitted to betting on Pistons games, the NBA suspended him indefinitely and subsequently refused to reinstate him as a player. Molinas ultimately sued the NBA for $3 million – a tidy sum in the early 1960s. He alleged that his suspension was unreasonable because he never bet against the Pistons. He always bet on them to cover the point spread. Although this argument has some surface appeal, the court disagreed. In light of some gambling scandals, it was imperative that the NBA preserve its image and protect the integrity of the competition on the court. The court explained precisely why gambling by participants is an ill that a league can seek to eradicate. The court decided that the NBA's

> disciplinary rule invoked against gambling seems about as reasonable a rule as could be imagined. Furthermore, the application of the rule to the plaintiff's conduct is also eminently reasonable. Plaintiff was wagering on games in which he was to play, and some of these bets were made on the basis of a "point spread" system. Plaintiff insists that since he bet only on his own team to win, his conduct, while admittedly improper, was not immoral. But I do not find this distinction to be a meaningful one in the context of the present case. The vice inherent in the plaintiff's conduct is that each time he either placed a bet or refused to place a bet, this operated inevitably to inform bookmakers of an insider's opinion as to the adequacy or inadequacy of the point-spread or his team's ability to win. Thus, for example, when he chose to place a bet, this would indicate to the bookmakers that a member of the Fort Wayne team believed that his team would exceed its expected performance. Similarly, when he chose not to bet, bookmakers thus would be informed of his opinion that the Pistons would not perform according to expectations. It is certainly reasonable for the league . . . to conclude that this conduct could not be tolerated and must, therefore, be eliminated. The reasonableness of the league's action is apparent in view of the fact that, at that time, the confidence of the public in basketball had been shattered, due to a series of gambling incidents. Thus, it was absolutely necessary for the sport to exhume gambling from its midst for all time in order to survive.
>
> The same factors justifying the suspension also serve to justify the subsequent refusal to reinstate. The league could reasonably conclude that in order to effectuate its important and legitimate policies against gambling, and to restore and maintain the confidence of the public vital to its existence, it was necessary to enforce its rules strictly, and to apply the most stringent sanctions.[6]

This ruling is significant because it endorses severe sanctions for gambling by athletes in professional sports. The suit involved the NBA, but the court's logic would seem to apply to all sports.

In Major League Baseball (MLB), gambling on baseball by players, coaches, managers, and even owners is construed as *misconduct* and punished severely. Early in the 1943 season, William Cox, the owner of the Philadelphia Phillies, made 15 to 20 bets of $25 to $100 each on baseball games. After Cox admitted to the gambling, Commissioner Kennesaw Mountain Landis ordered him to sell the team. In 1970, another commissioner, Bowie Kuhn, suspended Denny McClain (Detroit Tigers) for three months for being involved in bookmaking. Pete Rose, as most fans know, was banned for life for betting on baseball while managing the Cincinnati Reds. Rose is ineligible for the Hall of Fame because of his betting on baseball.

[6] *Molinas v. National Basketball Association*, 190 F. Supp. 241 (S.D.N.Y., 1961).

Although baseball does not have an explicit rule on gambling on other sports, it finds illegal gambling problematic. Accordingly, when Lenny Dykstra admitted to having lost $50,000 in illegal poker games, he was put on a one-year probation by Commissioner Fay Vincent.

Box 10.1 ***That's My Story and I'm Sticking to It***

The *New York Daily News* reported that Paul Lo Duca, the Mets' All-Star catcher, had bet with illegal bookmakers.* According to the *Daily News*, the illegal bookmakers took steps at least twice to "encourage" Lo Duca to pay his gambling debts. When he was with the Marlins, a bookie allegedly complained to the Marlins management that Lo Duca owed some money to the bookie. The Marlins reported this to the MLB. Presumably, this was investigated by MLB, and Lo Duca was cleared.

Lo Duca admitted that he gambles legally on horse races. He owns several horses and has an interest in horse racing. Lo Duca maintained that he bets only on horse racing with a legal, online account. He denied incurring any gambling debts. He steadfastly stuck to that story.

Under MLB's policy, if a player bets on baseball, he is subject to a one-year suspension. If he bets on a game involving his own team, he is subject to a lifetime ban. However, when a player gambles legally on anything else, MLB may not like it, but it has no explicit policy on such gambling.

* For another newspaper account regarding Paul Lo Duca's alleged gambling, see Ben Shpigel, "Mets Support Lo Duca as Gambling Stories Swirl," *New York Times*, Aug. 12, 2006.

The Arena Football League (AFL) has taken a strong stand against gambling on AFL games by players. The player contract expressly provides that a player not "bet legally or illegally, anything of value on the result or margin of victory on any AFL game." The contract further provides that the player will not "knowingly associate with gamblers or gambling activities." If the AFL has a sound foundation for believing that a player has violated the prohibition on gambling, the sanctions may be severe: "suspension, dismissal, and/or permanent disqualification . . . from any further association with the AFL."

4.1 The Added Risks of Betting on Baseball

On the basis of economic reasoning, one would predict that very few MLB players bet on baseball. The reason is that it makes no sense to do so because doing so carries a lifetime ban (if you bet on your own team). It is hard to imagine that the benefits could outweigh the expected costs. To illustrate, suppose a player has a career of T years in front of him. An average MLB player will earn considerably more as a baseball player than in his next best occupation. This difference is known as *rent* because it is a return that need not be paid to keep the player in MLB. We can denote the difference in income as ΔI. At a discount rate of r, the present value of the increased income is[7]

$$PV(\Delta I) = \sum_{t=1}^{T} \Delta I_t/(1+r)^t.$$

In 2009, the average MLB player's salary was nearing $3 million. For purposes of illustration, suppose that $\Delta I = \$2.75$ million, $T = 10$, and $r = 0.06$. In that event, the present value of the rents earned by the average player would be

$$\sum_{t=1}^{10} \$2.75\ million/(1.06)^t = \$20{,}240{,}000.$$

Thus, a lifetime ban would cost the average player more than $20 million. This, of course, must be discounted by the probability of getting caught. But if the chances of getting caught were only one in a hundred, gambling would have to be worth more than $200,000 to make any sense even if the player were risk neutral. If the player is a risk seeker, which is likely because he is a gambler, the value need not be so high, but it would still have to be considerable.

5 NCAA AND GAMBLING ON COLLEGE SPORTS

The NCAA takes a hard line on gambling. Its policy on gambling by players and coaches is set out quite clearly in the NCAA Bylaws. Its attitude toward gambling on NCAA athletics by nonparticipants is reflected in its efforts to persuade Congress to prohibit gambling on NCAA events.[8]

5.1 NCAA Policy on Gambling

The NCAA's hostility toward gambling by participants is spelled out clearly in the *NCAA Division I Manual.* Bylaw 10.3, Gambling Activities, categorically forbids gambling by coaches, student-athletes, and athletic department staff members:

Staff members of a member conference, staff members of the athletics department of a member institution and student-athletes shall not knowingly:

(a) Provide information to individuals involved in organized gambling activities concerning intercollegiate athletics competition;
(b) Solicit a bet on any intercollegiate team;
(c) Accept a bet on any team representing the institution;

[7] These calculations were explained in some detail in Chapter 2.

[8] The NCAA apparently believes that if intercollegiate games are removed from the sports books in Las Vegas that all gambling will cease. It would like to have betting on college sports banned throughout the country. It has sought help from Congress, but to no avail – at least so far. For arguments against such legislation, see Jon Saracano, "Outlawing College Odds a Bad Fix," *USA Today,* April 25, 2001. Also, see Doris Dixon, "Bid to Outlaw Betting on College Sports Faces Very Long Odds," *Wall Street Journal,* Sept. 3, 2001, p. 9.

(d) Solicit or accept a bet on any intercollegiate competition for any item (e.g., cash, shirt, dinner) that has tangible value; or
(e) Participate in any gambling activity that involves intercollegiate athletics or professional athletics, through a bookmaker, a parlay card or any other method employed by organized gambling.

There is little room for confusion regarding this blanket prohibition. No coach or student-athlete can reasonably claim to be confused about the NCAA policy against gambling on athletic competition. It is absolutely forbidden. Those who engage in gambling activities do so at their own peril.

Box 10.2 ***The Franchione Newsletter***

Dennis Franchione, head coach of Texas A&M's football team, had a secret newsletter, the *VIP Connection.* About a dozen Aggie supporters paid $1,200 each to receive the e-mail newsletter. This newsletter contained confidential information on injuries and scouting reports. Because Franchione's salary in 2007 was about $2 million, it is unlikely that he needed an extra $14,000 or so. Franchione asked subscribers not to use the confidential information for gambling purposes, but he was in no position to monitor that. The fact of the matter is that such inside information is very useful for making decisions on gambling opportunities. As a result, it is reasonable to ask whether the *VIP Connection* violated NCAA rules.*

* At the end of the 2007 season, after a stunning win over arch rival Texas, Franchione resigned. The *Dallas Morning News* identified the *VIP Connection* as one of five reasons that Franchione had failed at Texas A&M.

5.2 NCAA Sanctions for Gambling

Because "rules were made to be broken," there must be penalties for rules violations, or the rule will be disregarded. This is certainly true for those student-athletes who gamble and are caught. NCAA Bylaw 10.3.1, Sanctions, sets out some severe penalties:

The following sanctions for violations of Bylaw 10.3 shall apply as follows:

(a) A student-athlete who engages in activities designed to influence the outcome of an intercollegiate contest or in an effort to affect win-loss margins (i.e., "point shaving") or who solicits or accepts a bet or participates in any gambling activity through a bookmaker, a parlay card or any other method employed by organized gambling that involves wagering on the student-athlete's institution shall permanently lose all remaining regular-season and postseason eligibility in all sports.
(b) A student-athlete who solicits or accepts a bet or participates in any gambling activity that involves intercollegiate athletics or professional athletics, through

> a bookmaker, a parlay card or any other method employed by organized gambling, shall be ineligible for all regular-season and postseason competition for a minimum of a period of one year from the date of the institution's determination that a violation has occurred and shall be charged with the loss of a minimum of one season of competition. A request for reinstatement may be submitted on behalf of a student-athlete who has participated in such activity only upon fulfillment of the minimum condition indicated above. If the student-athlete is determined to have been involved in a subsequent violation of any portion of Bylaw 10.3, the student-athlete shall permanently lose all remaining regular-season and postseason eligibility in all sports.

Given the severity of the sanctions, one would expect that sensible athletic departments would counsel their athletes regarding the gambling prohibition. At the University of Florida, for example, the athletic director regularly admonishes all head coaches to educate their players on the NCAA policies on gambling.

Given the NCAA's clear prohibition of gambling, the counseling efforts of the member schools, and the heavy sanctions for gambling, one would expect athletes to steer clear of the local bookie. Sadly, they do not always do so. The NCAA conducted a year-long study that covered 21,000 athletes.[9] It found that nearly 35 percent of the male athletes and 10 percent of the female athletes engaged in some form of sports wagering during the previous year. Among the male athletes, golfers, wrestlers, lacrosse players, and football players were more likely to gamble than athletes in other sports. Among the women, golfers, lacrosse, basketball, and field hockey players were more apt to gamble than athletes in other sports.

NCAA President Myles Brand found the results both startling and disturbing. He said that "sports wagering is a double-threat because it harms the well-being of student athletes and the integrity of college sports."

On the integrity issue, there can be no doubt that gambling can create serious problems. The NCAA study uncovered some alarming facts. Some 2.3 percent of the football players surveyed had been asked to affect the outcome of a game because of gambling debts. About 1.4 percent admitted that they had affected the outcome of a game because of gambling debts, and 1.1 percent admitted to having taken money to play poorly in a game. This is cause for serious concern. If fans routinely suspect that college football games are fixed, interest will fade quickly, and big-time college football will be a thing of the past. For example, in 1996, 13 Boston College football players were suspended for betting on college and professional football as well as MLB games.[10] Two of the players bet *against* their own team in a loss to Syracuse. If such conduct were widespread, it would surely undermine the integrity of the game.

[9] NCAA News Release, "NCAA Study Finds Sports Wagering a Problem Among Student-Athletes," May 12, 2004.

[10] Associated Press, "Sports Gambling Scandals," *Toronto Star*, Feb. 9, 2006.

Table 10.1. Gambling Activity by Game Officials

Gambling Activity	Number	Percent
1. Casino gambling	420	66.0
2. Lotteries	325	51.0
3. Slot machines	318	50.2
4. Super Bowl squares	211	33.2
5. Bowling, pool, golf	196	30.8
6. Card games	168	26.4
7. NCAA basketball tournament	138	21.6
8. Horses, dogs	114	17.9
9. Dice games	109	17.1
10. Sports	68	10.7
11. Bingo	34	5.3
12. Internet gambling	4	0.6
Summary	540	84.4

There have been point-shaving incidents in a few NCAA basketball programs.[11] Following their NCAA championship in 1951, Kentucky fell prey to a point-shaving scandal that resulted in the suspension of the program for the 1952–1953 season. In the wake of point-shaving allegations, Tulane shut down its basketball program in 1985. It did not resume play until the 1989–1990 season. In 1997, Steven Smith and Isaac Burton, Jr., former Arizona State players, pleaded guilty to conspiring to commit sports bribery that fixed four Arizona State basketball games. As with football, if fans suspect that games are fixed, confidence in the integrity of the game will suffer, and fan interest will diminish.

The NCAA has other worries as well. A University of Michigan study uncovered some possibly disturbing information about the gambling activities of football and basketball game officials.[12] Most of their gambling was not related to NCAA athletic events, but some of it was. The authors sent out 1,642 questionnaires to NCAA Division I football, men's basketball, and women's basketball game officials. They received 640 completed questionnaires, which were anonymous. The survey revealed the gambling activity displayed in Table 10.1.

The prevalence of some form of gambling is not too surprising. It is a little unsettling, however, to find that officials bet on NCAA basketball tournament games.

The really bad news that the study uncovered involved issues of integrity. First, 2.2 percent of the officials admitted that they placed bets with bookies. Recall that the court in the *Molinas* case pointed out the dangers of a player's

[11] *Ibid.*

[12] Ann G. Vollano and Derrick L. Gragg (2000), "NCAA Division I Officials: Gambling with the Integrity of College Sports?" Department of Athletics, University of Michigan.

Box 10.3 ***For Rick Neuheisel, All's Well That Ends Well****

The NCAA manual makes it pretty clear that coaches, staff, and athletes may not knowingly "solicit or accept a bet on any intercollegiate competition for any item (e.g., cash, shirt, dinner) that has tangible value." As March Madness approached, the University of Washington cautioned the coaches about gambling. They were reminded that they could not place bets with bookies or organize an office pool. However, they were advised that they could participate in basketball pools organized outside the intercollegiate athletic staff, for example, a pool organized by neighbors.

Rick Neuheisel, head football coach at Washington, bet $5,000 and won about $20,000 by picking Maryland in 2002. When the NCAA got wind of this, he was investigated by the NCAA and the Pacific-10. The University of Washington fired him as a result. This raises a troubling question: If participation was improper, who should be sanctioned – Washington or Coach Neuheisel? After all, Coach Neuheisel adhered to the advice of the University of Washington athletic director's office. One could argue that he relied on those who are supposed to know the precise interpretation of the NCAA Bylaws.

Interestingly, the NCAA cleared Coach Neuheisel some time after he was fired.† Although he had initially lied to Washington's athletic director about having participated in the basketball pool, the memora from Washington's compliance officer misled Coach Neuheisel. The NCAA could find no evidence that he deliberately broke the rules on gambling. This raises an interesting question: What recourse did Rick Neuheisel have for an arguably improper breach of his employment contract? The answer: file a wrongful termination suit against the University. Neuheisel did and won $4.5 million.

Following his stormy departure from Washington, Neuheisel did not coach for a year. He then served as quarterback coach for two years for the Baltimore Ravens. He was promoted to offensive coordinator for the 2007 season. At the end of the season Neuheisel returned to his alma mater, the University of California – Los Angeles (UCLA), as head coach.

* "NCAA Clears Neuheisel, Punishes UW," MSNBC.com, Oct. 20, 2004.

† Associated Press, "NCAA Clears Neuheisel." http://nbcsports.msnbc.com/id/6290995/.

betting even on his own team to win. Given the fact that game officials are in a unique position to influence a game's outcome, the court's concern clearly extends to game officials. Nearly 2.0 percent of the officials indicated they knew that other officials had not called games fairly because of gambling. Two referees even reported that they had been approached about fixing the outcome of games. If there were only two incidents, this is a good news–bad news thing, but there may have been unreported incidents as well.

The results of the study raise some obvious questions: What should be the limits (if any) on gambling by referees? Should there be a total ban on gambling – including bets on the golf course, weekly poker games, and the like? This seems too broad, but where should the line be drawn? It seems clear that the limitations on NCAA officials should be at least as stringent as those that apply to the players and coaches.

6 AN NBA NIGHTMARE

In July 2007, a federal grand jury began reviewing the case of Tim Donaghy, a former NBA referee who had resigned after 13 years in the league. The inquiry involved allegations that Donaghy may have made calls that affected the outcome of games that he had officiated. This was a bombshell that threatened the credibility of the NBA. All referees recognized that their calls would be scrutinized and their integrity questioned. Donaghy's disgrace spilled over onto all referees. For the innocent, their reputations were damaged by the misdeeds of a rogue official.

In August 2007, Donaghy surrendered and pleaded guilty to two felony charges. It turns out that Donaghy had bet on NBA games. He even bet on games that he had officiated and, therefore, was in a position to influence for his own benefit. From December 2006 through April 2007, Donaghy was an advisor to professional gamblers regarding which team to bet on. For each correct pick, he was paid $2,000 at first and later received $5,000. He also gave them confidential information about referee assignments, the health of players, and relationships between players and referees.[13] It is unclear how much he was paid for this kind of information. The charges against Donaghy did not involve point-shaving or game-fixing allegations.

For the two felonies, Donaghy faced a maximum fine of $250,000 and up to 25 years in prison. He entered into a cooperation agreement with the government to provide all information that he had on gambling.

NBA Commissioner David Stern was extremely upset when the Donaghy story broke. If Donaghy's behavior had been widespread, the credibility of the NBA would have been destroyed. Stern acted swiftly in several ways. First, he started an extensive and intensive investigation of all NBA referees to determine whether anyone else had broken the NBA's antigambling rules. This investigation disclosed that about half of the referees had committed minor violations such as betting on the golf course. Second, the NBA hired a former referee to evaluate the performance of the NBA's crew chiefs. Third, Stern revisited the NBA's gambling rules for referees. He found that they were outdated and unrealistic. The rules were detailed in an eight-page pamphlet: *Bad Bet: Understanding the NBA's Antigambling Rules.* This pamphlet was given to every NBA referee. The NBA had an absolute prohibition on all gambling – casinos, golf course wagers, horse racing, and so on. This, Stern concluded, was too broad. The revised rules will permit some gambling, but will still prohibit all gambling on sports through sports books or brokers. Fourth, Stern had decided to use

[13] Howard Beck and Michael S. Schmidt, "N.B.A. Referee Pleads Guilty to Gambling Charges," *New York Times*, August 16, 2007.

the NBA's data on every call made by a referee to monitor performance and to detect any suspicious behavior.

7 CONCLUDING REMARKS

In this chapter, we have explored the economics of gambling. The expected utility model developed in Chapter 3 proved useful. Gambling results from a risk-seeking attitude. It is rational to gamble even though the expected return is negative. For sports leagues, organizations, and the NCAA, there is a concern for the image of the game and integrity of the competition. If players, coaches, or game officials are induced by gambling interests to impair the integrity of the competition, fans may abandon the sport for other forms of entertainment. As a result, all major leagues and organizations, including the NCAA, have fairly strict rules about gambling. There is evidence, however, that some sports gambling by participants continues to exist.

PROBLEMS AND QUESTIONS

1. Gamblin' Gary is a risk seeker and often accepts actuarially unfair gambles.
   a. What is an actuarially unfair gamble?
   b. Why does Gary accept them?
   c. Will he accept all gambling opportunities? Explain.
2. Could an insurance company sell insurance to a risk lover?
3. Why does the NCAA have a rule that forbids gambling by student-athletes and their coaches? Why should athletes be treated differently from other students?
4. A University of Michigan study found that a large number of football and basketball referees gamble. What should be done about referees who gamble?
   a. Does it matter where and when they gamble?
   b. How about betting with their buddies on the golf course or at their weekly poker game?
5. Does the NCAA prohibition of gambling mean that the Oklahoma coach and the Texas coach cannot bet a steak dinner on the outcome of their annual football game? If so, does this make any sense? What dangers do such "friendly" wagers pose?
6. Do you think that Pete Rose should be kept out of the Hall of Fame for having gambled on baseball while still in the game? Justify your view.
7. In Figure 10.1, find the expected utility of the gamble and compare that to the utility of the risk-free wealth. Explain this result and why a convex utility function leads to risk taking.
8. In the following figure, U(W) is Patrick Passer's utility function. If Patrick suffers a serious injury, his wealth will be $1 million, but if he does not suffer

such an injury, his wealth will be $10 million. His expected wealth is $8.2 million.

a. What is the probability of a serious injury?

b. Patrick can buy insurance for $10,000 per million dollars of coverage. Will he buy a $9 million insurance policy?

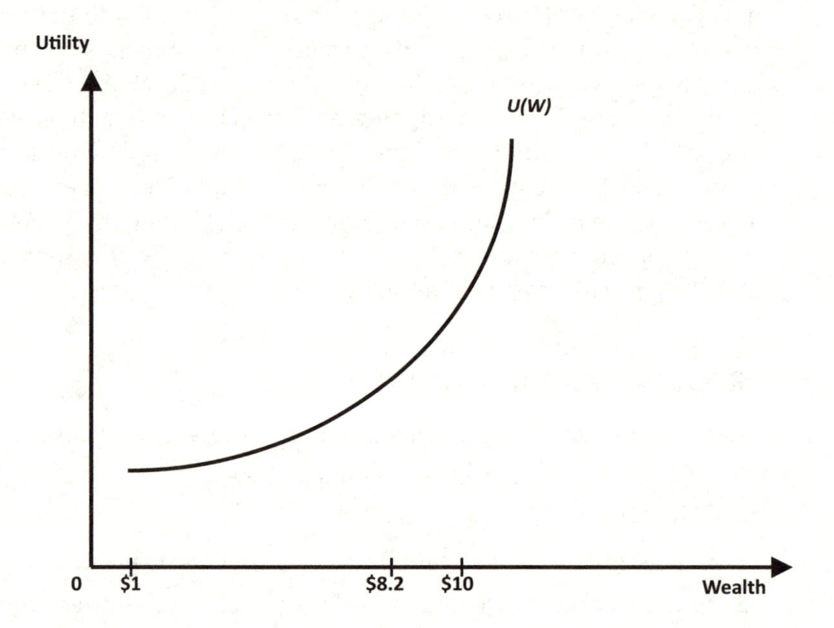

9. Apparently, the NCAA prohibits the organization of a basketball pool by a university athletic department (see Rick Neuheisel Box). Should it? What potential dangers are posed by such pools?

10. Should coaches and athletes be prohibited from all gambling activity including weekly poker games, betting with their friends on the golf course, buying lottery tickets, betting at the race track, and gambling in Las Vegas casinos? If so, why? If not, why not?

11. Those people who conspire to fix basketball games face prison if they are convicted. What is the basis for sending them to prison?

12. Myles Brand said that gambling *harms* student-athletes. How does it harm them?

13. Betting on your own team in baseball carries a lifetime ban for players, coaches, and managers. For an average MLB player, that is worth more than $20 million (assuming a 10-year career and a 6.0 percent discount rate). Explain the danger of being blackmailed by a bookie.

14. Do you believe that Jack Molinas deserved a lifetime ban from the NBA for betting on his own team to win? Explain.

15. Is there any reason why a professional bookmaker would want a player to shave points?

16. Explain why imbalances in the sums wagered on a college basketball game create an incentive for a bookie to try to induce point shaving.
17. Professional basketball players earn millions of dollars a year. Referees in the NBA earn $150,000–200,000 a year. Who is apt to be more approachable targets of gambling interests?

RESEARCH QUESTIONS

1. Teddy Dupay was supposed to have a big senior season in 2001–2002 at the University of Florida. Amid rumors of a gambling investigation, Dupay gave up his senior season. Develop the details of what was known and not known about Dupay's alleged gambling.
2. In 1981, Rick Kuhn was found guilty of fixing basketball games in the 1978–1979 season. He was sentenced to 10 years in prison. Find the details of his scheme, how he got caught, and the basis for a severe penalty.
3. In June 2003, Rick Neuheisel was fired for gambling, but the NCAA cleared him in October 2004. Neuheisel expressed a hope that he could return to college coaching. Finally, UCLA hired Neuheisel as its head coach for the 2008 season. What happened to Neuheisel's career between 2003 and 2008?
4. Connie Hawkins was a legend in New York City basketball. Although he was probably innocent of any wrongdoing, Hawkins essentially lost his career because of some hazy links to gambling. Trace the trials and tribulations he endured during his career after high school.

REFERENCES AND FURTHER READING

Forrest, D., and R. Simmons. (2003). "Sport and Gambling." *Oxford Review of Economics Policy*, 19, 598–611.

Wolfers, J. (2006). "Point Shaving: Corruption in NCAA Basketball." *American Economic Association Papers and Proceedings*, 96, 279–283.

11

Cheating in Sports

1 INTRODUCTION

In sports, to cheat is to violate the rules dishonestly. This definition distinguishes inadvertent infractions of the rules from deliberate or intentional infractions. It is the element of deliberateness that makes it cheating. Sports leagues and organizations have multiple concerns with cheating by players and coaches. First, cheating confers an unfair advantage on the cheater and thereby impairs the integrity of the competition. The best player or team may not win. Second, when cheating leads to suspect results, fans may lose interest in the game. This, of course, would have serious economic consequences for the players and their clubs. Unfortunately, cheating of one sort or another is all around us. Most of us are well aware of some common forms of cheating. Currently, the most prominent form of cheating involves the use of steroids and other performance-enhancing substances.[1] Also, there are the all-too-familiar college recruiting violations and impermissible payments to student-athletes. Cheating comes in all shapes and sizes, however. The silver medalist in the women's 800 meters at the 2006 Asian Games failed a gender test.[2] The International Olympic Committee suspended a senior Bulgarian official for his role in a vote-peddling scheme for bid cities.[3] Two players at the World Open, the largest chess tournament of the year, were suspected of cheating by using computers to help them.[4] Even NBC had to admit that some plagiarism had occurred in its script for a lead-in to the Kentucky Derby.[5]

[1] Performance-enhancing substances have plagued Major League Baseball, the National Football League, international track, and especially cycling. Because of the widespread concern with performance-enhancing drugs, Chapter 14 is devoted to that topic.

[2] "Runner Fails Gender Test, Loses Medal," Herald.com, Dec. 18, 2006.

[3] Associated Press, "IOC Suspends Member Mired in Bid Scandal."

[4] Dylan Loeb McClain, "Cheating Accusations in Mental Sports, Two," *New York Times*, Aug. 8, 2006.

[5] Richard Sandomir, "NBC Admits Plagiarism in Feature Before Derby," *New York Times*, May 11, 2006.

Cheating to win confers an unfair competitive advantage on the cheater. This could cause retaliatory cheating, so no one would be playing by the rules. As a result, the best team or the best athlete may not win, which can lead to fan dissatisfaction. As reprehensible as cheating to win may be, we can appreciate (if not approve of) the motivation. Cheating to lose, however, seems much worse. The boxer who takes a dive, the basketball player who shaves points, and the tennis player who tanks in a match are all involved in the most reprehensible cheating. Cheating to lose denies fans true competitive contests, which is what they are buying. In either event, cheating threatens the integrity of the contest, which may result in fan dissatisfaction and loss of interest. This is not good for the teams, the athletes, and the fans. Cheating must be controlled to protect the popularity of the sports involved. In this chapter, we examine cheating to win and cheating to lose. Our focus is on the economic incentives and economic consequences of cheating. We begin by developing an economic model of deterrence to illustrate how governing bodies can deter cheating. The economic approach to deterrence is not to point to the immorality of cheating and appeal to a player's conscience and sense of fair play. Instead, the economic approach is to make cheating "unprofitable" or otherwise unattractive so that players will elect to compete honestly.

2 DETERRING CHEATING

If a player or coach cheats and the cheating goes undetected, he gains an unfair competitive advantage.[6] For example, if a golfer moves his ball to a more favorable position, he improves his chances of a desirable score. This, however, violates the rules and calls for a penalty of two strokes, which defeats the purpose of cheating in the first place. However, the cheating golfer must be caught for the penalty to be imposed. Thus, when a golfer cheats in this fashion, there is a reward if he does not get caught and a penalty if he does get caught. The cheater, therefore, engages in risky behavior and will be influenced by the expected utility associated with that risky behavior. Taking steps to adjust the expected utility of the risky behavior is the key to deterring cheating.

2.1 A General Model of Deterrence

Cheating confers some benefit (B) on the cheater but exposes him to a punishment (F) if he is caught.[7] If the probability of detection and punishment is p, then the corresponding probability of avoiding detection and punishment is $(1 - p)$. Starting at an initial wealth of W_0, which the athlete will enjoy by competing honestly, the expected wealth when one cheats is:

$$E[W] = p(W_0 - F) + (1 - p)(W_0 + B).$$

[6] This section is an adaptation of the modern economic approach to crime, which stems from Gary S. Becker (1968), "Crime and Punishment: An Economic Approach," *Journal of Political Economy*, 76, 169–217.

[7] This model employs the expected utility model that we developed in Chapter 8.

We assume that the potential cheater is an expected utility maximizer: he will cheat if doing so makes him better off in the sense that his expected utility exceeds the utility of wealth. In other words, if

$$E[U(W)] > U(W_0),$$

then the expected utility of wealth exceeds the utility of wealth that he would experience without cheating, and he will cheat.

On the basis of this relationship, we can construct a deterrent function:

$$D = U(W_0) - E[U(W)],$$

which after substitution can be written as

$$D = U(W_0) - [pU(W_0 - F) + (1 - p)U(W_0 + B)].$$

If D is positive, cheating will be deterred. This result does not depend on the potential cheater's sense of fairness or morality (although we can incorporate that into the model). Instead, cheating is deterred because there is no net gain from cheating. In fact, the opposite is true: on average, the cheater will be worse off by cheating. In other words, cheating does not pay. When D is positive, the utility of the wealth without cheating exceeds the expected utility of wealth with cheating, and therefore the potential cheater will elect to compete honestly because it is in his or her best interest to do so. In contrast, if D is negative, then cheating makes economic sense because the expected utility of wealth exceeds the utility of wealth that can be enjoyed without cheating. In this case, cheating "pays" – at least on average. The economic approach to deterring cheating does not rely on preaching to the coach or athlete about fair play and what is the right thing to do. Instead, the economic approach is to make D positive so that it is in the coach's or athlete's interest to compete honestly.

2.2 Control Variables

If a sports organization (or society at large) wants to deter cheating, it must alter the variables under its control to reduce the expected utility. If we examine D, we see that there are five elements: W_0, U, B, F, and p. Now, a sports organization cannot change the shape of the utility function (U), nor can it change the initial wealth (W_0) or the benefits of cheating (B). It can, however, change the probability of detecting cheating (p) and the penalties for cheating (F). The use of these instruments can be illustrated graphically.

Figure 11.1 describes a situation in which the potential cheater is indifferent between cheating and competing honestly. Here $D = 0$, because $U(W_0) = E[U(W)]$ when the expected wealth is $\overline{W}$.

In this case, the expected punishment, which is $(p)F$, is such that expected wealth from cheating is $\overline{W}$, as shown in Figure 11.1. Because the height of the utility function at W_0 is $U(W_0)$ and the height of the chord at $\overline{W}$ is $E[U(W)]$, we can see that $U(W_0) = E[U(W)]$ and, therefore, $D = 0$. As a result, the potential cheater is indifferent between cheating and not cheating.

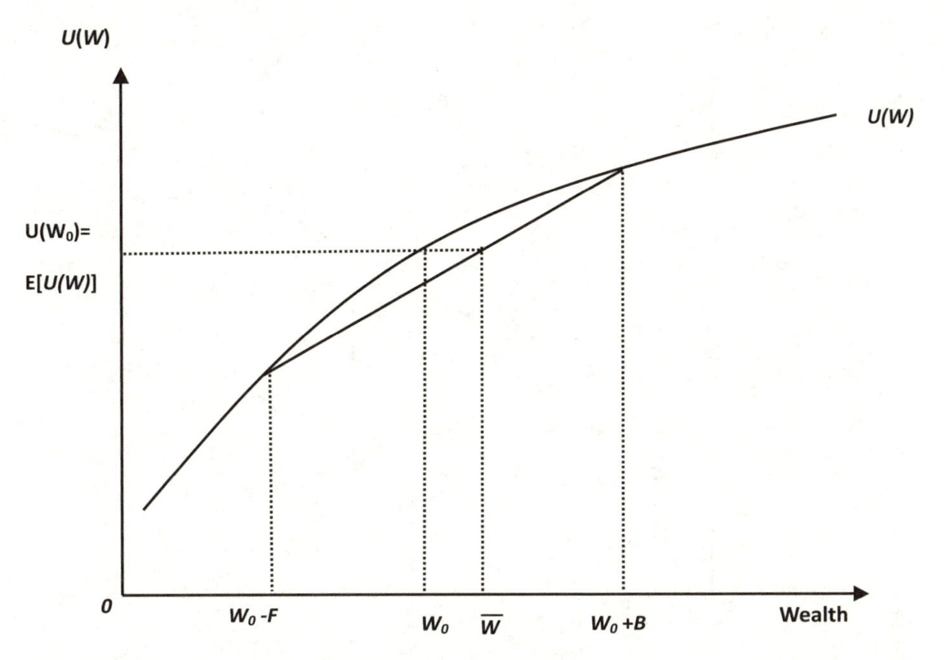

Figure 11.1. A potential cheater is indifferent about cheating when $U(W_0) = E[U(W)]$.

2.3 Changing the Probability of Detection

Suppose that we decide to pour more resources into detecting cheating. This will increase (p). How does this affect deterrence?

The effect of an increase in (p) is to reduce the expected wealth even if the punishment remains the same. Because the chord does not change, the expected utility will now be lower than before the increase in (p). As the $E[W]$ moves to the left of $\overline{W}$ on the wealth axis, the height of the chord at that lower $E[W]$ necessarily falls. As a result, increasing (p) will deter cheating.

We see evidence of increased expenditures designed to increase the probability of catching cheaters. The ATP is concerned about the possibility of rigged tennis matches. It has responded by hiring security firms and analysts in an effort to detect irregularities. The National Association for Stock Car Auto Racing (NASCAR) does more extensive testing to be sure that everyone's car conforms to the rules. In professional basketball, there used to be two referees, but there are now three. In PGA Tour events, there are rules officials all over the course. Unfortunately, sports leagues and organizations must invest resources designed to increase the probability of detecting cheating. If all competitors were honest, such expenditures would be unnecessary. Thus, cheating leads to socially unproductive expenditures. However, such expenditures are worthwhile in the sense of improving or preserving the integrity of the competition on the field.

2.4 Changing the Penalty for Cheating

What happens to D if the penalty is increased? The answer to this question can be found in Figure 11.2. First, note that the chord rotates downward to reflect

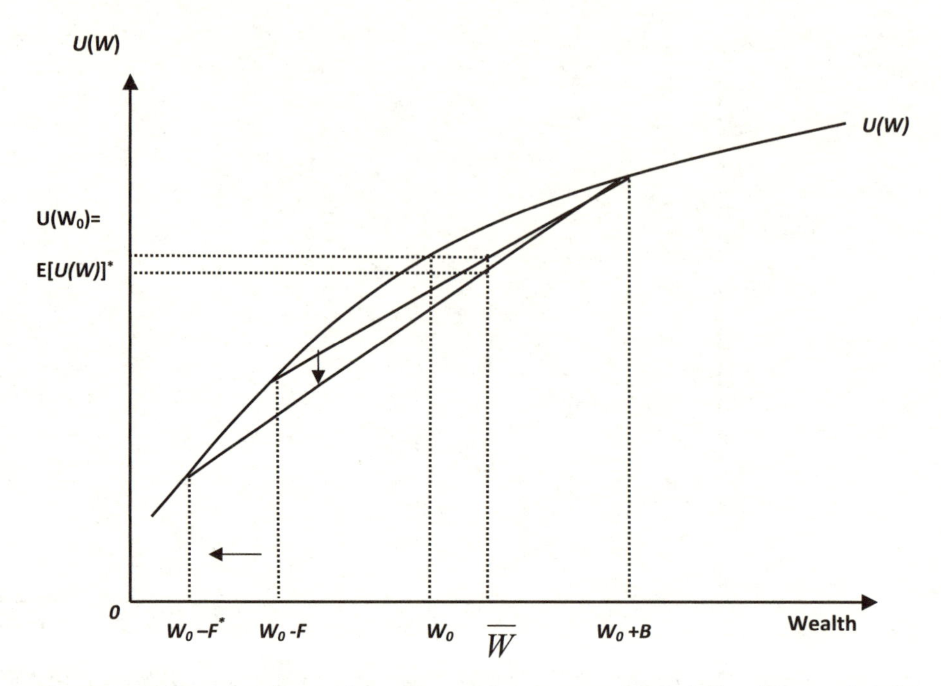

Figure 11.2. Increasing the punishment for a violation causes the $E[U(W)]$ to fall even if $E[W]$ is unchanged.

the fact that the wealth will be lower if the athlete or coach cheats and the cheating is detected. Second, if p is unchanged, an increase in F will lead to a reduction in $E[W]$; since

$$E[W] = p(W_0 - F) + (1 - p)(W_0 + B),$$

an increase in F to F^* will decrease expected wealth to

$$E[W] = p(W_0 - F^*) + (1 - p)(W_0 + B).$$

For example, suppose that W_0 is \$100,000, B is \$50,000, and F is \$25,000. If the probability of detection is 0.2, then the expected wealth is

$$E[W] = (0.2)(75{,}000) + (0.8)(\$150{,}000),$$

which means that $\overline{W}$ is equal to \$135,000.

If the punishment for cheating is increased to, say, \$50,000, the expected wealth will fall to

$$E[W] = (0.2)(\$50{,}000) + (0.8)(\$150{,}000),$$

which is only \$130,000.

To focus on the effect of increasing F, we will assume that the expected punishment remains unchanged, that is, $(p)F = (p^*)F^*$, which requires an offsetting decrease in (p) as F is increased. In our example, we can decrease the probability of detection from 0.2 to 0.15, which increases the probability of avoiding detection from 0.8 to 0.85. Now, with the enhanced penalty, the expected wealth is

$$E[W] = (0.15)(\$50{,}000) + (0.85)(\$150{,}000) = \$135{,}000,$$

as it was originally. Even in that case, $E[U(W)]$ falls, because the new chord is lower than the original chord at $\overline{W}$. Now, $U(W_0)$ exceeds $E[U(W)]$, and the potential cheater will be deterred. In short, $D > 0$.

If we are concerned about cheating, we can adjust p or F to improve deterrence. First, we can increase the penalty and decrease enforcement efforts and still enhance deterrence. Alternatively, we can increase the resources devoted to detecting cheating. In either event, the idea is to make cheating "unprofitable" so that coaches and athletes elect to compete honestly.[8]

It is clear that leagues and organizations are not apt to be indifferent between the two options. Increasing the probability of detection is expensive, whereas increasing the penalties is pretty cheap. This latter option appears to be attractive because it reduces the costs of enforcement, but there are limits. If penalties appear excessive, there will be a tendency not to impose them. Moreover, there will be a general disapproval by fans and society at large. For example, the National Collegiate Athletic Association (NCAA) could impose the death penalty for minor recruiting violations. Players could be ejected from National Football League (NFL) games for holding. Pitchers could be banned for life from Major League Baseball (MLB) for doctoring a ball. These punishments do not seem to fit the crime, so we do not see them.

3 CHEATING TO WIN

The word *cheat* has several meanings, but the most appropriate for our purposes is "to violate rules dishonestly." Some rules are violated inadvertently or unknowingly. A baseball player may fail to touch all the bases; a football player may line up offsides; a basketball player may walk with the ball; a golfer may sign an incorrect scorecard. These are examples of unintentional or inadvertent rules violations. Some rules violations occur because the athlete does not know the rules. For example, a golfer may be entitled to move his or her ball, but drops it in the wrong place. Although such rules infractions do not constitute cheating, this is not to say that unintentional rules violations should go unpunished because the rules are there for a reason. In this chapter, however, we are concerned with deliberate (that is to say, dishonest) rules violations that are intended to give the cheater an unfair advantage in competing against his or her opponents.

There are a variety of ways that cheating can occur in sports. Here, we focus on the following forms of cheating: deliberately violating the rules of play, using illegal equipment, and NCAA recruiting violations.

[8] For the 2007 season, National Association for Stock Car Auto Racing officials seemed to have increased their efforts to detect cheating and increased the penalties to those who are caught. This double whammy ought to improve deterrence.

3.1 Violating the Rules of Play

There are many instances of conduct that violate the rules of play. We examine three of them in this section: Jane Blalock's alleged cheating on the golf course, Rosie Ruiz's dubious behavior at the Boston Marathon, and deliberate rules violations.

3.2 Jane Blalock and the Ladies PGA Tour

Golf is an unusual game; each golfer is honor-bound to abide by the rules. In the vast majority of cases, when penalties are assessed for a rules violation, it is the golfer who imposes the penalty. Reports of cheating by professionals are rare. There are, however, some notable exceptions. Mark McCumber was accused of cheating by Greg Norman, who thereafter refused to play with him. Vijay Singh was accused of cheating while he was playing on the Asian Tour early in his career. A prominent cheating allegation that resulted in legal action by the accused athlete involved Jane Blalock, one of the top golfers on the Ladies PGA (LPGA) tour at the time. In 1969, Blalock was the LPGA's Rookie of the Year. Although she never won a major championship, she did win 27 tour events between 1970 and 1985. Early in her career, however, Blalock hit a bump in the road.

Several fellow competitors complained that Blalock had cheated by moving her golf ball while it was still in play. Every serious golfer knows that this is a clear rules violation that carries a two-stroke penalty. As a result of the complaints, the LPGA decided to monitor her play and thereby increase the probability of detecting any cheating. During a tournament in Louisville, the monitors decided that she had indeed moved her golf ball. More specifically, after cleaning her golf ball on the green (which is permitted), she did not replace it in its original position (which is not permitted). Instead, she replaced the ball closer to the hole and thereby improved her chance of success with the next stroke. Clearly, such rules violations are intended to give the golfer an unfair competitive advantage. Moreover, every professional golfer knows that moving one's golf ball at all, much less to a more advantageous location, violates the rules. Thus, one would have to conclude that such a violation was intentional. In Blalock's case, the Executive Board of the LPGA suspended her for one year.[9] This, of course, was a heavy penalty.

3.3 Rosie Ruiz and the Boston Marathon

The marathon is one of the most taxing events in track because competitors must run 26.2 grueling miles over what can be a hilly course. There are few rules in the marathon, but one rule stands out: a participant must run the entire course. No detours, no shortcuts, no cab rides. One of the most infamous examples of cheating occurred at the Boston Marathon in 1980. Rosie Ruiz qualified

[9] Blalock sued successfully for reinstatement, alleging that her suspension amounted to an illegal group boycott. See *Blalock v. Ladies Professional Golf Association*, 359 F. Supp. 1260 (N.D.Ga.1973). We will return to this case in Chapter 25.

for that year's Boston Marathon because of her performance in the New York City Marathon – a performance of dubious validity. In Boston, she appeared to have won the women's competition in record time. Although she was awarded the winner's medal, people were suspicious. In the first place, Ruiz did not have a history of world-class times in the marathon, but this victory was suspicious for other reasons as well: no one recalled seeing her run except at the end, no one could find her on the videotape of the race, and some people claimed to have seen her sneak into the race about a mile or so from the finish line. Eventually, the Boston race officials concluded that Ruiz had not run the entire course. Accordingly, they stripped her of the title but could not get her to return the medal. After more than a quarter of a century, Ruiz maintains that she did not cheat.

The Ruiz scandal resulted in heightened surveillance to prevent cheaters from cutting the course. At the Boston Marathon and other big races, there is far more video monitoring than there used to be. In addition, runners are subject to electronic surveillance. Chips are used to make sure that a runner passes through various check points along the route. For race organizers, then, deterrence has largely been a matter of increasing the probability of detecting cheating. The punishment for cheating has remained the same: disqualification and future bans. Sadly, the possibility of cheating has caused race organizers to incur higher costs. The resources used to prevent cheating are not socially productive.

Box 11.1 *Tracking Chip Does Its Job**

In 2006, Roberto Madrazo suffered a humiliating defeat in Mexico's Presidential race. He followed that up with a disgraceful attempt to cheat in the Berlin Marathon. At first, Madrazo appeared to win the men's age-55 category in Berlin in the remarkable time of 2:41:12. A few months earlier, Madrazo completed the San Diego marathon in 3:44:06 – an hour slower than his Berlin time.

The tracking chip revealed the secret to Madrazo's success. He took a shortcut. The chip revealed that he skipped two checkpoints. They also revealed that he passed through two checkpoints some 9 miles apart in only 21 minutes, which is an average of about 2:20 per mile. This was clearly impossible because the world record for the mile is 3:43.13. Thus Madrazo was far from clever in his attempt to cheat.

Madrazo also failed to dress for the part he wanted to play. Although the temperature was a comfortable 60 degrees, Madrazo crossed the finish line wearing a hat, a windbreaker, and long running pants, which was far too much clothing for the conditions. Everyone else was wearing T-shirts and shorts.

Outcome: Race officials disqualified Madrazo.

* SI.com, "Politician DQed from Marathon," October 9, 2007.

3.4 Deliberate Rules Violations

There are times when participants deliberately break the rules. For example, when a wide receiver has beaten a safety and is headed for a sure touchdown, the safety may deliberately interfere with the receiver. He knows two things. First, taking the penalty is better than giving up a score. Second, the pass interference may go undetected by the game officials and therefore go unpunished. Similarly, in basketball, a defender may be beaten on a fast break. By deliberately fouling the opponent, a sure two-point basket will be avoided. The fouled player will have the opportunity of getting those two points at the free-throw line. On average, however, the foul makes sense because no one makes 100 percent of his free throws.

Technically, the rule against holding in football is fairly clear. However, the application of the rule is somewhat murky. In fact, the conventional wisdom is that holding could be called on every play. This, of course, would make for a boring game. Thus, there is a tolerance for some holding when it is not too egregious. If an offensive lineman essentially tackles a defensive player who is about to sack the quarterback, he is apt to draw a flag. In this case, holding is a rational rules violation because (1) it may go undetected and (2) if detected, it may go unpunished.

Box 11.2 *Sometimes Cheating Pays**

There is much wisdom in the old adage that "honesty is the best policy." There are times, however, when cheating can have a substantial reward. Venus Williams's first-round victory in the 2007 Wimbledon championship provides a good example.

Venus Williams, a three-time champion at Wimbledon, was headed for the exit in her first-round match. Despite repeated reminders by her father to relax, she was down a set and a break in the second set. Her younger sister, Serena, came to the rescue. Apparently, Venus was rushing and not staying down on her shots. Although coaching during a match is not permitted under the Rules, Serena coached continuously. She shouted "V! Take your time," and "Stay low!" She shouted encouragement, which is permissible, and tactical advice, which is not. When Venus finally won, she gave Serena a good deal of credit for her victory.

We will never know what might have happened if she had not had Serena's coaching. Had she lost in that first-round match, she would have won $20,000. But she did not lose that match and went on to win the prestigious grand slam event along with $1.4 million.

* Liz Clarke, "Family Business: Serena Helps Venus Take Care of Things," *Washington Post*, June 27, 2007.

3.5 Using Illegal Equipment

Are Some Golfers Cheating? At the 2003 U.S. Open, Tiger Woods alleged that some golfers were using "nonconforming" drivers. These metal drivers have very thin faces that provide a trampoline effect when a golf ball is hit. The resulting spring propels the ball at a faster rate than the United States Golf Association (USGA) rules permit. Currently, however, the drivers actually in the players' bags are not tested for the spring effect. The USGA performs tests on samples provided by the manufacturers. If a specific make and model passes the test, it is deemed "conforming" and can be used in competition. If a golfer uses a club that has been deemed conforming, the club in the player's bag is presumed to be conforming and is not subject to testing.

In response to its concern with "hot-face" drivers, the PGA Tour decided it would provide testing equipment at every tournament site for *voluntary* testing. Because golfers are honor-bound to follow the rules, voluntary testing preserves the integrity of the game and fairness on the course. Tiger Woods and Jim Furyk, however, think that testing should be mandatory to make sure that everyone's driver conforms. Some golfers have suggested that they would be reluctant to have their drivers tested because the club might be damaged in the process. Although this may sound self-serving, a touring pro's driver is one of the most important clubs in the bag. If a favorite driver were damaged, this could adversely affect his performance and cost him a considerable amount of money. Thus, the expressed reluctance to put a favorite driver at risk is understandable.

Sammy Sosa's Corked Bat. On June 3, 2003, Sammy Sosa's bat exploded. Upon inspection, it was clear that Sosa had filled the barrel of the bat with cork to reduce the weight and increase his bat speed. Such an alteration, which is supposed to improve power, is not permitted under the rules. Sosa was ejected from the game for that rules violation. He claimed that he doctored the bat only for batting practice purposes but mistakenly used it in the game. Although the 76 bats that he had in the club house passed muster, as did those he had donated to the Hall of Fame, he was suspended for seven games. Because his salary that year was $16 million, the suspension amounted to an implicit fine of $691,358.[10]

Sosa had been voted the most popular player in MLB, but this episode tarnished his image and may have cost him a substantial sum of money.[11] At the time, he was earning $4 million per year for endorsing products and services of Pepsi, Easton Sports, ConAgra Foods, Armour Hot Dogs, and MasterCard. His future with these companies was dependent on how fans reacted to this incident. No doubt, some fans would suspect that Sosa's on-field performance had been an artifact of corked bats.

[10] Based on a 162-game season, seven games amount to more than 4.3 percent of the season. Multiplying 7/162 times $16 million yields an implicit fine of $691,358.

[11] Sosa's reputation took another hit because of his alleged use of steroids. The steroid scandal is examined in Chapter 14.

Strategic Complaints: Bat-gate. In a tight game with the Yankees, Akinori Iwamura was at the plate with two men on base. When the count got to 2–2, Yankees manager, Joe Torre, asked the umpire if Iwamura's bat was legal. Because of its unusual design, it was confiscated and sent to the league headquarters for review. In the next inning, in an admittedly retaliatory gesture, Tampa Bay's manager, Joe Maddon, asked the umpire to check Alex Rodriguez's bat, which was also confiscated. Both bats proved to be legal.[12]

Doctored Baseballs. Some major league pitchers in every era have doctored baseballs. Spit, slippery elm, tobacco juice, sandpaper, emery boards, tacks, and pine tar have all been used to help pitchers get an edge over opposing hitters. According to Hall of Famer, Bob Feller, this has been going on since Day 1.[13] This practice is against the rules and has been for quite some time. Nonetheless, some pitchers continue to cheat by doctoring the ball.[14] When pitchers are caught, they are ejected from the game and are subsequently suspended for short periods. In some cases, pitchers may be ejected before the game even starts. In 2005, for example, Brendan Donnelly, a relief pitcher for the Los Angeles Angels, was thrown out of a game before he could throw a pitch when the umpire found pine tar on his glove. The league suspended him for 10 days, which cost him more than 6 percent of his salary.

In the 2006 World Series, Kenny Rogers won game 2 and caused considerable commotion in doing so. In the first inning, Rogers appeared to have a brown substance on the palm of his hand. He later claimed that it was just "mud, resin, sweat, and spit" – not pine tar. Whatever it was, it was gone after the first inning because Rogers washed it off.

Did Rogers cheat? When Bob Feller was asked what Rogers had been doing, he said, "He was trying to cheat"[15] by using pine tar to get more spin on the ball. Gaylord Perry, who won 314 major league games in a 22-year career and was a Hall of Famer himself, disagreed. His reaction: "Oh, well, he probably just used a little pine tar. There's nothing wrong with that."[16] During his career, Perry did not use pine tar, which is quite sticky. Perry preferred slippery substances – spit, Vaseline, baby oil, hair tonic – which would make the ball move more. As a result, his perspective on what is cheating and what is not may be warped.

The smudge on Kenny Rogers's hand was picked up on the Fox telecast. One of the St. Louis Cardinals immediately told manager Tony La Russa, who could have asked the umpires to check Rogers's hand. Had he been caught with pine tar, he would have been ejected, and Detroit would have lost their best pitcher in the postseason. La Russa never asked the umpire to inspect Rogers' hand, however. After the game, he refused to explain why not. Cardinals pitching

[12] Associated Press, "Yankees, Devil Rays Say Bat-Gate Over," MSNBC.com, September 2, 2007.

[13] Tyler Kepner, "At 88, a Hall of Famer Who's Still in There Pitching," *New York Times*, March 7, 2007.

[14] Editorial, "Mischief on the Mound: An Abridged History," *New York Times*, Oct. 24, 2006.

[15] Kepner, note 15.

[16] Jack Curry, "In Perry's Book, a Brown Smudge Is Not a Black Mark," *New York Times*, Oct. 24, 2006.

coach Dave Duncan observed that La Russa could have asked if he had wanted to be a jerk about it.[17] Apparently, it is not good form to call someone on it when he is cheating.

3.6 Cheating at the Daytona 500

NASCAR officials were determined to clamp down on cheating during the 2007 season. Their approach was to increase the probability of detection through careful inspections and to increase the penalties for cheating with fines, suspensions, and deductions of Nextel Cup points.

The Daytona 500 was NASCAR's opening race of the 2007 season. Before the race began, NASCAR punished six race teams for cheating. Four crew chiefs were suspended when their cars failed NASCAR's inspection. In each instance, NASCAR found impermissible adjustments that improved the aerodynamics of the car, which would improve the car's speed. Two of the four crew chiefs were suspended for four races and fined $50,000 each. The other two were suspended for two races and fined $25,000 each. The drivers were neither suspended nor fined, but they were assessed Nextel Cup point penalties. At the end of the season, these penalties could affect their standing and, therefore, cost them monetarily.

Jeff Gordon, a three-time winner at Daytona, was feeling pretty good about his starting position after the qualifying race. NASCAR officials, however, found that his car was about an inch too low in a postrace inspection. They quickly announced that the problem with his car was inadvertent. However, NASCAR put Gordon in the 42nd starting spot for the Daytona 500. No driver had ever won the race from as far back as 42. Gordon was no exception: he finished in 10th place. As a result of a part failure that caused his unintentional rules violation, Gordon surely finished further back than he would have otherwise, which cost him Nextel Cup points.

Box 11.3 ***The Cheerleader Problem***

The NFL has every reason to protect the integrity of the competition on the field. After all, it is a multibillion dollar business. Some teams are known for trying to get any competitive advantage that they can any way that they can. Apparently, some teams instructed their cheerleaders to warm up in front of the visiting team's bench just before the game. Needless to say, some players found this distracting, which interfered with last-minute coaching instructions. To prevent home teams from gaining an unfair advantage, the NFL sent a memo to all teams ordering them not to allow their cheerleaders to warm up in front of the visiting team's bench. The NFL remains ever vigilant.*

* "NFL Blows Whistle on Sideline Passes Orders Home Cheerleaders to Keep away from Visiting Players," FOXNEWS.com, September 25, 2007.

[17] Tom Verducci, "A Series of Unusual Events," SI.com.

Michael Waltrip, a two-time winner at Daytona, had his car confiscated by NASCAR officials when a postrace inspection revealed the presence of a fuel additive. Waltrip was forced to use a backup car for the qualifying and for the Daytona 500. His crew chief was suspended indefinitely and fined $100,000. Waltrip wound up finishing the race in 30th place, which was one of his worst finishes ever. NASCAR also docked him 100 Nextel Cup points.

3.7 NCAA Violations

Members of the NCAA are required to adhere to the NCAA bylaws. For example, there is a limit of 85 full grants-in-aid (that is, scholarships) for football. The student-athlete may not receive more than the NCAA maximum stipend: room, board, tuition, and books. Thus, the members agree not to compete on the basis of player compensation. Instead, they agree to compete for athletes on a nonprice basis: quality of the coaching staff, quality of the facilities, quality of the education, and so on. The football program may have lower costs because of their agreement not to engage in price competition.[18] As with any other cartel agreement, there is an incentive for individual members to cheat on this agreement. Thus, there is a need to police the agreement and punish anyone who cheats by offering a higher price. The NCAA fills the role of policeman, prosecutor, and judge. Interestingly, it is in the interest of the member schools that the NCAA do just that.

As an example, consider the incentives facing two schools, say, Ohio State and the University of Michigan. If the schools limit the number of football scholarships to 85 and limit the "pay" of the athletes to room, board, tuition, and books, each program will earn a profit of $20 million on the football program. If OSU disregards these limits and UM follows them, OSU will have a more successful program and will earn $25 million, whereas UM will earn $8 million. Similarly, if UM ignores the limits and OSU adheres to them, UM will earn a $25 million profit and OSU will earn only $8 million. If both disregard the limits, each earns $10 million. These payoffs are shown in the following matrix:

		Ohio State: Ignore	Ohio State: Adhere
Michigan	Ignore	UM: $10 OSU: $10	UM: $25 OSU: $8
	Adhere	UM: $8 OSU: $25	UM: $20 OSU: $20

[18] If the NCAA members engage in vigorous nonprice competition, they could dissipate all of the benefits through the higher costs that they will incur on weight rooms, tutoring facilities and services, practice facilities, and the like. See George J Stigler (1968), "Price and Nonprice Competition," *Journal of Political Economy*, 72, 149–154, for a general discussion.

The optimal – that is, joint profit maximizing – outcome is for both UM and OSU to adhere to the limits as each will earn $20 million. Unfortunately for UM and OSU, both schools have an independent incentive to ignore the limits – that is, to *cheat*. Moreover, under some circumstances, cheating is perfectly rational. If UM ignores the NCAA limits and OSU adheres to the limits, UM earns $25 million, which is better than the $20 million that it would have earned if it had also adhered to the limits. If UM ignores the limits and OSU also ignores them, UM will earn $10 million instead of the $8 million that it would have earned if it had adhered to the limits. Thus, cheating is UM's best strategy irrespective of what OSU does. For precisely analogous reasons, OSU's dominant strategy is also to cheat – that is, to ignore the NCAA limits. Thus, left to their own devices, the result is that both schools "cheat," and each earns $10 million instead of the potential of $20 million.[19]

The NCAA can impose sanctions on cheaters that make cheating unprofitable. These sanctions may include the following:

> loss of scholarships, which reduces team quality and may reduce revenue, loss of bowl appearances and bowl money, loss of TV appearances, which reduces program visibility and revenue, and in extreme cases, the "death penalty", which completely shuts down the offending program.[20]

Thus, both schools – UM and OSU – want the NCAA to enforce their agreement not to compete on price for their mutual benefit. The NCAA, in effect, polices the cartel agreement and reduces the return to cheating. As we know from reading the sports section of our newspaper, this enforcement does not deter all cheating. Every year, some program or other is sanctioned by the NCAA for rules violations.

3.8 The NFL's Spygate Episode

The element of surprise is often important to success on the field. If the offense knows what the defense is going to do, it can select a play that is best suited to defeat the defense. If the defense knows what play the offense is going to run, it can adjust to minimize the chances of that play being successful. Playbooks, game plans, and signals are kept as secret as possible to protect that element of surprise.[21] So important is secrecy to NFL coaches that security consultants

[19] This is a classic *prisoner's dilemma* in which the least preferred outcome emerges. See, for example, Jack Hirshleifer, Amihai Glazer, and David Hirshleifer, *Price Theory and Applications*, 7th ed., New York: Cambridge University Press (2005), pp. 281–283.

[20] The death penalty is not too likely. It was imposed on the football program at Southern Methodist University in 1987. The adverse effects of the two-year absence have persisted until today. Because the punishment proved to be too severe, it has never been imposed again.

[21] Concerns over the improper theft of signals are not limited to the NFL. In 2008, the Philadelphia Phillies won the National League Championship and the World Series. In 2009, they repeated as National League Champions but not as the World Series Champions. Their successes in 2008 and 2009 were tarnished by accusations of cheating. The Phillies allegedly

sweep offices and meeting rooms for electronic bugs. Notes on game plans and other sensitive information are routinely shredded. Nearby buildings are inspected for evidence of spying. Many NFL coaches, a secretive lot by nature, appear to be paranoid about security.[22]

Contributing to this paranoia are incidents like the so-called Spygate episode involving the New England Patriots.[23] There are NFL rules regarding the taping of games by the teams. On more than one occasion, the NFL has reminded all teams about the rules. Despite those reminders, the New England Patriots used handheld video equipment on the opponent's sideline to steal defensive signals.[24] This was a clear violation of the NFL's rules. During the 2006 season, the Detroit Lions and the Green Bay Packers caught Patriots personnel taping them. Both clubs simply told them to stop. In the 2007 opener against the New York Jets, however, the Patriots' taping efforts were reported to the NFL commissioner's office. The consequences for the culprits were pretty stiff. Patriots coach Bill Belichick was fined $500,000. The club was also fined $250,000 and stripped of its first-round draft pick in the 2008 NFL draft. These sanctions seem severe for an infraction so early in the season that could not affect the outcome of the game in which the infraction occurred. However, there were rumors that the Patriots had done similar things in earlier seasons. In addition, the word on the street was that they were not the only ones involved in spying. Finally, Roger Goodell, NFL commissioner, was in the midst of a general crackdown on misbehavior, and the Patriots' taping was almost in defiance of the league's two memos on the subject of impermissible taping.

Interestingly, there were consequences for Eric Mangini, the Jets coach, as well. Mangini broke one of the NFL coaching fraternity rules – do not snitch.[25] Some in the NFL found Mangini's conduct troubling. Bill Belichick hired him and was his mentor for many years, finally promoting him to defensive coordinator. Thus, it appeared that Mangini betrayed his former friend and mentor. One coach's reaction: "I didn't think that he [Mangini] was that kind of guy."[26]

stole the signs of opposing teams by using binoculars from the bull pen. Although stealing signs is an age-old tactic, using binoculars is not permitted. The commissioner's office reviewed game tapes and found no evidence of illegal spying.

[22] For more about this, see Greg Bishop, "Paranoia Strikes Deep, into Your Headset It Will Creep," *New York Times*, Nov. 13, 2007.

[23] Among many articles on this spying scandal, see Chris Mortensen, "Sources: Camera Confiscated After Claims of Pats Spying on Jets," ESPN.com, September 10, 2007; Mike Reiss, "NFL Reportedly Faults Patriots," Boston.com, September 12, 2007; and Jimmy Golen, "NFL Fines Patriots, Belichick for Spying," SFGate.com, September 14, 2007.

[24] For the offense, signals are unnecessary because the quarterback has a radio receiver in his helmet. For the defense, however, hand signals are important.

[25] The other two rules involve trying to take free agents or coaches from one's former team; see Peter King, "The NFL's Mob Mentality," *Sports Illustrated*, Sept. 19, 2007.

[26] Judy Battista, "For Some, Video Taping Incident Raises Questions About Mangini," *New York Times*, Sept. 20, 2007.

Box 11.4 ***McLaren Receives a Record Fine***

Spying can occur in any sport; it is not confined to football.* In 2007, Formula One racing was rocked by an industrial espionage scandal involving the top team, McLaren Mercedes, and its main rival, Ferrari. After an extensive investigation, the International Automobile Federation (Formula One's governing body) imposed a $100 million fine on McLaren.

In 2006, Michael Schumacher, a Formula One superstar, retired from the Ferrari team. This resulted in the team's technical director, Ross Brown, going on leave. This left Brown's right-hand man, Nigel Stepney, disgruntled. In March 2007, Stepney began communicating with Mike Coughlan who was McLaren's chief designer. At some point, he gave Coughlan nearly 800 pages of data and strategy from Ferrari. Unfortunately for Stepney and Coughlan, an employee at the copy shop where the documents were copied happened to be a Ferrari fan. He was suspicious and blew the whistle. Ferrari filed a complaint with the International Automobile Federation and filed a criminal suit in Italy. When all the information came to light, it was clear that the data and other information had been used by McLaren to gain an unfair advantage.

McLaren was fined $100 million by the International Automobile Federation. It was also stripped of all points in the constructor's (manufacturer's) competition and disqualified for the 2007 season.

* Brad Spurgeon, "McLaren Is Fined; Took Data from Rival," *New York Times*, Sept. 14, 2007; Brad Spurgeon, "Details of McLaren Spying Reveal Widespread Involvement," *New York Times*, Sept. 15, 2007.

4 CHEATING TO LOSE

Every athlete who has ever competed at any level has cheated – or at least has been sorely tempted to do so – to win.[27] In tennis, club players and juniors make bad line calls, which can lead to vigorous disputes and sullied reputations. In golf, some players impermissibly improve their lie to enhance their chance of success. Basketball players hand check their opponents, football players hold, and baseball players doctor balls. Although we disapprove of cheating to win, all of us can appreciate the urge and the temptation to do so. However, cheating to lose is truly reprehensible. This kind of cheating requires deliberately giving less than one's best effort to let an opponent win. In most instances, the motivation for cheating to lose is pure greed. The cheater is being paid in some form or another to lose. This sort of behavior cheats the fan because competition on the field is debased.

There have been a few examples of cheating to lose, but there have been numerous stories over the years of boxers taking a dive. Since 1951, there

[27] Some people cheat at solitaire, which is almost inexplicable.

have been intermittent point-shaving episodes in college basketball. These sad affairs are usually motivated by gambling interests.

Consider the Black Sox scandal.[28] In 1919, gamblers hit on a scheme to win money by betting heavily on Cincinnati to beat the Chicago White Sox in the World Series. They bribed key players to throw the World Series. Although rumors of a fix began to circulate before the Series began, the players went through with their plan. Following the subsequent trial, the commissioner, Kennesaw Mountain Landis, banished those who were in on the fix as well as one player who knew about it but failed to report it.[29]

4.1 Point Shaving in Basketball

Arizona State University (ASU) was hit with a point-shaving scandal in the 1994–1995 season.[30] Steven Smith, one of ASU's star players, apparently had been gambling on sports and owed $10,000 to Benny Silman. As a way of getting out of debt, Smith agreed to shave points in four ASU games. He was paid $20,000 per game. Smith also involved a teammate, Isaac Burton, who was paid $4,300 for helping to fix two games. Silman and his co-conspirators bet more than $500,000 on the fixed games. As a result, they had a net profit of more than $400,000 on an "investment" of less than $100,000. When they got caught, the scheme, once so profitable, turned into a disaster for all of the participants. Benny Silman, who was the main architect of the sports bribery scheme, received a 46-month sentence in federal prison. The players, of course, have no future in professional basketball.

Box 11.5 *A Statistical Analysis of Point Shaving**

From time to time, point-shaving scandals in college basketball have been uncovered through the investigative efforts of the police. These efforts produce a few specific examples with names, dates, and other pertinent details. Justin Wolfers has taken a broader approach to the point-shaving inquiry. He used economic theory to figure out what he should be looking for. He then performed an econometric analysis on a large sample of NCAA basketball games to detect point shaving. His results are alarming.

Wolfers began by observing that the incentive for point shaving derives from the point-spread system of betting on basketball. Suppose the favorite is expected to win by 10.5 points. If you bet on the favorite, you only win if the favorite wins by 11 or more points. If you bet on the underdog, you win if the underdog wins or even if it loses by 10 points or less. This betting system creates an opportunity for mischief. A gambler could offer a bribe to a key player on the

[28] For an interesting account, see Eliot Asinof (2000), *Eight Men Out: The Black Sox and the 1919 World Series*, New York: Holt Paperbacks.

[29] A box of documents detailing the fix surfaced at an auction house outside Chicago in 2007. When these are analyzed, we may get new insights into the scandal. Associated Press, "Black Sox Documents Will Be Up for Auction," *New York Times*, Nov. 26, 2007.

[30] "Silman Gets 46 Months for His Part in ASU Point Shaving Scandal," June 30, 1998. Available at http://sportsillustrated.cnn.com/basketball/college/news/1998/06/30/asu_shaving.

favored team to shave points, so the favorite would fail to cover the spread. The gambler would then bet heavily on the underdog. A player on the favored team can reduce the team's margin of victory without actually losing the game but still collect the bribe. At the same time, a bet on the underdog wins because the favorite team failed to cover the point spread. It appears to be a win–win situation.

Wolfers predicts that point shaving is apt to occur when one team is a strong favorite – that is, favored to win by 12 or more points. He analyzed the outcomes of nearly 74,000 NCAA basketball games over 16 seasons to test this prediction. If betting markets are efficient, one would expect the favorite to cover the point spread half of the time and fail to cover the other half. Wolfers found that the favorite failed to cover the point spread significantly more than half of the time. Thus, the data confirmed his prediction: too few strong favorites covered the point spread.

On the basis of his statistical analysis, Wolfers found that about 1 percent of all games were fixed. This is a disturbing result to say the least.

* Justin Wolfers (2006), "Point Shaving: Corruption in NCAA Basketball," *American Economic Review*, 96, 279–283.

4.2 Corruption in Sumo Wrestling

Largely unknown elsewhere, sumo wrestling is an incredibly popular sport in Japan.[31] Elite sumo wrestlers are revered as athletic icons. In a society in which bad behavior leads to a loss of face and brings dishonor to one's entire family, we would expect sumo wrestlers to be incorruptible. Some former wrestlers, however, have rocked the sumo world with allegations that matches have been rigged. Interestingly, sumo officials have dismissed these allegations as being untrue. However, this dismissal may be unwarranted given Duggan and Levitt's economic and statistical analysis of sumo wrestling. They found powerful evidence of corruption in their study.

Duggan and Levitt explained that the institutional structure of sumo wrestling provides a substantial economic incentive for corruption. There are 66 wrestlers in a sumo tournament, and each wrestler has 15 matches. If the wrestler wins 8 or more matches (i.e., has a winning record), he improves his ranking. If a wrestler has a losing record, he falls in the rankings. For sumo wrestlers, rankings matter a great deal because they are the source of prestige, the basis for higher salaries, and influence other benefits. For example, those wrestlers below the top 66 have menial chores to do at the sumo stable – cleaning and cooking – that higher ranked wrestlers do not have to perform. The really elite wrestlers even have servants.

There is a sharp nonlinearity in the payoff for tournament wins. A wrestler with a 7–7 record gains far more by winning his final match than a wrestler with

[31] This section depends on Mark Duggan and Steven D. Levitt (2002), "Winning Isn't Everything: Corruption in Sumo Wrestling," *American Economic Review*, 92, 1594–1605.

an 8–6 record loses by losing that match. Moving up one spot in the rankings is worth about $3,000, so there are substantial gains from trade through fixing a match in the final days of a tournament.

Duggan and Levitt studied 10 years' worth of data and found convincing statistical evidence that match rigging near the end of tournaments did occur. The central statistical result was that wrestlers on the bubble win far more often than one would expect. This, of course, is also consistent with additional effort. However, there was other evidence that was inconsistent with such an explanation.

First, whereas the wrestler who is on the margin for an eighth win is victorious with inordinate frequency, the next time that those same two wrestlers face each other, it is the *opponent* who has an unusually high winning percentage. This result suggests that the "payment" used in match rigging is the explicit or implicit promise of throwing future matches in return for taking a fall today. *Second*, win rates for wrestlers on the bubble vary in accordance with factors predicted by economic theory to support implicit collusion. For example, success rates for wrestlers on the bubble rise throughout their careers (consistent with the development of a reputation for being cooperative), but those success rates fall in the last year of a wrestler's career. The economic reason for this fall is simple: there is no tomorrow. If the wrestler needing a win is owed one but does not get it, he cannot punish the opponent by refusing to cooperate in the future. If the wrestler needing a win is not owed one, there is no time for him to pay back a cooperative opponent. *Third*, match rigging disappeared during times of increased media attention and scrutiny. *Fourth*, some wrestling stables appear to have worked out reciprocity agreements with other stables such that wrestlers from either stable do exceptionally well on the bubble against one another. *Finally*, wrestlers identified as "not corrupt" by two former sumo wrestlers who have alleged match rigging do no better in matches on the bubble than in typical matches, whereas those accused of being corrupt are extremely successful on the bubble. It is difficult to reconcile all of these findings with added effort as the primary explanation for success on the bubble.

4.3 Fixing Matches in Tennis

A professional tennis player is relaxing in his hotel room when the telephone rings. An unfamiliar voice asks, "Would you like to make some money?" Among others, Dmitry Tursunov, Janko Tipsarevic, Paul Goldstein, and Novak Djokovic have all been approached by people who were willing to pay substantial sums for tanking a match. Djokovic, for example, was offered over $200,000 to lose a first-round match in a tournament in St. Petersburg, Russia.[32] The number three player in the world at the time, Djokovic refused the offer and did not play in the tournament. Although no one has been caught, there have been some suspicious incidents.

[32] A Belgian player, Gilles Elseneer, reported that he was offered $141,000 to throw a first-round match at Wimbledon in 2005. "ATP Says Sport Is Clean in Light of Recent Gambling Reports," ESPN.com, Sept. 27, 2007.

Yevgeny Kafelnikov, a former number one player in the world, played a match against Fernando Vicente in Lyons, France. Even though Vicente had lost his last dozen matches, a substantial amount was bet on Vicente to win. And win he did in straight sets. This raised suspicions and heightened scrutiny of future Kafelnikov matches.

The most recent episode involved Nikolay Davydenko, who was ranked number four in the world at the time. On August 2, 2007, Davydenko was playing a second-round match against Martin Vassallo Arguello in a tournament in Poland. At the time, Arguello was ranked 87th in the world. *After* Davydenko won the first set in a three-set match, an inordinate number of bets were placed on Arguello to win. Betfair, the largest online bookmaker in England, voided all bets on the match and reported the incident to the ATP. The ATP launched an investigation but failed to discover anything conclusive one way or the other.

Although Davydenko denied any wrongdoing, a cloud of suspicion hung over him. In the first round of the St. Petersburg Open in Russia, Davydenko, the top seed, lost to Marian Cilic in three sets after easily winning the first set 6–1. During the third set, the chair umpire chided Davydenko for not playing hard. Later, the ATP fined Davydenko for "lack of effort."

The ATP's investigation took a heavy toll on Davydenko through the rest of the 2007 season. His matches were scrutinized as were his telephone records. Questions about his character persist, even though no conclusive proof has surfaced. After examining all of the evidence that it could obtain, the ATP cleared Davydenko.[33] Whether this will restore his reputation and allay any lingering suspicions is open to question. Only time will tell.

Box 11.6 ***Tennis Australia – Zero Tolerance***

In the aftermath of the suspicious Davydenko affair, Tennis Australia took an aggressive approach at the 2008 Australian Open.* Players were greeted with a firm admonition: "Tennis Australia has a zero tolerance policy on illegal gambling, match fixing and the communication of sensitive information which may affect the outcome of a match and will investigate all reported instances." Australia's governing body set up an integrity hotline and displayed the number prominently.

For those accustomed to betting on tennis matches, there must have been some disappointment because the organizers shut down the on-site gambling window and also prevented access to real-time gambling websites. Laptop computers were banned in the stands. Tennis Australia even considered banning cell phones but abandoned that idea.

* Christopher Clarey, "At Open, an Aggressive Stance on Gambling," *New York Times*, Jan. 15, 2008.

[33] Joe Drape, "Inquiry into Betting Clears Davydenko," *New York Times*, Sept. 13, 2008.

5 CONCLUDING REMARKS

In this chapter, we have examined the problem of cheating in sports. There are many examples of athletes and coaches cheating in one way or another to win. We have examined a few examples in this chapter. We also considered cases of cheating to lose. Both types of cheating undermine the integrity of the competition and may reduce fan interest. This, of course, would have adverse consequences for everyone – clubs, coaches, athletes, and, of course, consumers.

On the basis of the expected utility model developed in Chapters 3 and 11, we presented an economic approach to deterring cheating. The focus was on how to make cheating unprofitable so that all participants will elect to compete honestly.

PROBLEMS AND QUESTIONS

1. In the model of deterrence, there is no guilt associated with cheating. How could feelings of guilt be incorporated in the deterrence function?
2. "Cheaters never win." In a world of risk averters, this old saying must be false. Explain why.
3. If the competitors are risk seekers, will they cheat no matter what we do to deter cheating?
4. If a coach is risk neutral, what is his or her deterrence function?
5. Base runners often try to steal the catcher's signals to the pitcher and tip off the batter as to what sort of pitch to expect. This is not considered cheating. If a team puts a spotter in the stands with binoculars to steal signs and relays them to the team, that is considered cheating. What is the difference?
6. In USTA amateur tennis tournaments, the participants must make their own line calls. If a player believes that his or her opponent is cheating, a lines judge can be summoned. Any bad calls made before the lines judge arrives go unpunished. Would you expect to see cheating under this system? Explain.
7. There is an old adage: *Honesty is the best policy.* In the case of cheating in sports, we see all sorts of violations being committed: recruiting violations, tampering with coaches, illegal equipment, and so on. In a world of risk averters, this adage must be wrong. True or false? Explain.
8. If everyone can acquire a "hot-face" driver, no one will have an unfair advantage. Why worry about hot-face drivers?
9. If a golfer knows that his driver is nonconforming but the USGA has not determined that the club is illegal, is he cheating by using it?
10. The end result of a rules infraction is to confer a competitive advantage on the one breaking the rule. Unintentional violations, such as being offsides in football, are punished less severely than intentional violations, such as holding. From an economic perspective, does this make sense?

11. Given the possible loss of an entire year's eligibility for gambling, it is surprising to find that 35 percent of male athletes gamble. Why does the heavy sanction fail to deter them?
12. For its part in the spying scandal, McLaren Mercedes was fined $100 million and was disqualified from the constructors' championship in 2007. In the aftermath, morale within the McLaren team was shattered. In addition, McLaren found it virtually impossible to generate investments in the team. How would you assess the full penalties that McLaren suffered for spying?
13. In 2006, a harness-racing driver tried to fix a race at Cal Expo. He was convicted of bribery, conspiracy, and grand theft. As a result, he could receive a three-year prison sentence and a lifetime ban from horse racing. How would you calculate the economic value of such a punishment?
14. Known cheaters often suffer a loss of reputation. How would you incorporate this into our model of deterrence? As a result, should we publicize the identity of those found guilty of cheating?
15. Arguably, the Patriots got no actual advantage from their spying efforts at the start of the 2007 season, but the team was punished severely and so was their coach. What is the purpose of such heavy penalties in a case where there was no actual injury?
16. At the start of the 2007 Ginn Tribute, Michelle Wie was hurting – a sore wrist and no energy – and headed for an astonishing 88. She withdrew after 16 holes complaining of a wrist injury. Under an obscure LPGA rule, had Wie shot an 88 or worse, she would not have been permitted to play again for a full calendar year. This rule only applies to non-LPGA members.
    a. If Wie was not really injured, is withdrawing "cheating"?
    b. What purpose is behind the LPGA's rule?
    c. What is the penalty for simply walking off the course in frustration when playing badly?

RESEARCH QUESTIONS

1. Examine the disciplinary actions taken by the NCAA over the past 10 years. Can you map out a schedule of sanctions for various violations to see whether the punishment fits the crime?
2. Trace the history of the "Black Sox" scandal in MLB.
3. Examine the history of scandals involving the International Olympic Committee's (IOC's) selection of host cities for future Olympics.
    a. How have potential host cities attempted to buy approval?
    b. How has the IOC attempted to prevent future scandals?
    c. Evaluate the IOC's effectiveness.
4. NASCAR drivers lose Nextel Cup points for rules violations. How much money does this cost them?

5. Compare the NCAA's disciplinary actions regarding A. J. Green (University of Georgia), Cam Newton (Auburn University), and Terrell Pryor (Ohio State University) in 2010. Can you explain the variation?

REFERENCES AND FURTHER READING

Associated Press. "Black Sox Documents Will Be Up for Auction." *New York Times*, November 26, 2007.

Associated Press. "IOC Suspends Member Mired in Bid Scandal."

Associated Press. "Yankees, Devil Rays Say Bat-Gate Over." MSNBC.com, September 2, 2007.

Balsdon, Ed, Lesley Fong, and Mark A. Thayer. (2007). "Corruption in College Basketball? Evidence of Tanking in Postseason Conference Tournaments." *Journal of Sports Economics*, 8, 19–38.

Battista, Judy. "For Some, Video Taping Incident Raises Questions About Mangini," *New York Times*, September 20, 2007.

Becker, Gary S. (1968). "Crime and Punishment: An Economic Approach." *Journal of Political Economy*, 76, 169–217.

Curry, Jack. "In Perry's Book, a Brown Smudge Is Not a Black Mark." *New York Times*, Oct. 24, 2006.

Drape, Joe. "Inquiry into Betting Clears Davydenko." *New York Times*, September 13, 2008.

Duggan, Mark, and Steven D. Levitt. (2002). "Winning Isn't Everything: Corruption in Sumo Wrestling." *American Economic Review*, 92, 1594–1605.

Heckelman, J. C., and A. J. Yates. (2003). "And a Hockey Game Broke Out: Crime and Punishment in the NHL." *Economic Inquiry*, 41, 705–712.

Hirshleifer, Jack, Amihai Glazer, and David Hirshleifer. (2005). *Price Theory and Applications*, 7th ed. New York: Cambridge University Press, pp. 281–283.

Kepner, Tyler. "At 88, a Hall of Famer Who's Still in There Pitching." *New York Times*, March 7, 2007.

Loeb McClain, Dylan. "Cheating Accusations in Mental Sports, Two." "*New York Times*, August 8, 2006.

Preston, I., and Szymanski, S. 2003. "Cheating in Contests." *Oxford Review of Economic Policy*, 19, 612–624.

"Runner Fails Gender Test, Loses Medal." Herald.com, December 18, 2006.

Sandomir, Richard. "NBC Admits Plagiarism in Feature Before Derby." *New York Times*, May 11, 2006.

Stigler, George J. (1968). "Price and Nonprice Competition." *Journal of Political Economy*, 72, 149–154, for a general discussion.

12

Misconduct and Discipline

1 INTRODUCTION

We encountered two kinds of misconduct in the preceding chapters – gambling and cheating. In this chapter, we turn our attention to an array of misconduct on and off the field. Misconduct on the field can be relatively minor – excessive celebration, taunting opponents, and arguing with game officials are common examples. It can also be more serious and far more dangerous – helmet-to-helmet hits, stick-wielding incidents, kicking opponents, and starting brawls. Off the field, misconduct has taken many forms – dog fighting, domestic violence, DUIs by the dozen, weapons charges, drug dealing, and assaults. These forms of misconduct can have an adverse impact on the image and popularity of professional sports. If fans begin to think that athletes are thugs and criminals, the stars will no longer shine so brightly and no longer be heroes in fans' eyes. When fans begin to turn away, the turnstile stops clicking, and the money stops flowing. As a result, sports leagues and organizations as well as the athletes themselves have an economic interest in controlling such behavior for the good of the game.

In this chapter, we begin with the personal conduct policy of the NFL, which is representative of the other major sports leagues and organizations. Once again, we analyze the economics of deterring undesirable conduct. Following that, we examine several examples – fighting, excessive violence, off-field legal problems, and even some relatively minor forms of misconduct that may draw the ire of the league officials. In all of these examples, our focus is on punishment that is designed to deter others from misdeeds.

2 DISCIPLINING PLAYERS FOR MISCONDUCT

On-field and off-field misconduct is appalling to league and club officials as well as to fans. Players can be disciplined by their clubs as well as by the league. As we will see, punishment can be severe – at least in financial terms, because players can be fined or suspended without pay for considerable periods. With so much to lose, it is a wonder that misconduct continues. Anthony Munoz is

Table 12.1. Arrests of National Football League Players, 2000–2010

Year	2000	2001	2002	2003	2004	2005	2006	2007	2008	2009	2010[4]
DUI	9	8	14	18	16	9	14	12	15	13	6
Domestic Violence	4	8	2	4	1	10	11	2	5	1	2
Assault[1]	5	6	7	3	6	2	7	13	8	5	1
Drugs[2]	4	5	4	6	2	1	4	9	14	6	1
Weapons	2	2	4	4	1	5	4	5	4	3	2
Disorderly Conduct	4	5	3	2	4	7	8	7	5	5	1
Traffic	5	2	11	2	3	2	10	2	5	0	0
Resisting Arrest	1	0	2	0	1	1	7	5	6	5	0
Burglary[3]	4	1	1	2	1	2	1	1	0	0	0
Total	38	37	48	41	35	39	66	56	62	38	13

[1] Sexual assaults were combined with other physical assaults.
[2] This includes possession, use, and dealing.
[3] This category includes robbery and other property crimes.
[4] Through May 8, 2010.

Note: New crimes were added upon first violation. Also, this may overstate actual number because multiple infractions decomposed (DUI manslaughter means DUI *and* manslaughter). Lastly, instances in which crime was not explicitly stated were put in most likely category (for example, hitting someone in the head with a bottle was classified as assault).

Source: San Diego Union-Tribune Arrests Database (available at: http://www.signonsandiego.com/nfl/arrests-database/?appSession=279273349166650&RecordID=&PageID=2&PrevPageID=2&cpipage=10&CPISortType=desc&CPIorderBy=Date) and letter from Mark G. Trigg, dated May 1, 2007, to the National Football League on behalf of Adam "Pacman" Jones.

a Hall of Fame lineman who played for the Cincinnati Bengals. When he was asked about the rash of run-ins with the law by current Bengal players, he was direct and succinct: "I don't think there's any way to sugarcoat it. It's just pure stupidity."[1] Both the leagues and the clubs expect the players to adhere to personal conduct codes. If they fail to do so, they are subject to disciplinary action. In this section, we focus on the NFL's personal conduct policy and its enforcement by National Football League (NFL) Commissioner Roger Goodell.

2.1 Personal Conduct Policy of the NFL

Players, coaches, and clubs can be disciplined by the NFL under its Personal Conduct Policy.[2] This became increasingly necessary as criminal behavior by NFL players mounted and media attention increased. In Table 12.1, the arrests of NFL players over the 2000–2010 period are shown. The dramatic increase in the number of arrests since 2006 emphasized the need for firm measures.

[1] *Honolulu Advertiser*, June 29, 2007.
[2] The details of the policy were taken from NFL Players Association, "Rules and Regulations: Conduct Policy," available at http://astro.berkeley.edu/~kalas/ethics/documents/nfl.pdf.

As a result of the crime wave that reached the NFL in 2006 and early 2007, the NFL and the NFL Players Association (NFLPA) agreed that strong measures needed to be taken. The image of the NFL was suffering from repeated reports of fights, illegal gun possession, drug use, domestic violence, and DUIs. When millionaire athletes appear to be out of control, it draws unfavorable attention to and criticism of the NFL as a whole. The NFL and the NFLPA decided to put the NFL commissioner in charge of enforcing a tougher personal conduct policy. This policy applies to the athletes under contract as well as prospective players. It also applies to all league and club personnel. As we will see, the NFL policy is clear and covers many types of misconduct.[3]

2.2 General Policy of the NFL

Engaging in violent and/or criminal activity is unacceptable and constitutes conduct detrimental to the integrity of and public confidence in the National Football League. Such conduct alienates the fans on whom the success of the League depends and has negative and sometimes tragic consequences for both the victim and the perpetrator. The League is committed to promoting and encouraging lawful conduct and to providing a safe and professional workplace for its employees.

2.3 Prohibited Conduct

It will be considered conduct detrimental for Covered Persons to engage in (or to aid, abet or conspire to engage in or to incite) violent and/or criminal activity. Examples of such Prohibited Conduct include, without limitation: any crime involving the use or threat of physical violence to a person or persons; the use of a deadly weapon in the commission of a crime; possession or distribution of a weapon in violation of state or federal law; involvement in "hate crimes" or crimes of domestic violence; theft, larceny or other property crimes; sex offenses; racketeering; money laundering; obstruction of justice; resisting arrest; fraud; and violent or threatening conduct. Additionally, Covered Persons shall not by their words or conduct suggest that criminal activity is acceptable or condoned within the NFL.

2.4 Persons Charged with Criminal Activity

Any Covered Person arrested for or charged with conduct prohibited by this policy will be required to undergo an immediate, mandatory clinical evaluation and, if directed, appropriate counseling. Such evaluation and counseling must be performed under the direction and supervision of the NFL Vice President of Player and Employee Development. Failure to cooperate with evaluation and counseling (including being arrested for or charged with additional criminal activity during the evaluation and counseling period) shall itself be conduct detrimental to the National Football League and shall be punishable by fine or suspension at the discretion of the Commissioner.

2.5 Persons Convicted of Criminal Activity

Any Covered Person convicted of or admitting to a criminal violation (including a plea to a lesser included offense; a plea of nolo contendere or no contest; or the

[3] In the NFL's policy statement, the term "Covered Person" refers to the athletes, prospective athletes, and league and club personnel who are subject to the policy.

acceptance of a diversionary program, deferred adjudication, disposition of supervision, or similar arrangement) will be subject to discipline as determined by the Commissioner. Such discipline may include a fine, suspension without pay and/or banishment from the League. Any Covered Person convicted of or admitting to a second criminal violation will be suspended without pay or banished for a period of time to be determined by the Commissioner.

2.6 Persons Engaged in Violent Activity in the Workplace

Every employee is entitled to a safe and professional workplace free of criminal behavior, violence and threats against personal safety. Criminal conduct in the workplace or against other employees is prohibited. Any Covered Person who commits or threatens violent acts against coworkers, regardless of whether an arrest is made or criminal charges are brought, shall be subject to evaluation, counseling and discipline, including termination of employment.

2.7 Duty to Report Prohibited Conduct

To ensure the effective administration of the policy, the League must be advised when a Covered Person engages in Prohibited Conduct. The obligation to report an arrest or criminal charge extends to both the person involved and to the Club or League entity for which he or she works. Persons subject to this policy who are arrested or charged with Prohibited Conduct must report that incident to their Clubs or to NFL Security at (800) NFL-1099. Failure to report an incident will constitute conduct detrimental and will be taken into consideration in the final determination of discipline under this policy.

2.8 Appeal Rights

Any person disciplined under this policy shall have a right of appeal, including a hearing, before the Commissioner or his designee. Except for the enforcement of discipline, no other requirements set forth in the policy will be stayed pending the completion of the appeal.

The biggest stars are not exempt from the NFL's personal conduct policy. It should also be noted that embarrassing brushes with the law can lead to suspensions even if no charges are filed. Ben Roethlisberger won two Super Bowls with the Pittsburgh Steelers but found himself in trouble with Roger Goodell over an accusation of sexual assault. Even though Roethlisberger was not charged, he was suspended for the first six games of the 2010 season. Given his salary, the suspension cost him more than $2 million.[4] The message should be clear: if you tarnish the image of the NFL, you will be punished by the NFL. The idea, of course, is to deter others from similarly bad behavior.

3 DETERRING MISCONDUCT

We saw in the previous chapter that cheating – a form of undesirable conduct – can be deterred. The kinds of misconduct examined in this chapter can also

[4] For details, see Judy Battista, "Roethlisberger Suspended for 6 Games," *New York Times*, April 21, 2010, and related articles in the days leading up to the suspension.

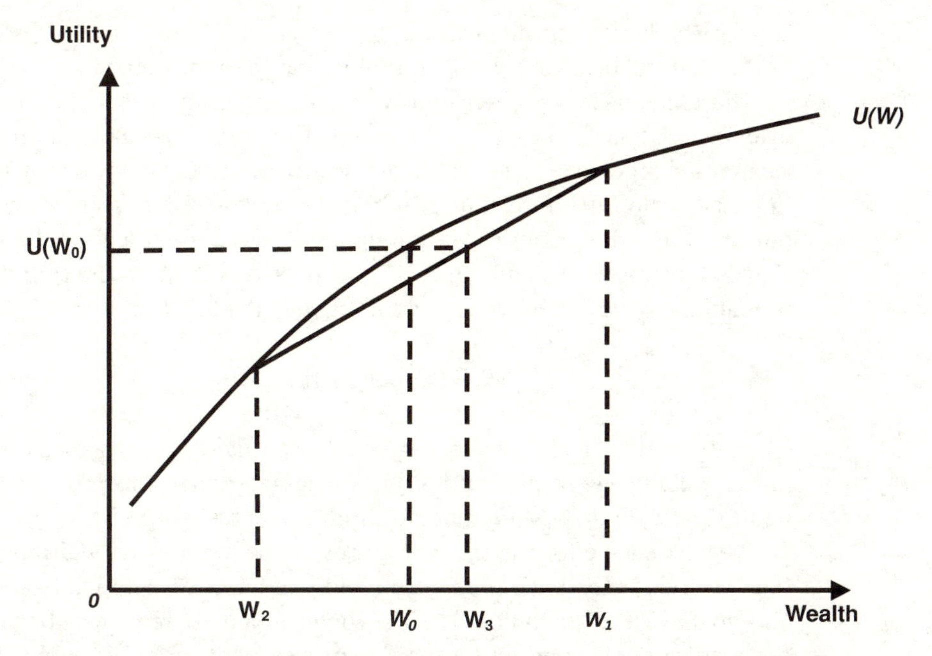

Figure 12.1. Deterring undesirable behavior requires a punishment that makes $U(W_0)$ larger than $E[U(W)]$.

be deterred – not by preaching to those engaged in such conduct but by making the misconduct unattractive. Sports leagues and organizations can impose sanctions with predictable regularity to reduce the expected benefits of misconduct and thereby deter that conduct. This approach to deterring undesirable behavior does not depend on attitudes toward risk. It can work on anyone.

3.1 Deterring Risk Averters

Presumably, the athlete or coach derives some benefit from the objectionable conduct. When a player drives while drunk or a coach publicly berates game officials, some benefit is derived from that conduct. The economic approach to deterring such conduct is to impose penalties so the player or coach finds himself better off by not engaging in that behavior. In fact, this is the approach taken by most leagues and organizations. Figure 12.1 illustrates this.

Suppose a coach has an initial wealth of W_0. He has an opportunity to engage in misconduct that will provide some benefit (B) to him. If he engages in the misconduct, the value of his wealth rises to W_1, which is equal to W_0 plus the monetary value of B. If the misconduct is detected, it will be punished by an amount F, which will reduce wealth to W_2. Now the coach who engages in misconduct embraces a risk that can be avoided by not misbehaving. Absent the misconduct, the coach will enjoy $U(W_0)$. If he misbehaves, he will enjoy $U(W_2)$ with probability p or $U(W_1)$ with probability $(1 - p)$. Misconduct will be deterred if the $U(W_0)$ exceeds the $E[U(W)]$. That is, the coach will engage in the objectionable conduct or not, as the deterrent function is negative or positive, if

$$D = U(W_0) - E[U(W)],$$

is positive, the coach will elect not to engage in misconduct. If D is negative, however, it will be economically rational for him to misbehave.

The kinds of misconduct that we are considering in this chapter are easily detected. It is hard to hide a bench-clearing brawl or an arrest on an illegal weapons charge. In practice, then, deterrence depends largely on the sanctions imposed, which are pretty much limited to monetary fines or suspensions without pay. If the fine is not heavy enough, the misconduct will not be deterred. This is illustrated in Figure 12.1. The expected wealth is determined by the probability of punishment (p) and the value of the fine (F):

$$E[W] = pW_2 + (1 - P)W_1,$$

where $W_2 = W_1 - F$. If the expected wealth exceeds W_3, an expected utility maximizer will engage in misconduct. If F is large enough to make the expected wealth lower than W_3, then that misconduct will be deterred.

We have seen efforts in the NFL, for example, to improve deterrence. Under Roger Goodell's leadership, the probability of being disciplined has increased and so have the penalties. He was determined to reduce substantially, if not eradicate, misconduct by making punishment more probable and more severe.

Box 12.1 *Paying the Price for Misconduct*

In the Roger Goodell era, NFL clubs have become more concerned with character issues when drafting and signing players. As a result, there can be heavy financial penalties for bad conduct. Marcus Thomas, a great defensive tackle at the University of Florida, is a good example. Thomas failed two drug tests at the university and was suspended from the team. He was reinstated and played with a vengeance. However, he was dismissed permanently when he failed to live up to the terms of his reinstatement.

Jarvis Moss, a teammate and a mid-first-round draft pick in 2007, said Thomas was the best player on the team. Moss believed that Thomas was a top-10 pick on the basis of his ability. Instead, Thomas was drafted by the Denver Broncos in the fourth round with the 121st pick. Thomas signed a four-year contract with Denver that will pay Thomas a total of $3 million. Now, an average of $750,000 per year is not exactly chump change, but it is a far cry from top-10 money. His failure to comply with the terms of his reinstatement probably cost him $10 million.

3.2 Deterring the Risk Seeker

Many athletes do not appear to be risk averse or even risk neutral. They appear to be aggressive risk takers – that is, risk seekers. Misconduct by risk seekers

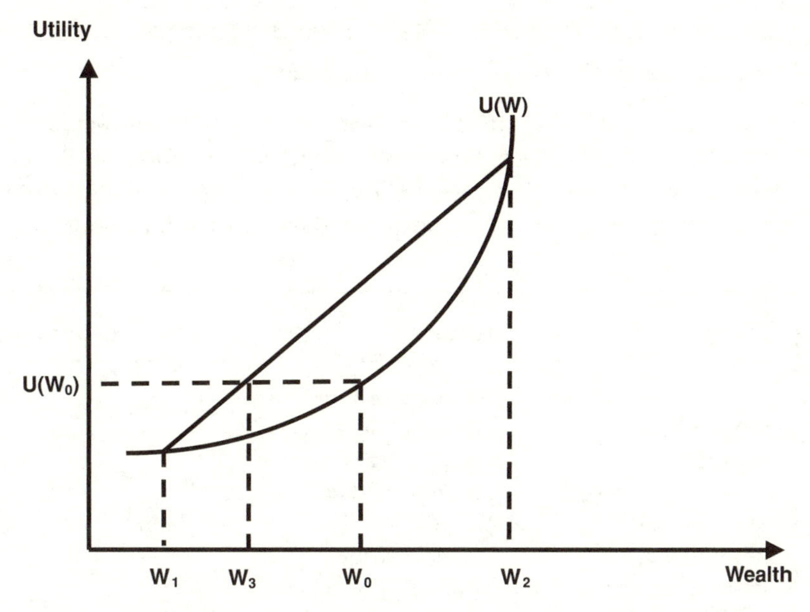

Figure 12.2. Deterring a risk seeker requires some care in picking the sanctions.

is more difficult to deter, but it can be done. This can be seen in Figure 12.2, where W_0 is the athlete's wealth without any misconduct. If the athlete engages in some form of misconduct – on-field or off-field – and is not caught, his wealth will be W_2. Thus, W_2 is equal to W_0 plus the monetary value of the misconduct to the athlete. If the misconduct is detected and punished, the athlete's wealth will be W_1. Thus, W_1 is equal to W_2 minus the monetary value of the punishment. After the misconduct has occurred, the athlete experiences the benefit and, therefore, the monetary value of that benefit. The punishment must then exceed the value of the benefit to push W_1 below W_0. If the punishment were precisely equal to the benefit, misconduct could not be deterred.

In Figure 12.2, we can see that misconduct will occur if the expected wealth exceeds W_3. This follows from the fact that the expected utility of wealth will exceed the utility of W_0 for all values of expected wealth above W_3. The key to deterrence then is to reduce the expected wealth below W_3. This, of course, can be achieved by increasing the probability of punishment or by increasing the punishment.

There is some evidence that the NFL, for example, has increased the probability of being punished for misconduct. In an effort to reduce serious injuries from unnecessary roughness on the field, the NFL now reviews game film with this in mind. There have been suspensions imposed for particularly violent or dangerous hits even when the player was not ejected from the game. The league's zero-tolerance policy for off-field misconduct, such as DUIs, also raises the probability of being punished. These increased probabilities should improve deterrence even for risk seekers.

Box 12.2 *Suspensions in the Roger Goodell Era*

When Roger Goodell became Commissioner of the NFL, he decided to improve the image of the NFL. Discipline was going to be swift and stiff. To get the message across, Goodell has suspended players for various violations of the NFL's personal conduct policy. Those suspended include the following:

Player	Team	Number of Games
Adam "Pacman" Jones	Tennessee Titans	16
Chris Henry	Cincinnati Bengals	8
Tank Johnson	Chicago Bears	8
Albert Haynesworth	Tennessee Titans	5
Michael Vick	Atlanta Falcons	Indefinite[1]
Roy Williams	Dallas Cowboys	1
Jerramy Stevens	Tampa Bay Buccaneers	1[2]
Odell Thurman	Cincinnati Bengals	16

[1] In 2009, Vick was reinstated.
[2] Stevens was also fined an additional game check.

3.3 Suspensions and Implicit Fines

When a player is suspended, he does not get paid for the games missed. This amounts to an implicit fine that amounts to the lost salary. In the National Basketball Association (NBA), some hefty implicit fines have been handed out for egregiously bad behavior. This outrageous behavior includes assaulting a coach (Latrell Sprewell), severely injuring an opponent (Kermit Washington), kicking a television photographer (Dennis Rodman), hitting a fan (Vernon Maxwell), and participating in brawls. In Table 12.2, the longest suspensions are shown. As is plain to see, bad behavior can cost a player plenty of money. This strong action on the part of the NBA should serve as a deterrent to future undesirable conduct.

In some cases, the financial consequences of suspensions can be mitigated to some extent. Consider the case of John Daly, who has won two major golf titles – the PGA Championship and the British Open. His booming drives and aggressive style make him a fan favorite, but his tumultuous lifestyle has gotten him in trouble with the PGA Tour on many occasions. His antics in 2008 resulted in a six-month suspension in 2009. The suspension would cost Daly the (expected) winnings on the PGA Tour if he has no alternatives. But Daly did have options. He could go to the Asian Tour or to the European Tour. Any winnings on these tours would reduce the financial consequences of his suspension by the PGA Tour.

Table 12.2. Suspensions in the National Basketball Association

Player	Season	Games
Ron Artest[1]	2004	72
Latrell Sprewell	1997	68
Gilbert Arenas	2010	50
Javaris Crittenton	2010	38
Kermit Washington	1977	26
Jermaine O'Neal[1]	2004	15
Carmelo Anthony	2006	15
Dennis Rodman	1997	11
Nate Robinson	2006	10
J.R. Smith	2006	10
Vernon Maxwell	1995	10
Lindsey Hunter	2007	10
Darius Miles	2008	10
Rashard Lewis	2009	10
Delonte West	2010	10
Steven Jackson	2007	7
J.R. Smith	2009	7
Mardy Collins	2006	6

[1] Does not include the immediate suspension (one game) handed down on Nov. 20.

Source: Associated Press, "Painful Moments for the NBA," *New York Times*, December 19, 2006.

4 FIGHTING

Fighting instead of competing on the field of play can tarnish the image of a sport. To the extent that this may reduce fan interest, there will be economic consequences: reduced attendance, lower ticket prices, fewer stadium revenues, lower fees for broadcast rights, and so on. As a result, leagues have an economic incentive to keep this form of misconduct to a minimum. In addition to financial concerns, leagues are also concerned about player (and even fan) safety.

From time to time, tempers flare during athletic competition. In some instances, fights erupt and on occasion a fight turns into a bench clearing brawl. We have seen this in all of the major sports. In 2006, a brawl erupted involving the Denver Nuggets and the New York Knicks. Bench clearing fights occur from time to time in Major League Baseball (MLB). The National Collegiate Athletic Association (NCAA) is not immune – a particularly distressing fight occurred during the Clemson–South Carolina game in 2004. The brawl so embarrassed the two teams that they both withdrew from bowl consideration. In the National Hockey League (NHL), fighting is not uncommon, to say the least, but the league has tried to reduce the frequency of fights. The league would prefer to focus on hockey rather than on fighting. In the NFL, fighting seems to be much less of a problem. Few fights break out and brawls are basically nonexistent.

Some leagues are more concerned about fighting than others. The NHL is obviously the least concerned. A fight leads to some penalty minutes but not much else. In the NFL, however, a brief scuffle results in a penalty against the team, which hurts the team's chances of winning. It may also result in the player's ejection from the game and possible fines from the league. Similar fates await players in the NBA and in MLB when they get into fights.

Recently, the NBA has started to get tougher on fighting during games. In 2004, a major brawl erupted in a game between the Indiana Pacers and the Detroit Pistons. That fight actually spilled into the stands and threatened fan safety. As a consequence, several players received heavy suspensions: Ron Artest was suspended for 72 games, Stephen Jackson for 30 games, and Jermaine O'Neal for 25 games, which was later reduced by an arbitrator to 15 games. Such suspensions obviously hurt the team's performance when key players are unable to play. The players, of course, lose money because they are not paid for the games that they miss. There are 82 games in an NBA season. For Artest, then, he lost 87.8 percent of his salary for that season because of the suspension. Jackson lost 36.6 percent of his salary, and O'Neal lost 18.3 percent. These turn out to be substantial financial penalties. Obviously, the more a player makes, the more he loses when he is suspended.

As noted earlier, another brawl broke out in a game between the Denver Nuggets and the New York Knicks during the 2006–2007 season. Fortunately, that fight did not threaten fan safety. As a result, the suspensions were not as long: Carmelo Anthony lost 15 games, and Nate Robinson and J. R. Smith both lost 10 games.

The NBA is trying to reduce incidents that could lead to fighting. Getting the message across to the players has been difficult, but the league is determined. During the 2006–2007 season, Kobe Bryant served three one-game suspensions. These were all prompted by "unnatural basketball moves" that resulted in contact with another player that could have led to retaliation. By clamping down on this kind of behavior, the NBA hopes to stop fights before they get started. The league wants to deter fighting rather than punish it.

5 VIOLENCE IN SPORTS

Many sports are inherently violent. Football, hockey, and even basketball involve collisions that can be quite violent. To some extent, we recognize, tolerate, and even admire this violence,[5] but there is a limit to how violent these collisions need to be. When the level of violence becomes "unnecessary," it should be controlled for player safety. Otherwise, there is an incentive to disable the star players, which will reduce fan interest.[6] In some cases, the violence occurs

[5] For the dark side of this issue, see William C. Rhoden, "In N.F.L. Violence Sells, but at What Cost?" *New York Times*, Jan. 20, 2007. We examine the long-term dangers of concussions later in this chapter.

[6] Dave Anderson, "Knock out the Star and Lose 15 Yards? Hmm, Let Me See," *New York Times*, Oct. 28, 2006.

outside the scope of play and could have no other purpose than to deliberately injure an opponent.[7] For example, just before the end of a game between the New England Patriots and the New York Giants, Vince Wilfork stuck his hand inside Brandon Jacobs' face mask and deliberately poked him in the eye. This was clearly extracurricular and not an inherent part of football violence. In other cases, however, the violence occurs within the scope of play and therefore can be controlled through changes in the rules. For example, late hits on quarterbacks, blocks below the knees, and helmet-to-helmet contact can occur within the normal play of the game but can be controlled through rules against such conduct. We examine these in turn.

5.1 Intentionally Hurting an Opponent

There have been some incidents in which players have deliberately tried to injure an opponent. In the NFL, Albert Haynesworth, a Pro Bowl defensive tackle for the Tennessee Titans, received a five-game suspension for "flagrant unnecessary roughness." During a game between the Dallas Cowboys and the Titans, Haynesworth was enraged when Dallas scored to take a 20–6 lead. On the play, Dallas guard Andre Gurode lost his helmet. Haynesworth kicked the unprotected Gurode in the face twice. Everyone involved – even Haynesworth – was appalled by what had happened. That five-game suspension cost Haynesworth about $190,000, which does not seem like much considering the possible injury that Haynesworth might have inflicted on Gurode.[8] Fortunately, Gurode was not severely injured. He considered suing Haynesworth but ultimately decided against it.

The NHL is also beginning to crack down on excessive violence. For example, Colton Orr (New York Rangers) cross-checked Alexander Ovechkin (Washington Capitals). The NHL characterized Orr's action as "reckless and dangerous." Although Ovechkin did not get hurt, Orr received a five-game suspension, which cost him 6.1 percent of his salary.

A more violent and potentially more dangerous stick violation involved Chris Simon. During a game between the New York Islanders and the New York Rangers, Simon took a vicious, two-handed swipe at Ryan Hollweg's face with his stick. Simon was promptly suspended indefinitely by the NHL.[9] Fortunately, Simon's deliberate attempt to injure Hollweg resulted in only a few stitches in Hollweg's chin. It could have been much worse if Simon's aim had been a bit better. After a hearing, the NHL suspended Simon for 25 games. As a result, he lost the final 15 games of the regular season and all of the postseason games. Because the Islanders only played five playoff games, Simon's suspension carried over to the 2007–2008 season.

[7] Before the Dallas Cowboys played the Detroit Lions in 2007, Dallas cornerback Terence Newman threatened Jon Kitna's safety. The NFL got wind of the threatened mayhem and warned Newman that he was being watched.

[8] The financial consequences for Haynesworth could have been more severe if the Titans had reclaimed a proportional share of Haynesworth's signing bonus.

[9] When Simon's suspension eventually became definite, this violent incident cost Simon more than 30 percent of his salary for the season.

Apparently, Simon did not learn from his first suspension. In a game against the Pittsburgh Penguins, Simon deliberately stomped on Jarko Ruutu's right foot. This time, the NHL suspended Simon for 30 games, which is 36.7 percent of the season. The Islanders put Simon on an indefinite leave of absence so he could get counseling. At 35 years old, it is unclear whether Simon will ever play again. The penalty, however, puts all players on notice that excessive violence will not be tolerated.

These heavy punishments are supposed to deter other players from committing similar violent acts, but some folks are not easily deterred. After Simon's first suspension for hitting an opponent in the face with his stick, Jesse Boulerice cross-checked Ryan Kesler (Montreal Canadiens) in the face. He also received a 25-game suspension for this violent and dangerous act. Apparently, his club, the Philadelphia Flyers, had had enough of the 29-year old Boulerice and put him on waivers.

As a final example, consider the Dallas Cowboys safety Roy Williams. Because of Williams's dangerous "horse-collar" tackles, the NFL specifically addressed this dangerous practice. There is now a rule, popularly referred to as the "Roy Williams Rule," that prohibits horse-collar tackles. A defensive player may not grab the collar of an opposing player from the back or from the side and yank him down. Such a tackle results in a 15-yard penalty, which hurts the defender's team. It also leads to review by the NFL and possible fines.

One might suppose that Roy Williams would be wary of breaking a rule that is named in his (dis)honor, but one would then be mistaken. Williams was fined $100,000 during the 2006 season for breaking "his" rule. During the 2007 season, Williams was fined $12,500 for the first horse-collar tackle of 2007, $15,000 for the second one, and received a one-game suspension for the third. That suspension cost Williams $35,000. It is interesting to speculate about the size and scope of the penalty that Williams will receive for his next horse-collar tackle.

Box 12.3 *Big Hits, Big Fines*

There is increasing evidence that concussions have long-term consequences including depression, dementia, and Alzheimer's disease. The NFL and NFLPA, as well as Congress, have become concerned about player safety. As a result, the NFL has taken an aggressive approach to reducing the number of helmet-to-helmet hits and other unnecessary, brutal contact. The implementation of this program has been somewhat controversial – some people are concerned that violence is an essential element of football.

There are two parts to the NFL's effort to deter dangerous hits. First, game officials are calling penalties for helmet-to-helmet hits. These 15-yard penalties can have a decisive effect on the outcome of a game. Second, and perhaps more effective, the NFL is reviewing game tapes and imposing stiff fines on offending players. A few $25,000 fines ought to have a deterrent effect. If not, the NFL can raise the fines.

---

6 PROBLEMS WITH THE LAW

Some players embarrass the league, their clubs, and ultimately themselves with legal problems. These problems may involve drunk driving, narcotics use, domestic violence, weapons charges, and dog fighting. They can also be even more serious – sexual assault, drug trafficking, and murder. A league does not want its image marred by such behavior and may impose penalties beyond those imposed by the judicial system. Here, we review several kinds of legal problems that have resulted in disciplinary action by league officials.

6.1 Drunk Driving

The NFL has taken a hard line on drunk driving. This offense falls under the league's substance abuse policy. A first offender is subject to a fine of $20,000 and subsequent monitoring. Beyond that, players are subject to suspensions without pay and additional fines. For example, Jerramy Stevens, a Tampa Bay Bucs tight end, was convicted of "extreme" DUI because his blood alcohol level was above 0.15. In Arizona, the minimum sentence for such an offense is 30 days in jail. The NFL imposed its own penalty: a one-game suspension without pay plus a fine equal to another game check.

Dante Stallworth, a premier wide receiver for the Cleveland Browns, killed a man while drunk driving. In court, he was sentenced to only 29 days for doing irreparable harm to the victim and his family. The NFL suspended him for the entire 2009 season. When a player is a repeat offender, he will find even stiffer sanctions. Odell Thurman, a Cincinnati Bengals linebacker, was on a four-game suspension for alcohol abuse when he was charged with a DUI. The NFL extended the suspension to a full year. Because of Thurman's conduct during the NFL's rehabilitation program, the NFL expressed some doubt about reinstating him at the end of his one-year suspension.

The NHL has also cracked down on players who abuse alcohol and thereby embarrass the league. For example, following a no-contest plea to drunk driving and hit-and-run charges, Mark Bell (Toronto Maple Leafs) was suspended for 15 games. He was surprised by the length of the suspension, but respected the NHL Commissioner Gary Bettman's decision. The NHLPA characterized the punishment as "excessive." Because Bell faced jail time during the off-season and other suspensions, the union believed that an additional 15 games served no purpose. But that is not true. The purpose of the punishment is not to "get even" with Bell. Instead, it is to deter others from committing similar violations that impair the image of the NHL. As Gary Bettman pointed out, "Playing in the National Hockey League is a privilege, and with that privilege comes a corresponding responsibility for exemplary conduct."[10] Bell's conduct was hardly exemplary.

6.2 Repeat Offenders

Adam "Pacman" Jones has been called the most notorious NFL player.[11] Pacman Jones, a superb cornerback for the Tennessee Titans, always seemed to

[10] www.thestar.com/sports/NHL/article/256122.

[11] A columnist for the *New York Times* called Jones the NFL's most notorious player, but Jones lost that dubious distinction to Michael Vick.

be in the right place on the field, but often in the wrong place off the field. After five arrests and 10 encounters with the police over a two-year period, NFL Commissioner Roger Goodell had had enough. He suspended Jones for the entire 2007 season.[12] This, of course, meant that Jones did not receive the $1.3 million salary that he was scheduled to earn in 2007. Initially, Goodell had indicated that Jones's suspension might be reduced to 10 games, which would have reduced the forgone income to "only" $812,500. Jones's suspension was not reduced, however.

Pacman Jones had quite a resume at the time of his suspension. The Tennessee Titans used the 6th overall pick in the 2005 NFL draft on Jones. Some two months later, marijuana was found in Jones's hotel room, but someone else took the blame. Later, Nashville police confiscated Jones's car because it was being used by a drug ring. Jones was not charged, but he had to buy his car back at a police auction. Three days later, he was at a gas station where shooting broke out. He apparently was not involved but was questioned as a witness. Three separate incidents involved fights at nightclubs or strip clubs. In each case, the charges against Jones were dropped or dismissed.

Although one might think that Jones would have figured out how to avoid trouble, he apparently did not. During the NBA All-Star Weekend in Las Vegas, Jones visited a strip club and began to scatter thousands of dollar bills around. In the ensuing mêlée, serious trouble began brewing. Outside the strip club, shots rang out. Three people were shot. One of the three is paralyzed from the waist down. Las Vegas police wanted Jones tried on several felony counts for starting the fight inside the club. Luckily for Jones, he was able to plead no contest to a gross misdemeanor charge of "conspiracy to commit disorderly conduct." For that plea deal, he was to get a one-year suspended sentence.

Roger Goodell reviewed Jones's notorious behavior and concluded that he had had enough of Pacman Jones. To protect the integrity of the NFL, Goodell suspended Jones for the entire 2007 season. Goodell informed Jones that his behavior had "brought embarrassment and ridicule upon yourself, your club, and the NFL, and has damaged the reputation of players throughout the league." Goodell went on to point out that Jones had "engaged in conduct detrimental to the NFL and failed to live up to the standards expected of NFL players."[13] Goodell also made it clear that subsequent problems could lead to more penalties and even a lifetime banishment from the NFL.[14]

6.3 Weapons Charges

Tank Johnson was an important member of the defensive line for the Chicago Bears. Although he was talented on the field, he had some serious off-field problems with the law.

[12] Chris Henry, a talented wide receiver for the Cincinnati Bengals, was also suspended for repeatedly being arrested on various charges. His suspension was for eight games.

[13] www.thegrio.com/opinion/nfl-needs-to-sack-roethlisberger-double-strandard.php.

[14] TheThe Titans also concluded that they had had enough of Pacman and traded him to the Dallas Cowboys. Eventually, Goodell reinstated Jones for the 2008 season. He played as brilliantly as ever but succumbed to alcoholism and entered a rehab program less than halfway through the season.

In 2005, Johnson was charged with misdemeanor gun possession. He was put on probation for that offense. In December 2006, while he was still on probation, the police raided Johnson's Chicago-area home. They found three handguns, three rifles, and 500 rounds of ammunition. None of the guns were registered and were therefore illegal. As a result, Johnson was in violation of his probation and was facing a new weapons possession charge.[15] Following his guilty pleas, he was sentenced to four months in prison. Johnson lamented, "I have lost my freedom . . . all my endorsements, my dream home, a dog and peace of mind."[16] Johnson's troubles were not over, however.

After serving half of his sentence, Johnson was released from prison. Not long after, NFL Commissioner Roger Goodell suspended Johnson for the first half of the 2007 season for his past legal problems. Goodell announced at the time that if Johnson had no further problems off the field, his suspension could be reduced from eight games to six. This, of course, would reduce the financial consequences by 25 percent. Johnson was scheduled to earn $510,000 with the Bears in 2007. In effect, he was "fined" half of that, which amounts to $255,000. If the suspension had been reduced to six games, the "fine" would have been reduced by $63,750.

Johnson was confident that his suspension would be reduced because he was determined to stay out of trouble. In late June, however, he was stopped for speeding – 40 MPH in a 25 MPH zone – at 3:30 in the morning. He was then arrested on suspicion of drunken driving.[17] The Chicago Bears were already embarrassed by Johnson's legal problems, and this was the last straw. He was released by the Bears, and his suspension was not reduced by the NFL.

Johnson remained unemployed for nearly three months before he was signed by the Dallas Cowboys. He was reinstated by the NFL in November and began playing for the Cowboys in their ninth game of the season.

6.4 Dog Fighting

Michael Vick was the face of the Atlanta Falcons. A superb athlete, Vick was the most exciting quarterback in the NFL, and he was paid accordingly. After being selected as the number one overall pick in the 2001 draft, Vick earned about $30 million during the 2001–2004 period, but that was just the beginning. Following the 2004 season, Vick signed a 10-year contract with the Falcons for $130 million. Of this, $37 million was in the form of signing bonuses and guarantees. In 2005 alone, Vick was paid $23.1 million. Life was good for Michael Vick.

Vick's world began to unravel in April 2007, however, when federal agents raided a home owned by Vick. This raid produced evidence of organized dog

[15] Two days after the police raid, Johnson and his bodyguard, William Posey, were in a nightclub. Posey got in a fight and was shot to death. Although Johnson was not involved, Bears executives were furious that Johnson was at the nightclub.

[16] Judy Battista, "Bears' Johnson Gets 4-Month Prison Sentence," *New York Times*, March 16, 2007.

[17] It turned out that Johnson's blood alcohol level proved to be .072, which is just below the legal limit of .08. By the time these test results came back, the damage had already been done.

fighting, which resulted in a second raid. Initially, Vick claimed that although he owned the house, he rarely visited the property because he let a relative live there. Subsequently, however, it became clear that Vick had been an active participant in the dog-fighting activities. He was indicted on federal charges in July 2007. Vick maintained his innocence and pleaded not guilty.

The indictment put the NFL in a tough spot. It had already suspended Pacman Jones for an entire season and could not show favoritism toward Vick just because he was a bigger star. The cases, however, were different, and Vick had not been found guilty – yet. The Falcons had decided to suspend Vick for four games. Under the Collective Bargaining Agreement, a team cannot impose a heavier punishment. Before the Falcons could act, the NFL stepped in and told Vick not to report to training camp.

Vick's not-guilty plea took some hits during the investigation. One by one, his three codefendants accepted plea deals. The required cooperation incriminated Vick as a financier and a willing participant. Under mounting evidentiary pressure, Vick accepted a plea agreement. The NFL immediately suspended him for the 2007 season. As one would expect, sponsor after sponsor – Nike, Reebok, Upper Deck – severed ties with Vick.

Vick's income from the Falcons stopped with his suspension. His endorsement income had dried up. Legal bills were mounting. He was facing a one-year prison sentence, according to his plea agreement, and perhaps a further suspension from the NFL. Things did not look as though they could get any worse, but they did. The federal district judge was not obligated to accept the prosecution's recommendation of a 12-month sentence. Appalled by Vick's conduct and his lying about it, the judge sentenced him to 23 months in prison.[18]

7 OTHER FORMS OF MISCONDUCT

There are various forms of misconduct that may seem relatively minor but still result in punishment. In many cases, the sanctions are simply penalties assessed against the team during the game. In other cases, the athlete or coach may be subject to fines. There are even cases in which institutions may be punished. Here, we consider a few examples: criticizing game officials, using offensive language, violating dress codes on the field, and failing to ensure safety.

7.1 Criticizing Game Officials

The NCAA and the major sports leagues have policies against public criticism of game officials. There are procedures for lodging complaints about officiating with the league or conference headquarters. Public criticism, however, is prohibited because it raises doubt about the integrity of the outcome on the field, which impairs the image of the sport. As an example, consider the events that occurred in the NBA playoffs between the Dallas Mavericks and the Miami

[18] After serving his sentence, Vick was eventually signed by the Philadelphia Eagles. In the 2010 season, Vick performed spectacularly and appeared to be rehabilitated.

Heat in 2006.[19] Before the playoffs even started, Mavericks coach Avery Johnson criticized the NBA for inconsistency in penalizing players and even suggested that the league favored some players.

Mark Cuban, the Mavericks' owner, began by criticizing the selection of the officials for the playoffs. For that and running onto the court to complain about some calls, Cuban was fined $200,000. In Game 5 of the playoffs, the Mavericks lost 101–100, and Cuban was irate. He berated the officials on the court right after the game using profane language. In media interviews, he continued his profanity-laced complaints about the officials. This outburst cost him another $250,000.

NBA Commissioner David Stern pointed out that the athletic competition on the court was great. The players were performing at a high level. The focus of attention was not on the competition, however. Stern said that "it's with some consternation that we find the airwaves are loaded with discussions about owners, coaches and referees."

NBA players also get fined for publicly criticizing the referees. Following a 91–90 loss to the Detroit Pistons, the New Jersey Nets' Jason Kidd referred to the officiating crew as the three blind mice. That remark cost him $20,000.[20]

The NFL also protects its game officials from verbal abuse and public criticism. In a Monday night game, the New England Patriots beat the Baltimore Ravens in a close game. Near the end of the game, some calls went in favor of the Patriots.[21] Ravens linebacker Bart Scott lost it and wound up with two consecutive unsportsmanlike conduct penalties and a subsequent $25,000 fine. After the game, three Ravens players questioned the integrity of the officials. Those ill-advised comments cost them $15,000 each.

In college football, each conference has its own rules regarding public criticism of game officials. The Big 12, for one, is serious about this.[22] In the aftermath of a 59–43 loss to Texas, Texas Tech coach Mike Leach severely criticized the officiating. His remarks challenged the integrity and competence of the officials. As a result, Leach received the largest fine in Big 12 Conference history. The Big 12 also issued a public reprimand. Leach was also informed that a repeat performance would result in even higher fines and perhaps a suspension.

7.2 Offensive Language and Gestures

Using language or making gestures that some fans might find offensive can lead to fines and other penalties. National Association for Stock Car Auto Racing (NASCAR) driver Tony Stewart found this out the hard way.[23] Following his

[19] Liz Robbins, "Cuban Is Fined $250,000 by N.B.A. for 'Misconduct'," *New York Times*, June 21, 2006.

[20] David Picker, "Nets' Kidd Fined $20,000 for Criticizing Officials," *New York Times*, Dec. 28, 2006.

[21] Judy Battista, "Officials Defended, 4 Ravens Are Fined," *New York Times*, Dec. 8, 2007.

[22] Brandon George, "Texas Tech's Leach Hit with Record Fine," *Dallas Morning News*, Nov. 14, 2007.

[23] "Stewart Docked 25 Points, Fined 25k," FOX Sports on MSN, 2007.

winning performance in 2007 at the Indianapolis Motor Speedway, Stewart was interviewed by ESPN on camera. During the interview, Stewart used an expletive that might offend some fans. NASCAR officials found that Stewart spoiled ESPN's first NASCAR broadcast since 2000. ESPN condemned the language as "inappropriate," and NASCAR agreed. Finding Stewart's actions detrimental to stock car racing, NASCAR fined Stewart $25,000.

Rex Ryan, the Jet's coach, made an obscene gesture at a mixed martial arts competition. The Jets fined him $500,000 for embarrassing the team.

7.3 On-Field Dress Code Violations

In order to ensure appearance standards, the NFL has rules regarding apparel and equipment.[24] Infractions can result in fines. Players, and even some teams, have expressed their individuality in ways that violate these rules. As part of Roger Goodell's efforts to shore up discipline, the NFL is enforcing its rules and imposing fines on players. A recent list of apparel and equipment violations included the following:

Not completely buckling chin straps, which must be white in color.
Wearing gloves with contrasting color piping.
Wearing jerseys that are too small and do not cover the shoulder pads and other equipment.
Wearing sleeves of improper lengths.
Wearing "extremely high pants" that don't cover the player's knees.
Wearing wrist bands that are not black or white.
Wearing tape on hands and arms that is not opaque white. No black or team colors are permitted.
Wearing uncovered "What Would Jesus Do?" – style or Lance Armstrong "Live Strong" – style bracelets.

According to the late NFLPA leader Gene Upshaw, fines for apparel and equipment violations are the source of considerable griping by the players, but if the rules are there for a reason, then they should be enforced.

7.4 Some Safety Concerns

There are many safety issues that arise in sports. Concerns for fan and participant safety may result in rules or policies that attempt to influence behavior. For example, fans often celebrate stunning victories in ways that are dangerous. When Vanderbilt played Florida during the 2006–2007 season, Florida was the defending NCAA champion in men's basketball and was ranked number 1. At the conclusion of the game, which Vanderbilt won 83–70, Vanderbilt fans rushed onto the court. The Southeastern Conference strictly forbids such celebrations out of concern for the safety of the athletes. As a result of this exuberant display, Vanderbilt faced a $25,000 fine for failing to control the fans.

[24] Liz Mullen and David Kaplan, "Upshaw: Apparel Fines from NFL 'Out of Hand,'" *Sports Business Journal*, Oct. 8, 2007.

The SEC policy is quite clear: "access to competition areas shall be limited to participating student-athletes, coaches, officials, support personnel, and properly-credentialed individuals at all times."[25] This, of course, applies to football fields as well as basketball courts. The University of Kentucky apparently had a hard time grasping this. Kentucky's long-suffering football fans rushed onto the field after Kentucky beat Georgia in 2006. This cost Kentucky $5,000. As the team got better, so did fan enthusiasm. In 2007, Kentucky beat Louisville. This time, the fine was $25,000 when the fans rushed onto the field. Later that same year, Kentucky won a thrilling triple overtime game against top-ranked LSU, which eventually won the Bowl Championship Series National Championship game. Again, fans stormed the field. This time, the fine was $50,000. Eventually, the expected fine will become large enough to get Kentucky's attention.

Box 12.4 *Is This Cheating or Misconduct?**

At the end of every season in every sport, athletes are tired, injured, or both. Rest is most welcome, and coaches usually try to provide some relief.

In women's soccer, the NCAA tournament follows on the heels of the Atlantic Coast Conference (ACC) tournament. Because the NCAA tournament is more important, the Florida State University coach decided to rest several starters and therefore did not send his best team to the ACC tournament. Predictably, FSU did not do well and lost in the first round. ACC officials cried foul as FSU had undermined the integrity of the ACC tournament. The ACC fined FSU $25,000 and denied travel reimbursement expenses of $15,000. The coach was suspended for one game.

This raises (at least) two interesting questions. First, does such a decision constitute cheating or some other form of misconduct? Second, did the strategy work? (Check FSU's success in the 2010 Women's Soccer tournament.)

* Jere Longman, "After Reprimand College Coach Receives Support from Soccer Peers," *New York Times*, Nov. 18, 2010.

8 CONCLUDING REMARKS

Although there are several reasons owners and players may object to the misconduct of some participants, the leagues are justifiably concerned about the league's image. To protect that image and the fan loyalty that goes with it, leagues have taken steps to deter objectionable conduct. The actions that have been taken are consistent with the economics of deterrence. The more probable punishment is and the more severe that punishment, the less likely is bad behavior. To the extent that we continue to observe misconduct, that simply means that more work needs to be done to improve deterrence.

[25] www.nmnathletics.com/ViewArticle.dbml?DB_OEM_ID=8800&ATCLID=537230.

PROBLEMS AND QUESTIONS

1. Even though Utah was leading Wyoming 43–0, Utah attempted an onside kick, which infuriated the Wyoming coach. In an emotional outburst, he made an obscene gesture toward the Utah players. For that, the Mountain West Conference reprimanded him. Analyze the deterrent effect of such sanctions.
2. Why does the NBA suspend players for undesirable behavior, thereby hurting the team's competitiveness, rather than just imposing the equivalent fine?
3. Domestic violence cuts across all racial and socioeconomic lines in U.S. society. This behavior is subject to criminal law and punishment within the judicial system. Why do professional sports leagues impose additional punishments?
4. In the NFL, a large part of a player's compensation may be in the signing bonus. In the event that a player is suspended for misconduct, should the club be able to recover a proportional part of the signing bonus? How would this affect deterrence?
5. When Damon Stoudamire was arrested at the Tucson airport for marijuana possession, it was his third arrest on a drug charge. The Portland Trail Blazers suspended him and fined him $250,000. The club wanted to void his contract entirely, but was not sure that the contract would allow it to do so. Should an NBA team be permitted to void a player's contract if the player is arrested on criminal charges? How would that affect deterrence?
6. The penalty for "unnecessary roughness" in the NFL is 15 yards. However, such conduct may injure an opposing player and thereby reduce the quality of the team. Is there an incentive for engaging in unnecessary roughness to sideline an opponent's star quarterback? How can the NFL deal more effectively with such conduct?
7. Mike Price was fired as the head football coach at the University of Alabama following some partying that Alabama found objectionable. His unsigned seven-year, $10 million deal went up in smoke. Price claims that *Sports Illustrated*'s article about the incident defamed him because of various alleged inaccuracies. He filed a $20 million lawsuit demanding $10 million in compensatory damages and another $10 million in punitive damages.
   a. Under what circumstances should he recover compensatory damages?
   b. Assuming that there were some inaccuracies in the *Sports Illustrated* article, do you think that he should receive punitive damages? Why or why not?
8. Mattias Ohlund, a Vancouver defenseman, was suspended for four games by the NHL. He swung his stick at Minnesota's Mikko Koivu hitting him in the leg and breaking a bone in Koivu's leg.
   a. How much did the suspension cost Ohlund?
   b. Is the penalty severe enough given the injury Ohlund caused?

c. How much might the injury cost Koivu's team?

d. Should Ohlund be subject to criminal prosecution?

9. In many cases, repeat offenses result in increased punishments. For example, the Big 12 fined Mike Leach for criticizing game officials after a loss. He was warned that a second episode would be punished more severely. Why do repeat offenses warrant increased sanctions?

10. New York Yankees rookie Joba Chamberlain threw two wild pitches near the head of Boston's Kevin Youklis. For that, he was ejected from the game, suspended for two games, and fined. He insists that he had not tried to hit Youklis and that there was no malicious intent. What is the rationale for punishing Chamberlain for being wild?

11. Jason Richardson missed a shot and fell out of bounds in the waning seconds of a Golden State Warriors playoff loss to the Dallas Mavericks in 2007. He then had "improper interaction" with a fan. The result of his heated verbal exchange was a $35,000 fine imposed by the NBA.

    a. Why was this conduct a punishable offense in the NBA?

    b. Was the fine excessive in your opinion? If so, why?

12. In April 2008, Ron the Receiver, a star wide receiver on the State University football team, a Division I-A powerhouse, was arrested for carrying a concealed handgun and possession of marijuana. After pleading guilty in court, his coach somberly suspended him from the first two games of the 2008 season. The opponents were two Division II schools.

    a. Will such punishment serve as much of a deterrent?

    b. Does the team suffer much with such a suspension?

    c. Could the suspension come back to haunt Ron come NFL Draft day?

RESEARCH QUESTIONS

1. How much did their suspensions cost Carmelo Anthony, Nate Robinson, and J. R. Smith?

2. In December 1977, Kermit Washington, a forward for the Los Angeles Lakers, punched Rudy Tomjanovich. At the time, Tomjanovich was a star forward for the Houston Rockets. Compare Tomjanovich's performance before and after his serious injury. Was Washington's two-month suspension a suitable punishment?

3. Examine the terms of the personal conduct policy of one of the following: MLB, NBA, NHL, PGA Tour, Association of Tennis Professionals, Women's Tennis Association, Ladies PGA.

    a. Are the prohibitions specific or general?

    b. If they are general, will they catch all (or nearly all) forms of objectionable behavior?

    c. Are the terms specific enough so a reasonable person would know that a particular act would be punished?

4. Read Karen Crouse, "USA Swimming Outlines Plan to Stop Misconduct," *New York Times*, April 20, 2010. Examine the plan and analyze its deterrent effect.

REFERENCES AND FURTHER READING

Allen, W. David. (2002). "Crime, Punishment, and Recidivism: Lessons from the National Hockey League." *Journal of Sports Economics*, 3, 39–60.

Becker, Gary S. (1968). "Crime and Punishment: An Economic Approach." *Journal of Political Economy*, 76, 169–217.

Humphreys, B. R., and J. E., Ruseski. (2006). "Financing Intercollegiate Athletics: The Role of Monitoring and Enforcing NCAA Recruiting Regulations." *International Journal of Sport Finance*, 1, 151–161.

Kendall, Todd D. (2008). "Celebrity Misbehavior in the NBA." *Journal of Sports Economics*, 9 (2008), pp. 231–249.

Winfree, Jason A., and Jill J. McCluskey. (2008). "Incentives for Post- Apprehension Self-Punishment." *International Journal of Sport Finance*, 3, 196–209.

13

Steroids and Other Performance-Enhancing Drugs

1 INTRODUCTION

Drug use has long been a serious problem in the sports world. For many years, the central concern was over the use of illegal "street" drugs such as marijuana, cocaine, and heroin. More recently, however, attention has shifted to performance-enhancing drugs: anabolic steroids, human growth hormone, stimulants, and erythropoietin (EPO).[1] There are almost daily allegations and revelations regarding the use of performance-enhancing drugs across all sports – amateur as well as professional. These reports appear so often we are hardly surprised to find that one of our heroes – Marion Jones, Justin Gatlin, Shawne Merriman, Alex Rodriguez – has feet of clay. Some athletes have been temporarily suspended, and others have been banned for life. Suppliers have gone to prison, paid heavy fines, or both. Surveillance is increasing, and sanctions are becoming more severe. In this chapter, we examine the health risks associated with using performance-enhancing drugs. We also review the policies of several sports leagues and organizations and the sanctions they impose for using banned substances. We then employ the expected utility model to identify the potential for deterrence.

2 PREVALENCE OF ABUSE

No one can be quite sure just how prevalent the use of steroids has become in the sports world. Athletes do not want to admit to steroid use. In fact, several prominent athletes have lied about it. Some have persistently and vehemently denied using steroids when, in fact, they did use them.

The World Anti-Doping Agency (WADA) conducts tests all over the world. Over the 2003–2009 period, the frequency of failed drug tests rose from 1.62 percent in 2003 to more than 2.0 percent in 2005 then fell below 2.0 percent for

[1] In some quarters, the focus has shifted in the other direction. The Australian Rugby Union may begin out-of-competition testing for recreational drugs as well as steroids. James Mac-Smith, "Sailor Affair Prompts ARU Crackdown," May 21, 2006, http://www.rugbyheaven.smh.com.au.

Table 13.1. Frequency of Failed Drug Tests, 2006–2009

Year	Tests	Positives	Percent
2006	198,143	3,887	1.96
2007	223,898	4,402	1.97
2008[1]	274,628	5,053	1.84
2009	277,928	5,610	2.02

[1] It should be noted that 2008 is an extrapolation. The numbers were extrapolated from the following statement: "Approximately 3,300 additional samples were analyzed in 2009 compared to 2008, with a slight increase in Adverse Analytical Findings (AAFs) and Atypical Findings (AF's) from 1.84% (2008) to 2.02% (2009)."
Source: World Anti-Doping Agency, 2006, 2007, and *2009 Adverse Analytical Findings Reported by Accredited Laboratories.*

2006–2008 but rose again above 2.0 percent in 2009. Table 13.1 shows this. Thus, the failure rate seems to be settling at about 2.0 percent.

Newspaper, magazine, and broadcast news reports have made us well aware of the steroid use in baseball, cycling, and football. However, nearly all sports are plagued by drug cheats. Table 13.2 shows the number of tests, the number of failed tests, and the failure rate for several sports for 2009. As we can see, the failure rate was highest in baseball followed closely by golf, boxing, cycling, and football. The failure rates in these sports are somewhat above and below the 2 percent mark. Football players were tested most frequently – more than 23,000 times – but the failure rate was only .5 percent. Tennis and volleyball players were not tested frequently, and their failure rates were fairly low. A review of WADA's complete list contains the failure rates for a wide array of sports. The

Table 13.2. Frequency of Failed Drug Tests by Sport,[1] 2009

Sport	Tests	Positives	Percent
Baseball	19,560	541	2.51
Basketball	11,150	341	1.99
Boxing	3,231	85	1.64
Cycling	21,835	724	1.46
Football	32,526	569	0.50
Golf	1,530	40	2.16
Hockey	2,118	45	1.23
Ice Hockey	6,065	151	1.27
Tennis	3,945	54	0.43
Volleyball	5,121	89	0.80

[1] These data were extracted from World Anti-Doping Agency, *2009 Adverse Analytical Findings Reported by Accredited Laboratories.* See this report for a complete listing of all sports tested.

use of banned substances is undeniable but hardly "rampant." On the basis of these test results, it does not appear to be of epidemic proportions.

We should also note that it is not just steroids that are on the banned substances list. WADA tests for many things – and finds them in use. As the box shows, athletes liked steroids but did not rely on them exclusively.

Box 13.1 *It's Not All Steroids**

The WADA tests urine samples for a whole host of banned substances. The numbers and percentages of failed tests in 2005 by substance group were as follows:

Substance Group	Number	Percentage
Anabolic agents	1,864	43.4%
Beta-2 agonists	609	14.2%
Stimulants	509	11.8%
Cannabinoids	503	11.7%
Glucocorticosteroids	325	7.6%
Diuretics and other masking agents	246	5.7%
Hormones and related substances	162	3.8%
Beta-blockers	42	1.0%
Narcotics	17	0.4%
Agents with antiestrogen activity	21	0.5%

As one can see, steroids were the banned substance of choice, but clearly not the only cause of a failed test.

* World Anti-Doping Agency, *2005 Adverse Analytical Findings Reported by Accredited Laboratories.*

3 BANNED SUBSTANCES: BENEFITS AND RISKS

There are many substances that are on the WADA's list of prohibited substances.[2] All can enhance performance, but all have short-run, undesirable side effects. The long-run side effects are less understood but could be even worse.

3.1 Anabolic Androgenic Steroids

These steroids reduce the recovery time after exercise by increasing the rate of protein synthesis. As a result, athletes may increase the intensity and length of their training. Thus, the benefits of training increase, as do both muscle mass

[2] This section relies on the World Anti-Doping Code; the 2007 Prohibited List International Standard; and Committee on Sports Medicine and Fitness, Policy Statement, "Use of Performance Enhancing Substances," *Pediatrics*, 115, 1103–1106.

and strength. There is a long list of steroids that fall into this banned category. Steroids have some undesirable side effects that could be quite serious: jaundice and liver damage, heart problems, and psychological problems such as depression and paranoia. They can also lead to very aggressive behavior – *'roid rage* – that can lead to unfortunate events.[3] In extreme cases, the results may be truly tragic. Chris Benoit provides an example of one such tragedy. Benoit was a professional wrestler who was a heavy steroid user. He received prescriptions for a 10-month supply of steroids every 3 to 4 weeks from May 2006 until May 2007. In June 2007, he killed his wife, his seven-year old son, and himself. At the time of this murder-suicide, Benoit's testosterone level was 10 times normal.

3.2 Beta-2 Agonists

These drugs are commonly used by asthma sufferers but may be misused by athletes to increase muscle and reduce body fat. The undesirable side effects include heart palpitations, dizziness, headaches, nausea, and muscle cramps.

3.3 Stimulants

There are various stimulants – caffeine, amphetamines, ephedrine – that are used by athletes to improve alertness and reduce fatigue. They can also enhance competitiveness and aggression. Stimulants operate on the central nervous system to achieve these results. Unfortunately, stimulants can be addictive. Side effects may include increased blood pressure, increased heart rate, breathing problems, insomnia, and a variety of other discomforts. Ironically, they can also cause problems for athletic success as they can cause balance and coordination difficulties.

3.4 Diuretics

Athletes use diuretics to produce additional urine. For some athletes, this is a way to reduce their weight so that they meet weight restrictions in sports such as boxing, weightlifting, and wrestling. For others, they are hoping to dilute their urine samples to hide their use of anabolic steroids. The excessive use of diuretics can result in dehydration, which can cause kidney or heart failure in some instances. The other side effects are uncomfortable and hamper athletic performance but are not really dangerous. These include dizziness, headaches, nausea, and muscle cramps.

3.5 Hormones

Although the most discussed hormone being abused is human growth hormone (HGH), there are a wide array of hormones that are banned. These hormones have various effects on the body and various side effects. Most of them are used for a familiar end result: to build muscle and strength. Some of them,

[3] For a brief discussion of anabolic steroids, see Daniel De Noon, "Why Steroids Are Bad for You," WebMD.com, March 16, 2005.

most notably HGH, are impossible to detect in urine tests. In the case of HGH, one serious side effect is heart disease.

3.6 EPO

EPO is used to increase the production of red blood cells, which increases the amount of oxygen that the blood carries to the muscles. Athletes who must rely on endurance for success – cyclists, distance runners, distance swimmers – may use EPO to improve their endurance. Using EPO tends to thicken the blood, which increases the chance of blood clots, which thereby increases the risk of heart attacks and strokes.

3.7 Blood Doping

Some athletes infuse extra blood into their bodies. The idea is much the same as EPO – get more red blood cells so the athlete's blood will deliver more oxygen to the muscles. Possible side effects of blood doping include blood clots, stroke, heart failure, and shock.

3.8 Austrians Get Tough on Blood Doping[4]

The Austrian Olympic Committee lowered the boom on 13 officials who played some part in the blood doping scandals at the 2006 Winter Olympics in Turin. Each is banned for life from the Olympics. The AOC will deny them accreditation. Moreover, the AOC decided that any Austrian athlete or coach found guilty of a doping violation would receive a lifetime ban from all future Olympics.

4 STEROID POLICIES IN SPORTS

Most sports leagues and organizations have policies that prohibit the use of steroids and other performance-enhancing substances such as HGH, EPO, and various stimulants.[5] In addition to the general prohibitions, the policies set out the sanctions for violating the policy. Interestingly, these sanctions vary widely across sports. We examine in this section the policies of several prominent leagues and organizations.

4.1 National Collegiate Athletic Association Policy

The National Collegiate Athletic Association (NCAA) is committed to fair and equitable competition at its championships and postseason certified events.[6] It is also concerned about the health and safety of student-athletes. The NCAA

[4] Associated Press, May 30, 2007.

[5] Except in Iowa, race horses can be treated legally with anabolic steroids. The horse-racing industry appears to be rethinking that policy. Bill Finley, "Horse Racing Officials Move Toward Steroid Ban," *New York Times*, Feb. 28, 2007.

[6] For a useful summary, see *NCAA Drug-Testing Program*, available at http://www.ncaa.org/wps/portal/ncaahome?WCM_GLOBAL_CONTEXT=/ncaa/NCAA/Legislation+and+Governance/Eligibility+and+Recruiting/Drug+Testing/drug_testing.html. Much less user-friendly is the *NCAA Division I Manual of Operations.*

drug-testing program was created so that (1) no athlete might have an artificially induced competitive advantage, (2) no athlete would be pressured into using chemical substances to remain competitive, and (3) the health and safety of the athletes would be protected. The NCAA has a list of banned substances that includes performance-enhancing drugs as well as "street" drugs. This list is much the same as the WADA list.

The NCAA conducts tests at its championships. The NCAA member institutions also conduct random tests during the year. For the individual institutions, the drug-testing programs may vary considerably from one school to another. The NCAA does not demand that each institution have a testing program. It does require, however, that an institution carry through on any program that it puts in place. In other words, star players cannot receive special treatment.

The NCAA sanctions for testing positive are fairly severe. First-time offenders lose eligibility in all sports for one calendar year. They are not eligible for regular season or postseason play, including bowl games, while on suspension. A second offense for performance-enhancing drugs results in the total loss of all remaining eligibility in all sports. This amounts to a lifetime ban at the college level. A second offense for "street drugs" is somewhat less severe – the second offense leads to another one-year period of ineligibility, which would still permit a return to competition.

4.2 Major League Baseball

Due to congressional pressure, Major League Baseball (MLB) somewhat reluctantly adopted a steroid policy. Currently, every player is tested at least twice during the season. All players are also subject to additional random tests no matter how many times they have been tested. Testing continues throughout the off-season. The scheduling of tests, supervision of the sample collection process, transportation of the sample to the WADA-Certified Laboratory, oversight of the laboratory, and reporting of positive test results are handled by an independent person, not affiliated with MLB or the MLB Players Association. The penalties for players who test positive for steroids are as follows:

First-time offenders will be suspended for 50 games.

Second-time offenders will be suspended for 100 games.

Third-time offenders will be banned from MLB for life.

These possibilities amount to pretty hefty fines because suspended players are not paid. For a 50-game suspension, a player will lose about 30.9 percent of his salary. For a player earning $4.0 million per year, the implicit fine is $1,236,000. A 100-game suspension would double that amount to $2,472,000. A lifetime ban would cost the player the present value of his future earnings in baseball minus the amount that he could earn outside baseball.

The MLB season is long and involves a substantial number of night games. Combined with extensive travel, this schedule is energy draining. As a result, some players have used amphetamines to perk themselves up. As a consequence, MLB developed an amphetamine policy as well. The penalties for players who test positive for amphetamines are as follows:

First-time offenders will be subject to mandatory evaluation and follow-up testing, but not suspended.[7]

Second-time offenders will be suspended for 25 games.

Third-time offenders will be suspended for 80 games.

Fourth-time offenders will receive a punishment determined by the commissioner, which could amount to a lifetime ban.

Players who are banned for life have the opportunity to seek reinstatement after serving a minimum suspension of two years.

Mike Cameron was a Gold Glove center fielder for the San Diego Padres. Following the 2007 season, Cameron was suspended for the first 25 games of the 2008 season for testing positive for a banned stimulant. He blamed the positive test on a tainted nutritional supplement. The suspension cost Cameron more than 15 percent of his 2008 salary.

4.3 National Football League

Given the obvious benefits of added bulk and strength, it is not surprising that steroid use has become a problem in the NFL, which has an extensive substance abuse program. All players who are either under contract to an NFL club or are seeking a contract with an NFL club are subject to testing.[8] All players under contract to an NFL club will be tested once during the "preseason," which runs from April 20 to August 9. The cornerstone of the NFL's antidrug program is its Intervention Program, which players are required to enter after a positive test result for a prohibited substance. In this program, players are tested, evaluated, treated, and monitored for substance abuse. Fines and suspensions may be imposed by the player's club for a positive test result. Players who are suspended for positive test results are suspended without pay. Players who repeatedly fail to comply with the Intervention Program will be banned for at least one year by the NFL. After the banishment is completed, the commissioner determines if and when the player can return to the NFL. Once a player is reinstated, he will remain in the highest stage, Stage 3, of the Intervention Program for the rest of his NFL career. In Stage 3, the player is subject to continued testing and may be suspended indefinitely for repeat offenses.

During the 2006 season, a failed substance test carried a four-game suspension. In 2006, several prominent NFL players received four-game suspensions.

[7] In 2006, MLB conducted 3,000 amphetamine tests. It has been reported that Barry Bonds tested positive for amphetamines. It is unclear how many players tested positive once. No one tested positive more than once because no punishments were imposed. Michael S. Schmidt, "3,000 Tests for Amphetamines, but Only Bonds Is in the Spotlight," *New York Times*, Jan. 12, 2007.

[8] Arena Football League Players are subject to rules on steroids, but it is not clear just what they are. Article XL, Substance Abuse Policy of the Collective Bargaining Agreement says, "AFL players shall be subject to such substance abuse policies – covering both drugs of abuse and anabolic steroids and related substance – as the AFL and the AFLPA may agree upon."

For example, Shawne Merriman, a Pro Bowl linebacker with the San Diego Chargers, was suspended for four games. Defensive linemen Shaun Rogers (Detroit Lions) and Hallis Thomas (New Orleans Saints) were also suspended. Given a 16-game season, a four-game suspension amounts to a fine equal to 25 percent of the player's salary. For Merriman, the fine amounted to $81,500 because his base pay was $350,000. He also had substantial bonuses amounting to $6,352,970. It is unclear whether he lost any of that bonus money. If so, the fine could have been much larger. For Shaun Rogers, the fine was $212,500. For Hallis Thomas, his four-game suspension cost him $177,500. These implicit fines should serve as something of a deterrent to steroid use.

4.4 National Basketball Association

All National Basketball Association (NBA) players are subject to random testing for prohibited substances at any point in the season without prior notice. There are limits on the frequency of testing: a player will not be tested more than four times in a season. All testing is conducted by the NBA or the medical director and is in compliance with specifically accepted analytical techniques. The tests are then analyzed by laboratories that are selected by the NBA and the Players Association (NBAPA), approved by the medical director, and certified by the WADA, the Substance Abuse and Mental Health Services Administration, or the International Olympic Committee (IOC). If a player's test is positive, the player's penalties include enrollment in the NBA's SPED (Steroid and Performance-Enhancing Drug) program, which involves education, treatment, and counseling. The SPED program was established by the NBA's medical director in consultation with the NBA and NBAPA. Specific penalties for testing positive for any of the prohibited steroids, performance-enhancing drugs, or masking agents are as follows.

For the first violation, the player is suspended for 10 games without pay and is required to enter the SPED program.

For the second violation, the player is suspended for 25 games without pay and required to enter the SPED program if he is not already enrolled.

For the third violation, the player is suspended for one year without pay and required to enter the SPED program if he is not already enrolled.

For the fourth violation, the player is immediately dismissed and disqualified from any association with the NBA and any of its teams.

If a first-year player is dismissed and disqualified, he may apply for reinstatement to the NBA after one year. Other players who have been dismissed and disqualified must wait for two years before applying for reinstatement. The decision on reinstatement is made by the NBA and NBAPA.

4.5 National Hockey League

Every hockey player is subject to two "no-notice" tests from the start of training camp through the end of the regular season. The sample-collecting authority is Comprehensive Drug Testing, a Long Beach, California, entity. Positive tests for performance-enhancing substances result in the following mandatory disciplines:

For the first positive test, a 20-game suspension without pay and mandatory referral to the NHLPA [National Hockey League Players Association]/NHL Substance Abuse & Behavioral Health Program for evaluation, education, and possible treatment.

For the second positive test, a 60-game suspension without pay.

For the third positive test, a player receives a permanent suspension from the League.

Players with a third positive test and a consequent permanent suspension are eligible to apply for reinstatement after two years. The application for reinstatement is then considered by a committee appointed by the NHL.

4.6 U.S. Track and Field

There is a long history of drug testing in track and field. Currently, the testing is conducted by the United States Anti-Doping Association, the WADA, and International Doping Test and Management. Every athlete participating in a meet is subject to in-competition testing. Athletes who are ranked in the top 50 in the world in their respective events are subject to out-of-competition testing. If an athlete is ranked in the top 15 domestically, he or she is also subject to out-of-competition testing. Regardless of the number of times an athlete has been selected for in-competition or out-of-competition testing, that athlete must provide a sample each time he or she is selected for testing. Athletes found to have committed a doping violation are subject to the following penalties for *stimulants*:

A first offense for using a stimulant results in a public warning, a disqualification from the event in which the sample was taken, and a loss of any award or prize money received.

A second offense for using a stimulant results in a 2-year period of ineligibility.

A third offense results in a lifetime ban.

In the 2003 Pan American Games, Mickey Grimes led a U.S. sweep of the 100-meter dash. After the race, however, he failed a doping test. He had an excessive amount of ephedrine in his blood. Grimes was stripped of his gold medal. Earlier, the women's 800-meter gold medalist tested positive for excessive amounts of caffeine and lost her medal as well.

The penalties for using anabolic steroids or certain amphetamines are more severe:

A first offense warrants a 2-year period of ineligibility.

A second offense carries a lifetime ban.

There have been some spectacular athletic performances wiped out by positive drug tests. Perhaps the most spectacular was Ben Johnson's at the 1988 Olympics in Seoul. Carl Lewis of the United States and Ben Johnson of Canada met in the finals of the 100 meters to determine the world's fastest man.

Johnson burst away from Lewis and the rest of the field in a world-record time of 9.79 seconds. Lewis finished a distant second in 9.92 seconds. However, Johnson's postrace test was positive for steroids. As a result, he was stripped of both his medal and his world record. Carl Lewis received the gold medal, and his time of 9.92 seconds was recognized as the world record at that time.[9]

4.7 Men's and Women's Professional Tennis

The Tennis Anti-Doping Program is a comprehensive and internationally recognized drug-testing program that applies to all players competing at tournaments sanctioned by the Association of Tennis Professionals (ATP), the Women's Tennis Association (WTA) Tour, and the International Tennis Federation (ITF). Any player who enters or participates in a competition, event, or activity organized, sanctioned, or recognized by the ITF or who has an ATP Tour or WTA Tour ranking is subject to both in-competition and out-of-competition testing. All drug testing is conducted on behalf of the ITF by qualified personnel authorized by the ITF. The ITF began overseeing all drug testing at WTA tournaments in January 2007. The number of tests was scheduled to increase by 150 percent in 2007 in an effort to improve enforcement. The ITF also manages the antidoping program for the ATP tour. If a player's test is positive, the following penalties are imposed:

First offense: Two years of ineligibility.
Second offense: Lifetime ineligibility.

In addition, the doping offenses will lead to disqualification of all of the player's individual results obtained in the other matches in the tournament. There are substantial consequences of being disqualified, including forfeiture of all medals, titles, computer ranking points, and prize money (without deduction for tax). Before the period of ineligibility begins, a player with positive test results is afforded an opportunity to appeal. To be successful, the appeal must establish a basis for eliminating or reducing the penalty.

It should be noted that these punishments may be appealed and are often modified. For example, Mariano Puerta failed a drug test for the second time following his loss in the 2005 French Open. He faced a lifetime ban from ATP and ITF competition. He appealed on the basis that he did not intentionally take any banned substances. The Court of Arbitration for Sports ruled that Puerta's suspension be two years. He also had to forfeit all prize money won during and after the 2005 French Open.

4.8 Men's and Women's Golf

Until 2008, there was no real drug policy for either the Professional Golf Association (PGA) or the Ladies PGA (LPGA). Because golf is a game based on

[9] Ben Johnson now claims that a friend of Carl Lewis spiked Johnson's beer with the banned steroid, which is why he failed the postrace drug test. Johnson does admit having used steroids but claims that he would not have tested positive without someone tampering with his beer. Associated Press, "Johnson Claims Lewis Sabotaged Him in 1988," MSNBC.com, Dec. 5, 2006.

accuracy, distance control, and feel, this absence may be because of the possibly mistaken notion that there are no drugs that will enhance a golfer's performance. There was a time when some professional golfers had been known to use beta-blockers in an effort to slow down their heart rates and calm their nerves for pressure-packed situations. Craig Parry, the 2002 WGC-NEC Invitational champion, alleged that several top golfers had won important tournaments while taking beta-blockers. Most golfers who have tried beta-blockers, however, have discounted their advantage. In fact, they claimed that the side effects actually impaired their performance. As a result, there did not appear to be any concern regarding such abuse.

The idea that power is not a critical ingredient in the success of the top professionals is undermined by the dominant presence of powerful golfers at the top of the world rankings: Tiger Woods, Phil Mickelson, Vijay Singh, Ernie Els, and several others are very long hitters. Physical fitness and strength training are now a part of professional golf. With that new emphasis comes concerns that steroids may also arrive on the scene.[10] It is undeniable that using steroids will increase strength and permit a golfer to practice longer. PGA Tour Commissioner Tim Finchem had always emphasized that using performance-enhancing drugs constitutes cheating under the rules. "It's no different taking steroids to prepare for a golf tournament than it is kicking your ball in the rough."[11] Because golfers are honor-bound to follow the rules, there seemed to be no need for a testing program. Not everyone was convinced, however. Notably, at the 2006 WGC-Bridgestone Invitational, Tiger Woods advocated testing golfers for performance-enhancing drugs.[12] Although Tim Finchem did not believe that golfers would cheat by using steroids, he may have been kidding himself. In 2005, an NCAA survey found that 1.3 percent of its golfers had used steroids in the past.

At the 2007 British Open, Gary Player revealed that he knew for a fact that some professional golfers were using performance-enhancing drugs. He did not disclose the names of those who were using HGH, creatine, or steroids, but he was adamant that it was happening. At that time, golf's governing bodies in Great Britain and the United States were already working on a drug-testing policy. In September 2007, the PGA Tour and other golf organizations announced that the use of certain substances was prohibited. The list was much the same as the WADA list. Abandoning its reliance on the honor system, random testing began in 2008 on the PGA Tour.

The LPGA had earlier announced that it would begin a testing program in 2008. Although everyone appeared confident that there was no steroid problem on the LPGA Tour, there was support for the testing proposal. The attitude seemed to be that the tour was clean and the drug testing would simply confirm that for all the world to see.[13]

[10] Damon Hack, "In Steroid Era, Will Golf's Integrity Stand Test?" *New York Times*, Aug. 14, 2006.

[11] *Ibid.*

[12] Alan Shipnuck, "Does Power Corrupt?" SI.com, Aug. 29, 2006.

[13] Damon Hack, "L.P.G.A. to Begin Drug Testing in 2006," *New York Times*, Nov. 15, 2006.

Box 13.2 *A New Industry: Steroid-Free Supplements – Guaranteed*

As testing for steroid use increases across all sports and punishments become more severe, a new industry has emerged: steroid-free nutritional supplements. GlaxoSmithKline, a pharmaceutical company, offers a line of sports drinks, energy bars, and carbohydrate gels that are all but guaranteed to be free of banned substances or anything that might be mistaken for a banned substance. Many athletes who have tested positive for steroids claim that they have never *knowingly* taken any banned substance. They contend that a trainer or even a fellow competitor must have put the steroid in their drink. To prevent someone else from spiking a drink, the Glaxo products are sold in sealed, single-portion containers. Glaxo carefully monitors production to prevent contamination by a banned substance.

The ATP (men's tennis tour) has entered into an agreement with Glaxo in response to a number of failed drug tests by ATP members. The new products should minimize the danger of an athlete's inadvertently taking a banned substance. It will also eliminate claims that someone else did it when an athlete fails a test.

Abbot Nutrition produces the EAS brand of sports supplements. It guarantees that its products do not contain any substances banned by the NBA drug policy. These EAS products have been widely used by NFL players with no problems.*

* Liz Robbins, "N.B.A. Union Strikes Deal for Supplements," *New York Times*, Nov. 17, 2006.

5 SANCTIONS AND DETERRENCE

In all the sports that prohibit the use of performance-enhancing drugs, a steroid user incurs risk.[14] Consider the expected costs and benefits of steroid use by an athlete. When an athlete uses steroids, the short-run benefit is enhanced performance. This improved performance will lead to greater rewards and therefore to higher wealth related to higher salary, bonuses, bigger prizes, more endorsements, and space. However, steroid use is prohibited because it confers an unfair advantage on the user, and sanctions are imposed on those users who are caught. This makes steroid use risky because the outcome is uncertain. Wealth is improved if the steroid use goes undetected but wealth will decline if the steroid use is detected and the athlete is punished. Punishments are often severe – 50-game suspensions in MLB, four-game suspensions in the NFL, two-year bans in track. No one wants to see those punishments actually imposed because the fans suffer, too. As an economic matter, however, the purpose of punishment is to deter undesirable behavior. To the extent that steroid use is deterred, actual punishment will be unnecessary. This, of course, is the goal.

[14] This section is an adaptation of the analysis presented in the previous chapter.

As we saw in the last chapter, we can work on an athlete's expected utility to alter his or her choices. Suppose that an athlete's performance without using steroids will generate a wealth of W_1. Steroids greatly improve athletic performance, which leads to wealth of W_2 that exceeds W_1. Because steroid use is prohibited, there are sanctions for using steroids. In some cases, the athlete may be fined, but in most cases, the athlete will be suspended without pay. Suspensions therefore involve implicit fines due to the loss of income. We will treat the monetary value of all sanctions as a fine. Thus, if the athlete gets caught using steroids, his or her wealth will be $W_1 - F$. By using steroids, the athlete trades a certain wealth of W_1 for a risky prospect.

If the athlete uses steroids, his actual wealth is random, but the *expected* wealth is

$$E[W] = p(W_1 - F) + (1 - p)(W_2),$$

where p is the probability that the athlete gets caught using steroids.

This formulation is most appropriate when steroid use leads to a reward of $W_2 - W_1$, which the athlete does not get if he or she is caught and a punishment F is also imposed. For example, when Ben Johnson failed his drug test, he did not get the Olympic gold medal and did not enjoy the other financial benefits that would have gone with it. If the steroid use leads to monetary returns that cannot be taken back (such as endorsement income), then we might say that the athlete gets $W_2 - F$ if he or she is caught. In that event, it is possible that $W_2 - F$ could exceed W_1 if F is not large enough. If $W_2 - F$ exceeds W_1, steroid use cannot be deterred because the athlete is better off using steroids whether he is caught or not. For the analysis to be interesting, $W_2 - F$ must be below W_1. One way to think about our formulation here is that F exceeds any gain that cannot be recovered so that $W_1 - F$ can represent the outcome when a steroid user is caught.

Ignoring the long-term health risks of using steroids as well as any moral qualms about violating rules, we assume that the athlete is an expected utility maximizer. Thus, he or she will use steroids if the expected payoff from doing so is large enough to make him or her better off than would be the case without the steroid use. Put differently, if the expected utility associated with steroid use exceeds the utility of wealth that would be enjoyed without it, then the athlete will use steroids. Using the notation, if

$$E[U(W)] > U(W_1),$$

then steroids will be used.

5.1 Deterrent Function

There are various punishments for steroid use: suspensions, lifetime bans, fines, loss of awards and records, and loss of reputation. For purposes of our simple model, assume that these can be expressed in dollars and cents and treated as a fine, which we have denoted as F. For example, suppose an offensive lineman has a salary of $1.6 million. A 4-game suspension without pay for steroid use translates into a $400,000 fine because the NFL has a 16-game

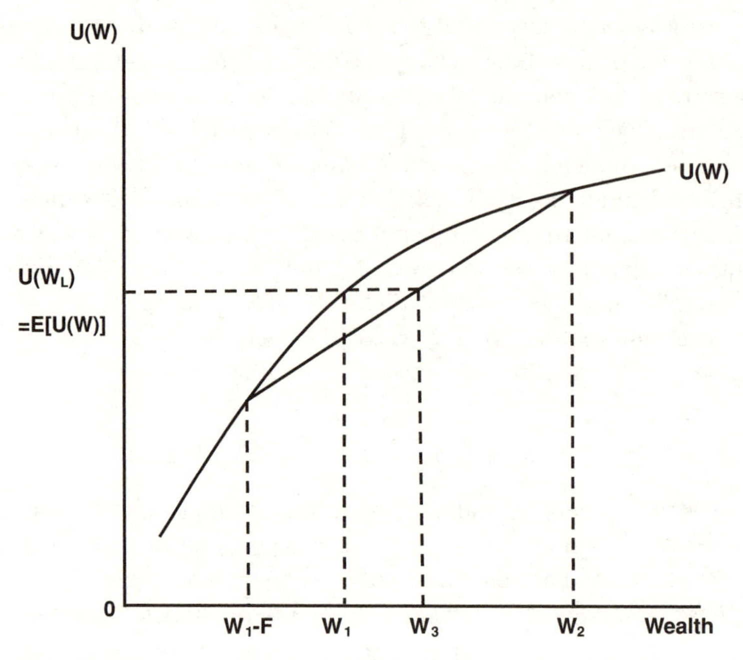

Figure 13.1. To deter the use of steroids, the expected wealth must be reduced below W_3 by increasing p or F.

schedule. In this case, F equals \$400,000. As a general matter, we can write the *deterrent function* as

$$\begin{aligned} D &= U(W1) - E[U(W)] \\ &= U(W_1) - \{pU(W_1 - F) + (1-p)U(W_2)\}, \end{aligned}$$

where p is the probability of detection, W_1 is the athlete's wealth without steroids, and W_2 is the illegitimate wealth with steroid use.

If $D > 0$, the potential steroid user will be deterred from using steroids because he or she is better off without the steroid use. If $D < 0$, then the athlete will use the steroids because he or she is better off with their use.

Figure 13.1 describes a situation in which the potential steroid user is indifferent between using and not using steroids. We know this because the height of the utility function at W_1 is equal to the height of the chord at the expected wealth, which is denoted as W_3. In short,

$$U(W_1) = E[U(W)],$$

and $D = 0$ when expected wealth is equal to W_3.

In this case, the expected punishment, which is $p \cdot F$, is such that expected wealth from using the steroids is W_3. Because the height of the utility function at W_1 is $U(W_1)$ and the height of the chord at an expected wealth of W_3 are the same, we can see that the potential violator is indifferent between using steroids and not doing so. Now consider what happens if the probability of detection is increased. For example, if MLB increases the testing frequency, it is more likely that steroid users will be caught. As a result, the expected wealth will fall. Starting from a point where an athlete is indifferent between using steroids and not using them, an increase in enforcement will tip the scales toward not using steroids. The reduction in $E[W]$ causes the $E[U(W)]$ to fall below $U(W_1)$. In that event, $D > 0$ and a potential user is deterred.

Box 13.3 ***Deterring Steroid Use in High School***

There is mounting evidence that steroid use has spread to high school athletes. In response, Florida,* New Jersey,† and Texas intend to test high school athletes for steroid abuse. The commitment is well intentioned but probably futile because the probability of getting caught is actually quite small. In New Jersey, only athletes competing in state playoffs are subject to testing. Random testing of these athletes will result in about 500 tests. Because there are about 240,000 high school athletes in New Jersey, only 0.2 percent will be tested. In Texas, the proposal is to select 30 percent of the high schools on a random basis and then test 3.0 percent of their athletes. This means that Texas will test about 0.9 percent of all athletes in Texas high schools. In Florida, 1 percent of all baseball players, football players, and weightlifters will be tested. Consequently, those competing in track, swimming, wrestling, and basketball will go untested.

In New Jersey, the probability of an athlete's being tested is 0.002, in Texas, it is 0.009, and it is 0.01 in Florida. In our model of deterrence, the probabilities of avoiding detection are large: 0.998 in New Jersey, 0.991 in Texas, and 0.99 in Florida. Given these probabilities, it is doubtful that many will be deterred from using steroids.

* The 2007–2008 State of Florida/ FHSAA Anabolic Steroid Testing Program.

† Michael S. Schmidt, "Critics Question the Effectiveness of New Jersey's High School Drug Tests," *New York Times*, Nov. 22, 2006.

Alternatively, consider what happens to D if the penalty is increased. For example, in March 2007, European track officials increased the penalty for doping violations. If an athlete receives a two-year ban from the International Association of Athletics Federations (IAAF) , he or she will be banned from all European indoor and outdoor championships for an additional two years beyond the IAAF ban. This, of course, does not apply worldwide, but the added sanction is severe. Not many track and field athletes will compete successfully after a four-year absence from competition and the training that such competition demands.

This result can be seen in Figure 13.2. First, note that the chord rotates downward to reflect the fact that the wealth will be lower if the athlete uses steroids and is caught. Second, if p is unchanged, an increase in F will lead to a reduction in $E[W]$. Because

$$E[W] = p(W_1 - F) + (1 - p)(W_2),$$

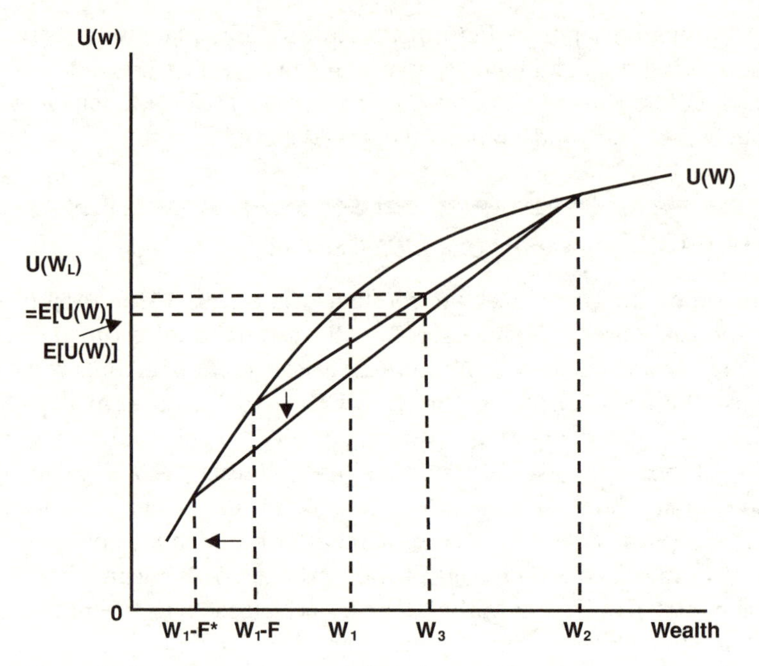

Figure 13.2. An increase in the punishment for steroid use decreases expected wealth and increases the variance in wealth.

an increase in F to F^* will reduce expected wealth to

$$E[W] = p(W_1 - F^*) + (1 - p)(W_2).$$

Alternatively, note that $\partial E[W]/\partial F = -p$, which must be negative because p must be positive.

To focus on the effect of changing F, we may assume that the expected wealth remains unchanged. In other words, if the expected wealth remains equal to W_3, which requires an offsetting *decrease* in p as F is increased, $E[U(W)]$ falls as is plain to see in Figure 13.2. Now, $U(W_1)$ exceeds $E[U(W)]^*$, and the potential steroid user will be deterred.

There is some anecdotal evidence of deterrence. For example, at the end of 2006, Lyubov Ivanova was banned for two years by the Russian track and field federation for steroid use. She was the ninth athlete banned in 2006. In 2005, there were 23 athletes who failed their drug tests. This suggests that enforcement is having a deterrent effect. Deterrence in baseball appears to be getting better, too. In 2005 and 2006, 15 major league players and 119 minor league players had positive steroid tests. The number in 2006 was lower than in 2005, which suggests reduced use.[15] But there is also evidence of lingering problems. Despite the systematic testing, which should make the probability of detection approach one, there are numerous indications of continued problems. Alberto Contador won the 2010 Tour de France and failed a drug test. Brandon Spikes, the New England Patriots second-leading tackler, missed the last four games of

[15] *Ibid.* Unfortunately, it might also suggest that new designer steroids have been developed, which are harder to detect.

the 2010 season because of a failed drug test. The owner of the Houston Texans ordered club personnel to search his team's locker room for banned substances during the 2010 season.

5.2 The Trade-Off between *p* and *F*

If a league or organization wants to increase deterrence, it can increase p or it can increase F. It is tempting to increase F because that does not require any resources. In contrast, the only way to increase p is by investing resources in monitoring, policing, testing, and so on. This added expense can be avoided by increasing the punishment instead of increasing the probability of detection. However, there is a limit to using punishment to deter the use of banned substances. At some point, the punishment does not "fit the crime." To see the problem, suppose that an athlete gets some benefit B from the use of a banned substance. The expected punishment for doing so is

$$E[F] = pF + (1 - p)(0),$$

which is just pF. Now, we can adjust p and F so the expected punishment is equal to the benefit:

$$pF = B.$$

If we decide to save resources by decreasing p and increasing F, the actual value of F will be much larger than B. For example, suppose $p = 0.01$ and $B = \$100$. To make pF equal B, F must be \$10,000. In principle, there is no problem with this, but most people would feel that the punishment was disproportionate to the violation.

Another reason to be cautious about raising the punishment to extreme levels is the danger of false positives. Marion Jones, for example, tested positive for EPO following the U.S. Track and Field Championships in June 2006. The retest results were negative, which cleared her. However some damage had already been done. The first test result led to a provisional suspension, which caused her to miss several important – and potentially lucrative – track meets in Europe. By the time the second test cleared her, she was no longer in racing shape. Her season was over, along with any appearance fees or prize money that she might have earned.

In November 2005, there were House and Senate bills that would have made the policy in professional sports uniform.[16] The most popular proposal among lawmakers was to adopt the Olympic standard: first-time offenders receive a two-year ban; second-time offenders are banned for life. These legislative proposals met with resistance from league officials and the players' unions. The main objection was that the penalties limit the sanctions, but this ignores the fact that the expected punishment can still be increased by testing more frequently and thereby increasing the probability of detection. At this point, there has been no federal legislation regarding mandatory sanctions. The threat of

[16] Associated Press, "Penalties Decreased to Get Support for Steroids Bill," ESPN.com, Nov. 8, 2005.

federal legislation has undoubtedly had an effect on the enforcement policies of the various leagues and organizations.

Box 13.4 *Attacking the Supply of Drugs in Italy*

Sports leagues and organizations try to deter the use of performance-enhancing drugs by punishing the users. Penalties reduce the expected net benefit for the athlete, and this should deter some use. Governmental authorities can also attack the supply. Spain, for example, has attacked the supply side with its "Law to Protect Health and Combat Doping in Sports." Under this law, anyone who prescribes, dispenses, or facilitates the use of performance-enhancing drugs can be imprisoned for six months to two years. Such penalties raise the expected cost and thereby reduce the supply.

In the following figure,

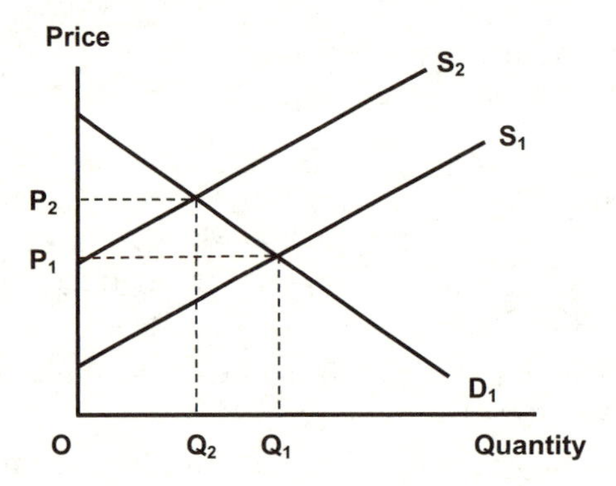

D_1 is the demand for steroids given the current sanctions on the athletes who use them, and S_1 is the initial supply. The result is a quantity of Q_1 and a price of P_1. With increased penalties for suppliers, costs of being in that business rise. The increased costs lead to a shift in supply to S_2, which causes the quantity to decline to Q_2 and the price to rise to P_2. Thus, law enforcement complements the efforts of sports leagues and organizations in reducing steroid use.

5.3 Olympian Efforts at Deterrence

The IOC already imposes the maximum penalty at its disposal: disqualification. To further deter steroid use, it must increase the probability of detection. This, it seems, is precisely what it has been doing. The number of doping tests is increasing with every Olympics. The IOC conducted approximately 4,600 doping tests at the 2008 Olympics in Beijing. This total is about 25 percent more than the number of tests conducted at the 2004 Athens Games and double the number conducted at the 2000 Sydney Games.

A large part of the increase will be devoted to precompetition tests. This seems like a good idea because it reduces the chances that an athlete will be stripped of a medal, which is embarrassing for everyone involved. It also prevents the true winner from being deprived of an appropriate award ceremony. To appreciate the significance of this, consider the following question: Who is Oscar Pereiro? He was the winner of the 2006 Tour de France. However, he did not get the yellow jersey until October 2007 when Floyd Landis was officially stripped of his title.

6 ADDITIONAL SANCTIONS

There are specific sanctions for a positive test result, but the adverse consequences do not necessarily end there. Additional financial consequences may result. In addition, an athlete can experience a stunning loss of reputation.

6.1 Financial Consequences

At the end of the 2006 season, Guillermo Mota became a free agent. He had a good record as a relief pitcher for the Mets: 18 appearances, 18 innings pitched, 3 wins, 1.00 ERA. No doubt, he was looking forward to a big pay day during the free agency period. Unfortunately, Mota tested positive for some performance-enhancing drug and was suspended for the first 50 games of the 2007 season. The Mets were disappointed that Mota had made an error in judgment, but they applauded his taking responsibility for his actions. The Mets decided to re-sign Mota to a two-year contract. The contract was still lucrative, and he earned $1.8 million in 2007 minus about $550,000 for the suspension and $3.2 million in 2008. Aside from the suspension, Mota's contract probably was quite a bit lower than what he would have commanded in free agency had he not been caught.

6.2 Lost Reputation

Another real and substantial punishment for steroid use is loss of reputation.[17] Some prominent and highly regarded athletes test positive, and fans realize that their accomplishments were chemically induced. They are suddenly labeled as "juicers" or "drug cheats." As we will see, this can even happen without a positive test on the basis of circumstantial evidence.

Mark McGwire is an excellent example of a baseball hero who has lost his reputation (see Box 13.5). Without revelations of steroid use, McGwire would have been a certain Hall of Famer, but steroids have muddied his reputation. In his first year of eligibility, McGuire received only 23.5 percent of the votes, falling well short of the necessary 75 percent. The annual votes for McGuire have not gotten any better. In fact, in 2010, he received even fewer votes than in some earlier years. Rafael Palmeiro is another example. After a long, distinguished career, he joined the very exclusive 3,000-hit club. Two months later, he was driven into retirement because of a positive steroid test. Now, it is doubtful that he will ever enter the Hall of Fame. Barry Bonds was always a hard guy to

[17] This matters a good deal to many athletes. See, for example, Karen Crouse, "For Swimmer, Ban Ends, but Burden Could Last," *New York Times*, Aug. 7, 2010.

like. Unfriendly and unaccommodating, Bonds was never confused with Mr. Personality. Nonetheless, his performance on the field commanded admiration and respect. In the wake of the Bay Area Laboratory Co-Operative (BALCO) scandal, however, there were stories of his using steroids and HGH.[18] Now his records are tainted by the steroid allegations. Bonds is an embarrassment to the baseball establishment because he holds the most acclaimed records for home runs in a single season and most home runs in a career.

Box 13.5 *A Fallen Hero: Mark McGwire*

Mark McGwire was due to earn millions of dollars for the final year of his contract with the St. Louis Cardinals, but he was wracked with injuries and knew he could not play effectively. He did the honorable thing – he retired. McGwire had a Hall of Fame career. Although his production was somewhat inconsistent, McGwire was an awesome power hitter with 583 career home runs. He hit a home run every 10.61 times he batted, which is the best of all time. In 1998, he set a new single-season home run record with 70. Friendly, accessible, polite, everyone liked Mark McGwire. He was clearly a first-ballot Hall of Famer.

At the end of the five-year waiting period, his name appeared on the ballot. Needing 75 percent of the votes, he received only 23.5 percent. The reason was clear: McGwire was a steroid user.

A former teammate, Jose Canseco, accused McGwire of steroid use back in their days together in Oakland, but accusations by someone not known for his honesty would not have shut the door to the Hall of Fame. McGwire did that himself when he refused to "talk about the past" at a congressional hearing on steroid use. His evasiveness and lack of candor were his undoing. As Dave Anderson of the *New York Times* put it, if McGwire does not want to talk about his past, "then I don't want to guess how many of the 583 home runs in his past were steroid-aided."* This steroid cloud could keep him out of the Hall of Fame forever.

* Dave Anderson, "Hall-Ful Who Belong, Minus One," *New York Times*, Dec. 28, 2006.

Track is littered with disgraced athletes. Ben Johnson is a prominent example, but a more recent example is Justin Gatlin. Gatlin was the shining star of U.S. track. He held the world record in the 100-meter dash and seemed poised for continued success. Then came the stunning news that he had tested positive for steroids. He received a two-year suspension. Many fans felt as though they had been betrayed by Gatlin. Given his blinding speed and a more forgiving attitude in the NFL, Gatlin tried to catch on as a wide receiver. These efforts did not lead anywhere.

Marion Jones, with her dazzling smile, was the darling of the Sydney Olympics in 2000. One could see her image everywhere after winning a fistful

[18] For an extended view, see Mark Fainaru-Wada and Lance Williams (2006), *Game of Shadows*, New York: Gotham Books.

of medals, three gold and two bronze. Soon, however, her reputation began to fade. Her former husband, her boyfriend, and her coach had the steroid taint. When the BALCO scandal broke, her name was mentioned prominently. Of course, she steadfastly denied ever using steroids, and, in fact, she had never failed a drug test. Nonetheless, her considerable accomplishments were then clouded with suspicion. As it turns out, Jones had been lying all along. Having lied to federal investigators, she faced prosecution. Under pressure, she finally confessed and pleaded guilty. On March 7, 2008, Marion Jones began serving a six-month prison sentence for having lied about her steroid use.

In all of these cases and many more, the loss of reputation is a very real punishment. In some cases, it is well deserved; in others, it may not be.

Box 13.6 ***Punishing the Innocent***

At the Sydney Olympics in 2000, Marion Jones was aiming for five gold medals. She came up short, but not by much. She won gold medals in the 100 meters, 200 meters, and 1,600-meter relay. She also won bronze medals in the long jump and 400-meter relay. It was a remarkable performance by a charismatic athlete with charm and grace. The drug tests of the day could not detect her secret: designer steroids from BALCO.

Jones was accused of steroid use in the BALCO investigation. For years, she denied having used steroids. When Jones finally admitted that she had been doping at the Sydney Olympics, she was disqualified retroactively. All of her results were wiped out along with her records. The IOC demanded that she surrender the five medals – three gold and two bronze – that she had won. One gold medal was won in the 1,600-meter relay, and one bronze was won in the 400-meter relay. Because Jones participated in those finals and had subsequently been disqualified, the IOC disqualified the entire team. In April 2008, the IOC wanted the medals awarded to her relay teammates returned. This seems somewhat unfair to her teammates who had done nothing wrong. Yet Jones was on the team and contributed to the team's performance – a performance that was enhanced by steroids. Would these medals have been won without Jones? Would they have won with Jones if she had not been on steroids? We will never know.

7 CONCLUDING REMARKS

In this chapter, we have examined the problem posed by steroids and other performance-enhancing drugs. We have noted the varied policies of the major sports leagues, some sports organizations, and the NCAA. The details of the policies are not uniform, but steroids are uniformly prohibited. To put the enforcement policies in an analytical framework, we relied on the expected utility model. The control variables in that model are the probability of detection and punishment and the sanction. Deterring steroid use requires increasing the probability of detection and/or the magnitude of the punishment. The actual behavior of sports leagues and organizations is consistent with the economic theory of deterrence.

PROBLEMS AND QUESTIONS

1. Suppose an athlete is risk neutral.
   a. What is his or her deterrent function?
   b. What must be true for a violation to be committed?
2. On January 21, 2003, the *Gainesville Sun* reported that a Texas A&M basketball player was arrested for two counts of possessing a controlled substance. The police found a plastic bag containing syringes and what appeared to be vials of anabolic steroids. This player apparently was undeterred by the potential sanctions for steroid use. Does the fact that he was caught prove that he failed to maximize his expected utility?
3. Some professional golfers believe that a drug code is needed on the PGA Tour. Although the usual performance-enhancing drugs – steroids and HGH – may not prove popular or even very useful to golfers, there are reports that some golfers have taken beta-blockers, which are prescribed for hypertension, to calm their nerves for pressure-packed situations. This raises several interesting questions.
   a. Should golfers be precluded from using beta-blockers? Why or why not?
   b. How should the PGA Tour deal with those golfers who suffer from hypertension and need the medication?
4. Suppose that a potential steroid user is a risk seeker. How does this affect deterrence?
5. The use of steroids and other performance-enhancing drugs gives the user a competitive advantage over "clean" athletes. Dealing with this problem is a costly nightmare: thousands of tests and retests, policing, suspensions, and so on. Why not just permit the use of performance enhancers and put all athletes on the same competitive footing?
6. If MLB is satisfied that Barry Bonds used steroids and HGH to increase his strength and speed, should his home run records carry an asterisk? Or should they just be eliminated altogether? How should other records set in MLB's steroid era be treated?
7. In response to the designer drug revelation, USA Track and Field (USAT&F) officials proposed stiffer sanctions for first-time steroid offenses. These included a lifetime ban and a $100,000 fine.
   a. If an athlete is banned for life, how would USAT&F collect the fine?
   b. Should an athlete be deprived of earning a living for life for a youthful error in judgment?
8. Suppose there were 200 athletes in an event. Six athletes were tested for banned substances. All of the test results were negative (i.e., were clean). If

5 percent of the athletes actually used some banned substance, what is the probability of drawing a random sample of six that were clean?

9. If an NFL player receives a four-game suspension for using steroids, should the team be able to recover part of his signing bonus? Why or why not?
10. A penalty for steroid use may deter risk averters but not risk lovers. Explain.
11. Fans appreciate great performances. Why should a professional sports league care about the use of performance-enhancing drugs?
12. At the Olympics, every gold medalist is tested for banned substances. This occasionally leads to spectacular disqualifications (e.g., Ben Johnson). Because the athletes must know that they will be tested, why do they take banned substances anyway?
13. Jerry "the Juicer" knows that he will win $100,000 in an athletic event if he takes steroids and is not caught. If he is caught, he will win nothing. Without steroids, he would win $50,000. If 5 percent of all contestants are tested, will Jerry take the steroids? Explain.
14. For the current NFL season, Larry Linebacker was scheduled to earn $2 million. Ron Receiver was scheduled to earn $800,000. Both players failed random drug tests and were suspended for four games. The same offense cost Larry $500,000, whereas it only cost Ron $200,000.
    a. Is this "fair"?
    b. Is there an economic explanation for the disparity?
15. Justin Gatlin, a 2004 Olympic champion, was suspended from track for four years. When his suspension ended, he discovered that the organizers of major European track meets barred him from competing. (Dave Ungrady, "As Suspension Ends, Gatlin Faces New Obstacles," *New York Times*, July 21, 2010.) Show how Gatlin's experience will affect deterrence and explain.

RESEARCH QUESTIONS

1. Identify the NFL players who were suspended last season for drug violations. Based on the length of their suspensions, calculate the implicit fine imposed by the league.
2. Trace the history of MLB's reluctant development of a steroid policy. Examine the increasing severity of the sanctions for steroid use.
3. With respect to performance-enhancing drugs, what is the policy of the following leagues and organizations:
    a. Major League Soccer
    b. Professional Bowling Association
    c. WTA
    d. United States Golf Association
    e. National Association for Stock Car Auto Racing
4. Find out the short-run and long-run health risks of (a) steroids, (b) HGH, and (c) EPO.

5. The Associated Press reported that "Spanish cyclist Aitor Gonzalez was banned for two years for doping by the highest tribunal in world sports. The Court of Arbitration for Sport ruled Gonzalez was at fault for taking a food supplement that he claimed was contaminated and led to his positive test for a steroid compound during last year's Spanish Vuelta."

   What are the estimated financial consequences for Gonzalez?
6. What is *genetic doping*? Has it been successful? Can it be detected? Is it impermissible under the steroid policies of MLB, the NBA, and the NFL?
7. Pick a major college conference – Southeastern Conference, Big Ten, Atlantic Coast Conference – and examine its drug-testing policy. If it does not have one, examine the policies (if any) of the member schools.
8. Compare the policy of the NFL regarding the use of "street drugs" (marijuana and cocaine, for example) with the policy on steroids and HGH. If there is a difference, what explains the difference?
9. Identify the MLB players who have been suspended for steroid use.
   a. How long were their suspensions?
   b. How much did it cost them in forgone salary?
10. Compare the reported failure rates in Table 13.2 with those in 2005. Does it appear that drug use is being deterred?

REFERENCES AND FURTHER READING

Bradbury, J. C. (2007). *The Baseball Economist: The Real Game Exposed* (chapter 9). New York: Penguin Group.

Digler, Alexander, Bernd Frick, and Frank Tolsdorf. (2007). "Are Athletes Doped? Some Theoretical Arguments and Empirical Evidence." *Contemporary Economic Policy*, 25, 604–615.

Dinardo, John E., and Jason A. Winfree. (2010). "The Law of Genius and Home Runs Refuted." *Economic Inquiry*, 48, 51–64.

Eber, N. (2008). "The Performance-Enhancing Drug Game Reconsidered: A Fair Play Approach." *Journal of Sports Economics*, 9, 318–327.

Haugen, K. K. 2004. "The Performance-Enhancing Drug Game." *Journal of Sports Economics*, 5, 67–86.

Fainaru-Wada, Mark, and Lance Williams. (2006). *Game of Shadows*. New York: Penguin Group.

Maennig, Wolfgang. (2002). "On the Economics of Doping and Corruption in International Sports." *Journal of Sports Economics*, 3, 61–89.

Tainsky, Scott, and Jason A. Winfree. (2008). "Financial Incentives and League Policy: The Example of Major League Baseball's Steroid Policy." *European Sport Management Quarterly*, 8, 67–80.

FACILITIES, FRANCHISES, AND PUBLIC POLICY

14

Competing for Sports Franchises and Events

1 INTRODUCTION

Many cities have an unmet demand for a professional sports franchise in their midst. Whenever an existing franchise expresses an interest in relocating to greener pastures, there is no apparent shortage of willing hosts. The same is true when one of the major sports leagues contemplates expansion. For strategic reasons, the major sports leagues make sure that there are a few viable locations that go unserved. In this way, they ensure the presence of excess demand and thereby improve the credibility of threats by existing franchises to move. This excess demand also provides leverage when either a new or existing franchise is bargaining with a city for benefits.

Cities also compete for major sports events. Major cities around the world compete with one another to host the Olympics or the World Cup. On a somewhat smaller scale, Omaha pursued the College World Series. Some U.S. cities compete to host the NFL player draft, which has turned into a media event. Cities compete in the only way they can by providing benefits to the organizers. Usually these are legitimate, but there have been instances of corruption.

In this chapter, we examine some of the explanations offered for why cities want to host a professional sports franchise or major sports event. We find that most of these reasons sound good but lack much empirical support. In addition, we examine the ways in which a sports franchise can exploit the excess demand for sports franchises. Finally, we examine the use of eminent domain powers in acquiring the land needed for sports facilities.

2 THE ECONOMIC INCENTIVES TO BE A HOST

There are many economic benefits that allegedly flow from hosting a major league sports franchise. These include the following: (1) job creation, (2) greater tax revenues, (3) enhanced prestige, and (4) consumption benefits. These are all sound reasons for wanting to attract or retain a professional sports franchise, but it is not at all clear that these benefits actually materialize.[1]

2.1 Job Creation

This, of course, has a wonderful ring to it. After all, more jobs are always good for a city (and its mayor) as they result in more employment and (perhaps) higher wages. However, is it true that a professional sports franchise creates much employment?

The sad truth is that a sports franchise does not produce much in the way of increased employment opportunities. By and large, the players, coaches, and top management are not local residents. These people move into the community when the team locates there. Those who lived there before the team arrives are unlikely to land any of the really attractive jobs with the club. No doubt, there will be a few local residents hired to provide clerical support, maintenance, and low-level management services. There are part-time jobs for game days – parking lot attendants, food and beverage servers, concession workers, cleanup crews, and the like. For the most part, these are unattractive, low-paying jobs, but not all of them are actually *additional* jobs. Most fans who attend a game would have spent their money on other things if the franchise had not been there. In other words, spending at the game substitutes for spending elsewhere in the local economy. If the franchise had not been there, fans might spend their money on dinner and a movie, playing golf, attending a rock concert, buying a new sweater, and a host of other alternatives. These forms of economic activity generate employment opportunities. Consequently, many of the part-time jobs associated with the game would still exist in other forms elsewhere in the local community, but it is not always obvious where these jobs would be because they would be dispersed throughout the local economy. The bottom line is that there would be some substitution of employment at the game for employment elsewhere, but no real additional employment.

There is little empirical support for the proposition that the presence of a major league sports team creates significant net new job opportunities. Moreover, any new jobs come with a price tag. The host city typically incurs substantial costs in attracting or retaining a team. Thus, each job created may cost far more than it is worth.[2]

2.2 Greater Tax Revenue

Some proponents may argue that a professional sports franchise will lead to greater tax revenues for the local community. After all, the team's operation will lead to an increase in economic activity, and with presumably enhanced economic activity, state and local tax revenues should grow. In addition, property tax receipts will also increase and thereby benefit the community by providing

[1] For an exceptionally good treatment that explodes many myths, see Roger G. Noll and Andrew Zimbalist, eds. (1997), *Sports, Jobs, and Taxes*, Washington, DC: The Brookings Institution, 1997.

[2] For an analysis, see Robert A. Baade and Allen Sanderson, "The Employment Effects of Teams and Sports Facilities," in Noll and Zimbalist, *ibid.*

more money for education and the community's infrastructure (roads, parks, and the like). But is there any evidence that a pro team leads to greater tax revenue?

The empirical evidence does not support the proposition that the presence of a major league franchise will significantly increase the community's tax revenues. In fact, property taxes are apt to fall due to tax concessions made to the club. For example, suppose that a city decides to build a stadium and parking facilities for a pro team. To do so, it acquires the land from local residents and businesses that were paying property taxes. This revenue stream disappears when the city acquires the land. If the displaced residents and businesses relocate within the city in existing properties, the revenue is also lost. The same results occur if the club owns the stadium, but the city exempts it from property taxes.

Claims that sales taxes will rise may be hollow as well. Sales tax receipts will only rise if the club's presence leads to increased retail spending. But a good deal of the retail spending at the ballpark simply substitutes for retail spending elsewhere and, therefore, is not *increased* spending. In other words, the spending is relocated, but not necessarily increased.

Box 14.1 ***Is the Pro Bowl Worth It?***

Following the Super Bowl, the NFL puts on an all-star game known as the Pro Bowl. For many years, the Pro Bowl has been played in warm, sunny Hawaii at a time when most of the country is shivering. Many players bring their families and enjoy a working vacation.

In 2004, Hawaii paid some $5.4 million for the privilege of hosting the Pro Bowl. Was it worth it? Well, the Hawaii Tourism Authority estimated that the game attracted about 22,000 out-of-state visitors. Obviously, these visitors spent money on food, hotels, transportation, and other things. Spending was estimated at $29.5 million, which is an average of about $1,350 per person. The state collected additional tax revenues of $2.84 million. The NFL claimed that the state's exposure was worth another $12.1 million based on the cost of media advertising. Well, was it worth it?

2.3 Prestige/Exposure

It is often claimed that a city with a professional sports franchise enjoys greater prestige and media exposure than a comparable city without a sports franchise. One alleged benefit of being "prestigious" is the increased willingness of businesses to relocate in the city. This, of course, would be beneficial as additional business creates even more jobs for the local citizens. But is there any empirical support for this claim?

Again, there is scant support for this proposition. It is difficult to confirm or deny the claim of added prestige, but it is possible to examine the claim about attracting businesses. Did any businesses leave Los Angeles when the

Rams moved to St. Louis? Did businesses flock to Phoenix because the Suns and the Diamondbacks came to town?

2.4 Consumption Value

There is an undeniable benefit to having "our" team. Even those who do not attend the games benefit from having a home team to root for, brag about, and sometimes to complain about. No one wants to be the mayor of a city that loses an existing franchise. Irrespective of what else that mayor accomplishes during his or her tenure, losing the home team will always be a blight on that politician's legacy.

The consumption benefits associated with a local pro team cannot be dismissed in a serious counting of the costs and benefits of allocating or retaining the home team. These consumption benefits are intangible and nonpecuniary. They are, therefore, very difficult to measure and incorporate in an otherwise quantitative analysis. The weight accorded to consumption benefits is bound to be controversial. Advocates of efforts to attract or retain a team have an obvious incentive to overvalue the benefits. Opponents have an equally obvious incentive to minimize their significance.

Box 14.2 *The Value of Our Team*

Given several budget problems in many states, some have questioned the wisdom of spending millions of dollars on the State University's athletic programs. There is little doubt that it would be better if State University's Athletic Departments were fiscally sound (i.e., not running deficits). In response to the critics, proponents of college sports claim that there are important intangible benefits. One such proponent offered the following rationale for athletics: "...schools, especially in states where there are no pro sports teams have looked upon college athletics as a vehicle to raise visibility and draw community and alumni contributions." He went on to point out that "when State University's sports teams do well, they can rally an entire state in touch times, witness the effect of national championships and NCAA exploits." This argument has some merit as we all enjoy rooting for the home team. But it raises some questions:

1. How much should the state spend on raising public morale?
2. How should the state finance the expenditure?

3 THE COMPETITION FOR FRANCHISES AND EVENTS

As Noll and Zimbalist point out, the major sports leagues are monopolies.[3] In order to maximize their profits, they restrict the number of teams in the league.

[3] Roger G. Noll and Andrew Zimbalist, "Sports, Jobs, and Taxes: The Real Connection," in Noll and Zimbalist, *ibid.*

As a result, there is unmet demand for being a host city, which causes cities to compete with one another to host sports franchises. In addition to extending a warm greeting and generous hospitality to prospective franchises, cities compete on the basis of the economic benefits that they offer to the club. These may include a variety of economically attractive inducements.

3.1 Stadiums, Ballparks, and Arenas

To one extent or another, host cities participate in financing the construction of football stadiums, ballparks, and sports arenas for the benefit of the franchise. The team is then given a sweetheart deal on the rent.

3.2 Stadium Leases

Professional teams often rent the venue in which they play their home games. The terms of the lease vary widely. Some fortunate teams pay little or no rent, whereas others pay relatively significant amounts. The contract terms can vary in other ways as well. The lease payment can be tied to ticket sales with or without guarantees. Some payments are based on sharing stadium revenues from concessionaires or parking.

If a team enjoys a real sweetheart deal, the stadium investment is almost sure to be a financial disaster for the state or local government involved. For example, the Chicago White Sox pay the grand sum of $1 per year to use Comiskey Park. The Cleveland Cavaliers, Phoenix Suns, and Milwaukee Bucks pay no rent at all. The San Antonio Spurs pay $205,000, which seems like a lot in contrast to the Cavaliers, Suns, and Bucks but is still peanuts.

There are some interesting lease contracts in Cleveland. Major League Baseball's (MLB's) Indians share ticket revenue with the Gateway Economic Development Corporation, which oversees Cleveland's major league sports facilities. The Indians pay $1.25 per ticket to Gateway if total attendance exceeds 2.5 million fans for the season. If attendance is between 1.85 million and 2.5 million, the Indians pay only $1 per ticket. In a year when attendance dips below 1.85 million, the Indians pay nothing at all. For the past few years, the Indians have had to pay some rent but not much compared with ticket revenues. In Table 14.1, attendance, average ticket price, and ticket revenue are shown for the 2003–2010 seasons. In 2003 and 2004, the Indians paid no rent even though ticket revenues amounted to $37.7 million and $36.8 million, respectively. In 2005, 2006, 2007, and 2008, attendance exceeded 1.85 million but fell below 2.5 million so the Indians had to pay a dollar a ticket. On the basis of the average ticket price, Cleveland's share of the Indians' ticket revenue was less than 5 percent. In 2008, the lease payments were less than 4 percent of ticket revenue. Although the lease payments are substantial in an absolute sense, they are relatively small compared with the ticket revenue.

Interestingly, the National Basketball Association's (NBA's) Cavaliers have the same deal as the Indians. The Cavaliers, however, play only 41 home games in Quicken Loans Arena (formerly Gund Arena), which holds 20,562 fans. Since the maximum total attendance is 843,042, which is obviously less than

Table 14.1. Attendance, Ticket Prices, and Gate Receipts for the Cleveland Indians, 2003–2010

Year	Attendance[1]	Average Ticket Price[2]	Ticket Revenues[3]
2003	1,730,001	$21.82	$37.7 million
2004	1,814,401	$20.29	$36.8 million
2005	2,013,763	$21.17	$41.8 million
2006	1,997,995	$21.54	$43.0 million
2007	2,275,916	$21.32	$48.5 million
2008	2,169,760	$25.72	$55.8 million
2009	1,776,904	N/A	N/A
2010	1,394,812	$22.12	$30.8 million

[1] Attendance information is from ESPN.com.
[2] Average ticket price information is from teammarketing.com.
[3] Gate receipt information is simply attendance multiplied by the ticket price.

1.85 million, the Cavaliers pay no rent at all even though the lease does not specify that result.

The National Football League's (NFL's) San Diego Chargers have a stadium deal with decidedly perverse incentives. The Chargers pay 10 percent of their gross ticket revenue as a stadium lease payment. San Diego, however, has agreed to pay the Chargers for all unsold tickets. As a result, the Chargers earn far more on unsold tickets than they do on sold tickets. In the NFL, gate receipts are split 60–40 with the visiting team getting the 40 percent. Now, suppose that a ticket cost $100. If sold, 10 percent or $10 goes to the city. Forty percent of what is left, or $36, goes to the visiting team. The Chargers then keep the remaining $54. If the ticket goes unsold, however, the city reimburses the Chargers for the full price of $100, which is not shared with the visiting team. Thus, the Chargers receive $46 *more* on an unsold ticket than they retain on a sold ticket. This provides a perverse incentive because the Chargers appear to be better off with lower ticket sales. It is important, however, not to overstate this point. Unsold tickets do not generate parking fees or concession sales. When attendance is off, merchandise sales may also be off. As a result, the team may be better off selling out the stadium.

In many cases, major league sports franchises have extremely attractive leases that generate little or no rent. In such instances, it is clear that net revenues for the municipality are going to be low and in some cases even negative. Nonetheless, it may be *economically* sensible to subsidize a facility that does not pay for itself. It depends on whether the team's presence generates enough consumer surplus.

4 THE DARK SIDE OF CITY COMPETITION

In most cases, the competition for hosting a team or an event may be fierce, but it is ethical. There are, however, some unfortunate examples of corrupt, or at least unethical, practices.

4.1 The "Need" for New Facilities

There are many instances in which incumbent franchises demand new facilities. If a new facility is not built, the franchise threatens to leave town for greener pastures. At times, these threats are supplemented by pressure from the league. For example, the Falcons have been pressing Atlanta for a new stadium. The NFL has told Atlanta that it will not get a Super Bowl if there is no new stadium. Even though an existing facility may provide a perfectly good sports venue, a franchise may insist on something new for a very good reason: money.

It has been estimated that new facilities increase revenues by some $25 million per year. The increased revenues flow from (1) luxury suites, other premium seating, and personal seat licenses; (2) increased ticket prices; and (3) increased attendance.

First, luxury suites sell for $30,000 to $65,000 per season. Club seats and premium seating are not quite as expensive, but there is a price premium that falls straight to the bottom line. Personal seat licenses (PSLs) act like insurance policies that guarantee renewal rights for future seasons. PSLs may cost as much as $16,000. Interestingly, these revenues are not subject to revenue sharing with other teams, which makes them even more attractive. Furthermore, ticket prices at new facilities tend to be higher.

Second, enhanced amenities increase gate receipts because they increase demand and thereby permit higher ticket prices. This is because the new facility is attractive in many ways, and more people come to the game even though ticket prices are higher.

Third, higher attendance leads to more parking, merchandise, and concession revenues because they are complements to attendance at the venue. Some of the most valuable franchises are in relatively new stadiums.

4.2 Revenue Guarantees

Some cities will reduce uncertainty for the new franchise by providing revenue guarantees. Once again, revenue guarantees can create perverse incentives depending on the contract terms. This problem should not be overstated because clubs ordinarily have plenty of incentives to avoid the need to exercise the guarantee.

4.3 Stadium Revenues

Even though a city may be financing the sports facility, it will typically permit the club to capture the revenues associated with naming rights, parking, concessions, luxury seating, and personal seat licenses. These revenues are very attractive to a club for two reasons. First, there are few (if any) costs required to generate those revenues. Consequently, they are nearly all pure profit. Second, these revenues usually are not shared with the rest of the league.

5 THE WINNER'S CURSE

In its zeal to attract (or retain) a sports franchise, the winning city may suffer the *winner's curse*, that is, it may "pay" more for the franchise than it is worth to the community. In a bidding war, the winner may offer the highest bid for one of several reasons. First, it may be able to make more profitable use of the sports franchise than rival cities. One city may be larger than a rival bidder and therefore will have more residents who will enjoy having a home team. The residents of one city may be more interested in, say, hockey than the residents of another. One city may have a suitable facility, whereas another would have to build something new. Second, the winner may have overestimated the benefits or underestimated the costs. This, of course, is a mistake. Third, some have argued that the bidding process may induce aggressive bidding such that the bidding becomes a contest in and of itself. When this happens, each city decides that it must win for the sake of winning. In that event, it raises its bid to beat the other bidders rather than to acquire a franchise that will confer net benefits on the community. This explanation is somewhat dubious, but those who are bidding in that way are not acting as profit-maximizing firms would act. (Why not?) At bottom, the winner may simply be the most optimistic or least risk averse regarding the value of the franchise to the community. Having won the bid, however, the winner has to wonder why he was so much more optimistic than the others. Did they know something that he did not know?

The winner may have made a mistake by offering too much. The decision may well have been sound, but events intervene to make the *ex post* results unfavorable. It is not clear that we should refer to this as the winner's curse. Forecasting the future is necessarily imprecise and fraught with risks. Labels really do not matter much. If a city host committed more than the club's presence or an event is worth, it is a mistake and the taxpayers suffer the consequences. Presumably, the taxpayers will get even at the next election and oust those who paid too much.

6 SHOULD A SPORTS FRANCHISE BE SUBSIDIZED?

Not all sports franchises are profitable. The Buffalo Bills and the New Orleans Saints, for example, have had financially marginal operations. The Montreal Expos (now the Washington Nationals) floundered in MLB. The National Hockey League's (NHL's) Phoenix Coyotes were bankrupt. Despite their local monopoly status, some franchises do not earn positive profits, or at least they claim that they are losing money. It is hard to pin this down because most franchises are privately held corporations, which means that there is no public disclosure of the financial statements. Suppose, however, that it is, in fact, true that the club is unprofitable. This raises the question of whether it should be subsidized by the local community. This is not without controversy.

Consider the franchise depicted in Figure 14.1. Given the demand and marginal cost, the best that the club can do is operate where marginal revenue and marginal cost are equal. At a quantity of Q_1, the corresponding price is P_1. Revenues will be P_1 times Q_1. Unfortunately, cost will be equal to AC_1 times Q_1, which is larger than total revenue because AC_1 is greater than P_1. The very best that the team can do with simple monopoly pricing is *lose* a sum equal to

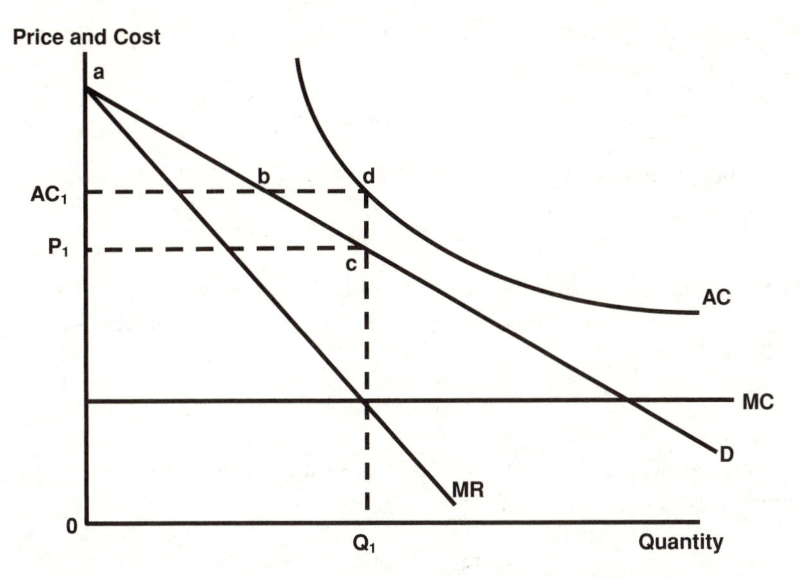

Figure 14.1. Teams that cannot earn a profit may be subsidized if they provide enough consumer surplus.

$(AC_1 - P_1)Q_1$. To retain the team, the local community will have to provide a subsidy of some sort to cover the loss. It makes sense to do so if the consumer surplus exceeds the subsidy.

At the profit-maximizing price and output, consumer surplus is equal to the triangular area acP_1, whereas the necessary subsidy is the rectangular area AC_1dcP_1. These two areas overlap to some extent. Consumer surplus will exceed the loss if triangle $abAC_1$ is larger than triangle *bdc*. If so, the community is better off subsidizing the team rather than losing it to another city.

In many cases, the owners of sports franchises are billionaires. If the losses are not too steep, the billionaire owner could absorb the loss and not burden the community with it, but there is no reason to expect the owner to do so. Just because an owner can afford to absorb a loss is no reason to expect this. If the owner can move to greener pastures, he or she will want to unless the local fan base steps up and supports the franchise in some way that eliminates the loss.

7 COMPETITION, SUBSIDIES, AND TEAM LOCATION

In an interesting article, Porter and Thomas show that the competition among cities for professional teams does not materially influence the ultimate location of those teams.[4] That competition does result in substantial subsidies for the billionaire owners of the teams. Put differently, the competition results in a redistribution of wealth from taxpayers in the host city to the wealthy owners. The geographic distribution of teams, however, will be largely unchanged by these subsidies. We can see this result using some familiar tools.

[4] Philip K. Porter and Christopher R. Thomas (2010), "Public Subsidies and the Location and Pricing of Sports," *Southern Economic Journal*, 76, 693–710.

Suppose that there are two cities that want to host a professional team. In City *A*, the demand for tickets is

$$P = 100 - 0.001\,Q,$$

and the corresponding marginal revenue is

$$MR = 100 - 0.002\,Q.$$

The marginal cost is constant and equal to 10. As a result, locating in City *A* will maximize the profits by operating where marginal revenue equals marginal cost:

$$100 - 0.002\,Q = 10,$$

which requires $Q = 45{,}000$. Substitution into the demand yields a price of $55, which results in a profit of

$$\Pi = (55 - 10)(45{,}000) = \$2{,}025{,}000$$

per game.

In City *B*, demand is somewhat higher,

$$P = 120 - 0.001\,Q,$$

the corresponding marginal revenue is

$$MR = 120 - 0.002\,Q,$$

and marginal cost is still equal to 10. Profit maximization in City *B* requires operating where

$$120 - 0.002\,Q = 10,$$

or at $Q = 55{,}000$. This leads to an optimal price of $65. The team profits in City *B* will be

$$\Pi = (65 - 10)(55{,}000) = \$3{,}025{,}000 \text{ per game.}$$

Clearly, the team will opt for City *B* because it will earn $3,025,000 per game there, whereas it would only earn $2,025,000 per game in City *A*. With no subsidies, City *B* will have a team and City *A* will not have a team.

City *A* has an unmet demand for a professional team and decides to compete by offering a subsidy to the team. If the city assumes that the team will maximize profits once it gets there, it will anticipate a $55 price and ticket sales of $45,000 per game. This will leave consumer surplus of

$$CS = \tfrac{1}{2}(100 - 55)(45{,}000),$$

which amounts to $1,012,500. The city can therefore offer a subsidy that amounts to a bit over a million dollars per game. With that subsidy, the team will earn $3,037,500 per game in City *A* and will locate there if City *B* does not respond. However, City *B* will respond by offering a subsidy that makes the team more profitable in City *B*. Even at monopoly prices, City *B* enjoys consumer surplus of

$$CS = \tfrac{1}{2}(120 - 65)(55{,}000),$$

which is equal to $1,512,500. Because City *B* is already far more profitable than City *A*, its subsidy need not be large. If its subsidy were only, say, $25,000, the team profit in City *B* would be $3,050,000 and the team would locate there.

Box 14.3 *The Seattle SuperSonics*

In 2006, Howard Schultz sold the NBA's Seattle SuperSonics to a group of Oklahoma businessmen led by Clay Bennett. At the time, the SuperSonics had a lease that bound them to Key Arena in Seattle through the 2009–2010 season. Although it was likely that the Bennett group wanted to move the team to Oklahoma City, they tried to get a new arena in Seattle. Having already spent a good deal of money on facilities for MLB's Mariners and the NFL's Seahawks, the state and local governments refused to build a new arena. The Bennett group argued that a new arena is essential to make the franchise profitable. In Key Arena, the team had lost $55 million dating back to 1999.

Oklahoma City served as the temporary home of the New Orleans Hornets following Hurricane Katrina. It demonstrated an enthusiasm for professional basketball, which impressed NBA Commissioner David Stern. Moreover, Oklahoma City promised a $121.6 million renovation of its Ford Center Arena. No doubt the Sonics move was met with a sweetheart lease on the renovated arena. Because Seattle did not come up with a competitive offer, the Sonics moved to Oklahoma City.

Box 14.4 *Florida versus Arizona*

In the distant past, most MLB clubs had spring training facilities in Florida.* There has been, however, an exodus of clubs that are relocating to Arizona. The clubs find drier weather, closer proximity to one another, and permanent excise taxes on car rentals to finance sweetheart stadium deals for the teams. At this point, half of the clubs are in the Grapefruit League in Florida and half are in the Cactus League in Arizona. The intensity of the competition to host the Chicago Cubs illustrates the benefits of competition enjoyed by MLB clubs.

The Chicago Cubs have been going to Arizona for spring training for more than 50 years. Their stadium lease, which expires in 2016, has an opt-out provision if the club is dissatisfied with the stadium and the city's failure to update it. This provision kicks in after the 2011 season. Because of the impending deadline, the city of Mesa began negotiating with the Cubs over a new facility. At the same time, government officials and private investors in Naples, Florida, began urging the Cubs to relocate to Naples. Naples offered a new stadium, training facilities, and an area around the stadium for commercial development. The funding for all of this would come from a combination of public and private sources. Mesa responded in kind. It offered to buy a 110-acre site for the stadium, offices and training facilities, and a commercial development zone at a cost of some $84 million in public money.

Query: In a time of tight budgets, should public dollars be spent to subsidize privately owned MLB clubs?

* Ken Belson (2010), "Promises and Perks to Try to Lure Cubs from Arizona," *New York Times*, Jan. 29, 2010.

The bottom line is that competition between cities does not alter the ultimate location, but it does make the team more profitable at the expense of the taxpayers who bear the cost of the subsidy.

8 THE USE OF EMINENT DOMAIN

Suppose that a popular sports team threatens to relocate to greener pastures unless the city builds a new stadium. If the city wants to acquiesce to the team's demand, it must find some land that will be large enough to accommodate the stadium and the necessary parking for the fans. In many urban areas, this will pose a serious problem because all of the land is being used for something: housing, office buildings, stores, and parks, among other things. There is precious little vacant land that is large enough for a stadium. The city will then have to buy land from several landowners. This leads to the dreaded *land assembly problem*.

When many small parcels of land must be purchased to assemble enough land for a stadium, there is the danger that one (or more) landowner will hold out for a price that is well above market levels on comparable property in a different location. For example, suppose that 10 separately owned parcels of land must be assembled to build a baseball park. Operating the ballpark will generate a surplus of, say, $50 million. If the club has acquired nine parcels for $1 million each, there is $41 million left. The 10th landowner recognizes that his parcel is worth up to $41 million because the project cannot proceed without his parcel. Of course, the club wants to pay the fair market value of $1 million. The holdout is in a position to extract all of the surplus, which infuriates the club. If that last landowner gets a very large share of that surplus, that is of no real economic concern. The ballpark is built and one of the landowners receives a windfall. However, the problem is that every landowner has an incentive to hold out. If the aggregate demands by the landowners exceed $50 million, the project will fall through. The solution lies in the exercise of eminent domain.

Eminent domain refers to the right of the state to take private property for public use. This right is limited by the Fifth Amendment to the United States Constitution:

> Nor shall private property be taken for public use without just compensation.

Although the takings clause permits the government to take private property without the owner's consent, there are two limitations on this power. First, the property must be put to public use, and second, the government must pay *just compensation.* In fact, almost any use can be justified as *public.* For example, private property can be taken so a *private* developer can build a shopping mall or office complex that will increase property tax revenue. Taking private property so a city can build a sports facility to be leased at sweetheart rates to a professional sports team would seem to be easy to justify. Thus, the public use requirement would not seem to be much of a limitation.

Because the government cannot take the property without just compensation, one might think that property owners will not be hurt by the taking. Such is not usually the case. The courts have defined *fair market value* to constitute *just compensation.* This, of course, is incorrect from an economic perspective because the value to the property owners must exceed the fair market value or they would have sold the property willingly. As a result, property owners are not fully compensated by receiving fair market value because their subjective (perhaps idiosyncratic) value exceeds fair market value. There does not seem to be a solution without abandoning eminent domain, however. Fair market value is observable, whereas subjective value is not. Thus, an owner can misrepresent the subjective value. Its true value can neither be proved nor disproved.

The bottom line is that those property owners who are compelled to sell their land at fair market value pursuant to eminent domain proceedings are not fully compensated. As a result, there is a cost of a sports facility that they bear disproportionately.

9 CONCLUDING REMARKS

In this chapter, we have been concerned with the demand by cities to host a sports franchise or an event. Cities compete with one another on the basis of the benefits that they are willing to provide to the team. These benefits often involve sports facilities, which are ultimately paid for by the taxpayer. We have also seen that the competition among cities causes a redistribution of wealth from the taxpayer to wealthy team owners without affecting the ultimate location of the team. In the end, the team winds up in the most profitable location because that city will be able to provide the most benefits to the team.

PROBLEMS AND QUESTIONS

1. Competition among cities for a sports franchise should lead to a socially optimal location decision. Why?
2. The Seattle SuperSonics had to pay a $30 million fee to the NBA for its approval to move from Seattle to Oklahoma City. Why would the NBA impose such a tax on a financially struggling franchise?
3. The Seattle SuperSonics wanted to move from the 14th largest market to Oklahoma City, which is 62 percent smaller. Should other NBA owners care about that? If so, why?

4. Some city leaders seem to think that attracting a professional sports franchise will make it a "big league" city. What is the benefit of being a big league city?
5. Some cities finance their basketball arena with hotel occupancy taxes, whereas others use taxes on admission. Does it make a difference? If so, how?
6. How could one measure the benefit of the positive exposure that a city gets from being an event host?
7. The demand facing a sports franchise located in City A is

$$P = 100 - 0.005\,Q.$$

But if it moved to City B, the demand would be

$$P = 150 - 0.01\,Q.$$

If marginal and average cost would be equal to 10 in either city, which location would be the most profitable? Show that competition from the other city could not lead to a different choice of location.
8. Explain why those who must sell their property to the government for fair market value are invariably injured in the bargain.
9. Why does the government have to rely on eminent domain rather than market transactions?
10. Suppose that the demand facing the local franchise is

$$P = 100 - 0.001\,Q.$$

Marginal revenue is $MR = 100 - 0.002Q$, and marginal (and average) cost is 20.

   a. What price and output will maximize the franchise's operating profit?
   b. If average total cost is equal to 70 at the optimal price and output, will profit be negative? If so, should the franchise be subsidized?
11. Suppose that the Philadelphia Phillies decide to build a new ballpark that they want to own. Christina owns a piece of land that is just the right size and is perfectly located. The Phillies want to buy her land, but balk at her asking price, which they claim is above fair market value.
   a. Should Philadelphia be able to take her land through eminent domain proceedings and then sell it to the Phillies?
   b. Is the answer any different if the city is going to own the ballpark?
   c. If Christina is forced to sell her land at fair market value, is she hurt by this? Why or why not?
12. Prominent sports economists, such as Roger Noll and Andrew Zimbalist, have characterized the major leagues (NFL, MLB, NBA, and NHL) as *monopolists*.
   a. Define monopoly.

b. Can the NFL, for example, be a monopoly given the presence of college and high school football?

c. Can the NFL be a monopoly given other forms of sports entertainment (e.g., baseball and basketball)?

RESEARCH QUESTIONS

1. In eminent domain proceedings, is the seller subject to capital gains taxes? How would that influence the discussion in the text?
2. What steps has the International Olympic Committee (IOC) taken to prevent bribery from determining the location of a Summer or Winter Olympics?
3. What new facilities were required for the Summer Olympics in Beijing, China? Find estimates of the costs to the Chinese taxpayers.
4. What did Oklahoma City do to persuade the Seattle SuperSonics to move?
5. Vancouver hosted the 2010 Winter Olympics in the midst of a major recession. Citing reduced TV revenues and international sponsorships, the organizing committee projected a deficit (Katie Thomas, "I.O.C. Pledges to Help Balance Vancouver's Budget," *New York Times*, August 29, 2009).

   a. Did Vancouver experience a loss?

   b. How much of the loss was covered by the IOC?
6. China constructed a large number of venues for the 2008 Summer Olympics. To do this, it needed to acquire land. How did it do this? Who bore the cost?

REFERENCES AND FURTHER READING

Baade, Robert A., and Allen Sanderson. "The Employment Effects of Teams and Sports Facilities," in Roger G. Noll and Andrew Zimbalist, eds. (1997). *Sports, Jobs, and Taxes*. Washington, DC: The Brookings Institution, 1997.

Barget, Eric, and Jean-Jacques Gouguet. (2007). "The Total Economic Value of Sporting Events: Theory and Practice." *Journal of Sports Economics*, 8, 165–182.

Bradbury, J. C. (2007). *The Baseball Economist: The Real Game Exposed* (chapter 4). New York: Penguin.

Clapp, Christopher M., and Jahn K. Hakes. (2005). "How Long a Honeymoon? The Effect of New Stadiums on Attendance in Major League Baseball." *Journal of Sports Economics*, 6, 237–263.

Coates, Dennis. "Stadiums and Arenas: Economic Development or Economic Redistribution?" *Contemporary Economic Policy*, 25, 565–577.

Coates, D., and B. R. Humphreys. (2000). "The Stadium Gambit and Local Economic Development." *Regulation* 23, 15–20.

Depken, Craig A., II. (2000). "Fan Loyalty and Stadium Funding in Professional Baseball." *Journal of Sports Economics*, 1, 124–138.

Greenberg, M. J. (2000). "Stadium Financing and Franchise Relocation Act of 1999." *Marquette Sports Law Journal*, 10, 383–399.

Johnson, A. T. (1983). "Municipal Administration and the Sports Franchise Relocation Issue." *Public Administration Review*, 6, 519–528.

Johnson, Bruce K., Peter A. Groothuis, and John C. Whitehead. (2001). "The Value of Public Goods Generated by a Major League Sports Team: The CVM Approach." *Journal of Sports Economics*, 2, 6–21.

Johnson, Bruce K., Michael J. Mondello, and John C. Whitehead. (2006). "Contingent Valuation of Sports: Temporal Embedding and Ordering Effects." *Journal of Sports Economics*, 7, 267–288.

Noll, Roger G., and Andrew Zimbalist, eds. (1997). *Sports, Jobs, and Taxes.* Washington, DC: The Brookings Institution, 1997.

Owen, J. G. (2003). "The Stadium Game: Cities Versus Teams." *Journal of Sports Economics*, 4, 183–202.

Porter, Philip K., and Christopher R. Thomas. (2010). "Public Subsidies and the Location and Pricing of Sports." *Southern Economic Journal*, 76, 693–710.

Quirk, James, and Rodney D. Fort. (1997). *Pay Dirt: The Business of Professional Team Sports* (chapters 2 and 3). Princeton, NJ: Princeton University Press.

Walton, Harry, Alberto Longo, and Peter Dawson. (2008). "A Contingent Valuation of the 2012 London Olympic Games: A Regional Perspective." *Journal of Sports Economics*, 9, 304–317.

15

Economic Impact of Sports Events

1 INTRODUCTION

Major sports events undeniably bring with them large crowds of fans and media. The Super Bowl, Major League Baseball's (MLB's) All-Star Game, the Masters Golf Tournament, and big home football games in College Station, Auburn, Tallahassee, and Clemson all attract hordes of people and an apparent burst of economic activity. Thousands of people flock to these events, and they spend plenty of money in the local area. In addition to their spending at the event (tickets, concessions, and souvenirs), these fans spend substantial sums at local hotels and motels, car rental agencies, bars and restaurants, gas stations, T-shirt shops, and so on. This first round of spending provides income to residents in the local community, which results in subsequent rounds of spending. There is a multiplied effect of the initial spending, which is the economic impact of the sports event. Sports leagues and organizations often grossly exaggerate this economic impact for their own purposes. The National Football League (NFL), for example, claims that the impact of the Super Bowl is hundreds of millions of dollars. As we will see, however, such claims are dubious.

In this chapter, we examine the fundamentals of economic impact analysis. We begin with a simple multiplier model and explain why the impact of an event is not as large as some leagues and organizations would have us believe. We also review and evaluate some empirical studies that have been conducted to test the reliability of some claimed impacts.

2 ECONOMIC IMPACT ANALYSIS: FUNDAMENTALS

As a general matter, it is easy to say how one should perform an economic impact study. The first step is to measure all of the net spending in the local area (suitably defined) that is the result of hosting the sports event in question. Care must be taken to include only incremental spending that can be attributed to the event. This means that adjustments must be made to account for *displacement* and *substitution*. Displacement occurs when the out-of-town visitors who attend the event cause other would-be visitors to go elsewhere. Substitution occurs when local residents buy hot dogs at the ballpark instead of lunch at their usual place. Once all of the net incremental spending has been identified, local impact multipliers are then applied. The total economic impact is the product of the net incremental spending and the multiplier. From this total, one should deduct any local costs of being a host. These added costs would include overtime pay for police and emergency personnel, cleanup costs, congestion costs, and any other costs that arise due to the event.

Although it is relatively easy to summarize the appropriate steps to take, it is difficult to implement them in practice. Difficulties surface at both major steps. First, identifying the correct net incremental spending is difficult because actually controlling for displacement and substitution is nearly impossible. Second, the correct multiplier is hard to isolate. We explore these issues with some care in what follows, but do so in reverse order. First, we examine local impact multipliers, and second, we explore the difficulties in determining the net incremental expenditures.

Box 15.1 ***Impact of the Indianapolis Motor Speedway***

In 2000, there were three major events at the Indianapolis Motor Speedway (IMS): the Indy 500, NASCAR's Brickyard 400, and a Formula One race, the U.S. Grand Prix.* An economic impact study estimated the contribution to the central Indiana economy at $727 million. This was broken down as follows:

Indy 500	$336.6 million
Brickyard 400	$219.5
U.S. Grand Prix	$170.8
Total	$726.9

In addition, IMS needed some renovation to accommodate the Formula One race, and this added another $80.9 million, for a grand total of $807.8 million. The study also estimated an employment effect of 16,000 jobs.

The study found that visitors spend an average of $187 per day on food, drinks, souvenirs, local transportation, and lodging. It predicted that sales taxes would amount to $17.7 million and state income taxes would be $7.3 million.

* "IMS Worth $727M in Impact Study," *Sports Business Journal*, Sept. 11, 2000, p. 57.

3 MULTIPLIERS: SIMPLE ECONOMIC THEORY

A sporting event often attracts fans from far and wide. These fans spend money on hotel rooms, meals, drinks, car rentals, souvenirs, and a host of other things. Those who sell these goods and services then have money to spend on food, clothing, new cars, appliances, and a wide array of other goods and services. This second round of spending generates the income necessary for a third round of spending, which leads to a fourth round. This process does not lead to an infinite increase in the income of a local economy because there are leakages from the local economy that make each successive round of spending somewhat smaller than the preceding round. This makes the impact converge to a finite number.

3.1 Simple Multipliers

Suppose that we want to find the economic impact of a Penn State home football game. If 100,000 fans attend the game, they may spend an average of, say, $200 each on tickets, food, lodging, gasoline, and souvenirs. Thus, the first round of spending amounts to $20 million. If the marginal propensity to consume is 80 percent and the marginal propensity to save is 20 percent, then $4 million will leak out of the spending stream and into savings accounts, and $16 million will be spent in the second round. Some 20 percent of this (or $3.2 million) will go into savings, and $12.8 million will be spent. Each successive round of spending gets smaller because of the leakage into savings. These leakages put a limit on the total economic impact of a Penn State home game. In the limit, the simple multiplier for an exogenous spending shock is

$$M = \frac{1}{1 - mpc},$$

where *mpc* is the marginal propensity to consume.[1] In the appendix to this chapter, we show why this is true.

In our example, the marginal propensity to consume is 0.80, which means that we spend 80 percent of any additional income on consumption and save the remaining 20 percent. Then the effect of a one dollar increase in local spending will be:

$$M = \frac{1}{0.2} = 5.$$

Consequently, the total economic impact will be the initial increase in spending times the multiplier. In our example, the $20 million in initial spending yields a multiplied impact of $100 million, which would be most welcome in any local economy.

Table 15.1 summarizes the subsequent rounds of spending following a Penn State home game. An initial jolt of exogenous spending of $20 million leads to $16 million in the second round for a total of $36 million. In the third round, expenditures increase by another $12.8 million, for a total of $48.8 million. This table shows that total expenditures climb to nearly $73.8 million after only six rounds of spending. It also shows that spending in each successive round gets smaller and smaller. In the limit, an *mpc* of 0.80 will result in a total impact of $100 million.

3.2 Two Caveats

There are two caveats to bear in mind when thinking about spending multipliers. First, there is an implicit assumption that all supply curves are perfectly

[1] See Michael Parkin (2007), *Economics*, 8th ed., Boston: Addison-Wesley.

Table 15.1. Spending Multiplier

Round	Spending	Saving	Total Spending
1	$20	–	$20
2	$16	$4	$36
3	$12.8	$3.2	$48.8
4	$10.24	$2.56	$59.04
5	$8.19	$2.05	$67.23
6	$6.55	$1.64	$73.78
∞			$100

Note: These calculations are based on the assumption that the *mpc* is 0.80 and savings is the only leakage. The spending and saving in the final round are so small they are effectively zero.

elastic (that is, horizontal). This means that we are assuming that the increased economic activity has no effect on prices. This assumption may not be realistic in the short run. If anything, we would expect prices to rise in the short run when demand increases because short-run supply curves are usually positively sloped. Usually, hotel room rates shoot up when a major event comes to town. Promotional discounts disappear, and other prices rise. Second, the full multiplied impact may take an awfully long time. In principle, the number of rounds of spending is infinite, which would obviously take forever. We do not want to overstate the importance of this numerical fact because the vast majority of the total impact will be realized with just a few rounds of spending. In Table 15.1, we can see that nearly 74 percent of the total impact in that example is realized in just six rounds of spending.

3.3 More General Multipliers

For the analysis of local multipliers used to conduct serious economic impact studies, we have to account for (at least) two other factors that reduce spending at each successive round. First, income is subject to taxation. As a result, the money available for spending must be reduced by the taxes paid on the income, as well as any sales taxes that may apply. Tax revenues reduce the consumption possibilities as the tax goes into the government's coffers rather than into local cash registers. Second, imports into the local economy cause another leakage that reduces the amount spent in subsequent rounds. Locally, much of what we buy is "imported" into the local economy from other areas of the country or from foreign countries. Spending on imports obviously reduces local spending in subsequent rounds. As a result, a more general multiplier can be derived as follows. First, we start by observing that income is the sum of consumption (c), investment (i), government spending (g), and exports (x) less imports (m):

$$Y = c + i + g + x - m.$$

Consumption is equal to the marginal propensity to consume times after-tax income:

$$c = mpc(1 - t)Y,$$

where t is the tax rate and, therefore, $(1 - t)Y$ is the after-tax income. Imports equal the marginal propensity to import (*mpm*) times after-tax income:

$$m = mpm(1 - t)Y.$$

By substitution, we can write income as:

$$Y = mpc(1 - t)Y + I + G + X - mpm(1 - t)Y.$$

This can be rearranged algebraically as follows:

$$Y - (1 - t)(mpc - mpm)Y = i + g + x$$
$$Y[1 - (1 - t)(mpc - mpm)] = i + g + x.$$

We can solve this equation for Y and write income as

$$Y = \frac{i + g + x}{1 - (1 - t)(mpc - mpm)}.$$

The multiplier for an exogenous shock to the level of exports is given by the derivative of Y with respect to X:

$$M = \frac{1}{1 - (1 - t)(mpc - mpm)}.$$

Suppose that the combined tax rate on incremental spending is 25 percent. This would account for income taxes and any sales taxes. In that case, $t = 0.25$. In a local economy, a good deal of what we buy is imported from elsewhere. Most food, drinks, clothing, household goods, cars, toys, and much more originate outside the local economy. For illustrative purposes, suppose that imports account for 50 percent of what we buy. In that case, *mpm* equals 0.50. The economic impact multiplier would then be

$$M = \frac{1}{1 - (0.75)(0.80 - 0.50)}$$
$$M = \frac{1}{1 - 0.225}$$
$$M = 1.29$$

Instead of a naïve multiplier of 5 when $mpc = 0.80$, we now have a multiplier of only 1.29. This obviously reduces the economic impact of any sports event – the Super Bowl, Masters Golf Tournament, World Series, or Penn State home game – to a more modest level. In our Penn State example, the initial spending of \$20 million now results in a total impact of 1.29 times \$20 million, or \$25.8 million, which is much smaller than our initial estimate of \$100 million. This is not to say that such an event is unwelcome, but only that the economic impact is apt to be considerably smaller than some analysts might claim.

3.4 Estimating Local Multipliers

Estimating a numerical value for the multiplier is an enormous undertaking. No one who conducts an economic impact study actually estimates multipliers from scratch. Instead, the analyst starts with an estimate from a government agency and tweaks it for the purpose at hand.

Good starting points for local multipliers are the regional multipliers estimated by the Bureau of Economic Analysis at the U.S. Department of Commerce. Using massive amounts of data, their Regional Impact Multiplier System (RIMS) produces multipliers for various expenditure categories. These multipliers vary across expenditure categories because the leakages will vary. For example, the multiplier for expenditures on salaries is quite low because of income taxes, Social Security and Medicare taxes, sales taxes, and the significance of spending on imports. The multiplier for spending on food is somewhat higher because a good deal of service goes into food preparation and sales. Even these RIMS multipliers are generally too large for a local area sports event because there is more leakage from a local area than from a state or a region. Consequently, even these multipliers should be reduced further.

4 MEASURING INCREMENTAL SPENDING

Even if an analyst uses the appropriate multiplier, he or she may still make an error if the exogenous spending shock is measured incorrectly. For example, suppose that we did a careful survey of spending by attendees at the Super Bowl in Miami and the spending was $100 million. Given a multiplier of 1.29, we would conclude that the economic impact on the Miami economy was $129 million.[2] However, this presupposes that the presence of the Super Bowl's attendees did not displace other visitors. In other words, if the Super Bowl attendees crowded out other visitors to the Miami area, then their spending overstates the net incremental spending. For illustrative purposes, suppose that tourists who would otherwise have been in Miami went somewhere else because of the Super Bowl crowd. If they would have spent $20 million, then the net initial impact of the Super Bowl would only be $80 million rather than $100 million. Suppose further that a convention was held in Orlando that would have been held in Miami except for the Super Bowl congestion. If this displaced expenditure amounted to $15 million, then the net initial spending would have to be reduced even further to $65 million. With a multiplier of 1.29, the economic impact of the Super Bowl would be only $83.85 million rather than $129 million. This, of course, is still important to the local community, but it is far less than originally estimated.

In many cases, analysts erroneously fail to account for displaced expenditures and compound this error by using an inflated multiplier. In the Super Bowl example, suppose one used a multiplier of 2.5 and ignored displacement. The claimed impact would then be $250 million, whereas the actual sum is the

[2] I do not mean to suggest that the correct numerical value is 1.29. That number is purely hypothetical based on an *mpc* of 0.80, a tax rate of 0.25, and an *mpm* of 0.50.

much smaller value of $83.85 million. In practice, this compound error is not rare.

Displacement is a tricky issue because some displacement may only be temporary. For example, suppose that the Super Bowl is being held in New Orleans on January 30. If the Super Bowl were being played elsewhere, the American Numismatic Society would have held its annual convention in New Orleans on that date. Crowded out for that date, the numismatists postpone the convention for one week, but still go to New Orleans. This displacement is not really relevant because there is no loss that should be deducted from the Super Bowl spending. In contrast, if the American Numismatic Society decided to go elsewhere, then their loss should be offset against any Super Bowl gain. These are easy cases to see and perhaps measure, but there could be numerous individual decisions that would be more difficult to identify. Even in this case, we may not know about the displacement. The Super Bowl schedule is known well in advance, and convention planners may simply plan on going elsewhere. There is no way of knowing about such displacement.

4.1 Substitution

Some spending at a sports event is a substitute for other local spending. As a general proposition, spending by local residents should be excluded from careful economic impact studies, but not always. Consider a San Francisco native who attended the 2007 MLB All-Star Game. Suppose her expenditure on a ticket; food and drinks before, during, and after the game; a souvenir; and parking amounted to $300. If she had not spent $300 at the game, she would have spent $100 on two dinners, $50 on a round of golf, $25 on a Giants T-shirt, $25 on a concert ticket, and the remaining $100 on odds and ends over the next month or so. In this case, spending on the All-Star Game substituted for these other local expenditures. From the perspective of economic impact, she contributed no incremental spending; she simply substituted one local expenditure for another. Thus, none of her spending should be included in the analysis.

Excluding all spending by local residents may not be correct either. Suppose another local resident also spent $300 at the All-Star Game. In the absence of the game, however, this fan would not have spent the money locally. If this fan would have spent that $300 during a trip to New York, then that out-of-area expenditure would have substituted for the local spending at the All-Star game. In that event, it would be correct to include her local spending in the economic impact of the All-Star Game.

4.2 Attribution

There is also a problem of attribution. Consider the Capital One Bowl in Orlando. In 2006, Auburn (Southeastern Conference) played Wisconsin (Big Ten) and attracted a big crowd. Some of the attendees were local residents whose spending ordinarily should not count because of the substitution effect. Those who were from out of town, primarily from Alabama and Wisconsin, were the ones whose spending should have been counted. Even though the game

Table 15.2. Triple Crown of Surfing: Direct Spending[1]

Type	Number	Days	Expenditures[2]
Contestants	164	30	$228,000
Companies	31	30	31,000
Media	223	10	417,010
Visitors I[3]	1,539	21.5	6,189,254
Visitors II[4]	1,650	1.0	308,575
Organizers	–	–	1,050,000
Corporate	–	–	640,000
Total			$8,863,839

[1] These data were estimated for Vans Triple Crown of Surfing by Markrich Research.
[2] Based on Markrich surveys and data from the State of Hawaii.
[3] Visitors I were in the Hawaii area only because of the surfing competition.
[4] Visitors II were in Hawaii anyway but budgeted a day for watching the surfing competition.

was played on January 2, surveys showed that the average fan stayed for six days. During that time, perhaps some of these fans visited Disney World for two days, Universal Studios for one day, Sea World for one day, and a variety of other area attractions – in addition to spending one day at the game. How much of their total spending should be attributed to the Capital One Bowl? One could argue that none of them would have been in Orlando if it had not been for the game, and, therefore, all of their spending should be attributed to the game. But one could just as easily argue that the Wisconsin folks would not have made the long trip to Orlando just for the game. It was really the Orlando area attractions that lured them from the Wisconsin snow to the Florida sunshine. In that event, the game should receive far less credit for the infusion of spending. Short of an extraordinarily detailed and in-depth survey, this problem of attribution cannot be resolved. Thus, there is an element of ambiguity that will remain.

5 PROFESSIONAL SURFING CONTESTS: AN EXAMPLE FROM HAWAII

There are many examples of economic impact studies that overstate the benefits to a host city, but not all of them are irresponsible. In this section, we review a study that seems to reach reasonably conservative conclusions.

At the end of the 2006 professional surfing season, the Triple Crown of Surfing is held on Hawaii's famed North Shore. The international field competed on three North Shore beaches. As a result, thousands of people – contestants, industry people, and fans – visited Hawaii and spent money in the local economy. In fact, they spent a lot of money, which is summarized in Table 15.2.

The contestants and their companions stayed in Hawaii for about 30 days. The media people apparently came and went for each event and, consequently, they stayed for only 10 days. Visitors who came specifically for the surfing competition and would not have been in Hawaii otherwise stayed an average of 21.5 days. There were some attendees who were visiting Hawaii primarily for other reasons but set aside a day for watching the surfing competition. As a result, they were included in the study for one day. Now, one could argue that this treatment is appropriate only if they actually stayed an extra day because of the surfing contest. If they did not extend their stay specifically for the surfing, then they would have done something else – visit Maui, play golf, sip tropical drinks, or lie on the beach at Waikiki.

In addition to visitor spending, the organizers spent $1,050,000 that they would not have spent otherwise. Finally, some $640,000 was spent by participating companies. The grand total of direct spending associated with the Triple Crown of Surfing in 2006 was estimated to have been $8,863,839.

The study estimated a multiplied impact of some $14.6 million. This implies a local impact multiplier of 1.65, which seems fairly reasonable and may even be a little conservative.[3]

6 ESTIMATION AND VERIFICATION

In this section, we examine some examples of empirical analyses of economic impact studies. Most analysts are quite critical of the work that has been done on behalf of leagues and event organizers with vested interests in pumping up the numbers. They are skeptical about claims of large impacts because large impacts are not consistent with other economic evidence.

6.1 Economic Impact of the Super Bowl

Of all the annual mega-events in sports, the biggest in the United States is the Super Bowl.[4] According to the NFL and the economic impact studies that they commission, the Super Bowl's economic impact on the host city is in the $250 to $300 million range. Such numbers are impressive to say the least and would surely warrant some spending and some concessions by the host city. After all, as the saying goes, "you have to spend money to make money." These estimates, however, do not appear to withstand much scrutiny.

Visitors to a host city are present for a very short period of time. During their stay, they spend money at bars, restaurants, hotels and motels, car rental agencies, and a wide assortment of retail outlets. Most of this spending is subject to sales taxes. If the NFL's claims were accurate, we would expect to see a spike in sales tax receipts for the month of January in the county where the Super

[3] Apparently, thousands of local surfing fans attended the competition. None of their spending was included. This, of course, is appropriate, but is not always done in economic impact studies.

[4] This discussion depends on Phillip Porter, "Mega-Sports Events as Municipal Investments: A Critique of Impact Analyses," in J. Fizel, E. Gustafson, and L. Hadley, eds., *Sports Economics: Current Research*, New York: Praeger, 1999. See also Phillip Porter, "Super Bowl Impact Figures a Super Stretch," *Sports Business Journal*, Jan. 15, 2001; and Andrew Zimbalist, "NFL Mixes Hype and Reality in Assessing Super Bowl's Economic Impact," *Sports Business Journal*, Feb. 2, 2006.

Bowl was played. Accordingly, one way to verify the NFL's claims is to examine sales tax receipts. If they are not consistent with an increase in taxable sales of $250 million, then it is reasonable to infer that the actual impact differed from the claimed amount. This is precisely the verification effort adopted by Phillip Porter. Porter examined sales tax receipts in the month during which a Super Bowl was held (January) for the years preceding and succeeding a Super Bowl game. A careful statistical analysis showed no significant impact of the Super Bowl on sales tax receipts. In other words, Porter did not find a significant increase in the sales tax receipts for January in a Super Bowl year over the January receipts in the preceding year, nor did he find a significant decrease in the following January. As a consequence, there could hardly be much net incremental spending during the Super Bowl year. Part of the explanation is that spending by Super Bowl attendees displaced spending by those who would have spent money if the Super Bowl had not been there.

Porter also subjected the claims made for Super Bowl XXXV, which was played in Tampa, to a reality check. The alleged economic impact was supposed to be $250 million, which Porter characterized as a "gross exaggeration." He backed up this assessment by pointing out that Hillsborough County (which is where Tampa is located) normally experienced about $1 billion in sales per month. This amounts to about $65 million every two days. If the actual Super Bowl spending were only about one-fourth of the NFL's estimate, Hillsborough County sales would have had to double on Super Bowl weekend. Sales of everything – cars, clothes, food, toys – would have had to double. This obviously could not happen, and therefore, the NFL's claim should be viewed with considerable skepticism.

The NFL also predicted that 100,000 people would be visiting Tampa for the Super Bowl, but Porter pointed out that there could not be a net increase of 100,000 people. First, assuming double occupancy, Tampa would need 50,000 hotel rooms to house them, but the city did not have that many vacant hotel rooms. Second, how could there be 100,000 net new arrivals in a short period of time? The number of flights into all Tampa Bay area airports would have had to more than double to deliver an extra 100,000 people. Thus, the NFL's estimates failed Porter's reality checks.

6.2 MLB's All-Star Game

MLB's midseason classic – the All-Star Game – is a short-term event.[5] Played on a Tuesday, the players and many out-of-towners arrive on Monday and leave on Wednesday.[6] Even for that brief spurt of economic activity, MLB's estimates of the economic impact ranged from $62 million to $75 million for the 1999 game in Boston. In 1999, MLB predicted an impact of at least $70 million for Milwaukee for the 2002 All-Star Game. According to Baade and Matheson, such

[5] This section is based on Robert A. Baade and Victor A. Matheson (2001), "Home Run or Wild Pitch?" Assessing the Economic Impact of Major League Baseball's All-Star Game," *Journal of Sports Economics*, 2, 307–327.

[6] MLB has tried to add some extra activities to prolong the event, so it may take up to five days for some visitors.

Table 15.3. Hosts of Major League Baseball All-Star Games, 2000–2012

Year	Host	Year Built
2000	Turner Field (Atlanta)	1996
2001	Safeco Field (Seattle)	1999
2002	Miller Park (Milwaukee)	2001
2003	U.S. Cellular Field* (Chicago)	1991
2004	Minute Maid Park (Houston)	2000
2005	Comerica Park (Detroit)	2000
2006	PNC Park (Pittsburgh)	2001
2007	AT&T Park (San Francisco)	2000
2008	Yankee Stadium (New York)	1923
2009	Busch Stadium (St. Louis)	2006
2010	Angel Stadium* (Anaheim)	1966
2011	Chase Field (Phoenix)	1998
2012	Kauffman Stadium* (Kansas City)	1973

* These ball parks were substantially renovated prior to the award of the All-Star Game.

estimates are dubious at best. This raises a serious question: Does MLB deliberately mislead people about the All-Star game's economic impact? If so, why would they do that?

There is no real evidence that MLB does not actually believe the inflated estimates that it puts forward, but there is an interesting pattern. MLB promises the All-Star Game to host cities if they build new ballparks for the home team. Apparently, they deliver on those promises. Between 1970 and 1997, 15 new ballparks were built. All but two of them were awarded an All-Star game within five years of construction.[7] MLB's demand for new facilities is not inflexible. For example, the 2008 All-Star Game was awarded to Yankee Stadium because that was the final year that the Yankees played in the "House That Ruth Built" before moving to their new ballpark.[8] But there is an apparent pattern. Table 15.3 shows the host stadium and the year it was built for All-Star games played during the 2000–2009 period. Some are old, but most are new.

A good deal of the financial support for the construction of new ballparks comes from public coffers. MLB's claims of a $70 million economic impact of an All-Star Game may soothe concerns about the wisdom of investing in a stadium. Not all cities buy into the MLB hype. Miami, for example, dragged its feet for years about building a new ballpark for the Marlins.

Baade and Matheson tested MLB's claims by looking at the effect of hosting an All-Star Game on employment growth in the host city. To do this, they constructed a multiple regression model in which the dependent variable was the

[7] The new Comiskey Park in Chicago lost out because it had hosted an All-Star Game within the preceding 10 years. Miami lost out because of the uncertainty of the Marlins' future location.

[8] Jack Curry, "Yankee Stadium Gets One Last All-Star Game," *New York Times*, Feb. 1, 2007.

percentage change in employment in a city. They used a number of explanatory variables including a dummy variable for the year in which a city hosted an All-Star Game.[9] If MLB's claims were correct, one would expect the coefficient on the All-Star Game dummy variable to be positive and statistically significant. If the claims were empty, the coefficient would not be statistically significant and therefore would be considered equal to zero.

Baade and Matheson analyzed the effect of 23 All-Star Games played during the 1973–1997 period. The All-Star Game coefficient was statistically significant in only one case, but the sign was negative, which would indicate a *decline* in employment growth. After further careful consideration, the authors concluded that there was no empirical support for the claims made by MLB regarding the economic impact of the All-Star Game.

Baade and Matheson conducted another empirical test using taxable sales data in California. During the sample period, there were three All-Star Games in California. The host cities were Oakland in 1987, Anaheim in 1989, and San Diego in 1992. The authors examined the ratio of taxable sales for the county in which we find the host city to taxable sales for the state. If the All-Star Game had a substantial impact on the local economy, it should have caused a positive jump in that ratio when the All-Star Game came to town. If the presence of the All-Star Game caused congestion that crowded out other tourists and spending by local residents, there would have been no effect on the ratio.

In fact, the authors found a *decrease* in the ratio for each All-Star Game. This again suggests that the presence of MLB's All-Star Game does not have a large positive net effect on the local economy.

6.3 Impact of College Football

At the National Collegiate Athletic Association Division I-A level, college football is big business.[10] Attendance is high, TV ratings are high, coaches' salaries are high, investments in facilities are high, and bowl payouts are high. On a football weekend, many fans pour into college towns for the game. At first blush, one would suppose that all this activity would have a large, positive effect on the local economy. After all, the hotels are full, the restaurants are crowded, and the cash registers seem to be ringing constantly.

Baade, Baumann, and Matheson used statistical techniques to estimate the economic impact of college football on the economy of the host city. The authors examined football programs in 63 Metropolitan Statistical Areas over the 1970–2004 period. These 63 areas include every team in a Bowl Championship Series conference. The results of their statistical analysis are somewhat surprising given the apparent game-day spending. Neither real personal income nor employment received a statistically significant boost from college football games. Again, displacement and substitution seem to be at work here.

[9] A dummy variable equals one for an All-Star Game year and zero otherwise.

[10] This section depends on Robert A. Baade, Robert Baumann, and Victor A. Matheson (2008), "Assessing the Economic Impact of College Football Games on Local Economics," *Journal of Sports Economics*, 9, 628–643.

7 CONCLUDING REMARKS

Ex ante economic impact studies, which are usually commissioned by a party with an ax to grind, estimate direct spending at an event and then apply a multiplier to obtain the predicted economic impact. When economists do an *ex post* analysis, the *ex ante* claims are almost never confirmed. These *ex post* studies examine taxable sales, sales tax revenues, employment, and real personal income. The economic effect of a sports event – Super Bowl, All-Star Game, Final Four – may be there in the local economy, but if it is, it is buried. Statistical efforts to unearth those economic effects have proved largely futile. Thus, one is forced to the conclusion that the bloated claims of those with a vested interest cannot be trusted. If a large impact were there, we should be able to measure it. Thus, the economic benefits appear to be largely illusory.

PROBLEMS AND QUESTIONS

1. It is clear that the "displacement" issue poses a serious problem for accurately calculating the economic impact of a sporting event.
   a. Explain why this is true.
   b. How could an analyst estimate the extent of displacement?
2. Explain why local economy multipliers are apt to be much smaller than national economy multipliers.
3. Following the 2007 Super Bowl in Miami, the owner of the Sleep Cheap motel found that by gouging the Super Bowl attendees, he made enough money in one week to buy a new Toyota Camry. How much of the Camry's $25,000 purchase price leaked out of the Miami economy, and how much stayed for subsequent rounds of spending?
4. "It is doubtful that a new NFL team in Los Angeles will have much economic impact." Do you agree or disagree? Explain.
5. Local hotel room rates increased from $150 per night to $250 per night during the Super Bowl week. If Christina went to Tampa for the Super Bowl, but Laura did not go to Busch Gardens because of the Super Bowl, what is the appropriate amount to attribute to the Super Bowl?
6. During the 1996 Summer Olympic Games in Atlanta, many law firms simply closed for two weeks because of the crowds and traffic congestion. How would you include this in an economic impact study of those Olympic Games?
7. A noted critic of the NFL's economic impact boasts found fiscal shortfalls for cities hosting Super Bowls. For example, he pointed out that the Super Bowl in Miami led to a net increase of some 5,525 visitors. If they stayed for four days and spent $400 per day, the direct impact would be $8.8 million. At a 6.5 percent sales tax rate, tax receipts would increase by $572,000. "But the additional fiscal costs associated with hosting the game were estimated at $4 million. Net impact: minus $3.4 million." If you were an NFL official, how would you respond?

8. In the mood for Chinese food, a University of California–Berkeley faculty member and his family were headed for San Francisco's famed Chinatown. Someone remembered that there was apt to be quite a crowd because of the All-Star Game. As a result, they took a detour to Oakland's less famous Chinatown. How would this affect the economic impact of the All-Star Game? How would a serious analyst discover the extent of these decisions to go elsewhere?
9. Review the estimated impact of the three races at the Indianapolis Motor Speedway. What sorts of reality checks and empirical verification would you suggest?
10. Suppose that merchants hid some taxable sales during mega-sports events. How would this affect empirical verification of the claimed impact?

APPENDIX: DERIVATION OF THE SIMPLE MULTIPLIER

In principle, there is no end to the rounds of successive spending because the leakage in each round is partial. However, spending in each successive round does get smaller – it is equal to the *mpc* times the spending in the preceding round. The final total spending (S) attributable to an initial spending shock of Δy is equal to

$$S = \Delta y + mpc\Delta y + (mpc)^2\Delta y + (mpc)^3\Delta y + \cdots,$$

which can be written as

$$S = \Delta y(1 + mpc + (mpc)^2 + (mpc)^3 + \cdots).$$

Thus, S is the product of an initial jolt of spending (Δy) and the infinite series in parenthesis. The term in parentheses is the multiplier, which we can write as M:

$$M = 1 + mpc + (mpc)^2 + (mpc)^3 + \cdots.$$

Now multiply both sides by *mpc* to get

$$mpc^* M = mpc + (mpc)^2 + (mpc)^3 + \cdots.$$

Subtracting $mpc * M$ from M yields:

$$M - mpc^* M = 1.$$

Solving for M, we have

$$M = \frac{1}{1 - mpc},$$

and

$$S = \left(\frac{1}{1 - mpc}\right)\Delta y.$$

REFERENCES AND FURTHER READING

Baade, R. A., R. W. Baumann, and V. A. Matheson. (2008). "Assessing the Economic Impact of College Football Games on Local Economies." *Journal of Sports Economics*, 9, 628–643.

Baade, R. A., and R. F. Dye. (1988). "An Analysis of the Economic Rationale for Public Subsidization of Sports Stadiums." *Annals of Regional Science*, XXII, 37–47.

Baade, R. A., and Matheson, V. A. (2001). "Home Run or Wild Pitch? Assessing the Economic Impact of Major League Baseball's All-Star Game." *Journal of Sports Economics*, 2, 307–327.

Baade, R. A., and Matheson, V. A. (2004). "The Quest for the Cup: Assessing the Economic Impact of the World Cup." *Regional Studies*, 38, 343–354.

Carlino, G., and N. E., Coulson. (2004). "Compensating Differentials and the Social Benefits of the NFL." *Journal of Urban Economics*, 56, 25–50.

Coates, D., and B. R. Humphreys. (2002). "The Economic Impact of Postseason Play in Professional Sports." *Journal of Sports Economics*, 3, 291–299.

Coates, D., and B. R. Humphreys. (2003). "Professional Sports Facilities, Franchises, and Urban Economic Development." *Public Finance and Management* 3, 335–357.

Crompton, J. L. (1995). "Economic Impact Analysis of Sports Facilities and Events: Eleven Sources of Misapplication." *Journal of Sport Management*, 9, 14–35.

Hudson, I. (2001). "The Use and Misuse of Economic Impact Analysis: The Case of Professional Sports." *Journal of Sport & Social Issues*, 25, 20–39.

Lavoie, M., and G. Rodriguez. (2005). "The Economic Impact of Professional Teams on Monthly Hotel Occupancy Rates of Canadian Cities: A Box-Jenkins Approach." *Journal of Sports Economics*, 6, 314–324.

Lentz, B. F., and D. N. Laband. (2009). "The Impact of Intercollegiate Athletics on Employment in the Restaurant and Accommodations Industries." *Journal of Sports Economics*, 10, 351–368.

Lertwachara, K., and J. J. Cochran. 2007. "An Event Study of the Economic Impact of Professional Sport Franchises on Local U.S. Economies." *Journal of Sports Economics*, 8, 244–254.

Matheson, Victor A. "Contrary Evidence on the Economic Effect." *Journal of Sports Economics*, 6, 420–428.

Noll, Roger G., and Andrew Zimbalist. (1997). *Sports, Jobs, and Taxes: The Economic Impact of Sports Teams and Stadiums.* Washington, DC: The Brookings Institution.

Parkin, Michael. (2007). *Economics*, 8th ed. Boston: Addison-Wesley.

Quirk, James, and Rodney Fort. (1999). *Hard Ball: The Abuse of Power in Pro Team Sports* (chapter 7). Princeton, NJ: Princeton University Press.

Siegfried, J., and Andrew Zimbalist. (2002a). "The Economics of Sports Facilities and Their Communities." *Journal of Economic Perspectives*, 14, 95–114.

Siegfried, John, and Andrew Zimbalist. (2002b). "A Note on the Local Economic Impact of Sports Expenditures." *Journal of Sports Economics*, 3, 361–366.

Walton, Harry, Alberto Longo, and Peter Dawson. (2008). "A Contingent Valuation of the 2012 London Olympic Games: A Regional Perspective." *Journal of Sports Economics*, 9, 304–317.

16

Financing Sports Facilities

1 INTRODUCTION

There is a wide array of sports facilities: bowling alleys, golf courses, tennis courts, multiuse athletic fields, parks, public school facilities, and, of course, the professional venues. Some of these facilities are privately financed, and many others are publicly financed. In the vast majority of cases, privately owned facilities are privately funded. For example, privately owned bowling alleys, golf courses, racquetball courts, health and fitness centers, and tennis clubs are financed by the owners of those facilities with private debt and equity. Similarly, governmentally owned facilities are publicly funded. For example, municipal golf courses, community swimming pools, high school athletic facilities, and parks are publicly financed through bonds and taxes. This, of course, makes perfect sense: facilities for private use are privately owned and privately financed, and those for public use are governmentally owned and publicly financed. When it comes to professional team sports, however, we often have public ownership and private use. For the most part, the stadium, ballpark, or arena is at least partially funded by local and/or state government, which then leases the facility to the professional club on very favorable terms. These "sweetheart" deals are designed to attract pro teams to a city and to keep them there.

In this chapter, we begin with some principles of sound investment decisions. We examine the case for public subsidies of privately owned facilities and explore some political realities. Then we turn our attention to the nature and extent of public funding for the benefit of professional clubs. We also examine some issues of fairness as they relate to paying for sports facilities that are used by few people in the community that is paying for them. Along the way, we analyze the ways in which state and local governments can raise the money necessary to pay for sports facilities. As we will see, local governments often use eminent domain to acquire the needed land, and that imposes added costs on some members of the community.

2 INVESTING IN A SPORTS FACILITY

For a private investor, investing in a sports facility – a stadium, ballpark, arena, bowling alley – is like any other investment that has initial costs and future payoffs. From an economic perspective, a new facility will be built if the net present value (*NPV*) of the investment is positive.[1] More formally, it makes economic sense to build a sports facility if

$$NPV = \sum_{t=1}^{T} R_t/(1+i)^t - I > 0,$$

where R_t is the net profit on operations in period t, T is the useful life of the facility, i is the discount rate, and I is the initial investment to acquire the land and construct the facility. The facility will be profitable over its life because the present value of the operating profits exceeds the initial construction cost. In such cases, no public subsidy is necessary to make the project economically viable. We can illustrate this basic principle with a numerical example.

2.1 A Numerical Example

Suppose that the initial construction cost for a baseball park is $500 million. The useful economic life of the new ballpark is 20 years, and the appropriate discount rate is 10 percent. Finally, assume that the expected operating profit is $60 million per year. These values can be substituted into the net present value expression:

$$NPV = \sum_{t=1}^{20} \$60/(1.10)^t - \$500.$$

From the Table A2.3 showing the present value of an annuity of $1 (see Chapter 2), we know that a dollar per year for 20 years at a 10 percent discount rate has a present value of $8.514. As a result, $60 million per year for 20 years has a present value of (8.514)($60 million), which is $510,840,000. Thus, this project has a net present value of $10.84 million, which means that it is economically viable.

2.2 Some Further Considerations

A more complete picture of the investment decision must include considerations of taxes on the operating profits, depreciation, and scrap values.[2] These alter and somewhat complicate the net present value calculations but do not change the fundamental message: if the net present value is positive, the investment is viable; otherwise it is not. For the sake of improved realism, we incorporate these considerations here.

Suppose that the corporate tax rate on profits is represented by τ. This means that the investor will get to keep $(1-\tau)R_t$ in each period and will turn

[1] Recall that we developed the mathematics of present value calculations in Chapter 2.

[2] Some people prefer to use the term *residual* value. Whatever term we use, the idea is the same; s represents the value of what is left at the end.

over τR_t to the government. The tax rules permit the investor to deduct depreciation of the ballpark from R_t. We can represent the depreciation in each period as D_t. Because depreciation is deductible, the tax is levied on $R_t - D_t$, and therefore, the tax bill will be $\tau(R_t - D_t)$ in each period. The investor then gets to keep $R_t - \tau(R_t - D_t)$, which we can write as $(1 - \tau)R_t + \tau D_t$. As a result, the net present value of the ballpark project is

$$NPV = \left((1 - \tau)\sum_{t=1}^{T} R_t/(1 + i)^t + \tau \sum_{t=1}^{T} D_t/(1 + i)^t - I\right).$$

If the after-tax *NPV* is positive, then the investment makes economic sense. In a case where the pretax *NPV* is positive but the posttax *NPV* is negative, the investment will not be viable because investors must respond to after-tax returns.

2.3 Scrap Value

The scrap value is what the land and facility are worth at the end of the facility's useful life. In principle, the scrap value could be positive or negative. In many cases, the scrap value is positive. First, over a long period of time, land tends to appreciate. As a result, once an aging stadium is removed, the land can be used for an office building or shopping complex. In other cases, the land may be useful for housing projects. Second, some of the rubble may command fairly high prices. For example, when historic facilities are dismantled, some fans will buy pieces as memorabilia. The rest of the rubble may be sold as well. However, the scrap value may be negative in other situations. It is possible for land values to appreciate only slightly in some blighted neighborhoods and for the costs of demolition to be large. Thus, S could be negative if the cost of tearing the facility down and hauling the rubble away exceeded the market value of the rubble and the land. Whether it is positive or negative, one would have to discount the scrap value to the present. Letting S represent the scrap value, the NPV of the facility would then be

$$NPV = (1 - \tau)\sum_{t=1}^{T} R_t/(1 + i)^t + \tau \sum_{t=1}^{T} D_t/(1 + i)^t + S/(1 + i)^T - I.$$

Now we can return to our numerical example. Let's assume that a straight line depreciation schedule is used. This means that one-twentieth of the initial investment can be deducted from the operating profit each year. In this case, that amounts to \$25 million. Let's also assume that there is a scrap value of \$50 million and that the corporate tax rate is 20 percent. The net present value of the ballpark project is now

$$\begin{aligned} NPV &= (0.80)\sum_{t=1}^{20} \$60/(1.10)^t + (0.20)\sum_{t=1}^{20} \$25/(1.10)^t + \$50/(1.10)^{20} - 500 \\ &= (0.80)(\$510{,}849{,}000) + (0.20)(\$212{,}850{,}000) \\ &\quad + \$7{,}450{,}000 - \$500{,}000{,}000. \end{aligned}$$

We can then do the arithmetic to find that the net present value is a negative \$41,308,000. Thus, the once profitable investment is now unprofitable and will be abandoned by private investors.

2.4 The Giants–Jets Stadium

The calculation of the *NPV* also can be somewhat complicated by a multiperiod investment. Consider, for example, the new Giants–Jets stadium in the Meadowlands, which opened in 2010. The total construction cost was estimated to be \$1.6 billion. For purposes of this illustration, suppose that the \$1.6 billion was spent as follows: \$200 million in 2007, \$500 million in 2008 and 2009, and \$400 million in 2010. In that event, the I in the *NPV* expression is the present value of that stream of payments. Assuming a discount rate of 12 percent, we have

$$I = \frac{\$200}{1.12} + \frac{\$500}{(1.12)^2} + \frac{\$500}{(1.12)^3} + \frac{\$400}{(1.12)^4}.$$

Thus, at the point of committing to the investment, the present value of the investment expenditure was

$$I = \$1{,}187{,}270{,}000.$$

The operating profits do not start to flow until 2010.[3] If the new stadium has a useful life of 30 years, then the present value of the operating profits will be

$$PV(R) = \sum_{t=4}^{33} R_t/(1.12)^t.$$

For the investment in the stadium to make any economic sense, the present value of the operating profits must exceed the initial investment of \$1,187,270,000. For this to be true, R_t must be at least \$231,888,671.[4] This operating profit is necessary to recover the initial construction costs. These necessary annual operating profits seem very high, but that is because they do not start until four years after the investment was made. Another factor that drives up the necessary operating profit is the discount rate of 12 percent. If we had used a lower discount rate, the minimum operating profits would have been lower.

3 PRIVATE AND PUBLIC FINANCING

In the distant past, sports facilities were funded by the clubs that used them. In other words, the facilities were privately owned and privately funded. As cities became concerned about keeping their team or attracting a team, they began

[3] This may not be literally true because personal seat licenses (PSLs) may be sold in advance. Revenue from naming rights could possibly begin before 2010. However, the vast majority of the revenues will not start until 2010.

[4] To calculate this sum, find the present value of \$1 for 34 years and subtract the present value of \$1 for 4 years; then divide that number into the present value of the initial construction costs.

Table 16.1. Financing of American League Ballparks

Team	Stadium	Date	Cost ($ millions)	Public ($ millions)	% Public
Baltimore Orioles	Oriole Park	04/06/1992	$100	N/A	N/A
Boston Red Sox	Fenway Park	04/20/1912	$0.65	N/A	N/A
Chicago White Sox	U.S. Cellular Field	04/18/1991	$167	$167	100.0
Cleveland Indians	Progressive Field	04/04/1994	$175	$91	52.0
Detroit Tigers	Comerica Park	04/11/2000	$300	$115	38.3
Kansas City Royals	Kauffman Stadium	04/10/1973	$320	$0	0
Los Angeles Angels	Angel Stadium of Anaheim	04/19/1966	$142	$0	0
Minnesota Twins	Target Field	04/03/2010	$544.4	$392	72.0
New York Yankees	New Yankee Stadium	04/03/2009	$1,300	$220	16.9
Oakland Athletics	Cisco Field	2012	$400[1]	$0	0
Seattle Mariners	Safeco Field	04/15/1999	$517.6	$340	65.7
Tampa Bay Rays	Tropicana Field	04/03/1990	$208	$0	0
Texas Rangers	Rangers Ballpark	04/01/1994	$191	$135	70.7
Toronto Blue Jays	Rogers Centre	06/05/1989	$600	$60	10.0

[1] The entire $400 million cost of Cisco field is privately financed with government assistance.
Note: Cisco Field was cancelled as of February 2009.
Source: http://www.ballparks.com/baseball/index.htm.

to offer support for stadium construction. At this time, there is a mixture of private and public funding. Tables 16.1 and 16.2 provide some information on this mix for baseball parks in the American League and National League, respectively. Some ballparks are funded entirely by private investors. For example, AT&T Park, home of the San Francisco Giants, was privately funded. At the other extreme, Nationals Park, home of the Washington Nationals, was funded almost entirely by Washington, D.C. The club was on the hook only for any cost overruns. In some other cases, the club and the city split the cost 50–50 (or nearly so). For example, Citizens Bank Park, home of the Philadelphia Phillies, cost $346 million. The city picked up $174 million of the total, and the club picked up the remaining $172 million. There are, however, other splits that are decidedly less even. For the new Yankee Stadium, the club is investing $1.1 billion, whereas the city is putting in "only" $200 million. In Minneapolis, the Twins are getting a lot of public support: $392 million out of the $544.4 million price tag. The final column in Tables 16.1 and 16.2 shows the percentage of the total cost provided from governmental sources. It is plain to see that there is considerable variation.

Table 16.2. Financing of National League Ballparks

Team	Stadium	Date	Cost ($ millions)	Public ($ millions)	% Public
Arizona Diamondbacks	Chase Field	03/31/1998	$349	$238	0.68194842
Atlanta Braves	Turner Field	03/29/1997	$235	$0	0
Chicago Cubs	Wrigley Field	04/23/1914	$250		0
Cincinnati Reds	Great American Park	10/04/2000	$325	$280	0.86153846
Colorado Rockies	Coors Field	04/26/1995	$215	$168	0.78139535
Florida Marlins	Miami Ballpark	04/2012	$525	$370	0.7047619
Houston Astros	Minute Maid Park	03/30/2001	$250	$180	0.72
Los Angeles Dodgers	Dodger Stadium	04/10/1962	$23		0
Milwaukee Brewers	Miller Park	03/30/2001	$400	$310	0.775
New York Mets	Citi Field	04/03/2009	$600	$164.4	0.274
Philadelphia Phillies	Citizens Bank Park	04/09/2004	$346	$174	0.50289017
Pittsburgh Pirates	PNC Park	04/17/1964	$262		0
San Diego Padres	Petco Park	04/2004	$456.8	$153	0.3349387
San Francisco Giants	AT&T Park	04/31/2000	$357	$0	0
St. Louis Cardinals	Busch Stadium	04/04/2006	$365	$45	0.12328767
Washington Nationals	Nationals Park	03/29/2008	$610.8[1]	$610.8	0.99996726

[1] Any cost overruns are privately covered.
Source: http://www.ballparks.com/baseball/index.htm.

The split between private and public funding depends to some extent on a city's willingness to pay and a club's willingness to move if the city does not pay. If a city is desperate enough to attract a club, it will be forced to pay dearly. The Nationals Park is a good example of a city's having to pay a great deal for a team.

3.1 Nationals Park

For years, the Washington Senators were just awful. Finally, they moved to Minnesota, changed their name to the Twins, and improved substantially. Their departure left Washington, D.C., without a baseball team. Despite their dismal experience with the Senators, there was an unsatisfied hunger for Major League Baseball (MLB) in the District. After many years, a ray of sunshine appeared in the form of the Montreal Expos, which had fallen on hard times and was owned by MLB. To get the Expos, the District had to put together a stadium deal. After some tough negotiations, the city agreed to buy the land and build the ballpark for its new team. The deal was struck.

The financially floundering Montreal Expos moved to Washington, D.C., in 2005 and were renamed the Washington Nationals. For three seasons, the Nationals shared the 46-year-old RFK Stadium with a Major League Soccer team, D.C. United. The Nationals, of course, wanted their own ballpark and got it in 2008. The Nationals Park, which was built on land along the Anacostia River, opened on March 30, 2008. The ballpark was financed entirely by the District of Columbia and cost $611 million. This financial commitment occurred at a time when the public school system in Washington was in disarray.

The city sold 30-year municipal bonds to cover the entire cost of the land and the ballpark. To cover the interest on the bonds as well as their redemption, the city found three revenue sources:

rent to be paid by the Nationals of $5.5 million per year;

in-stadium taxes on tickets, concessions, and merchandise sales of $11–14 million; and

taxes on businesses in the city of $21 to $24 million.

The revenues from rent and in-stadium taxes impose burdens on the team and those fans who directly benefit from the ballpark and the presence of the Nationals. The gross receipts tax, which is levied on city businesses with revenues in excess of $3 million, is another matter. First, it is doubtful that all of these businesses derive much benefit from the presence of the Nationals. Second, these taxes are apt to influence the price and output of those businesses. A gross receipts tax is essentially a sales tax, and sales taxes ordinarily cause the prices paid by consumers to rise and output to fall.

3.2 Stadium Financing in the National Football League[5]

Because of substantial revenue sharing and the enormous importance of national broadcast revenues, cities of rather modest size can now support a National Football League (NFL) franchise. As a result, franchises can relocate quite easily if an aggressive city puts together a sufficiently attractive stadium deal. There are several examples: the Los Angeles Rams moved to St. Louis, the Cleveland Browns became the Baltimore Ravens, and the Houston Oilers turned into the Tennessee Titans. Andrew Zimbalist has pointed out that the individual club's pursuit of the best financial deal that it can get has a potential downside for the league. The movement from larger media markets such as Los Angeles, Cleveland, and Houston to smaller media markets like St. Louis, Baltimore, and Nashville could lead to a reduction in future broadcast licensing fees. Each club has an incentive to hunt down the best deal for itself and should be expected to do so. If all clubs made such moves, however, the effect on the league as a whole could be a reduction in popularity with severe financial consequences. The league therefore has an incentive to find ways of dampening a club's incentive to move.

[5] Andrew Zimbalist (2006), *The Bottom Line*, Philadelphia: Temple University Press, pp. 139–140.

Table 16.3. National Football League (NFL) Stadium Disbursements

Year	Club	Disbursement ($ millions)
1999	Broncos	$50.0
1999	Patriots	150.0
1999	Eagles	150.0
2000	Lions	102.0
2000	Seahawks	50.0
2000	Bears	100.0
2001	Packers	13.0
2001	Cardinals	50.0
2005	Cowboys	76.5
2005	Colts	34.0
2006	Chiefs	42.5
2006	Jets/Giants	300.0

Note: The "G-3" fund that the NFL used to subsidize stadiums dried up and is no longer in use. At the beginning of 2007, the NFL announced that the fund was no longer viable.

Source: Daniel Kaplan, "NFL Owners Give $300M for N.Y. Stadium," *Sports Business Journal*, Dec. 11, 2006, p. 3.

In response to the departure of the Browns, Cleveland prepared an antitrust suit against the NFL. Not wanting to fight that battle, the NFL settled the suit by expanding into Cleveland. This experience showed that the NFL might not be able to control its expansion in an orderly fashion and thereby maximize the value of the franchises.

For those reasons, the owners decided to try to protect the larger media markets from defections by incumbent clubs. The plan was for the NFL to lend up to 50 percent of the private share of the cost of a new stadium. These loans are interest-free and can be repaid over a 15-year period with revenues generated by personal seat licenses and premium seating in the new stadium. Although this program was designed to protect the six largest media markets, everyone seems to be eligible for support. Table 16.3 shows the sums that have been disbursed and to whom the disbursements were made. It is clear that smaller markets such as Denver, Kansas City, Indianapolis, and Green Bay have benefited from this program. The largest commitment has been $300 million for the new stadium that the Giants and Jets share.[6] The Giants and Jets each received the maximum amount of $150 million under the so-called G-3 funding program. The loan will be repaid with revenues from 9,000 club seat sales at $4,500 per year. In addition to the $300 million in G-3 funding, each club borrowed $650 million to cover the expected stadium construction cost of $1.6 billion.

4 FUNDING AND SUBSIDIES FOR OTHER FACILITIES

The most prominent municipal funding deals involve professional sports venues – stadiums, arenas, and ballparks – because the dollars are large and sports are popular. However, subsidies and funding are not limited to professional sports facilities. Municipalities provide golf courses, tennis courts, swimming pools, jogging trails, athletic fields, and many other facilities that may be heavily subsidized. In some instances, that is a good idea, but in others, it is not.

[6] Richard Sandomir, "N.F.L. Loans $300 Million for Stadium," *New York Times*, Dec. 8, 2006; Daniel Kaplan, "NFL Owners Give $300M for N.Y. Stadium," *Sports Business Journal*, Dec. 11, 2006; and Daniel Kaplan, "Giants, Jets to borrow $650M Each," *Sports Business Journal*, March 19, 2007.

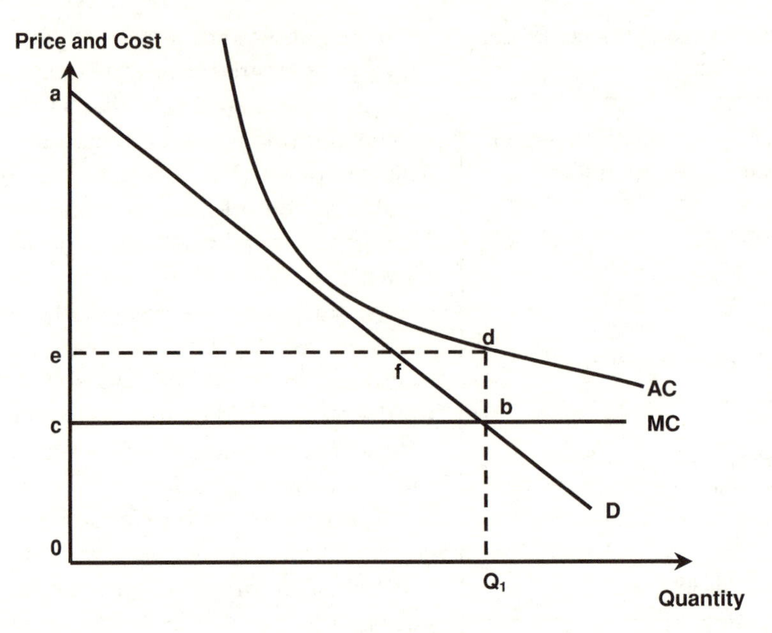

Figure 16.1. Even though no price will make this project profitable, it may make sense to subsidize it if it generates enough consumer surplus.

4.1 Subsidizing Community Facilities

Under some circumstances, it is socially optimal to subsidize a municipally owned sports facility that cannot be operated profitably. Consider Figure 16.1 in which *D* represents the demand for using a swimming pool, *MC* is the marginal cost of using the pool, and *AC* is the average cost. Because *AC* lies above *D* at every quantity, there is no single price that will generate enough revenue to cover the cost of the pool. If the owner of the swimming pool cannot use some creative pricing scheme,[7] the pool may close and swimmers could then be worse off. However, it may make economic sense to subsidize the pool if the social value of the pool exceeds the social cost.

Suppose that the city charges the socially optimal user fee to swim in the pool. Price will then be equal to marginal cost and the number of swimmers will be Q_1. Total cost will exceed total revenue by the rectangular area *edbc*. However, consumer surplus is equal to the triangular area *abc*. If the area of triangle *abc* exceeds the area of rectangle *edbc*, then consumer surplus will exceed the loss. As one can see, these two areas overlap. Focusing on the difference between the two areas, if area *afe* is smaller than area *fdb*, then consumer surplus is less than the revenue shortfall and the pool should not be subsidized. In contrast, if the consumer surplus generated with marginal cost pricing exceeds the revenue shortfall, then the community will benefit by subsidizing the pool. The subsidy will have to be equal to the revenue shortfall of *edbc* to cover all of the pool's costs. In principle, the swimmers could get together and chip in enough money to cover the necessary amount. In practice, however,

[7] For some creative pricing, see Chapter 7.

these efforts are usually organized by the government. In that event, the government will have to generate tax revenue to cover the subsidy. This, of course, can cause problems because of the effect of taxes on incentives and choices. The incidence of the tax is another important consideration. Sales taxes, for example, tend to be regressive, which means that they will fall disproportionately on those with lower incomes. The wisdom of subsidizing a facility with sales taxes should take the tax incidence into account. If the distributional consequences are sufficiently objectionable, it may be wise to abandon the subsidy. Moreover, collecting taxes is not without cost. These transaction costs must be taken into account in deciding whether to subsidize. In other words, if the difference between the consumer surplus and the necessary subsidy is smaller than the costs of administering the tax, then the subsidy will not provide a net benefit and should be abandoned.

4.2 Political Realities and Municipal Commitments

Political decisions are often bewildering to say the least. Politicians increase the minimum wage when they must know that reduced employment will result. They impose rent controls when they must know that a reduced supply of rental units will result. They provide public support for sports facilities that seems unwarranted at times. It is not useful to attribute these decisions to stupidity. Politicians are not generally stupid, even though they do dumb things from time to time. It is also not useful to proceed on the assumption that politicians will always act in our interest. Although politicians may be generally well intentioned, they are not selfless servants of their constituents. Instead, they are rational utility maximizers just like the rest of us. To understand their decisions, one must examine their utility functions and the arguments in those utility functions. We assume that a politician's utility function (U) may be written as

$$U = U(W, P, R, C, \dots),$$

where W is personal wealth, P is power, R is reelection, and C is constituent welfare. This view is not cynical; it is just realistic. After all, politicians are human beings and we should expect them to act accordingly, that is, as utility maximizers. This formulation makes it easier to understand some political decisions that appear to be irrational at first blush.

Organized groups have disproportionate political influence as they can focus attention on what interests them most. With respect to funding a stadium, which organized groups are most likely to support a team owner? Although there may be a few others, several groups are obvious. First, construction contractors will benefit from landing a major job involving large sums of money. Second, materials suppliers and subcontractors have a similar interest. Third, labor unions in the construction trades will also profit from a stadium contract. These organized groups can provide campaign financing and blocks of votes when reelection time rolls around. Consequently, currying favor with these groups makes sense even when doing so may reduce constituent welfare.

Table 16.4. Costs and Benefits of Two Municipal Projects

	Sports Facility	Arts Center	Net
East	−$500	−$300	$200
Central	−$300	−$300	−$600
West	−$300	$500	$200
Net	−$100	−$100	−$200

In other words, some governmentally financed projects may be ill advised on the basis of social welfare.

Things could be worse. There are times when multiple projects receive governmental support when none of the projects can be justified on social welfare grounds. This comes about through *logrolling*. Logrolling refers to the practice among legislators of trading votes: I vote for your program and then you reciprocate by voting for mine. This practice can lead to socially undesirable outcomes that make perfect economic sense for utility-maximizing politicians. Consider the economic consequences of two municipal projects. Project 1 is a sports facility, and Project 2 is a performing arts center. The monetary benefits of each project for three residential areas within the community are shown in Table 16.4. The sports facility confers $500 million of net benefits on those living in the East neighborhood. This facility imposes net costs of $300 million on Central residents and another $300 million on West residents. For the community as a whole, the result is negative: the combined net cost of $600 million to Central and West residents outweighs the net benefits of $500 million to East residents. Thus, a democratic vote will reject the project as it should on welfare grounds. Much the same can be said for the performing arts center. West residents enjoy a net gain of $500 million, whereas East and Central residents each lose $300 million. Again, a democratic vote will defeat this project – as it should because the net costs outweigh the net benefits for the community as a whole.

In this example, neither project should pass on majority voting grounds:

Central and West will vote against the sports facility.

Central and East will vote against the performing arts center.

More important, in a social sense, neither should pass because both of them have negative effects on the community.

Through logrolling, however, both may pass because there are net benefits for East and West if this occurs. East gains $500 million from the sports facility and loses $300 million from the performing arts center, for a net gain of $200 million. West also has a net gain of $200 million: a $300 million loss from the sports facility and a $500 million gain from the performing arts center. By trading votes, East and West will form a coalition and vote for both projects. Thus, East and West impose losses on Central to their net benefit. East and West have net gains of $200 million each, and Central loses $600 million. For the community, the net loss is $200 million. Thus, through logrolling, two projects that do not make sense from a social perspective gain public support. The politicians who vote for these projects are promoting the interests of their constituents at the expense of someone else's constituents.

5 PUBLIC FINANCING OF SPORTS FACILITIES

State and local governments must use taxes to pay for just about anything that they buy. To be sure, they may issue bonds – that is, they may borrow the money – but bonds require interest payments and ultimately must be redeemed. If the sports team occupying the facility is not paying enough to cover this, the public must do so through taxation. In some cases, local governments impose taxes on tourists and business travelers in an effort to "export" the tax burden and thereby get something for nothing. It is, however, very difficult to get something for nothing. As an example, consider Orlando's plan for a new downtown facility for the Orlando Magic.

5.1 Taxing the Tourists in Orlando

To keep the Orlando Magic in Orlando, city and county officials agreed to build a new arena in downtown Orlando with a price tag of $480 million.[8] To their credit, the Magic agreed to put in $50 million in cash. The Magic also agreed to pay $64 million in advance for lease payments and operational support for the new arena. Finally, the Magic agreed to provide a $100 million guarantee on the municipal bonds that were to be issued to finance the project. Such guarantees reduce the interest rate on the bonds because of the reduced risk of default.

Part of the money needed for the arena came from the Tourist Development Tax, which is a misnomer of the first order. Taxes on tourists are apt to retard tourism rather than develop it. Orlando's plan was to impose a dollar per night bed tax at hotels and motels in the area. Because those who stay in hotels and motels are visitors – business travelers and tourists – it looks like Orlando is exporting the tax burden. As we know, however, this is not entirely accurate as a general proposition. Unless the demand for hotel and motel rooms is perfectly inelastic, which is highly doubtful, the tax will cause some reduction in the number of rooms booked. As a result, some portion of the tax is absorbed by the hotels and motels in the Orlando area. The less elastic the demand, the greater the proportion of the tax that is exported. This economic fact of life is easy to demonstrate.

Consider the supply and demand curves shown in Figure 16.2. The demand for hotel rooms is D and the pretax supply is S. The original equilibrium price and output are P_1 and Q_1, respectively. When a unit tax is imposed, the posttax supply shifts from S to S^*. The vertical distance between S and S^* is the amount of the unit tax. After the tax is imposed, the quantity falls to Q_2 and the price paid by consumers rises to P_2, whereas the price received by hotel operators falls to P_3. The difference between P_2 and P_3 is the unit tax. A comparison of the pretax and posttax results reveals that a portion of the tax is paid by the consumers: $P_2 - P_1$. The rest of the tax, $P_1 - P_3$, is absorbed by the hotel operator. Thus, not all of the tax burden is exported to tourists and business travelers. In addition, when the number of rooms booked falls, sales of complements

[8] David Darron and Mark Schlueb, "City, County Announce Deal on New Facilities," *Orlando Sentinel*, Sept. 29, 2006.

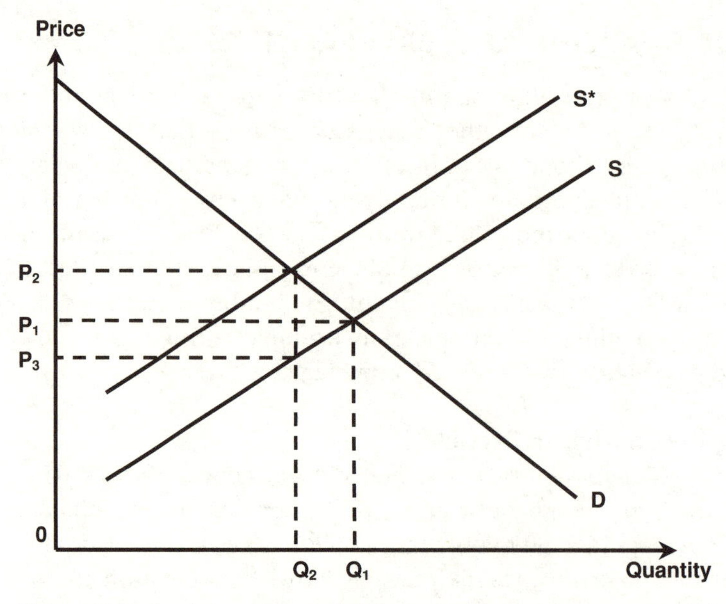

Figure 16.2. A unit tax puts a wedge between the price consumers pay (P_2) and the price sellers receive (P_3). The tax burden is shared but not necessarily equally.

also fall. Fewer cars will be rented, fewer restaurant meals will be eaten, and fewer souvenirs will be sold. Although these drains on local businesses are predictable, they are diffused throughout the local economy and difficult to see.

The ability of a local government to export the tax burden depends on supply and demand elasticities. The more elastic the demand, the greater the share of the tax that the hotel operators will have to absorb. In addition, the more elastic the demand, the greater the reduction in quantity, which means that the adverse effect on the local restaurants, tourist attractions, car rental agencies, and other providers of complementary goods and services will be greater. We can see this in Figure 16.3. The original equilibrium price and output are P_1 and Q_1, respectively. When a unit tax is imposed, supply shifts from S to S^*. If demand is D_1, more of the tax is passed on to consumers than would be the case if demand were D_2. Note that D_1 is less elastic than D_2 at the original equilibrium (proof by assignment). We can also see that the more elastic the demand, the larger the reduction in quantity: $Q_1 - Q_{22}$ is larger than $Q_1 - Q_{12}$.

The basic lesson here is that taxing the tourists is not a way to get some sports facility for free. If demand is relatively elastic, a good deal of the tax burden falls on the local economy. Analogously, the less elastic the supply, the greater the tax burden on the local economy (proof by assignment). Exporting the tax burden may seem like an appealing way to pay for a new ballpark, but great care must be taken when trying to do so.

5.2 Alternative Sources of Tax Revenues

There may be great resistance to taxing the tourists by local businesses that fear the consequences. Moreover, some cities do not have all that many tourists. For Miami, New Orleans, and Orlando, there are plenty of tourists, but Cincinnati

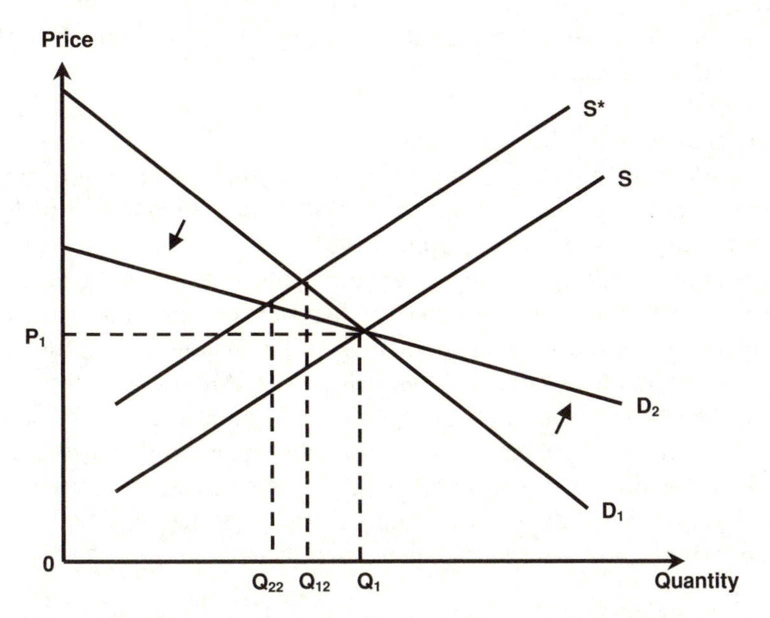

Figure 16.3. The tax burden on local business changes as demand becomes more (or less) elastic.

and Kansas City are not similarly blessed (or cursed). Consequently, a city may need to consider alternative sources of tax revenues to cover the debt service on bonds sold to fund a sports facility. Generally, cities like to tax items with relatively inelastic demand because consumers do not substitute away from those products in great quantities. This makes it easier to raise the necessary revenue. The problem is often an equity issue because these taxes may be regressive.

Alcohol and Cigarettes Sales. Taxes on alcohol and cigarettes are attractive because demand tends to be relatively inelastic for these goods. Thus, the tax does not decrease in quantity much, and therefore, it is a good revenue generator. The problem is the tax incidence: the tax falls disproportionately on those who do not benefit directly from the sports facility. If these people tend to have low incomes, then the tax is *regressive* and may be objectionable on that basis.

Taxing the Lottery. Many states have lotteries that are actually operated by the government. The payoffs in these lotteries are huge, but the gamble is far from being actuarially fair. As a result, the lottery generates substantial surpluses (or profits) that can be earmarked for education or for general purposes. Some portion of the surplus can be directed toward funding a new stadium, ballpark, or arena. All else being equal, siphoning off lottery proceeds to support a sports facility takes money away from something else receiving state support. It could mean, for example, that less money will be available for education. Again, it is very difficult to get something for nothing. Sacrifices usually must be made, and it should matter who makes them.

When lottery proceeds are diverted from their current use to fund a football stadium, it is reasonable to ask who pays for this. As the state spends less on other programs, the beneficiaries of those programs are worse off. These are the people who are paying for the stadium, but who are they? The answer will vary from state to state and over time within each state. Unless we know the incidence of this "tax," it is difficult to evaluate the wisdom of public funding for a football stadium.

5.3 Debt Financing and Equity

When cities fund a sports facility, the cost is too high to pay out of current tax revenues without causing serious disruptions. Cities, therefore, usually borrow the necessary funds by issuing municipal bonds. Municipal bonds are attractive for debt financing because the interest is not subject to federal income taxation. As a result, the interest rate is equal to the post tax interest rate on a corporate bond of equivalent risk. Thus, the cost of debt financing is lower for cities than for corporations. This raises an interesting issue of fairness. To the extent that the interest income on municipal bonds is not subject to federal income taxation, taxpayers all over the country are subsidizing local sports facilities. To make matters worse, the owners of major league sports teams are among the wealthiest people in the United States. As a result of the tax policy, then, those of modest means actually subsidize the wealthy.

Box 16.1 *Citi Field Municipal Bond Funding*

When the New York Mets decided that it had to abandon Shea Stadium for a modern venue, Citi Field was the result. The construction costs were estimated at $800 million. To finance the construction, the New York City Industrial Development Agency issued 40-year tax-free bonds with a coupon rate of 5 percent. These bonds were issued on behalf of the Queens Ballpark Company, which was created to finance construction. Interestingly, the Mets are responsible for the debt payments. This suggests that the Mets were indirectly able to obtain funding at municipal bond rates rather than at taxable corporate bond rates. Because the interest received on the Citi Field bonds is tax exempt, U.S. taxpayers appear to be subsidizing the Mets. Does this sound like sensible public policy?

---

6 CONCLUDING REMARKS

In this chapter, we have been concerned with financing sports facilities. By examining net present values, we identified those facilities that can support themselves and those that will require some help. If the *NPV* is positive, no support is necessary, but if the *NPV* is negative, the project needs help or will be abandoned. Despite their unprofitability, some facilities can be justified on social welfare grounds. If the consumer surplus generated by the facility exceeds the loss on operations, then a subsidy is justified.

Government provision of sports facilities or government subsidies require money. Usually, that money comes from taxes. Taxes, however, have both allocative and distributive consequences. These must be considered when weighing the sensibility of financing or subsidizing sports facilities.

PROBLEMS AND QUESTIONS

1. Show that all of a unit tax is passed on to consumers if demand is perfectly inelastic. Who bears the tax burden if demand is negatively sloped and supply is perfectly inelastic?
2. Suppose that demand is given by $P = 120 - 3Q$, and supply is given by $P = 10 + Q$.
   a. What are the competitive equilibrium price and output?
   b. If a per unit tax of $10 is imposed, what happens to the price paid by consumers, the price received by suppliers, and the quantity consumed?
   c. How much total tax is generated?
   d. Who bears the burden of the tax?
   e. How much is the deadweight social welfare loss due to the tax?
3. Suppose a stadium costs $400 million to build and had a useful life of 30 years. How much operating profit is necessary each year to break even? Assume a 10 percent interest rate, no scrap value, and no taxes on the operating profit.
4. Although subsidies make team owners better off, they will not necessarily lead to improved team quality. Why not?
5. Municipalities issue bonds to pay for stadiums and rely on general sales taxes to pay the interest on those bonds. Why are general sales taxes apt to favor the fan at the expense of the general public?
6. When the Hogtown City Commission was considering a $5 per night bed tax on all hotel and motel rooms to pay for some recreational facilities, the commissioners were concerned about opposition to the tax. Who in the local community would you expect to be opposed to the tax? Explain.
7. Show that all of an *ad valorem* tax – that is, a tax that is a percentage of the price – will be passed on to the consumer if demand is perfectly inelastic.
8. Many private golf clubs charge annual dues to their members, who can then play as often as they wish with no user fees. The dining room often loses money and therefore must be subsidized by the members. Although there may be some grumbling, no one quits the club. Can you explain what is going on here?
9. The text claims that many pro teams have extremely favorable lease arrangements for the venue in which they play.
   a. What does it mean to say that a lease is “favorable”?
   b. How can one tell whether a lease is “favorable”?
10. Examine Figure 16.3. Prove that D_1 is less elastic than D_2 at the original equilibrium.
11. What influences the elasticity of demand for hotel and motel rooms in Orlando?

12. Will hotel operators in Tampa, Miami, and West Palm Beach benefit from an increase in Orlando's room tax?
13. When the original Cleveland Browns abandoned Cleveland and moved to Baltimore, Cleveland threatened the NFL with an antitrust suit. What do you think Cleveland could have claimed as an antitrust violation?
14. Suppose that a municipal golf course will confer net benefits to Westside residents of $200 but will impose net costs on Eastside and Central residents of $75 each. A public park will provide net benefits to Eastside residents of $200 while imposing costs of $75 each on Westside and Central residents.
    a. Will either project pass on individual votes?
    b. Should either pass on social welfare grounds?
    c. Will logrolling lead to passage of both?
    d. If so, is this a good thing?
15. In the text, we analyzed the operating profit necessary to make the new Giants-Jets football stadium viable. Suppose that the appropriate discount rate was 6 percent instead of 12. How would that affect the calculations?

RESEARCH QUESTIONS

1. Select a sports facility and find out how its construction was financed. How are operating costs being financed? How much rent and operational support are paid by the team?
2. Find out why the Yankees had an easier time getting a stadium deal than the Marlins.
3. Sports facilities for professional teams used to be privately funded. There was then a period of heavy public subsidies, but the trend recently appears to be away from public funding. Examine the extent of public funding for NFL stadiums from 1970 to the present.
4. Examine the extent to which eminent domain has been used to acquire the land necessary for the construction of sports facilities. Have the previous landowners received fair market value for the land that they were compelled to sell?

REFERENCES AND FURTHER READING

Baade, R. A., and V. A. Matheson. (2006). "Have Public Finance Principles Been Shut Out in Financing New Stadiums for the NFL?" *Public Finance and Management*, 6, 284–320.

Kaplan, Daniel. "NFL Owners Give $300M for N.Y. Stadium." *Sports Business Journal*, Dec. 11, 2006.

Kaplan, Daniel. "Giants, Jets to Borrow $650M each." *Sports Business Journal*, March 19, 2007.

Miller, P. (2007). "Private Financing and Sports Franchise Values: The Case of Major League Baseball." *Journal of Sports Economics*, 8, 449–467.

Noll, Roger G. (1974). *Government and the Sports Business* (chapter 9). Washington, DC: The Brookings Institution.

Noll, Roger G., and Andrew Zimbalist. (1997). *Sports, Jobs, and Taxes: The Economic Impact of Sports Teams and Stadiums.* Washington, DC: The Brookings Institution.

Owen, Jeffrey G. (2003). "The Stadium Game: Cities Versus Teams." *Journal of Sports Economics*, 4,183–202.

Pickard, J. L., and I. C. Araujo. (1989). "Financing Toronto's SkyDome: A Unique Partnership of Public and Private Funding." *Government Finance Review* (December), 7–12.

Quirk, James, and Rodney Fort. (1992). *Pay Dirt: The Business of Professional Team Sports* (chapter 4). Princeton, NJ: Princeton University Press.

Quirk, James, and Rodney Fort. (1999). *Hard Ball: The Abuse of Power in Pro Team Sports* (chapter 7). Princeton, NJ: Princeton University Press.

Quinn, Kevin G., Paul B. Bursik, Christopher P. Borick, and Lisa Raethz. (2003). "Do New Digs Mean More Wins? The Relationship Between a New Venue and a Professional Sports Team's Competitive Success." *Journal of Sports Economics*, 4, 167–182.

Shubnell, L. D., J.E. Petersen, and C. B. Harris. (1985). "The Big Ticket: Financing a Professional Sports Facility." *Government Finance Review* (June), 7–11.

Szymanski, Stefan. (2009). *Playbooks and Checkbooks: An Introduction to the Economics of Modern Sports* (chapter 6). Princeton, NJ: Princeton University Press.

Zimbalist, Andrew. (2003). *May the Best Team Win* (chapter 6). Washington, DC: The Brookings Institution.

Zimbalist, Andrew. (2006). *The Bottom Line.* Philadelphia: Temple University Press, pp. 139–140.

Zimbalist, A., and J. G. Long. (2006). "Facility Finance: Measurement, Trends, and Analysis." *International Journal of Sport Finance*, 1, 201–211.

17

Salary Determination: Competition and Monopsony

1 INTRODUCTION

The average salary in major league sports is substantial to say the least. For the 2010 season, the average salary in Major League Baseball (MLB) was $3.33 million and was $1.87 million in the National Football League (NFL). In the National Basketball Association (NBA), the average salary was $4.58 million, and it was $2.4 million in the National Hockey League (NHL). The salaries of the superstars were even more astonishing:

Alex Rodriguez (MLB)	$33.0 million
Kobe Bryant (NBA)	$24.8 million
Peyton Manning (NFL)	$15.0 million
Roberto Luongo (NHL)	$10.0 million

Even die-hard sports fans often wonder aloud how someone can be worth so much money for playing a game.[1] The answer, of course, is supply and demand. At the highest levels, there are very few athletes, but there is a substantial demand for their talents because of the popularity of pro sports as a form of entertainment. The salaries of the 10 highest-paid players in each major league sport for the 2010 season are shown in Table 17.1.

In this chapter, we examine the determinants of player salaries. We will also take a look at how the major leagues have tried to exercise buying power to keep salaries down. Some empirical evidence of their success in doing so will be examined as well.

[1] It is not just the players who are earning huge salaries. For 2003, Bud Selig earned $11.6 million as commissioner of MLB. In his last year as NFL commissioner, Paul Tagliabue earned more than $10.3 million. Some union executives do quite well, too. Gene Upshaw, for example, earned more than $6 million in 2006 as head of the NFLPA. Coaches are also paid handsomely.

Table 17.1. Top 10 Salaries

Major League Baseball (2010)	
1. Alex Rodriguez	$33,000,000
2. CC Sabathia	$24,285,714
3. Derek Jeter	$22,600,000
4. Mark Teixeira	$20,625,000
5. Johan Santana	$20,144,708
6. Miguel Cabrera	$20,000,000
7. Carlos Beltran	$19,401,571
8. Ryan Howard	$19,000,000
9. Carlos Lee	$19,000,000
10. Alfonso Soriano	$19,000,000
National Basketball Association (2010)	
1. Kobe Bryant	$24,800,000
2. Rashard Lewis	$20,500,000
3. Kevin Garnett	$18,800,000
4. Tim Duncan	$18,700,000
5. Michael Redd	$18,300,000
6. Pau Gasol	$17,800,000
7. Andrei Kirilenko	$17,800,000
8. Gilbert Arenas	$17,700,000
9. Yao Ming	$17,700,000
10. Zach Randolph	$17,300,000
Source: www.forbes.com.	
National Football League (2010)	
1. Peyton Manning	$15,800,000
2. Nnamdi Asomugha	$14,300,000
3. Donovan McNabb	$11,500,000
4. Champ Bailer	$9,500,000
5. Sam Bradford	$8,300,000
6. Ndamukong Suh	$8,000,000
7. Elvis Dumervil	$7,200,000
8. Julius Peppers	$7,000,000
9. Matthew Stafford	$6,900,000
10. Gerald McCoy	$6,600,000
Source: www.forbes.com.	
National Hockey League (2010–2011 Season)	
1. Roberto Luongo	$10,000,000
2. Vincent Lecavalier	$10,000,000
3. Sidney Crosby	$9,000,000
4. Evgeni Malkin	$9,000,000
5. Alexander Ovechkin	$9,000,000
6. Chris Drury	$8,000,000
7. Scott Gomez	$8,000,000
8. Dany Heatley	$8,000,000
9. Duncan Keith	$8,000,000
10. Jason Spezza	$8,000,000
Source: www.forbes.com.	

2 DEMAND FOR ATHLETIC TALENT

We begin our analysis of the sports labor market by assuming that it is competitively structured. For the most part, however, sports labor markets are not competitive. Nonetheless, the competitive model provides a useful benchmark for comparison with the actual results. In addition, it introduces a way of measuring a player's value to his club.

Athletes are employees of their respective clubs, which are business firms that produce athletic competition that is sold to the fans. We begin our analysis with the principles that drive the employment decisions of profit-maximizing firms. In general, labor is an input in the production process. No one demands labor services for their own sake. Instead, labor is demanded because it can be used to produce something that the employer can sell. Consequently, the demand for labor is a *derived* demand – it is derived from the demand for the output that the labor is used to produce. In the sports business, players, coaches, and managers are employed by their clubs to produce athletic competition, which is what the clubs sell to the fans. The demand for athletic talent is derived from the fans' demand for watching the games that the athletes play.

The production function of the firm tells us the maximum quantity of output that can be produced for any given combination of inputs. In the simplest case, the firm's output may be a function of the labor and capital employed. For that case, we may suppose that the firm's production function can be written generally as

$$Q = Q(L, K),$$

where Q is output, L is labor, K is capital, and $Q(\cdot)$ is the production function – or the technology – that converts inputs into outputs. In the short run, we may assume that capital is fixed at $\overline{K}$ whereas labor is variable. Consequently, changes in output are made by changing the amount of labor that is combined with the fixed quantity of capital. As usual, the firm's profit is the difference between total revenue and total cost. By incorporating the production function explicitly, the firm's short-run profit function can then be written as

$$\Pi = P(Q)\,Q(L, \overline{K}) - wL - r\overline{K},$$

where π is profit, $P(Q)$ is the demand function, and w and r are the input prices. In this formulation, the firm's decision variable is the quantity of labor. Because capital is fixed, the decision on how much labor to employ determines the quantity of output and therefore the total revenue. It also determines the expenditures on labor and thereby determines the total variable costs. The fixed cost, $r\,\overline{K}$, has already been determined.

To maximize profits, the firm will expand its employment of labor until the increment in profit vanishes. In other words, as long as an increase in the quantity of labor employed increases profit, the firm will continue to expand

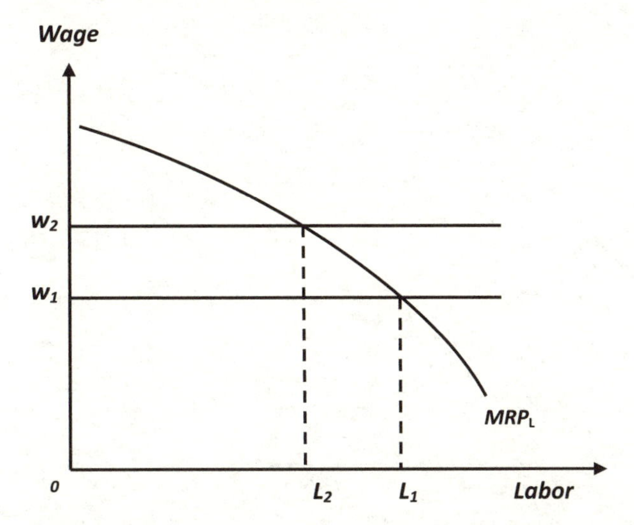

Figure 17.1. The firm's demand curve for labor is the marginal revenue product curve (MRP_L).

employment. This expansion stops when there is no further increase in profit. Specifically, profit maximization requires that

$$\frac{\Delta \Pi}{\Delta L} = \frac{\Delta PQ}{\Delta Q} \times \frac{\Delta Q}{\Delta L} - w = 0.$$

Because $\frac{\Delta PQ}{\Delta Q}$ is marginal revenue and $\frac{\Delta Q}{\Delta L}$ is the marginal product of labor (MP_L), profit maximization requires that

$$MR \cdot MP_L = w.$$

This makes sense from an economic perspective. When the firm increases employment slightly, output will increase by the marginal product of labor. The monetary value of that increased output is determined by the marginal revenue generated by the sale of that increment in output. The product of MR and MP_L gives us the marginal benefit of the increase in employment, which we usually refer to as the *marginal revenue product.* The marginal cost of the increase in labor is the wage (w) that must be paid. Thus, employment is expanded until the marginal benefit of doing so equals the marginal cost of doing so.[2]

For convenience, we write $MR \cdot MP_L$ as MRP_L and call it the marginal revenue product of labor. The MRP_L is the firm's demand curve for labor given the fixed quantity of capital ($\overline{K}$). For example, in Figure 17.1, the firm will demand L_1 units of labor services at a wage rate of w_1. If the wage were to rise to w_2, the quantity of labor services demanded would fall to L_2. This exercise can be repeated for other values of w. From this, we can see that the firm's MRP_L curve constitutes its demand for labor. At any wage, the quantity of labor demanded is found on the MRP_L curve.

[2] This condition for profit maximization can be rearranged into a more familiar expression:

$$MR = w/MP_L,$$

when we recognize that w/MP_L is the marginal cost.

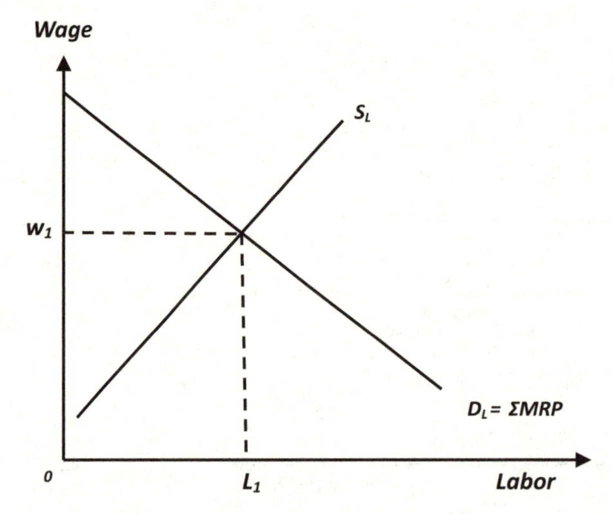

Figure 17.2. Equilibrium in the competitive labor market requires the equality of supply (*S*) and demand (*D*).

A professional team's focus on marginal revenue product is illustrated by the Cincinnati Reds' assessment of Ken Griffey, Jr.'s presence in 2000.[3] The team expected to gain $20 million in new revenues due to his presence in the lineup. Attendance rose by some 500,000 fans during the 2000 season, which translated into $16 million in additional gate receipts and concession revenues. Merchandise sales rose another $1.9 million. Arguably, Griffey's MRP was nearly $18 million, which was less than the Reds had hoped for but more than Griffey was paid, which was $7 million.

2.1 Market Demand for Labor

The market demand for labor is found by summing the demands of the individual firms. This is the usual horizontal summation: for each wage, find the amount of labor that each employer wants to hire and sum these quantities. This wage and total quantity demanded are the coordinates of one point on the market demand curve. The process can be repeated for other values of w to trace out the market demand curve.

2.2 Equilibrium Wage

The equilibrium wage is found at the intersection of supply and demand. In Figure 17.2, the equilibrium wage is w_1, and total employment by all firms is L_1. The market clears because supply and demand are equal at that wage; everyone who is willing to work for w_1 is employed. Note that the wage equals the marginal revenue product for all employers. In other words, in equilibrium every firm operates where $MRP_L = w$. This, of course, means that $MRP_L^1 = MRP_L^2 = \& = MRP_L^n = w$.

That is, the marginal revenue product of labor is the same across all firms.

[3] John Rofe, "'Griffey Factor' Revenue Wasn't as Big as Forecast," *Sports Business Journal*, October 2, 2000, p. 3.

2.3 Numerical Example

Suppose that the supply of linebackers can be expressed as

$$w = \$100{,}000 + 5{,}000L,$$

where w is the wage and L is the number of linebackers. The marginal revenue product of linebackers – the demand – is as follows:

$$MRP_L = \$1{,}000{,}000 - 4{,}000L.$$

The equilibrium number of linebackers employed is found where supply and demand are equal. Accordingly, we have

$$\$100{,}000 + 5{,}000L = \$1{,}000{,}000 - 4{,}000L.$$

Solving for L, we find that there will be 100 linebackers employed. The wage can be found by substituting $L = 100$ into either the supply or the demand:

$$\$100{,}000 + 5{,}000(100) = \$600{,}000,$$

or,

$$\$1{,}000{,}000 - 4{,}000(100) = \$600{,}000.$$

Either way, the equilibrium wage is $600,000.

3 MONOPSONY IN THE LABOR MARKET

At times, sports teams and leagues may exercise *monopsony* power, that is, power on the buying side, in the sports labor market. Before examining specific instances of monopsony, we will develop the basic economic model of monopsony to understand the economic consequences of this market structure.

If a firm is the only purchaser of an input, it is a monopsonist by definition. If, in addition, the supply of that input is positively sloped, the monopsonist will enjoy monopsony power, which is the power to depress the price paid below the competitive level.[4] Now the monopsonist does not force prices down through heavy-handed, abusive practices. As we shall see, a monopsonist simply reduces its purchases and thereby slides down the supply curve to a lower price.

In the preceding section, we found that the profit-maximizing employment level required that the firm's marginal revenue product of labor be equal to the wage: $MRP_L = w$. In that case, however, the wage was constant and equal to the competitive wage. For a monopsonist, the marginal cost of an additional unit of labor will exceed the wage paid because an increase in employment leads to an increase in the wage. This can be seen clearly in Figure 17.3

The supply of labor (S) is positively sloped and, as a result, when employment rises from L_1 to $L_1 + 1$, the wage must rise from L_1 to L_2 to induce the

[4] This is the flip side of monopoly power, which is the ability to take the output price above the competitive level.

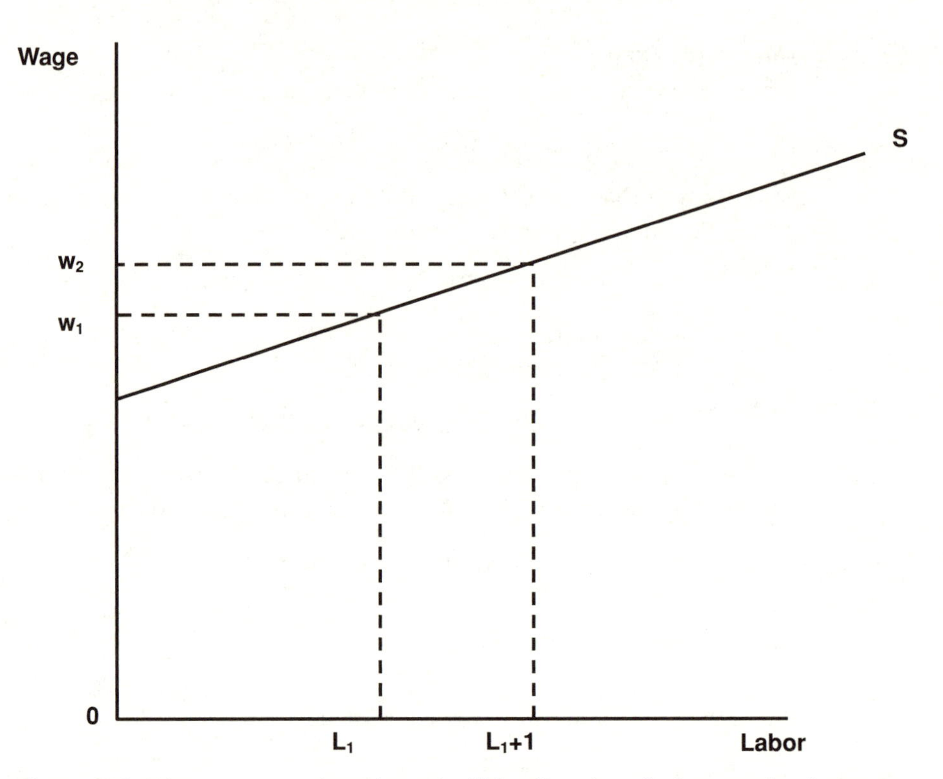

Figure 17.3. When a monopsonist adds a unit of labor (L_1 to $L_1 + 1$), the wage rises from w_1 to w_2. All workers receive the higher wage. The wage bill rises from $w_1 L_1$ to $w_2(L_1 + 1)$.

provision of that increment in labor. If the monopsonist cannot discriminate, all labor will command the higher wage. The firm's total wage bill rises from $w_1 L$ to $w_2(L_1 + 1)$. The difference can be decomposed to reveal the marginal cost of expanded employment. First, adding one unit requires paying w_2 for that unit. Second, the original L_1 units now must be paid w_2, so there is an increase of $(w_2 - w_1)L_1$ in the wage bill. Thus, expansion leads to a change in the wage bill of $w_2 + (\Delta w/\Delta L)L_1$ where $\Delta w/\Delta L$ is the change in the wage brought about by the expanded employment. This impact is called the marginal factor cost (MFC):

$$MFC = w + (\Delta w/\Delta L)\,L.$$

Because $\Delta w/\Delta L$ is positive, the MRC exceeds the wage. As a result, MFC lies above S in Figure 17.4.

To maximize its profits, the monopsonist will expand its employment of labor until the marginal benefit equals the marginal cost. That is, the monopsonist will operate where the MRP_L is equal to the MFC. Because the marginal factor cost exceeds the wage, the monopsonist will find it profitable to reduce employment below the point where MRP_L equals w.

These observations can be seen in Figure 17.4 where MRP_L is the demand for labor, S is the supply of labor, and MFC is the associated marginal factor

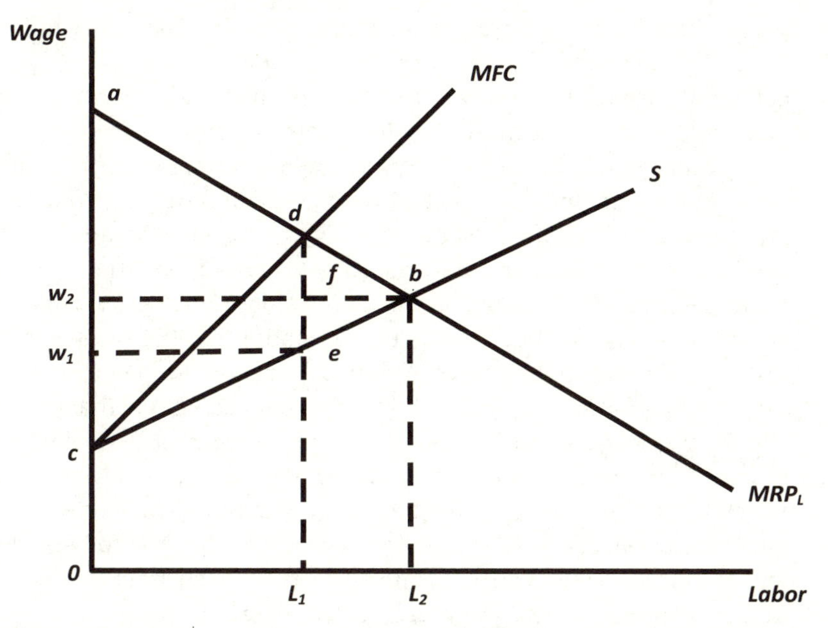

Figure 17.4. Monopsony leads to a reduction in employment and a loss in social welfare.

cost.[5] The firm maximizes profit by employing L_1, which is determined by the equality of MRP_L and MFC. The wage that the monopsonist pays is determined by the height of the supply curve at L_1, which is shown as w_1. As is plain to see, the marginal revenue product exceeds the wage at the firm's optimum. It is *privately* optimal for the firm to employ labor at a quantity where the marginal value to the firm exceeds the wage that it pays.[6] This is necessary to maximize the profits of the firm, but this employment level is not *socially* optimal.

3.1 Social Welfare Loss of Monopsony

The exercise of monopsony power leads to a deadweight social welfare loss, which is analogous to that associated with monopoly.[7] Because the monopsonist operates where the MRP_L equals the MFC rather than where the MRP_L equals the supply, the employment level is allocatively inefficient. The social cost of employing another unit of L is given by the height of the supply curve, and the value to society of the added output that would have been produced is given by the height of the demand for labor (i.e., the height of MRP_L). At L_1, the added social value exceeds the added social cost. From a *social welfare*

[5] For a linear supply curve, the marginal factor cost has the same intercept on the wage axis and is twice as steep as the supply. For example, if $w = a + bL$, then $wL = aL + bL^2$. A small change in L is then $\Delta wL/\Delta L = a + 2bL$; thus, the slope of MFC is 2b, and the slope of S is b.

[6] The excess MRP over w gave rise to charges of "monopsonistic exploitation"; see Joan Robinson, *The Economics of Imperfect Competition*, London: Macmillan (1933) at p. 281. This concept of exploitation has been employed in analyses of sports labor markets as we will see later in the chapter.

[7] For a compact statement of the welfare effects, see George J. Stigler (1987), *The Theory of Price*, 4th ed., New York: Macmillan, at pp. 216–218.

perspective, then, the employment of labor should expand beyond L_1. In fact, social welfare would be maximized at an employment level of L_2, which would call for a wage of w_2. However, the monopsonist finds it *privately* optimal to employ L_1 because this maximizes its profits.

We can identify the social welfare loss due to monopsony in Figure 17.4. The competitive outcome – $w = w_2$ and $L = L_2$ – yields a surplus equal to the triangular area *abc*. Part of this is profit (or buyer surplus): area abw_2. The rest is producer surplus: area w_2bc. Monopsony leads to a reduction in employment from L_2 to L_1 and a reduction in the wage paid from w_2 to w_1. This reduces the surplus to area *adec*, but it alters the distribution of the surplus as well. Area w_2few_1 had been producer surplus but is now profit to the buyer. Because this area exceeds the loss in profits due to the reduced employment of labor, area *dbf*, the buyer is better off at the expense of the suppliers. Usually, these distributional consequences are of no concern regarding social welfare.[8] However, the allocative inefficiency of the monopsony solution can be seen as the triangular area *dbe* in Figure 17.4. This area represents a loss in profit (buyer surplus) and producer surplus, which no one receives. It results from the allocative inefficiency of monopsony: too few units of labor are being allocated to the production of the monopsonist's output.

3.2 Numerical Example

Suppose that the supply of *NFL* quality quarterbacks is given by

$$w = \$1{,}000{,}000 + 600{,}000(QB),$$

where w is the wage and QB is the number of quarterbacks. The marginal revenue product of such quarterbacks is

$$MRP = \$10{,}000{,}000 - 300{,}000(QB).$$

If the market were competitive, the wage and employment level would be determined by the equality of supply and demand (which is the marginal revenue product). In this case, we would have

$$\$1{,}000{,}000 + 600{,}000(QB) = \$10{,}000{,}000 - 300{,}000(QB).$$

Solving for the employment level, we find QB equals 10. The wage can be found by substituting $QB = 10$ into either the supply or the demand. In either case, we find that the competitive wage is \$7 million.

If there is monopsony power in the *NFL*, then the number employed will be determined by the equality of the marginal revenue product and the marginal factor cost. Given the supply of quarterbacks, the marginal factor cost will be

$$MFC = \$1{,}000{,}000 + 1{,}200{,}000(QB).$$

Profit maximization requires the equality of MRP and MFC:

$$\$10{,}000{,}000 - 300{,}000(QB) = \$1{,}000{,}000 + 1{,}200{,}000(QB),$$

[8] Of course, the suppliers care a great deal about this redistribution and take steps to try to prevent it. We address this issue later.

which yields an optimal number of quarterbacks: $QB = 6$. This value must be substituted into the supply curve to determine the wage:

$$w = \$1{,}000{,}000 + 600{,}000(6),$$
$$= \$4{,}600{,}000.$$

The result of monopsony is to reduce the wage from \$7.0 million to \$4.6 million and the employment from 10 to 6.

Monopsonistic exploitation is the difference between MRP when $QB = 6$ and the wage paid, which is \$4,600,000. Substituting $QB = 6$ into MRP yields an MRP of \$8,200,000. Thus, the extent of monopsonistic exploitation is \$3,600,000.

The social welfare loss is given by

$$\tfrac{1}{2}(MRP - w)(QB_L - QB_M) = 1/2(\$3{,}600{,}000)(4),$$

which is equal to \$7,200,000.

4 SOURCES OF MONOPSONY POWER

In professional sports, the major leagues historically have used a variety of tactics to obtain and retain monopsony power over the players. These tactics include (1) incorporating the reserve clause in the standard player contracts, (2) the use of reverse-order player drafts, and (3) outright collusion.

4.1 Reserve Clause

As we saw in the discussion of competitive balance, the reserve clause in the standard player contract bound a player to one team for as long as that team wanted to employ the player's services. The player's only alternative was to retire from the league and change occupations. Once under contract, then, a player dealt with a pure monopsonist. There was no one else who could or would bid for his services. For most premier athletes, there are no alternative occupations that are even close in terms of compensation. A few athletes can play other sports and can credibly threaten to go elsewhere, but not many. Bo Jackson and Deion Sanders played football and baseball at the major league level. Danny Ainge played basketball and baseball. Not many athletes can do that. Michael Jordan, arguably the best basketball player of all time, tried his hand at baseball. He was mediocre and could not play at the major league level. Most successful professional athletes stick to one sport. Because these athletes have no reasonable alternatives outside that one sport, the reserve clause put them at the mercy of the teams that owned their contracts. Each team, then, was a pure monopsonist with respect to the players it had under contract. As we will see subsequently, there is empirical evidence that the teams showed little mercy in their dealings with players subject to the reserve clause.

4.2 Player Drafts

The four major sports leagues in the United States employ a reverse-order player draft. Players entering the league are chosen by the teams in an orderly fashion. The team with the worst record picks first, the next worst team picks second, and so on.[9] In principle, the reason for the reverse order is to help the weaker teams improve the quality of their roster and thereby improve competitive balance. In practice, however, draft choices are often traded. As a result, some strong teams get to move up in the draft and thereby protect the strength of their rosters. The draft therefore does not necessarily improve competitive balance.

From a competitive perspective, the draft eliminates competition for the best young players. Without the player draft and other constraints imposed through collective bargaining, one can only imagine how much some NBA team would have paid for Greg Oden in 2007. As it turns out, Oden did fairly well by most standards, but for the kind of big man like him who comes along once in a blue moon, his initial contract was paltry.

4.3 Collusion among the Clubs

With the demise of the reserve clause, players gained a measure of freedom. There are still some limits, which are part of the Collective Bargaining Agreement, but there are completely unrestricted free agents in all major league sports. Free agents should get the benefit of competition for their services, which would mean higher salaries. Faced with that prospect, owners have simply colluded at times to avoid competing in the player market. The owners may simply agree not to raid the rosters of rival teams. In other words, they may agree not to bid competitively in free-agent markets. By agreeing not to compete, they reduce a player's options and maintain each club's monopsony power. In the next section, we examine collusion in MLB's free-agent market to illustrate this strategy.

5 COLLUSION IN MLB'S FREE-AGENT MARKET

For decades, the owners of Major League Baseball teams were protected from competition by the reserve clause, which bound a player to the team that brought him to the majors. The validity of the reserve clause was challenged several times as a violation of the antitrust laws. These challenges, however, were unsuccessful.[10] Eventually, the Collective Bargaining Agreement between MLB and the MLBPA, the players' union, basically eliminated a player's right to file an antitrust suit. Instead, the agreement allowed for arbitration to resolve what would otherwise be antitrust suits. In 1975, a labor arbitrator set pitchers Dave McNally and Andy Messersmith free, which spelled the end of the reserve clause in MLB. Players became free agents and began receiving salaries more in line with their market value.

Salaries in MLB began to rise dramatically. During the 1976–1980 period, average salaries increased by 279 percent. In the subsequent five-year period,

[9] In the NBA, the worst teams are subject to a lottery system, which complicates matters. The idea, however, is the same: the worst teams pick first.

[10] The history of these unsuccessful antitrust challenges is examined in Chapter 22.

1980–1985, average salaries increased by another 287 percent. From relatively meager beginnings, multiyear million-dollar contracts began to appear. For example, during the 1984–1985 free-agency period, Bruce Sutter signed a six-year contract with the Atlanta Braves that was reportedly worth $10.1 million, which was an unheard of sum at the time. Rick Sutcliffe signed a five-year contract with the Chicago Cubs that was worth $9.6 million.[11] From the owners' perspective, it was clear that something had to be done to halt the salary stampede and restore some semblance of fiscal order. The owners were not used to sharing so much of the surplus with their hired hands.

The owners decided to collude rather than compete in the free-agent market. Apparently, they decided simply not to make serious offers to free agents from other teams. In 1985–1986, there were 29 free agents on the market. In stark contrast to earlier years, only one player received an offer from a new team. In the following free-agency period of 1986–1987, there were 19 players available, but no one received a serious offer from a new team. In 1987–1988, the experience was about the same, and this pattern continued in subsequent years as well. How did the owners orchestrate this conspiracy to deny the players the benefits of a competitive free-agent market?

Among other things, the owners established a salary offer data bank. Each team agreed to report any offers that it made to free agents. The anticompetitive potential for such a reporting commitment is fairly obvious. The owners had agreed among themselves to refrain from competitive bidding. Reports to the data bank revealed whether a club was cheating on the agreement. An owner who was tempted to cheat knew that retaliation could be swift if he succumbed to the temptation. Moreover, when each club made its offers known to the other owners, the offers tended to be lower. The result has been described as "quiet cooperation." The players refused to put up with the lack of competitive bidding in the free-agent market.

Unable to file an antitrust suit because of the Collective Bargaining Agreement, the players filed a grievance with a labor arbitrator. This grievance pertained to the 1985–1986 free-agency period. Although the owners steadfastly denied that they had been colluding and argued that they were unilaterally (and simultaneously) practicing fiscal restraint, arbitrator Tom Roberts found the lack of interest in free agents to be "inexplicable." Accordingly, he ruled in favor of the players. The owners were outraged and demanded that a new arbitrator be appointed to deal with the grievances for subsequent years. This demand was met, and George Nicolau replaced Tom Roberts, but the change did not help the owners.

As each subsequent year was examined, the new arbitrator continued to rule in favor of the players. The owners quickly saw the handwriting on the wall and agreed to settle all cases for all years for $280 million. Splitting this sum among the players proved to be difficult. Some 843 players filed 3,173 claims for losses due to the collusion. These claims totaled $1.3 billion, which was more than 4.5 times the total settlement fund.

[11] These values are incorrect from an economic standpoint. Why?

6 MEASURING MONOPSONY POWER

The essence of monopsony power in the labor market is the ability of a large employer to influence wages by restricting employment. Basically, the monopsonist recognizes that the supply curve is positively sloped and that it can move down along that supply curve to a lower wage by decreasing its employment. In this way, the monopsony wage deviates from the competitive wage. A measure of monopsony power should reflect this deviation. One way to do this is to adapt the Lerner Index of monopoly power to the case of monopsony.[12]

6.1 Lerner Index of Monopsony Power

Following Lerner, we want to measure the percentage deviation of the wage actually paid from the competitive wage at the quantity employed, which would equal the marginal revenue product (MRP). Put differently, the Lerner Index of monopsony measures the monopsonistic exploitation ($MRP - w$) relative to the wage (w). consequently, the Lerner Index (λ) would then be

$$\lambda = \frac{MRP - w}{w}.$$

To maximize profit, the monopsonist will restrict its employment to that quantity where the marginal revenue product is equal to the marginal factor cost:

$$MRP = MFC = w + L(\Delta w/\Delta L).$$

If we subtract w from both sides, we have

$$MRP_L - w = L(\Delta w/\Delta L).$$

Now, divide both sides by w to get the Lerner index:

$$\lambda = \frac{MRP_L - w}{w} = \frac{L}{w} \cdot \frac{\Delta w}{\Delta L}.$$

Because the elasticity of supply is $\varepsilon = (\Delta L/\Delta w)(w/L)$, we see that the Lerner Index is the reciprocal of the elasticity of supply of *labor:*

$$\lambda = \frac{1}{\varepsilon}.$$

Intuitively, this is an appealing result. Increases in the supply elasticity decrease monopsony power. This makes economic sense because the greater the quantity response of labor to changes in the wage, the less influence on wages the monopsonist will have. Put differently, the greater the elasticity of supply, the larger the reduction in employment will have to be to reduce the wage

[12] See Abba Lerner (1934), "The Concept of Monopoly and the Measurement of Monopoly Power," *Review of Economic Studies*, 1, 157–175. For an adaptation to monopsony, see Roger D. Blair and Jeffrey L. Harrison (1992), "Cooperative Buying, Monopsony Power, and Antitrust Policy," *Northwestern University Law Review*, 86, 331–366.

Table 17.2. The Influence of Supply and Elasticity on the Lerner Index

ε	0.5	1.0	2.0	5.0	∞
λ	2.0	1.0	0.5	0.2	0

by a given amount. The effect of ε on λ can be seen in several numerical examples, which are contained in Table 17.2.

Thus, when supply is inelastic ($\varepsilon = 0.5$), there is a 200 percent deviation from the competitive result. The more elastic the supply, however, the smaller the deviation. In the limit, when supply is perfectly elastic ($\varepsilon = \infty$), the buyer is essentially in a competitive market and the deviation is zero.[13]

7 MONOPSONISTIC EXPLOITATION: THEORY AND EMPIRICAL EVIDENCE

The term *monopsonistic exploitation* sounds pejorative, but it only refers to the fact that a profit-maximizing monopsonist will hire athletes to the point where $MRP = MFC$ rather than where $MRP = w$. Because $MRP = MFC = w + L\Delta w/\Delta L$, it follows that $MRP > w$ because $L\Delta w/\Delta L > 0$. This is *exploitation* in the sense that the player is paid less than his value to the club. The extent of this exploitation is determined by the supply elasticity. As we will see, the exploitation and the Lerner Index are closely related. Because profit maximization requires

$$MRP = w + L\Delta w/\Delta L,$$

the monopsonistic exploitation will be

$$MRP - w = L(\Delta w/\Delta L).$$

If we multiply the right-hand side by w/w, we have

$$MRP - w = w(L/w)\Delta w/\Delta L,$$

or

$$MRP - w = \frac{w}{\varepsilon}.$$

Thus, the smaller the elasticity of supply, the greater the exploitation.

Whether athletes are exploited in the sense that their *MRP* exceeds the wage that the team pays them is an empirical question. The evidence is that athletes indeed have been exploited: they have been paid less than they were worth to the team. Some athletes are still being exploited in this sense even though salaries are extremely high for many of them.

7.1 Empirical Evidence

Gerald Scully produced the first – truly pioneering – work on this difficult subject.[14] His research provided valuable insights into the dramatic disparity

[13] Jonathan Jacobson and Gary Dorman (1991), "Joint Purchasing, Monopsony, and Antitrust," *Antitrust Bulletin*, 36, 1–90, make the point that if supply is flat (i.e., $\varepsilon = \infty$), there is no monopsony power because price cannot be depressed.

[14] Gerald W. Scully (1974), "Pay and Performance in Major League Baseball," *American Economic Review*, 64, 915–930.

between pay and performance in MLB before the advent of free agency. Scully started from the proposition that team revenues increase when the team's winning percentage rises. This makes sense because fans do not get too excited about their favorite team when it is constantly losing. Players contribute to their teams' winning percentages through their performance on the field. As a result, Scully proceeded by estimating the impact of player performance on a team's winning percentage, which is akin to the player's marginal product. He then estimated the effect of an improved winning percentage on the team's revenue, that is, the marginal revenue. In this way, he estimated the marginal revenue product of a player's performance.

Using data for the 1968 and 1969 seasons, Scully estimated marginal revenue products and compared them with the actual salaries paid. He found that the star players fared the worst. The stars received salaries that were about 15 percent of their MRP. Average players did somewhat better because they received salaries that were about 20 percent of their MRP. Interestingly, mediocre players actually were slightly overpaid. In sum, Scully concluded that monopsonistic exploitation was significant. It is important to recognize that Scully's estimates pertained to a period before free agency. During 1968 and 1969, the players were still subject to the reserve clause and therefore had no real options. They were at the mercy of their club. The empirical evidence suggests that mercy was in short supply before free agency.

Things changed when a labor arbitrator set baseball players free. With free agency, one should expect that those players who were free agents would be paid their market value – that is, their MRP, or something very close to it.[15] This is the approach taken by Krautmann, who assumed that free agents received salaries equal to their MRPs.[16] He then estimated a wage equation in which the salary received by a free agent was a function of performance using data on players eligible for free agency. Next, he used that equation to estimate what the wage of those players subject to reserve restrictions would have been had they been free agents. Using the estimated wage, Krautmann substituted a player's actual performance data to get an estimate of that player's wage had he been a free agent. Krautmann then compared the estimated salaries with the actual salaries paid to measure the extent of any monopsonistic exploitation that remained.

For the free agents, there was presumably no difference between their salary and their MRP – that is, no exploitation. Veterans with at least three seasons in *MLB*, but less than six seasons, were not free agents, but they were protected to some extent by final offer arbitration.[17] When a player and his club cannot agree on a new contract, the player can file for arbitration and have a third party choose between the player's final demand and the club's final offer. The arbitrators look at pay and performance of other players to aid their decision. As a

[15] This inference depends on there being no collusion among the teams. Collusion, of course, could lead to exploitation of free agents.

[16] Anthony C. Krautmann (1999), "What's Wrong with Scully – Estimates of a Player's Marginal Revenue Product," *Economic Inquiry*, 37, 369–381.

[17] We examine final offer arbitration in more detail in Chapter 21.

result, the players should get pretty close to market value. Indeed, Krautmann estimated that these players received about 85 percent of their *MRP*. This, of course, is much better than the 15 to 20 percent of *MRP* that players received before free agency. Final offer arbitration, therefore, introduced some market forces and improved those player's fortunes, even though it did not completely eliminate monopsonistic exploitation. For those players with less than three seasons in MLB, there was no market mechanism to protect them. As one would expect, the clubs were somewhat less than generous. Those players who were wholly restricted were paid about 27 percent of their *MRP*. This is somewhat better than Scully's estimate but a far cry from fair market value.

7.2 A Broader Look at Market Value

Performance measures are easy to find: home runs, batting average, rushing yards, receiving yards, points per game, and so on. For some players, however, their value to a team cannot be captured fully by these performance measures. Consider the case of Terrell Owens, who has been an on-field superstar in the NFL and an off-field negative influence during his career. Despite his unquestioned talent on the field, Terrell Owens was dumped first by the San Francisco 49ers and then by the Philadelphia Eagles for his disruptive attitude off the field. Nonetheless, the Dallas Cowboys signed a three-year deal with Owens. The contract included a $5 million signing bonus and salaries of $5 million for 2006, $8 million in 2007, and $7 million in 2008. At the end of 2006, Cowboys coach Bill Parcells retired. Although the Cowboys could have cut Owens at the end of 2006, they kept him.[18] The Owens example raises an interesting question: How much income has he lost due to the negative influence he brings to the locker room? It is hard to say specifically, but one way to gauge this is to compare his contract to those of other wide receivers after adjusting for performance differences.

For another example, consider the case of Randy Moss, who has always been a controversial athlete. He experienced legal problems while in high school, which led to the withdrawal of a scholarship offer at Florida State University. Moss was a star wide receiver at Marshall University and was drafted by the Minnesota Vikings. Despite complaints about his work ethic and focus during games, Moss was a superstar. After much on-field success and a few off-field problems, Moss moved on to the Oakland Raiders – the last refuge of troubled and troublesome players. Unfortunately, the Raiders had fallen on hard times on the field, and Moss's productivity waned. During the 2006 season, Moss caught only 42 passes for 553 yards, and he scored only three touchdowns. Moss was dissatisfied and complained constantly. He loafed at times and made it clear that he was unhappy and wanted to leave Oakland.

Moss was due to earn $9.25 million in 2007 and $11.25 million in 2008 with the Raiders. During the 2007 NFL draft, however, Moss was traded to the New England Patriots for a fourth-round draft choice.[19] Because of a combination

[18] Owens wore out his welcome in Dallas, moved on to the Buffalo Bills, and in 2010 landed in Cincinnati with the Bengals and Ochocinco – another controversial player.

[19] Judy Battista, "Patriots Accelerate an Overhaul by Trading for the Raiders' Moss," *New York Times*, April 30, 2007.

of factors – his age (30), his recent lack of productivity, and the limited demand for a troublesome player – Moss agreed to play for the Patriots in 2007 for $3 million. Arguably, the price that Moss paid for his attitude was more than $6 million per year.[20]

In contrast to Moss and Owens, the Yankees valued Roger Clemens for more than mere numbers.[21] Starved for quality pitching, the Yankees signed Clemens to an extraordinary contract in 2007. The total value was $28,000,022, which was prorated over the portion of the season he played. Although Clemens had more wins than any living pitcher and more Cy Young Awards than any pitcher who ever lived, he was no longer the dominating power pitcher of earlier years. Nonetheless, Clemens improved the attitude and demeanor of the Yankees. Although some pitchers excuse losses due to poor run production, Clemens was not among them: "When you have guys scuffling at the plate, you're [still] supposed to get it done." When the Yankees needed it, Clemens volunteered to pitch in relief, which showed other players that a real professional athlete will do whatever will help the team win.[22]

Clemens also brought some good old-fashioned toughness to the Yankees. Some pitchers fail to protect their teammates, but Clemens was not among them. The Toronto Blue Jays were repeatedly throwing at Alex Rodriguez during 2007, so Clemens responded in kind. Even after a warning from the umpire, Clemens hit Alex Rios with a pitch and was ejected from the game, fined, and suspended for a game. Presumably, the message was not lost on the Blue Jays or on Clemens's Yankee teammates.

8 CONCLUDING REMARKS

In this chapter, we found that a player's worth to a team is his marginal revenue product. After setting out the competitive benchmark, we focused on monopsony in general and in the sports labor market. Empirical research shows that players can be underpaid – even while earning millions of dollars – when the clubs wield monopsony power.

PROBLEMS AND QUESTIONS

1. A few years ago, the University of Hawaii (UH) increased the ticket prices to its home football games. At about the same time, the UH head football coach received a $400,000 per year raise in salary. UH officials quickly claimed that the salary increase had nothing to do with the increased ticket prices. Is this claim believable? Does it make sense from an economic perspective?

[20] In New England, Moss was a model citizen. His attitude was exemplary, and his performance was outstanding. He caught an NFL-record 23 touchdown passes in 2007. When he re-signed with the Patriots, he received a $12 million signing bonus as part of a three-year $27 million contract.

[21] Tyler Kepner, "Measured by More than Numbers," *New York Times*, July 2, 2007.

[22] This, of course, can be excessive. As we saw in Chapter 14, Clemens was implicated in MLB's steroid scandal.

2. When Michelle Wie was 13 years old, she was a golf prodigy from Honolulu. Not only did she drive the ball nearly 300 yards, but she was charismatic beyond her years. Her presence in a tournament sparked immediate interest. When she played in an Ladies Professional Golf Association event, the requests for media credentials doubled and the organizers actually ran out of daily tickets. How would you asses her MRP for these tournaments?
3. In 2000, Ken Griffey, Jr.'s MRP appeared to be some \$18 million and his salary was only \$11 million. Can you explain why Cincinnati was able to pay Griffey so much less than his MRP?
4. In 2002, Tiger Woods agreed to play in the New Zealand Open for the first time. The organizers offered to pay him a \$2 million appearance fee. When the organizers dramatically increased ticket prices, fans and other professional golfers howled in protest. The organizers explained that "ticket prices are higher because of Tiger's presence, but not because of his appearance guarantee." Does this make sense from an economic perspective?
5. Suppose that the supply of NFL caliber punters (P) is given by

$$w_s = 100{,}000 + 3{,}000P,$$

where w_s represents the wage and P is the number of punters. Given the supply, the marginal factor cost is $MFC = 100{,}000 + 6{,}000P$. The marginal revenue product of punters can be expressed as

$$MRP_P = 460{,}000 - 3{,}000P.$$

   a. What are the competitive wage and employment level?
   b. What are the wage and employment under monopsony?
   c. What is the extent of monopsonistic exploitation in this market?
   d. What is the social welfare loss of monopsony?
   e. Illustrate all of the above in a graph.
6. Scully found that the salaries paid in MLB before free agency were about 20 percent of a player's MRP. Suppose this is accurate. What was the elasticity of supply of those players?
7. Suppose that the labor supply is given by:

$$w_s = 25 + 5L,$$

where w_s is the wage on the supply curve and L represents the units of labor. The marginal factor cost is then $MFC = 25 + 10L$. The demand (MRP) is given by

$$w_D = 100 - 5L,$$

where w_D is the wage on the demand curve.

   a. Find the competitive wage and quantity.
   b. Find the wage and quantity under conditions of monopsony.
   c. Calculate the deadweight social welfare loss of monopsony.

8. In the 1950s, MLB teams often paid big bonuses to sign amateur stars. The owners imposed a rule that such "bonus babies" could not be sent to a minor league team and had to be placed on the team's 25-man roster. Why would the owners deliberately hinder the development of these "bonus babies"?
9. Despite the talent, desire, and grit that it takes to be a world-class speed skater, a *New York Times* headline proclaimed "Speedskating's Olympic Rewards Fail to Pay the Bills." Why are world-class speed skaters broke?
10. Tiger Woods decided to end his self-imposed absence from the PGA Tour at the 2010 Masters Tournament. This caused a slight surge in ticket prices in the secondary market. What does this say about Tiger Woods's *MRP* for this particular tournament?
11. Some NCAA coaches have found that their schools have no tolerance for losing. Despite following the rules and graduating their players, coaches who fail to win fail to keep their jobs. Should they be surprised?

RESEARCH QUESTIONS

1. The owner of the Los Angeles Clippers has a history of letting free agents go rather than paying them their market value. Keeping free agents can be very expensive. Elton Brand, for example, has been offered an $84.2 million multiyear contract. The Collective Bargaining Agreement permits a team to pay 25% of the contract value as a signing bonus. In this case, that would be about $21 million. In addition, a player can receive 70% of the first-year salary as an upfront payment. In Brand's case, this could be another $7 million. Thus, the Clippers would have to pay Brand as much as $28 million just to prevent his leaving. Find out which players have left the team for more money. How have the Clippers fared on the court with their strategy of letting free agents go elsewhere?
2. Review the facts in *Brown v. Pro Football Inc.*, 518 U.S. 231 (1996). Discuss the source of the owners' collective monopsony power and its exercise in this case.
3. In the 2006 season, the rookie minimum salary in the NFL was $260,000. How many rookies played for the minimum? Construct a schedule of salaries for all first-year players. If a player received a signing bonus, prorate the bonus over the life of his contract.
4. Examine how rookie salaries vary with place in the draft. Look at the salaries for the players chosen in the first three rounds.

REFERENCES AND FURTHER READING

Baade, R. A., and V. A. Matheson. (2006). "Have Public Finance Principles Been Shut Out in Financing New Stadiums for the NFL?" *Public Finance and Management*, 6, 284–320.

Kaplan, Daniel. "NFL Owners Give $300M for N.Y. Stadium." *Sports Business Journal*, Dec. 11, 2006.

Kaplan, Daniel. "Giants, Jets to borrow $650M each." *Sports Business Journal*, March 19, 2007.

Miller, P. (2007). "Private Financing and Sports Franchise Values: The Case of Major League Baseball." *Journal of Sports Economics*, 8, 449–467.

Noll, Roger G. (1974). *Government and the Sports Business* (chapter 9). Washington, DC: The Brookings Institution.

Noll, Roger G., and Andrew Zimbalist. (1997). *Sports, Jobs, and Taxes: The Economic Impact of Sports Teams and Stadiums.* Washington, DC: The Brookings Institution.

Owen, Jeffrey G. (2003). "The Stadium Game: Cities Versus Teams." *Journal of Sports Economics*, 4, 183–202.

Pickard, J. L., and I. C. Araujo. (1989). "Financing Toronto's SkyDome: A Unique Partnership of Public and Private Funding." *Government Finance Review* (December), 7–12.

Quirk, James, and Rodney Fort. (1992). *Pay Dirt: The Business of Professional Team Sports* (chapter 4). Princeton, NJ: Princeton University Press.

Quirk, James, and Rodney Fort (1999). *Hard Ball: The Abuse of Power in Pro Team Sports* (chapter 7). Princeton, NJ: Princeton University Press.

Quinn, Kevin G., Paul B. Bursik, Christopher P. Borick, and Lisa Raethz (2003). "Do New Digs Mean More Wins? The Relationship Between a New Venue and a Professional Sports Team's Competitive Success." *Journal of Sports Economics*, 4, 167–182.

Shubnell, L. D., J. E. Petersen, and C. B. Harris. (1985). "The Big Ticket: Financing a Professional Sports Facility." *Government Finance Review* (June): 7–11.

Szymanski, Stefan. (2009). *Playbooks and Checkbooks: An Introduction to the Economics of Modern Sports* (chapter 6). Princeton, NJ: Princeton University Press.

Zimbalist, Andrew. (2003). *May the Best Team Win* (chapter 6). Washington, DC: The Brookings Institution.

Zimbalist, Andrew. (2006). *The Bottom Line.* Philadelphia: Temple University Press, pp. 139–140.

Zimbalist, A., and J. G. Long. (2006). "Facility Finance: Measurement, Trends, and Analysis." *International Journal of Sport Finance*, 1, 201–211.

SPORTS LABOR MARKET

18

The National Collegiate Athletic Association as a Collusive Monopsony

1 INTRODUCTION

The National Collegiate Athletic Association (NCAA) has been characterized as a cartel, that is, "a combination of independent commercial or industrial enterprises designed to limit competition."[1] As we will see, this is an accurate characterization, especially as it relates to the labor market for student-athletes and coaches. More precisely, the NCAA acts as a buyer cartel or collusive monopsony. Under the auspices of the NCAA, the member institutions collude to reduce competition among themselves in an effort to reduce costs and thereby generate more profit for their athletic programs. As we saw in the preceding chapter, *monopsony* is the awkward label attached to the market structure in which there is a single buyer of a good or service. In the United States, this market structure is rare indeed, but *collusive* monopsony is not so rare. Examples can be found throughout the economy, but the NCAA is a particularly good example.[2]

The NCAA's members collude on two key inputs in the production of athletic competition: the student-athletes themselves and their coaches. With respect to athletes, the agreement restricts quantities by placing a ceiling on the number of scholarships that a school may award in each sport. In addition, in the name of amateurism, the compensation of these athletes is limited to room, board, tuition, books, and incidentals.[3] Bonuses for winning conference championships are limited to relatively inexpensive rings or watches. There have been several legal challenges to the NCAA's monopolistic behavior

[1] *Webster's New Ninth Collegiate Dictionary*, Springfield, MA: Merriam-Webster, 1988. For a detailed study, see Arthur A. Fleisher, Brian L. Goff, and Robert D. Tollison, *The National Collegiate Athletic Association: A Study in Cartel Behavior*, Chicago: University of Chicago Press, 1992. The present chapter depends on Roger D. Blair and Richard E. Romano (1997), "Collusive Monopsony in Theory and Practice: The NCAA," *Antitrust Bulletin*, 42, 681–719.

[2] For a thorough treatment of antitrust law and the economics of monopsony, *see* Roger D. Blair and Jeffrey L. Harrison (2010), *Monopsony in Antitrust Law and Economics*, New York: Cambridge University Press.

[3] For an interesting analysis, see Lawrence M. Kahn (2007), "Markets: Cartel Behavior and Amateurism in College Sports," *Journal of Economic Perspectives*, 21, 209–226.

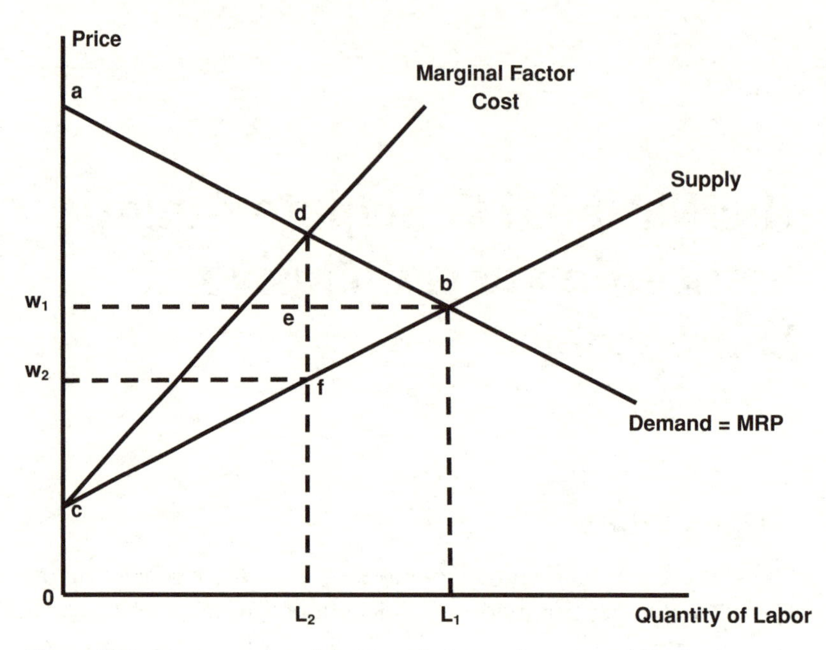

Figure 18.1. Monopsony is exploited by reducing employment and thereby depressing price below the competitive level.

by student-athletes, which we examine here. With respect to coaches, the number employed in each sport is limited by NCAA Bylaws. In this connection, we examine the *Hennessey v. NCAA* litigation.[4] The compensation of coaches is typically unconstrained, although there have been attempts to restrict the earnings of some coaches. In this connection, we examine the *Law v. NCAA* litigation,[5] which led the NCAA to rescind its rule restricting the earnings of some assistant coaches.

In this chapter, we explore the economic theory of collusive monopsony. In doing so, we explain how the NCAA deals with the problems inherent in organizing a cartel, coordinating the efforts of the members, and enforcing the terms of their agreement. We also explore the implications of collusive monopsony for price and quantity as well as the returns to the colluders. In this regard, we show the effect of collusive monopsony on average and marginal cost as well as on profit. Finally, we examine the welfare consequences and the implications for antitrust policy.

2 THE INCENTIVE TO COLLUDE

When buyers behave independently, the forces of supply and demand will typically lead to a price and quantity that maximize social welfare. Figure 18.1 shows the market for labor services L, which is an input in production. The

[4] *Hennessey v. National Collegiate Athletic Association*, 564 F. 2d 1136 (5th Cir. 1977).
[5] *Law v. National Collegiate Athletic Association*, 902 F. Supp. 1394 (1995).

independent decisions of buyers and sellers of labor will lead to a price of w_1 and a quantity of L_1. Now, consumer surplus is the difference between the most that buyers are *willing* to pay for the labor services and the amount that the market *requires* them to pay. Analogously, producer (or supplier) surplus represents the difference between the lowest price that suppliers are *willing* to accept and the actual market price. Social welfare is the sum of supplier surplus (area w_1bc) and consumer surplus (area abw_1), which is represented by area *abc* in Figure 18.1. In the absence of market failure, unfettered competition leads to the maximization of social welfare. Although the buyers enjoy consumer surplus, or profits, equal to area abw_1, they may be able to collude and use their collective buying power to increase their profits at the expense of the suppliers and to the detriment of society. If the formerly independent buyers pool their demands and coordinate their purchases, they can exploit whatever buying power they possess. By acting together to limit their employment decisions, the former competitors can act as a monopsonist would act. The collusive monopsonist will maximize profits in precisely the same way as a single-firm monopsonist would. As we saw in the preceding chapter, a profit-maximizing monopsonist will restrict employment and thereby depress the wage below the competitive level.

Box 18.1 ***Protecting Amateurism or Exploiting Monopsony Power?***

The NCAA would like the public to believe that it is dedicated to defending *amateurism*.* It is pretty clear, however, that the only amateurs are the student-athletes. Certainly, neither the coaches nor the athletic directors are amateurs. They are handsomely paid professionals. Moreover, college athletics are big business, not amateur events. For the major sports programs, there are multimillion-dollar payoffs: TV revenues, bowl revenues, stadium revenues, endorsements deals, and licensing fees for intellectual property. The NCAA may actually have to share some of these revenues with the so-called amateurs.

Student-athletes have a property right in their images and likeliness that can be used in TV advertising, posters, calendars, apparel, video games, film clips, and rebroadcasts of classic games. As a condition of eligibility, all student-athletes must grant these rights to the NCAA. All licensing fees go to the NCAA or the member institution rather than to the athlete. Clearly, an athlete's willingness to surrender potentially valuable property rights in exchange for NCAA eligibility is a function of the NCAA's collusive monopsony power. Two former athletes have filed separate lawsuits objecting to the NCAA's licensing of their images and likenesses without compensating the athletes. These court decisions could result in a significant reallocation of those licensing fees.

* For a compact analysis, see Jeffrey L. Harrison and Casey C. Harrison (2009), "The Law and Economics of the NCAA's Claim to Monopsony Rights," *Antitrust Bulletin*, 54, 923–949.

As we can see in Figure 18.1, to maximize the benefits of their collective buying power, the colluding employers will restrict their total employment to L_2, which is the quantity at which the marginal factor cost equals the marginal revenue product. The collusive monopsony will then pay only w_2, which is the price on the supply curve that corresponds to quantity L_2. This hiring restriction is generally supported by an agreement on hiring quotas among the members; the sum of the quotas is equal to L_2. The lower input price is, of course, the motive for collusion. In comparison to the competitive outcome, buyer surplus increases by the excess of area w_1efw_2 over area *dbe*. This difference must be positive because we have found the profit-maximizing solution for the buyer cartel. As is apparent from Figure 18.1, the cartel converts supplier surplus equal to area w_1efw_2 into profit for the cartel members. Thus, the gains to the NCAA members come solely at the expense of the athletes. Unfortunately, social welfare falls by area *dbf*, which is the deadweight social welfare loss of monopsony. This is the economic foundation for an antitrust policy that proscribes collusive monopsony.

3 EFFECT OF COLLUSIVE MONOPSONY ON COSTS

When members of the NCAA agree among themselves to restrict their demands for athletes and coaches, one might suppose that this would reduce their costs and thereby benefit consumers through lower output prices. Sadly, however, this is not the case. A complete understanding of this result is important for an informed analysis of the NCAA's conduct.

When a buying cartel exercises monopsony power, it pays a lower price for the input in question. This might seem to reduce the cartel's costs, which in turn should lead to greater output and lower prices for consumers. In fact, the opposite occurs – the exercise of monopsony power leads to a reduction in output and therefore higher prices for consumers.[6] This can be derived from the effect of monopsony power on the cartel's cost curves.[7] Because final output declines, there is no consumer welfare rationale for encouraging the NCAA's collusive monopsony.

3.1 Marginal Cost

The formation of a collusive monopsony will cause the industry marginal cost curve to shift upward rather than downward. To see this, we will compare the marginal cost of a competitor with the marginal cost of a monopsonist increasing the employment of labor.

Marginal cost is defined to be the change in total cost when output is increased by one unit. Assuming that the only variable input in the short run is labor, a one-unit increase in output requires hiring additional labor at the competitive wage, which is constant for the competitive employer. When the

[6] Because a monopsonist depresses the price it pays by reducing employment, we should suspect that output will fall. After all, if a producer uses fewer inputs, the quantity of output must decline.

[7] These results are derived mathematically in the appendix to this chapter.

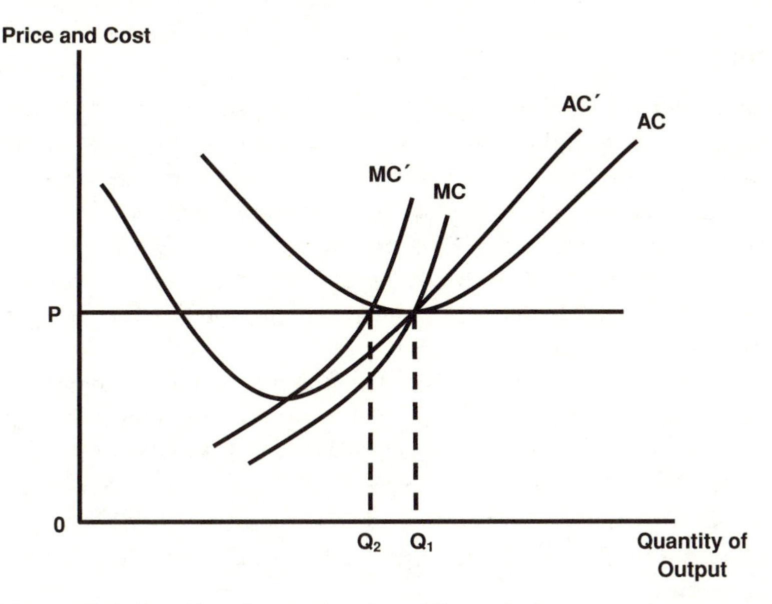

Figure 18.2. The effect of monopsony is to shift marginal cost up and average cost down and to the left.

monopsonist expands employment to increase output by one unit, it moves along a positively sloped labor supply curve and therefore must pay a higher wage to the added labor and to everyone else who is employed.

Consequently, the monopsonist's marginal cost curve *MC′* lies above the competitive marginal cost *MC* in Figure 18.2. This is the result because a monopsonist cannot simply pay the marginal worker a higher wage. All workers must be paid the higher wage when employment expands.

3.2 Average Cost

The profit incentive for behaving as a collusive monopsony flows from the effect on average cost. Whereas the marginal cost curve shifts upward because of the exercise of monopsony power, the average cost falls below that of a competitor in the labor market at outputs below the competitive level. This, of course, is why profit rises: monopsony creates a gap between the output price and the per unit cost.

The average cost of a firm with no monopsony power is determined by constant competitive wages. If a firm with monopsony power were to increase output, it would increase employment and pay a higher wage. The result would be an increase in average cost above that of the competitive employer. If the monopsonist reduced output, it would hire less labor, and wages would fall below the competitive level. The result would be a decrease in the average cost relative to that of a competitive firm. Thus, the exercise of collusive monopsony is to shift the average cost curve down and to the left for output levels below the competitive quantity. The effect of monopsony on the average cost curve is shown in Figure 18.2. The clear implication is that a lower-than-competitive output yields greater profits for the cartel.

4 THE NCAA: A COLLUSIVE MONOPSONY

The NCAA behaves like a collusive monopsony in acquiring two crucial inputs: student-athletes and coaches.[8] As a result, it faces the usual problems confronted by all buyer cartels: deciding on payments, imposing hiring quotas, limiting nonprice competition, sharing the resulting profits, coordinating activities, and deterring cheating.[9] The structure of the NCAA is designed to deal with all of these problems. The NCAA's durability, resilience, and enormous success are proof of its ability to adjust as necessary to cope with the changing needs of its member institutions.

Before intercollegiate athletics became big business, there was a need for uniform rules regarding the games being played, especially football, which was brutal. As a result, a precursor to the NCAA was formed in 1905. Between then and now, the NCAA has evolved in size, scope, and power.[10] Now that intercollegiate sports, particularly football and men's basketball, are big business, a good deal of the NCAA's attention is centered on business matters: revenues, costs, and profits.

4.1 Limits on Prices and Quantities

The NCAA members – some 1,000 educational institutions – meet annually to vote on a variety of matters. If necessary, special sessions can be called between the annual meetings. There are various committees that advise the NCAA members at large on specific issues of interest. Once agreement is reached, the policies of the NCAA are set out in Bylaws that are binding on all members. Among these are those that deal with student-athletes and with coaches. There are rules governing the compensation of student-athletes. Generally, athletes may not receive more than a "full grant-in-aid," which is defined as "financial aid that consists of tuition and fees, room and board, and required course-related books."[11] In addition to the limits on compensation, the NCAA limits the number of grants-in-aid that can be awarded in each sport.[12] These limitations are summarized in Table 18.1. As one might expect, there are detailed rules regarding how one counts the student-athletes in the various sports and how to deal with those who participate in two sports. These details are important

[8] The NCAA has been so successful that "the NCAA is the clear and deserving winner of the first annual prize for best [monopsony] in America." Robert J. Barro, "Let's Play Monopoly," *Wall Street Journal*, Aug. 27, 1991. The *Antitrust & Trade Regulation Report*, Jan. 30, 1997, reported that the NCAA "continues in many regards to operate as a cartel."

[9] For an examination of cartels and their problems, see Roger D. Blair and David L. Kaserman (2009), *Antitrust Economics*, New York: Oxford University Press, 2nd ed.

[10] For a more detailed historical account, see Fleisher, Goff and Tollison, *supra* note 2.

[11] 2006–2007 NCAA Division I Operating Manual, article 15.2.5.1. The specific definition of each component of a full grant-in-aid is contained in article 15.2. It has been estimated that a "full grant-in-aid" is some $2,500 short of the actual cost. This obviously causes problems for student-athletes whose families cannot provide supplemental financial support. See ESPN.com, *NCAA Might Face Damages in Hundreds of Millions*, Feb. 20, 2006.

[12] The limitations for men's and women's basketball are found in the NCAA Manual, at article 15.5.4; the limit for football is in article 15.5.5. For the other sports, see article 15.5.3.

Table 18.1. Maximum Number of Grants-in-Aid

Men's Sports	Number	Women's Sports	Number
Baseball	11.7	Archery	5
Basketball	13.0	Badminton	6
Cross Country/Track	12.6	Basketball	15
Fencing	4.5	Bowling	5
Football	85.0	Cross Country/Track	18
Golf	4.5	Equestrian	15
Gymnastics	6.3	Fencing	5
Ice Hockey	18.0	Field Hockey	12
Lacrosse	12.6	Golf	6
Rifle	3.6	Gymnastics	12
Skiing	6.3	Ice Hockey	18
Soccer	9.9	Lacrosse	12
Swimming and Diving	9.9	Rowing	20
Tennis	4.5	Rugby	12
Volleyball	4.5	Skiing	7
Water Polo	4.5	Soccer	14
Wrestling	9.9	Softball	12
		Squash	12
		Swimming and Diving	14
		Synchronized Swimming	5
		Team Handball	10
		Tennis	8
		Volleyball	12
		Water Polo	8

Source: 2010–11 NCAA Division I Operating Manual.

for closing loopholes. There are, for example, 85 grants-in-aid available to football players. One way around this limitation is to recruit some football players and put them on track scholarships. The rules prevent this subterfuge. There are also detailed rules regarding recruiting. All of this is fully consistent with cartel theory.

If restrictions on prices and quantities are to be fully effective, a cartel must prevent cheating in the agreement. The old saying "there is no honor among thieves" certainly holds for members of a cartel. Consequently, indirect means of skirting the agreed upon restrictions must be foreclosed. If a cartel does not limit other ways of competing, costs will rise and cartel profits will be eroded. The costs of nonprice competition can easily get out of hand and erode an athletic program's profits. In competing for the best athletes, schools can compete by hiring the best coaches who earn salaries in the $2 to $5 million range. They also compete by offering lavish training facilities, plush athletic dorms, upgraded training tables, extensive educational counseling and tutoring, frequent campus visits with first-class plane tickets, and so on. As a program spends ever more dollars to attract the best players, its cartel profits fall. As a result, it is in the collective interest of the NCAA's members to implement rules that curtail such expenditures. They have been somewhat successful in this effort.

Box 18.2 ***Should NCAA Athletes Be Paid?***

In a sense, NCAA athletes who receive a full grant-in-aid are being paid. Those who attend prestigious private schools, such as Duke, Northwestern, Notre Dame, and Vanderbilt, are being paid around $50,000 per year. The payment is considerably less at state-supported schools where tuition is substantially lower, but the fact remains that those athletes on scholarship are being paid.

Usually, when the issue of payment arises, the question is whether student-athletes should be paid something approaching their marginal revenue products. As elsewhere in the real world, this would lead to very uneven payments. NCAA champions in sports such as golf, lacrosse, soccer, swimming, and tennis would receive next to nothing. Star football and basketball players would earn substantial sums: hundreds of thousands of dollars.

To the extent that profits earned in revenue-generating sports such as football and men's basketball are paid to student-athletes in those sports, the non-revenue sports (in most cases, all the rest) will not be subsidized. This, however, is not the end of the world. There are many student-athletes participating at schools that provide no scholarships. This may not be such a bad thing.

Box 18.3 ***Monopsonistic Exploitation by the NCAA***

The NCAA puts strict limits on the compensation of student-athletes. No one – even the premier players – may receive more than a full-grant-in-aid, which is defined as tuition and fees, room and board, and books. Because the NCAA is a buying cartel, one should expect some monopsonistic exploitation, that is, a gap between an athlete's marginal revenue product and the monetary value of the grant-in-aid.

Brown estimated the marginal revenue product of premium college football players.* First, he estimated team quality, as measured by the number of players selected in the NFL draft, as a function of a team's recruiting efforts, market characteristics, and conference revenue-sharing policies. Second, team revenues were then estimated as a function of the number of players drafted by the NFL. Using data for the 1988–1989 season, Brown estimated that a premium college player's marginal revenue product was $538,760. The difference between this and the monetary value of a full grant-in-aid is a measure of the monopsonistic exploitation of premium college football players.

* Robert W. Brown (1993), "An Estimate of the Rent Generated by a Premium College Football Player," *Economic Inquiry*, 31, 671–684.

Table 18.2. Maximum Number of Coaches[1]

Men's Sports	Number	Women's Sports	Number
Baseball	3	Archery	2
Basketball	4	Badminton	2
Cross country/track	3	Basketball	4
Fencing	2	Bowling	2
Football[2]	12	Cross Country/Track	3
Golf	2	Equestrian	3
Gymnastics	3	Fencing	2
Ice Hockey	3	Field Hockey	3
Lacrosse	3	Golf	2
Rifle	2	Gymnastics	3
Skiing	2	Ice Hockey	3
Soccer	3	Lacrosse	3
Swimming	2	Rifle	2
Swimming and Diving	3	Rowing	3
Tennis	2	Rugby	3
Volleyball	3	Skiing	2
Water Polo	2	Soccer	3
Wrestling	3	Softball	3
		Squash	2
		Swimming	2
		Swimming and Diving	3
		Synchronized Swimming	2
		Team Handball	2
		Tennis	2
		Volleyball	3
		Water Polo	2

[1] In addition to the numbers listed, a weight or strength coach may also be employed.
[2] In football, two graduate assistant coaches are also permitted.
Source: 2010–11 NCAA Division I Operating Manual. Each entry shows the number of head and assistant coaches.

As one might suspect, the limitations on the number of coaches by sport are fairly detailed for football but are less so for the other sports. A "countable" coach is anyone who "participates (in any manner) in the coaching of the intercollegiate team in practice, games, or organized activities directly related to that sport."[13] For Division I-A football, there is a limit of one head coach, nine assistant coaches, and two graduate assistant coaches. In addition, an institution may employ a strength and conditioning coach who does not count against the number of football coaches. The limitations on the number of coaches for the other sports are summarized in Table 18.2.

[13] Operating Manual, *supra* note 13, at article 11.7.1.1.1.

4.2 Revenue Sharing

In simple, textbook cartel models, there is no real need to worry about revenue sharing. When all the cartel members are identical, the restrictions on output or employment can usually be spread proportionately. As a result, each member simply keeps the excess profit that its own operation generates, and equal profit sharing results. In the real world, of course, college athletic programs are not identical, and this may pose problems in sharing the cartel's spoils. In intercollegiate athletics, gate receipts are shared with opposing teams, bowl revenues are shared within conferences, television revenues are shared, and the NCAA basketball tournament revenues are shared. This revenue sharing is not complete. For example, individual institutions keep private donations, trademark licensing fees, concession revenues, and most of the gate receipts (net of payments to visiting teams), which means that some cartel members are going to be much better off financially than others. This financial imbalance cannot be eliminated entirely because there is a danger that the most powerful athletic programs could defect from the NCAA. In fact, the revenue-sharing formula has evolved over time to prevent the defection of a coalition of the most powerful athletic programs.

4.3 Sanctions for Cheating

The NCAA has developed sanctions to deal with cheating on the cartel rules by member institutions. For example, when the NCAA found the University of Washington guilty of recruiting violations, it imposed substantial penalties: (1) a 2-year ban on bowl participation, (2) a 1-year ban on receiving television revenue, (3) a reduction in football scholarships for 2 years, (4) a reduction in the number of permissible football recruiting visits for 2 years, and (5) a 2-year probation. The purpose of such sanctions is to deter cheating by making it unprofitable to cheat.[14] Being able to impose such penalties on cartel members that cheat gives the NCAA an enormous advantage over most cartels that have limited enforcement options.

4.4 The Evolution of Sanctions

In the 1946–1953 period, the major conferences met and decided on rules for recruiting and limitations on financial aid. Earlier efforts had been largely unsuccessful, but this time they also created an enforcement mechanism. Committees were established to investigate cheating and to impose punishment on the guilty. Unfortunately, the only available punishment was expulsion, which is a rather blunt instrument. Eventually, however, the NCAA refined the sanctions to include the elimination of revenue sharing and reductions in the number of grants-in-aid, television appearances, bowl appearances, and eligibility for championships. In extreme cases, the NCAA may issue the "death penalty" by suspending a program for a period of one or two years. As Southern Methodist University's (SMU's) experience shows, it is extremely difficult to recover from the death penalty.

[14] For a more detailed model of deterrence, see Chapter 11.

4.5 Consequences of the Death Penalty: SMU

If a school is found guilty of a "major violation" of NCAA rules within five years of being on probation for rules violations, it may receive the "death penalty." If so, the school cannot compete in the sport involved in the major violation for one or two seasons. The death penalty can have a devastating impact on once-proud programs that run afoul of NCAA rules. This is illustrated by the consequences suffered by SMU's football program.

SMU's football program – featuring the Pony Express of Eric Dickerson and Craig James – enjoyed remarkable success in the early 1980s. After a modest record of 8–4 in 1980, SMU went on a splendid four-year run: 10–1 in 1981, 11–0–1 in 1982, 10–2 in 1983, and 10–2 in 1984. Then things began to unravel as suspicions of NCAA violations began to surface. In 1985, the NCAA put SMU on three years probation. While on probation, SMU paid players from $50 to $750 per month, which is a major violation. SMU received extremely heavy punishment.

First, SMU's 1987 season was cancelled, and all of its players were allowed to transfer without penalty. Not surprisingly, most did so. Second, all of SMU's 1988 home games were cancelled. Because it had so few remaining players, SMU cancelled its away games as well. Third, SMU's scholarships were reduced by 55 over a four-year period. Fourth, the SMU coaching staff was reduced from 10 to 6. Finally, SMU was banned from bowl games and TV appearances in 1988 and 1989.

SMU has still not recovered from the death penalty. Even though its team was back at full strength by 1992, its record since has been abysmal. From 1981 to 1984, the Mustangs' record was 41–5–1. For the 1992–1995 seasons, SMU's record was 9–32–3. It has not gotten much better in subsequent years. For 1996–2000, SMU was 23–33; for 2001–2005, they were 15–42; and for 2006–2010, SMU was 23–40.

The message for member schools is loud and clear: flagrant cheating will be punished severely, and the consequences may extend well into the future. The SMU example should serve as a powerful deterrent to such rules violations. Most people doubt that the death penalty will be imposed again because the consequences for SMU were so severe, but the NCAA has not taken that sanction off the table.

The penalties recently imposed on the University of Southern California (USC) may be a more realistic indicator of things to come. The NCAA infractions committee concluded that football star Reggie Bush and basketball star O. J. Mayo received improper benefits that violated the amateurism principle. Moreover, the NCAA found USC guilty of a "lack of institutional control."

The football program was hit the hardest. First, it was deemed ineligible for a bowl appearance in either 2010 or 2011. Second, it lost 10 scholarships for each of the three years, 2010 through 2012. Third, it had to forfeit all games in which Reggie Bush played after December 2004, which included its Bowl Championship Series Championship win in 2005. These penalties, especially the loss of scholarships, will weaken USC on the field, which will extend into the future. This is not the death penalty, but nor is it a slap on the wrist.

5 ANTITRUST CHALLENGES BY COACHES

We examine two antitrust cases that demonstrate the NCAA's behavior as a collusive monopsonist. These cases also illustrate the judiciary's failure to understand some fundamental economic concepts regarding monopsony. In the first case, economic misconceptions mattered, but not in the second.

5.1 *Hennessey v. NCAA*

At a special session in 1975, the NCAA members agreed to limit the maximum number of assistant football and basketball coaches. This restriction applied only to Division I schools. As a result of the restriction, Hennessey was demoted to part-time status after being an assistant coach for 16 years. His compensation was reduced by 90% from $20,000 to $2,100. This cost saving for the university was a crippling financial blow to Hennessey. In response, Hennessey filed an antitrust suit alleging that the NCAA's agreement on the number of coaches violated Section 1 of the Sherman Act, which forbids "contracts, combinations, and conspiracies in restraint of trade." As a victim of the alleged conspiracy, Hennessey could recover three times the damages that he suffered plus his attorney's fees.

The court found that the NCAA Bylaw limiting the number of coaches resulted from an agreement among the member institutions that obviously restrained trade because they agreed not to compete by hiring more coaches. However, the question was whether the agreement constituted an *unreasonable* restraint of trade. In this connection, the court noted an absence of specific intent to injure the named plaintiffs or other assistant coaches, either individually or as a group. This observation reveals a lack of understanding of supply. If the supply function of assistant coaches has a positive slope, an agreement to reduce the number of assistant coaches hired has two effects. First, some coaches will lose their jobs entirely or be demoted as Hennessey was. Second, there is movement along the supply curve to a lower wage for those who remain employed. As a consequence, the record may be devoid of any evidence that this was the unabashed intent of the restriction, but it nonetheless is true that the restraint would have an adverse effect on the community of assistant coaches. The fact that the NCAA members apparently were concerned about the welfare of those whom they knew would be hurt seems to have influenced the court.[15] To see how silly this is, one need only ponder whether similar expressions of concern would get price fixers in the output market off the hook.

[15] "There was, to be sure, an awareness by the members of the association that there would be some adversely affected by the Bylaw, but the attitude expressed was one of concern, not indifference." *Hennessey*, 564 F. 2d at 1153. In this court, at least, a good attitude saves bad deeds.

The court clearly understood the nature and purpose of the NCAA's endeavor: "Bylaw 12–1 was . . . intended to be an 'economy measure.' In this sense, it was both in design and effect one having commercial impact." What were, then, the redeeming virtues of the restraint that saved it from being deemed "unreasonable"?

Apparently, some member institutions were experiencing financial difficulty. Those colleges with athletically and economically more successful programs were seen as taking (unfair) advantage of their success by expanding their programs. This sounds very much like more output or higher quality output is a bad thing. The acknowledged concern was that the less successful programs were having a hard time catching up to and keeping up with the more successful programs. Success had to be harnessed so all could enjoy being mediocre. This is not to say that competitive balance is undesirable, but the goal should be to raise quality to a common level. It should not be to reduce the quality of superior programs so inferior programs can compete.

The NCAA has had a measure of success in peddling the line that it is concerned with preserving amateurism. This, of course, is a sham. Everything about Division I football and basketball is big business. The only amateurs (arguably) are the players. As for Hennessey and his fellow coaches, restricting their number was deemed necessary to preserve "the competitive and amateur nature of the programs." Incredibly, the court found that "the fundamental objective [of the Bylaw] was to preserve and foster competition in intercollegiate athletics by curtailing . . . potentially monopolistic practices by the more powerful and to reorient the programs into their traditional role as amateur sports operating as part of the educational process." However, there was no proof that this restraint would save intercollegiate athletics, and the court did not demand any such proof. One would think that the NCAA should have had to shoulder the burden of proving that a plainly anticompetitive restraint would have redeeming features that result in net *social* benefits. It should not have been allowed to point to some vague ideal of preserving amateurism. However, this court was "of the view *admittedly bordering on speculation* that the Bylaw will be of value in achieving the ends sought." In effect, the court was willing to trade Hennessey's undeniable injury for some pie-in-the-sky benefit.

Finally, the court fashioned a "ruinous competition" defense for the NCAA members. The restraint, according to the court, may have beneficial effects for the assistant coaches by preserving employment opportunities. Without the restraint – and the consequent cost saving – financially strapped athletic programs might have shut down. Thus, the restraint would have the long-run effect of increasing the number of potential employers above the free market level. Talk about speculation.

5.2 *Law v. NCAA*

Despite a few methodological slips along the way, Judge Kathryn Vratil got to the correct result in *Law v. National Collegiate Athletic Association.*[16] This case

[16] 902 F. Supp. 1394 (1995).

involved a collusive effort on the part of the NCAA and its members to reduce the salaries paid to certain assistant coaches. The explicit purpose of the resultant NCAA Bylaw 11.02.3 was to stabilize and depress the compensation of the coaches designated as *restricted earnings coaches.* At least since 1940, such interference with the price mechanism has been illegal *per se.*[17] In this case, however, the court engaged in a rule-of-reason analysis to determine whether the restraint was unreasonable after considering all of the anticompetitive and procompetitive evidence.

Apparently, a large number of NCAA members were still experiencing financial difficulties of one sort or another in the late 1980s. In 1989, the NCAA formed the Cost Reduction Committee to explore alternative ways of reducing the costs of the intercollegiate athletic programs. The goal was to reduce cost without sacrificing competitive balance or curtailing access to higher education by student-athletes. At the same time that some schools were eliminating certain nonrevenue sports, there were pressures to spend even larger sums to recruit the most talented athletes and coaches. To do otherwise would have meant becoming less competitive on the field.

The NCAA decided that a collaborative effort to reduce costs was necessary. Of course, each school could have acted unilaterally to reduce its costs in any number of ways – reducing the number of sports offered, the number of scholarships, the value of a scholarship, the number of coaches, the salaries of the coaches, travel budgets, equipment budgets, and the like. However, a unilateral cost-reduction effort, if unmatched by rival schools, would have created an uneven playing field. The cost cutter would have become less competitive on the field than its rivals that did not reduce costs, and competitive balance would have been impaired. As a school began to lose on the field, spectator interest would wane, and revenues would fall, thereby worsening the school's financial position. The net result might not be improved financial viability if revenues fell by more than the cost savings.

The NCAA's Cost Reduction Committee decided that cost savings could be realized by reducing the number of coaches in all Division I sports. In addition, in every sport other than football, one coach would be designated a *restricted earnings coach.* A restricted earnings coach's compensation could not exceed $12,000 during the academic year and $4,000 during the summer. Some of the coaches who were affected had been earning $60,000 to $70,000 annually. The adverse impact on these coaches was undeniable and obvious for all to see.

The court began its analysis by noting that an agreement fixing the maximum salaries that will be paid to one class of employees attracts antitrust attention. In fact, in most circumstances, one would expect such an agreement to be a *per se* violation of section 1 of the Sherman Act. However, the NCAA enjoys rule of reason treatment because the NCAA and its members

[17] In *United States v. Socony-Vacuum Oil Co.*, 310 U.S. 150 (1940), the Supreme Court held that "[a]ny combination which tampers with price structures is engaged in an unlawful activity." Later, the Court pointed out that this applied to depressing prices as well as raising them.

sell competition: athletic contests between rival schools. Consequently, some horizontal restraints on competition in the market are deemed necessary to make the output possible. The court conceded that the NCAA plays a vital role in making intercollegiate athletic events available to the public, and therefore, its restraints should be examined for their reasonableness. At the same time, however, the court expressed its belief "that the Supreme Court [did not intend] to give the NCAA *carte blanche* in imposing restraints of trade on its member institutions or other parties because of its role in the marketplace. There can be no doubt that the NCAA is subject to the antitrust laws."

It is clear on its face that the Restricted Earnings Coach Rule had an adverse anticompetitive effect in the market. As noted earlier, some of the restricted earnings coaches had earned salaries of $60,000 to $70,000 before the rule,[18] which reduced their maximum compensation to $12,000 from $16,000. Presumably, the higher salaries resulted from market forces that were blunted by the agreement. Thus, the adverse anticompetitive impact of the rule was apparent to the court:

> Because the Restricted Earnings Coach Rule specifically prohibits the free operation of a market responsive to demand and is thus inconsistent with the Sherman Act's mandates, it is not necessary for the Court to undertake an extensive market analysis to determine that the rule has had an anticompetitive effect on the market for coaching services.

The NCAA responded by arguing that the rule was necessary to maintain "a level playing field in the sports arena, retaining and fostering the spirit of amateurism..., and protecting NCAA member institutions from self-imposed, ruinous cost increases." In part, the NCAA pointed to its success in *Hennessey*, which we may recall challenged an NCAA Bylaw restricting the number of football and basketball coaches that member institutions could employ. There, the court found that the plaintiffs failed to prove that the intent was to hurt them. The court found that the NCAA's motivation was more noble: "to preserve and foster competition in intercollegiate athletics . . . and to reorient the programs into their traditional role as amateur sports operating as part of the educational process." However, it is the *athlete* – not the coach – who is supposed to be an amateur. It is not apparent that the rule at issue in *Law v. NCAA* would level any playing field or contribute to competitive balance. It would, of course, tend to weed out competent, experienced coaches and to weaken the quality of the coaching staff. This would tend to reduce the quality of the athletic performance. Because this is what they sell, the rule would reduce the quality of the output and thereby reduce social welfare.

In *Law v. NCAA*, the court found that the Restricted Earnings Coach Rule may be intended to further some legitimate goals of the NCAA, but the NCAA failed to do more than assert that the rule would, in fact, further these goals. No evidence was presented to support the NCAA's claims. Given this finding,

[18] 902 F. Supp. at 1405.

the court did not have to consider whether the rule was the least restrictive way of achieving the stated goals. Accordingly, the court found in favor of the plaintiffs.[19]

From an economic perspective, the *Law* and *Hennessey* decisions are inconsistent. According to *Hennessey*, the NCAA members can agree to reduce the number of coaches hired, which will have a predictable effect on coaches' salaries. According to *Law*, the NCAA members cannot agree on a salary reduction, which would also have a predictable effect on the number of coaches employed. It is unclear what this inconsistency means for future challenges to restraints of trade by the NCAA and its members.

6 ANTITRUST CHALLENGES BY STUDENT-ATHLETES

There have been some antitrust challenges by student-athletes regarding the NCAA's exercise of monopsony power. Because the individual claims are fairly small, these challenges usually take the form of class actions, which pose some legal problems.

At the outset, we note that the conduct of the NCAA and its members is usually evaluated under the rule of reason. The rationale for this is that to offer a competitive product in the form of collegiate athletics, the NCAA must have some leeway to impose rules that are designed to promote rough parity among teams. These rules do restrict competition in the market, but without parity, games would be lopsided and less attractive to both live and broadcast audiences.[20] In each of the cases discussed in this section, the underlying antitrust question should be whether the restraint in question is necessary for the NCAA to compete with other sellers of entertainment products.

6.1 *In re: NCAA I-A Walk-on Football Players Litigation*

One of the recent efforts to curb the NCAA's use of monopsony power came in the form of a class action challenge to its limits on the number of football player grants-in-aids.[21] Walk-on players (those not paid) argued that but for the limit, they would have received scholarships. Along with the cap on what may be paid to scholarship players, the limit on the number of players limits a school's labor costs and limits the means of competing for players.

In terms of a pure antitrust analysis, the question would be whether increasing the number of scholarships would jeopardize the quality of the product sold by the NCAA, which is competition on the field. The answer to this is not clear. A walk-on player at one school may be a scholarship player at another. Limiting the number of scholarships may prevent some wealthier schools from stockpiling players. On the other hand, walk-on players who excel are often

[19] The jury awarded more than $22 million to 1,900 restricted earnings coaches. This sum was automatically tripled to about $67 million plus the lawyer's fees. The member schools had to chip in to pay the tab for their ill-fated efforts to control costs.

[20] *NCAA v. Board of Regents*, 468 U.S. 85 (1984).

[21] 2006 WL 1207915 (W.D. Wash, 2006).

subsequently awarded scholarships, and a school would have little interest in stockpiling those who do not excel. Thus, it is not clear what the ultimate damage to competition in the sports entertainment market would be.

These questions were not addressed, however, because the NCAA was able to prevail with an argument that the class of plaintiffs should not be certified.[22] One of the requirements for class certification is that the plaintiffs bringing the case on behalf of the class be able to fairly and adequately protect the interests of the class. The court noted that the fact that an individual was a walk-on does not mean that that player would have received a scholarship "but for" the NCAA rule. This fact set up an internal conflict among the representatives of the class and other class members. For example, if it was determined that a school, in the absence of the regulation, would have offered 20 additional scholarships, the class members would then compete to determine which of them would have been awarded the scholarship. Although the court did not certify the class, the underlying antitrust issue remains undecided.

6.2 *White v. NCAA*

In *White*,[23] the issue was not the number of scholarships but the amount paid per scholarship to football and basketball players since February 2002. The plaintiffs claimed that collusion among NCAA members led to a grant-in-aid cap that was less than the actual cost of attending college. Consequently, they sought the difference between the actual costs of attending college and the grant-in-aid cap. The plaintiffs, perhaps wisely, avoided the bigger issue of whether players should be paid at levels that would prevail in the absence of any collusion at all. Had the issue been framed in this matter, it is quite likely the NCAA would have prevailed under the rule of reason.

Although the class was certified, as with the limitation on the number of scholarships, a judicial decision on whether the cap violated the antitrust laws was avoided. This time, it was the result of a settlement between the NCAA and the class. Although denying any wrongdoing, the NCAA agreed to make available a fund totaling $218 million for the purpose of aiding student-athletes with "demonstrated financial and/or academic needs." In addition, a $10 million fund was established to reimburse former players for a variety of expenses to be incurred in the future in connection with career development.

6.3 *O'Bannon v. NCAA*[24]

Not content simply to restrict the number of student-athletes employed and their compensation, the NCAA requires student-athletes to surrender their

[22] For a class to receive certification, a court must find that (1) the class is so numerous that joinder of all members is impractical, (2) there are questions of law and fact common to all members of the class, (3) the claims of the representative plaintiffs are typical of the class members and the representative parties will fairly and adequately protect the interests of the class.

[23] No. CV06–0999 (C.D. Cal. 2008).

[24] O'Bannon v. N.C.A.A., CV 09 3329 United States District Court, Northern District of California, July 21, 2009.

property rights in their own images. For most athletes, these property rights are not worth much, but, for the elite few – Tim Tebow, for example – these rights may be worth a good deal. Tim Tebow jerseys, Cam Newton coffee mugs, Sam Bradford posters, and Mark Ingram T-shirts sell for premium prices due to the image of the premier student-athlete. The NCAA extracts these benefits from the student-athlete by exercising its monopsony power.

To be eligible to participate, each student-athlete must sign Form 08–3a, which authorizes the NCAA, member schools, conferences, and organizing committees to use the player's name and picture. The student-athlete receives no compensation for these uses.

Another NCAA regulation permits the use of an athlete's likeness, picture, or name in school and conference promotions, but all money goes directly to the school or conference. If the athlete receives any compensation, he or she jeopardizes his or her eligibility.[25]

In *O'Bannon*, the complaint does not involve athletes who are still participating in NCAA athletics. Instead, *O'Bannon* challenges the NCAA's presumption that it can use the likenesses in perpetuity. This issue will be sorted out in the courts, or it will be settled. The point here, however, is that the NCAA secures these property rights because of its monopsony power. If an athlete refuses to surrender those rights, he or she cannot compete and will be denied a grant-in-aid.

7 CONCLUDING REMARKS

In this chapter, we have seen that the NCAA and its member schools behave like a buying cartel. In this regard, we analyzed collusive monopsony. We also debunked the notion that a monopsony passes on the lower prices that it pays in the form of lower prices that it charges. Specifically, we saw that the exercise of monopsony power causes the marginal cost curve to shift upward, which leads to less output. At the same time, the reduced payments lead to lower average costs at the optimal output, which results in profits for the monopsonists. After examining the unique characteristics of the NCAA cartel, we turned our attention to two antitrust challenges – one successful and one unsuccessful.

PROBLEMS AND QUESTIONS

1. Is there a market for Division I basketball coaches that is separate from the markets for (a) high school coaches, (b) professional basketball coaches, and (c) Division II coaches? How would you go about defining the market (see Chapter 9)?
2. How would an NCAA restraint on the number of coaches affect the salaries of those coaches who remained employed?

[25] §12.5.1.1 Institutional, Charitable, Educational or Non-Profit Promotions.

3. Because only one coach per sport was designated a "restricted earnings" coach, this NCAA Bylaw would not have affected the other coaches. True or false? Explain.
4. When the NCAA depressed coaching salaries, it reduced costs and thereby enhanced efficiency. True or false? Explain.
5. As we saw, a group of Division I-A "walk-on" football players tried to sue the NCAA. Their complaint was that but for the NCAA limit on grants-in-aid, they would have had scholarships.
   a. How could they have proved their contention?
   b. If they had proved it, what would their damages have been?
6. In light of the *Law* decision, does the *Hennessey* decision make any sense from an economic perspective? Explain.
7. Using Figure 18.1, show that any movement away from $w = w_1$ and $L = L_1$ will reduce social welfare. Show that any movement away from $w = w_2$ and $L = L_2$ will reduce the collusive profits.
8. Division I schools limit the number of scholarships and the amount of the stipend to earn profits on their football programs, which they use to support men's and women's nonrevenue sports: golf, tennis, gymnastics, fencing, and so on. Why, as an economic matter, should we be opposed to collusive efforts that yield these benefits?
9. How would you measure damages in the *Law* case?
10. If a coach were willing to take a job as a restricted earnings coach, would he have suffered any damages as a result of the NCAA Bylaw limiting his or her compensation?
11. In the *O'Bannon* case, how would you measure the damages suffered by the student-athlete?
12. When Des Bryant, Oklahoma State wide receiver, "misled" NCAA investigators about his relationship with Deion Sanders, he lost a whole year of eligibility. When Bruce Pearl, the University of Tennessee head basketball coach, "misled" NCAA investigators about a recruiting violation, the university fined him, and the Southeastern Conference suspended him for eight conference games. Is this consistent treatment of players and coaches?

RESEARCH QUESTIONS

1. Trace the history of the NCAA's restrictions on the number of football scholarships. Track down the official explanations for any changes. Do these explanations make economic sense?
2. Estimate the dollar value of a full grant-in-aid at the following Division I schools:

   Notre Dame University
   Vanderbilt University

Texas A&M University
University of Virginia
Are some athletes getting a bigger grant-in-aid than others?

3. There have been sporadic efforts to unionize student-athletes. Examine these efforts and explain why they have failed.
4. Examine SMU's football success before and after the death penalty was imposed for repeated violations of NCAA rules.

APPENDIX: MONOPSONY, MARGINAL COST, AND AVERAGE COST

The exercise of monopsony power causes marginal cost to shift up and average cost to shift down and to the left. In this appendix, we derive these results.

A.1 Monopsony and Marginal Cost

Marginal cost is defined to be the change in total cost when output is increased by one unit:

$$MC = dTC/dQ.$$

Assuming that the only variable input in the short run is labor, the marginal cost for a competitive buyer will necessarily be

$$MC = d(wL)/dQ,$$

which will be

$$MC = w(dL/dQ).$$

Because dL/dQ is the reciprocal of the marginal product of labor, the competitive firm's short-run marginal cost curve is then

$$MC = w/MP_L.$$

Now, let us compare this with the marginal cost of a monopsonist.

For a monopsonist, short-run marginal cost is

$$MC = d(wL)/dQ,$$

which is complicated by the fact that the wage increases when employment increases. In this case, we have

$$MC = (w + Ldw/dL)dL/dQ.$$

Again, dL/dQ is the reciprocal of the marginal product of labor, so we have

$$MC = \frac{w + Ldw/dL}{MP_L}.$$

Because Ldw/dL is positive, the marginal cost for a monopsonist lies above the marginal cost of a competitive firm:

$$\frac{w + Ldw/dL}{MP_L} > \frac{w}{MP_L}.$$

A.2 Monopsony and Average Cost

The average cost of a competitive firm is given by

$$AC = \frac{F + w_1 L(Q)}{Q},$$

where w_1 is the wage in competitive equilibrium, F is the fixed capital cost, and $L(Q)$ is the labor input necessary to produce output Q. The average cost of the monopsonist is given by

$$AC' = \frac{F + w(L)\, L(Q)}{Q},$$

where $w(L)$ is again the labor supply, which is positively sloped. Because $w(L) < w_1$ if L is less than L_1 (the competitive labor input), $AC' < AC$ for outputs below the competitive output. Analogously, because $w(L) > w_1$ if L is greater than L_1, AC' is greater than AC when output is above the competitive output. Thus, the exercise of collusive monopsony is to shift the average cost curve down and to the left for output levels below the competitive quantity.

REFERENCES AND FURTHER READING

Berri, David, Martin Schmidt, and Stacey Brook. (2007). *The Wages of Wins.* Stanford, CA: Stanford University Press.

Blair, Roger D., and Jeffrey L. Harrison. (2010). *Monopsony in Antitrust Law and Economics.* New York: Cambridge University Press, 2010.

Blair, Roger D., and David L. Kaserman. (2009). *Antitrust Economics,* 2nd ed. New York: Oxford University Press.

Blair, R. D., and R. E. Romano. (1997). "Collusive Monopsony in Theory and Practice: The NCAA." *Antitrust Bulletin,* 42, 681–719.

Brown, R. W. (1993). "An Estimate of the Rent Generated by a Premium College Football Player." *Economic Inquiry,* 31, 671–684.

Brown, R. W. (1994). "Measuring Cartel Rents in the College Basketball Player Recruitment Market." *Applied Economics,* 26, 27–34.

Eckard, E. W. (1998). "The NCAA Cartel and Competitive Balance in College Football." *Review of Industrial Organization,* 13, 347–369.

Fleisher, Arthur A., III, Brian L. Goff, and Robert D. Tollison. (1992). *The National Collegiate Athletic Association: A Study in Cartel Behavior.* Chicago: University of Chicago Press.

Harrison, Jeffrey L., and Casey C. Harrison. (2009). "The Law and Economics of the N.C.A.A.'s Claim to Monopsony Rights." *Antitrust Bulletin,* 54, 923–949.

Kahn, L. M. (2007). "Cartel Behavior and Amateurism in College Sports." *Journal of Economic Perspectives,* 21, 209–226.

Lambrinos, James, and Thomas D. Ashman. (2007). "Salary Determination in the National Hockey League: Is Arbitration Efficient?" *Journal of Sports Economics,* 8, 192–201.

Leonard, J., and J. Prinzinger. (1984). "An Investigation into the Monopsonistic Market Structure of Division One NCAA Football and Its Effect on College Football Players." *Eastern Economic Journal*, 10, 455–467.

Zimbalist, Andrew. (1999). *Unpaid Professionals: Competition and Conflict in Big Time College Sports*. Princeton, NJ: Princeton University Press.

19

Salary Determination: Bidding and Bargaining

1 INTRODUCTION

When star players are free agents, several teams may bid for their services in a kind of auction.[1] Barry Zito is a good example of this. Several Major League Baseball (MLB) teams were interested in signing Zito when he became a free agent after the 2006 season. In the end, the San Francisco Giants and the New York Mets battled down to the wire over Zito. The Giants ultimately won the battle and Zito's services by outbidding everyone else. Zito, of course, was the real winner: $126 million over seven years. In this instance, Zito's salary was determined through competitive bidding. In other cases, however, salaries are determined through bilateral bargaining between one team and one player (or his agent). Top NFL draft choices for example, bargain over the terms of their initial contracts with the teams that selected them in the draft. Some players who are currently under contract bargain over multiyear contract extensions. At the end of the 2010 season, for example, Derek Jeter and the New York Yankees engaged in a very public bargaining struggle. Jeter wanted more than his market value, and the Yankees wanted to pay less than his market value. In the end, they settled on a three-year contract for $51 million. Some National Football League (NFL) players bargain over restructuring their current contract because of salary cap constraints.

In this chapter, we develop the simple economics of bidding at auctions and how it applies to professional sports. We also develop the basics of bargaining. Several examples illustrate the applicability of bargaining theory. Finally, we examine the posting system that applies to players under contract with professional baseball teams in Japan. As it applies in the United States, the posting system combines bidding at one stage with bargaining at the next stage.

[1] For that matter, much the same can be said for star coaches.

2 AUCTIONING PLAYER TALENT

The market for free agents is a private value auction.[2] In a *private value* auction, the value of what is being sold varies across potential buyers. A player's value is his marginal revenue product (MRP), which is the product of the player's marginal product and the marginal revenue associated with the player's contribution to the team's performance: $MRP = MR * MP$. Now a player's MRP will vary across teams for two reasons. First, a player's productivity – that is, his marginal product – will vary across teams because one player's productivity depends upon his teammates. A pitcher will win more games for a high-scoring team than for a low-scoring team. No matter how good a hitter is, one slugger cannot win games all by himself. Each player's productivity depends on the productivity of his teammates and the quality of the coaches. Even the home field can make a big difference in a player's performance. Fenway Park, for example, is a friendlier place for right-handed hitters than for left-handers.

Second, the marginal revenue of additional wins that may be attributed to a player's productivity will vary across teams because of different local market conditions. In combination, the variation in marginal productivity and in marginal revenue leads to variation in MRPs for the same player across different teams. As a result, we have a private value auction.[3]

The player auction's bidding rules resemble an *English auction*, which means that the offers by clubs rise as teams try to outbid one another to sign the player. The player's agent receives the offers (bids) from various clubs that are interested in his client. He then rejects low bids and waits for the rejected teams to increase their offers. This continues until there are no further increases in the offers. This is not to say that the agent is a passive auctioneer. On the contrary, agents are often marketing their clients throughout the entire process, extolling their client's virtues, and suggesting to each interested club that there is a lot of interest in their client. Agents may even suggest that there are other bidders when they are actually bluffing.

2.1 Economic Results of an English Auction

From an economic perspective, there are two important characteristics of English auctions that are worth noting. First, when an asset is sold at an English auction, it goes to the potential buyer who values it most. Suppose that an antique chest is being sold at auction. As the bids rise, those who place the lowest values on the chest drop out of the bidding. It would be foolish to bid more than one's maximum value because that bid might win. At the end, there will

[2] There are many compact treatments of the fundamentals of auctions. Among these are Hal Varian (2006), *Intermediate Microeconomics* (chapter 17), New York: W.W. Norton; R. Preston McAfee (2002), *Competitive Solutions* (chapter 12), Princeton, NJ: Princeton University Press; and Louis Philips (1988), *The Economics of Imperfect Information* (chapter 4), New York: Cambridge University Press.

[3] The alternative is a *common value* auction. In that case, the value of what is being sold is the same for all potential buyers even though the actual value may not be known *ex ante*. For example, the actual value of the oil-drilling rates in a particular location may not be known in advance, but the value is the same for all petroleum companies and therefore is common.

be two bidders left. Suppose that Laura places a value of $5,000 on the antique chest and Melissa's value is $5,500. Suppose further that Laura bids her maximum price of $5,000. Melissa will then bid more than $5,000 and win the bidding. She will not pay $5,500, however, because there is no other bidder to compel her to go that far. She will bid as little over $5,000 as the auction's bidding rules permit her to bid.[4] The important point here is that the antique chest goes to Melissa who values it the most. This is economically efficient because it maximizes value.

In the context of bidding for free agents and coaches, the player or coach tends to wind up with the club that values him the most. This will always be the case if the player or coach is indifferent about who employs him. In that event, he will go to the highest bidder, and that will be the club that values him the most. Unlike antique chests and rare paintings, however, players and coaches often care who employs them. Some players prefer the West Coast, whereas others prefer New York or Boston. Some players may value the tradition of the Boston Celtics or the Green Bay Packers. For others, the prospect of winning championships is of paramount importance, and others value certain communities. For example, Kirby Puckett, the great Minnesota Twins outfielder, stayed with the Twins for less money than he could have earned elsewhere because he preferred to live and play in Minneapolis. The fact is that there is more to a job than just the money, and that means that some players will not go where they are most valued. The Mets, for example, may have valued Barry Zito more than San Francisco did, but living and playing in San Francisco are not the same as living and playing in New York. Barry Bonds, for example, has often said that he wanted to play for the San Francisco Giants because his father (Bobby Bonds) and his godfather (Willie Mays) had played for the Giants. Moreover, he was returning home since he grew up in San Francisco. However, there is no doubt that money matters a good deal. It is probably no coincidence that San Francisco was the only club that was willing to pay Bonds more than $7.1 million a year for six years.[5] In a similar vein, Andy Pettite left the New York Yankees after the 2003 season as a free agent. He chose to play for his hometown team, the Houston Astros. The Astros paid him $31.5 million over three years. For the 2007 season, the Astros offered Pettitte $12 million. Rather than stay in Houston, where he and his family lived, he returned to the Yankees for $16 million.[6]

The second feature of English auctions is that the seller usually cannot extract the full value for what is being sold. For our antique chest, the full value is the value to Melissa: $5,500. However, Melissa will rationally bid as little over $5,000 as the bidding rules permit. As a result, she may buy the chest for, say, $5,100, which is less than the full value of $5,500. The seller cannot extract all of the consumer surplus from Melissa with this kind of auction. The only exception is when the seller knows Melissa's reservation value. In that event, the seller

[4] Most auctions have minimum increments so that bids do not increase one penny at a time. How large the increment is depends on the price range.

[5] Murray Chass, "Love for San Francisco a Contractual Affair," *New York Times*, June 20, 2006.

[6] Murray Chass, "For Pettite, Home Is Where the Money Is," *New York Times*, December 12, 2006.

can set a *reserve* price equal to that value. If no one meets the reserve price, the seller can remove the item from the auction. However, it is rare indeed that the seller will know the true private values that the bidders place on an antique.

The same is true for players and coaches. Despite the wallet-busting deals that we read about in the newspaper, the winner might not pay the maximum because a club just has to bid a bit more than the next highest bidder. This is where a skilled agent may earn his keep. Unlike antique and art auctions where all of the bids are usually public, the bids for players and coaches are privately communicated. An agent does more than field competing offers. He engages in negotiations that are designed to induce higher offers from rival clubs. Whether the agent can get full value for his client is unclear, but they certainly try to do so.

2.2 Barry Zito Moves across the Bay

Barry Zito became a free agent at the end of the 2006 MLB season. A big (6′4″) left-handed starter with an exceptional curveball, Zito was highly prized in the free-agent market. It is not completely clear just why Zito was such a hot commodity. Although he won the Cy Young Award in 2002, his performance after that was not nearly as impressive. Over 2003–2006, Zito's record was 55–46 with a good, but unspectacular, earned run average (ERA) of 3.86. To be sure, he was consistently durable, however, starting 35 games per year and pitching about 220 innings per season. In any event, armed with Scott Boras as his agent, Zito was assured of a fat contract with some team. Many teams with notoriously low payrolls – Tampa Bay, the Marlins – were never in the running for Zito, and several others had reliable starting rotations already. However, there were enough clubs competing to sign Zito that Boras could play one team against another. By December 2006, the four major bidders were the New York Mets, the San Francisco Giants, the Seattle Mariners, and the Texas Rangers. Zito and Boras met with these clubs and began considering the offers. Rumors were flying. There was a report, which turned out to be false, that the Rangers had offered a six-year $100 million deal. The Mets apparently were interested in a five-year $75 million deal.

Not everyone was in love with Zito. The New York Yankees, for example, never got into the bidding. First, Boras wanted a contract befitting a number one starter in the rotation, but the Yankees were skeptical about Zito's being a dominant pitcher in the Pedro Martinez–Roger Clemens mold. In 2006, Zito's ERA against the Yankees was a whopping 8.16. Against the Red Sox, it was 5.51, and against the Toronto Blue Jays, it was 5.40. Fortunately for Zito and Boras, the four major contenders for Zito's services were not similarly skeptical about his talent.

In the end, Zito landed a seven-year, $126 million contract with the San Francisco Giants. The six-year $84 million offer from the Rangers[7] and the five-year, $75 million offer from the Mets fell well short of the Giants' offer. Zito's contract details are presented in Table 19.1.

[7] The Rangers added a seventh year option at $15 million to bring the total to $99 million.

Table 19.1. Barry Zito's Contract Details

Salaries: 2007–2013	
2007	$10.0 million
2008	$14.5 million
2009	$18.5 million
2010	$18.5 million
2011	$18.5 million
2012	$19.0 million
2013	$20.0 million
Option Year: 2014	
The club has an option for 2014 at $18 million with a $7.0 million buyout if it does not exercise its option. The option becomes guaranteed if Zito (a) pitches 600 innings during 2011–2013, (b) pitches 400 innings during 2012–2013, or (c) pitches 200 innings in 2013 and 180 innings in 2011 or in 2012. If the option becomes guaranteed, Zito can void the option and receive $3.5 million.	
Incentives/Bonuses	
All Star	$100,000
Gold Glove	100,000
National League Championship Series MVP	100,000
World Series MVP	200,000
League MVP	250,000
Cy Young Award	500,000
Perks	
Zito stays in a suite on road trips.	

Source: MLB.com, January 2, 2007.

As the table shows, Zito's biggest pay days are in the future. Accordingly, his contract is not really worth $126 million because the future payments have to be discounted to present value. Nonetheless, the bidding for Zito resulted in a handsome return.

Nearly every year, a similar story can be told for some star. Following the 2010 season, the big prize was Cliff Lee. Lee has an awesome postseason record, and any contender would welcome him to the pitching rotation. Following the bidding in the newspaper and television accounts, it became clear that the race was down to the Texas Rangers and the New York Yankees. Much to the surprise of everyone, especially the Yankees, the Philadelphia Phillies came out of nowhere and signed Lee. He accepted a bit less money from the Phillies, but he got to rejoin his old team and be part of the most impressive starting rotation in all of MLB.

2.3 Bidding for Coaches

Coaches are also pursued in an auction-like fashion. As with players, however, coaches are utility maximizers just like everyone else. In bidding for a coach, an NFL club or a university athletic department will try to appeal to what interests coaches. For most coaches, money and an opportunity to win are important considerations. Some coaches have specific geographic preferences that come into play. In college coaching, recruiting is of paramount importance for success. If a coach neither likes nor is good at recruiting, a college job may not suit him. There is no recruiting in the pro ranks, but a coach must deal with players who earn more than he does, which may make it difficult to coach them. If a coach does not cope well with indifferent attitudes, the pro ranks may not be ideal for him.

Some coaches are intensely loyal to their teams and routinely deflect any interest from other teams or schools. However, loyalty is only one variable in a coach's utility function. For example, Dennis Erickson began his head coaching career at the University of Idaho in 1982. Between 1982 and 2006, Erickson moved around quite a bit with several college jobs and two NFL jobs. In 2006, he returned to Idaho presumably to finish out his career. No doubt, Erickson's intentions were sincere, but then Arizona State came calling. The opportunity to win in the Pac-10 and earn considerably more money in the attempt won out over mere loyalty to Idaho. Erickson left Idaho after a single year.

Urban Meyer, Florida's former fair-haired boy, started his head coaching career at Bowling Green in 2001. After two very successful seasons, he moved on to the University of Utah, where he was even more successful and more visible. Following two great years, Meyer moved to Florida, where he won a national championship at the end of the 2006 season and another one following the 2008 season. Given his lucrative, long-term contract and the wealth of football talent in Florida, Meyer was expected to stay put for a while. However, keeping the job that one has depends on the options available. After all, coaching is a profession, and a successful coach must do what is in his best interest.[8]

Florida's experience with Steve Spurrier should have taught Florida fans and university officials a valuable lesson. Spurrier won the Heisman Trophy in 1966 while playing at the University of Florida. After an NFL career as a player and several coaching jobs, Spurrier returned to his alma mater in 1990 and brought instant success to the program. Spurrier won six Southeastern Conference (SEC) titles and the national championship in 1996. Nearly every year, one NFL team or another would make overtures, but Spurrier deflected them all. However, the pursuit of successful coaches never ends. Finally, following a successful year in 2001, Spurrier stunned everyone by accepting the head coaching job of the Washington Redskins. The challenge of trying to win in the NFL and a $5 million a year salary were too attractive to pass up.[9]

2.4 Nick Saban's Comings and Goings

Nick Saban was the head football coach at Louisiana State University when the Miami Dolphins came knocking on his door. Saban went to Miami for fame

[8] In Meyer's case, health issues and family interests led him to resign from Florida at the end of the 2010 season. He was hired by ESPN to be a football analyst.

[9] Spurrier's "fun and gun" offense did not work in the NFL, and after two dismal seasons, he resigned. He returned to college coaching with the University of South Carolina in 2005.

and fortune in the NFL. Two years later, the job with the Miami Dolphins did not look so attractive. Under Saban, the Dolphins went 9–7 in 2005 and 6–10 in 2006. Then the University of Alabama came calling and bailed Saban out of the NFL. After steadfastly denying that he was going to Tuscaloosa, Saban broke the news to Dolphins owner Wayne Huizenga that he was indeed going to leave with three years still remaining on his contract. Alabama offered Saban an eight-year contract reportedly worth more than $30 million.[10] In this case, Saban gave up $4.5 million per year with the Dolphins for slightly less money. However, living in Tuscaloosa and coaching at Alabama where Saban does not expect any losing seasons are different from coaching in the NFL where no one routinely wins 75 percent of their games.

2.5 Billy Gillispie Hits the Big Time

After an extremely successful career as an assistant coach, Billy Gillispie took over as head coach of the University of Texas – El Paso (UTEP) men's basketball program in 2002. He inherited an awful team that went 6 and 24 during the 2002–2003 season. But then Gillispie began to work his magic. UTEP was the most improved team in the country in 2003–2004 with a record of 24–8. Following that stellar season, Gillispie's coaching talent was noticed by many schools in need of an extreme makeover. One of the schools most in need of a revamped program was Texas A&M. The following year, Gillispie moved to Texas A&M, which had won no games in the Big-12 during 2003–2004. Again, Gillispie coached the most improved team in the country as the Aggies enjoyed a respectable 21–10 record in 2003–2004. The team was 8–8 in Big-12 play, which was a remarkable turnaround from a winless season a year earlier. Gillispie continued to be successful at Texas A&M with records of 22–9 in 2005–2006 and 27–7 in 2006–2007. The Aggies finished ninth in the nation in the final 2007 poll. During his three seasons in College Station, Gillispie was named Big-12 Coach of the Year each year. Such success meant a lot of attention in the coaching labor market.

Although the University of Kentucky's (UK's) first choice to replace Tubby Smith was Florida's Billy Donovan, Donovan made it clear that he would not leave the Gators for the Wildcats. Kentucky quickly turned to Gillispie. The UK job offered a rich tradition and a commitment to return UK to its glory days. In addition, they offered Gillispie a lucrative multiyear contract: seven years at $2.3 million per year. Sadly, things did not work out in Lexington. After several disappointing seasons and some personal problems, Gillispie was replaced by John Calipari.

[10] Saban's contract has an array of bonuses: $75,000 for playing in the SEC Championship and another $50,000 if Alabama wins the SEC Championship, $65,000–$90,000 for a non–Bowl Championship Series (BCS) bowl, $125,000 for a BCS bowl, $200,000 for playing in the BCS title game, and $400,000 for winning the BCS title. There are bonuses – much smaller – for getting Alabama's graduation rate into the top half of the SEC. ESPN.com, "Saban's Deal Limits Required Public Appearances, Does Not Include Buyout Clause," June 14, 2007.

Table 19.2. Top 20 Highest Paid College Football Coaches, 2010[1]

	School	Coach	Salary ($)
1	Alabama	Nick Saban	5,997,349
2	Texas	Mack Brown	5,161,500
3	Oklahoma	Bob Stoops	4,375,000
4	Florida	Urban Meyer	4,010,000
5	LSU	Les Miles	3,905,000
6	Ohio State	Jim Tressel	3,888,389
7	Iowa	Kirk Ferentz	3,781,000
8	Georgia	Mark Richt	2,937,740
9	Arkansas	Bobby Petrino	2,713,000
10	Missouri	Gary Pinkel	2,550,000
11	Michigan	Rich Rodriguez	2,525,280
12	Mississippi	Houston Nutt	2,509,000
13	Oregon	Chip Kelly	2,400,000
14	California	Jeff Tedford	2,305,000
15	Georgia Tech	Paul Johnson	2,300,000
16	South. Methodist	June Jones	2,142,056
17	Virginia Tech	Frank Beamer	2,128,000
18	Tennessee	Derek Dooley	2,121,391
19	Auburn	Gene Chizik	2,103,500
20	Kansas	Turner Gill	2,101,200

[1] List may be incomplete because salaries at private schools – Notre Dame, Stanford, and others – are not available.

Source: http://www.usatoday.com/sports/college/football/2010-coaches-contracts-table.htm.

2.6 Head Coach Salaries

The salaries of the head football coaches at the traditional powerhouses are remarkable. In 2010, Alabama's Nick Saban topped the list with a salary of $5,997,349. Mack Brown (Texas) also topped the $5 million mark. Bobby Stoops (Oklahoma) and Urban Meyer (Florida) were paid more than $4 million. At the bottom end of the top 20, the coaches earned more than $2 million.

These salaries are high because college football is a big business, and there is a substantial demand for coaches who can win. In many cases, the athletic director renegotiates existing contracts of the head coach to preempt competition. These deals occur because offers are anticipated by the athletic director and are therefore driven by perceived market forces. This is the upside for successful coaches. The downside is impatience. If a coach is not successful almost immediately, he will not keep his job long. At Michigan, for example, Rich Rodriguez had three lackluster years with some embarrassing loses. Rodriguez was fired at the end of the 2010 season.

Box 19.1 *The Rich Get Richer**

In 2010, Ohio State's Jim Tressel was paid handsomely – $3,888,389. In addition, to his salary, Tressel enjoys many other benefits under the terms of his contract. These include the following:

1. Free Tickets
   - Two seats in the former athletic director/coaches booth of Ohio Stadium
   - Four seats in the writing press area of the Ohio Stadium press box
   - One season parking permit for all home football games
   - Two season tickets and one parking permit for all Ohio State home men's and women's basketball games
   - Upon retirement from Ohio State, coach gets all tickets free for life
2. Personal use of private jet for 20 hours per year
3. Country club membership and dues for him and his wife

The contract also provides a $3 million buyout if Tressel is terminated.†

* "What You Give the Man Who Has Everything: Ohio State's Jim Tressel," Dec. 9, 2010, at http://www.usatoday.com/sports/college/football/bigten/2010-12-07-ohio-state-jim-tressel_N.htm.

† In 2011, Coach Tressel was forced to resign from Ohio State due to alleged misrepresentations to the NCAA.

3 BARGAINING

Bargaining over salary, incentives, and other contract terms arises in many situations in sports. As a simple example, consider what happens when a tournament sponsor wants a star like Tiger Woods or Phil Mickelson to play in its golf tournament. If it is not a PGA Tour stop, the tournament organizer can offer an appearance fee plus whatever that star player happens to win.[11] The sponsor wants the star because his appearance will boost attendance and improve TV ratings. The star is willing to participate because it is lucrative to do so. The problem is deciding on the size of the fee. The two parties bargain over the terms, that is, the amount of the fee. In this section, we develop a simple bargaining model that will help us understand how such bargaining yields a solution.[12]

In a simple bargaining setting, two parties try to reach agreement on how to split a sum of money that will exist if they reach an agreement but will

[11] The PGA Tour does not permit the payment of appearance fees at its sanctioned events. Why do you suppose that appearance fees are not permitted?

[12] This section relies on the extremely clear presentation of Avinash Dixit and Susan Skeath (2004), *Games of Strategy* (chapter 17), 2nd ed., New York: W.W. Norton.

disappear if they fail to reach an agreement. For example, suppose that the golf tournament will earn a \$5 million profit if Tiger Woods is in the field and only a \$1 million profit if he is not. Reaching an agreement on an appearance fee therefore creates a surplus of \$4 million. The bargaining is aimed at dividing that surplus between Tiger and the sponsor. Each party would like to get as much of that surplus as possible without jeopardizing Tiger's participation because the surplus disappears if he decides to go fishing instead of playing in the tournament.

What do we know about the possible solutions? First, there are a lot of them. If t is Tiger's share of the surplus and s is the sponsor's share, we know that $t+s$ must be equal to one. If we represent the net surplus with Tiger present as Π, then we know that

$$t\Pi + s\Pi = \Pi,$$

but there is an infinite number of values for t and s that sum to one. Tiger's share, t, can be any fraction between zero and one, which means that the sponsor's share s will be $1 - t$.

John Nash analyzed this problem and came up with a solution that falls out of a constrained maximization problem.[13] In particular, Nash proved that the amount going to Tiger Woods (T) and the amount going to the sponsor (S) were the solutions to maximizing the product of T and S subject to the constraint that $T + S = \Pi$. This formulation is the simplest case in which Tiger and the sponsor have equal bargaining power. If we want to maximize TS subject to the requirement that $T + S = \Pi$, we can substitute and write

$$Z = T(\Pi - T).$$

Now,

$$\frac{dZ}{dT} = \Pi - 2T = 0,$$

which means that $T = 1/2\Pi$. In that event, $S = 1/2\Pi$, too. Thus, with equal bargaining power, the two parties split the surplus evenly.

3.1 Greg Maddux: An Example

Greg Maddux had been the ace of a great Atlanta Braves pitching staff for many years.[14] In the 2002 season, Maddux won 16 games and lost only 6. His ERA was a more than respectable 2.62. He and his agent, Scott Boras, negotiated with the Braves over his salary for the 2003 season but seemed to be at an impasse. After a careful review of his performance and those of other pitchers, Maddux asked for \$16 million in arbitration. The Braves looked at the same data but offered only \$13.5 million. Thus, Maddux and the Braves were \$2.5 million apart. Before

[13] John F. Nash, Jr. (1950), "The Bargaining Problem," *Econometrica*, 18, 155–162. This is an advanced paper by Nash, who won a Nobel Prize for his work in game theory.

[14] "Maddux Gets \$14.75 Million," *New York Times*, Feb. 18, 2003. We will take an extensive look at arbitration in MLB in the next chapter.

the arbitration panel could review this case, Maddux and the Braves settled for $14.75 million. Thus, they split the difference.

These bargaining results are plausible if we assume equal bargaining power. More generally, however, we cannot assume equal bargaining power. In the more general case, the surplus will be split in proportion to the bargaining power of the participants. This vagueness is not very comforting, but it is the best that can be done.

3.2 Carlos Zambrano Negotiates an Extension

Before the 2007 MLB season, Carlos Zambrano tried in vain to extend his contract with the Chicago Cubs. Going into the season, Zambrano was in the final year of his contract. Without a new contract, Zambrano bore all of the risk of injury. Zambrano tried to pressure the Cubs by vowing that he would not be interested in negotiating during the season and would not re-sign with the Cubs if he were forced to play in 2007 without an extension. The Cubs stubbornly refused to extend his contract before the season, but they did continue to negotiate with Zambrano's agent. In the end, the Cubs gave him a five-year deal in August 2007.

The terms of the extension were the best a pitcher had ever gotten in a multiyear contract. He received a $5 million signing bonus and annual salaries as follow:

2008	$15.0 million
2009	17.75 million
2010	17.875 million
2011	17.875 million
2012	18.0 million

At the end of the 2012 season, Zambrano has an option for a sixth year at $19.25 million provided that he is healthy and finishes in the top four in Cy Young voting in 2012.

3.3 Larry Johnson's Holdout

In 2007, Larry Johnson was heading into the final year of his contract with the Kansas City Chiefs. Although Johnson was due to earn $1.8 million for the 2007 season, he was concerned about his future. During the 2006 season, Johnson set an NFL record for total carries in a season. Assuming a similar workload in 2007, he had to be concerned about injuries and general wear and tear on his body. There was always a danger that 2007 could be the end of his career. All of the risk was being borne by Johnson, and he did not like it. He insisted on a contract extension. When the Chiefs refused, Johnson decided to hold out.

Johnson failed to report for duty when training camp opened. The fine for holding out is $14,300 per day. So the cost of bargaining was piling up for Johnson. For the Chiefs, it is hard to say just what it cost them. They could see that their running game would suffer substantially without Johnson. Moreover, the longer Johnson held out, the less productive he would be when he did come back. Eventually, they reached an agreement on a five-year extension that removed a lot of financial uncertainty. Johnson received a $12 million signing bonus and another $7 million in guaranteed salary.[15] The value of the total deal was put at $43.3 million. Because the holdout lasted 25 days, Johnson was fined about $357,000, but that seems like a good investment given the return. The result was not good for the Chiefs as they soon parted ways with Johnson.

3.4 Brady Quinn's Holdout

The two top quarterbacks in the 2007 NFL draft were JaMarcus Russell of Louisiana State University and Notre Dame's Brady Quinn. Leading up to draft day, there was endless speculation about which one would be selected as the overall number one draft selection. The final consensus seemed to be that Russell would go first to Oakland. Calvin Johnson, Georgia Tech's spectacular wide receiver, was expected to go second to the Detroit Lions if the Lions had the courage to select yet another receiver with their first pick. Quinn was expected to go shortly after that. The first two predictions held up, but Quinn had to endure an agonizingly long day. By the time Cleveland selected him, he had fallen to number 22. When his name was called, one could see on his face sheer relief that his downward slide was over. Now, all he had to do was sign his Browns contract and get on with his NFL career.

As it turned out, this was not so easy. Quinn and his agent took the position that he should have been drafted higher and therefore was worth more than the typical 22nd pick. The Browns, of course, disagreed.[16] During the bargaining process, Quinn's value to the Browns was falling because he was not in camp learning how to play in the NFL. For Quinn, the cost of delay was much less. In the end, after an 11-day holdout, they reached an agreement on a five-year contract reportedly worth $20.2 million including a $7.75 million signing bonus.

3.5 Darrelle Revis's Holdout

Darrelle Revis was recognized as a premier cornerback in the NFL and an important cog in the New York Jets defense for the 2010 season. Revis was unhappy with his contract, however, which would have paid him $21 million over the 2010–2012 seasons. Revis believed that he has a commitment from the Jets to make him the highest paid cornerback in the league. Revis wanted an extension and, of course, more money. The Jets wanted him to honor his contract. They were at an impasse, so Revis ultimately decided to hold out.

Following the 2009 season, Revis and the Jets engaged in a nasty, seven-month contract dispute to no avail. During the bargaining process, the Jets offered two big contracts. On was a 10-year deal worth a total of $120 million. The other was a four-year at $40 million. However, neither offer has much guaranteed money, and therefore, both were risky for Revis. Revis's agent asked

[15] ESPN.com, "Johnson Guaranteed $19M in New Chiefs Contract," Aug. 21, 2007.

[16] William C. Rhoden, "Brown's Quinn Shouldn't Need to Apologize," *New York Times*, Aug. 11, 2007.

for a 10-year deal for $162 million with $40 million in guarantees. These proposals were rejected.

Revis began his holdout by refusing to show up for training camp. As time passed and the season opener approached, the two sides got increasingly concerned about the season. After a 35-day holdout with accumulated fines of $578,300, Revis agreed to a new four-year deal that would pay him a total of $46 million. Thus, the bargaining process permitted Revis to replace a three-year deal at $7 million per year for a four-year deal at an average of $11.5 million per year. Importantly, some $32 million of the $46 million is guaranteed.

3.6 Coaches' Contracts

It is not just players who negotiate multiyear contracts. College coaches usually have four-year or five-year contracts. These are necessary for recruiting purposes. Although coaches are often fired or elect to resign before their contracts expire, a coach with a two-year contract cannot credibly promise to be there for a recruit's entire career. Some college contracts are longer than five years. Nick Saban, for example, received an eight-year contract from the University of Alabama. In 2005, Urban Meyer agreed to a seven-year contract at the University of Florida, which he did not fulfill. Charlie Weis had a 10-year contract at Notre Dame, which was cut off because of his failure to win often enough.

Many times, universities extend an existing contract and change the terms to be sure of retaining the coach. Rick Pitino's contract as head men's basketball coach at the University of Louisville is a prime example. Pitino had three years remaining on his contract when Louisville extended it for an additional three years. Louisville also improved Pitino's salary on the old contract by $600,000 per year. The details of Pitino's contract are set out in Box 19.2.

Box 19.2 ***Rick Pitino's New Contract****

Rick Pitino, men's basketball coach at the University of Louisville, signed a three-year contract extension in May 2007. The new deal increased his base salary in every year as well as the "loyalty" bonuses he was scheduled to receive as deferred compensation. The terms of his new contract were as follows:

Base Salary

Season	Old	New
2007–2008	$1,650,000	$2,250,000
2008–2009	$1,650,000	$2,250,000
2009–2010	$1,650,000	$2,250,000
2010–2011		$2,250,000
2011–2012		$2,250,000
2012–2013		$2,250,000

Deferred Compensation ("Loyalty" Bonuses)

Date	Old	New
July 1, 2007	$1,000,000	$1,750,000
July 1, 2010	$3,000,000	$3,600,000
July 1, 2013	–	$3,600,000

No doubt, Pitino benefited from the lucrative contract signed by the new University of Kentucky coach, Billy Gillispie, who started a seven-year deal in 2007 at $2.3 million per year.

Rick Barnes at the University of Texas signed a 2007 contract at $2 million per year. Former Pitino protégé, Billy Donovan, also signed a new six-year contract at Florida after winning back-to-back National Collegiate Athletic Association Championships that is worth $3.5 million per year.

* Michael Grant, "Pitino Signs On Through 2013," *The Courier-Journal,* May 4, 2007.

Professional coaches also have multiyear contracts. Many of these are in the same four- to five-year range that is customary in college coaching. The purpose has nothing to do with recruiting because professional coaches do not recruit. In this case, both sides want some semblance of stability.

3.7 Incentives and Bonuses

Most coaches' contracts have incentive provisions. In fact, these incentives are really bonuses for achieving certain goals. At the margin, however, these provisions will call forth some extra effort on the coach's part. A good example of contractual incentives is provided by Phil Fulmer's contract. Phil Fulmer, the former head football coach of the Tennessee Volunteers, earned a salary of $2.05 million for the 2007 season. There were several incentives in his contract as well:

Going to a non-BCS bowl	$37,500
Tying for first place in the SEC East	$50,000
Appearing in the SEC Championship	$75,000
Winning the SEC or going to a BCS bowl	$100,000
Playing for BCS Championship	$150,000
Winning the National Championship	$250,000

By including these incentive provisions, the University of Tennessee made Fulmer's compensation somewhat uncertain. The salary was certain, but the possible additional compensation was not.[17]

[17] Fulmer failed to qualify for enough of these incentive payments and was fired after the 2008 season.

4 THE POSTING SYSTEM IN MLB

The *posting system*[18] is used when a Japanese baseball player wants to play in the United States but is not yet a free agent in Japan.[19] The player informs his team that he wants to be considered by MLB. If the team agrees, it will post his name with the commissioner of MLB, who then informs all MLB teams that the player is available – if the price is right. Because the player is not a free agent, his club has property rights that must be purchased by any team that wants to sign the player.

Once a player has been posted and the MLB commissioner has informed all 30 teams, the teams have four business days to decide whether to bid and, if so, how much to bid. Each interested MLB club submits a sealed bid to the commissioner who opens them and informs the Japanese club what the highest bid was. At this stage, the teams are bidding for the exclusive right to negotiate a deal with the player. The Japanese club is not told which MLB team submitted the highest bid. The Japanese club then has four days to decide whether to accept the posting fee offered or to reject it. If it rejects the offer, the process stops, and the player remains in Japan. The player can be posted again in the following year but not before then. If the team accepts the posting fee, the winning bidder and the player then have 30 days to reach agreement on a contract. If they cannot reach agreement, then the whole deal is off, the property rights revert to the Japanese club, the player remains in Japan, and the posting fee is not paid to the Japanese club. If an agreement is reached during the bargaining phase, the Japanese team receives the posting fee, and the player gets the benefits of his bargain with his new club.

The posting system dates back to a concern that MLB teams could raid the Japanese leagues and take the best players without compensating the Japanese team.[20] Because MLB would only be interested in the very best Japanese players, teams that were raided stood to lose valuable assets. Teams that lost their star players could suffer a drop in attendance, with the consequent loss in gate receipts and stadium revenues. Television ratings could also fall and lead to a reduction in broadcast license fees as well. To guard against such losses, MLB and the Japanese baseball leagues agreed to the posting system.

Although the system has been around since 1999, it has not been used very often. Table 19.2 contains the entire history of transactions pursuant to the posting system. It is clear that 2006 was a banner year as Kei Igawa went to the Yankees, Akimori Iwamura went to the Tampa Bay (Devil) Rays, and Daisuke

[18] See Duane W. Rockerbie, *Peculiarities of the Major League Baseball Posting System* (November 2006). Available at SSRN. http://ssrn.com/abstract=946399. For a critical view, see Andrew Zimbalist, "Red Sox-Matsuzaka Saga Highlights Flaws in MLB's Posting System," *Sports Business Journal*, January 15, 2007.

[19] In Japan, a player must have nine years of service in Japan's top leagues before he becomes an unrestricted free agent.

[20] There was cause for concern. In 1995, Hideo Nomo was the property of the Kintetsu Buffaloes. Ineligible for free agency, Nomo retired from baseball and then promptly signed with the Los Angeles Dodgers. The Buffaloes were not amused by this subterfuge.

Table 19.3. History of the Posting System, 1999–2010

Year	Player	Japanese Team	MLB Team	Bid
1999	Alejandro Quezada	Hiroshima Toyo Carp	Cincinnati Reds	$400,001
2000	Ichiro Suzuki	Orix Blue Wave	Seattle Mariners	$13,125,000
2002	Kazuhisa Ishii	Yakult Swallows	Los Angeles Dodgers	$11,260,000
2003	Akinori Otsuka	Chunichi Dragons	San Diego Padres	$300,000
2003	Ramon Ramirez	Hiroshima Toyo Carp	New York Yankees	$350,000
2005	Shinji Mori	Seibu Lions	Tampa Bay Devil Rays	$750,000
2005	Norihiro Nakamura	Kintetsu Buffaloes	Los Angeles Dodgers	Unknown
2006	Kei Igawa	Hanshin Tigers	New York Yankees	$26,000,194
2006	Akinori Iwamura	Yakult Swallows	Tampa Bay Devil Rays	$4,500,000
2006	Daisuke Matsuzaka	Seibu Lions	Boston Red Sox	$51,111,111
2010	Tsuyoshi Nishioka	Chiba Lotte Marines	Minnesota Twins	$5,329,000

Matsuzaka went to the Red Sox. The next player to move to the United States under the posting system was Tsuyoshi Nisjioka, who was signed by the Minnesota Twins in 2010. The terms varied widely as Table 19.2 clearly shows.

4.1 Akimori Iwamura – Tampa Bay (Devil) Rays

The transfer fee for Iwamura was only $4.5 million.[21] The Rays then negotiated a three-year deal with an option. Iwamura's contract called for salaries of $1.8 million in 2007, $2.4 million in 2008, and $3.5 million in 2009. The Rays can keep Iwamura for 2010 at a salary of $4.25 million. If they fail to exercise their option for 2010, they must pay Iwamura $250,000. In this case, the Japanese team – the Yakult Swallows – received $4.5 million and Iwamura received a stream of future payments with a present value of at least $6.42 million assuming a discount rate of 10 percent and a failure to exercise the fourth-year option.[22] From this, we can conclude that the Rays valued Iwamura's services at $10.92 million. This sum was split between the original team and the player: 58.8 percent to Iwamura and 41.2 percent to the Swallows.[23]

4.2 Kei Igawa – New York Yankees[24]

The Yankees won the auction for the exclusive negotiating rights to Kei Igawa with a bid of $26 million. This gave them the exclusive right to negotiate a deal

[21] See Associated Press, "Devil Rays Agree to Deal with Iwamura," *Gainesville Sun*, December 16, 2006, for contract details.

[22] To calculate this amount, compute the present value of the salaries plus the buyout.

[23] In his first season, Iwamura appeared to have been a good choice with a very respectable batting average of .285 in 123 games.

[24] Murray Chass, "In New Bidding, Price is Right for The Yankees," *New York Times*, November 29, 2006; Tyler Kepner, "Igawa's Bronx Arrival Met with Tampered Expectations," *New York Times*, January 9, 2007.

with Igawa. The result of the subsequent negotiations was a five-year $20 million contract. The cost of Igawa's services for five years to the Yankees was the present value of the payments:

$$PV(Contract) = \$26.0 + \sum_{t=1}^{5} \$4.0/(1+i)^t.$$

If we assume a 10 percent interest rate, the present value of the cost of obtaining Igawa's services for five years amounted to

$$\begin{aligned} PV(contract) &= \$26.0 + (3.7908)(\$4.0) \\ &= \$41{,}163{,}200. \end{aligned}$$

This seems like a big commitment for a pitcher whom the Yankees did not expect to be a dominant starter. Although Igawa led his Japan league in strikeouts several times, the Yankees never believed that he would blow away major league hitters. In fact, they did not really know just what they were getting for that average of $8.2 million per year. Nor would they know until Igawa actually faced MLB competition. During the 2007 and 2008 season, Igawa was a major disappointment to the Yankees. So far, the Yankees have gotten precious little for their money. In 2007, Igawa started only 12 games, won only twice, and had an ERA of 6.25. As disappointing as this may have been, 2008 was worse: one start, no wins, and an ERA of 13.5. Igawa has been a flop in the majors and not much better in the minor league.[25]

4.3 Daisuke Matsuzaka – Boston Red Sox

The most notable of the three players recruited from Japan in the 2006 posting season was Daisuke Matsuzaka.[26] Following an excellent 2006 season in which Matsuzaka had a 17–5 record and an earned run average of only 2.13 while playing for the Seibu Lions, all of the expectations were that he would be a top-of-the rotation starter at the MLB level. Given the thin free-agent market for starting pitchers, several teams were clearly interested in Matsuzaka. These clubs included the Yankees, the Mets, the Cubs, the Rangers, and the Red Sox. Perhaps warned off by Scott Boras, Matsuzaka's agent, the Dodgers and the Mariners announced that they would not submit a bid.

The word on the street was that the bidding would probably peak at around $20 million. What a poor prediction that was! The New York Yankees' sealed bid was $33 million and the New York Mets' bid was $39 million. Both New York clubs were well behind the record-shattering bid of the Boston Red Sox: $51,111,111. For this untidy sum, the Red Sox had the pleasure of bargaining with Matsuzaka's agent, the notoriously tough Scott Boras, over the terms of Matsuzaka's contract (see the box setting out the final terms).

[25] In 2007, Igawa pitched in the minors to gain experience. In AAA ball, his ERA was a discouraging 5.72.

[26] The most accomplished player is Ichiro Suzuki. His posting fee in 2000 was $13.2 million, which must look like an enormous bargain to the Seattle Mariners.

The two sides had 30 days to reach an agreement or the whole deal would be off. The Seibu Lions would not get any of the $51.1 million posting fee if no agreement were reached, the Boston Red Sox would have to pursue championships without him, and Matsuzaka would have to return to Japan. When salary negotiations bogged down, Boras actually recommended that Matsuzaka return to Japan and either try the posting system the next year or play two more years in Japan and become a free agent. If Matsuzaka had become a free agent, then there would be no posting fee, and that money would presumably go to Matsuzaka (minus Boras's commission, of course). Matsuzaka, however, was determined to start his MLB career in 2007, which reduced what little leverage he had in dealing with Boston. Although the deal was only finalized at the last moment, it did get finished, and Matsuzaka was under contract to Boston for six years. The salary dollars amounted to $52 million before discounting.[27]

Box 19.3 *Matsuzaka Strikes It Rich**

Even though the Seibu Lions got a big chunk of Daisuke Matsuzaka's market value, he still struck it rich with his six-year contract. The Boston Red Sox agreed to a hefty six-year deal that included some handsome (and handy) perks. Considering the money first, Boston agreed to pay $2 million as a signing bonus plus the following salaries:

Season	Salary ($millions)
2007	6.0
2008	8.0
2009	8.0
2010	8.0
2011	10.0
2012	10.0

The contract also includes incentive provisions. If Matsuzaka finishes among the top three in Cy Young Award voting or among the top five in Most Valuable Player (MVP) Award voting, his 2009 and 2010 salaries could rise to $10 million and his 2011 and 2012 salaries could increase to $12 million. The contract also includes a host of award bonuses for being named Rookie of the Year, MVP of the league championship series, and MVP of the World Series, winning a Gold Glove award, being named to the All-Star team, and starting an All-Star game.

Moving on to the perks, the contract provides an assortment of extras to make life easier (and cheaper):

[27] It is hard to say that Matsuzaka was a big success in 2007. He gave Boston 32 starts, but had a 15–12 record and an ERA of 4.40. In the postseason, Matsuzaka made 4 starts, had a 2–1 record, and pitched 19.2 innings with an ERA of 5.03.

Travel:

Use of a Lincoln Town Car or equivalent
Eight first-class round-trip tickets between Boston and Japan

Housing Allowances

Spring training: $25,000
Boston: $75,000

Services

Interpreter
Assistant to deal with Japanese media

Miscellaneous

Uniform number 18
Red Sox player ticket package
Cannot be sent to minors

No trade without approval

* Boston.com, "Matsuzaka Contract Details," December 15, 2006.

4.4 Tsuyoshi Nishioka – Minnesota Twins

In 2010, Tsuyoshi Niskioka was a star infielder for Chiba in the Pacific League of Nippon Professional Baseball. He led the league in batting average (0.346) and runs scored (121). Niskioka also had 32 doubles, 8 triples, 11 home runs, and 22 stolen bases.

The Minnesota Twins were interested in adding more speed to their lineup and were attracted to Niskioka based on reports from Japan. When Chiba posted Niskioka, the Twins were ready to bid for negotiating rights.

The Twins won the bidding phase with a bid of $5,329,000. In the bargaining phase, the Twins and Niskioka settled on a three-year deal that will pay Niskioka $3.0 million from 2011 through 2013. The Twins have a club option for 2014 at $4.0 million. If they fail to exercise the option, they must pay a $250,000 buyout.

4.5 Gaming the Posting System

For the posting system to work the way it was intended, all parties must participate in good faith. There are many potential loopholes in the system that may alter the results. First, one team could block another from getting a player it wants. In the Matsuzaka case, suppose that the Yankees had bid $70 million. It would have denied the Red Sox access to Matsuzaka. The Yankees could then offer Matsuzaka $20 million for six years. If Matsuzaka refused, it would cost the Yankees nothing but would keep Matsuzaka away from the Red Sox for at least another year. The Red Sox might contend that the Yankees had not bargained in good faith, and therefore, they were entitled to pursue him without waiting another year. However, the Yankees could reasonably point out that they were offering an average of $15 million per year in total – most of it going to the Seibu Lions. How could MLB conclude that that was bad faith – even if, in fact, it was a ploy to keep Matsuzaka away from Boston?

Second, the player might refuse to bargain in good faith in the hope of getting some of the posting fee from his old team. Again, Boston's bid was about $12 million more than the next highest bid. Rather than lose its opportunity to cash in, the Seibu Lions could have offered to split that $12 million with Matsuzaka rather than have the deal fall apart. Although there is no evidence that this occurred in Matsuzaka's case (or any other), it could have. There is no way of knowing.

Third, a variant on this side deal would be a rebate from Seibu to Boston. Again, if the deal seemed to be falling apart, Seibu could offer to help Boston get a deal done by giving up some of the $12 million surplus.

5 CONCLUDING REMARKS

In this chapter, we have taken another look at salary determination. This time, we have considered how teams bid for a player's services in a kind of English auction. We found that this process leads to the efficient allocation of resources; the team that values a player most highly will actually wind up with that player. We also examined how a team and a player or coach may bargain over contract terms. Finally, we examined the posting system in MLB that pertains to players under contract to baseball teams in Japan. This system involves bidding in the first stage and bargaining in the second stage.

PROBLEMS AND QUESTIONS

1. Ignoring the perks in Matsuzaka's contract and assuming an 8 percent discount rate, how much did Boston commit for six years of Matsuzaka's services? Don't forget the posting fee.
2. Because the second highest bid for Matsuzaka was $39 million, Boston could have won with a bid of, say, $39,111,111. Had they bid that sum, they would have saved $12 million. Is this correct?
3. Under the posting system, is it likely that the club that values the player the most will actually wind up with the player on its roster? Explain why or why not.
4. In a private value English auction, the seller cannot get the highest value unless he sets the reserve price equal to that value. Why don't all sellers set such reserve prices?
5. Suppose there are two bidders for Larry Linebacker. The two clubs collude (i.e., agree to not compete). Under these circumstances, Larry will not maximize the salary he receives, but he will play for the team that values him the most. Explain.
6. Boston committed a nominal total of $103.1 million over six years to Daisuke Matsuzaka. This amounts to about $17.2 million per year. Because of baseball's 40 percent luxury tax and Boston's already bloated payroll, Matsuzaka would not have received an annual salary of $17.2 million had he been an unrestricted free agent. Explain.

7. Assume that Daisuke Matsuzaka could have earned $3 million per year for the 2007 and 2008 seasons playing for the Seibu Lions. Had he done so, he would have been an unrestricted free agent following the 2008 season and not subject to the posting system. Should he have followed Scott Boras's advice and done this? Examine the pros and cons.
8. Describe the bargaining phase of the posting system:
   a. What are the payoffs to the player and the club if they fail to reach an agreement?
   b. What is the surplus that they are trying to divide?
   c. How does the 30-day bargaining deadline influence behavior?
9. The Yankees have considered trading Kei Igawa but would also like to recoup some of the $26 million posting fee they paid to the Hanshin Tigers. Explain why that payment should be irrelevant in deciding whether to trade Igawa.
10. After a productive season in 2007, Boston Red Sox third baseman Mike Lowell wanted a four-year contract. Boston offered him a three-year $37.5 million contract. Even though the Philadelphia Phillies offered Lowell $50 million over four years, Lowell stayed with Boston. Explain why.
11. Players picked in the NFL draft have two choices: sign with the team that drafted them or sit out a year and reenter the draft. Michael Crabtree, the San Francisco 49ers' first choice in the 2009 draft, threatened to sit out the entire season even though the 49ers offered him $16 million guarantees. Under what circumstances would sitting out an entire year be sensible?
12. The major college football powers include Alabama, Florida, the University of Southern California, and Ohio State, among others. In 2010, the salaries of the head football coaches at these places were in the $2 to $5 million range. Explain how the use of monopsony power makes these salaries possible.

RESEARCH QUESTIONS

1. Brian Cashman has been the General Manager of the New York Yankees for many years. During his tenure, the Yankees have signed many free agents. Their success has been mixed to say the least. Identify Cashman's free-agent signings, the contract terms, and the subsequent productivity of the players.
2. Examine the history of the posting system. How have these players performed in MLB?
3. On occasion, bargaining breaks down. Following the 2007 season, the Yankees manager, Joe Torre, began discussions over his contract. In the end, they failed to reach an agreement. Torre left the Yankees and began managing the LA Dodgers. Examine the *New York Times* reports of the negotiations and explain the breakdown.

4. Review Barry Zito's performances from 2007 to the present and compare them with his contract (see Table 19.1). How many of the incentive provisions has Zito cashed in on?
5. In 2006, the Boston Red Sox won the bidding war and signed Daisuke Matsuzaka. How has he performed? Did the Red Sox make a mistake?

REFERENCES AND FURTHER READING

Berri, David, Martin Schmidt, and Stacey Brook. (2007). *The Wages of Wins.* Stanford, CA: Stanford University Press.

Bradbury, J.C. (2007). *The Baseball Economist: The Real Game Exposed* (chapter 13). New York: Penguin.

Conlin, M. (2002). "Reputation in Bargaining: National Football League Contract Negotiations." *Economic Inquiry,* 40, 241–259.

Dixit, Avinash, and Susan Skeath. (2004). *Games of Strategy* (chapter 17), 2nd ed. New York: W.W. Norton.

Farmer, A., P. Pecorino, and V. Stango. (2004). "The Causes of Bargaining Failure: Evidence from Major League Baseball." *Journal of Law & Economics,* XLVII, 543–568.

Faurot, David J. (2001) "Equilibrium Explanation of Bargaining and Arbitration in Major League Baseball." *Journal of Sports Economics,* 2, 22–34.

Marburger, D. R. (1994). "Bargaining Power and the Structure of Salaries in Major League Baseball." *Managerial and Decision Economics,* 15, 433–441.

McAfee, Preston R. (2002). *Competitive Solutions* (chapter 12). Princeton, NJ: Princeton University Press.

Nash, John F., Jr. (1950). "The Bargaining Problem." *Econometrica,* 18, 155–162.

Philips, Louis. (1988). *The Economics of Imperfect Information* (chapter 4). New York: Cambridge University Press.

Surdam, David G. (2006). "The Coase Theorem and Player Movement in Major League Baseball." *Journal of Sports Economics,* 7, 201–221.

Varian, Hal. (2006). *Intermediate Microeconomics* (chapter 17). New York: W.W. Norton.

20

Economic Value of Multiyear Contracts

1 MULTIYEAR CONTRACTS

Before the demise of the reserve clause, there was no need for multiyear contracts because players never became free agents. Now, however, many athletes and coaches have multiyear employment contracts. The terms of these contracts may vary widely.[1] Some contracts are guaranteed, which means that the club must pay the player regardless of his or her performance, or even if the player is injured and cannot perform at all. In the case of losing coaches, they must be paid or bought out in order to hire a new coach. Other contracts are not guaranteed. Some contracts have buyout provisions, some have option years, some have incentive provisions, and so on.[2] One thing is certain about multiyear contracts, however: none of them are valued correctly in newspaper and TV reports. For example, Rick DiPietro, the New York Islanders goaltender, recently agreed to a 15-year contract extension that was reported to be worth $67.5 million. National Hockey League (NHL) star Patrick Elias signed a seven-year deal with the New Jersey Devils that the *New York Times* reported as a $42 million contract. Carmelo Anthony, when he was a Denver Nuggets star, signed a five-year contract extension in 2006 that was estimated to be worth $80 million. Alfonso Soriano signed an eight-year contract with the Chicago Cubs reportedly worth $136 million. In November 2010, Donovan McNabb signed a five-year contract extension with the Washington Redskins that could be worth more than $80 million according to some reports. All of these reports are misleading because they report the total *nominal* dollars in the contract.

The mistake that is invariably made by the news media is that they simply add up all of the future payments without regard to when, or even if, those payments will be received. The news reports would only be correct if all of the payments were received at the time the contract was signed. This, of course, is never the case, and therefore, these reports are always misleading. DiPietro's

[1] This chapter is filled with specific examples. Some of them are a bit old, but they are included to illustrate an economic principle. The examples are not intended to be current events.

[2] Buyouts, options, and incentives are defined and more thoroughly examined later in this chapter.

contract calls for annual payments of $4.5 million, which add up to $67.5 million over 15 years. However, the last payment of $4.5 million will not be received until the 15th year of the contract. The last payment is worth far less than $4.5 million on signing day.

In this chapter, we examine the economic value of multiyear contracts. This necessarily involves the calculation of present values[3] with and without uncertainty depending on the circumstances. We also include considerations of guarantees, player and club options, signing bonuses, and incentives.

2 FUNDAMENTALS OF CONTRACT VALUATION

All multiyear contracts necessarily involve future payments. To assess the economic value of the contract at the time it was signed, we have to find the present value of those future payments. In most cases, this is pretty straightforward, but in some cases, it can be a bit complicated. For example, when Tom Glavine pitched for the New York Mets, he earned $7.5 million for the 2006 season. He received $2.25 million during the season and deferred the remaining $5.25 million at 6 percent interest. If he received that deferred payment four years later, we can calculate the value of $1 at 6 percent in four years and multiply that value by $5.25 million. In other words, we first must find

$$(\$1.00)(1.06)^4 = 1.2625,$$

(from Table 1 in the appendix to Chapter 2) and then multiply by $5.25 million:

$$(\$5.25 \text{ million})(1.2625) = \$6{,}628{,}125$$

As a result, Glavine will receive $6,628,125 at the end of four years. To determine the value of this sum on signing day, the present value must be found. If the appropriate discount rate exceeds 6 percent, the present value will fall below $5.25 million. If, in contrast, the discount rate is below 6 percent, the present value will exceed $5.25 million. The present value of salaries that will not be received until well into the future can fall far short of the nominal dollar amount. For example, suppose Patrick Elias is scheduled to receive a salary of $5 million in the final year of his seven-year contract. If the appropriate discount rate is 6 percent, the present value of that future salary payment would be

$$PV = \frac{\$5{,}000{,}000}{(1.06)^7},$$

which is $3,325,286. Thus, the difference between the nominal dollars ($5 million) and the discounted dollars is $1,674,714.

The further into the future that a payment is received, the larger the difference between the nominal sum and the present value. As another hockey

[3] For a refresher on present value calculations, see the appendix to Chapter 2.

example, the present value of the $4.5 million that Rick DiPietro will receive in the 15th year of his contract is

$$\begin{aligned} PV &= \frac{\$4{,}500{,}000}{(1.06)^{15}} \\ &= \$1{,}877{,}693, \end{aligned}$$

which is substantially less than half of the nominal value of $4.5 million.

It should be noted that we have assumed that players receive their salaries at the end of the year. This, of course, is a simplification. Players are actually paid throughout the season according to conventions in the sport. In the National Football League (NFL), for example, players receive weekly checks during the season. To avoid computational complications, we have assumed that payment is received at the end of the year.

Some contracts include advances rather than deferred compensation. As a concrete illustration, consider Donnell Harvey, who enjoyed a brilliant freshman year as a power forward at the University of Florida. Following that season, Harvey left for the National Basketball Association (NBA). The New York Knicks drafted him and immediately traded him to the Dallas Mavericks, which signed him to a three-year contract. He received $646,920 of his $718,800 first-year salary in advance. He received $772,800 in his second season and $826,700 in his third season. The economic value of this contract on signing day is the present value of these payments. Assuming that the discount rate is 10 percent, the calculations are as follows:

$$\begin{aligned} PV &= \$646{,}920 + \frac{\$71{,}880}{1.10} + \frac{\$772{,}800}{(1.10)^2} + \frac{\$826{,}700}{(1.10)^3} \\ &= \$646{,}800 + 65{,}346 + 638{,}678 + 621{,}112 \\ &= \$1{,}911{,}936. \end{aligned}$$

Because Harvey received an advance of $646,920, this amount is not discounted. The balance of his first-year salary, $71,880, is discounted for one year. His Year 2 and Year 3 salaries are discounted for two and three years, respectively. Although the *Gainesville Sun* reported that Harvey's three-year contract was worth $2.3 million, it was actually worth less than that because of the discounting.

If the annual payments are the same, the present value calculation is a little easier. Rick DiPietro's 15-year contract calls for annual payments of $4.5 million. Thus, the present value of the contract is

$$\begin{aligned} PV &= \sum_{t=1}^{15} (\$4.5\ mil)/(1.06)^t, \\ &= (\$4.5\ mil) \sum_{t=1}^{15} 1/(1.06)^t \end{aligned}$$

where $\sum_{t=1}^{15}$ denotes summation over the period from Year 1 to Year 15. In this case, the value of DiPietro's 15-year contract is as follows:

$$PV = (\$4.5\ mil)(9.7122),$$

which is about $43.705 million. Although this is a substantial sum, it is far less than the reported amount of $67.5 million.

When the annual payments are the same, we can use Table A2.3 in the appendix to Chapter 2. This table shows some sample values for the present value of an annuity of $1 per year for *n* years. For DiPietro's contract, we can find the entry for 15 years and 6 percent interest, which is 9.7122. If we multiply this by the $4.5 million annual salaries, we get $43,704,900. Compare this to the $67.5 million value reported by the media.

Box 20.1 *Urban Meyer's Initial Contract*

Coaches also have multiyear contracts. Following two successful head coaching performances at Bowling Green and at Utah, Urban Meyer was hired at the University of Florida in 2005. His seven-year contract provided the following compensation:

Year	Income
2005	$1,985,000
2006	$1,741,750
2007	$1,998,702
2008	$1,980,863
2009	$2,238,238
2010	$1,745,835
2011	$2,353,660

Following Florida's impressive victory over Ohio State in the 2007 Bowl Championship Series (BCS) National Championship game, Meyer was rewarded with a new contract that increased his salary to more than $3 million per year. When the Gators defeated Oklahoma in the 2009 BCS championship game, Meyer's contract was revised again to $4 million per year.

3 CONTRACTS WITH UNCERTAIN TERMS

Some multiyear contracts have employment terms that are subject to uncertainty. In the NFL, for example, future years of the contract are not usually guaranteed. If a player suffers an injury during one season, he will be paid for that season, but he may be cut from the team for future years, essentially voiding the remainder of his contract.

In some cases, by the time a player reaches the end of a multiyear contract, his skills have succumbed to wear and tear. The salary specified in the contract may be well above the player's fair market value. Rather than paying the salary in the contract, the team may renegotiate for a lower sum or may simply cut the player. Emmitt Smith, the great Dallas Cowboys running back, was due to earn $7 million in 2003. The Cowboys, believing that Smith was no longer an elite back, released him, and he signed a two-year contract with the Arizona Cardinals reportedly worth $7.5 million (he received a $2.5 million signing bonus, and his base salaries were $2.5 million each for 2003 and 2004).[4]

Box 20.2 *Not So Fast, My Friend**

Jamal Lewis, the great Baltimore Ravens running back, has been a big part of the Raven's meager offense. Baltimore used its first pick in the 2000 NFL draft to get Lewis. His productivity and compensation over his seven seasons with the Ravens are as follows:

Year	Games	Carries	Yards	Salary
2000	16	309	1,364	$1,878,000
2001	On injured reserve			$1,692,720
2002	16	308	1,327	$2,038,000
2003	16	387	2,066	$4,310,900
2004	12	235	1,006	$4,765,029
2005	15	269	906	$3,833,760
2006	16	314	1,132	$6,000,220

In 2003, Lewis was the Offensive Player of the Year when he rushed for more than 2,000 yards. As we can see, however, Lewis's productivity has declined recently. He suffers from recurring ankle problems.

Lewis was due to earn a $5 million roster bonus on March 3, 2007, and a $5 million salary for the 2007 season. However, as Lee Corso would say, "Not so fast, my friend." The Ravens cut Lewis on February 28. The Ravens had hoped to re-sign Lewis to a more "cap friendly" contract at about $2 million. Lewis signed a one-year contract with the Cleveland Browns for $3.5 million. With incentives, this deal could be worth $5 million.

* "Lewis stops waiting on Ravens, signs with Browns," ESPN.com, March 7, 2007.

In contrast to NFL contracts, multiyear contracts are guaranteed in Major League Baseball (MLB) but some contain option years. It is not certain that a team will exercise its option for the final year, and this introduces uncertainty into the value of the contract. For example, Tom Glavine's contract made 2007 an option year. If the team had exercised its option, Glavine would have been paid $12 million unless he pitched 180 innings or more in 2006. In that event, he would earn $14 million. Thus, uncertainty arises from two sources. First, it is

[4] Pasquarelli, Len, "Emmitt's Deal Keeps Him in Elite Salary Group," espn.com, March 23, 2003, at http://sports.espn.go.com/espn/print?id=1531692&type=columnist.

uncertain whether the team will exercise its option. Second, it is uncertain how many innings Glavine would pitch in 2006.

Box 20.3 *A Coach's Tenure Is Never Secure*

When a team fails to live up to expectations, the coach's head may roll. It is startling how quickly a coach can fall out of favor. Consider the case of Mike Shula, former head coach of Alabama's Crimson Tide.

Mike Shula, a former quarterback at the University of Alabama, replaced Mike Price, who was fired for off-the-field misbehavior. At the time, Alabama was on probation for NCAA violations, and Shula had only four months to get his team ready for the 2004 season. The Tide had a 4–9 season in 2003. Shula led his team to a record of 6–6 in 2004. In 2005, Alabama enjoyed a 10–2 season, a Cotton Bowl victory, and a top 10 ranking.

Alabama was ecstatic with Shula's performance. His contract was extended for two additional years through 2012. He received an increase in salary of $650,000 per year to put his annual salary at $1.55 million.

Shula said, "I'm excited about our future at Alabama and I love the university." Mal Moore, Alabama's athletic director, was similarly pleased, and said, "We are certainly happy to know that Mike Shula will be our coach for many years to come."

Following a 6–7 season in 2006 and a fourth straight loss to arch rival Auburn, Mal Moore fired Mike Shula.

4 VALUE OF MULTIYEAR CONTRACTS WITHOUT GUARANTEES

Larry Linebacker signs a three-year contract calling for salaries of w_1, w_2, and w_3 in years 1, 2, and 3, respectively. The salary in the first year is guaranteed. The salaries for years 2 and 3 are not guaranteed, which is the norm in the NFL. As a result, the value of the contract is uncertain. There is risk associated with the future payments. For simplicity, assume that Larry could be cut at the end of the first year and therefore would not receive w_2 or w_3. If Larry is cut after the second year, then he would not receive the third-year payment of w_3. Thus, the possible payments would be as follows:

1. w_1, w_2, w_3
2. w_1, w_2
3. w_1

There is a probability associated with each possible outcome: p_1, p_2, p_3. Now, we can calculate the *expected present value* of Larry's contract:

$$E[PV] = p_1[(w_1/(1+i) + w_2/(1+i)^2 + w_3(1+i)^3] \\ +p_2[(w_1/(1+i) + w_2/(1+i)^2] + p_3[(w_1/(1+i)],$$

where p_1 is the probability of playing all three years under the contract, p_2 is the probability of playing two years under the contract, and p_3 is the probability of playing just one year under the contract. Recalling that $p_1 + p_2 + p_3 = 1$, we can rearrange this expression algebraically:

$$E[PV] = w_1/(1+i) + (p_1 + p_2)(w_2/(1+i)^2) + p_1 w_3 (1+i)^3.$$

A numerical example will help to illustrate the influence of uncertainty. Suppose that $p_1 = .60$, $p_2 = .25$, and $p_3 = .15$. Assume that $w_1 = \$1{,}000{,}000$, $w_2 = \$1{,}500{,}000$, and $w_3 = \$2{,}000{,}000$. At a discount rate of 10 percent, the expected value of the contract would be calculated as follows:

$$\begin{aligned} E[PV] &= \$1{,}000{,}000/(1.10) + (.85)(\$1{,}500{,}000)/(1.10)^2 \\ &\quad + (.60)(\$2{,}000{,}000)(1.10)^3 \\ &= \$909{,}091 + 1{,}053{,}719 + 901{,}578 \\ &= \$2{,}864{,}388. \end{aligned}$$

This is a lot lower than the simple sum of \$4,500,000, which is what the news media would report. It is lower for two reasons. First, some of the payments (w_2 and w_3) are not certain. As a result, these sums are reduced by the probability of their being received. Second, the payments are discounted to reflect the fact that the sums will be received in the future.

A real-life example of Larry Linebacker and the uncertainty of NFL contracts is the contract of LaVar Arrington, a Pro Bowl linebacker who signed with the New York Giants in April 2006 after six seasons with the Washington Redskins. The contract was reportedly for seven years and valued at \$49 million, or \$7 million per year.[5] Arrington's contract included a relatively small signing bonus of \$5.25 million, and his deal was heavily laden with performance incentives.[6] Less than a year later, however, the Giants released Arrington. Arrington played in just six games for the Giants before suffering a season-ending Achilles tendon injury. It has been reported that Arrington was to make only \$900,000 in his first season. This salary, along with his signing bonus, is a far cry from the \$49 million dollars that was reported by the media.[7]

5 CONTRACTS WITH OPTION YEARS

Some multiyear contracts contain options for the teams. If the team exercises its option to employ the player in a future year, it will pay the salary specified

[5] http://www.nytimes.com/2006/04/23/sports/football/23giants.html?adxnnl=1&ref=lavararrington&adxnnlx=1311283511-LK0bEzEBb2tJoEikTzaHfw.

[6] Compare this deal to the deal of a similar player, Julian Peterson, a linebacker who signed a seven-year deal worth \$54 million with the Seahawks a month before Arrington signed with the Giants. His signing bonus was \$11.5 million, and in total about \$18 million was guaranteed – more than three times the amount of guaranteed money Arrington received. Ironically, Peterson and Arrington share the same agents, Carl and Kevin Poston. (http://articles.philly.com/2006-03-22/sports/25416057_1_free-agent-signings-contract-kevin-poston)

[7] http://query.nytimes.com/gst/fullpage.html?res=9E0CE5D61F3FF930A25751C0A9619C8B63&ref=lavararrington.

in the contract. If it elects not to employ the player, it pays a buyout amount, which is also specified in the contract. As an example, consider Billy Wagner's contract. The Houston Astros signed Billy Wagner, a relief pitcher, to a four-year contract. The contract called for the following annual payments:

Year 1: $8 million
Year 2: $8 million
Tear 3: $8 million
Year 4: $9 million or $3 million

For Year 4, the Astros had the option of keeping Wagner on the team and paying him $9 million or releasing him with a buyout of $3 million.

If the appropriate discount rate is 10 percent and the (subjective) probability of the team's exercising the option to employ Wagner in Year 4 is 0.60, we can calculate the expected present value of Wagner's contract as follows:

$$E[PV] = \frac{\$8\text{ million}}{1.10} + \frac{\$8\text{ million}}{(1.10)^2} + \frac{\$8\text{ million}}{(1.10)^3} + \frac{(.60)(\$9\text{ million}) + (.4)(\$3\text{ million})}{(1.10)^4}$$

$$E[PV] = \$7{,}272{,}727 + 6{,}611{,}570 + 6{,}010{,}518 + 4{,}507{,}889$$

$$E[PV] = \$24{,}402{,}704$$

This, of course, is much less than the reported value of $33 million.

6 CONTRACTS WITH SIGNING BONUSES

Typically, when a contract is prepared, the signing bonus is *earned* simply by signing the contract. The actual payment of the signing bonus can be structured in any fashion that fits the needs of the team and the player. For example, Barry Bonds received a $10 million signing bonus that was paid in four installments. Derek Jeter's signing bonus was paid in equal annual installments over eight years. If the language of the contract is clear, no part of the signing bonus should be refundable. That is, the entire bonus is earned upon signing the contract, but the life of the contract can be more complicated. In some cases, however, a team may recover part of the signing bonus if the player fails to live up to the terms of his contract. In Chapter 12, we examined Michael Vick's misconduct and an arbitrator's decision that he had to return some of his signing bonus to the Atlanta Falcons.

7 GUARANTEES

Whether salary payments in future years are guaranteed is a matter of tradition and the Collective Bargaining Agreement in each sport. In the NBA and MLB, future years are guaranteed unless there are explicit option years in the player's contract. In the NFL, future years usually are not guaranteed, but as a percentage of the entire package, the signing bonuses tend to be larger. Thus, the signing bonus acts like a guarantee of sorts.

There are several reasons for nonpayment that override guarantees. These include (1) engaging in hazardous activity and being injured or disabled, (2) being on a drug suspension, and (3) being imprisoned. In cases in which future payments are not guaranteed, the usual reasons for nonpayment include (1) salary cap, (2) deterioration in skill, (3) injury (not in the NBA), and (4) illness.

8 CONTRACTS WITH INCENTIVE PROVISIONS

Some contracts contain incentive clauses that may increase the total payment to the player. Contracts may provide for (1) *award bonuses* (e.g., Most Valuable Player [MVP]), (2) *attendance* bonuses, and (3) *team performance* bonuses.

Curt Schilling's one-year deal with the Boston Red-Sox for the 2008 season had some interesting incentive provisions.[8] In 2007, Schilling was not in great condition and finished the regular season with a 9–8 record, an earned run average of 3.87, and 151.0 innings pitched. Nonetheless, at 40, he was his usual reliable postseason self, going 3–0. To stay in Boston, Schilling bypassed the free-agent market and accepted a one-year contract for $8 million. If he pitched 200 innings, he received another $3 million. If he hit his desired weight at six weigh-ins, he received an additional $2 million. Finally, if he received a vote for the Cy Young Award, the Red Sox would pay him an additional $1 million.

Barry Zito's already lucrative contract contains some substantial incentives. Zito will receive $100,000 for being named to the National League All Star team, for winning a Gold Glove Award, or for being the MVP in the National League Championship Series. Being selected as the World Series MVP is worth $200,000, and being the National League MVP is worth $250,000. The biggest prize of all, however, comes with being the Cy Young winner: $500,000.

The contracts of college coaches often contain incentives tied to the team's success. Consider, for example, the contract of Phil Fulmer, former head coach of the Tennessee Volunteers. He earned a salary of $2.05 million for the 2007 season. There were incentives in his contract as well:

Going to a non-BCS bowl	$37,500
Tying for first place in the Southeastern Conference (SEC) East	50,000
Appearing in the SEC Championship	75,000
Winning the SEC or going to a BCS bowl	100,000
Playing for the BCS Championship	150,000
Winning the National Championship	250,000

Given Fulmer's salary of $2.05 million and a coach's inherent interest in winning anyway, it is not obvious that incentives are needed. Nonetheless, the incentives are there.

9 CONCLUDING REMARKS

Many players and coaches have multiyear contracts, which obviously involve future payments. Some future payments are guaranteed, and others are not. To

[8] Tyler Kepner, "Red Sox Retain Schilling," *New York Times*, November 6, 2007.

value such contracts properly, we introduced the fundamentals of present value calculations. To include considerations of uncertainty, we also introduced some elementary concepts of probability. For the most part, we focused our attention on player contracts in this chapter. As we will see in subsequent chapters, present value calculations are useful in understanding franchise valuations, naming rights contracts, and other multiyear contracts.

PROBLEMS AND QUESTIONS

1. In Section 20.4, what would be the value of Larry's contract if the payments had been guaranteed?
2. Along with Joe Namath, Curtis Martin has been described as "perhaps the greatest player in Jets history." After seven seasons, Martin was still improving; his rushing average of 4.6 yards per carry in 2001 was his career best. In addition, Martin was a role model on and off the field. He signed a new contract that contained some impressive numbers. Martin received a $10 million signing bonus before the 2002 season. His 2002 salary was $3.5 million, and his 2003 salary was $650,000. The contract was for five years with a team option for an additional three years. The option had to be exercised by March 1, 2003. If it was exercised, Martin would get a $10 million bonus. If it was not exercised, he would get a default payment of $2.9 million. For 2003 and 2004, he received $1 million roster bonuses, which he received for "making the team" – that is, by not being cut. Assuming Martin's salary for 2004 would be $950,000 and that the probability of the Jets exercising its option was 0.9, what was the value of the first three years of Martin's contract? Make whatever other assumptions you need.
3. When David Ball was a free agent, he signed a four-year contract with the Phillies. The terms included a signing bonus of $800,000 and annual salaries of $3.0 million for Year 1, $4.2 million for Year 2, and $4.5 million for Years 3 and 4.
   - **a.** Assuming that the appropriate discount rate was 10 percent, what was the economic value of Ball's contract at signing?
   - **b.** Suppose that Year 4 was an option year in David Ball's contract – that is, the Phillies could have released him. How does that alter the value of his contract?
4. During the 2006 free-agent period, the New Jersey Devils re-signed Patrick Elias to a seven-year contract that the *New York Times* reported as a "$42 million contract." The payment schedule is $7.5 million in each of the first two seasons, $6 million in the third and fourth seasons, and $5 million in seasons five through seven.
   - **a.** Suppose that the appropriate discount rate is 7.5 percent. How much is the contract worth on signing day?
   - **b.** If the discount rate were 10 percent, how much would it be worth?
5. In his first full season in MLB, Aubrey Huff was an offensive powerhouse for the Tampa Bay Devil Rays. He was in the top 10 in batting average, home runs, and runs batted in. He set numerous club records. In recognition of

his performance, he received a three-year contract calling for a $500,000 signing bonus, and salaries of $2.5 million in Year 1, $4.75 million in Year 2, and $6.75 million in Year 3. The *Gainesville Sun* headline said it was a $14.5 million contract.

a. Is this correct?

b. Explain why or why not.

c. If not, make any necessary assumptions and calculate the correct value.

6. In the 2001 draft, Leonard Davis was the second pick overall. His six-year contract was reported to be worth $52 million. Here are the details:

Signing bonus: $12.125 million; $9.5 million paid upon signing balance during Year 1.

Salary payments:

1. $209,000
2. $892,000
3. $951,000
4. $5,815,000
5. $6,839,000
6. $7,169,000

If the appropriate discount rate were 6 percent, what was the economic value of Little's contract?

7. Derek Jeter's 10-year contract with the New York Yankees was reported to be worth $189 million. His signing bonus was $16 million payable in equal installments over the 2001–2008 seasons. Jeter's annual salary payments were as follows:

2001	**$11 million**	**2006**	**$19 million**
2002	$13 million	2007	$20 million
2003	$14 million	2008	$20 million
2004	$17 million	2009	$20 million
2005	$18 million	2010	$21 million

If the appropriate discount rate was 5 percent, what was the value of Jeter's contract? What is the value if the discount rate had been 8 percent?

8. The former football coach at the University of Tennessee (UT), Phillip Fulmer, got a raise in his salary to $1.65 million. The contract was broken down as follows:

Base salary	$225,000
Radio and TV	$675,000
Endorsements	$550,000
Retention bonus	$200,000

The retention bonus was deferred. If Fulmer stayed at UT for five years, he would receive a $1 million bonus; if he left, he forfeited the bonus. There is also a buyout provision in his contract. If he left during 2002, he would pay UT $500,000. If he left during 2003, he would pay UT $250,000.

   a. Assuming he stayed for five years, what was the economic value of his contract? Assume a discount rate of 6 percent.

   b. Suppose there is a 10 percent chance that he would leave in 2002. What is the economic value of his 2002 salary?

9. Following one of the greatest seasons in baseball history, Barry Bonds tried the free-agent market and found a lukewarm reaction. At 37 years old, his age may have worked against him. The Giants offered salary arbitration, but before actually getting to arbitration, they settled on a five-year deal, which the *Gainesville Sun* reported as being a $90 million deal: signing bonus of $10 million; $2.5 million now and $2.5 million per year for 2002–2004. Salary: $13 million in 2002 and 2003, $16 million in 2004, $20 million in 2005, and $18 million in 2006. Assuming that the appropriate discount rate was 8.0 percent, what was the value of the contract?

10. Lefty Larry, an All-American pitcher from the University of Florida, just signed a three-year contract that was reportedly worth $7 million. The details of the contract are as follows: signing bonus: $2 million, year 1 salary: $1 million, year 2 salary: $2 million, and year 3 salary: $2 million.

   a. What is the true economic value of Larry's contract? Explain what you are doing and make any necessary assumptions.

   b. How would the value change if the third year were an option year and the team had to pay Larry $500,000 if they decided not to exercise their option? Show how the revised calculation would be done and explain what you are doing. Make any necessary assumptions.

11. Ted Lilly, a left-handed starting pitcher for the Toronto Blue Jays, had a 15–13 record with an earned run average of 4.31 in 2006. He signed a four-year contract with the Chicago Cubs with the following terms:

Signing bonus:	$4.0 million
Salary	
2007	$5.0 million
2008	$7.0 million
2009	$12.0 million
2010	$12.0 million

At a discount rate of 6 percent, what is the economic value of the contract?

12. At the end of Mike Mussina's six-year contract with the New York Yankees, the team elected not to exercise its option for a seventh season at $17 million. Instead, it paid Mussina a $1.5 million buyout. As a free agent, Mussina signed a new two-year deal with the Yankees for 2007 and 2008. Under the new contract, Mussina has received $11.5 million each year. Of this, $2 million per year will be deferred without interest. Mussina was then paid $1.0 million per year for 2009–2012.

What was the value of the new contract on December 1, 2006? (Assume an interest rate of 6 percent.)

RESEARCH QUESTIONS

1. Compare signing bonuses in the NFL and MLB as a percentage of the total contract value. What might account for the differences?
2. Identify an NFL player who signed a multiyear contract. Compare the contract terms with what the player actually earned.
3. When Barry Sanders abruptly retired shortly after receiving a large signing bonus, the Detroit Lions wanted some of it back. Find out what happened and why.
4. When Ricky Williams retired, the Miami Dolphins sued to recover some money he had previously received. What happened and why?
5. Compare the contract values of the 10 highest paid football coaches at publicly funded universities. Does performance matter?
6. Signing bonuses are earned by simply signing the contract, but this raises several questions. What happens if someone signs a contract, receives a $10 million signing bonus, and retires a week later? What happens if he is injured a week later? Examine the cases of Eric Crouch, Barry Sanders, and Ricky Williams.

REFERENCES AND FURTHER READING

Kahn, L. M. 1993. "Free Agency, Long-Term Contracts and Compensation in Major League Baseball: Estimates from Panel Data." *Review of Economics and Statistics*, LXXV, 157–164.

Maxcy, J. 2004. "Motivating Long-Term Employment Contracts: Risk Management in Major League Baseball." *Managerial and Decision Economics*, 25, 109–120.

21

Final Offer Arbitration in Major League Baseball

1 INTRODUCTION

Final offer arbitration is a mechanism for resolving salary disputes in Major League Baseball (MLB) when a player and his club cannot agree on a salary. In MLB, rookies and veterans with only one or two years experience in MLB are not eligible for final offer arbitration. To a large extent, they are at the mercy of their clubs. Those players with six years' experience are free agents unless they are under contract. These players are protected by the market. Those veterans in between who have three to five years' experience are eligible for final offer arbitration. If a player's agent and the general manager of the team cannot reach agreement on a salary, the player is entitled to put the dispute before a three-person arbitration panel. The three arbitrators are neutral – that is, none of them will favor one side or the other. "Final" offers are submitted by both sides to the arbitrators along with supporting documentation. After considering the evidence presented by the player and that submitted by the team, the panel must select one of the two offers; no compromises are permitted. If the evidence shows that the player's demand is closer to market value than the team's offer, the panel will award the salary demanded by the player. If the evidence shows that the team's offer is closer to the player's market value, then the panel must award that lower number to the player. The decision of the panel is binding on the two parties. If the panel chooses the team's offer, the player is obligated to sign a one-year contract for that salary. If the player wins, the team must pay the higher salary demanded by the player.

In this chapter, we examine final offer arbitration. Very few cases that are filed are actually heard by the arbitration panel; the vast majority of these disputes are settled. There is an economic reason for this result, which we develop in some detail. We also present brief accounts of some empirical results.

2 ARE "FINAL" OFFERS REALLY FINAL?

In principle, the offers submitted to the arbitration panel are *final*, but are the offers really final? For the 2006 season, the Chicago Cubs paid Carlos Zambrano

$6,650,000. Zambrano had a good year with a 16–7 record, an earned run average (ERA) of 3.41, and 210 strikeouts. When he and the Cubs could not agree on a salary for the 2007 season, Zambrano filed for arbitration. His final offer was $15.5 million, and the Cubs' final offer was only $11,025,000. As it turned out, these offers were not really final on either side because the two sides reached an agreement on a one-year deal for $12.4 million.

In 2006, Joe Mauer was one of the biggest bargains in all of baseball. For a salary of only $400,000, the Minnesota Twins got a catcher who hit .347 to lead all of MLB in batting. Eligible for arbitration for the first time, Mauer's final offer was $4.5 million, and the Twins final offer was $3.3 million. Had the case been heard, Mauer would have gotten either $4.5 million or $3.3 million in a one-year contract for the 2007 season. However, before the arbitration panel heard his case, Mauer settled with the Twins and signed a four-year contract: $3.75 million in 2007, $6.25 million in 2008, $10.5 million in 2009, and $12.5 million in 2010. All of these sums were guaranteed, so Mauer was protected from injury or an off year.[1]

There are many examples of settlements occurring after final offers have been exchanged. The fact of the matter is that the final offers are not really "final" in most cases because the vast majority of the salary disputes submitted to arbitration are resolved (that is, settled) before the panel acts on the case. In Table 21.1, we can see the actual history over the 1990–2010 period. The number of cases filed varied over that period from a low of 40 in 2005 to a high of 162 in 1990. During the entire period, 1,987 cases were filed, but most of these cases settled before the panel did its work. Only 220 cases were actually heard, and 1,772 were settled. Thus, nearly 90 percent of the cases settled. Table 21.1 shows that the settlement rate varied from year to year. The lowest settlement rate was 80 percent in 1994, and the highest rate was 97.3 percent in 2009.

As we will see in the next section, there is a good economic reason for settlements to occur frequently. In fact, the real mystery is why all arbitration cases do not settle.[2]

3 THE ECONOMICS OF SETTLEMENTS IN FINAL OFFER ARBITRATION

When Greg Maddux filed for arbitration in 2003, he asked for $16 million, whereas the Atlanta Braves offered only $13.5 million. The arbitration panel would then have started their analysis with the *break point*, or the midpoint between the two offers. In this case, the break point was $14.75 million. If the evidence put before the panel indicated that Maddux was worth a penny more than $14.75 million, he would have been awarded the $16 million that he requested. If the evidence indicated that he was worth a penny less, he would

[1] Maurer continued to play well, and during spring training in 2010, he signed a $194 million contract extension. This made Maurer the highest paid catcher in MLB history.

[2] For an answer to this question, see Amy Farmer, Paul Pecorino, and Victor Stango (2004), "The Causes of Bargaining Failure: Evidence from Major League Baseball," *Journal of Law and Economics*, 47, 543–568. We return to this later in the chapter.

Table 21.1. Final Offer Arbitration, 1990–2010

Year	Filed	Heard	Settled	% Settled
1990	162	24	138	85.2
1991	157	17	140	89.2
1992	147	20	127	86.4
1993	118	18	100	84.8
1994	80	16	64	80.0
1995	61	8	53	86.9
1996	76	10	66	86.8
1997	80	5	75	93.8
1998	81	8	73	90.1
1999	62	11	51	82.3
2000	90	10	80	88.9
2001	102	14	88	86.3
2002	93	5	88	94.6
2003	72	7	65	90.3
2004	65	7	58	89.2
2005	40	3	37	92.5
2006	96	6	90	93.8
2007	56	7	49	87.5
2008	110	8	102	92.7
2009	111	3	108	97.3
2010	128	8	120	93.8
Total	1987	220	1772	89.2

have been awarded the $13.5 million offered by the club. Thus, Maddux was going to get a contract for either $16 million or $13.5 million. The salary dispute then was over the difference, which was $2.5 million.

To facilitate our economic analysis,[3] we will adopt the following notation: p represents the player's estimate of the probability that he will win; q is management's estimate of the probability that the player will win; C_P and C_M are the costs of arbitration to the player and to management, respectively; and D is difference between the two offers. The model proceeds on the following basis: the player can accept management's offer, or he can go to arbitration. From this perspective, he has something to gain if he believes that management's offer is below his market value.

The player and his club are really fighting over the difference between the two offers. In this example, Maddux and the Braves were fighting over the difference between $16 million or $13.5 million. Thus, Maddux and the Braves were fighting over the $2.5 million. When a player goes to arbitration, he faces risk.

[3] This section relies on the work of William M. Landes (1971), "An Economic Analysis of the Courts." *Journal of Law and Economics*, 14, 61–107; and John Gould (1973), "The Economics of Legal Conflicts," *Journal of Legal Studies*, 2, 279–300.

He will win the difference (D) with probability p or will lose D with probability $(1 - p)$. The player's expected value of going to arbitration is:

$$E[A]_P = p(D) + (1 - p)(0) - C_P,$$

or

$$E[A]_p = p(D) - C_P.$$

That is, the expected value of arbitration equals the probability of winning (p) times the difference (D) in salary that the player will receive if he wins less the costs of engaging in the arbitration process (C_P), which are incurred whether he wins or loses his case.

For management, there is no upside. If management wins, it avoids paying more than its final offer, but it still incurs arbitration costs (C_M). If management loses, the team will have to pay the difference plus the arbitration costs that it will incur. Thus, the management faces an expected *loss* from the arbitration process, which is

$$E[A]_M = q(D) + (1 - q)(0) + C_M,$$

or

$$E[A]_M = q(D) + C_M.$$

In other words, for management, the expected loss is its estimate of the probability of the player's winning (q) times the difference in offers (D) plus its cost of participating in the arbitration process (C_M), which it incurs whether it wins or loses.

For the moment, we will assume that the parties are *risk neutral*, which means that they are only concerned with the expected outcome; neither party is concerned about the variance in the outcomes.[4]

3.1 The Economic Condition for Settlements

The player expects to win $E[A]_P$ and management expects to lose $E[A]_M$ in the arbitration process. Settlements occur when management expects to lose more than the player expects to win. In other words, when $E[A]_M > E[A]_P$, a settlement should occur. Intuitively, this is like any market transaction – an asset flows to the party that values it most highly. In this case, the player's right to go to arbitration is an asset that the player owns. The player places a value of $E[A]_P$ on that asset. The value of that asset to management is $E[A]_M$. If $E[A]_M$ exceeds $E[A]_P$, then management values the asset more highly than the player. As a result, management will "buy" the asset from the player for some price between $E[A]_M$ and $E[A]_P$. Whenever $E[A]_M > E[A]_P$, the parties should settle because management is willing to pay more than the player's reservation price, and the player is willing to accept less than the maximum that management is

[4] You will recall that attitudes toward risk were examined in some detail in Chapter 3.

willing to pay. In other words, there are gains from trade. Because $E[A]_M > E[A]_P$, there is some amount, X, at which the parties will settle because

$$E[A]_M > X > E[A]_p.$$

A numerical example will help to make these general observations more concrete. In the Maddux case, the difference (D) was \$2.5 million. Suppose that Maddux believed that his probability of winning was 0.9 and his cost of arbitration was \$100,000. Then his expected value would have been

$$\begin{aligned} E[A]_p &= (0.9)(\$2.5) - \$100,000 \\ &= \$2,125,000. \end{aligned}$$

Now suppose that management believed that the probability that Maddux would win was 0.85, and its costs of arbitration would be \$150,000. Then management's expected loss would be

$$\begin{aligned} E[A]_M &= (0.85)(\$2.5) + \$150,000 \\ &= \$2,275,000. \end{aligned}$$

In this case, management expects to lose \$2,275,000 in arbitration and should settle for anything less than this amount. Maddux expects to win \$2,125,000 and should settle for anything more than this amount. If they agreed on, say, \$2,200,000, Maddux would be better off, and management would be better off in an expectations sense. Thus, they should settle for some amount between \$2,125,000 and \$2,275,000.[5]

3.2 Condition for Settlements

It is useful to analyze the conditions that are necessary for settlements to occur, so we can tell what went wrong when settlements do not materialize. If $E[A]_M > E[A]_p$, then by substitution, we have

$$q(D) + C_M > p(D) - C_P,$$

which can be rearranged algebraically as

$$q(D) + C_M - p(D) + C_P > 0,$$

or we may write this as

$$(q - p)(D) + C_M + C_p > 0.$$

Now, if the parties agree on the probability of the player's winning the arbitration, then q equals p, and we are left with

$$C_M + C_p > 0,$$

which must always hold because arbitration costs are necessarily positive. In that event, the player and the management will settle for a sum between the

[5] In fact, Maddux and the Braves settled at the break point, thereby splitting the difference equally.

expected award ($p(D)$) plus the management's arbitration cost (C_M) and the expected award minus the player's arbitration cost (C_P).

An example will help to illustrate this result. Suppose that the player's final offer is $3,000,000, and the team's final offer is $2,000,000. As a result, D is equal to $1,000,000. Suppose that $q = P = .60$ and the arbitration costs are $C_M = C_p =$ $25,000. Then

$$E[A]_M = (0.60)(\$1{,}000{,}000) + \$25{,}000$$
$$= \$625{,}000,$$

while

$$E[A]_p = (0.60)(\$1{,}000{,}000) - \$25{,}000$$
$$= \$575{,}000.$$

Because the player expects to win $575,000 if he goes through the arbitration process, he will settle for anything above $575,000. Management, on the other hand, expects to lose $625,000 if it goes through the arbitration process and therefore should settle for anything below $625,000. In effect, because $p = q$, there is a positive bargaining range. As a result, the player and the management should settle for an amount between $575,000 and $625,000. If they agree on, say, $610,000, then the player's salary would be $2,610,000 – despite the fact that the "final" offers of the player and management were $3,000,000 and $2,000,000, respectively.

3.3 Problems in Reaching Settlements

Optimism can pose problems for resolving salary disputes. By *optimism*, we mean that p is high because the player strongly believes that he will win, and q is low because management strongly believes that the player will lose. The effect of optimism is to make $(q - p)$ negative.

Doing this will make $(q - p)(D)$ negative. It is then possible for $(q - p)(D) + C_M + C_P$ to be negative. In that event, the two sides will not settle. Suppose, for example, that $p = .7$, $q = .6$, $D = \$1{,}000{,}000$, and $C_M = C_P = \$25{,}000$. In that event,

$$(q - p)D + C_M + C_P = -.1(\$1{,}000{,}000) + \$50{,}000,$$

or

$$-100{,}000 + 50{,}000 < 0.$$

This salary dispute will not settle because the $E[A]_M$ is less than the $E[A]_P$, that is, management's expected loss is less than the player's expected gain. In other words, the player values his right to go to arbitration more highly than management values it. Consequently, management will not be interested in buying that asset from the player.

Although a negative value of $(q - p)$ is necessary for arbitration to occur, it does not guarantee that settlement will not be reached. Even if $(q - p)$ is negative and, therefore, $(q - p)(D)$ is negative, that sum may still be smaller in absolute value than the sum of the arbitration costs. In other words, it may still be true that $(q - p)(D) + C_p + C_M$ is positive even when $(q - p)$ is negative. For example, suppose that $D = \$500{,}000$, $C_p = C_M = \$25{,}000$, $p = 0.75$, and $q = 0.70$. In that event, $(q - p) = -0.05$ and

$$E[A]_M - E[A]_p = -0.05(\$500{,}000) + \$50{,}000$$
$$= -\$25{,}000 + \$50{,}000 > 0.$$

Thus, if the difference in the probabilities is not too large, there may still be settlement possibilities, but not always as we saw here.

3.4 Some Summary Remarks

First, because there can be no dispute over the value of D, arbitration can only occur if $(q - p) < 0$. Given a negative value for $(q - p)$, arbitration is more likely the larger the difference is between the final offers. To see why, consider this example. Suppose $(q - p) = -0.05$, and the sum of the arbitration costs is \$50,000. If the difference in the offers is \$1,000,000, then the player and management are indifferent between settling and going to arbitration because $(q - p)D + C_M + C_P = 0$. Put differently, the $E[A]_M$ is precisely equal to $E[A]_P$. Each party therefore values the player's right to go to arbitration equally. There are then no gains from trade. If D exceeds \$1,000,000, they will not settle, but if D is less than \$1,000,000, then they will settle. Thus, given that $(q - p)$ is negative, the larger D is, the less likely that the parties will settle.

Second, a settlement is more likely the larger the arbitration costs $(C_p + C_M)$ are. Why? A significant cost of baseball arbitration is the hard feelings that may develop when the team explains why the player is not really worth what he thinks he is worth. It will be hard for a proud player not to take it personally, even though it may just be business to the team. *Sports Illustrated* referred to salary arbitration as MLB's equivalent of divorce court.

Third, *pessimism* always leads to settlements. By pessimism, we mean that q is large and p is small. As a result, $(q - p) > 0$, which implies that a settlement is going to occur. This would appear to be consistent with our intuition because a high value of q increases the $E[A]_M$ (management's expected loss) and a low value of p reduces the $E[A]_P$ (the player's expected gain), thereby widening the bargaining range.

3.5 Costs of Reaching Settlements

So far, we have included the cost of arbitration, but we have ignored the cost of reaching a settlement. These costs can be quite substantial – especially if the parties delay (serious) settlement talks until the eve of the arbitration hearing. The player's expected value of arbitration is

$$E[A]_p = pD - C_p,$$

where D is again the difference between the final offers. Thus, the player will settle for an amount X provided that

$$X - R_p > pD - C_p,$$

or if

$$X > pD - (C_p - R_p),$$

where R_p is the player's cost of settling. For management, the calculations are similar. Management will pay a sum X to settle provided that

$$X + R_M < qD + C_M,$$

or

$$X < qD + (C_M - R_M).$$

Now a settlement will occur provided that

$$qD + (C_M - R_M) > pD - (C_A - R_A),$$

or

$$(q - p)D + (C_p + C_M) - (R_P + R_M) > 0.$$

If $p = q$, then the condition for a settlement always holds provided that the cost of settling is less than the cost of arbitration.

Box 21.1 ***Mariano Rivera and Arbitration***

Mariano Rivera is no stranger to final offer arbitration. The great Yankee closer earned $750,000 in 1998. Rivera appeared in 54 games with 36 saves and an ERA of 1.91. Following this stellar year, the Yankees offered him a substantial salary increase to $3 million for the 1999 season. Rivera, however, wanted $4.25 million. Unable to reach a settlement, they went to arbitration. For that year, Rivera won at arbitration and received the $4.25 million that he had requested. In 1999, Rivera appeared in 66 games as a closer. He had 45 saves and an ERA of only 1.83. Following that great year, the Yankees offered a whopping salary increase to $7.25 million for the 2000 season. Once again, Rivera had other ideas as he had his heart set on $9.25 million for the 2000 season. This time, however, he was too aggressive, and he lost. Although he "lost," Rivera recognized that he was still a rich man. When he was informed that he had lost, Rivera was philosophical about it. He reminded his associates that no one had died. He then remarked, "I'm not upset at all. It's good money. I'm happy to be here."* In 2000, Rivera again pitched in 66 games. This time he had 36 saves and an ERA of 2.86. The Yankees offered still another substantial raise for 2001 to $9.0 million, but as usual, Rivera wanted more. He asked for $10.25 million. Before the arbitration panel heard this case, Rivera and the Yankees settled on a four-year $39.99 million contract.

In 2004, Rivera no longer needed arbitration. The Yankees settled with him on a two-year extension at $10.5 million per year. Rivera earned a third-year option for 2007 at $10.5 million.

* "Yankees' Pitcher Loses in Arbitration, Gets $7.25 million," *Gainesville Sun*, February 20, 2000.

Table 21.2. Percent Lost by Player, 1990–2010

Year	Heard	Lost	% Lost
1990	24	10	41.7
1991	17	11	64.7
1992	20	11	55.0
1993	18	12	66.7
1994	16	10	62.5
1995	8	6	75.0
1996	10	3	30.0
1997	5	4	80.0
1998	8	5	62.5
1999	11	9	81.8
2000	10	6	60.0
2001	14	8	57.1
2002	5	4	80.0
2003	7	5	71.4
2004	7	4	57.1
2005	3	2	66.7
2006	6	4	66.7
2007	7	4	57.1
2008	8	6	75.0
2009	3	1	33.3
2010	8	5	62.5
Total	212	129	52.2

4 SOME EMPIRICAL EVIDENCE ON ARBITRATION RESULTS

For 1990–2010, Table 21.2 reports the number of arbitration cases that were heard and lost by the player. Over this period, only 215 cases were heard. The players lost 130 times, which is 60.5 percent of the time. In only three years (1990, 1996, and 2009) did the players win more often than they lost. In each of the other years, management won more than half of the decided cases.

It is not clear why players lose more often than they win. One explanation could be that an athlete's natural aggressiveness could hinder his objectivity and lead to mistakes at the bargaining table. The player may overestimate his probability of winning. Alternatively, supreme self-confidence may lead to an excessive demand. When a player increases his final offer, he raises the break point and thereby reduces the likelihood that the panel will decide in his favor. Another explanation may be that management makes a more realistic final offer, which moves its offer closer to the player's market value with the same results. Without a lot more information, we cannot provide a definitive explanation for management's disproportionate success rate.

The fact that the clubs win more than half of the time may miss an important issue: the economic importance of the wins. In the 2007 arbitration season, for example, management won four and lost three. However, the players won

Table 21.3. Wins and Losses in 2007 Arbitration

Players	Amount Awarded
Winners	
Miguel Cabrera	$7,400,000
Chad Cordero	$4,150,000
Todd Walker	$3,950,000
Losers	
Joe Beimel	$912,000
Kevin Gregg	$575,000
Josh Patterson	$850,000
Josh Paul	$625,000

the "big" ones, whereas the clubs won the "little" ones. As Table 21.3 shows, Miguel Cabrera won an award of $7.4 million, Chad Cordero won $4.15 million, and Todd Walker won $3.95 million. In contrast to these big winners, Joe Beimel lost and received $912,000. Kevin Gregg lost and received $575,000; John Patterson received $850,000; and Josh Paul received $625,000. The clubs won four "small" ones, and the players won three "big" ones.

In the 2008 arbitration season, all the cases that were heard were big ones. These are summarized in Table 21.4. There were eight cases heard, and the players won only two. Ryan Howard was a big winner. The Phillies offered him $7 million, but the panel awarded him his salary request of $10 million. The only other player to win was Oliver Perez, who received $6.5 million instead of the Mets' offer of $4.275 million. The rest of the players lost. One interesting thing that happened in 2008 is a couple of cases involved very small differences. Felipe Lopez and his club were only $300,000 apart, Chien-Ming Wang and the Yankees were only $600,000 apart. Being this close, one might expect that they would have settled rather than gone through with the arbitration, but that did not happen.

Farmer, Pecorino, and Stango analyzed the results of final offer arbitration for the 1990 through 1993 seasons.[6] Their statistical results are consistent with the model of settlements presented above. When players are too aggressive in their demands, settlement failure occurs and the cases go to arbitration hearings. This aggressiveness is reflected in an excessive estimate of the probability of winning or in an excessive demand that increases the difference between the offers. As one might expect, aggressive players must pay for that attitude and they apparently do as they lose more often than they win. Farmer, Pecorino, and Stango found that the players wind up with lower salaries than they would have received if they had been less aggressive.

Management tends to win more arbitration cases than they lose irrespective of the time frame examined. From the inception of final offer arbitration in 1974 through 2010, management won 285 cases while the players won only 210. Thus, management has won 57.5 percent of the time. Since this is not too far from a 50–50 split, there has been some speculation that baseball arbitrators try to split their decisions evenly between management and the players. This proposition has been tested by Burgess, Marburger, and Scoggins.[7] Their statistical analysis rejects the hypothesis that arbitrators decide cases arbitrarily in an effort to achieve a 50–50 split. Put differently, the statistical analysis

[6] Amy Farmer, Paul Pecorino, and Victor Stango, *supra* note 2.

[7] Paul Burgess, Daniel Marburger, and John Scoggins, "Do Baseball Arbitrators Simply Flip a Coin?" in John Fizel, Elizabeth Gustafson, and Lawrence Hadley, eds. (1996), *Baseball Economics*, Westport, CT: Praeger.

Table 21.4. Wins and Losses in 2008 Arbitration (in $millions)

Player	Request	Offer	Awarded
Brian Fuentes	$6.5	$5.05	$5.05
Ryan Howard	$10	$7	$10
Felipe Lopez	$5.2	$4.9	$4.9
Mark Loretta	$4.9	$2.75	$2.75
Oliver Perez	$6.5	$4.275	$6.5
Francisco Rodriguez	$12.5	$10	$10
Jose Valverde	$6.2	$4.7	$4.7
Chien-Ming Wang	$4.6	$4.0	$4.0

supports the proposition that the arbitrators behave in a neutral fashion and simply call them as they see them.

5 THE THREAT OF FINAL OFFER ARBITRATION PROTECTS PLAYERS

Dustin Pedroia, the diminutive second baseman of the Boston Red Sox, was one of the biggest bargains in MLB. In 2007, Pedroia won Rookie of the Year honors in the American League (AL). He batted .317 with 8 home runs and 50 runs batted in (RBIs) while playing stellar defense. That year he earned $380,000. In 2008, Pedroia got a pretty big raise to $457,000 but was an even bigger bargain. He had 213 hits (tied for the AL lead), led the majors with 56 doubles, and finished second in the AL with a .326 batting average. He increased his home run total to 17 and his RBI total to 83 while winning a Gold Glove Award.

The Red Sox had one more year in which to exploit Pedroia's inability to get any protection from the market. After the 2009 season, however, Pedroia would be entitled to final offer arbitration for three years and would become an unrestricted free agent in 2013. The Red Sox decided that they would be better off to remove this possibility by entering into a multiyear contract. Despite the fact that Pedroia recognized he was sacrificing some money, he also wanted a multiyear contract so he could remain in Boston with financial security.

The result was a six-year contract with a club option for a seventh season. Although many considered the terms to be a bargain for the Red Sox, Pedroia was satisfied:

Signing Bonus	$1.5 million
2009	$1.5 million
2010	$3.5 million
2011	$5.5 million
2012	$8.0 million
2013	$10.0 million
2014	$10.0 million

If the Red Sox exercise their option for the 2015 season, Pedroia will earn $11 million for that year.

Several other players have signed multiyear contracts before they were eligible for arbitration. These include Marlins shortstop Hanley Ramirez, who signed a six-year deal reportedly worth $70 million. David Wright, the Mets third-baseman, signed a six-year deal at $55 million, and Ryan Braun, the Brewers left fielder, signed an eight-year deal for $45 million.

6 CONCLUDING REMARKS

A player with three to five years' experience in MLB is eligible for final offer arbitration if he and his club cannot agree on a contract. Although each side submits its final offer to the arbitration panel, these offers are not really *final* in most cases. Typically, the player and his club settle for an amount between the two offers. We explored the economic reason for the fact that the vast majority of salary disputes are settled before an arbitration hearing has been held. We also examined some reasons why settlements might fail.

PROBLEMS AND QUESTIONS

1. Because neither management nor the player is penalized for losing the arbitration, there is an incentive for management to make unrealistically low final offers and for the player to make outrageous demands. True or false? Explain.
2. If the player and management are risk averse, will settlements be more or less likely than when they are risk neutral? Explain.
3. If the player and management are risk lovers, does the settlement range expand or shrink relative to the case when both are risk neutral? Explain.
4. Suppose that the difference in offers is $1 million and the player believes that his probability of winning is 0.90. The player's arbitration costs are $100,000. Management believes that the player's probability of winning is only 0.60. Management's arbitration costs are also $100,000.
   a. Assuming no settlement costs, will there be a settlement in this case?
   b. If $R_P = R_M =$ $30,000, would there be a settlement?
5. "As a general proposition, the larger the difference between the final offers, the less likely that the parties will settle." True or false? Explain.
6. Slugger Sam's final offer was $7.5 million, but the Hogtown Hens offered $5.5 million. Sam is pretty confident he will win and thinks that the probability of his winning is 0.85. The Hens think that their chances of winning are only 0.30. Sam's arbitration costs are $50,000, whereas the Hens' arbitration costs are $75,000.
   a. What is the expected value of arbitration to Sam?
   b. What is the expected value to the Hens?
   c. Will they settle? Explain.

   d. Suppose the Hens' final offer had been $6.5 million. Answer questions (a)–(c) under that assumption.

7. During the 2006 season, Carlos Zambrano compiled a 16–7 record with the Chicago Cubs. Eligible for arbitration, he asked for $15.5 million for the 2007 season. The Cubs offered $11,025,000. Explain why Zambrano and the Cubs settled before the arbitration panel settled it for them.
8. Adam Dunn and the Cincinnati Reds were scheduled for an arbitration hearing but agreed at the last minute on a two-year deal that would pay Dunn $7.5 million for 2006 and $11.0 million for 2007. The Club has an option for the 2008 season at $13 million. If it does not exercise the option, it must pay Dunn $500,000. If the probability that the option will be exercised is .75 and the discount rate is 10 percent, what is the value of the contract?

REFERENCES AND FURTHER READING

Bodvarsson, O. B., and K. Banaian. (1998). "The Value of Arbitration Rights in Major League Baseball: Implications for Salaries and Discrimination." *Quarterly Journal of Business and Economics*, 37, 65–80.

Burgess, P. L., and D. R. Marburger. (1993). "Do Negotiated and Arbitrated Salaries Differ Under Final-Offer Arbitration?" *Industrial and Labor Relations Review*, 46, 548–559.

Burgess, Paul, Daniel Marburger, and John Scoggins. (1996). "Do Baseball Arbitrators Simply Flip a Coin?" In John Fizel, Elizabeth Gustafson, and Lawrence Hadley, eds. *Baseball Economics*. Westport, CT: Praeger.

Farmer, Amy, Paul Pecorino, and Victor Stango. (2004). "The Causes of Bargaining Failure: Evidence from Major League Baseball," *Journal of Law and Economics*, 47, 543–568.

Faurot, David J. (2001). "Equilibrium Explanation of Bargaining and Arbitration in Major League Baseball." *Journal of Sports Economics*, 2, 22–34.

Faurot, D. J., and S. McAllister. (1992). "Salary Arbitration and Pre-Arbitration Negotiation in Major League Baseball." *Industrial and Labor Relations Review*, 45, 697–710.

Fizel, J. (1996). "Bias in Salary Arbitration: The Case of Major League Baseball." *Applied Economics*, 28, 255–265.

Fizel, J., A. C. Krautmann, and L. Hadley. (2002). "Equity and Arbitration in Major League Baseball." *Managerial & Decision Economics*, 23, 427–435.

Gould, John. (1973). "The Economics of Legal Conflicts." *Journal of Legal Studies*, 2, 279–300.

Hadley, L., and E. Gustafson. (1991). "Major League Baseball Salaries: The Impacts of Arbitration and Free Agency." *Journal of Sport Management*, 5, 111–127.

Lambrinos, J., and T. D. Ashman. (2007). "Salary Determination in the National Hockey League: Is Arbitration Efficient?" *Journal of Sports Economics*, 8, 192–201.

Landes, William M. (1971). "An Economic Analysis of the Courts." *Journal of Law and Economics*, 14, 61–107.

Marburger, D. R. (2004). "Arbitrator Compromise in Final Offer Arbitration: Evidence from Major League Baseball." *Economic Inquiry*, 42, 60–68.

Miller, Phillip A. (2000a). "An Analysis of Final Offers Chosen in Baseball's Arbitration System: The Effect of Pre-Arbitration Negotiation on the Choice of Final Offers." *Journal of Sports Economics*, 1, 39–55.

Miller, Phillip A. (2000b). "A Theoretical and Empirical Comparison of Free Agent and Arbitration-Eligible Salaries Negotiated in Major League Baseball." *Southern Economic Journal*, 67, 87–104.

Scully, G. W. (1978). "Binding Salary Arbitration in Major League Baseball." *American Behavioral Scientist*, 21, 431–450.

Sommers, P. M. (1993). "The Influence of Salary Arbitration on Player Performance." *Social Science Quarterly*, 74, 439–443.

22

Players' Unions and Collective Bargaining

1 INTRODUCTION

Workers in many occupations and industries have felt the need to band together in unions so that they could bargain collectively with management. In this way, the workers sought to level the playing field in negotiating wages, hours, benefits, and working conditions with large, powerful employers. Much the same has been true in professional sports: the players have formed unions to offset the collective monopsony power of the team owners.[1] These players' unions, however, are somewhat different from the traditional craft unions or industrial unions. We explore some of the differences here.

We begin this chapter by introducing the players' unions in the four major sports leagues. We then turn our attention to the economics of unions. Successful unions are labor cartels, which would ordinarily be illegal under the antitrust laws. There is, however, an explicit antitrust exemption for organized labor, which we outline briefly. When the union meets the league management negotiators, we have a market structure known as bilateral monopoly. We develop a simple model of bilateral monopoly and relate it to professional sports. We then examine minimum salaries in the major professional sports leagues, salary caps and luxury taxes, revenue sharing, and free agency. All of these issues are subject to collective bargaining and are largely protected from antitrust scrutiny.

2 ORGANIZING THE PLAYERS' UNIONS IN THE MAJOR LEAGUES

No employer embraces the prospect of dealing with a union. When workers are not organized into a union, the employer largely has the upper hand in any labor–management negotiation. This is not to say that employers are immune to market forces, but whatever power exists is in management's hands as long as the workers are not organized. Consequently, management typically resists efforts at unionization. Things are no different in the major sports leagues.

[1] For some reason, the players' unions are generally referred to as players' associations rather than unions, but they are unions nonetheless.

All of them eventually became unionized, but the early going was pretty rough. In the balance of this section, we examine briefly the early organizational struggles of the four major players' unions.

2.1 Major League Baseball Players Association

From the inception of the reserve clause in the late 1880s, club owners had all the power in any labor–management negotiation. The players knew this and tried to organize to fight the reserve clause as far back as 1885 with the formation of the Brotherhood of Professional Baseball Players, which was the first union. This initial effort failed. In 1900, the players tried again and formed the Players' Protective Association, which also failed to defeat the reserve clause. The Fraternity of Professional Baseball Players of America, formed in 1912, and the American Baseball Guild, organized in 1946, were similarly unsuccessful. This, of course, resulted in continuing frustration for the players.

The modern Major League Players Association began in 1965 when the players organized under Marvin Miller's guidance. In 1968, Miller's effort resulted in the first Collective Bargaining Agreement (CBA) between MLB and the MLB Players Association (MLBPA). The gains for the players were small but significant. The league minimum salary rose from $6,000 to $10,000. This does not seem like much today, but it was an important first step. In 1970, the MLBPA negotiated the right to have a player's grievance heard by an independent arbitrator. This turned out to be extremely important in 1975 when Andy Messersmith and Dave McNally challenged the reserve clause. The independent arbitrator, Peter Seitz, ruled that the reserve clause could only provide the club with one added year of service. After that second year, the player would become a free agent. Free agency, of course, provides protection for the player – free market forces would determine compensation. As a result, clubs began to offer multiyear contracts at much higher salaries.

The MLBPA has been successful in many regards. The MLB minimum salary has increased over time. In 2006, the league minimum reached $380,000. In addition, average salaries have soared. In 2007, the average salary in MLB was $2.82 million. Players have health benefits, pension plans, generous travel per diems, and guaranteed contracts.

2.2 National Football League Players Association

Dissatisfied players began to organize the National Football League Players Association (NFLPA) in 1956. The players were concerned about several things: a league minimum salary of $5,000, a standard per diem for all players, and a requirement that the club had to provide equipment for the players. There was one more request that was extremely important to the players. They wanted a contract that required the club to pay injured players for the balance of the season. The NFLPA was met with passive resistance by the owners – no one would meet with them. The NFLPA got the owners' attention by threatening an antitrust suit. The NFLPA was prepared to charge the owners with collusive monopsony, which would be a violation of Section 1 of the Sherman Act. If successful, such a suit would expose the owners to treble damages.

The NFL recognized the NFLPA but essentially reneged on its agreements. For example, they agreed to the injury protection clause but did not put it in the standard player contract. They also agreed to pay the players an extra $50 for each preseason game, but then simply did not pay the players. Other demands for employee benefits, such as pension and health insurance, were basically ignored by the owners. Another threat of an antitrust suit in 1958 once again got the owners' attention, and the NFLPA made some progress.

The gains were slow and things were complicated by the merger between the NFL and the American Football League (AFL). Even after the NFL-AFL merger, the NFLPA and the AFLPA remained separate. Initially, the owners divided and conquered them. In 1970, however, the two unions joined forces. The new NFLPA applied for and received certification as a union by the National Labor Relations Board (NLRB). This was important because NLRB certification comes with some added legal protections for unions. The NFLPA continued to face many struggles but eventually achieved its most significant objectives: free agency; hospitalization, health and life insurance, and pension benefits; and (limited) injury protection.

2.3 National Basketball Players Association

Bob Cousy, the great Boston Celtics guard, began organizing National Basketball Association (NBA) players into the National Basketball Players Association (NBPA) in 1954. For 10 years, the owners stalled the NBPA's efforts at gaining formal recognition. Finally, in 1964, the owners bowed to the players' collective threat to refuse to play in the first televised All-Star Game. The NBPA's early demands were fairly modest: a league minimum salary, health benefits, pension benefits, and a per diem for meals on travel days. Progress on these goals was slow because the owners were not inclined to share the wealth.

The players recognized that the reserve clause in their contracts was limiting the salaries that they could negotiate. Bound to one team, a player had only two choices: play or retire. In 1970, a group of NBA players filed a class action lawsuit alleging that the uniform adoption of the reserve clause by all clubs was an antitrust violation. Because of the glacial pace of antitrust litigation, a settlement was not reached until 1976. The clubs continued to limit free agency through various means, which frustrated the players. This frustration resulted in further litigation in 1987, but this time, a settlement was reached quickly. With the settlement of the lawsuit, the NBA players enjoyed true, unrestricted free agency. Now, when an individual player's contract expires, the player is completely free to sign with the highest bidder or any other team willing to hire him. As long as the clubs do not collude in the free-agent market, a player can negotiate a contract that will pay him something very close to his marginal revenue product.

As a result of collective bargaining and several lawsuits, the NBA players enjoy substantial salaries, substantial benefits, and free agency. There has been some labor strife over the years with strikes and lockouts threatened. On balance, however, the NBPA has done a good job for its members.

2.4 National Hockey League Players Association

Players in the National Hockey League (NHL) are represented by the NHL Players Association (NHLPA), which was formed in 1967. The union was organized by player representatives from the six original NHL clubs: Montreal and Toronto in Canada and Boston, Chicago, Detroit, and New York in the United States. When the fledgling union met with management, it warned them that a refusal to recognize the union would result in an appeal to the Canadian Labour Relations Board. Such an appeal was unnecessary, however, as the owners agreed to recognize the NHLPA.

The NHLPA has had some internal problems but appears to be on relatively solid ground now. As with the other leagues, NHL players have the usual array of benefits. Their salaries are substantial as they are protected by market forces through free agency.

2.5 Executive Directors

The executive directors of the major players' unions are well paid: Don Fehr (MLBPA) earned $1 million before he stepped down in 2010. Almost immediately, Fehr was hired by the NHLPA at a salary of $3 million. Billy Hunter (NBPA) earned $3.4 million, and Gene Upshaw (NFLPA) earned $3.7 million in 2008 before his death.

3 UNIONS AND ANTITRUST POLICY

A players' union is a cartel. Instead of competing against one another on all terms of their employment as professional athletes, the players join together and agree to bargain collectively with management. The union acts on behalf of the players as a group. This player cartel can then behave somewhat like a monopoly supplier of athletic talent. Cartels and monopolizing behavior are usually illegal under the Sherman Act. Section 1 of the Sherman Act forbids collective action that restrains trade:

> Every contract, combination . . . or conspiracy, in restraint of trade or commerce . . . is hereby declared to be illegal.

This, of course, would seem to apply to players' unions because they are combinations of independent athletes that restrain trade in the sense that the union members agree not to compete in the labor market with one another. This, of course, does not mean that they refrain from competing on the field or in the arena during games. It simply means that they will not agree to play under less favorable economic conditions than those that the union and management agree on. In the event that the union and management cannot agree on the terms of employment, the union may organize a strike. In that event, all of the union members agree to refuse to play. This looks like an obvious restraint of trade, which could be challenged as a violation of the Sherman Act.

In the early enforcement of the Sherman Act, which was passed in 1890, the courts found that unions did, in fact, violate Section 1 of the Sherman Act.

Congress, however, wanted union activity to be lawful and therefore exempted labor in 1914 when it passed the Clayton Act. In particular, Section 6 appeared to eliminate labor unions from antitrust scrutiny by definition:

> The labor of a human being is not a commodity or an article of commerce. Nothing in the antitrust laws shall be construed to forbid the existence and operation of labor... organizations... nor shall such organizations... be held or construed to be illegal combinations or conspiracies in restraint of trade, under the antitrust laws.

Despite this plain language, the Supreme Court interpreted this exemption very narrowly. Frustrated by the Supreme Court's apparent determination to impede union activity, Congress passed the Norris-La Guardia Act in 1932. This act reasserted Congress' original intentions in the Clayton Act to immunize union activity from antitrust prosecution. This immunity is not absolute, however; it is limited to organizing activity and unilateral decisions of the union and its members.

In addition to the statutory labor exemption provided by the Norris-La Guardia Act, the courts have developed a nonstatutory labor exemption that permits unions to reach agreements with nonlabor entities. This exemption is limited to agreements between a union and a nonlabor entity that involve core labor market issues such as wages and working conditions. Other than through their effect on labor costs, these agreements should not influence competition in the output market.[2] In other words, a union cannot agree with one employer to reduce a rival employer's ability to compete in the output market. As a result of the labor exemption, players' unions are legal and can behave like a labor cartel.

4 UNIONS AND COLLECTIVE BARGAINING

Labor unions represent the collective interests of their members. As a general proposition, unions focus their attention primarily on (1) wages and salaries; (2) benefits such as vacation and sick leave, heath insurance, and pension plans; and (3) working conditions such as hours and safety. These issues are, of course, the concerns of professional athletes as well as of workers in other occupations. No matter how much a player loves his sport, playing is his or her job. Professional athletes cannot lose sight of that fact. There is ample evidence that the players are well aware of the need to protect their self-interest. Their unions help them achieve their personal economic goals.

4.1 Unions: Goals and Economic Consequences

A union is a monopoly supplier of labor, but its goals are unclear. Depending on the union's approach to supplying labor to employers, the wages and employment will vary. We can illustrate this in Figure 22.1. As usual, D represents the aggregate demand for a particular type of labor, and S represents the supply

[2] For a thorough examination of labor law and antitrust policy, see Phillip Areeda and Herbert Hovenkamp (2006), *Antitrust Law*, Vol. IB, 255–257, New York: Aspen Publishers.

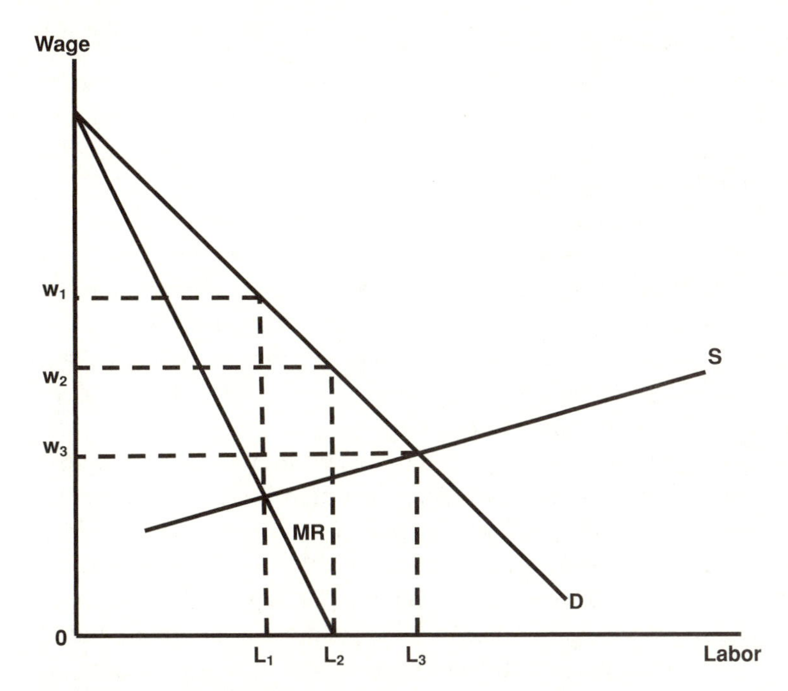

Figure 22.1. Employment at L_1 maximizes profit, employment at L_2 maximizes the wage bill, and employment at L_3 is the competitive result.

of these labor services. The competitive solution is found where supply and demand are equal. In Figure 22.1, we can see that L_3 workers will be employed at a wage of w_3. Presumably, the workers want something more than a competitive wage and form a union to get it. It is unclear what the union's objective is because selling labor services is not the same as selling merchandise. A LeBron jersey that is not sold does not care, but a worker who goes unemployed does care.

Profit Maximization. If the union maximized profit, it would act as though the supply of workers was its marginal cost curve. It would then provide L_1 workers because w_1 exceeds w_3. Those workers who are employed do quite well financially, but there are many who would like to work at a wage of w_1 who will not find a job. In fact, there are workers willing to work for the competitive wage (w_3) who will be unemployed. No doubt these unemployed workers will be disgruntled.

Maximizing the Wage Bill. An alternative to profit maximization is maximizing the wage bill, which is the total expenditure on labor. That is, the union may select a wage of w_2 where marginal revenue equals zero. There will be L_2 workers hired at w_2, and the total expenditure on labor will be maximized. As we can see, the wage will be w_2 rather than w_1 with this strategy. However, employment will be L_2 rather than L_1. A union may be satisfied that this trade-off of somewhat higher employment for a somewhat lower wage is well worth making. The wage is still above the competitive level, and therefore, there are still more people who want to work at w_2 than there are jobs for them.

4.2 Two Approaches to Excess Supply

When a union raises the wage above the competitive level, there will be excess supply. More people will want to work than will be able to find a job. Unions have to deal with this problem because disgruntled unemployed workers may disrupt the union's efforts.

Craft Union Strategy. Craft unions represent skilled workers such as carpenters, electricians, and plumbers. If the union's goal was to maximize the wage bill, it would recognize that it needed only L_2 members. The union would then limit the membership to L_2 and adjust that number over time as demand shifted. The union still faces a problem because there will be skilled workers who cannot get in the union. These nonunion workers may be able to compete with union workers for employment.

Industrial Union Strategy. The industrial union gathers together less skilled workers under the union umbrella. The union permits anyone to join. If it maximizes the wage bill, it will set a wage of w_2. At a wage of w_2, there will be excess supply. The union must deal with this excess supply because the unemployed members may take a nonunion job and compete with other union members. This, of course, would undermine the stability of the union. Industrial unions try to share the work by having shorter work weeks or rotating employment opportunities.

Players' Union Strategy. The players' unions employ a different strategy. The roster size for each team is determined through collective bargaining. Once the roster size, and therefore the total number of jobs, has been determined, it is entirely up to each club to decide who makes the team. The union has nothing to say about which players are retained and which players are cut. The clubs select the highest quality players from the available pool of talent according to their willingness to pay. Of course, mistakes are made, but few players of major league caliber fall through the cracks and go unemployed for very long.

The NFLPA, the NBPA, and the NHLPA bargain over the total wage bill. The results are expressed as salary caps, which limit the total payroll of each club. In MLB, there is no salary cap, but there is a luxury tax that is imposed on clubs that spend more than some threshold amount. The unions have little to do with the allocation of the salary dollars. Players bargain for salary dollars on their own (some with the help of an agent). Most of the other terms of employment – working conditions, pensions, contract terms – are subject to negotiations between the union and the league. The player's salary, however, is an individual matter between the club and the player.

5 BILATERAL MONOPOLY IN SPORTS

When the NFLPA sits down across the bargaining table from the NFL Management Committee, there is market power on both sides of the table. The union has something akin to monopoly power in the supply of major league quality football players. However, there is only one employer of such talent (the NFL) and, therefore, the NFL has an element of monopsony power. A market in which there is a single seller (the NFLPA) and a single buyer (the NFL) is called a

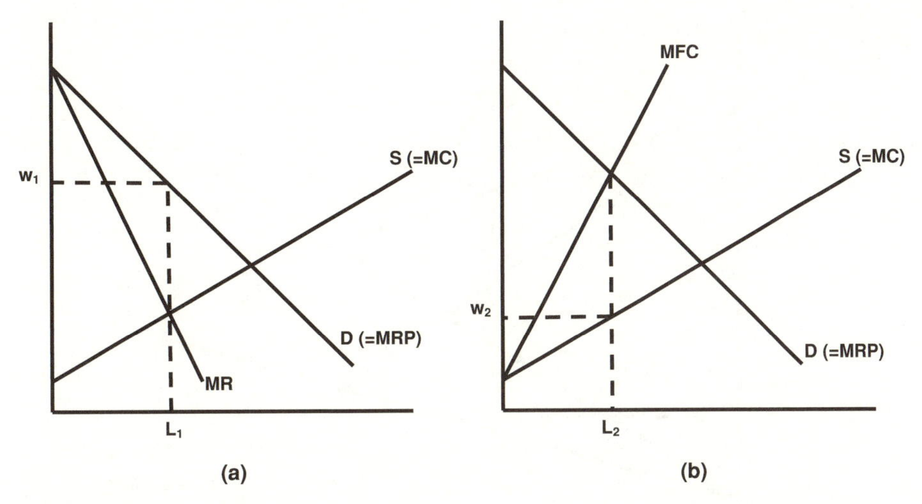

Figure 22.2. In panel (a), the monopoly union wants a wage of w_1. In panel (b), the monopsony league wants a wage of w_2. Neither the union nor the league can behave according to the usual marginal analysis.

bilateral monopoly. Because there is power on both sides of the market, the usual marginal analysis fails us here. We can see the problem in Figure 22.2. In panels (a) and (b), the demand and supply curves are precisely the same. In panel (a), the union will maximize profits by restricting the supply of players to L_1 and setting a wage of w_1. However, this only works if the NFL clubs act as though they have no buying power. In panel (b), the NFL wants to restrict employment to L_2 and set a wage of w_2. Now, w_1 does not generally equal w_2, and L_1 does not equal L_2. The NFL and the NFLPA cannot behave as the marginal analysis suggests that they should. Nonetheless, the parties are going to settle on some employment level and some wage. We just need to modify our thinking a bit to find the equilibrium solution. In this section, we develop the bilateral monopoly model and explain how it may apply to collective bargaining in the major sports leagues.

5.1 A Simple Model of Bilateral Monopoly[3]

There is a profit motive for cooperation to emerge between the sole buyer and the sole seller under conditions of bilateral monopoly. This profit incentive arises because the parties will wind up eventually splitting whatever profits materialize from the employer's business. This is not to say that they will split the profit evenly, but whatever the split turns out to be, each party is better off the larger the total profit. For example, suppose that the buyer gets 35 percent of the profit, and the seller gets the remaining 65 percent. If the maximum joint profit is, say, \$100 million, then the buyer will earn \$35 million and the seller will earn \$65 million. If the parties do not cooperate, the total profits may fall to, say, \$80 million. The buyer then earns only \$28 million (35 percent of

[3] For a more detailed analysis, see Roger D. Blair, David L. Kaserman, and Richard E. Romano (1989), "A Pedagogical Treatment of Bilateral Monopoly," *Southern Economic Journal*, 55, 831–841.

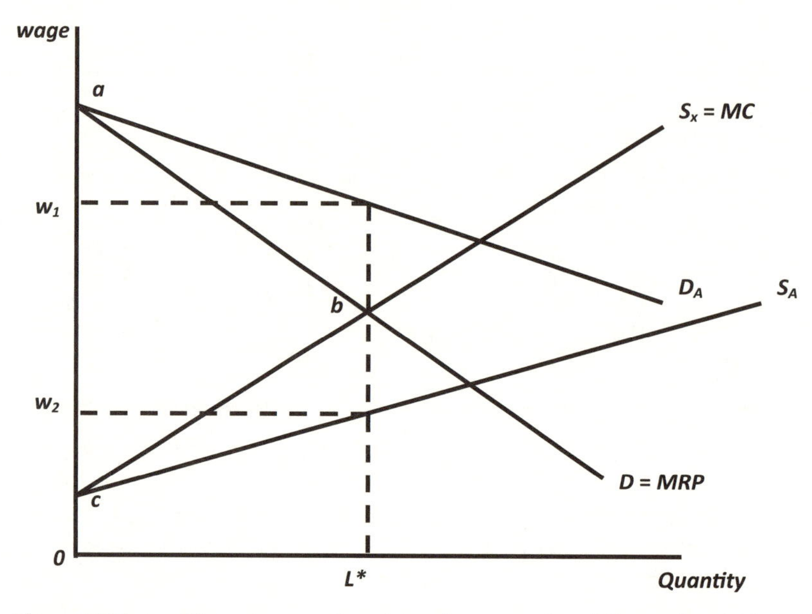

Figure 22.3. In a bilateral monopoly, a determinate quantity will be employed. The indeterminate price, which will be between w_1 and w_2, is a mechanism for sharing the profits.

$80 million), and the seller's profit falls to $52 million (65 percent of $80 million). Thus, a failure to cooperate costs the buyer $7 million and costs the seller $13 million. Failing to cooperate is not smart. It is therefore in the interest of both parties to cooperate with one another to maximize the joint profits. Such cooperation may take the extreme form of vertical integration, which is unlikely in a sports setting, or it may be accomplished through the bargaining process. For the latter, it is important to realize that the negotiations that take place involve a commitment on quantity and a sharing of the joint profits.

The solution can be found in Figure 22.3, which reproduces the demand and supply curves found in Figure 22.2. The area below demand (D) represents buyer surplus, whereas the area above the supply (S) curve represents the surplus enjoyed by the players. It is clear that the employment level that maximizes the total surplus is L^*. A larger value of L will not occur because the marginal cost of employing one more player exceeds the marginal benefit and therefore reduces the total surplus. A value of L below L* will leave money on the table because the marginal benefit of adding a player exceeds the marginal cost of doing so.

The NFLPA and the NFL will wind up splitting the surplus in some way. Consequently, they should reach agreement on L^*. Having reached that agreement, the remaining issue is how to split the pot of gold. This split is the result of bargaining. The wage that is agreed on does not have any *allocative* significance, which means that the wage does not influence employment decisions. The parties selected L^* to maximize the surplus, which is given by area *abc* in Figure 22.3. The wage is then a means of sharing that surplus between the clubs and the players.

To find the range of possible wages, we will use the all-or-none demand curve (D_A) and the all-or-none supply curve (S_A). The all-or-none demand shows price and quantity combinations that extract all of the consumer surplus. In this case, it shows wage and quantity combinations that give all of the surplus to the union for each value of L. Thus, a wage of w_1 leaves no surplus for the teams. This, of course, is the maximum wage that can be paid for an employment level of L^*. The all-or-none demand curve is half as steep as the regular demand curve. In other words, if the regular demand is $P = 100 - 2Q$, then the all-or-none demand would be $P = 100 - Q$.

The all-or-none supply is an analogous concept. Along the all-or-none supply, the employer extracts all of the surplus. The combination of L^* and w_2 leaves no surplus for the players. Consequently, w_2 is the lowest wage that the players can be paid and still get L^* players. The all-or-none supply is half as steep as the regular supply curve. In other words, if the regular supply curve is $P = 20 + Q$, then the all-or-none supply will be $P = 20 + 0.5Q$.

The bargaining range is then from w_1 to w_2. Any wage between w_1 and w_2 along with an employment of L^* will split the maximum surplus between the players and their clubs. The closer the negotiated wage is to w_2, the more of area *abc* goes to management. Similarly, the closer that the wage is to w_1, the more of the surplus goes to the players.

5.2 Bargaining in the Major Leagues

Bargaining between the players' union and the management committee in the major leagues is much more complicated than the simple bilateral monopoly model suggests. The negotiations involve a wide variety of issues including revenue sharing among the clubs, restrictions on free agency, salary caps, minimum salaries, reverse-order player drafts, and a host of other issues. We examine some of these issues in the remainder of the chapter.

Box 22.1 ***Strikes and Lockouts***

The economic analysis of bilateral monopoly predicts that both sides will agree to maximize the total surplus and then bargain over the division of the spoils. Failure to reach an agreement makes no sense because the surplus is reduced. In professional sports, however, we have witnessed strikes by the players and lockouts by the owners that are immediate results of bargaining failure.

There have been work stoppages in all of the major league sports. Many occur in the preseason and are resolved in time to start the regular season on time. There have been some serious disruptions in the regular season, however. In 1994, for example, there was a prolonged strike in MLB that caused the cancellation of the World Series. In 2005, the owners locked out the players, and the entire NHL season was lost. These examples of bargaining failure are difficult to explain.

---

6 FREE AGENCY

For decades, professional athletes in the major sports leagues were bound to one team through the reserve clause. The players were set free in a series of decisions in arbitration and the courts. As a result, the clubs could not agree among themselves to restrict free agency. Instead, they bargained with the union to impose some restrictions on free agency. These restrictions vary somewhat from league to league.

6.1 Major League Baseball

If a player is selected in the MLB draft, he is initially bound to the club that selected him for six years. The player can be traded to another club, which will then have exclusive rights to that player's services. For the first three years in the league, the player has only two choices: play for his club at whatever salary the team dictates or retire. The club cannot pay him less than the MLB minimum, which was $380,000 in 2006. After three years of service, the player is not free to negotiate with another club but is protected to some extent by final offer arbitration (see Chapter 21). After six years of MLB service, the player can become a free agent if he is not already under contract. As a free agent, the player can sign with any club that offers him a contract.

6.2 National Football League

There are several categories of free agency and one major exception in the NFL. If a player has four or more years of service in the NFL and is not under contract, he will be an *unrestricted free agent.*[4] He can then sign with any club that wants to sign him. If the unrestricted free agent has not signed with another club by June 1, his original club can offer him a contract that calls for a 10 percent increase in salary over the previous year. If the player is still unsigned by July 15, his original club has the exclusive right to sign him to a contract for the following season.

Players with three years of service, but less than four, are *restricted free agents.* Beginning on March 1, the restricted free agent has a 60-day window during which he can try to generate interest from other clubs. If he gets an offer, his original team can retain his services by matching the offer. If the original club decides not to match the offer, the player can sign with the new club, and his old team will get a draft choice as compensation.

Players with less than three years of service are *exclusive rights* players. These players must sign with their original club. The club must offer a one-year contract and must pay at least the league minimum. In 2010, the NFL rookie minimum was $325,000, a player with one year of service had to be paid at least $400,000, and a player with two years in the NFL had to be paid at least $475,000.

[4] The four years of service limit only applies in years when a salary cap is in place. In years without a salary cap, the player must have five years of service. Similar adjustments apply to restricted free agents.

There is one major exception to these free-agency categories: the *franchise player*. Each NFL club can put the franchise tag on an otherwise free agent. The club must then pay the franchise player the average of the five highest salaries paid to players at his position. A club cannot designate more than one player as a franchise player in a single season. Once the franchise player signs, the club cannot use the designation on anyone else until the franchise player's contract runs out or the franchise player suffers a career-ending injury.

6.3 National Basketball Association

In the NBA, there are two classes of free agents: unrestricted and restricted. An unrestricted free agent is free to sign with any club without restriction.[5] For restricted free agents, the original club can exercise its right of first refusal. When another club signs an offer sheet, it offers a contract for two or more years to the restricted free agent. The original club can retain the player by matching the offer.

6.4 National Hockey League

Following the lockout in 2005, the new CBA provided two ways of becoming an unrestricted free agent. Irrespective of age, a player can become an unrestricted free agent after seven seasons in the NHL. Alternatively, if a player is 27 years old and has played four seasons in the NHL, he can become an unrestricted free agent.

7 SALARY CAPS AND LUXURY TAXES

A salary cap is a limit on the total player payroll. The NFL, NBA, and NHL all have salary caps of one sort or another; the precise definition varies across leagues. There is no salary cap in MLB, but there is a hefty "luxury tax" when a club's payroll exceeds the tax threshold. The idea is to limit the payroll cost to improve each club's financial stability and increase competitive balance. Salary caps can be *hard* or *soft*.

7.1 Hard Salary Caps

The NFL has a hard cap, which means that a club's payroll cannot exceed the cap for any reason. The NFL's hard cap went into effect in the 1993 CBA, which has been extended several times. The NFLPA and the NFL have agreed to split the *designated gross revenue*. The players receive 64 percent of the total estimate of the designated gross revenue. This sum is then divided evenly among the 32 NFL teams. This is the maximum amount that a team can spend on the player payroll.

There is some maneuvering around the salary cap in the NFL. The NFL salary cap does not actually include all salary expenditures paid to players

[5] The contract must include a salary at least equal to the NBA minimum, which varies on the basis of years of experience. In no event can the salary be lower than $473,604, which was the rookie minimum in 2010.

Table 22.1. Player's Share of National Hockey League (NHL) Revenue

Revenue	Share
Less than $2.2 billion	54%
$2.2–2.4 billion	55%
$2.4–2.7 billion	56%
Over $2.7 billion	57%

Source: NHL–NHL Players Association Collective Bargaining Agreement.

in a given season. The most significant exceptions involve bonuses. Signing bonuses and roster bonuses are allocated equally over the length of the player's contract, even though the player is paid the bonus in one lump sum at the beginning of the contract. For example, suppose a player signs a four-year contract for $3 million with a $1 million signing bonus. For salary cap purposes, $250,000 of the signing bonus will be allocated to each of the four years. However, limits have to be imposed because a gaping loophole would otherwise exist. Suppose that a team wanted to pay a player $33 million for three years. The contract could call for a $30 million signing bonus and salaries of $1 million per year. For salary cap purposes, the bonus would be allocated evenly – $10 million per year. A clever club, however, could sign the player to a 15-year contract. Now, the bonus would only count $2 million per year. At the end of the three years, the club can cut the player. Such a strategy cannot be tolerated because it would undermine the purpose of the cap. To avoid the pairing of minimum base salaries with multimillion-dollar signing bonuses, the NFL adopted a rule, known as the "Deion Sanders Rule," that requires the signing bonus to be allocated over the first three years of any player's contract. In addition, incentives that are deemed too "likely to be earned" by the NFL are counted against the cap. In the event that the "likely to be earned" incentives are not earned, they become cap credits for the next year. This is how some teams can be technically under the cap yet be spending over the cap. Another of the rare ways a team can get around the salary cap is through the "Cap Relief for Veterans" rule. This allows a club to sign players with more than four years of experience to one-year contracts and have it count for only $450,000 against the cap.

The NHL cap, which is a recent development, is hard. Following a 301-day lockout, the NHL and NHLPA reached agreement on a new CBA just before the start of the 2005–2006 season. For the first time, there was a salary cap in the NHL. The exact payrolls depend on how well the NHL is doing financially. The players' share of league-wide revenue depends on how much revenue is generated by the NHL. According to the CBA, the players' share increases as revenue increases from 54 percent to 57 percent, as shown in Table 22.1. The resulting sum is divided evenly among the 30 NHL teams. For example, if the NHL league-wide revenues were $2.5 billion, the total salary pool would be 56 percent or $1.4 billion. Each team would then face a salary cap of $46.67 million. This sum must cover all salaries, signing bonuses, and performance bonuses paid to all players.

Some teams located in financially weak markets may not be able to afford the salary cap limit on their own. The NHL and the NHLPA recognized this and included a provision for revenue sharing among the clubs. By transferring revenue from the financially stronger teams to those in need, each club should have enough money to cover the salary cap. The parties also recognized the potential for opportunistic behavior on the part of some clubs. To mitigate such incentives, there are eligibility requirements for revenue sharing. To be a recipient, a club must be in the bottom half of the NHL in terms of league revenue. It must also be in a "small" market, which is defined as one with less than 2.5 million TV households.

In normal circumstances, a club is not allowed to exceed the salary cap. There is, however, an injury exception. If a player is injured severely enough to miss 24 days and 10 games, that player can be replaced on the roster with another player with a similar salary. This can put the club over the salary cap while the injured player is sidelined. Once the injured player returns, however, his replacement must be cut from the roster, and the club must meet the salary cap limitations.

7.2 Soft Salary Caps

The NBA has a *soft cap*, which means that there are plenty of exceptions so teams can sign the players that they want. The salary pool is determined by basketball-related income (BRI). Under the current CBA, which is a six-year deal signed in June 2005, the players received 49.5 percent of the BRI for the 2005–2006 season and 51 percent of BRI for the 2006–2007 season. The total pool is divided equally among all NBA clubs. Given the number of exceptions, the resulting salary cap hardly means anything.

The "Larry Bird Exception" pertains to teams that want to re-sign a veteran player who has played for that club for at least the three previous seasons. This player can be re-signed to a contract up to seven years long that calls for annual raises of up to 12.5 percent, even if doing so will put the club over the cap. There is also an "Early Bird Exception" for early qualifying veteran free agents who played the previous two seasons for the club that wants to re-sign the player. Even if the club is over the cap, it can re-sign such a player at a new salary up to 175 percent of his previous salary. This contract can also provide for annual raises of up to 12.5 percent. There is a Non-Bird Exception that pertains to veteran free agents who do not qualify for the Larry Bird or the Early Bird Exception. This could arise because the player had been traded or waived. These players can be re-signed at a salary up to 120 percent of the previous salary. Their contracts can call for annual increases of up to 10 percent.

There are other exceptions to the salary cap as well. One of the most common exceptions is the Mid-Level Exception, which allows a team to sign a player to a contract equal to the NBA average, even when the team will exceed the salary cap. This exception can be used on one player or split among players. Another exception is the Rookie Exception, which allows a team to sign rookies to contracts, even if they are over the cap. The $1 million exception is used to re-sign a free agent or another team's free agent. It is hard to see how the soft NBA salary cap imposes any limits on team payrolls given all of the exceptions.

7.3 Luxury Taxes

Alone among the four major sports leagues, MLB does not have a salary cap. Instead, it uses a *luxury tax* to keep payrolls down. The central purpose is to prevent wealthy teams from signing all the best players. In other words, the

Table 22.2. Rookie Minimum Salaries, 2010 Season

League	Rookie Minimum
National Football League	$325,000
Major League Baseball	$400,000
National Basketball Association	$473,604
National Hockey League	$500,000

luxury tax is supposed to improve competitive balance. Any club with a payroll that exceeds a predetermined tax threshold may be subject to the tax depending on that club's past history. The tax is levied on the difference between the actual payroll and the threshold. For example, suppose that the tax threshold is $150 million. If a club's payroll were, say, $170 million, the tax would apply to the difference of $20 million.

The luxury tax is designed to deal with chronic "overspending" by a club. As a result, occasional lapses are ignored. Under the terms of the CBA, the following assessments applied to clubs that exceeded the threshold:

First-time offenders were assessed no luxury tax.

Clubs that exceeded the threshold in 2006, but not in 2005, were assessed no luxury tax.

Clubs that exceeded the threshold in 2006, 2005, and 2003, but not in 2004, were assessed a 30 percent tax.

Clubs that exceeded the threshold in 2006 for either the third or fourth consecutive year were assessed a 40 percent luxury tax.

Thus, if a club's payroll exceeded the threshold by $20 million, a 40 percent luxury tax would increase the payroll cost from $170 million to $178 million. If the tax rate is 30 percent, then the cost increases to $176 million.

As a means of trying to equalize payrolls in MLB, the luxury tax is an abysmal failure. The only teams chronically over the threshold are the New York Yankees and the Boston Red Sox. Moreover, the range in player payrolls is enormous.

8 MINIMUM SALARIES

The players' unions were all concerned about minimum salaries for their members. Each of the major unions has been successful in negotiating a minimum salary. All of the major sports leagues now have minimum salaries for rookies. Interestingly, the minimum salaries seem to be inversely correlated with the popularity of the sport. The rookie minimum is lowest in the NFL and highest in the NHL. The figures for 2010 are displayed in Table 22.2.

Many rookies earn considerably more than the league minimum. Those players chosen early in the NFL draft, for example, usually earn much more than $1 million in the NFL. Jake Long was the number one overall pick in the

Table 22.3. Minimum Salary Schedules, 2010 Season

Years	National Basketball Association	National Football League
0	$473,604	$325,000
1	$762,195	$400,000
2	$854,389	$475,000
3	$885,120	$550,000
4	$915,852	$635,000
5	$992,6809	$635,000
6	$1,069,509	$635,000
7	$1,146,337	$760,000
8	$1,223,166	$760,000
9	$1,229,255	$760,000
10+	$1,352,181	$860,000

NFL's 2008 draft. He signed a five-year contract reportedly worth $57.75 million. Of this, $30 million was guaranteed. For Jake Long, the rookie minimum was, of course, irrelevant. However, it is not irrelevant for undrafted free agents, struggling for a spot on some team's roster.

In the NBA and the NFL, veterans must be paid minimum salaries based on their years in the league. It is interesting to note that the veteran minimum salaries are much higher in the NBA than in the NFL as shown in Table 22.3.

In individual sports – bowling, golf, tennis, track – athletes do not receive salaries. Prize money is awarded according to performance. Thus, there are no minimum salaries. A player could conceivably attempt to compete for an entire year and win no money at all. This, of course, is unlikely, but it is possible.

9 REVENUE SHARING

The major sports leagues all have some sort of revenue sharing. The idea is that all clubs contribute to the success of the league, but some clubs have better locations and therefore enjoy higher revenues. In a spirit of cooperation, the clubs agree to share revenues to some extent. The precise terms vary from one league to the next, but there is an effort in every league to redistribute the wealth. The players' unions care about this sharing of league revenue because it reduces the market value of a player.[6] A player's value to his club is his marginal revenue product, which is marginal revenue times marginal product. Revenue sharing acts like a tax on total revenue. Players contribute to total revenue by improving a club's winning percentage. An additional win increases total revenue by the marginal revenue, but with revenue sharing, the after-tax contribution is reduced from MR to $(1 - t)MR$, where t is the tax rate. As a result, a

[6] We examined this in Chapter 6 when we discussed competitive balance.

player's market value is reduced from *MRP* to $(1 - t)MRP$. Given the impact of revenue sharing, it is small wonder that the union wants to be involved in what might not look like their business.

Major League Baseball provides an excellent example, although it is a little complicated. MLB uses a combination of a Base Plan and a Central Fund Component supplemented by the Commissioner's Discretionary Fund. For the Base Plan, each club contributes 31 percent of its Net Local Revenue into a pool. The total amount collected is then shared equally. If a club gets back more than it put into the pool, then it is a net recipient. If it gets back less, it is a net contributor. MLB also has a Central Fund generated from other sources that provides net transfers to financially strapped clubs. These are designed to improve the financial position of those teams in weak markets to improve competitive balance. Finally, the commissioner has a Discretionary Fund that can be used to assist clubs that need a little extra help.

10 CONCLUDING REMARKS

Players' unions are concerned with protecting and promoting the economic interest of their members. Any aspect of league operations that affects the well-being of the players will spark the union's interest. As a result, things such as revenue sharing among the teams, which has an impact on a player's market value, will arouse the union and become a part of the CBA. Free-agency rules, salary caps, and luxury taxes are more obvious concerns for the union.

The players' unions in the NFL, the NBA, and the NHL all negotiate with their leagues over the total wage bill, that is, the total payroll. They do not negotiate individual salaries. Each player negotiates his own salary, which must come from the available salary pool. This is decidedly different from the case in other industries in which the union negotiates wages and salaries for its members.

PROBLEMS AND QUESTIONS

1. "Revenue sharing among teams leads to lower salaries for players." True or false? Explain.
2. In a typical union, all members with the same tenure earn the same wage. This is not true in the NFL. Why not?
3. The MLBPA represents all major league baseball players. The St. Louis Cardinals have a monopoly on the provision of major league baseball in St. Louis. Explain why this is not a bilateral monopoly situation.
4. A strike or lockout is the result of a labor impasse. The clubs suffer because they earn no profit, and the players suffer because they earn no income. Is there any reason why the government should intervene to resolve the matter?
5. There have been efforts to unionize National Collegiate Athletic Association student-athletes, but they have all failed. Why?

6. Because salary caps and luxury taxes depress the salaries that athletes can command, why do players' unions agree to them?
7. Suppose that the CBA expired in MLB and the prospects for successful negotiations appeared bleak. Could the players form a new league of their own? What *economic* and *logistical* problems would they face?
8. Suppose that the demand for wide receivers (WR) is w_D = \$2,000,000–25,000WR, which means that the marginal revenue (MR) is MR = \$2,000,000–50,000 WR. The supply of wide receivers is w_S = 200,000 + 10,000WR. Consequently, the marginal factor cost (MRFC) is MRC = \$200,000 + 20,000WR. Assume that the wide receivers are unionized, but they compete with one another in the wide receiver market.
   a. If the union tries to maximize profit, what wage will those who are employed earn? How many will be employed?
   b. If the union wants to maximize the wage bill, what wage will result? How many wide receivers will be employed?
   c. How many wide receivers will want to be employed at the wages found in (a) and (b)?
9. Suppose that the wide receivers in problem 8 are unionized and that the teams join together to bargain with the wide receiver union. Use the same supply and demand functions to answer the following questions.
   a. What employment level will result from the bargaining process?
   b. How much surplus will the players and the owners split?
   c. What is the range of equilibrium wages that results?
10. For the 2008–2009 season, an NHL club must have had average home attendance of at least 14,000 to be eligible for the revenue sharing plan.
    a. Why would the NHL impose such a minimum for eligibility?
    b. What are the consequences for competitive balance?
11. During the 2011 negotiations between the NFL and the NFLPA, one commentator ridiculed the parties for employing a mediator.
    a. How does a mediator help parties reach an accord?
    b. Is it shameful that they needed a mediator?

RESEARCH QUESTIONS

1. Find out what the objective is of unions. Do they maximize the wage bill, employment opportunities, or something else?
2. Examine the behavior of the unions in MLB, NFL, NBA, and NHL. What do their objective functions appear to be?
3. Go to www.mlbplayers.com and review the MLB–MLBPA Collective Bargaining Agreement. Identify the issues that are covered in the agreement.
4. In the 2010 season, the rookie minimum salary in the NFL was \$325,000. How many rookies played for the minimum? Construct a schedule of

salaries for all first-year players. If a player received a signing bonus, prorate the bonus over the life of his contract.

5. Examine how rookie salaries vary with place in the draft. Look at the salaries for the players chosen in the first three rounds.
6. What was the salary cap in the NBA for 2010? For each team, how did the actual payroll compare to the cap? How do you explain the deviations?
7. Has the salary cap in the NBA improved competitive balance?
8. Has the salary cap in the NFL improved competitive balance?

REFERENCES AND FURTHER READING

Areeda, Phillip, and Herbert Hovenkamp. (2006). *Antitrust Law*, Vol. IB, 255–257. New York: Aspen Publishers.

Bergmann, T. J., and J. B. Dworkin. (1978). "Collective Bargaining vs. the Rozelle Rule: An Analysis of Labor-management Relations in Professional Football." *Akron Business and Economic Review*, 9, 35–40.

Blair, Roger D., and Jessica S. Haynes. (2009). "Collusion in Major League Baseball's Free Agent Market: The Barry Bonds Case." *The Antitrust Bulletin*, 54, 883–906.

Blair, Roger D., David L. Kaserman, and Richard E. Romano. (1989). "A Pedagogical Treatment of Bilateral Monopoly." *Southern Economic Journal*, 55, 831–841.

Coates, Dennis, and Thane Harrison. (2005). "Baseball Strikes and the Demand for Attendance." *Journal of Sports Economics*, 6, 282–302.

Easton, Stephen T., and Duane W. Rockerbie. (2005). "Revenue Sharing, Conjectures, and Scarce Talent in a Sports League Model." *Journal of Sports Economics*, 6, 359–378.

Hill, J. Richard, and Peter A. Groothuis. (2001). "The New NBA Collective Bargaining Agreement, the Median Voter Model, and a Robin Hood Rent Redistribution." *Journal of Sports Economics*, 2, 131–144.

Kahn, L. M. (2009). "Sports, Antitrust Enforcement and Collective Bargaining." *The Antitrust Bulletin*, 54, 857–882.

Noll, Roger G. (1974). *Government and the Sports Business* (chapter 6). Washington, DC: The Brookings Institution.

Quirk, James, and Rodney Fort. (1999). *Hard Ball: The Abuse of Power in Pro Team Sports* (chapter 3). Princeton, NJ: Princeton University Press.

Scoville, James. (1974). "Labor Relations in Sports," chapter 6 in Roger G. Noll, ed., *Government and the Sports Business*. Washington, DC: The Brookings Institution.

Sloane, A. A. (1977). "Collective Bargaining in Major League Baseball: A New Ball Game and Its Genesis." *Labor Law Journal*, 28, 200–210.

Zimbalist, Andrew. (2003). *May the Best Team Win* (chapter 5). Washington, DC: The Brookings Institution.

Zimbalist, Andrew. (2009). "The BCS, Antitrust and Public Policy." *The Antitrust Bulletin*, 54, 823–856.

23

The Role of Sports Agents

1 INTRODUCTION

In a relatively short time, sports agents have become major participants in the sports industry. Mark McCormack began representing Arnold Palmer in 1960 when Palmer was at the top of his game and the peak of his popularity. McCormack helped Palmer cash in on his swashbuckling style and personal charisma. Although he could not help Palmer on the golf course, he provided plenty of assistance off the course in building Palmer's financial empire. McCormack's representation of Palmer was a major building block of the International Managerial Group, which McCormack founded and is now known as IMG. The value of IMG has been reported as being more than $1.5 billion.

Before the demise of the reserve clause in major league team sports, sports agents could not help much in dealing with the players' clubs. First, the players had no options other than retiring and therefore no real bargaining power. Second, many clubs simply refused to deal with a player's agent and might even punish players who had one. Once players were set free from the hated reserve clause, however, sports agents took center stage in dealing with the player's club. Today both athletes and coaches are represented by agents who negotiate deals on and off the field for their clients.

In this chapter, we begin with an overview of the role that sports agents play in representing their clients and managing their affairs. We then examine the extent to which there is some incompatibility between the agent's incentives and the interest of his client. This potential problem, which is known as the *principal–agent problem*, cannot be completely resolved, but it is important to recognize and understand the problem. The ultimate conflict arises when a corrupt agent is guilty of malfeasance. We examine that possibility and provide some examples. Finally, we turn our attention to various controls imposed on the behavior of agents by state laws and the players' unions.

2 ROLES OF SPORTS AGENTS

Sports agents help their clients both on the field and off the field. Obviously, their on-field contributions cannot involve playing and are limited to contract negotiations. Their off-field contributions to a player's financial well-being, however, can be substantial. For any given athlete, the more adept the agent, the more money the athlete earns in salary and other forms of compensation. Many top athletes earn more (sometimes far more) off the field than they do on the field, and it is the agent's job to make sure that his client optimizes his or her financial opportunities. This does not necessarily mean maximizing income. Athletes are utility maximizers, and some things, such as leisure and dignity, are more important than a few extra dollars.

2.1 On-Field Performance

A sports agent's contributions to his client's on-field performance are fairly limited. Scott Boras cannot throw strikes for Barry Zito, nor can Don Yee complete a pass for Tom Brady. For the most part, agents can only provide training support that improves on-field performance. For example, some agents will pay for predraft training for their NFL prospects. This training involves a conditioning and strength training program that is designed to improve a prospect's draft position. Each year, we read about players who vastly improve their draft position because of dazzling performances in the 40-yard dash, vertical leap, and high repetitions in the bench press. Moving from a midround draft pick to a top 10 position can mean millions of dollars in the initial contract. This increase is shared between the player and his agent.

2.2 Negotiating Salaries

Sports agents negotiate salaries and other contract terms with the club. The agent's leverage depends on the team's needs, its ability to pay, and whether the player is a free agent. There have been some substantial deals negotiated recently on behalf of free agents. Scott Boras, for example, negotiated a 10-year deal for Alex Rodriguez that was reported to be worth more than $250 million. As the first pick in the 2007 NFL draft, JaMarcus Russell really had only two options: sign with the dreadful Oakland Raiders or sit out a year and enter the 2008 draft. Nonetheless, his agent negotiated a six-year, $68 million contract that provided $31.5 million in signing bonus and other guarantees. Jake Long and Matt Ryan were in similar positions following the 2008 draft. The Miami Dolphins, coming off a dismal 1–15 season, desperately needed an anchor for their offensive line. Long received a five-year contract, with $30 million in guaranteed money. Ryan was drafted by the Atlanta Falcons, who were also desperate to find a new face of the Falcons with Michael Vick disgraced and in prison. Ryan's agent negotiated a six-year deal reportedly worth $72 million with $34.75 million of that being guaranteed.

2.3 Negotiating among Several Clubs

When a player is a free agent, he can sign with the team that offers the best deal. For some players, the deal with the most money is the best. For other players, however, money is not the only factor, although it is one of the most important. For example, there were several things that were important to Roger Clemens

Box 23.1 ***Where Was His Agent? Where Was He?***

Anthony Carter signed a three-year contract with the Miami Heat in 2001. The 2003–2004 season was to be the third and final year. Interestingly, the third year was an option, but it was his option, not the team's. Although Carter had not lived up to expectations – he was not a full-time starter and averaged only 5.5 points and 4.3 assists per game – he could have exercised his option for a third year and would have earned $4.1 million simply by notifying the Heat that he intended to do so.

Neither Carter nor his agent, Bill Duffy, notified the club by the June 30 deadline. As a result, Carter was not given a third year with the Heat. Instead, he caught on with the San Antonio Spurs but had to play for the league minimum, $688,679, for a veteran of his experience. Thus, the failure to exercise Carter's option cost him more than $3.4 million. According to Carter, his agent, Bill Duffy, is "going to take care of the rest of it."

Query: Was his agent guilty of malpractice?
How much blame should be put on Carter's shoulders?

when he was negotiating with the Yankees over his 2007 contract. In addition to a huge salary, these included reduced travel requirements and extended time away from the team. It is up to the player's agent to shop carefully and find the best offer according to the player's preferences. In 2007, Barry Zito was a free agent who attracted plenty of attention among MLB teams. A young, durable, former Cy Young Award winner, Zito was a hot prospect. His agent, Scott Boras, warned off clubs that did not interest Zito. In the end, there were four clubs in the final running – the New York Mets, the San Francisco Giants, the Texas Rangers, and the Seattle Mariners. Boras had hoped to get the New York Yankees interested in Zito so he could start a cross-town bidding war between the Mets and the Yankees. Unfortunately for Boras and Zito, this did not materialize, as the Yankees turned their attention elsewhere. However, with four finalists, Boras was able to play one club off against another and thereby force them to compete for Zito's services. Boras did his job admirably and landed a seven-year deal worth an erroneously reported $126 million.[1]

Scott Boras is a thorn in the side of any General Manager who has to deal with him. He is a tough, demanding negotiator. Many of his clients have profited handsomely from his representation, but he can make mistakes, too. A very visible example is his apparent mishandling of Alex Rodriguez's contract with the New York Yankees.

When Boras negotiated Rodriguez's original 10-year contract, it came with an opt-out provision at the end of the 2007 season. Threatening to exercise that option, Boras demanded a 10-year, $350 million contract extension for

[1] See Chapter 20 for a correct valuation of Zito's contract.

Rodriguez, who was 32 years old at the time. The Yankees were prepared to offer a five-year extension that would have increased Rodriguez's salary to about $30 million per year. To preserve their future credibility, the Yankees stuck to their position, and Rodriguez opted out. Now Boras had to find Rodriguez a new home. At $350 million for 10 years, this was going to be tough. In fact, the only team to show much interest was the Los Angeles Angels.

Boras exercised the opt-out provision without meeting with the Yankees and discussing their proposal. This turned out to be foolish for two reasons. First, it resulted in a lot of negative publicity for Rodriguez and tarnished his image. Second, Rodriguez's original contract was being subsidized by the Texas Rangers as part of the trade that brought Rodriguez to the Yankees from the Rangers. The balance of that subsidy on the remaining three years of the original contract was $21.3 million. By opting out, Boras ended the Rangers' obligation. If the Yankees signed Rodriguez to a new contract, there would be no subsidy.

Even though Rodriguez was a superstar, there was some doubt that Boras would find many teams that would be willing to pay $30 to $35 million a year, especially on a long-term contract. The skeptics were right. Boras did not find any teams willing to make that sort of commitment. At the same time, Rodriguez had serious misgivings about leaving the Yankees.

A few weeks passed and Rodriguez reached out to the Yankees without Boras. He definitely wanted to return to the Yankees and wanted a deal worked out that would allow him to do so. Ultimately, Rodriguez got a new 10-year deal with the team for $270 to $275 million, which was $80 million less than Boras's demand. Moreover, it was $21.3 million less than Rodriguez could have gotten if the Yankees had not lost the Rangers' subsidy. Arguably, Boras cost his client $21.3 million. Interestingly, Boras still received his hefty commission on the contract that he did not negotiate.[2]

To be fair to Boras, he does not have a reputation for making many mistakes. Boras has a large staff and about 130 clients. Some of the clients are journeymen, but Boras apparently works very hard on behalf of all clients. Even lesser-known players, such as Ron Villone, Chad Krueter, Craig Shiply, and David Newhan, appear to be quite satisfied with their representation by Boras and his staff. To be sure, Alex Rodriguez and Barry Zito get more personal attention than his journeymen clients. Boras may have made a strategic error in exercising Rodriguez's opt-out provision, but this is an exception.

2.4 Endorsements and Other Opportunities

Endorsements and other off-field income opportunities can be important sources of additional income for some athletes. In fact, endorsements may far exceed an athlete's earnings from competition. In 2005, for example, Tiger Woods won $10,628,024 playing golf. This tidy sum was swamped by his endorsement income of $80 million. In the same year, Andre Agassi won

[2] This is a bit too strong. Boras did not negotiate the financial terms, but he did work out the bonus terms, the no-trade clause, and the contract language.

$1,177,254 playing tennis, but earned a whopping $44.5 million in endorsements. Lance Armstrong's endorsements amounted to $17.5 million, which far exceeded his cycling winnings of $497,500. Of course, these large disparities are not true for all athletes, but the point is clear: endorsements can mean many extra dollars in an athlete's pocket, and the agent gets a piece of the action as well.

It is the sports agent's job to evaluate endorsement offers and make sure that a player's endorsement portfolio generates as much income as possible while preserving a desired image for the athlete and allowing him some time to enjoy it.

For athletes with a suitable image, sports agents can arrange appearance fees. In this way, the agent helps the athlete trade on his or her celebrity status. Much the same can be said for speaking engagements. A popular player who is well-spoken can join the "rubber-chicken" banquet circuit during the off-season and earn substantial fees for telling a few jokes and offering some inspirational advice.

The stars in individual sports are more visible in some ways than the stars in team sports. As a result, their endorsement potential is usually higher. In Table 23.1, we have the endorsement income generated by the top earners in baseball, basketball, and football for 2010. This table shows the top earners in golf and auto racing as well. These data show that the stars in team and individual sports have considerable endorsement opportunities. For NBA stars, the endorsement potential rivals that in individual sports, but this is not the case for baseball and football.

Box 23.2 *Illegal Immigration**

Some agents have gone so far as to smuggle baseball players into the United States from Cuba. In 2004, Gus Dominguez and Geoffrey Rodrigues went to Cuba and picked up 19 Cubans and smuggled them into the United States. The players were then loaded into a van and taken to Los Angeles, where the agents provided food, clothing, and housing. The baseball players then began training in the hopes of being signed by an MLB team.

Dominguez, Rodrigues, and others involved in the scheme were indicted for conspiring to bring immigrants illegally into the country, transporting them illegally, and concealing and harboring them from detection by law enforcement authorities.

An immigration official remarked that "[t]hough this case involves a Beverly Hills sports agent and talented baseball players, it is remarkably similar to human smuggling operations that ICE [Immigration and Customs Enforcement] encounters every day. The ring leaders put the lives of illegal immigrants at risk and sought to profit from their labor."

* The Associated Press, "Feds: Agent Smuggled Players from Cuba," Nov. 1, 2006.

Table 23.1. Endorsement Income for 2010

Sport/Athlete	Endorsements ($millions)
Baseball	
Derek Jeter	10.0
Albert Pujols	8.0
David Ortiz	4.5
Basketball	
LeBron James	30.0
Shaquille O'Neal	15.0
Dwayne Wade	12.0
Dwight Howard	12.0
Football	
Peyton Manning	15
Brett Favre	7.0
Eli Manning	7.0
Golf	
Tiger Woods	70.0
Phil Mickelson	52.0
Tennis	
Roger Federer	54.8
Rafael Nadal	18.5
Auto Racing	
Dale Earnhardt Jr.	22.0
Jeff Gordon	15.0
Jimmie Johnson	10.0
Boxing	
Floyd Mayweather Jr.	0.25

Source: SI.com: http://sportsillustrated.cnn.com/specials/fortunate50–2010/index.html

3 FINANCIAL MANAGEMENT

Some athletes allow their agents to manage their financial affairs: pay their bills, make investments for them, and manage their retirement plans. In most cases, this probably works out fine for the athletes, but not always. The player relies on his agent to work on his behalf. On occasion, however, agents appear to act in their own self-interest rather than in their client's interest. For example, the beleaguered Michael Vick filed a $2 million lawsuit against his former financial advisor, Mary Roy Wong, and her company, Williams and Bullocks L.L.C. He alleged "fraud, breach of contract, breach of fiduciary security, conversion, and negligence." In extreme cases, the agent may even cheat the player and steal some of the player's wealth. This happened to a number of NFL players who were represented by Tank Black.

3.1 The Tank Black Story

As a Securities and Exchange Commission lawyer pointed out, "professional athletes are prime candidates for financial fraud. Many are unsophisticated in financial matters and suddenly find themselves with six-or-seven figure salaries."[3] An unscrupulous agent can take advantage of young, trusting athletes. William "Tank" Black is a well-known example of such an agent.

Black founded Professional Marketing Incorporated (PMI) to represent professional athletes. It was slow at first, but Black signed some big-time players – Sterling Sharpe (Packers), Jevon Kearse (Titans), Fred Taylor (Jaguars), and Ike Hillard (Giants), to name a few. By May 1999, Black had 35 NFL clients and the NBA's Vince Carter. According to news reports, Black either stole from them or mismanaged their money by putting it into a large-scale Ponzi scheme.

Using his charm and personal charisma, Black was able to gain the trust of many clients. Fred Taylor considered him a second father. Black also endeared himself to some players by giving them money before their eligibility ran out. Many of those athletes lost considerable sums of money as a result of Black's representation. The biggest loser was Black's most ardent supporter: Fred Taylor. A premier running back out of Florida, Taylor turned over his entire signing bonus, which amounted to $3.6 million after taxes, to Black. Taylor lost it all. Taylor was not the only one, however. Vince Carter lost $300,000, Jacquez Green and Germane Crowell lost some $500,000 each, and Rae Carruth lost $300,000. In total, Black's clients lost an estimated $15 million.

Black was convicted in federal court of defrauding his clients. He also pleaded guilty in a separate suit to money laundering for a drug ring. Black was sentenced to almost seven years in prison, but that did not get his clients' money back.

4 THE PRINCIPAL–AGENT PROBLEM

The *principal* hires an *agent* to work on his behalf. When the goals of the principal and the goals of the agent are not perfectly aligned, the agent may pursue his own goals at the expense of the principal.[4]

When a player hires a sports agent to represent him or her, what is known as the *principal–agent problem* arises. The player, of course, is the principal and the sports agent is his agent. The root of the problem is asymmetric information: the player cannot completely monitor (observe) and/or evaluate the agent's efforts. Because sports agents are utility maximizers just like anyone else, they may act in their own best interest – at least to some extent – to the detriment of the player. This may take various forms. For example, an agent may take an afternoon off rather than work on behalf of the player. An agent

[3] This section depends on L. Jon Wertheim, Don Yaeger, and B. J. Schecter, "Web of Deceit," *Sports Illustrated*, May 2000, and other news accounts of Tank Black's fall from prominence.

[4] This section relies in part on Jeffrey M. Perloff (2007), *Microeconomics*, 4th ed., Boston: Addison Wesley, at pp. 666–694. This is an excellent, accessible treatment of the principal–agent problem.

Box 23.3 *Alabama Crackdown on Sports Agents**

In Alabama, sports agents better not interfere with a student-athlete's eligibility. State law requires sports agents to register with the state. Failure to do so is a felony, which could mean significant jail time for offenders.

National Collegiate Athletic Association (NCAA) rules prohibit student-athletes from being represented by a sports agent while still eligible. Unscrupulous sports agents who pay players, and thereby jeopardize their eligibility to participate, run the risk of prosecution. Even far less egregious behavior can lead to legal difficulties.

Tyrone Prothro, an outstanding wide receiver at the University of Alabama, broke his leg in three places while Mike Shula appeared to be running up the score against Florida in 2005. The government alleges that Raymond Savage, an agent, directed one of his employees, Jason Goggins, to visit Prothro in the hospital and give him a Savage Sports brochure. Both Savage and Goggins were indicted for failing to register and or contacting a player with remaining eligibility.

* Liz Mullen, "State of Alabama Says Agent Ran Afoul of Tough Recruiting Laws," *Sports Business Journal*, Nov. 10, 2008, p. 13.

may fail to return phone calls from potential sponsors. However, the agent's behavior could be more sinister as we saw in the previous section.

The player's problem can be formalized a bit by defining the player's payoff (π) as a function of the actions taken by the agent (a) and a random variable (θ) that describes the state of nature:

$$\pi = \pi(a, \theta).$$

To make this a bit more concrete, suppose that π represents a player's endorsement income. The amount of endorsement income will be determined by actions taken by his agent to attract and negotiate endorsement deals and by vagaries in the advertising world. Now the payoff to the player can be observed, but the action of the agent cannot. For example, the player will obviously be aware of how much he earns in endorsements during a year, but he will not be able to monitor his agent's efforts to solicit and then negotiate the best endorsement deals possible. If the player cannot observe his agent's actions (a), then he will be unable to determine whether a low endorsement total (π) was due to low effort (a) or bad luck (θ). This problem cannot be resolved entirely, but it can be mitigated by using contracts that improve the incentive compatibility between the player and his agent.

4.1 Principal–Agent Contracts

A contract between a principal and his agent determines how the random outcome (π) is split between them. There are three basic contract types: (1) fixed

Box 23.4 *It Was All a Misunderstanding**

There are times when a sports agent can act on his own behalf rather than on his client's behalf. This apparently happened to LaDamian Tomlinson.

Tomlinson's agent, Bill Henkel, should have been negotiating a memorabilia deal strictly on Tomlinson's behalf. It turned out, however, that Henkel received a side payment from the memorabilia company. In an affidavit, Tomlinson said that "Henkel had pressured the sports memorabilia company into paying him an improper, secret $75,000 kickback . . . for securing my services." Because this money (less Henkel's commission) should have gone to Tomlinson, Henkel was originally charged with felony commercial bribery and theft. As part of a plea agreement, Henkel pleaded guilty to criminal deprivation of property, which is a misdemeanor. After his guilty plea, Henkel claimed that it was all a misunderstanding. An assistant district attorney called Henkel's explanation "laughable."

* Liz Mullen, "Marketing Agent Henkel Pleads Guilty in Tomlinson Case," *Sports Business Journal*, Nov. 17, 2008, p. 10.

fee contracts, (2) hire contracts, and (3) contingent fee contracts. Each contract has some desirable and some undesirable properties.

Fixed Fee Contracts. Under a fixed fee contract, the fee that the agent receives does not depend on the payoff realized by the player or by the agent's efforts. Thus, the agent gets a fee of F and the player receives the payoff minus the agent's fee: π (a, θ) $- F$.

This contract can be used in all situations because the principal need not observe a or θ to pay his agent. Thus, even when the principal cannot observe his agent's efforts (a) or the state of nature (θ), he can use a fixed fee contract. A player can agree to pay an agent a fee of, say, $20,000 to line up endorsement deals. No matter how much or how little effort the agent expends and no matter how lucky or unlucky the player is, the agent receives $20,000.

Fixed fee contracts have an obvious flaw: the agent has no incentive to maximize the player's endorsement income. The agent gets his fee either way. If there were no uncertainty, the player would know what to expect in endorsement income. He could then agree on a fixed fee and simply not pay his agent until the job was completed satisfactorily. When there is uncertainty, however, the player will be unable to determine whether the work was satisfactory. As a consequence, a fixed fee contract is not economically efficient in the sense that its terms induce the agent to maximize the payoff.

Hire Contracts. In a hire contract, payment to the agent is purely a function of the agent's effort (a). The player and the agent agree on an hourly wage of w and the agent receives wa for his efforts. This kind of contract is most commonly used when the player can readily monitor the agent's effort.

With a hire contract, the agent is paid wa, where w is the hourly wage and a represents the hours worked, and the principal keeps the residual, which is

π $(a, \theta) - wa$. When Tim Duncan and Grant Hill came into the NBA, their agent (Lon Babby) represented them on an hourly basis. As a result, the players received the full value of their contracts minus their agent's fees, which were calculated as the product of the hourly wage times the number of hours that the agent spent negotiating their contracts.

This kind of contract can be beneficial to the player. Suppose, for example, that an agent spends 500 hours negotiating a $10 million contract for a player. At $300 per hour, the agent's compensation would be $150,000. This is obviously a lot of money, but it is only 1.5 percent of the contract value. The player gets to keep $9.85 million for himself. In contrast, suppose that an agent's fee would be 4 percent of the contract value. In that case, the agent's commission would be $400,000. The player would then keep $9.6 million, which is a difference of $250,000.

There is a downside to hire contracts: they do not provide an incentive for the agent to maximize the payoff. Suppose that the agreed-on wage w is the agent's opportunity cost. He is then indifferent about maximizing $\pi(a, \theta)$ because he gets no benefit from doing so. Assuming that the hourly wage represents the agent's opportunity cost means that he can work for someone else at the same wage. In the earlier example, suppose that the agent could increase the player's contract to $12 million by working an extra 100 hours. The agent, however, will earn that extra $30,000 whether he works for this player or for someone else. However, there is another problem: he may "steal" from the player by reporting excessive hours. If the agreed-on wage exceeds the agent's opportunity cost, he has an incentive to put forth too much effort. In other words, the actual value of a will be greater than the value of a that maximizes π (a, θ). The agent wants to maximize wa rather than $\pi(a, \theta)$.

Given the presence of uncertainty – and therefore risk – there is another problem with both the fixed fee and hire contracts. It should be noted that the player bears all of the risk in the hire contract as well as in fixed fee contracts. The agent's compensation is not a function of θ, which is where the risk lies. All of the uncertainty surrounding θ falls on the player when one of these contract types is used. It is probably not optimal (that is, value maximizing) to allocate all of the risk to the player. In an economically efficient contract, risk should be allocated to the party that minds it the least. For risk averters, risk is a cost that will be incorporated in the decision process. Thus, if one party is risk neutral and the other is risk averse, the risk-neutral party will have lower costs than the risk-averse party and therefore should bear the risk. If both parties are risk averse, the one who is the least risk averse should bear the risk.[5] By allocating risk in this way, the expected value of $\pi(a, \theta)$ will be larger than it would be otherwise.

Contingent Fee Contracts. In a contingent fee contract, the payments to the parties depend on the payoff that is realized and therefore on the agent's effort

[5] The less risk averse a person is, the less concave the utility function – that is, the closer it is to a straight line. For a more complete treatment of attitudes toward risk, recall the discussion of insurance in Chapter 8.

and the state of nature. For example, the reward to the agent may be a percentage of the player's endorsement income, which is uncertain. Thus, the agent gets a percentage share, α, of the endorsement income, and the player retains the rest. In that event, $\alpha \pi$ (a, θ) goes to the agent and $(1 - \alpha) \pi$ (a, θ) goes to the player. Obviously, the agent's share is between zero and one: $0 < \alpha < 1$. For sports agents, α is about 4 or 5 percent.

Contingent fee contracts are most common when it is difficult to observe (i.e., measure) the amount and quality of the agent's effort (a), but the state of nature (θ) can be observed after the fact. In this kind of contract, the principal and agent share the risk. For example, suppose that the player's agent spends 100 hours soliciting and negotiating endorsement contracts. If luck is with them, the deals will be worth \$5 million, but only \$3 million if they are not so lucky. Thus, the endorsement income is random. The player could get 95% of \$5 million, which is \$4.75 million, and the agent's commission would be \$250,000 in one state of the world. If things do not go so well, however, the player will receive only 95% of \$3 million, which is \$2.85 million, and the agent would then receive a commission of \$150,000. This uncertainty is beyond the control of the player or the agent.

There are two problems with contingent fee contracts. First, to the extent that the player and his agent have different attitudes toward risk, sharing may not make sense. In other words, the expected value of $\pi(a, \theta)$ may be larger if the least risk-averse party bears all of the risk. Second, sharing the proceeds alters the agent's incentives.

Suppose an agent is negotiating an endorsement deal that will produce some total revenue (TR). To fulfill the contract, the player will incur opportunity costs of *TC*. In that case,

$$\pi(a, \theta) = TR(a, \theta) - TC.$$

If the player and the agent share the revenue, the agent gets αTR while the player gets $(1 - \alpha) TR(a, \theta) - TC$. In this contract, we should note that the player gets only part of the revenue, $(1 - \alpha) TR$, but bears all of the cost. Thus the agent will work to maximize total revenue instead of net revenue. Because of asymmetric information, the agent may have an incentive to maximize $\pi(a, \theta)$, but only if he can steal some of it from the principal.

Alternatively, consider a profit-sharing contract. Now the player gets $(1 - \alpha)$ $\pi(a, \theta)$, which is $(1 - \alpha)(TR(a, \theta) - TC)$, and the agent gets $\alpha\pi(a, \theta)$, which is equal to $\alpha(TR(a, \theta) - TC)$. The agent will no longer have an incentive to maximize total revenue. However, he will not have an incentive to maximize net revenue either. Again, unless the agent can steal all of the profit, the incentive to maximize profit is absent. The problem is that the agent bears all of the cost of his marginal effort but receives only a portion of the incremental profit.

5 CORRECTIVE AND PREVENTIVE MEASURES

The principal–agent problem leads to a suboptimal outcome in the sense that the payoff to the player is not maximized. Thus, there is an inefficiency that creates an economic incentive for corrective or preventive measures to surface. If the cost of correction is less than the increase in the value realized, then these measures will be adopted. There are a number of safeguards that pertain to the contract between a player and his agent. These include reputation, supervision by the players' unions, and legal remedies.

5.1 Reputation

The principal–agent problem described in the preceding section did not consider the consequences of failing to maximize the player's payoff. Because the agent's incentives are not perfectly aligned with the player's interests, the compensation to the agent is lower than it would be if the player could be sure that the agent would actually maximize the player's payoff. For example, suppose that an agent charged an hourly fee for his services. Because of incentive incompatibility, that hourly fee is reduced. If an agent develops a reputation for providing more bang for the buck, his hourly fee will be bid up by other players who want to retain him. As long as the agent continues to perform at a high level, he will retain his reputation for acting in the interest of his client. He will be perceived as one who can be trusted to do his best. If he fails to live up to his reputation, he will lose that reputation, his business will fall off, and his fees will shrink.

An agent who contemplates behavior that will provide a short-term benefit must consider the consequences for his reputation. If the agent is rational, he will not engage in that behavior if

$$B - \sum_{t=1}^{T} \Delta F/(1+i)^t < 0,$$

where B is the short-term benefit and ΔF is the reduction in fees that result from his loss of reputation. If the present value of the fee reduction over the agent's career horizon (T) exceeds the benefit, he will be worse off if he sacrifices his reputation.

As an example, suppose that the agent could experience a benefit of $1 million by failing to work diligently on the player's behalf. If this opportunistic behavior damages his reputation and causes an annual reduction in fees of, say, $100,000 over the remaining 20 years in his career, the agent will be worse off if the appropriate discount rate is 7% or less, but he will be better off if the appropriate discount rate is 8% or more.[6]

5.2 Players' Union Supervision

The players' union is interested in protecting the players from opportunistic behavior by agents. Agents depend on union approval for their business as sports agents. The union can impose heavy financial penalties on unscrupulous sports agents by putting them out of business. When Tank Black was recruiting clients, he paid them while they were still in college. Some rival sports agents complained to the NFLPA; the union investigated the allegations and

[6] Revisit Chapter 2 and the annuity table in the appendix to verify these numbers.

concluded that they were accurate. The NFLPA threatened a lifetime suspension. Such a threat would end such behavior if it is profitable to do so. If we let Π_{tC} represent the profit that Black could earn each year by cheating and Π_{tN} be the (presumably) lower profit that he would earn without cheating, we can find the condition necessary to deter this behavior. If the present value of Π_{tc} exceeds the present value of Π_{tN}, the agent will cheat. In other words if

$$\sum_{t=1}^{\tau} \Pi_{tC}/(1+i)^t - \sum_{t=1}^{T} \Pi_{tN}/(1+i)^t > 0,$$

where τ is the year in which the agent is suspended and T is the agent's career life, the agent will cheat. If the difference is negative, he will not cheat.

It is not just the unions that impose sanctions on wayward agents. Some of the governing bodies in individual sports do much the same thing. For example, USA Track & Field (USAT&F), American track's governing body, screens sports agents and provides a list of authorized agents to the athletes. If it finds that an agent has acted improperly, the agent can be suspended. This is precisely what happened to Charles Wells, Marion Jones's former agent, when he pleaded guilty to money laundering. USAT&F suspended him for two years.

5.3 Contract Law

A player and his agent have a contract that should set out the agent's responsibilities. If the agent fails to satisfy his or her responsibilities, the common law of contracts will provide some remedies. The breach of contract may mean that the agent will not get paid at all. To the extent that the agent's failure to perform caused the player to lose opportunities, he or she may sue the agent for these lost opportunities.

Legal disputes between an athlete and his or her agent are not uncommon. Sometimes the agent sues the player. For example, Anthony Kim, a rising PGA Tour star, was under contract to Hambric Sports. Kim dismissed the firm some seven months before the contract was set to expire and then signed on with IMG. Hambric sued for breach of contract and sought to recover the income that it would have earned if Kim had not breached the contract.

6 CONCLUDING REMARKS

Sports agents play many roles in professional sports. The most visible roles involve negotiating player contracts and endorsement deals. Currently, there is so much income potential for professional athletes that a really good agent can make a significant financial difference.

Sports agents are ubiquitous – nearly every professional athlete and coach have one. Even the big-time college coaches have agents whose job it is to manage the client's earning potential. The problem lies in designing a compensation scheme that makes the agent's incentives compatible with the player's (or coach's) incentives. As we have seen, this cannot be done perfectly. The most common arrangement is a contingent fee contract. With a contingent fee contract, the agent receives a specified percentage of the value of any contract and

Box 23.5 ***Competing for Pro Prospects***

It is obvious that a sports agent cannot earn a living unless he or she has clients. Given the prevalence of contingent fee contracts between players and agents, the more prominent the athlete, the more money the agent earns. As a result, there is competition – often fierce competition – among agents to sign the top pro prospects. Although we usually applaud competition, this competition can have a dark side that may have serious consequences for amateur athletes.

In some cases, competition involves paying the prospects while they are still competing as amateurs. Such payments violate NCAA rules and therefore jeopardize the athlete's eligibility. The agent who makes such payments is obviously hoping to sign the favored athlete when he or she turns pro. This, of course, does not always work out because the athlete can take the money and then sign with another agent. When it works, however, the agent's investment of a few thousand dollars can pay handsome dividends.

When the improper payments are discovered, the consequences are not pleasant. For example, several college football programs were thrown into turmoil just as the 2010 season was about to start. NCAA investigators uncovered evidence that Georgia's star receiver, A. J. Green, received $1,000 from an agent for his jersey. Green was suspended from Georgia's first four games, and Georgia's offense floundered. The investigators also found that Marcus Dareus, Alabama's star defensive lineman, received $2,000 in benefits from an agent. Dareus was suspended for Alabama's first two games, which it won anyway. North Carolina lost 13 players for a variety of academic and agent-related violations. As a result, the team has struggled, and its coach is under fire.

the player (or coach) receives the rest. This helps align their interest but does not do so perfectly. In the end, the reputation effects of doing a good job and an expansion in the agent's business may go a long way in promoting the client's interest.

PROBLEMS AND QUESTIONS

1. What is the principal–agent problem? Explain why the standard sports agent contract, which provides a contingent fee for the agent, does not resolve the principal–agent problem.
2. Suppose the player is risk neutral and the agent is risk averse. Why should the player have to bear all of the risk?
3. Agents are often in a position in which they can steal from their clients. Stealing, however, is a risky business. How can we deter such behavior?
4. Explain how reputation effects reduce the incentive for a sports agent to cheat his client. Will this effect be larger or smaller for young agents compared with older agents?

5. Does a player have any remedy if he signs an undesirable contract because of his agent's incompetence?
6. Some sports agents induce college athletes to break rules by accepting money and gifts that would make the athlete ineligible under NCAA rules if it is discovered.
    a. How does the agent gain from this?
    b. How can such conduct be deterred?
7. Suppose that the contract between the player and his agent guarantees a payment of P to the player and the agent receives the residual of

$$\pi(a, \theta) - P.$$

For example, the agent may guarantee $2 million in endorsement income while keeping the difference between the total endorsement income and $2 million for himself. Will this contract be efficient? Explain. If so, why do you think that we do not observe these contracts very often?
8. Why do you think that the vast majority of player–agent contracts are contingent fee contracts? Is it because they are efficient?
9. Suppose an agent can earn $50,000 per year in his next best occupation. If he does his job honestly, he will earn $250,000 per year for 30 years. If he steals from his clients, he can "earn" $550,000 a year until he gets caught. Once he is caught, he will no longer be a sports agent! If the appropriate discount rate is 10 percent, how long must he get away with stealing from his clients for such behavior to be "profitable"?
10. Marion Jones's former agent was suspended for two years by USAT&F. How would you calculate the economic value of this punishment?
11. In 2007, the MLS Players' Union put together some draft regulations for sports agents. Some agents objected to the proposed regulations.
    a. Would you expect an honest agent to want rules to prevent unscrupulous agents from engaging in improper behavior?
    b. Why might an honest agent object to some of the proposed regulations?
12. There are far more people who want to be sports agents than there are positions. What does this imply about the average compensation of successful sports agents?

RESEARCH QUESTIONS

1. Analyze the efforts of one of the following tours in authorizing or certifying sports agents:
    a. Association of Tennis Professionals
    b. Ladies Professional Golf Association
    c. Professional Bowlers Association

How does the association investigate the qualifications of would-be agents? How are complaints handled? What disciplinary measures are used?

2. Examine the nature, scope, and potential sanctions of state laws that regulate the conduct of sports agents in their dealings with amateur athletes.

REFERENCES AND FURTHER READING

Dohrman, George. "Confessions of an Agent," *Sports Illustrated*, Oct. 18, 2010.

Mason, D. S., and G. H. Duqette. (2005). "Globalisation and the Evolving Player-Agent Relationship in Professional Sport." *International Journal of Sport Management and Marketing*, 1, 93–109.

Meggyesy, D. (1992). "Agents and Agency: A Player's View." *Journal of Sport and Social Issues*, 16, 111–112.

Miller, L. K., L. W. Fielding, and B. G. Pitts. (1992). "A Uniform Code to Regulate Athlete Agents." *Journal of Sport and Social Issues*, 16, 93–102.

Parkin, Michael. (2010). *Microeconomics*, 9th ed. Boston: Addison-Wesley.

Perloff, Jeffrey M. (2007). *Microeconomics*, 4th ed. Boston: Addison-Wesley, at pp. 666–694.

Roberts, G. R. (1992). "Agents and Agency: A Sports Lawyer's View." *Journal of Sport and Social Issues*, 16, 116–120.

Sappington, David E. M. (1991), "Incentives in Principal-Agent Relationships." *The Journal of Economic Perspectives*, 5, 45–66.

Steinberg, L. (1992). "Agents and Agency: A Sports Agent's View." *Journal of Sport and Social Issues*, 16, 113–115.

24

Should an Athlete Turn Pro "Early"?

1 INTRODUCTION

Following the University of Florida's (UF's) 2006 National Collegiate Athletic Association (NCAA) Championship in men's basketball, Gator fans held their collective breath. Four of UF's starters could have declared for the National Basketball Association (NBA) draft even though they had college eligibility remaining. To the great relief of the Gator Nation, they all decided to return for another season. Whether this was a wise decision *ex post*, only time will tell,[1] but the relevant issue is whether it was wise *ex ante*; after all, we all have 20-20 hindsight.

Every year, there are hundreds of athletes with college eligibility remaining who must decide whether to stay in school – or even to go to school in the first place. Star athletes – and even some who are not stars – agonize over whether they should take a shot at fame and fortune in professional sports before they have exhausted their college eligibility. No doubt, this is a difficult decision with many risks whether the athlete stays or leaves. There are some prominent examples of those who made the wrong choice.

Ed Chester (whom we met in Chapter 3) was a star defensive tackle at UF. Although he could have gone to the National Football League (NFL) after his junior year, he returned to UF. Sadly, he suffered a career-ending knee injury during his senior season. Chester had wisely purchased an insurance policy against this unfortunate eventuality. Following unsuccessful efforts to rehab his knee, he collected $1 million but was probably still far worse off financially for having stayed an extra year. In contrast, Chris Weinke, a quarterback at Florida State University, stayed for his senior season and won the Heisman Trophy. Weinke was drafted by the Carolina Panthers in 2001 in the fourth round. His decision to stay probably paid off, but even that is not certain.[2]

[1] Florida did repeat as NCAA champions in 2007, so their return was sensible from that perspective. Those four players – Joakim Noah, Al Horford, Corey Brewer, and Taurean Green – were all drafted by the NBA in the 2007 draft.

[2] Weinke received a $500,000 signing bonus and the rookie minimum salary of $209,000 for the 2001 season. The following year, his salary was $750,000. In 2003, he earned $800,000 in

In this chapter, we examine the decision calculus that an athlete should follow to reach an optimal decision *ex ante.* This calculus takes account of the costs and benefits of postponing a professional career. Some specific examples highlight the complexity of this decision process. We also examine some constraints imposed by sports leagues and organizations on "underage" athletes.

2 TO STAY OR NOT TO STAY?

When an athlete has an opportunity to turn pro before his or her NCAA eligibility runs out, an important and complicated decision must be made.[3] The decision should be made in as systematic a fashion as possible. Whether it is conducted formally or informally, in making a decision on turning pro "early," the athlete must conduct a benefit–cost analysis. After adding up the expected benefits of leaving school and turning pro, the expected costs of not staying in school are deducted. If the expected benefits outweigh the expected costs, then the athlete should not stay in school and should turn pro early. This decision process can be complicated because there are many factors to consider, and uncertainties abound. Some of the costs and benefits are not readily quantifiable, which further complicates things.

As we describe this decision process, it is important to recognize that everyone does this when making any decision. How carefully one proceeds depends on how important the decision is. Moreover, the process may involve nothing more formal than making a list of the pros and cons and then weighing them in a subjective way. There are two complicating factors in the process. First, some of the costs and benefits are difficult to express in monetary terms. For example, Colorado's great running back, Chris Brown, decided to head for the NFL instead of returning to the University of Colorado for his senior year. Brown explained his decision: "It was a childhood dream of mine to play in the NFL. I think I've accomplished a lot at CU and it's time for me to try it at the next level." For Brown, one cost of returning to CU would have been postponing the realization of his dream. It is obviously difficult to quantify that cost.

The second complicating factor is the uncertainty that surrounds the costs and benefits. For anyone who is risk averse, uncertainty reduces the value of the benefits and increases the value of the costs. The probabilities of various outcomes usually are not known in an objective sense, and one must depend on subjective probabilities that may be hard to assess for a young athlete.

2.1 Potential Costs of Leaving School

There are numerous benefits of staying in college rather than leaving for the pros. The costs of turning pro early must include these foregone benefits. *Athletic development* is one potential benefit of additional college training and

salary plus $2.6 million in bonuses. He earned over $1 million in 2004 and again in 2005. In 2006, he had a base salary of $600,000 with bonuses totaling $1.4 million.

[3] For a brief example, see Karen Crouse, "More Seek Seasoning Before Moving to the Pros," *New York Times,* Sept. 4, 2010.

Table 24.1. Larry Fitzgerald's Performance

Season	Games	Receptions	Yards	Touchdowns
2004	16	58	780	8
2005	16	103	1,409	10
2006	13	69	946	6
2007	15	100	1,409	10
2008	16	96	1,431	12
2009	16	97	1,092	13
2010	16	90	1,137	6

experience. Some athletes remain in college because they feel that they are not quite ready for professional competition. Others reach the opposite conclusion. For example, Larry Fitzgerald, Pitt's fabulous wide receiver, decided to turn pro after only two seasons. He said that the main reason for going to college in the first place was to improve his opportunity to earn a good living. He decided that he had done that and was ready for the NFL. His performance bears out his optimistic assessment, as shown in Table 24.1.

Fitzgerald was slowed with a hamstring injury in 2006 but has been an uncommonly productive receiver for the Arizona Cardinals.

Educational development is more important to some athletes than to others. There is no doubt that completing an undergraduate degree is far more difficult if one leaves early. The demands on a professional athlete's time during the season preclude college course work. Even during the off-season, time is scarce, and going to school is tough. Emmitt Smith, the Dallas Cowboys running back, left the University of Florida a year early in 1990. He fulfilled his promise to his mother that he would finish his degree when he graduated in 1996. What is surprising is not that it took so long but that he persevered and finished at all. There have been other prominent athletes who have similarly persevered and managed to graduate after leaving early. Shaquille O'Neal, for example, earned his degree eight years after leaving LSU for fame and fortune in the NBA.[4]

A third potential benefit of staying in school is simply growing up a bit more. *Physical and emotional maturity* may be gained by staying in school. Physical size, strength, endurance, and skill may all be improved before trying to compete with mature professional athletes. This is clearly more important in some sports than in others. In men's and women's professional tennis, for example, teenagers often compete quite successfully. Spain's Rafael Nadal reached number two in the world tennis rankings in 2006 while still a teenager. Maria Sharapova won Wimbledon at 17. In women's golf, Michelle Wie became a serious contender in Ladies Professional Golf Association (LPGA) events at 15. While

[4] O'Neal is not the only one in the NBA. Dozens of NBA players continue to pursue their degrees. Jonathan Abrams, "N.B.A. Players Make Their Way Back to College," *New York Times*, Oct. 6, 2009.

she is clearly an exception, other teenagers – Paula Creamer and Megan Pressel, for example – have been successful on the LPGA tour as well. In professional football, offensive and defensive linemen must grow in size and strength to compete effectively and few leave before completing their junior year. Wide receivers, in contrast, do not require as much physical growth because their position demands speed, good hands, and the discipline to run precise pass routes. As a result, they are more apt to leave early, as did Larry Fitzgerald and Mike Williams of the University of Southern California.

A fourth benefit is enjoying college life. Part of the reason Peyton Manning and Matt Leinert did not leave early was that they enjoyed being in college and wanted to experience their senior year. The value of this is hard to quantify *ex ante*. For some athletes, the cost of this experience can be substantial. Matt Leinert is a prime example because his position in the 2006 NFL draft was much lower than it would have been in the 2005 draft. As a result, his initial signing bonus may have been as much as $10–$15 million less than it would have been had he left early. It would be interesting to know if he would have made the same decision had he known that it would cost so much.

2.2 Potential Benefits of Leaving School

The potential benefits of leaving school are primarily financial and therefore quantifiable to some extent. However, quantification is not necessarily easy and is inevitably imprecise.

Professional Earnings. Suppose that a player remains in college and plays for free instead of turning pro and earning a salary of, say, $3 million.[5] If the player has only, say, six seasons left in his career, he may never recover this foregone income. Playing one of his six remaining seasons for free could be costly indeed. One benefit of turning pro early is the salary that early entry brings.

Cost of an Injury. In most sports, everyone experiences some sort of injury. In noncontact sports, such as golf, tennis, and swimming, various injuries are common, although rarely career-ending. In tennis, there is a tremendous amount of wear and tear on ankles, knees, backs, shoulders, and elbows that may diminish skill levels without ending a career. In contact sports, of course, injuries are both common and potentially far more serious. There are career-ending injuries, such as the knee injury suffered by Ed Chester, which ended his career. Such extreme injuries are not common, but when they occur, the impact on professional earnings is obvious. More subtle, and far more prevalent, are the injuries that may permanently impair a player's performance. If a sprinter loses a few hundredths of a second, he or she goes from world class to noncompetitive. A cornerback who loses a step goes from being an NFL star to being a backup at a greatly reduced salary. These potential injuries can be avoided before the money flows by leaving early. In 2005, Michael Bush rushed for 1,143 yards at Louisville. He led the NCAA with 23 touchdowns. He decided to return

[5] Section 4 provides a simple model that shows why this decision could well be a sound one in purely financial terms.

for his senior year because he thought that he and Oklahoma's Adrian Peterson would be the top two running backs in the 2007 NFL draft. In Bush's first game in 2006, he suffered a severe fracture in his leg. He had multiple surgeries but was still drafted by the Oakland Raiders in the fourth round. He received a four-year contract with a $500,000 signing bonus. Returning to school does not always turn out for the best. Bush is not disabled, but he may always be impaired to some extent.

Changed Market Conditions. For a professional athlete, market conditions can change in several ways. For example, a promising defensive end may look at who else is in the draft and decide to turn pro while the competition at his position is not too severe. Waiting a year could mean enhanced competition from other defensive ends or from prominent players at other positions. In some sports, market conditions may change because the Collective Bargaining Agreement between the league and the players' union may change the landscape. A new agreement could change eligibility requirements, impose caps on rookie salaries or signing bonuses, or change some other important term.[6]

Poor Team Performance. Even stars cannot shine brightly if the team they are on is no good. An athlete may look at his or her returning teammates and decide that the team will be weak and therefore reduce the athlete's performance. One of Larry Fitzgerald's concerns about returning to Pitt was the view of many that Pitt would not have a potent passing attack the following year. This, of course, would have reduced Fitzgerald's opportunities to showcase his talent.

Risk of Reduced Personal Performance. Finally, there is always the possibility of reduced personal performance. This happened to Brett Nelson, a guard on Florida's basketball team. In the 2000–2001 season, Nelson had a great sophomore year, and many believed that he would be a high draft choice. Nelson elected to return for his junior year, but his performance dropped off considerably. He was no longer a hot prospect and had to return again for his senior year. Another season fell short of his sophomore performance. Nelson went undrafted in the 2003 NBA draft.

2.3 In Principle, the Choice Is Simple

To make the best choice *ex ante*, the athlete has to weigh the expected costs of leaving school early against the expected benefits. If those expected benefits exceed the expected costs, then he or she should turn pro rather than remain in school. If the opposite is the case, then the athlete should not turn pro. Making this choice is simple to say, but not so simple to do.

3 HOW EARLY ENTRANTS HAVE FARED IN THE NFL DRAFT

All NCAA players with remaining eligibility can get advice from the NFL regarding their draft status. The information is necessarily somewhat imprecise but generally reliable. Apparently, some players do not seek this advice or choose

[6] We examined unions and collective bargaining in Chapter 22.

Box 24.1 *Did Kwame Brown Make a Mistake?*

Kwame Brown was the real jewel in the University of Florida's recruiting class of 2000, but he was also an attractive NBA prospect. Had Brown spent a year or two at UF, he would have gained from the experience in several ways. His game would have improved, and he would have matured physically, emotionally, and academically. In the end, the lure of the NBA – the money and the glamour – was too strong, and Brown opted for the NBA.

The Washington Wizards made Brown the first high school player to be chosen as the first overall pick in the NBA draft. Brown has been a mediocre player in his first five years in the NBA. In 325 games, he averaged just 7.6 points per game, one assist per game, and 5.7 rebounds per game. During his career, he has displayed a bad attitude and a poor work ethic. One could make an argument that Brown would have been better off going to UF for some growing up, but consider the money that he has made so far:

Season	Salary
2001–2002	$3,697,440
2002–2003	$3,974,760
2003–2004	$4,252,080
2004–2005	$5,361,873
2005–2006	$7,500,000
2006–2007	$8,287,500
2007–2008	$9,075,000
2008–2009	$4,000,000
2009–2010	$4,100,000

Did Kwame Brown make a mistake by turning pro early? The answer is far from obvious.

to ignore the advice that they get because a large number of early entrants do not do so well in the draft.

Table 24.2 summarizes the results of the 2006, 2008, and 2010 NFL drafts. In 2006, there were 49 early entrants. Twelve of the 49 were selected in the first round, and another eight went in the second round. These players thought that they were ready for the NFL, and the NFL apparently agreed. Fourteen more players were picked in rounds three through seven. Interestingly, 15 of the 49 early entrants went undrafted. The undrafted players can sign free-agent contracts with any team that is interested, but they cannot return to college football. These players may have been better off if they had remained in college, but that is not a certainty. For some players, the NFL is beyond their reach because they just are not good enough. If so, finishing their education should be a priority.

Table 24.2. Early Entrants in the National Football League Draft, 2006–2008

Round	2006	2008	2010
1	12	11	17
2	8	11	8
3	4	9	7
4	5	3	6
5	1	2	3
6	1	1	5
7	3	2	0
Undrafted	15	14	7
Total	49	53	53

Source: nfl.com.

In 2008, there were 53 early entrants – a big increase over the prior year. Once again, a large number were apparently ready for the NFL – 11 went in the first round, another 11 went in the second round, and 9 more were taken in the third round. However, 14 would-be pros were not drafted. In 2010, there were 53 early entrants. Nearly half were drafted in the first two rounds: 17 in round 1 and another 8 in round 2. Another 21 players were drafted in later rounds, but 7 were not drafted and had to seek a free-agent contract.

The bottom line is clear. The exceptional players who are drafted early probably made a wise choice by leaving school early, but a substantial number go undrafted and rarely have successful careers. For them, an education would probably have been a far better choice.

4 A SIMPLE ECONOMIC MODEL

In life, there are many factors that will influence an athlete's decision to turn pro or postpone turning pro for another year. To keep this analysis simple, we will focus on the effect on lifetime earnings of turning professional at various points in time. We will abstract from other considerations but still find numerous complications for the athlete.

We start when the athlete graduates from high school, and we assume that the athlete will have a professional career of T years whenever he or she turns pro. Remaining in school and preparing for that pro career cause earnings to grow at a rate of r. This growth rate varies from year to year, but we will assume here that the benefit of staying in school declines over time. In other words, we assume that $r_1 > r_2 > r_3 > r_4$, where r_1 is the growth rate during year 1, r_2 is the incremental growth during year 2, and so one. Initially, we also assume that these growth rates are both positive and known to the athlete. As you can appreciate, these are pretty strong assumptions, but they allow us to solve the easy problem first.

If an athlete turns pro right out of high school, the present value of his or her lifetime professional earnings can be written as[7]

$$V = \sum_{t=1}^{T} S_t/(1+i)^t,$$

where S_t is the athlete's salary for season t, i is the appropriate discount rate, and T is the length of his career. This base value provides the foundation for his or her decision to turn pro.

If the athlete goes to college for one year, the lifetime earnings will grow to $(1 + r_1)V$, but the athlete will have to postpone receipt of that money for a year, and therefore the present value will be

$$V_1 = \frac{(1+r_1)V}{1+i}.$$

From a lifetime earnings perspective, waiting a year makes sense whenever $r_1 > i$ because V_1 will be larger than V in that case. For example, suppose that V is \$5 million, r_1 is 10 percent and i is 8 percent. In that event,

$$V_1 = (1.10/1.08)(\$5 \text{ million}).$$

which is \$5,092,593. If, however, r_1 were only 5 percent, then delaying a year would cost the athlete \$138,889 because

$$V_1 = (1.05/1.08)(\$5 \text{ million}).$$

is only \$4,861,111.

Consider the effect of waiting two years:

$$\begin{aligned} V_2 &= \frac{(1+r_2)V_1}{(1+i)} \\ &= \frac{(1+r_2)(1+r_1)V}{(1+i)^2}. \end{aligned}$$

If delaying for one season made sense, delaying a second year makes sense provided that $r_2 > i$. The same analysis holds for years 3 and 4. Because r_t declines over time, it is more likely that $r_t < i$ the closer t gets to 4.

Some players could not realistically turn pro immediately after high school but face a decision at a later point. Consider Rex Grossman, who played quarterback for the University of Florida and subsequently for the Chicago Bears. After a sensational sophomore year, Grossman nearly won the Heisman Trophy. During 2001, Grossman's statistics were impressive: 3,896 yards passing, 65.6 percent completions, 34 touchdown passes, and only 12 interceptions. Steve Spurrier, Grossman's coach, left, along with his "fun and gun" offense. Grossman considered leaving, too, but the new head coach, Ron Zook, persuaded Grossman to return for another year. Although Grossman threw 108 more passes in 2002 than he had thrown in 2001, the passing yards fell to 3,402. His completion percentage fell to 57.1 percent, touchdowns dropped to 22, and interceptions jumped to 17. Following this far less spectacular junior season,

[7] Recall that we learned how to calculate present values in Chapter 2. In this application, V is simply the present value of lifetime earnings as a professional athlete.

Grossman had a one-year decision to make: stay for his senior year or leave "early." Grossman then had to compare:

$$V_4 = \frac{(1 + r_4)\,V_3}{(1 + i)},$$

with V_3. Again, staying would have made sense if $r_4 > i$. Apparently, he did not think so because he left for the NFL and the Chicago Bears.

4.1 Decision Rules

Given this simple model, decisions are straightforward:

If $r > i$, delay (stay in school)
If $r < i$, turn pro

This simple model raises (at least) two questions. First, what influences the value of r? Second, is r necessarily positive? The determinants of r will include experience, maturity, injury, competition from rivals, team quality, coaching quality, and so on. The value of r will clearly vary from one player to the next, and therefore, each case must be analyzed separately.

The growth rate can be negative as a few examples will illustrate. Jeff Morrison – a great tennis player at Florida – won the NCAA singles title as a sophomore. He was offered lucrative opportunities for turning pro at that time. In addition to substantial financial incentives, the governing bodies in tennis – the United States Tennis Association (USTA) and the Association of Tennis Professionals (ATP) – would have provided easy access (known as "wild cards") into many professional tournaments. Morrison stayed at UF and played superbly during his junior year but failed to defend his NCAA singles title. Most of the financial incentives disappeared. For Morrison, r_3 was negative.

Golfer Matt Kuchar, who won the U.S. Amateur in 1997, provides another example. His U.S. Amateur victory gave him an automatic invitation to the Masters in 1998. He played well and received a lot of favorable attention from the TV commentators and the news media for his refreshing demeanor and excellent play. He also played very well in the U.S. Open that year. After flirting with the lead for a few days, he finished 14th – a remarkable performance for an amateur. Once again, he received considerable – and favorable – media attention. Had he turned professional, his endorsements would have been worth about $2 million per year. In addition, he would have enjoyed celebrity status – courtesy cars, free housing, and other assorted benefits. Instead of turning pro, however, Kuchar decided to remain at Georgia Tech. His performance on the golf course subsequently sagged, and his star power faded quickly. When he finally turned pro at the beginning of 2001, he received no special treatment and no money. His agent expected to work out endorsements that would generate $500,000 per year – not exactly chump change, but still $1.5 million shy of what it could have been.

This raises an interesting question: Did Matt Kuchar make a mistake? From a purely financial perspective, it may appear so, but Kuchar does not think so, as he enjoyed his years at Georgia Tech and earned his degree.

4.2 Uncertainty

In our simple model, we assumed that the athlete knew all of the relevant variables: T, S_t, r_t and i. To make the analysis a little more realistic, we should recognize that there is uncertainty surrounding some of these variables.

Career Length. The length of an athletic career varies widely depending on injuries and interest. Some careers are cut short by injuries. Bo Jackson provides a good example. After a great career at Auburn University, Jackson won the Heisman Trophy following the 1985 season. Unwilling to play football for Tampa Bay, Jackson began his pro career in baseball. Later, he played football for the Oakland Raiders while continuing to play baseball. His professional career was cut short by a hip injury. Andrea Jaeger, who was a great tennis player, provides another example. A child prodigy, Jaeger turned pro at 14 and quickly rose to a ranking of number 2 in the world. At 19, when most pro careers are just starting, she suffered a career-ending shoulder injury.

Some careers are cut short because the athlete loses interest or suffers "burnout." Robert Smith, for example, appears to have lost interest in playing football. After a great career at Ohio State, he was drafted in the first round by the Minnesota Vikings in 1993. His early years in the NFL were plagued by assorted ailments, but he had a breakout season in 1997 when he rushed for 1,266 yards. In 2000, Smith led the NFC in rushing with 1,521 yards. At the end of his best season, Smith retired from the NFL. He was only 28 years old.

For purposes of the model, we can use the average or expected value of T, $E[T]$, rather than T. In the NFL, that average is extremely short. The NFL Players Association (NFLPA) analyzed team rosters over a 10-year period, 1987–1996. The average NFL career was just 3.3 years. The shortest careers were experienced by running backs at 2.57 years, wide receivers at 2.81 years, and cornerbacks at 2.94 years. The main cause of these short careers is the number of big hits these players take.

Future Salaries. There is no doubt that the value of future salaries is uncertain when deciding whether to turn pro. An athlete cannot know for sure what he or she will earn even in the first year without actually turning pro. To find out S_1 in the NFL or NBA, the player must actually be drafted, but that requires declaring for the draft and thereby making the decision to turn pro or at least surrendering his or her eligibility. For decision-making purposes, then, the athlete must rely on the experience of others and make an estimate of S_t. Again, for purposes of the model, we can use expected values, $E[S_t]$, instead of S_t, which is uncertain.

Growth Rates. The growth rates, r_t, are also uncertain and may even be negative as we saw earlier. In this simple model, we can again substitute expected values.

In deciding whether to stay in school for his senior year, Larry Linebacker will then look at

$$E[V_4] = \frac{(1 + E[r])}{(1 + i)} E[V_3].$$

We should point out that these expectations may be decidedly imprecise because they involve subjective probabilities.

5 AGE LIMITS IN PROFESSIONAL SPORTS

Nearly every professional sports league and organization puts some age limits on eligibility to participate. To some extent, those age limits are paternalistic efforts to protect young athletes from injury, "burnout," and the stress of professional competition. To some extent, the age limits protect incumbent participants from competition provided by newcomers. For the major leagues, amateur sports provide a free minor league. Consider the NFL's rule that a player's eligibility cannot begin until he has been out of high school for at least three years. This means that the player will have three years in which to grow physically, emotionally, and athletically while in some college program. This benefits the NFL because college football programs provide a free training ground for the NFL. It also reduces risks for NFL teams because each athlete's potential will be somewhat easier to assess.

Box 24.2 ***The NCAA's No-Agent Rule****

The NCAA has a rule that permits a baseball player to consult an advisor about his professional prospects, but the rule, known as the "no-agent rule," does not permit the advisor (i.e., agent) to negotiate on behalf of the player. As a result, the player is left with no firm information regarding the terms of a professional contract should he have decided to turn pro rather than continue to play as an amateur.

Presumably, the rule is designed to protect the NCAA's goal of amateurism, but the lack of solid information makes room for speculation and guesswork. Some student-athletes may overestimate their market value and turn pro prematurely. In other cases, an athlete may underestimate his market value and fail to turn pro at the optimal time. The source of these errors in judgment is the lack of full information.

Some athletes have fought back when the NCAA punished them for violating the rule. For example, when Oklahoma State suspended Andy Oliver in 2008, it alleged that Oliver has allowed an advisor to negotiate a contract on his behalf with the Minnesota Twins in 2006. Oliver sued the NCAA and received a $750,000 settlement. Oliver is now devoting his full attention to his budding professional baseball career.

* Pat Borzi, "Settlement Sheds Light on N.C.A.A. No-Agent Rule," *New York Times*, July 23, 2010.

5.1 Age Limits Vary by Sport

Nothing can prevent an athlete from turning pro at any age, but eligibility rules imposed by sports leagues and organizations can certainly dampen the economic incentive to turn pro. The major sports leagues have age limits in their eligibility requirements for the entry draft. An aspiring NFL or NBA player will not have much incentive to turn pro early if he cannot participate in the draft

Table 24.3. Age Limits on Eligibility[1]

League/Organization	Minimum Age
National Football League	20–21
Major League Baseball	18
National Basketball Association	19
National Hockey League	18
Professional Golf Association Tour	18
Ladies Professional Golf Association	18
Association of Tennis Professionals	14
Women's Tennis Association	14
Soccer	None
USA Track and Field	19

1. Each league or organization sets its own eligibility requirements for full participation. Most of the entries in this table are subject to qualification and exceptions.

because he will not find employment. In this way, athletes are discouraged from turning pro prematurely. The various age limits are summarized in Table 24.3.

These age limits are not as simple as the table suggests because most are subject to qualifications or exceptions of one sort or another. As noted earlier, to be eligible for the NFL draft, an athlete must be three years removed from high school. Maurice Clarett challenged this age limit under the antitrust laws but lost his suit on appeal. Larry Fitzgerald went to the NFL after only two years at the University of Pittsburgh, but he was eligible for the draft because he went to a prep school after he finished high school.

For the NBA, players used to be eligible for the draft as soon as their high school class graduated. After some criticism, the NBA revised its age limit. Now, a player must be at least 19 years old during the year of the draft and must be one year removed from high school if he is from the United States. In addition, a player can only play in the NBA if he has been eligible for at least one draft. In the NHL, all players who are 18 or older are eligible for the Entry Draft. Underaged players, such as Ricky Rubio, can gain professional experience in Europe.[8] When those players become eligible, they can try their hand at the NBA. In the MLB, a player must be 21 years old, or have graduated from high school and not yet attended college, or a college player who has completed his junior or senior year, or any junior college player regardless of how many years of school he has completed. This complicated age rule really means that a player who is 18 is eligible unless he is a freshman or sophomore in college. This would appear to be a concession to the NCAA. Major League Soccer appears to have no age limit. Freddy Adu, clearly an exceptional case, began his professional soccer career at 14. In Adu's first three years, he was somewhat inconsistent, but the talent was

[8] For a glimpse at Rubio, see Pete Thamel, "Ricky Rubio at 19: The Prodigy Is Coming of Age," *New York Times*, Aug. 28, 2010.

Box 24.3 ***The Maurice Clarett Story***

For a variety of reasons, Maurice Clarett, a running back from Ohio State, wanted to enter the NFL draft before he met the age requirement. When he was denied access to the draft, he sued the NFL. In his bid to challenge the draft rule, Clarett gained the support of U.S. Rep. John Conyers, Jr., and the Rev. Jesse Jackson. Although Jesse Jackson would have preferred that Clarett stay in school, he pointed out that Clarett was old enough to fight in Iraq and old enough to pay taxes. "If he can answer the call, then let him work!" Conyers criticized the NFL's paternalistic explanation for its rule: Clarett "is challenging a draft rule which the league tells us is designed to help kids, but really seems to institutionalize a farm system that reaps huge financial rewards for the colleges and pros, and operates primarily at the expense of African-American teenagers." The Maurice Clarett story raises some interesting questions. First, does the NFL gain at the expense of players like Clarett who have to wait to play and, if so, how? Second, does the NFLPA gain and, if so, how?

Clarett's case against the NFL failed due to labor law considerations. The rule against drafting a player before he has been out of high school for three years was the product of a collective bargaining agreement. Both the players' union and the NFL management agreed to the rule. In effect, the union bargained away Clarett's rights to employment in the NFL until he met the age requirement. This raises some serious equity issues. Should the union be permitted to bargain on behalf of *future* employees? Is it *fair* that Clarett (and others like him) had no say or vote in this matter? Do current NFL players benefit from the rule at the expense of younger players?

There are several interesting economic issues as well. First, what is the economic purpose of the rule? Second, absent the rule, how many "underaged" players would actually be drafted or signed?

there. In the midst of his fourth year, a Portuguese team bought his contract for $2 million. Adu signed a new four-year deal calling for annual salaries in the $550,000 to $600,000 range. At 18, Adu was not yet in his prime.

Sports organizations and tours also have age limits for full membership. The professional tennis tours – Women's Tennis Association (WTA) and ATP – have similar age limits. For the WTA, players under 14 years old may not participate in any professional WTA tournament. There are restrictions that follow for players in each age group from 14 to 18 years. For the ATP, players under 14 years old may not participate in any ATP tournament. Players aged 14 to 16 years are subject to entry restrictions.

The professional golf tours also have similar age limits for men and women. Players must be 18 years old to gain membership into the LPGA. However, the LPGA's age limit cannot prevent an athlete from turning pro. Michelle Wie, for example, turned pro at 16. Although Wie did not win an LPGA event until she was 20, she earned millions in endorsements. The 2010 phenom Alexis Thompson turned pro at 15. A month later, she finished in a tie for 10th at the U.S. Women's Open and won $72,000. Thompson also enjoys endorsement income from Puma, Cobra, and Red Bull. She may request an exemption to the age limit. The LPGA's age limit prevented her from becoming a member of the LPGA at 16, which limited her opportunities to compete. Through sponsors' exemptions and other means, she was able to compete on a limited basis in 2006 and still earn $718,343 in prize money to go along with millions in endorsements. For the PGA Tour, PGA players must be 18 years old for membership. This age limit also applies to being able to enter the Q-school. Players under 18 can play in PGA Tour events if they receive a sponsor's exemption. They can also play if they qualify through local and regional qualifying events.

In USA Track and Field, athletes are classified on the basis of age: Youths (18 and under), Open (19–39), and Masters (40 and up). Athletes in each group have separate events.

Finally, World Cup Skateboarding has no apparent age limit. Nyjah Huston was a professional "street and park" skateboarder at 11 years old. Before Huston, Ryan Sheckler was the youngest, having turned pro at 13. According to Don Bostick, president of World Cup Skateboarding, if Huston can make it through his teen years, "he's the future of street and park skateboarding."[9]

6 LEAVING HIGH SCHOOL EARLY

In 1995, Kevin Garnett went straight from high school ball to the NBA. Kobe Bryant followed suit in the following year. Although NBA teams recognized the risks in drafting young prospects, some of them were willing to take those risks. In the 2001 draft, Kwame Brown was the number one overall pick, and three more high school players were selected among the next seven. Kwame Brown has not fared so well (see Box 24.1), but other top picks have had spectacular success – LeBron James (2003) and Dwight Howard (2004). Starting with the 2006 draft, the NBA ended this experiment by imposing an age limit on draft eligibility. This has had some sad consequences.

Jeremy Tyler's experience may be instructive. By the end of his junior year at San Diego High School, Tyler looked like a pro: 6′11″ and 258 pounds. He possessed awesome talent averaging more than 28 points a game. He was also impatient to begin his pro career and decided to skip his senior year and go to Europe to play pro basketball. Tyler reasoned that he would improve his game more by playing against pros in Europe than by playing against high school and college players.

Tyler decided to sign with Haifa in Israel. According to Haifa, Tyler brought an arrogance and poor work habits to Israel that turned off his teammates. He had problems with being on time and had other off-court problems. His game was largely unproductive: in 10 games, he averaged 7.0 minutes, 2.1 points, and

[9] Matt Higging, "Navigating a Pro Career and the Preteen Scene," *New York Times*, July 17, 2006.

1.9 rebounds. Frustrated with his lack of playing time, lonely, and struggling with a different culture, Tyler quit and returned home. This experiment failed. Tyler was not mature enough for the life of a professional basketball player on and off the court.

Box 24.4 *Age Limits? "What Age Limit?"**

In 1995, Kevin Garnett went straight from high school to the NBA. This started a parade of precocious players following suit: Kobe Bryant, LeBron James, and Dwight Howard, among others. In 2006, the NBA required players to be 19, which drove many players to attend college for a year before heading to the NBA. This was the path taken by Greg Oden and O. J. Mayo, for example.

Some young players have found another way to turn pro early: go overseas. In 2008, Brandon Jennings decided to skip college and play in Europe. Between his salary and endorsements, Jennings made about $1.2 million for the 2008–2009 season.

* Pete Thamel, "Basketball Prospect Leaves High School to Play in Europe," *New York Times*, April 23, 2009.

7 CONCLUDING REMARKS

What do we mean when we say that an athlete turned pro "early"? We usually mean that the athlete left college without using all of his or her eligibility. At times, we mean that the athlete is not even out of high school. On occasion, an athlete turns pro prematurely – that is, before he or she is really ready to compete in professional sports. If an athlete is prepared in terms of athletic ability, emotional maturity, and experience to play with the pros, then he or she is ready, and the decision is not "early."

In this chapter, we have examined the decision to turn pro in a general sense by weighing the pros and cons of turning pro. We have also presented a simple model that formalizes the analysis. Finally, we have examined the age limits imposed by some of the sports leagues and organizations that are designed (at least in part) to protect young athletes from making a hasty decision.

PROBLEMS AND QUESTIONS

1. Following his junior year, Peyton Manning decided to return to the University of Tennessee for his senior year rather than head to the NFL. Manning explained that he enjoyed being in college. No doubt he also hoped to beat the University of Florida and perhaps win the Heisman Trophy. He neither won the Florida game nor the Heisman Trophy. Was staying at UT a mistake?

2. Dee Webb, a cornerback at the University of Florida, left after his junior year. "Someone" told him that he would be drafted in the first or second round. Actually, he was picked in the *seventh* round of the NFL draft as the 236th overall pick. Would he have been better off to have stayed at UF for his senior year? How did his pro career turn out?

3. The NFL has a rule that prohibits a player from being eligible for the NFL draft before he has been out of high school for at least three years. Maurice Clarett, the great running back from Ohio State, had serious NCAA eligibility problems. He wanted to play in the NFL, but was foreclosed by the NFL age rule. Clarett filed a suit against the NFL alleging that the rule violates the antitrust laws and harmed competition. This suit raised several questions:

   a. How does such a rule harm competition?
      i. On the field?
      ii. In the market?

   b. Should the NFL be able to specify eligibility standards?

   c. Is the rule a form of age discrimination?

4. Matt Leinert, quarterback from the University of Southern California, won the Heisman Trophy in 2004 at the end of his junior year. He returned for his senior year and played very well. A teammate, Reggie Bush, won the Heisman Trophy in 2005. Almost a certain number one overall pick after his junior year, Leinert was drafted 10th overall in the 2006 draft. The cost of staying an additional year has been estimated at $10 to $15 million. Should he have stayed?

5. If an NCAA athlete turns pro while he or she has college eligibility remaining, is that "early"? What do we mean by "early"? Did Bill Gates leave college "early"?

6. LeBron James was a high school sensation who considered turning pro after his junior year in high school. When he finished high school, James was drafted number one by the Cleveland Cavaliers in the 2003 NBA draft. He signed a four-year rookie contract with the following salary schedule:

Season	Salary
2003–2004	$4.02 million
2004–2005	$4.32 million
2005–2006	$4.62 million
2006–2007	$5.80 million (check option)

   a. What do you have to know to value this contract on signing day?

   b. From a purely financial perspective, did James make the right *ex ante* choice by going straight from high school to the NBA?

   c. Have things worked out for James?

7. When Larry Linebacker was selected as a first-team All-American after a sensational junior year at Hometown U., he was considering whether to go into the NFL draft. A local sportswriter claimed that Larry "owed" Hometown U. another year.
   a. Do you think that Larry owed something to Hometown U.?
   b. Can you make an economic argument for both sides?
8. Based on the difference in endorsement income, how much did Matt Kuchar's delay in turning pro cost him?
9. Near the end of his junior year, the great running back, Touchdown Tony, announced that if he had a strong finish that season, he would inquire about his NFL draft status. Presumably, if he was projected to go high enough in the NFL draft, he would leave after that year even though he had another year of eligibility. Tony expressed some concerns about leaving "early": "It's fine to go for the money, but then you have to live with the fact that you left and you weren't ready, and you weren't mentally ready to have that kind of a lifestyle . . . I want to leave when I am ready to go."

   Write a short memo to Tony explaining how he can determine whether he should leave early or stay for his senior year.
10. When an athlete plays a college sport, is he or she playing for "free"?
11. Congressman Steve Cohen of Tennessee is "deeply concerned" about the NBA's age eligibility rule. He contends that it is a "restraint on a person's freedoms and liberties."
    a. Can the same be said for the age limits in all sports?
    b. Is this really a matter of congressional interest?
    c. How many people does it restrain each year?
    d. Can you name 10 other restraints on freedom that are age related?

RESEARCH QUESTIONS

1. Every year, most major football programs lose players "early" to the NFL. In 2003, the following players declared for the NFL draft early:

   Onterrio Smith, running back, Oregon
   George Wrighster, tight end, Oregon
   Ian Scott, defensive line, Florida
   Clint Mitchell, defensive line, Florida

   a. Were they drafted? If so, what number? What team?
   b. Did they sign free-agent contracts? If so, with whom?
   c. How have they done so far?
2. Analyze the success of the early entrants in the most recent NFL draft.
   a. How many were drafted in each round?

   b. How many of the undrafted players made a roster as a free agent?
   c. Were those selected in the first three rounds successful?
3. On May 15, 2010, the *New York Times* proclaimed that "At 17, Baseball's Next Sure Thing, Bryce Harper" would probably be the first pick in the 2010 amateur draft. What has happened to Bryce Harper since then?

REFERENCES AND FURTHER READING

Groothuis, P. A., J. R., Hill, and Perri, T. J. (2007). "Early Entry in the NBA Draft: The Influence of Unraveling, Human Capital, and Option Value." *Journal of Sports Economics*, 8, 223–243.

McCann, Michael A. (2004). "Illegal Defense: The Irrational Economics of Banning High School Players from the NBA Draft." *Virginia Sports and Entertainment Law Journal*, 3, 113–225.

McCann, Michael A., and Joesph S. Rosen. (2006). "Legality of Age Restrictions in the NBA and the NFL." *Case Western Reserve Law Review*, 56, 731–768.

Spurr, S. J. (2000). "The Baseball Draft: A Study of the Ability to Find Talent." *Journal of Sports Economics*, 1, 66–85.

Winfree, Jason A., and Christopher J. Molitor. (2007). "The Value of College: Drafted High School Baseball Players." *Journal of Sports Economics*, 8, 378–393.

25

Discrimination in Sports

1 INTRODUCTION

In a nutshell, discrimination is the unequal treatment of equals. As objectionable as it may be, discrimination to one extent or another is all around us. It can be based on race, gender, ethnicity, religion, socioeconomic status, age, and other differences among people that should not matter. In the world of sports, discrimination may result in reduced job opportunities, lower salaries, more demanding performance standards, and fewer endorsement opportunities for those in the disfavored groups. In this chapter, we examine some aspects of discrimination in sports. As we will see, some differences in outcomes are based on merit, but others may not be.

We start by examining the definition and concept of discrimination and then move on to an economic analysis of discrimination. Following that, we analyze racial and gender discrimination in sports. Title IX is examined and its impact on both men and women is noted.

2 DISCRIMINATION: CONCEPT AND IDENTIFICATION

The essence of discrimination, as previously stated, is the unequal treatment of equals. As in U.S. society generally, there has been discrimination in sports. In addition to racial and gender discrimination, there has been some religious and ethnic intolerance as well. The economic effects are primarily reduced opportunities and reduced rewards. For example, if there are two players of apparently equal ability being considered for a position – one African American and one White – racial discrimination may foreclose that opportunity to the African American athlete. If two coaching candidates – one male and one female – have approximately equal potential, the opportunity may be foreclosed to the female candidate as preference is given to the male candidate. Rewards for similar performance may also vary in discriminatory ways. For example, if female soccer coaches systematically earn less than male soccer coaches with similar records, this may be discrimination.

Discrimination is a manifestation of prejudices, which are negative attitudes toward a group that are not based on meaningful characteristics.

Prejudice is a preference for one group over another that is not based on objective criteria. When a baseball team cuts a player who cannot hit, that is not based on prejudice. All baseball teams prefer players who can hit because this is an important attribute for team success. Cutting a player on the basis of race, ethnicity, or religious belief, however, is a display of prejudice because these characteristics have nothing to do with wins and losses.

2.1 Identifying Discrimination

Using some basic statistics, we can provide a systematic way of identifying the presence of discrimination.[1] Suppose we collect performance data on all outfielders in Major League Baseball (MLB). Using these data and the salaries earned by those players, we can estimate a wage equation. In this equation, the salary earned by the athlete is a function of performance variables as well as other variables. By including a race variable, we can see if race matters. For example, we can use actual data to estimate the coefficients in the following equation:

$$w = ß_0 + ß_1 HR + ß_2 RBI + ß_3 SLG + ß_4 AVE + ß_5 B + ß_6 L,$$

where w is the player's salary, *HR* is home runs, *RBI* is runs batted in, *SLG* is slugging percentage, and *AVE* is batting average. *B* is one if the player is African American and zero otherwise, and L is one if the player is Latin and zero otherwise.

We are primarily interested in the signs of β_5 and β_6. If β_5 is negative and statistically significant, then we infer that, all else being equal, an African American outfielder will earn less than a White player with comparable performance statistics. Similar inferences may be drawn for Latin players if β_6 is negative and statistically significant. These inferences are only as good as the wage equation that was estimated. It could be that the wage equation missed something important.

Suppose we did find that β_5 was negative. An inference of discrimination may be unwarranted because this wage equation may be incomplete: after all, we have not included the on base percentage, stolen bases, walks, fielding percentage, and games played. Expanding the model may change the sign and/or statistical significance of β_5. The moral of this story is to be very careful before drawing an inference of discrimination.

3 ECONOMICS OF DISCRIMINATION

Owners, fans, coaches, and players may harbor deep-seated prejudices against minorities. To act on those prejudices and, in fact, discriminate against those minorities, costs must be incurred. In other words, if a person wants to "consume" discrimination, he or she must "pay" for it. In many cases, the payment is in the form of a forgone opportunity. For example, a coach who refuses to

[1] The subject of econometrics is beyond the scope of this book, but the basic idea is relatively straightforward.

play an African American quarterback who is better than the White quarterback who does play reduces the quality of the team. This results in fewer wins over the course of the season. For the coach, who is paid for performance, fewer wins means a forgone bonus, a lower salary, or even dismissal. He ultimately must pay if he satisfies his taste for discrimination. Not much in life is free, and that goes for discrimination as well.

A similar fate awaits an owner whose discrimination reduces the quality of his team by failing to hire a better qualified minority coach or failing to draft a better qualified minority player. To the extent that reduced team quality leads to fewer wins, the team's fans will be less happy, and this may result in lower ticket sales, reduced stadium revenues, and lower profits. Again, the prejudiced owner pays a price for indulging his preference for discrimination.

It goes without saying that the group being discriminated against is worse off as a result of that discrimination. In most instances, this will show up in lower salaries, reduced employment opportunities, or both. Minority athletes may have to accept less money than an equally qualified nonminority player to get a spot on the roster. Thus, salaries may be lower for those minority players with jobs. However, some minorities may simply not get a job at all or get one for which they are overqualified.

3.1 Impact of Discrimination

The impact of discrimination can be illustrated with a simple model. Suppose that the supply of White candidates for defensive coordinator positions in the National Football League (NFL) is precisely the same as the supply of African American defensive coordinator candidates. In this model, all of the candidates, African American and White, are equally qualified. This is shown as $S_W = S_B$ in Figure 25.1. The total supply of candidates is shown as $S = S_W + S_B$. The positive slopes of S_B, S_W, and S reflect the fact that the candidates have different reservation wages. Because there are 32 teams in the NFL, there are 32 positions to fill. Over some range of salaries, the demand for defensive coordinators is inelastic – every team "needs" one. At some point, some teams can be priced out of the market, but that point is not displayed in Figure 25.1.

Initially, we assume that there is no racial bias among the head coaches or among the owners. The equilibrium salary is determined by the equality of supply and demand. At the point where S equals D, all the positions are filled, and the salary is w_1 for everyone who is hired. Because there is no discrimination, the number of African American coordinators is equal to the number of White coordinators: $B_1 = W_1$. Everyone earns the same salary, and everyone who is willing to be a defensive coordinator for a salary of w_1 is employed.

Now let's suppose there is discrimination against the African American candidates. One way to introduce this into our model is by assuming that the head coach or the owner incurs a psychic cost when an African American candidate is hired. The actual supply of African American candidates is still the same as the supply of White candidates. For the prejudiced employer, however, we have to add this additional cost to the salary that must be paid. As a result, the *perceived* supply shifts from S_B to $S_B{}^*$. Now the total supply that determines the

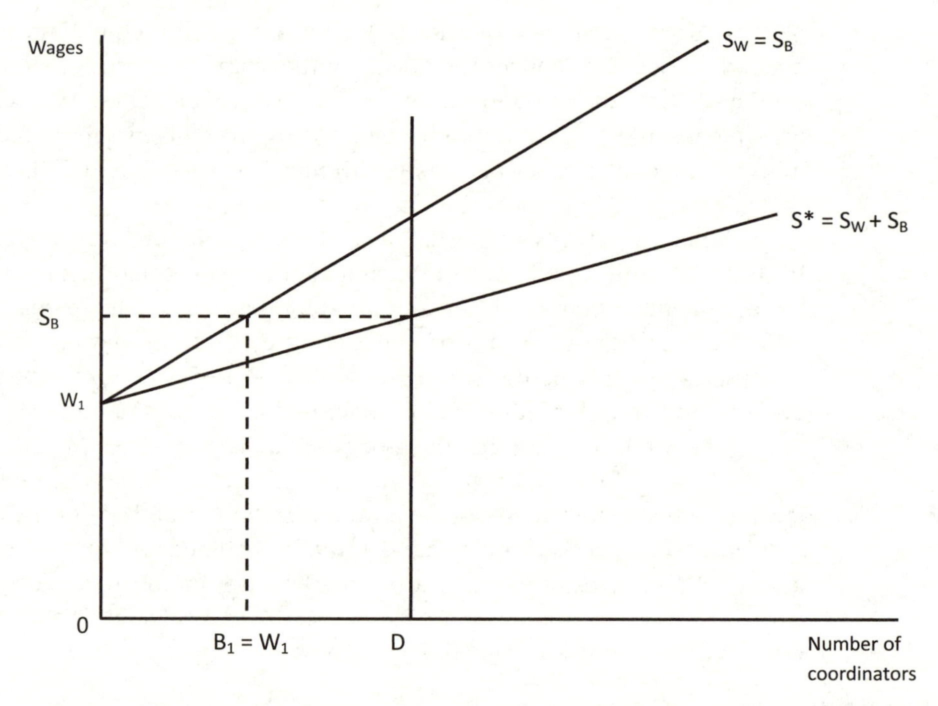

Figure 25.1. In the absence of discrimination, the number of White defensive coordinators equals the number of African American defensive coordinators, and their salaries are the same.

hiring decisions is $S^* = S_W + S_B{}^*$. As a result, the equilibrium occurs where S^* equals D. At that point, all of the positions are filled, but more than half of them are filled with White coaches. In this example, the number of African American defensive coordinators is B^*, whereas the number of White coordinators is W^*. Thus, one result of discrimination is that fewer African American candidates are hired even though we have assumed that African Americans and Whites are equally qualified. This is not the end of the story, however.

In equilibrium, the actual salary paid to the White coordinators is equal to the perceived salary paid to the African American coordinators. The actual salary received by the African American coordinators is given by the height of S_B, not the height of $S_B{}^*$. Consequently, the actual salary paid to African American coordinators, $w_B{}^*$ is less than $w_W{}^*$, which is the actual salary of the White coordinators. A second consequence of discrimination, then, is that salaries of the African American coordinators are lower than those of their equally qualified White counterparts. There is an interesting characteristic of this equilibrium: despite the prejudice, some African American defensive coordinators are hired. The reason for this is that the opportunity cost of indulging the preference for a white coordinator became large enough that some African American coaches become attractive candidates. In effect, the salary is depressed enough so that hiring a White coach is too expensive.

There is a third consequence of discrimination. The number of White coordinators rises with discrimination, but this is not free for the prejudiced owner. To increase the number of White coordinators, the salary must rise. In other

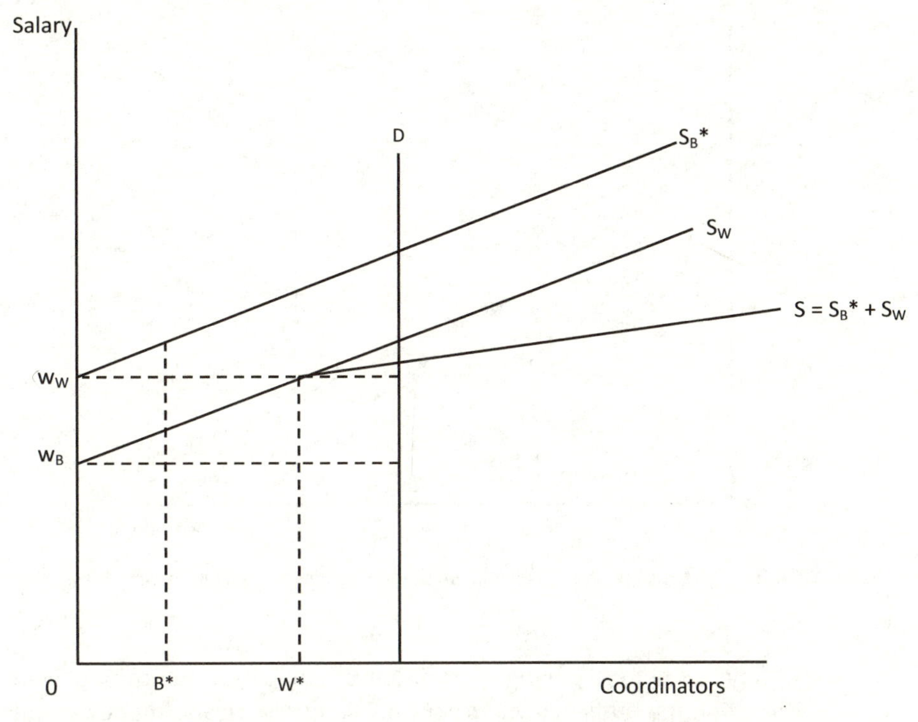

Figure 25.2. Discrimination leads to lower employment and lower salaries for minorities.

words, $w_w{}^*$ in Figure 25.2 exceeds w_1 in Figure 25.1. Thus, the White candidates benefit from discrimination in two ways: more of them are hired, and the salary is also higher.

There is a fourth consequence of discrimination. The teams who hire the White coordinators pay more than they would without discrimination. As we said before, indulging a taste for discrimination has a price. In this case, the price is the difference between w_1 and w_W. The teams that hire African American coordinators get a deal because the actual salary paid is lower than it would be without discrimination.

3.2 Competition and Discrimination

As we saw in Figure 25.2, discrimination leads to higher costs for the prejudiced employer. In equilibrium, White offensive coordinators have higher actual salaries than African American coordinators of equal ability. This, of course, reduces the profits of the teams practicing discrimination. Despite prejudice, some African American coordinators were hired, but at lower actual salaries. This salary differential shows up on the bottom line as higher profit even though the profits are not perceived to be higher because of the psychic cost of hiring an African American coordinator. For owners who are not prejudiced, the actual and the perceived profits are the same because there is no psychic cost associated with hiring an African American coordinator.

Over time, one would expect discrimination to diminish. Those potential owners who are not prejudiced will see a profitable opportunity in taking over

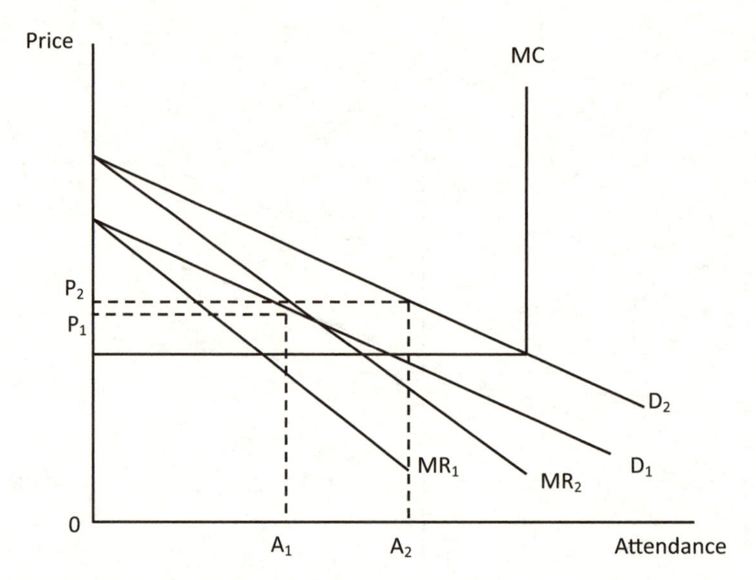

Figure 25.3. Fan prejudice can lead unbiased owners to avoid hiring minorities.

a franchise that is paying a premium by not hiring minority coaches. As the entry of unprejudiced owners continues, more African Americans will be hired, and therefore, their salaries will rise as we move along the supply curve. At the same time, fewer White coaches will be hired, and their salaries will fall as we slide down their supply curve. These pressures are blunted to some extent by monopoly power.

In the major professional sports leagues, there is ample competition on the field but considerable cooperation off the field. For the most part, the individual franchises have local monopoly power. Although football is only part of the overall entertainment industry, it is hard to believe that the Dallas Cowboys or the Washington Redskins do not have some market power. This power translates into positive economic profits and provides a cushion that does not force the teams to operate at minimum costs. Put differently, positive profits permit a team to absorb some inefficiency. It is still true, however, that a franchise with inefficiently high costs will be an attractive target for a more efficient operator.

3.3 Fan Discrimination

It is certainly possible for fans to be prejudiced. This means that they would be happier with a lower-quality team that has no minority players or coaches than with a better playing team that has some minority players or coaches. Alternatively, for two rosters of equal playing ability, the fans will pay more to watch the team that has no minorities than the team with minority players. In a sense, fans perceive a difference in quality between teams with and without minorities even when their performances are identical.

In the presence of fan prejudice, unbiased owners may not hire minorities as they strive to maximize profits. This is easy enough to see in Figure 25.3, where D_1 is the fan demand for an integrated team and D_2 is the fan demand for a

Table 25.1. Potential Role Discrimination in the National Football League, 2009

Position	White	African American
Quarterback	81%	16%
Wide Receiver	11%	87%

Source: 2010 Racial and Gender Report Card.

team without minorities. The marginal revenues corresponding to D_1 and D_2 are shown as MR_1 and MR_2, respectively. The marginal cost of fan attendance is shown as MC, which is horizontal until capacity is reached at A^*, and then it is vertical. To maximize profit, the team will want to operate where marginal cost equals marginal revenue and set prices accordingly. In Figure 25.3, we can see that the optimal attendance and price are A_1 and P_1 for D_1, and they are A_2 and P_2 for D_2. It is plain to see that both price and attendance will be higher for a nonintegrated team than for an integrated team. Thus, the operating profits will be higher without integration.

If the other costs are the same for integrated and nonintegrated teams, then overall profits will be higher for the nonintegrated team.

3.4 Role Discrimination

Role discrimination occurs when certain groups are systematically steered into specific positions. For example, if African American quarterbacks are steered into other positions – wide receiver, running back, defensive back – this may be the product of role discrimination. However, it may not be. In most high school football programs, the talent is pretty thin. Because quarterback is such an important position, the team's best athlete often plays quarterback. At the college level, there are fewer teams, and the talent pool gets deeper. Some former quarterbacks are converted to other positions where their skills can be used to better advantage. This is not role discrimination. Instead, it reflects the optimal allocation of scarce resources.

By the time players get to the NFL, the talent pool is so deep that the athletes must play where they have a comparative advantage. For the most part, the best athletes do not play quarterback in the NFL. The best athletes usually play other positions. This may look a bit like role discrimination, but we must be careful not to jump to conclusions.

In Table 25.1, the racial composition of quarterbacks and wide receivers in the NFL for the 2009 season is shown. In the NFL, some 29 percent of the players are White and 65 percent are African American. At quarterback, however, 81 percent are White, and only 16 percent are African American. At wide receiver, only 11 percent are White, and 87 percent are African American. These disparities could be the result of role discrimination at the college level but might also reflect the allocation of scarce athletic resources to their highest valued use.

Table 25.2. Racial Composition of Athletes, 2010

Race	Major League Baseball	National Football League	National Basketball Association
White	59.8%	30.0%	18.0%
African American	9.1%	67.0%	75.0%
Latino	28.3%	1.0%	3.0%
Asian	2.4%	2.0%	1.0%
Other	0.0%	<1.0%	1.0%

Source: 2010 Racial and Gender Report Card.

This is not to say that there is no role discrimination present. Rather, it is simply a reminder that economic forces push decision makers to allocate scarce resources efficiently.

4 RACIAL DISCRIMINATION

In college and professional sports, there is continuing concern regarding racial discrimination. Such discrimination could affect both players and coaches, but it is not limited to them. For example, there have been charges of racism in the United States Tennis Association (USTA). Following her dismissal as captain of the U.S. Fed Cup team, Zina Garrison alleged that the firing was due to racism. When Whitney Kraft, who is White, was named by the USTA to be the director of tennis at the National Tennis Center, Marvin Dent, who is African American, objected that the appointment was part of a pattern of racism at the USTA. There was even some concern that the selection of chair umpires lacked transparency.

4.1 Racial Discrimination: Players

Before the Brooklyn (now Los Angeles) Dodgers hired Jackie Robinson in the late 1940s, there were racial barriers in MLB, the NFL, and the National Basketball Association (NBA). Once MLB began integrating the "National Pastime," the NFL and the NBA were not far behind. At first, things moved slowly, but the teams that were more aggressive in hiring African American players were more successful. As great players such as Roy Campanella, Don Newcombe, and Joe Black followed Jackie Robinson to Brooklyn, the Dodgers began to dominate the National League. This was not lost on other teams, and racial discrimination in hiring began to disappear. Currently, there does not appear to be any racial bias in hiring players. As Table 25.2 reveals, there are many African American athletes in MLB, the NFL, and the NBA.

Although hiring discrimination may have ended, there is always the possibility that African American players are not paid as well as equally qualified White players. In other words, it is possible that if a White player and an African American player had equal performance statistics, the White player would be

Table 25.3. Racial Composition of Head Coaches, 2010

Race	Major League Baseball	National Football League	National Basketball Association
White	68%	81%	70%
African American	14%	19%	27%
Latino	17%	0%	3%
Asian	<1%	0%	0%

Source: 2010 Racial and Gender Report Card.

paid a higher salary. There is scant evidence of this. Several researchers have used performance data and salary data to estimate wage equations in professional sports. In general, they do not find any evidence of racial bias.

4.2 Racial Discrimination: Coaches

The major concern with racial discrimination in the coaching ranks involves foreclosed opportunities. There have been repeated expressions of concern about head coaching jobs in the National Collegiate Athletic Association (NCAA) as well as in the professional ranks. The numbers do not seem to add up.

Consider the three major sports leagues in the United States that have significant numbers of non-White athletes: MLB, the NFL, and the NBA. Table 25.2 shows the racial composition of the athletes. In MLB, for example, 59.8 percent of the players are White, 9.1 percent are African American, and 24.3 percent are Latino. Now let's examine the coaching ranks.

We can compare the racial composition of the athletes to that of the managers and coaches shown in Table 25.3. White managers account for 68 percent of the total, African Americans accounted for 14.0 percent, and Latinos had 17 percent of the jobs. Thus, Whites appear to be overrepresented, Latinos appear to be underrepresented, and African Americans appear to be just about right in baseball.

The differences are more pronounced in the NFL in which only 30 percent of the players are White, but 81 percent of the head coaches are White. In contrast, 67 percent of the players are African American, but only 19 percent of the head coaches are African American. Things are no more balanced in the NBA. Whereas 18 percent of the players are White, 70 percent of the coaches are White. As for African Americans, 77 percent of the players and only 27 percent of the head coaches are African American.

The disparity between the racial composition of the players and the racial composition of the coaches certainly suggests discrimination. It may or may not be racial (or ethnic) discrimination because players of major league caliber may or may not be the best coaches – the skills and abilities necessary for success are quite different. Some of the most successful head coaches in the NFL were not great players – Chuck Noll, Bill Belichick, Marv Levy, Joe Gibbs,

Bill Walsh. Nonetheless, it is somewhat remarkable that there is a substantial disparity between the racial composition of the players and that of the coaches.

At the college level, there is similar underrepresentation for head coaches in basketball and football. In 2007–2008, nearly 94 percent of the Division I head football coaches were White, whereas only 5.1 percent were African American. Things were somewhat better in basketball in which about 22.9 percent of the head coaches were African American, and about 75.8 percent were White. This imbalance suggests the presence of discrimination in the hiring process, but it does not prove it.

5 GENDER DISCRIMINATION

In sports, men and women are often treated differently. Whether this is discriminatory or not depends on whether one would judge men and women to be equals in that particular set of circumstances. This is difficult to say because of the many sources of discrimination. For example, men in the NBA earn far more than women in the WNBA. At one level, this disparity can be explained by the difference in popularity – NBA basketball is far more popular than the WNBA game. But is this outcome the product of fan discrimination? If so, the pay gap is discriminatory. Alternatively, the difference in popularity between the two games may be because the NBA game is faster, more physical, and more athletic. In other words, the games are different, and basketball fans prefer the game that the men play. If so, that is no more discriminatory than my preference for chocolate ice cream over vanilla ice cream. The message here is that the preference for men's basketball over women's basketball may be based on very real differences in the two games. Much the same can be said for figure skating, where the women are more popular than the men. In this case, the grace and beauty of women's figure skating seem to be preferred to the more athletic men's figure skating. Once again, this would not appear to be based on gender discrimination.

5.1 Men and Women in Professional Golf

In professional golf, the amount of money that golfers win in tournaments depends on how well they play relative to their competitors. Given the size of the total purse, winnings are based entirely on relative performance – the golfer with the lowest score wins more than the golfer with the next lowest score, and so on down to the last-place finisher. Winnings cannot be discriminatory because everyone plays by precisely the same rules of the game, and the payout formula is determined in advance of knowing who finished where in the scoring. In a PGA Tour event, the winner receives 18 percent of the total purse no matter who wins. If the purse is $5 million, whoever wins – be it Angel Cabrera, Tiger Woods, Phil Mickelson, or Vijay Singh – receives $900,000 for the victory. There is a substantial difference between the purses on the PGA Tour and those on the Ladies Professional Golf Association (LPGA) Tour. In Table 25.5, the difference is illustrated with a comparison of the total purses in the so-called major championships for 2010. For the United States Golf Association (USGA)

Table 25.4. Racial Composition of Division I Head Coaches (Men's Teams), 2007–2008

Race	Basketball	Football
White	75.8%	94.0%
African American	22.9%	5.1%
Latino	0.7%	0.5%
Asian	0.0%	0.0%
Native American	0.3%	0.0%

Source: 2009 Racial and Gender Report Card.

tournaments, the men were playing for $7.5 million, whereas the women were playing for only $3.25 million. In Great Britain, the men were playing for $7.3 million, whereas the women were playing for only $2.5 million. Similar disparities can be seen in the total purses for weekly events during the season.

The results of this disparity in total purses can be seen in the relative winnings of the top 15 money earners on the PGA Tour and the LPGA Tour during 2010. Table 25.6 shows that Matt Kuchar at number 1 won about three times the amount that Na Yeon Choi won. For those ranked 2 through 15, the same trend is true. These differences are purely a matter of the differences in the total purses.

Is this disparity the product of discrimination? If so, by whom? The answers are not obvious. The size of the purses is determined by attendance, TV coverage and ratings, and sponsorships. Women's golf generates lower attendance, lower TV ratings, and less generous sponsorships, and therefore, the purses are smaller on the LPGA Tour. Is the lower popularity of women's golf due to discrimination of some sort? Are golf fans discriminating against women? Television coverage of women's golf is largely relegated to cable. Are the TV networks discriminating against women's golf, or are women golfers treated unequally because they are unequal?

A case can be made that women golfers do not produce the same quality performance on the course as the men do. As a result, fans prefer men's golf to women's golf as a form of entertainment because the men play better. Stephen

Table 25.5. Purses in Golf's Majors (in millions): 2011 for Professional Golf Association (PGA), 2010 for Ladies PGA (LPGA)

Men		Women	
Masters	$7.5	Kraft Nabisco	$2.0
U.S. Open	7.5	U.S. Women's Open	3.25
British Open	7.3	Women's British Open	2.5
PGA Championship	7.5	McDonald's LPGA	2.25

Source: PGATour.com and LPGA.com.

Table 25.6. Top Money Winners: Professional Golf Association (PGA) Tour Versus Ladies PGA (LPGA) 2010

PGA Tour Money Leaders			LPGA Tour Money Leaders		
Rank	Player	Earnings	Rank	Player	Earnings
1	Matt Kuchar	$4,910,977	1	Na Yeon Choi	$1,871,166
2	Jim Furyk	$4,809,611	2	Jiyai Shin	$1,783,127
3	Ernie Els	$4,558,861	3	Cristie Kerr	$1,601,552
4	Dustin Johnson	$4473,122	4	Yani Tseng	$1,573,529
5	Steve Strickler	$4,190,235	5	Suzann Pettersen	$1,557,175
6	Phil Mickelson	$3,821,733	6	Ai Miyazato	$1,457,384
7	Luke Donald	$3,665,234	7	In-Kyung Kim	$1,210,068
8	Paul Casey	$3,613,194	8	Song-Hee Kim	$1,208,698
9	Justin Rose	$3,603,331	9	Michelle Wie	$888,017
10	Hunter Mahan	$3,574,550	10	Paula Creamer	$883,870
11	Tim Clark	$3,530,002	11	Inbee Park	$825,477
12	Jeff Overton	$3,456,356	12	Katherine Hull	$793,413
13	Bo Van Pelt	$3,336,258	13	Morgan Pressel	$767,455
14	Retief Goosen	$3,218,089	14	Amy Yang	$765,930
15	Bubba Watson	$3,198,998	15	Brittany Lincicome	$663,808

Source: ESPN.com and PGATour.com.

Shmanske examined the issue and found systematic differences between men and women in their quality of play.[2]

Shmanske used data from 1998 that were contained in the media guides published by the PGA Tour and the LPGA. He found that the men outperformed the women on every dimension. On average,

men played longer courses,
men played more rounds per tournament,
men played more tournaments per year,
men drove the ball farther,
men drove the ball straighter,
men hit more greens in regulation,
men had fewer putts per round,
men had more sand saves, and
men had lower average scores.

These differences in performance do not necessarily mean that men's golf is more entertaining and therefore should command higher earnings, but the data suggest that the differences in earnings do reflect these differences in skill levels. Shmanske's econometric analysis of earnings adjusts for the difference

[2] Stephen Shmanske (2000), "Gender, Skill, and Earnings in Professional Golf," *Journal of Sports Economics*, 1, 385–400.

in skill. His analysis indicates that there is no gender bias against women in professional golf.

Box 25.1 *Gender Bias at the USGA?*

A golfer on the Nationwide Tour, Brian Kontak, submitted an entry form for the 2003 U.S. Women's Open. His application was rejected because he was not "female at birth," which is an eligibility requirement for all participants. Kontak made noises about suing the USGA on the basis of gender discrimination.

The USGA defended its policy of limiting the field to golfers who were female at birth as being integral to preserving the competitive balance of the Women's Open. The USGA argued that admitting men would unalterably diminish the women's tournament.

This dispute seems somewhat silly, but it does raise some serious questions if public policies regarding discrimination are not handled sensibly. First, should the USGA have the right to admit only women to play in the U.S. *Women's* Open? Put differently, should a man have a "right" to play in women's tournaments? Second, what would happen to LPGA events if men could force their way into the field? Third, could some adult insist on being allowed to play in junior events on the basis of age equity?

5.2 Men and Women in Professional Tennis

There has been some disparity in the prize money available to men and women on the professional tennis tours but only at the very top. Table 25.7 shows the top 15 money winners on the Association of Tennis Professionals (men) and the top 15 on the Women's Tennis Association (women) tour in 2010. For the top three, the men won more than $21 million, whereas the top three women won only around $13 million. Below that, however, the prize money won is fairly equal. We might infer from this that men's tennis and women's tennis are fairly close in popularity among tennis fans.

The most prestigious and most lucrative professional tennis tournaments are the Grand Slam tournaments: the Australian Open, the French Open, Wimbledon, and the U.S. Open. These tournaments are played on different surfaces – clay courts at the French Open, grass courts at Wimbledon, and hard courts at the Australian and U.S. Opens. Before 1973, the men's prize money was higher than the women's prize money at these Grand Slam events. Starting in 1973, the prize money for men and women was equal at the U.S. Open but not at the other three. In an absolute sense, the women were doing fine, that is to say, they were making a lot of money. In 2000, for example, the first-place prize money at the Australian Open was $418,000, which is a tidy sum, but it amounted to only 95 percent of the men's prize money at $440,000. At the French Open, the women's prize was $597,000, which was again 95 percent of the men's prize of $628,000. At Wimbledon, the women's prize was only 90 percent of the men's prize: $668,500 as opposed to $740,125. The pay gap irritated the women, and

Table 25.7. Top Money Winners: Association of Tennis Professionals (ATP) Versus Women's Tennis Association (WTA), 2010

ATP Money Leaders			WTA Money Leaders		
Rank	**Player**	**Earnings**	**Rank**	**Player**	**Earnings**
1	Rafael Nadal	$10,171,998	1	Kim Clijsters	$5,035,060
2	Roger Federer	$7,698,289	2	Caroline Wozniacki	$4,466,488
3	Novak Djokovic	$4,278,857	3	Serena Williams	$4,266,011
4	Andy Murray	$4,046,805	4	Vera Zvonareva	$3,444,641
5	Robin Soderling	$3,731,527	5	Venus Williams	$2,614,782
6	David Ferrer	$2,593,353	6	Francesca Schiavone	$2,456,634
7	Tomas Berdych	$2,509,122	7	Jelena Jonkovic	$2,136,991
8	Jurgen Melzer	$2,037,084	8	Samantha Stosur	$2,090,340
9	Fernando Verdasco	$1,971,365	9	Elena Dementieva	$1,896,690
10	Andy Roddick	$1,917,612	10	Victoria Azarenka	$1,652,028
11	Mikhail Youzhny	$1,900,349	11	Justine Henin	$1,401,960
12	Gael Monfils	$1,303,546	12	Flavia Pennetta	$1,357,078
13	Sam Querrey	$1,252,096	13	Svetlana Kuznetsova	$1,345,564
14	Ivan Ljubicic	$1,251,609	14	Aravane Rezai	$1,282,538
15	Nicolas Almagro	$1,205,538	15	Na Li	$1,158,898

Source: Tennis.com.

they voiced their displeasure. Some players even talked about a boycott, but no boycott ever materialized because the sacrifice of a major payday (even with the gap) was too large for the principle of equality.

Through constant pressure and lobbying, all four Grand Slam tournaments now pay equal prize money for men and women. Most men applaud the change, but some resent it. They feel that the talent is deeper in men's tennis. They also point out the women's matches are best of three while theirs are best of five.

6 TITLE IX AND GENDER DISCRIMINATION

In 1972, Congress passed the Educational Amendments to the Civil Rights Act. As part of these amendments, Title IX dealt with gender equality. Its plain language seems eminently reasonable:

No person in the United States shall, on the basis of sex, be excluded from participation in, be denied the benefits of, or be subjected to discrimination under any educational program or activity receiving federal financial assistance.

Although we tend to think of Title IX in terms of athletics, it is clear that it applies to all educational programs. Women have experienced great benefits from Title IX in programs outside sports. The law schools and medical schools, for example, had almost no women in their classes when Title IX was passed. Now, at many schools, women now outnumber the men. Although there were plenty of growing pains, women now appear to be enjoying equal opportunity in most educational programs.

The economic approach to curtailing discrimination can be seen in Title IX. The statute does not preach about the inherent unfairness of discrimination on the basis of gender. It does not implore universities to end gender discrimination because that is the right thing to do. Instead, it warns that gender discrimination is not permitted in any program or activity at a university that receives federal funding. Because all major universities rely heavily on federal funding, the threat of losing that funding got their attention and gender discrimination began to fade.

Box 25.2 *Equal Rights Gone Awry**

The Massachusetts Supreme Court ruled that the state's constitutional amendment guaranteeing equal rights to all citizens applied to sports. One (presumably) unintended consequence of that ruling is that boys cannot be barred from participating in girls' high school sports.

This has caused some controversy. In 2001, the Mohawk Trail Regional High girls' field hockey team made the state semifinals on the broad shoulders of Ryan Sherburne, 6′5″ and 205 pounds. Being made to wear the same plaid skirt that his teammates wore, Sherburne no doubt dominated many a game because he was bigger and faster than the rival players, who were all girls. Sadly, Sherburne was not the only boy playing on a girls' team.

Consider the possibilities for other sports. How many girls would get to play basketball, softball, tennis, and golf if the boys played on the same team? What would happen to the girls' records in track and field and cross country if the boys competed in the girls' events?

Is there no room for reason in Massachusetts?

* Rick Reilly, "Not Your Average Skirt Chaser," *Sports Illustrated*, Nov. 26, 2001, at p. 100.

6.1 Compliance with Title IX

It is obvious that no one could have expected equal participation of men and women to result immediately at NCAA schools. Coaches would have had to be hired, schedules put together, athletes identified and recruited. Because there were only 295,000 girls participating in high school sports, it was clear that building up women's sports at NCAA institutions would take some time. No matter how good a school's intentions, complete equality was not feasible in the short run. Everyone recognized that it would take some time, but how much time?

Left to their own devices before Title IX, the NCAA member institutions had an array of men's and women's programs with no semblance of equality. Presumably, this is what they wanted to have. Title IX provided an incentive for them to want something different, but only if there was some enforcement of Title IX. This posed a real public policy problem because the law does not require equal outcomes. Instead, it requires equal opportunity. Under Title IX, gender discrimination is impermissible, but all schools will claim there is no discrimination. Each school can argue that it is doing its best to cope with Title IX's mandate in an orderly, expeditious fashion. The public policy problem is how best to judge the sincerity of those efforts.

6.2 Congressional Compliance Guidelines

In evaluating a school's compliance efforts, Congress has offered three measures. A school can be deemed in compliance if it satisfies any one of the three.

1. Proportionality Test. A university does not violate Title IX if the proportion of female athletes is equal to the proportion of females in the student body. For example, suppose there were 30,000 students enrolled in a university: 16,500 were women and 13,500 were men. In that case, women would make up 55 percent of the student body. To be in compliance with Title IX under the proportionality test, it is not necessary for precisely 55 percent of all athletes to be women. There is a tolerance of plus or minus 5 percent. Thus, the university would be in compliance if 50 to 60 percent of all athletes were women. This is a demanding standard for any school with men's football because football requires a large number of athletes. There are almost no major athletic programs that satisfy this test.

Approximate gender equity in the "plus-or-minus 5 percent" standard is under some attack. At the University of California – Davis, 50 percent of the athletes were women in 2007, but some 56 percent of the student body were women. A group of students started a class action suit in federal court. As part of a settlement, Davis agreed to get the proportion of female athletes to within 1.5 percentage points of the proportion of women in the student body. This effort may involve trimming the rosters in some men's nonrevenue sports, such as wrestling and gymnastics. Given the realities of athletic budgets, this may be unavoidable.

The Davis settlement would not be binding on any other university, but it suggests a benchmark that is stricter than the current 5 percent standard. If the federal courts were to adopt such a standard for compliance, more male athletes will lose the opportunity to compete.

Title IX is not limited to colleges and universities. It applies to high schools as well. In 2010, many high schools have not passed the proportionality test. The National Women's Law Center filed a complaint alleging that a dozen school districts have failed the proportionality test under Title IX.[3] These school districts included New York, Chicago, and Houston. The complaint, which was based on 2006 data submitted by the school districts, alleges that the gender gap in participation rates is about 10 percent on average but much higher in

[3] Katie Thomas, "Women's Group Cites 12 Districts in Title IX Complaint," *New York Times*, Nov. 10, 2010.

Box 25.3 *Draconian Measures at James Madison**

In 2006, James Madison University took a hard look at its athletic program and did not like what it saw. Based on the proportionality test, James Madison was not complying with Title IX. At the time, 61 percent of the 17,000 James Madison students were women, but only 50 percent of the athletes were women. The president of the university did not believe that it was setting a good example for his students by blatantly violating a federal law. He was determined to get the university into compliance.

Instead of adding women's teams and thereby adjusting the proportions, James Madison slashed men's and women's teams. The men lost seven teams: swimming, cross country, indoor and outdoor track, gymnastics, fencing, and archery. The women lost three teams: gymnastics, fencing, and archery. When the dust settled, three full-time coaches and eight part-time coaches had lost their jobs. In addition, 144 athletes no longer had a varsity team. The number of teams dropped from 28 to 18 – 12 women's teams and 6 men's teams were left. But James Madison was in compliance – 61 percent of the athletes were women. The move was abrupt and caused some serious dislocations, which resulted in some angry students – both men and women.

* Bill Pennington, "At James Madison, Title IX Is Satisfied, but the Students Are Not," *New York Times*, Oct. 7, 2006.

some instances. These school districts will have to get into compliance or risk all federal funding.

2. Program Expansion Test. Even if a school fails to meet the proportionality test, it can be in compliance if it is making progress in providing equal opportunities for women. One way to demonstrate progress is expanding women's programs over time. As a university adds women's soccer, softball, and lacrosse, for example, the number of female athletes will rise, and the proportion of female athletes will also rise. If a university does this too quickly, it will have to eliminate some men's programs because budget constraints. If it adds women's programs gradually, it may be able to do so without cutting any men's programs. It is a tough call because adding women's programs slowly delays the day of equal opportunity.

3. Interest Accommodation Test. If a university has not met the proportionality test and is not adding any new women's programs, there is a third way to satisfy Title IX. If a school's existing programs accommodate the interests of women in participating in athletics, then the school is in compliance. This makes sense because Title IX is not supposed to demand equal *participation*; it is supposed to ensure equal *opportunity* to participate. If all the women who want to participate are already doing so, then women would seem to have equal opportunity, but this can be seriously misleading. The male athletes at universities with major sports programs are there because they were recruited. If there is no women's golf team, for example, there may not be any NCAA-caliber women

Box 25.4 *Title IX and College Wrestling*

The Department of Education has adopted a proportionality test for Title IX compliance. The result has been the elimination of some men's sports and the addition of some women's sports. At many colleges and universities, men's wrestling has been a casualty of Title IX and been eliminated. Wrestling has been singled out because a wrestling team has a big roster, and therefore, elimination greatly improves the proportionality measure.

A group of college wrestling coaches filed suit alleging that the proportionality test for compliance amounted to a quota. As a result, Title IX, which is supposed to prohibit discrimination, has been turned into an affirmative action policy. Accordingly, the proportionality rule should be struck down as being inconsistent with other limitations on affirmative action.

The district court ruled that the coaches did not have *standing* to challenge Title IX regulations. This meant that the coaches were not proper parties and therefore had no legal recourse. The coaches lacked standing because the proportionality test had a direct impact on the wrestlers rather than on the coaches.

golfers at that school. They would have gone elsewhere. It would be true that no interested golfer is unaccommodated, but that is because there is no golf program for women and therefore, no women golfers.

None of these three tests is ideal, but they all have their uses. The proportionality test has an appearance of objectivity. It is possible, of course, for discrimination to persist in many ways that will not appear in a simple head count. Even if the proportionality test were satisfied, women's teams could suffer discrimination in housing quality, travel budgets, coaching quality, academic support, and so on. As for the program expansion test, progress can be steady at a reasonably rapid pace or it can be glacial. How fast is fast enough is obviously a difficult issue, and objective standards are hard to devise. It is clear, however, that a school may show some progress while dragging its feet on the road to gender equality. Finally, the accommodation of interest is ripe for abuse. It is also unclear just how we should think about this. Suppose State U. has 15,000 women and 10 of them want to participate in varsity basketball. Should State U. have to hire a coach and set a schedule to accommodate the interests of 10 students? Is there a continuing obligation after those 10 students graduate?

6.3 Impact on Coaching Opportunities

Over time, universities have added women's teams in an effort to comply with Title IX. As this has happened, many of the new coaching positions have gone to men rather than women. In 1971, fewer than 10 percent of women's teams were coached by men. That soon changed, however. By 1978, 42 percent of women's teams were coached by men. That percentage rose to 46 percent by 1984, to

Table 25.8. Gender of Head Coaches, Division I, 2007–2008

	Men	Women
Men's Teams	97.2%	2.8%
Women's Teams	59.7%	40.3%

Source: 2009 Racial and Gender Report Card.

53 percent by 1990, to 54 percent by 2000, to 56 percent by 2002, and to 60.4 percent by 2006. Initially, this shift may have been explained by the absence of women who were both qualified and interested in coaching. Because there were few women' teams and not much female participation, there would necessarily be a shortage of female coaches. Some 30 to 35 years later, however, that explanation no longer makes any sense.

In Table 25.8, we see that men coached 59.7 percent of the women's teams in Division I during 2007–2008. The remaining 40.3 percent were coached by women. For the men's teams, 97.2 percent were coached by men and only 2.8 percent were coached by women. This is obviously a large difference. It is an open question whether this pattern reflects discrimination by the athletic directors who make the hiring decisions. Each athletic director may firmly believe that he is hiring the best coach available, but such judgments are necessarily subjective. This, of course, leaves a lot of room for prejudices to result in discriminatory hiring practices, but without a careful analysis of specific decisions, it is dangerous to leap to conclusions.

6.4 Support for Title IX and Women's Sports

Intercollegiate athletics are very visible programs of many – if not most – major universities in the United States. As we have seen, Title IX applies with full force to those universities. In some circles, the impact of Title IX has been controversial to say the least. There are indications, however, that Title IX enjoys substantial public approval. First, polls have shown that 75 percent of parents want their daughters to participate in sports or at least have the opportunity to do so. The result of Title IX on female athletic participation in high schools has been dramatic. In 1971, the year before Title IX was enacted, about 295,000 girls participated in high school sports. In the same year, 3,667,000 boys participated. Thus, boys outnumbered girls by more than 12 to 1. Thirty years later, there were over 2.8 million girls participating in high school sports while there were about 3.96 million boys. The ratio of boys to girls had fallen from 12 to 1 to 1.4 to 1. No doubt, those parents with daughters were pleased with the progress toward gender equality.

Second, the *Chronicle of Higher Education* reported the results of a poll that showed substantial approval of Title IX. Some 68 percent of respondents approved of Title IX whereas only 20 percent disapproved. Given limited athletic budgets, it is often necessary to cut men's sports to support women's sports. The poll indicated that 66 percent of the respondents approved of cutting men's athletics to provide equivalent athletic opportunities for women. Only 27 percent of the respondents disapproved. Interestingly, 70 percent of the respondents wanted Title IX strengthened or left alone and only 21 percent wanted to see the law weakened.

7 CONCLUDING REMARKS

In this chapter, we have examined discrimination in sports. For players, job opportunities and compensation do not appear to be much affected, if at all, by racial considerations. The only significant qualification involves the possibility of role discrimination, which involves steering African Americans to certain positions and away from others.

When it comes to coaching positions, there appears to be a disparity. Relative to their presence among players, African Americans appear to be woefully underrepresented as head coaches. This is true in the NCAA as well as in the professional ranks. Whether this is discriminatory or not is a tough call, but the evidence is certainly suggestive.

We also examined gender discrimination. Disparities between earnings and opportunities may exist, but that is also difficult to determine. The impact of Title IX on options for women in the NCAA was examined. There can be no doubt that women are better off now than they were when Title IX was passed. The effect of Title IX on men and men's sports is controversial because accommodating women often requires some sacrifice of men's sports because of budgetary considerations.

Discrimination on the basic of religion or politics is not much concern in the United States, but it is not unheard of elsewhere. In 2009, for example, the United Arab Emirates refused to issue an entry visa to Shakar Peer, an Israeli tennis player who wanted to play in the Barclays Dubai Tennis Championship. As a protest, the Tennis Channel decided not to televise the tournament. Sadly, the other competitors did not boycott the tournament. Perhaps the lure of a big payday was too great.

PROBLEMS AND QUESTIONS

1. Some people have argued that the owners of sports teams who discriminate against minorities are worse off *economically* than those who do not discriminate. Do you agree?
2. If an athlete has a taste for discrimination, he discounts the actual wage paid if he has minority teammates. This means that he wants a wage premium. Some authors have argued that "an owner may be willing to pay the wage premium demanded by a top player with a taste for discrimination because there are no viable substitutes of equal ability." Does this make economic sense?
3. Fan discrimination occurs when fans feel as though their ticket costs more when minorities are on their favorite team – that is, the perceived price

is above the actual price. Would you agree that this "is the only form of discrimination that harms the group that is discriminated against without in turn damaging those with a taste for discrimination." Are they right?

4. Examine the distribution of prize money for men and women in the 2001 Ericsson Open tennis tournament. Is this evidence of discrimination? If so, is it the result of employer discrimination or fan discrimination?

2001 Sony Ericsson Open
Distribution of Prize Money

Finish	Men	Women
Champion	$444,000	$330,000
Finalist	233,000	162,000
Semifinalists	123,000	79,500
Quarterfinalists	64,640	39,000
Round of 16	34,000	19,000
Round of 32	17,900	9,300
Round of 64	9,400	4,600
Round of 128	4,960	2,300

6. Tickets to the NBA Championship series are scarce. Scalpers get thousands of dollars for them. There is an excess supply of tickets to the WNBA Championship series. Ticket prices are low, and there are many empty seats.
   a. Is this an example of fan discrimination? Why or why not?
   b. Provide an economic explanation that does not involve discrimination.
7. As an *economic* matter, we do not worry about the causes of discrimination. Instead, we focus on the consequences. Why?
8. If we did away with Title IX, would some men's wrestling programs be restored? Would some women's programs be cut? How would Athletic Directors decide what to cut, what to keep, and what to add?
9. In the NFL, 88 percent of running backs are African Americans. Are NFL owners or coaches discriminating against White running backs?
10. How does a salary cap affect the incentives for (a) owner discrimination, (b) player discrimination, and (c) fan discrimination?
11. In the NFL, there is extensive revenue sharing among the teams. How does revenue sharing affect owner discrimination?
12. Women are eligible to play in the U.S. Open Golf Championship, but men are not eligible to play in the U.S. Women's Open Golf Championship. Is this gender discrimination?
13. Annika Sorenstam and Michelle Wie have played on the PGA Tour through sponsor's exemptions, but no men have played in LPGA events. Is this discrimination?

14. At many NCAA Division I universities, the football program generates substantial profits. A good portion of these profits is not put back into the football program. Instead, it is used to subsidize women's golf, tennis, and soccer.
    a. Why should men's football support women's sports?
    b. Why do universities use football profits to support women's sports?
    c. Is there a better reason to use football profits to support men's golf, tennis, and soccer?
15. In considering the proportionality test for compliance with Title IX, can an argument be made for excluding men's football from the equation? If so, how would that work?
16. Few women are Athletic Directors at major universities. In Division I-A, only 5 percent of the Athletic Directors are women, and all of them are White. Is this a combination of gender and racial discrimination?
17. In the NFL, the Rooney Rule requires that an NFL team interview minority candidates when a head coaching vacancy exists. Will this help eradicate any racial bias harbored by NFL team owners?
18. Does the Rooney Rule do anything to correct prejudice or alleviate the economic effects of discrimination?
19. In 2010, Kye Allums played on the women's basketball team for George Washington University. (Katie Thomas, "Transgender Man Is on Women's Team," *New York Times*, Nov. 1, 2010)
    a. Should he be allowed to play on the women's team?
    b. Is this a gender equity issue?
20. The LPGA has an eligibility requirement that a golfer must be "female at birth." When Lana Lawless, a transgender woman golfer, was not permitted to participate in an LPGA qualifying tournament, she sued.
    a. Should women's sports organizations (LPGA, WTA, for example) be allowed to insist on members being female?
    b. Should they be allowed to exclude transgendered women?

RESEARCH QUESTIONS

1. At your school, how many women's teams are coached by men?
    a. Were any women candidates considered when the current male coach was hired?
    b. Has your school actively recruited female coaches?
    c. Are any men's teams coached by women?
2. Look at the number of African American head coaches in the NFL since the Rooney Rule went into effect. Has any progress been made?

REFERENCES AND FURTHER READING

Andersen, T. N., and S. J. La Croix. (1991). "Customer Racial Discrimination in Major League Baseball." *Economic Inquiry*, 29, 665–677.

Becker, Gary S. (1971). *The Economics of Discrimination.* Chicago: University of Chicago Press.

Bellemore, F. A. (2001). "Racial and Ethnic Employment Discrimination: Promotion in Major League Baseball." *Journal of Sports Economics*, 2, 356–368.

Bodvarsson, O. B., and R. T. Brastow. (1999) "A Test of Employer Discrimination in the NBA." *Contemporary Economic Policy*, 17, 243–255.

Bodvarsson, O. B., and M. D. Partridge. (2001). "A Supply and Demand Model of Co-Worker, Employer and Customer Discrimination." *Journal of Labor Economics*, 8, 389–416.

Brown, R. W., and R. T. Jewell. (1994). "Is There Customer Discrimination in College Basketball? The Premium Fans Pay for White Players." *Social Science Quarterly*, 75, 401–413.

Conlin, M., and P. M. Emerson. (2005). "Discrimination in Hiring Versus Retention and Promotion: An Empirical Analysis of Within-Firm Treatment of Players in the NFL." *Journal of Law Economics & Organization*, 22, 115–136.

Cymrot, D. J. (1985). "Does Competition Lessen Discrimination? Some Evidence." *Journal of Human Resources*, 20, 605–612.

Depken, C. A., II, and J. M. Ford. (2006). "Customer-Based Discrimination Against Major League Baseball Players: Additional Evidence from All-Star Ballots." *Journal of Socio-Economics*, 35, 1061–1077.

Findlay, D. W., and C. E. Reid. (1997). "Voting Behavior, Discrimination and the National Baseball Hall of Fame." *Economic Inquiry*, XXXV, 562–578.

Fort, Rodney, and Andrew Gill. (2000). "Race and Ethnicity Assessment in Baseball Card Markets." *Journal of Sports Economics*, 1, 21–38.

Gabriel, P. E., C. Johnson, and T. J. Stanton. (1999). "Customer Racial Discrimination for Baseball Memorabilia." *Applied Economics*, 31, 1331–1335.

Groothuis, P. A., and J. R. Hill. (2004). "Exit Discrimination in the NBA: A Duration Analysis of Career Length." *Economic Inquiry*, 42, 341–349.

Gwartney, J., and C. Haworth. (1974). "Employer Costs and Discrimination: The Case of Baseball." *Journal of Political Economy*, 82, 873–881.

Hanssen, A. (1998). "The Cost of Discrimination: A Study of Major League Baseball." *Southern Economic Journal*, 64, 603–627.

Hanssen, F. A., and T. Andersen. (1999). "Has Discrimination Lessened over Time? A Test Using Baseball's All-Star Vote." *Economic Inquiry*, 37, 326–352.

Humphreys, B. R. (2000). "Equal Pay on the Hardwood: The Earnings Gap Between Male and Female NCAA Division I Baseball Coaches." *Journal of Sports Economics*, 1, 299–307.

Jewell, R.T., R. W. Brown, and S. E. Miles. (2002). "Measuring Discrimination in Major League Baseball: Evidence from the Baseball Hall of Fame." *Applied Economics*, 34, 167–177.

Jones, G. A., W. M. Leonard, II, R. L. Schmitt, D. R. Smith, and W. L. Tolone. (1987). "Racial Discrimination in College Football." *Social Science Quarterly*, 68, 70–83.

Jones, J. C. H., S. Nadeau, and W. D. Walsh. (1999). "Ethnicity, Productivity and Salary: Player Compensation and Discrimination in the National Hockey League." *Applied Economics*, 31, 593–608.

Kahn, L. M. (1991). "Discrimination in Professional Sports: A Survey of the Literature." *Industrial and Labor Relations Review*, 44, 395–418.

Kahn, L. M. (2006). "Race, Performance, Pay and Retention Among National Basketball Association Head Coaches." *Journal of Sports Economics*, 7, 119–149.

Kanazawa, M. T., and J. P. Funk. (2001). "Racial Discrimination in Professional Basketball: Evidence from Nielsen Ratings." *Economic Inquiry*, 39, 599–608.

Lavoie, Marc. (2000). "The Location of Pay Discrimination in the National Hockey League." *Journal of Sports Economics*, 1, 401–411.

Lavoie, M., G. Grenier, and S. Coulombe. (1987). "Discrimination and Performance Differentials in the National Hockey League." *Canadian Public Policy*, 13, 407–422.

Lewis, M. (2006). *The Blind Side: Evolution of a Game.* New York: W.W. Norton.

Longley, N. (1995). "Salary Discrimination in the National Hockey League: The Effects of Team Location." *Canadian Public Policy*, XXI, 413–422.

Longley, N. (2000). "The Underrepresentation of French Canadians on English Canadian NFL Teams: Evidence from 1943 to 1998." *Journal of Sports Economics*, 1, 236–256.

Longley, N. (2003). "Measuring Employer-Based Discrimination Versus Customer-Based Discrimination: The Case of French Canadians in the National Hockey League." *American Journal of Economics and Sociology*, 62, 365–381.

Pedace, R. (2008). "Earnings, Performance, and Nationality Discrimination in a Highly Competitive Labor Market: An Analysis of the English Professional Soccer League." *Journal of Sports Economics*, 9, 115–140.

Scully, G. W. (1973). "Economic Discrimination in Professional Sports." *Law & Contemporary Problems*, 38, 67–84.

Scully, G. W. (1974). "Discrimination: The Case of Baseball," chapter 7 in Noll, Roger G., ed., *Government and the Sports Business.* Washington, DC: The Brookings Institution.

Shmanske, Stephen. (2000). "Gender, Skill, and Earnings in Professional Golf." *Journal of Sports Economics*, 1, 385–400.

Szymanski, S. (2000). "A Market Test for Discrimination in the English Professional Soccer Leagues." *Journal of Political Economy*, 108, 590–603.

Tainsky, S., and J. Winfree. (2010), "Discrimination and Demand: The Effect of International Players on Attendance in Major League Baseball." *Social Science Quarterly*, 91, 117–128.

Tygiel, Jules. (2008). *Baseball's Great Experiment.* New York: Oxford University Press.

Zimbalist, Andrew. (1999). *Unpaid Professionals: Competition and Conflict in Big Time College Sports.* Princeton, NJ: Princeton University Press.

Subject Index

Abbot Nutrition, 274
Adu, Freddy, 478–479
Advertising, promotion
  demand function, 118
  economic, demographic information in, 121–123, 123t
  endorsements, 129n, 129–130, 454–455, 456t
  expenditures, 120–121, 121t
  league-wide (public goods theory), 131–135, 132f
  naming rights, 24, 124–126, 127, 127n, 128n, 295
  of NCAA student-athletes, 377–378
  in NFL, 125t, 131–135, 132f
  optimal, 118–120, 119f
  overview, 7, 117, 135
  profit function, 118
  sponsorships, 124t, 128–129
  sports agents role in, 459
  sports publications, 124t, 124
  strategic behavior in, 121t, 130–131
African Americans. *See* Discrimination
Age limits, 478t, 477–480
Ainge, Danny, 347
Almagro, Nicolas, 498t
American Football League v. National Football League, 187–189
American League history, 60t, 59–60. *See also* National Football League (NFL)
American Needle v. National Football League, 183
Ameriquest Mortgage Company, 126
Amphetamines, 266, 269n, 271–272
Anabolic androgenic steroids, 265–266, 267n, 271–272
Anaheim Angels, 22t
Anaheim Ducks, 31t
Andrews, Erin, 129n
Anheuser-Busch advertising revenues, 130
Anthony, Carmelo, 249, 250, 405
Antiscalping laws, 112–113
Antitrust policy. *See also* Monopoly models
  American Football League v. National Football League, 187–189
  American Needle v. National Football League, 183
  broadcasting restraints, 184–185
  broadcast rights, 139, 139n
  challenges by coaches, 372–376
  challenges by league members, 184–187
  challenges by outsiders, 187–193
  challenges by student-athletes, 376–378
  Clayton Act of 1914, 435–436
  economic rationale for, 175–178, 176f, 177n
  enforcement, 179–182
  entry restrictions, 189, 193
  equipment restrictions, 191–193, 194
  exemptions, 184
  exemptions for players' unions, 435–436
  Herfindahl-Hirschman Index (HHI), 69, 69n, 70
  league rules in, 182–184
  legal rules, agreements in, 183
  market definition, 180
  monopoly power, 176f, 181–182
  Norris-La Guardia Act of 1932, 436
  overview, 9, 175
  public ownership ban, 185–186, 186n
  relevant geographic market, 181
  relevant product market, 180–181
  relocation restrictions, 186–187
  rent-seeking, 177n
  restrictions on schedules by organizations, 190–191
  rule of reason, 179–180, 182–183, 374–375
  Sherman Antitrust Act (*See* Sherman Antitrust Act)
  Sports Broadcasting Act of 1961, 139–141, 140t, 142t, 188
  ticket bundling in, 102

Antitrust policy (*cont.*)
  United States Football League v. NFL, 189–190, 190n
  walk-on players litigation, 376–377, 377n
Arena Football League (AFL), 208, 269n
Arenas, Gilbert, 249t, 339t
Arizona Cardinals, 27t, 28t, 327t
Arizona Diamondbacks
  broadcast revenues, payrolls 2001, 23t
  capital appreciation of, 34t
  franchise value 2010, 30t
  history of, 61t, 60–61
  stadium financing in, 325t
Arrington, LaVar, 411, 411n
Artest, Ron, 249t, 250
Asomugha, Nnamdi, 339t
Association of Tennis Professionals (ATP)
  age limits in, 478t, 479
  cheating in, 236n, 236–237
  commissioner's salaries, 52
  gender discrimination in, 497–498, 498t
  restrictions on schedules by organizations, 191
  steroid policies, 272
Athletic Propulsion Labs, 194
Atlanta Braves
  broadcast revenues, payrolls 2001, 23t
  broadcast rights monopoly by, 150–151
  capital appreciation of, 33–35, 34t
  final offer arbitration by, 419, 422n
  franchise value 2010, 30t
  history of, 61t
  payrolls in, 7t
  stadium financing in, 325t
  transfer of ownership, 50–51
Atlanta Falcons, 27t, 28t, 255–256
Atlanta Hawks, 29t
Atlanta Thrashers, 31t
Austrian Olympic Committee, 267
Azarenka, Victoria, 498t

Babby, Lon, 459–460
Bagwell, Jeff, 169t, 169–170
Bailer, Champ, 339t
Baltimore Orioles
  broadcast revenues, payrolls 2001, 22t
  capital appreciation of, 34t
  franchise value 2010, 30t
  history of, 60t
  stadium financing, 324t
  team insurance coverage for, 169
Baltimore Ravens
  attendance, performance 2010, 27t
  criticizing game officials penalties, 257
  franchise value 2010, 28t
  multiyear contracts with, 409
Barclay's, 4, 24, 126, 127
Barkley, Charles, 201
Barnes, Rick, 396
Basketball shoes, 194
Bat-gate, 228
Beamer, Frank, 390t
Beer advertising revenues, 121t, 130
Beimel, Joe, 427t, 426–427
Belichick, Bill, 232
Bell, Mark, 253
Belle, Albert, 169
Beltran, Carlos, 80, 339t
Benson, Kris, 168
Berdych, Tomas, 498t
Berri, D. J., 93–95
Beta-2 agonists, 266, 273
Bettman, Gary, 53t, 253
Bidding, bargaining (labor)
  for coaches, 387–388, 388n, 389n
  coaches' contracts of, 390t, 395–396
  economics of, 391–396
  head coach salaries, 390t, 390
  incentives, bonuses, 396
  overview, 12–13, 383, 402
  posting system (MLB), 397n, 397–402, 398t
  private value auctions (English auctions), 384n, 384–386, 385n
Big 12 conference, 257
Big Ten network, 153
Black, William "Tank," 457, 462–463
Black Sox scandal, 234
Blalock, Jane, 224, 224n
Blood doping, 267, 271
Board of Regents of the University of Oklahoma and University of Georgia Athletic Association, NCAA v., 184–185
Bodenheimer, George, 148
Bonds, Barry, 170–171, 281–282, 385, 412
Bookies, 204–205, 209n
Boras, Scott, 386, 452–454
Boston Bruins, 31t
Boston Celtics, 29t, 125–126
Boston Marathon, 224–225
Boston Red Sox
  broadcast revenues, payrolls 2001, 22t
  capital appreciation of, 34t, 33–35
  final arbitration settlements by, 428–429
  franchise values, 6t, 30t
  history of, 60t
  luxury tax, 79–81, 81t
  posting system use by, 398t, 399–402
  stadium financing, 324t
  ticket prices, 93–94
Boulerice, Jesse, 252
Bradford, Sam, 339t
Brady, Tom, 167
Brand, Myles, 211
Brewer, Corey, 467n
Broadcast rights
  antitrust litigation, 189–190
  antitrust policy restraints, 184–185

benefits of, 147–148
bidding, 140–149, 143f
contracts, transaction costs of, 152
market structure for, 138f, 138–139
overview, 8t, 8, 137, 153–154
ownership limits, 141
revenues, 22t, 23t, 21–23
revenue sharing, 54, 152
Sports Broadcasting Act of 1961, 139–141, 140t, 142t
sports networks, 140t, 152–153, 153t
United States Football League v. NFL, 189–190, 190n
vertical integration in, 138f, 149–152, 151f
winner's curse, 145–146, 146f, 147f, 295–296
Brown, Chris, 468
Brown, Kwame, 472, 480
Brown, Mack, 390t
Brown, R. W., 368
Brown, Shawn, 168
Bryant, Decory, 167
Bryant, Kobe, 250, 338, 339t, 480, 481
Buffalo Bills, 27t, 28t
Buffalo Sabres, 31t
Burgess, Paul, 427t
Burton, Isaac Jr., 212, 234
Bush, Michael, 166, 166n, 470–471
Business of sports. *See* Sports business

Cabrera, Miguel, 339t, 426–427, 427t
Calgary Flames, 31t
Cameron, Mike, 269
Cap Relief for Veterans rule, 444t
Carolina Hurricanes, 31t
Carolina Panthers, 27t, 28t
Carruth, Rae, 457
Carter, Anthony, 453
Carter, Vince, 457
Casey, Paul, 496t
Certainty equivalent, 164f, 164
The Challenge at Manele, 96t
Charlotte Bobcats, 29t, 93–94
Cheating
Bat-gate, 228
deterrence of, 219–220, 221f
distraction by cheerleaders, 229
doctored baseballs, 228–229
Formula One racing, 233
illegal equipment use, 227–233
to lose, 233–234
in NCAA, 230n, 230–231, 231n
overview, 9–10, 218–219, 238
penalties, changing, 221–223, 222f
player collusion in, 211
point shaving, 212, 234–235
probability of detection, changing, 221
sanctions (death penalty), 370–372
sumo wrestling, 235–236
in tennis, 236n, 236–237
violating rules of play, 224–226
to win, 223
Chester, Ed, 167, 167n, 467
Chicago Bears
attendance, performance 2010, 27t
franchise value 2010, 28t
stadium financing, 327t
ticket prices, 93–94
weapons charges policy, 254–255, 255n
Chicago Blackhawks, 31t, 78
Chicago Bulls, 6t, 29t
Chicago Cubs
broadcast revenues, payrolls 2001, 23t
capital appreciation of, 33–35, 34t
final offer settlement by, 418–419
franchise value 2010, 30t
history of, 61t
host city competition for, 299–300
multiyear contracts with, 405
stadium financing in, 325t
Chicago White Sox
Black Sox scandal, 234
broadcast revenues, payrolls 2001, 22t
capital appreciation of, 34t
franchise value 2010, 30t
history of, 60t
stadium financing, 324t
stadium lease agreement, 293
Chizik, Gene, 390t
Choi, Na Yeon, 495, 496t
Cincinnati Bengals, 27t, 28t
Cincinnati Reds
broadcast revenues, payrolls 2001, 23t
capital appreciation of, 34t
franchise value 2010, 30t
history of, 61t
posting system use by, 398t
stadium financing in, 325t
Citi Group, 7, 24, 126
Clarett, Maurice, 478, 479
Clark, Tim, 496t
Clayton Act of 1914, 435–436
Clemens, Roger, 170, 354t
Cleveland Browns, 27t, 28t
Cleveland Cavaliers, 29t, 293–294
Cleveland Indians
broadcast revenues, payrolls 2001, 22t
capital appreciation of, 34t
franchise value 2010, 30t
history of, 60t
stadium financing, 324t
stadium lease agreement, 293, 294t
Clijsters, Kim, 498t
Coaches
bidding, bargaining for, 387–388, 388n, 389n (*See also* Bidding, bargaining [labor])
contracts of, 390t, 395–396, 408, 410, 413

Coaches (*cont.*)
- incentives, bonuses, 396
- multiyear contracts of, 408, 410, 413
- racial discrimination, 493t, 493–494, 495t
- salaries, 390t, 390
- Title IX impacts on, 502–503, 503t

Coates, T., 93–95
Coca-Cola advertising revenues, 130
Collective bargaining. *See also* Players' unions
- overview, 13, 432, 441
- by players' unions, 436–438, 437f
- strikes, lockouts, 441

College conferences, 140t, 153t, 153. *See also* National Collegiate Athletic Association (NCAA)
Collins, Mardy, 249t
Collusive monopsony
- amateurism *vs.* exploitation, 363, 368
- antitrust challenges by coaches, 372–376
- antitrust challenges by student-athletes, 376–378
- average costs, 365f, 365, 381
- cheating sanctions (death penalty), 370–372
- coaches in, 367–369, 369t, 372–376, 376n
- effects on costs, 364n, 364–365, 365f, 380–381
- *Hennessey v. NCAA*, 372–373, 375, 376
- incentives, 362f, 362–364
- *Law v. NCAA*, 373–376
- marginal costs, 364–365, 365f, 380
- *O'Bannon v. NCAA*, 377–378
- overview, 12, 348–349
- price, quantity limitations, 366n, 366–367, 367t, 374n
- profit maximization in, 362–363
- restricted earnings coaches, 373–376, 376n
- revenue sharing in, 370
- student-athlete compensation, 366, 366n, 368
- walk-on players antitrust litigation, 376–377, 377n
- *White v. NCAA*, 377

Colorado Avalanche, 31t
Colorado Rockies
- broadcast revenues, payrolls 2001, 23t
- capital appreciation of, 34t
- franchise value 2010, 30t
- history of, 60–61, 61t
- stadium financing in, 325t

Columbus Blue Jackets, 31t, 125–126
Commissioners
- authority of, 52
- salaries, 52, 53t, 338n

Commodity bundling (season tickets), 102–103, 103t
Community facility subsidies, 328t, 329t
Competition for franchises, events. *See* Franchises, events demand
Competitive balance
- definition of, 65–66
- economic analysis of, 70–72, 71f, 73
- free agency in, 70–72, 71f, 73, 74
- Herfindahl-Hirschman Index (HHI), 69, 69n, 70
- luxury taxes (*See* Luxury taxes)
- measures of generally, 67, 70
- in New York Yankees, 75, 80–81, 81t
- Noll-Scully measure, 67n, 67–68, 68t
- overview, 6–7, 7t, 25, 65, 82
- reserve clause, 71–72, 73–75
- revenue sharing economic implications, 76–77
- revenue sharing generally, 75–76
- reverse-order player drafts, 79
- rules, procedures generally, 73
- salary caps, 77f, 77–78

Concussions, 252
Connecticut General Life Insurance, 169–170
Consumer surplus, 89–90, 90f, 91f, 91–92, 176, 177
Contador, Alberto, 277–279
Contracts
- broadcast rights, 152
- of coaches, 390t, 395–396, 408, 410, 413 (*See also* Coaches)
- contingent fee, 460–461
- fixed-fee, 459, 460
- hire, 459–460
- legal remedies, 463
- multiyear (*See* Multiyear contracts)
- principal-agent, 458–459
- stadium naming rights, 24, 124–126, 127, 127n, 295

Conyers, John Jr., 479
Coors Brewing advertising revenues, 130
Coral Creek Golf Course, 101t
Cordero, Chad, 426–427, 427t
Corso, Lee, 129n
Cousy, Bob, 434–447
Cox, Willilam, 207–208
Creamer, Paula, 469–470, 496t
Crittenton, Javaris, 249t
Crosby, Sidney, 339t
Crowell, Germane, 457
Cuban, Mark, 17–18, 168, 256–257

Dallas Cowboys
- attendance, performance 2010, 27t
- franchise values, 6t, 28t
- profit maximization by, 17–18
- stadium financing, 327t

Dallas Mavericks
- franchise value 2010, 29t
- misconduct penalties on, 256–257
- multiyear contracts with, 407

profit maximization by, 17–18
team insurance coverage for, 168
Dallas Stars, 31t
Daly, John, 201, 248
Dareus, Marcus, 464
Davis, Al, 186–187
Davydenko, Nikolay, 237
Daytona 500, 129, 229–230
Deadweight social welfare loss of monopoly, 178
Death penalty, 370–372
Deion Sanders Rule, 444t
Demand function, 118
Dementieva, Elena, 498t
Dent, Marvin, 492
Denver Broncos, 27t, 28t, 327t
Denver Nuggets, 29t, 250, 405
Detroit Lions
attendance, performance 2010, 27t
franchise value 2010, 28t
mismanagement of, 66, 66n
stadium financing, 327t
Detroit Pistons, 29t, 206–207, 250
Detroit Red Wings, 31t
Detroit Tigers
broadcast revenues, payrolls 2001, 22t
capital appreciation of, 34t
franchise value 2010, 30t
history of, 60t
luxury tax, 81t, 80–81
stadium financing, 324t
DiPietro, Rick, 405–407
Disability insurance, 166–167
Discount rate
importance, 43
selection, 32n, 43
Discrimination
competition impacts on, 489f, 489–490
concept, identification of, 485–486
economics of, 486–487
by fans, 490f, 490–491
gender, 494–498, 495t, 496t
impact of, 487–489, 488f, 489f, 491t
overview, 14, 485, 504
racial, 492t, 492–494, 493t, 495t
role, 491t, 491–492
Title IX (gender equality), 498–504
Diuretics, 266
Djokovic, Novak, 236, 498t
Dog fighting, 255–256, 256n
Dominguez, Gus, 455
Donaghy, Tim, 214–215
Donald, Luke, 496t
Donovan, Billy, 396
Dooley, Derek, 390t
Dr. Pepper/Seven Up, 130
Drew, J. D., 168n
Drury, Chris, 339t
Duffy, Bill, 453
Duggan, Mark, 235–236
Dumervil, Elvis, 339t
Duncan, Tim, 339t, 459–460

Earnhardt, Dale Jr., 456t
Economic analysis tools
Herfindahl-Hirschman Index (HHI), 69, 69n, 70
Lerner Index of monopoly, 176f, 181–182
overview, 4
power measurement (Lerner Index), 350–351, 351t
present value calculations (*See* Present value calculations)
uncertainty (*See* Uncertainty)
Economic impact analysis, 11
Edmonton Oilers, 31t
Educational Amendments, Civil Rights Act, 1972, 498–504
Elias, Patrick, 405, 406
Els, Ernie, 496t
Elseneer, Gilles, 236n
Eminent domain, 300–301
Endorsements, 129n, 129–130, 454–455, 456t
English auctions, 384n, 384–386, 385n
Enron, 126
Entry restrictions, 189, 193
EPO (erythropoietin), 267, 279
Equilibrium wage, 342f, 342–343
Equipment restrictions, 191–193, 194
Erickson, Dennis, 388
Erythropoietin (EPO), 267, 279
ESPN
business model, 149
Monday Night Football broadcast rights, 148
U.S. Open Tennis Championship broadcast rights, 146–147
ESPN Regional Television, 153
Events, competition for. *See* Franchises, events demand
Exceptional Student Athlete Disability Insurance, 166–167
Expected utility model
cheating deterrence of, 219–220, 221f
gambling, 203f, 203–204
measurement of, 164f, 163–164, 173–174, 175–196
performance-enhancing drugs, 274–281, 276f, 278f
risk aversion, 159–164, 161t, 162f, 163f
uncertainty calculations, 4–5

Facilities. *See also* Franchises
costs of, 5
financing of (*See* Financing of facilities)
naming rights, 24, 124–126, 127, 127n, 295
new facilities demands, 295
stadium lease agreements, 293, 294t, 294
subsidies, 296–297, 297f

Farmer, Amy, 427t
Favre, Brett, 456t
Federal Baseball Club of Baltimore, Inc. v. National League of Professional Baseball Clubs, 184
Federer, Roger, 129–130, 456t, 498t
Fehr, Don, 435
Feller, Bob, 228
Ferentz, Kirk, 390t
Ferrari, 233
Ferrer, David, 498t
Fighting, 249–250
Final Four tickets, 111
Final offer arbitration
  challenges in, 423–424
  conditions for, 422–423
  costs of, 424–425
  economic conditions for, 420–422
  empirical results of, 426t, 426–428, 427t, 428t
  negotiation of, 418–419, 420t
  overview, 13, 418, 429
  as player protection, 428–429
  settlement economics, 419–425
Financing of facilities
  alcohol, cigarette taxes in, 333t
  bonds, taxation, 331t, 332t, 333t, 334t
  community facility subsidies, 328t, 329t
  debit financing, equity, 334t
  as investment, 321–323
  logrolling, 330t
  lottery taxes in, 333t
  overview, 11, 320, 334t
  political decisions in, 329t
  private and public funding, 323–327, 324t, 325t, 327t
  scrap value, 322–323
Finchem, Tim, 52, 273
Finley, Michael, 168
First Union, 126
Fitzgerald, Larry, 468–469, 469t, 471, 478
Florida Marlins
  broadcast revenues, payrolls 2001, 23t
  capital appreciation of, 34t
  franchise value 2010, 30t
  history of, 60–61, 61t
  stadium financing in, 325t
Florida Panthers, 31t
Formula One racing, 233
Fort, Rodney, 67, 68
Fowler, Chris, 129n
Fox Entertainment Group, 153
Franchione, Dennis, 210
Franchises. *See also* Facilities
  celebrity benefit, 35
  competition for (*See* Franchises, events demand)
  financial disclosure by, 27–29, 28n
  financing of facilities (*See* Financing of facilities)
  location of, league policies on, 51
  profitability in, 26–31, 28t, 29t, 30t, 31t (*See also* Profitability)
  public ownership ban, 185–186
  relocation restrictions, 186–187
  as stand-alone investments, 32
Franchises, events demand
  competition influences on location, 297–300
  consumption value, 292
  economic incentives to host city, 289–292
  eminent domain in, 300–301
  job creation as incentive, 290
  naming rights, 24, 124–126, 127, 127n, 295
  new facilities demands, 295
  overview, 11, 289, 292–293, 301
  prestige, exposure as incentive, 291–292
  Pro Bowl, 291
  revenue guarantees, 295
  stadium, ballpark, arena construction/leasing, 293–294
  stadium revenues, 295
  subsidizing of franchise, 296–297, 297f
  tax revenue as incentive, 290–291
  winner's curse, 145–146, 146f, 147f, 295–296
Franco, John, 164–166
Free agency
  bidding, bargaining (labor) (*See* Bidding, bargaining (labor))
  collusive monopsony in, 348–349
  in competitive balance, 70–72, 71f, 73, 74
  in MLB, 442
  monopsonistic exploitation in, 352t
  in NBA, 443
  in NFL, 442–443
  in NHL, 443
  posting system (MLB), 397–402
  restrictions on, 442, 442n
Fuentes, Brian, 428t
Furyk, Jim, 205–206, 227, 496t
Future stream valuation, 41–42, 42t
Future values, 38–39, 41t

Gambling
  AFL, 208
  Donaghy case, 214–215
  economics of, 201–204, 202f, 203f
  expected utility model, 203f, 203–204 (*See also* Expected utility model)
  by game officials, 212t, 212–215
  horse racing, 208
  NCAA (*See under* National Collegiate Athletic Association (NCAA))
  Neuheisel case, 213
  overview, 9, 201, 215
  point spread wagers, 204–205

by professional athletes, 205–208
risk seeker utility function, 201–203, 202f
risks of in MLB, 208–209
sports books (bookies), 204–205, 209n
Garnett, Kevin, 339t, 480, 481
Garrison, Zina, 492
Gasol, Pau, 339t
Gate receipts, 20–21, 21t, 54, 75–76
Gatlin, Justin, 282
Gender equality. *See* Title IX (gender equality)
Gill, Turner, 390t
Gillispie, Billy, 389, 396
Glavine, Tom, 406, 409–410
GlaxoSmithKline, 274
Goggins, Jason, 458
Golden State Warriors, 29t
Golf. *See also* LPGA; PGA; PGA Tour
equipment restrictions in, 227
gender discrimination in, 494–497, 495t, 496t
peak load pricing, 99–102, 101f, 101t
price discrimination in, 96t
rules violations, cheating in, 224
sponsorships in, 128–129, 124t
steroid policies, 272–273
Gomez, Scott, 339t
Goodell, Roger
on broadcast rights ownership, 141
dress code violations policy, 258
misconduct policies, 244–246
repeat offenders policy, 253–254
salary, 52, 53t
suspensions of players by, 248t, 248–255
taping fines imposed by, 232
weapons charges policy, 254–255, 255n
Goosen, Retief, 496t
Gordon, Jeff, 229, 456t
Green, A. J., 464
Green, Jacquez, 457
Green, Taurean, 467n
Green Bay Packers
attendance, performance 2010, 27t
franchise value 2010, 28t
as publicly owned, 186n
stadium financing, 327t
Gregg, Kevin, 426–427, 427t
Griffey, Ken Jr., 342
Grimes, Mickey, 271
Grossman, Rex, 474–475
Gunter Harz, 191–192
Gurode, Andre, 251

Hambric Sports, 463
Harvey, Donnell, 407
Hawaii Kai Golf Course, 101t
Haynesworth, Albert, 248t, 248–251, 251n
Heatley, Dany, 339t
Henin, Justine, 498t
Henkel, Bill, 459
Hennessey v. NCAA, 372–373, 375, 376
Henry, Chris, 248t, 248–254, 254n
Herbstreit, Kirk, 129n
Herfindahl-Hirschman Index (HHI), 69, 69n, 70
Hill, Grant, 459–460
Hockey, 193
Hollweg, Ryan, 251
Horford, Al, 467n
Hormones, 266–267
Hornung, Paul, 206
Horse collar tackles, 252
Horse racing, 208
Hossa, Marian, 78
Hot face drivers, 227
Houston Astros
broadcast revenues, payrolls 2001, 23t
capital appreciation of, 34t
franchise value 2010, 30t
history of, 60–61, 61t
multiyear contracts with, 411–412
stadium financing in, 325t
team insurance coverage for, 169t, 169–170
Houston Rockers, 29t
Houston Texans, 27t, 28t, 124
Howard, Dwight, 456t, 481
Howard, Ryan, 339t, 427t, 428t
Hull, Katherine, 496t
Humphries, B. R., 93–95
Hunter, Billy, 435
Hunter, Lindsey, 249t
Huston, Nyjah, 480

Igawa, Kei, 398t, 398–399, 399n
Ilitch, Michael, 51
Image, integrity
cheating (*See* Cheating)
gambling (*See* Gambling)
overview, 9
participant misconduct (*See* Participant misconduct)
performance-enhancing drugs (*See* Performance-enhancing drugs)
Implicit fines, suspensions, 248, 249t
Indiana Pacers, 29t, 250
Indianapolis Colts, 27t, 28t, 327t
Insurance of player talent
certainty equivalent, 164f, 164
cooperation in, 170
decisions, 170–171
expected utility model (*See* Expected utility model)
failure to insure, 167
NCAA disability insurance, 166–167
overview, 8, 158–159, 171
premiums, 167–168
risk aversion, 159–164, 161t, 162f, 163f

Insurance of player talent (*cont.*)
  risk neutrality, 160–161, 161t, 163f, 163
  shifting risk, 164–166, 165f
  team purchases, 168n, 168–171, 169t
Interest accommodation test, Title IX, 501
International Automobile Federation, 233
International Olympic Committee (IOC), 145–146, 280–281
Ishii, Kazuhisa, 398t
Ivanova, Lyubov, 277–279
Iwamura, Akinori, 228, 398t, 398

Jackson, Bo, 347
Jackson, Jesse, 479
Jackson, Stephen, 250
Jackson, Steven, 249t
Jacksonville Jaguars, 27t, 28t
James, LeBron, 456t, 480, 481
James Madison University, 501
Jennings, Brandon, 481
Jeter, Derek, 13, 339t, 383, 412, 456t
John, Tommy, 158
Johnson, Ben, 271–272, 272n, 282
Johnson, Dustin, 496t
Johnson, Jimmie, 456t
Johnson, Larry, 393–394
Johnson, Paul, 390t
Johnson, Tank, 248t, 248–255
Jones, Adam "Pacman," 248t, 248–254, 253n, 254n, 255n
Jones, Jerry, 17–18
Jones, June, 390t
Jones, Marion, 279, 282–283
Jones, Pacman, 52
Jonkovic, Jelena, 498t
Jordan, Michael, 347

Kafelnikov, Yevgeny, 237
Kansas City Chiefs, 27t, 28t, 327t
Kansas City Royals
  broadcast revenues, payrolls 2001, 22t
  capital appreciation of, 34t
  franchise value 2010, 30t
  history of, 59–60, 60t
  payrolls in, 7t
  stadium financing, 324t
Karras, Alex, 206
Karsten Manufacturing Company, 192–193
Keith, Duncan, 339t
Kelly, Chip, 390t
Kerr, Cristie, 496t
Kesler, Ryan, 252
Kidd, Jason, 257
Kim, Anthony, 463
Kim, In-Kyung, 496t
Kim, Song-Hee, 496t
Kirilenko, Andrei, 339t
Kitna, Jon, 251n
Kontak, Brian, 497
Kovalchuk, Ilya, 78
Kraft, Whitney, 492
Krautmann, A. C., 93–95, 352t
Kuchar, Matt, 475, 495, 496t
Kuhn, Bowie, 207–208
Kuznetsova, Svetlana, 498t

Lacrosse stick head design, 193
La Frentz, Raef, 168
Landis, Kennesaw Mountain, 207–208, 234
Lanham Act, 23
Larry Bird Exception, 445t
Law v. NCAA, 373–376
Leach, Mike, 257
Leaf, Ryan, 79
Leagues, organizations. *See also specific franchises and organizations*
  athletic competition production, 52–53
  as cartels, 48
  commissioners, authority of, 52
  commissioner's salaries, 52, 53t, 338n
  consumer welfare in, 56–58, 59f
  cooperation off the field, 47
  expansion of, 58n, 58–61, 60t, 61t
  formation of, 47
  governance, 52, 53t
  as joint ventures, 47n, 47–48, 48n
  membership, 50n, 50–51
  as monopolies, 56–58, 57f, 57n (*See also* Monopoly models)
  overview, 5–6, 46–47
  players market, 53–54
  product marketing, 53
  profit maximization in (*See* Profitability; Profit maximization)
  revenue sharing in, 54–56 (*See also* Revenue sharing)
  rules, procedures in, 50–54
  sports networks, 140t, 152–153, 153t
  transfers of ownership, 50–51
League-wide advertising, 131–135, 132f, 133f
Lecavalier, Vincent, 339t
Lee, Carlos, 339t
Lee, Cliff, 387
Leinert, Matt, 470
Lerner Index
  of monopoly, 176f, 181–182
  monopsony power measurement, 350–351, 351t
Levitt, Steven, 235–236
Lewis, Carl, 271–272
Lewis, Jamal, 409
Lewis, Rashard, 249t, 339t
Li, Na, 498t
Lincicome, Brittany, 496t
Ljubicic, Ivan, 498t
Lockouts, strikes, 441
Lo Duca, Paul, 208
Logrolling, 330t

Long, Jake, 446–447, 452
Lopez, Felipe, 427t, 428t
Loretta, Mark, 428t
Los Angeles Angels of Anaheim
  capital appreciation of, 34t
  franchise value 2010, 30t
  history of, 59–60, 60t
  luxury tax, 80–81, 81t
  stadium financing in, 324t
Los Angeles Clippers, 29t
Los Angeles Dodgers
  broadcast revenues, payrolls 2001, 23t
  capital appreciation of, 33–35, 34t
  franchise value 2010, 30t
  history of, 61t
  posting system use by, 398t
  profit maximization by, 17–18
  stadium financing in, 325t
Los Angeles Kings, 31t
Los Angeles Lakers, 6t, 29t, 125–126
Los Angeles Open, 129
LPGA
  age limits in, 478t, 479–480
  commissioner's salaries, 52
  gender discrimination in, 494–497, 495t, 496t
  rules violations, cheating in, 224
  sponsorships in, 124t, 128–129
  steroid policies, 272–273
Luongo, Roberto, 338, 339t
Luxury taxes
  economic implications, 80–81
  overview, 77–80, 80t, 81t, 443, 445t

Maddon, Joe, 228
Maddux, Greg, 392–393, 419, 420–422, 422n
Madrazo, Roberto, 225
Mahan, Hunter, 496t
Major League Baseball (MLB)
  age limits in, 478t, 478–479
  antitrust policy exemptions, 184
  Bat-gate, 227n, 228
  Black Sox scandal, 234
  broadcast revenues, 21–23, 22t, 23t
  broadcast rights sales in, 140–141
  capital appreciation in, 33–35, 34t
  commissioner's salaries, 52, 53t, 338n
  competitive balance in, 6–7, 7t
  consumer welfare in, 56–58
  doctored baseballs, 228–229
  expansion of, 58n, 58–61, 60t, 61t
  fighting penalty, 250
  final offer arbitration in (*See* Final offer arbitration)
  franchise values, 6t, 30t
  free agency in, 442
  gambling restrictions in, 207–208
  gambling risks in, 208–209
  gate receipts 2009–2010, 21t
  illegal equipment use in, 227–229
  injury risks in, 158–159
  league membership policies, 51
  leagues as joint ventures in, 47n, 47–48, 48n
  luxury taxes in, 77–80, 80t, 81t, 443, 445t
  as monopoly, 56–58, 57f, 57n (*See also* Monopoly models)
  multiyear contracts in, 406, 409–410, 411–413
  payrolls in, 7t
  performance-enhancing drug penalty in, 10
  posting system in, 397n, 397–402, 398t
  pricing complements in, 109t
  racial discrimination in, 492t, 492–493
  reserve clause in, 71–72, 73–75, 433
  revenue sharing in, 54, 55–56, 447–448
  salary, average, 338
  salary, top ten 2010, 339t
  salary caps in, 77f, 77–78
  stadium financing in, 324t, 325t
  stadium lease agreements in, 293, 294t
  steroid policies, 268–269
Major League Baseball Players Association, 433
Major League Soccer (MLS), 137, 478t
Makaha Resort, 101t
Makaha Valley, 96t
Malkin, Evgeni, 339t
Mangini, Eric, 232
Manning, Eli, 456t
Manning, Peyton, 79, 338, 339t, 456t, 470
Marburger, Daniel, 427t
March Madness, 145
Marginal costs, 364–365, 365f, 380
Marino, Dan, 158
Massachusetts Supreme Court, 499
Masters golf tournament, 111–112
Matsuzaka, Daisuke, 398t, 399–402, 400n
Mauer, Joe, 419, 419n
Maxwell, Vernon, 248, 249t
Mayo, O. J., 481
Mayweather, Floyd Jr., 456t
McClain, Denny, 207–208
McCormack, Mark, 451
McCoy, Gerald, 339t
McGahee, Willis, 158
McGwire, Mark, 281–282
McLaren Mercedes, 233
McNabb, Donovan, 339t, 405
McNally, Dave, 433
Melzer, Jurgen, 498t
Memphis Grizzlies, 29t, 189
Merriman, Shawne, 269–270
Messersmith, Andy, 433
Meyer, Urban, 388, 388n, 390t, 390, 395, 408
Miami Dolphins, 27t, 28t, 50–51
Miami Heat, 29t, 256–257

Mickelson, Phil, 205–206, 456t, 496t
Mid-Level Exception, 445t
Miles, Darius, 249t
Miles, Les, 390t
Millen, Matt, 66n
Miller, Marvin, 433
Miller Brewing, 130
Milwaukee Brewers
  broadcast revenues, payrolls 2001, 23t
  capital appreciation of, 34t
  franchise value 2010, 30t
  history of, 60–61, 61t
  payrolls in, 7t
  stadium financing in, 325t
Milwaukee Bucks, 29t, 293
Minimum salaries, 443n, 446t, 447t, 447
Minnesota Hockey Inc., 193
Minnesota Made Hockey (MMH), 193
Minnesota Timberwolves, 29t
Minnesota Twins
  broadcast revenues, payrolls 2001, 22t
  capital appreciation of, 34t
  final offer settlement by, 418–419
  franchise value 2010, 30t
  history of, 60t
  posting system use by, 398t, 401
  stadium financing in, 324t
Minnesota Vikings, 27t, 28t
Minnesota Wild, 31t
Miyazato, Ai, 496t
Mohawk Trail Regional High School, 499
Molinas, Jack, 206–207
Monday Night Football, 148
Monfils, Gael, 498t
Monopoly models
  antitrust issues (*See* Antitrust policy)
  bilateral, 438–441, 439f, 440f
  deadweight social welfare loss of monopoly, 178
  leagues, organizations as, 56–58, 57f, 57n
  MLB, 56–58, 57f, 57n
  power, 176f, 181–182
  pricing, 90–92, 91f
  structural, 179
  successive, 149–151, 151f
Monopsony. *See also* Salary determination
  collusive (*See* Collusive monopsony)
  monopsonistic exploitation, 351t
  in NCAA, 12t, 12, 361–362, 366, 378 (*See also* Collusive monopsony)
  overview, 11–12, 343–345, 344f, 345f
  player drafts, 347–348
  power measurement (Lerner Index), 350–351, 351t
  power sources, 345n, 347–348
  profit maximization in, 340–341, 341f, 341n
  reserve clause, 347
  social welfare loss in, 345f, 345–347
Montreal Canadiens, 6t, 31t
Montreal Expos, 23t, 60–61. *See also* Washington Nationals
Mori, Shinji, 398t
Morrison, Jeff, 475
Moss, Jarvis, 244–246
Moss, Randy, 79, 353t, 354n, 354t
Mota, Guillermo, 281
Multiyear contracts. *See also* Insurance of player talent
  for coaches, 408, 410, 413
  economic value of, 13, 405–406, 413–414
  with guarantees, 412–413
  without guarantees, 410–411
  incentive clauses in, 413
  in NFL, 409, 411, 411n, 412–413
  option years in, 411–412
  as present value calculation, 4 (*See also* Present value calculations)
  signing bonuses, 412
  uncertain terms in, 408–410
  valuation fundamentals, 406–408
Munoz, Anthony, 241–242
Murray, Andy, 498t
Murray, Stephen, 170

Nadal, Rafael, 456t, 469–470, 498t
Nakamura, Norihiro, 398t
Naming rights, 24, 124–126, 127, 127n, 295
NASCAR
  cheating in, 233
  illegal equipment use in, 223n, 229–230
  offensive language, gestures policy, 257–258
  sponsorships in, 129
Nash, Steve, 168
Nashville Predators, 31t
National Basketball Association (NBA)
  age limits in, 478t, 478–479, 480
  commissioner's salaries, 52, 53t
  equipment restrictions in, 194
  fighting penalty, 250
  franchise values, 6t, 29t
  free agency in, 443
  gambling restrictions in, 206–207, 214–215
  gate receipts 2009–2010, 21t
  gender discrimination in, 494
  minimum salaries in, 443n, 446t, 447t, 447
  misconduct penalties, 256–257
  multiyear contracts in, 407, 412–413
  naming rights sale in, 125–126
  racial discrimination in, 492t, 492–493
  reserve clause challenges in, 434
  revenue sharing in, 54
  revenue sources, 19
  salary, average, 338
  salary, top ten 2010, 339t
  salary caps in, 13–14, 77f, 77–78, 445t

stadium lease agreements in, 293–294
steroid policies, 270
suspensions, implicit fines, 248, 249t
National Basketball Player's Association, 434, 438
National Collegiate Athletic Association (NCAA)
broadcasting restraints, 184–185
broadcast revenues, 153t
business of generally, 16
cheating in, 230n, 230–231, 231n
cheating sanctions in (death penalty), 370–372
disability insurance, 166–167
equipment restrictions, 193
Final Four tickets, 111
Franchione newsletter, 210
gambling policy, 209n, 209–210
gambling sanctions, 210–213
monopsony in, 12t, 12, 361–362, 366, 378 (*See also* Collusive monopsony)
multiyear contracts in, 413
point shaving, 212, 234–235
profit maximization in, 50
revenues, top programs, 12t
safety policies, 258–259
sports agents in, 458, 464, 477
steroid policies, 267–268
Title IX compliance, 499–500
National Football League (NFL)
advertising, promotion in, 125t, 131–135, 132f
age limits in, 477, 478t, 478, 479
American Football League v. National Football League, 187–189
as bilateral monopoly, 438–441, 439f, 440f
broadcast revenues, 21–23, 22t, 23t, 137
broadcast rights ownership limits, 141
broadcast rights pooling by, 138f, 138–139
commissioner's salaries, 52, 53t, 338n
criticizing game officials policy, 257
distraction by cheerleaders, 229
dog fighting policy, 255–256, 256n
draft results, 471–473, 473t
dress code violations policy, 258
drunk driving policy, 253
fighting penalty, 250
franchise value growth in, 28t, 32–33, 33t
franchise values in, 6t, 33t
free agency in, 442–443
gambling restrictions in, 206
gate receipts, 20–21, 21t
horse collar tackles, 252
injury risks in, 158–159
intentionally hurting opponent, 251, 252
league expansion antitrust ligitation, 187–189
minimum salaries in, 446t, 447t, 447
multiyear contracts in, 409, 411, 411n, 412–413
performance-enhancing drug penalty in, 10
personal conduct policy, 242t, 242–243
practice facility naming rights, 124
preseaon games in, 103t
public ownership ban, 185–186
racial discrimination in, 492t, 492–493
relocation restrictions, 186–187
revenue sharing in, 54
reverse-order player drafts, 79
salary, average, 338
salary, top ten 2010, 339t
salary caps in, 13–14, 77f, 77–78, 443–444, 444t
sponsorships in, 128
spygate, 52, 231n, 231–232, 232n
stadium financing in, 326–327, 327t
stadium lease agreements in, 294
stadiums in, 125t
steroid policies, 269–270
team quality, attendance in, 26, 27t
ticket bundling in, 102, 103t
trademarks rights in, 183
weapons charges policy, 254–255, 255n
National Football League, American Football League v., 187–189
National Football League, American Needle v., 183
National Football League Players Association, 433–434, 438, 462–463, 479
National Hockey League (NHL)
age limits in, 478t
broadcast revenues, 21–23, 22t, 23t
commissioner's salaries, 52, 53t
drunk driving policy, 253
fighting penalty, 250
franchise values in, 6t, 31t
free agency in, 443
gate receipts, 20–21, 21t
intentionally hurting opponent, 251–252
minimum salaries in, 446t, 447t, 447
multiyear contracts in, 406–407
naming rights sale in, 125–126
revenues, player's share of, 444t
salary, average, 338
salary, top ten 2010, 339t
salary caps in, 13–14, 77f, 77–78, 444t
steroid policies, 270–271
National Hockey League Players Association, 435, 438
National League, 60–61, 61t. *See also* Major League Baseball (MLB)
National League of Professional Baseball Clubs, Federal Baseball Club of Baltimore, Inc. v., 184
NBC, 145–146, 170
NCAA, Hennessey v., 372–373, 375, 376

NCAA, Law v., 373–376
NCAA, O'Bannon v., 377–378
NCAA, White v., 377
NCAA v. Board of Regents of the University of Oklahoma and University of Georgia Athletic Association, 184–185
Nelson, Brett, 471
Neuheisel, Rick, 213
New England Patriots
  attendance, performance 2010, 27t
  broadcast rights ownership limits, 141
  franchise values, 6t, 28t
  public ownership ban, 185–186
  spygate, 52, 231n, 231–232, 232n, 233n
  stadium financing, 327t
New Jersey Devils, 31t, 78, 405
New Jersey Nets
  franchise value 2010, 29t
  stadium naming rights, 4, 24, 126, 127
Newman, Terence, 251n
New Orleans Hornets, 19, 29t
New Orleans Saints, 27t, 28t
New York Giants
  attendance, performance 2010, 27t
  broadcast rights ownership limits, 141
  franchise value 2010, 28t
  multiyear contracts with, 411, 411n
  stadium financing, 327t
New York Islanders, 31t, 405
New York Jets
  attendance, performance 2010, 27t
  franchise value 2010, 28t
  practice facility naming rights, 124
  spygate, 52, 231n, 231–232, 232n
  stadium financing, 327t
New York Knicks
  fighting penalty, 250
  franchise value, 6t
  franchise value 2010, 29t
  multiyear contracts with, 407
  ticket prices, 93–94
New York Mets
  bidding for Zito by, 386
  broadcast revenues, payrolls 2001, 23t
  capital appreciation of, 34t
  final arbitration settlements by, 427t
  franchise values, 6t, 30t
  history of, 60–61, 61t
  multiyear contracts with, 406
  shifting risk, 164–166, 165f
  stadium financing, 325t, 334t
  stadium naming rights purchase, 7
New York Rangers, 6t, 31t
New York Yankees
  bidding for Zito by, 386
  broadcast revenues, payrolls 2001, 22t
  capital appreciation of, 33–35, 34t
  competitive balance in, 75, 80–81, 81t
  final offer arbitration by, 425, 427t
  franchise values, 6t, 30t
  history of, 60t
  luxury tax, 79–81, 81t
  payrolls in, 7t, 75, 81t
  posting system use by, 398t, 398–399, 401–402
  profit maximization by, 17–18
  Rodriguez negotiation, 453–454
  stadium financing in, 324t
  team insurance coverage for, 170–171
NFL, United States Football League v., 189–190, 190n
Nike, 129n, 129–130
Nishioka, Tsuyoshi, 398t
Niskioka, Tsuyoshi, 401
Nissan, 129
No agent rule, 458, 464, 477
Noah, Joakim, 467n
Noll, Roger, 67
Noll-Scully measure, 67n, 67–68, 68t
Nomo, Hideo, 397n
Norris-La Guardia Act of 1932, 436
Northern Trust, 129
Nowitzki, Dirk, 168
Nutt, Houston, 390t

Oakland A's, 22t
Oakland Athletics
  capital appreciation of, 34t
  franchise value 2010, 30t
  history of, 60t
  stadium financing in, 324t
Oakland Raiders, 27t, 28t, 186–187
O'Bannon v. NCAA, 377–378
Oden, Greg, 481
Oklahoma City Thunder, 29t
Oliver, Andy, 477
Olomana Golf Links, 96t
O'Neal, Jermaine, 249t, 250
O'Neal, Shaquille, 456t, 469, 469n
Orlando Magic
  franchise value 2010, 29t
  stadium financing, 331t, 332t, 333t
Orr, Colton, 251
Ortiz, David, 456t
Otsuka, Akinori, 398t
Ottawa Senators, 31t
Ovechkin, Alexander, 251, 339t
Overton, Jeff, 496t
Owens, Terrell, 353n, 353t

Palmeiro, Rafael, 281–282
Palmer, Arnold, 451
Pan American Games, 144
Park, Inbee, 496t
Parry, Craig, 273
Participant misconduct
  appeal rights, 244
  cheating, 211, 259 (*See also* Cheating)

criticizing game officials, 256–257
deterrence, 244–248, 245f
disciplining players for, 241–242
dog fighting, 255–256, 256n
dress code violations, 258
drunk driving, 253
duty to report, 244
fighting, 249–250
gambling (*See* Gambling)
intentionally hurting opponent, 251–252
legal problems, 253
offensive language, gestures, 257–258
off-field, 52, 253
overview, 10, 241, 259
personal conduct policy, NFL, 242t, 242–243
persons charged with criminal activity, 243
persons convicted of criminal activity, 243–244
point shaving, 212
prohibited conduct, 243
repeat offenders, 253n, 253–254, 254n
safety concerns, 258–259
spygate, 52, 231n, 231–232, 232n
steroid use (*See* Performance-enhancing drugs)
suspensions, implicit fines, 248, 249t
violence on field, 250–251, 251n
violent activity in workplace, 244
weapons charges, 254–255, 255n
Patterson, John, 426–427, 427t
Paul, Josh, 427t, 426–427
Pavano, Carl, 158–159, 159n, 168
Peak load pricing, 99–102, 101f, 101t
Pecorino, Paul, 427t
Pedroia, Dustin, 428–429
Pennetta, Flavia, 498t
Peppers, Julius, 339t
Pepsi-Cola advertising revenues, 130
Perez, Oliver, 427t, 428t
Performance-enhancing drugs
abuse prevalence, 263–265, 264t, 269n
anabolic androgenic steroids, 265–266, 267n, 271–272
banned substance benefits, risks, 265–267
beta-2 agonists, 266, 273
blood doping, 267, 271
diuretics, 266
EPO (erythropoietin), 267, 279
financial sanctions, 281
hormones, 266–267
loss of reputation, 281–282
overview, 10, 218, 218n, 227n, 263, 283–284
sanctions, deterrence, 274–281, 276f, 278f
steroid-free nutritional supplements, 274
steroid policies generally, 267 (*See also specific organizations*)
stimulants, 266, 269n, 271–272
Perry, Gaylord, 228
Personal conduct policy, NFL, 242t, 242–243
Personal seat licenses (PSLs), 295, 323n
Peterson, Adrian, 470–471
Peterson, Julian, 411n
Petrino, Bobby, 390t
Pettersen, Suzann, 496t
Pettite, Andy, 385
PGA
advertising expenditures by, 120, 122t
age limits in, 478t, 479–480
commissioner's salaries, 52
restrictions on schedules by organizations, 190–191
sponsorships in, 124t, 128–129
steroid policies, 272–273
PGA Tour
appearance fees, 391n
equipment restrictions, 192–193, 227
gambling restrictions in, 205–206
gender discrimination in, 494–497, 495t, 496t
suspensions, implicit fines, 248
Philadelphia Eagles
attendance, performance 2010, 27t
franchise value 2010, 28t
practice facility naming rights, 124
stadium financing, 327t
Philadelphia 76ers, 29t
Philadelphia Flyers, 31t, 125–126
Philadelphia Phillies
broadcast revenues, payrolls 2001, 23t
capital appreciation of, 34t
final arbitration settlements by, 427t
franchise value 2010, 30t
gambling litigation involving, 207–208
hand signal theft by, 231n
history of, 61t
payrolls in, 7t
stadium financing in, 325t
Phoenix Coyotes, 31t, 125–126
Phoenix Suns, 29t, 293
Ping Eye 2 Irons, 192–193
Pinkel, Gary, 390t
Pitino, Rick, 395–396
Pittsburgh Penguins, 31t
Pittsburgh Pirates
broadcast revenues, payrolls 2001, 23t
capital appreciation of, 34t
franchise value 2010, 30t
history of, 61t
payrolls in, 7t
stadium financing, 325t
Pittsburgh Steelers, 27t, 28t, 124
Player, Gary, 273
Player drafts, 347–348

Players' unions. *See also* Collective bargaining
- antitrust exemptions for, 435–436
- collective bargaining by, 436–438, 437f
- excess supply approaches, 438
- executive directors, 435
- goals, economic consequences of, 436–437, 437f
- Major League Baseball Players Association (MLBPA), 433
- minimum salaries, 443n, 446t, 447t, 447
- National Basketball Players Association (NBPA), 434, 438
- National Football League Players Association (NFLPA), 433–434, 438, 462–463, 479
- National Hockey League Players Association (NHLPA), 435, 438
- organization of, 432–433
- overview, 13, 432, 448
- sports agents supervision by, 462–463

Player talent. *See* Insurance of player talent
Point shaving, 212, 234–235
Point-spread wagers, 204–205
Portland Trail Blazers, 29t
Posting system (MLB), 397n, 397–402, 398t
Present value calculations. *See also* Profitability
- discount rate importance, 43
- discount rate selection, 32n, 43
- equal amount streams, 42–43
- equations, 39t, 39–40
- future stream valuation, 41–42, 42t
- future values, 38–39, 41t
- overview, 4, 38
- present-future relationship, 40

Pressel, Megan, 469–470
Pressel, Morgan, 496t
Price discrimination, 95–99, 96t, 98f, 100f
Pricing complements, 21
Pricing decisions
- commodity bundling (season tickets), 102–103, 103t
- competition *vs.* monopoly, 92
- competitive pricing, 89–90, 90f
- complements, 107–109, 109t
- demand elasticity in, 93–95
- empty seats in, 93f, 93–94
- Final Four tickets, 111
- monopoly pricing, 90–92, 91f
- overview, 7, 89, 113
- peak load pricing, 99–102, 101f, 101t
- price discrimination, 95–99, 96t, 98f, 100f
- student tickets, 110–111
- ticket scalping, 110f, 110–113, 113n
- two-part pricing, 104t, 106f, 107

Principal–agent problem, 451, 457–461
Private value auctions (English auctions), 384n, 384–386, 385n
Pro Bowl, 291
Producer surplus, 176, 177
Profitability. *See also* Present value calculations
- capital appreciation, MLB, 33–35, 34t
- defined, 24–25
- franchise value growth in NFL, 28t, 32–33, 33t
- in franchise values, 26–31, 28t, 29t, 30t, 31t
- as goal, 16–17
- as stand-alone investments, 32
- team quality in, 25–26, 27t

Profit function, 118
Profit maximization
- athletic talent (monopsony), 340–341, 341f, 341n
- in collusive monopsony, 362–363
- overview, 48–50, 49f, 50n
- by player's unions, 436–437, 437f
- price discrimination in, 97
- revenues in, 17–19
- ticket pricing, 97–99, 98f, 100f

Program expansion test, Title IX, 501
Proportionality test, Title IX, 500
Prothro, Tyrone, 458
Public goods theory, 131–135, 132f, 133f
Public ownership ban, 185–186, 186n
Puckett, Kirby, 385
Puerta, Mariano, 272
Pujols, Albert, 456t

Querrey, Sam, 498t
Quezada, Alejandro, 398t
Quinn, Brady, 394
Quirk, James, 67, 68

Ramirez, Ramon, 398t
Randolph, Zach, 339t
Redd, Michael, 339t
Reliant Stadium naming rights contract, 126
Relocation restrictions, 186–187
Reserve clause
- challenges to, 433, 434
- competitive balance, 71–72, 73–75
- in MLB, 71–72, 73–75, 433
- monopsony, 347

Revenues
- broadcast, 21–23, 22t, 23t
- gate receipts, 20–21, 21t, 54, 75–76
- generating costs, 24
- naming rights, 24, 124–126, 127, 127n, 295
- pricing complements, 21
- in profit maximization, 17–19
- sharing (*See* Revenue sharing; *specific organizations*)
- sources of, 19
- stadium, 21
- trademark licensing fees, 23
- transfer to weaker teams, 54–55

Revenue sharing
broadcast rights, 54, 152
in collusive monopsony, 370
economic implications, 76–77
in NBA, 54
in NFL, 54
overview, 54–56, 75–76, 447–448
Reverse-order player drafts, 79
Revis, Darrelle, 394–395
Rezai, Aravane, 498t
Richt, Mark, 390t
Risk aversion, 159–164, 161t, 162f, 163f
Risk neutrality, 160–161, 161t, 163f, 163
Risk seeking, 201–203, 202f
Rivera, Mariano, 425
Robinson, Nate, 249t, 250
Roddick, Andy, 498t
Rodman, Dennis, 248, 249t
Rodrigues, Geoffrey, 455
Rodriguez, Alex, 228, 338, 339t, 452, 453–454
Rodriguez, Francisco, 428t
Rodriguez, Rich, 390t
Roethlisberger, Ben, 244
Rogers, Kenny, 228–229
Rogers, Shaun, 269–270
Rookie Exception, 445t
Rooney, Dan, 50–51
Rose, Justin, 496t
Rose, Pete, 207–208
Roy Williams Rule, 252
Rubio, Ricky, 478–479
Ruiz, Rosie, 224–225
Rule of reason, 179–180, 182–183, 374–375
Russell, JaMarcus, 452
Ruutu, Jarko, 252
Ryan, Matt, 452
Ryan, Rex, 257–258

Saban, Nick, 388–389, 389n, 390t, 390, 395
Sabathia, C. C., 339t
Sacramento Kings, 29t
Salary caps
Cap Relief for Veterans rule, 444t
Chicago Blackhawks, 78
in competitive balance, 77f, 77–78
Deion Sanders Rule, 444t
hard, 442n, 443–445, 444t, 445t
Larry Bird Exception, 445t
Mid-Level Exception, 445t
minimum salaries, 443n, 446t, 447t, 447
in MLB, 77f, 77–78
in NBA, 13–14, 77f, 77–78, 445t
New Jersey Devils, 78
in NFL, 13–14, 77f, 77–78, 443–444, 444t
in NHL, 13–14, 77f, 77–78, 444t
overview, 443
Rookie Exception, 445t
soft, 445t
Salary determination. *See also* Monopsony
athletic talent demand, 340–342, 341f, 341n
bidding, bargaining (labor) (*See* Bidding, bargaining (labor))
equilibrium wage, 342f, 342–343
market demand for labor, 342
overview, 11–12, 338, 339t
San Antonio Spurs, 29t, 293
Sanders, Deion, 347
San Diego Chargers, 27t, 28t, 294
San Diego Padres
broadcast revenues, payrolls 2001, 23t
capital appreciation of, 34t
franchise value 2010, 30t
history of, 60–61, 61t
posting system use by, 398t
stadium financing in, 325t
San Francisco 49ers, 27t, 28t
San Francisco Giants
bidding for Zito by, 386
broadcast revenues, payrolls 2001, 23t
capital appreciation of, 34t
franchise value 2010, 30t
history of, 61t
stadium financing in, 325t
San Jose Sharks, 31t
Santana, Johan, 339t
Savage, Raymond, 458
Scarborough Research, 121
Schiavone, Francesca, 498t
Schilling, Curt, 413
Scoggins, John, 427t
Scott, Bart, 257
Scott, Ian, 167
Scrap value, 322–323
Scully, Gerald, 67, 73, 351t
Season tickets, 102–103, 103t
Seattle Mariners
bidding for Zito by, 386
broadcast revenues, payrolls 2001, 22t
capital appreciation of, 34t
franchise value 2010, 30t
history of, 59–60, 60t
payrolls in, 7t
posting system use by, 398t
stadium financing in, 324t
Seattle Seahawks
attendance, performance 2010, 27t
franchise value 2010, 28t
multiyear contracts with, 411n
practice facility naming rights, 124
stadium financing, 327t
Seattle Supersonics, 299
Seitz, Peter, 433
Selig, Bud, 53t, 338n
Sharapova, Maria, 469–470
Sherburne, Ryan, 499

Sherman Antitrust Act
  on broadcast rights, 139, 139n
  on entry restrictions, 193
  history, purpose of, 178
  Section 1 (collusive efforts to emulate monopoly), 178, 178n, 182, 374–375, 435–436
  Section 2 (prevention of emergence of monopoly), 179
Shin, Jiyai, 496t
Shula, Mike, 410, 458
Silman, Benny, 234
Simon, Chris, 251n, 251–252
Smith, Emmitt, 469
Smith, J. R., 249t, 250
Smith, Steven, 212, 234
SMU (Southern Methodist University), 371
Soccer, 137, 478t
Social welfare, 176, 177
Social welfare loss
  in monopoly, 178
  in monopsony, 345f, 345–347
Socony-Vacuum Oil Co, United States v., 178n, 374n
Soderling, Robin, 498t
Soft drink advertising revenues, 121t, 130
Soriano, Alfonso, 339t, 405
Sosa, Sammy, 227, 227n
Spaghetti racquets, 191–192
Spezza, Jason, 339t
Sponsorships, 124t, 128–129
Sports agents
  Alabama regulation of, 458
  appearances, 455
  competition among, 464
  contract law, 463
  contracts (*See* Contracts)
  corrective, preventive measures, 461–464
  endorsements, 129n, 129–130, 454–455, 456t
  financial management by, 456–457
  multiple club negotiations, 452–454
  in NCAA, 458, 464, 477
  on-field performance improvement, 452
  overview, 13–14, 451, 463–464
  player smuggling by, 455
  player's union supervision, 462–463
  principal–agent problem, 451, 457–461
  reputation of, 462
  role of, 14, 451–452
  salary negotiation, 452
Sports books (bookies), 204–205, 209n
Sports Broadcasting Act of 1961, 139–141, 140t, 142t, 188
Sports business
  advertising, promotion (*See* Advertising, promotion)
  antitrust policy (*See* Antitrust policy)
  broadcast rights (*See* Broadcast rights)
  competitive balance (*See* Competitive balance)
  insurance of player talent (*See* Insurance of player talent)
  leagues, organizations (*See* Leagues, organizations)
  overview, 5, 6t, 16–17
  pricing decisions (*See* Pricing decisions)
  profit (*See* Profitability)
  revenues (*See* Revenues)
Sports economics generally, 3
Sports networks, 140t, 152–153, 153t
Sports publications, 124t, 124
Sprewell, Latrell, 248, 249t
Spurrier, Steve, 388, 388n
Spygate, 52, 231n, 231–232, 232n
St. Louis Blues, 31t
St. Louis Cardinals
  broadcast revenues, payrolls 2001, 23t
  franchise value 2010, 30t
  history of, 61t
  stadium financing in, 325t
St. Louis Rams, 27t, 28t
St. Petersburg Paradox, 160–161, 161t
Stadium naming rights, 24, 124–126, 127, 127n, 295
Stafford, Matthew, 339t
Stallworth, Dante, 253
Stango, Victor, 427t
Staples Center, 126
Steinbrenner, George, 17–18
Stern, David, 53t, 214–215
Steroid-free nutritional supplements, 274
Stevens, Jerramy, 248t, 248–253
Stewart, Tony, 257–258
Stimulants, 266, 269n, 271–272
St. Louis Cardinals, 34t
Stoops, Bobby, 390t, 390
Stosur, Samantha, 498t
Strickler, Steve, 496t
Strikes, lockouts, 441
Student tickets, 110–111
Subsidies
  community facility, 328t, 329t
  franchise, 296–297, 297f
Suh, Ndamukong, 339t
Sullivan, Billy, 185–186
Sumo wrestling, 235–236
Sunday Night Football, 142–143, 143f
Suspensions, implicit fines, 248, 249t
Suzuki, Ichiro, 398t, 399n

Tagliabue, Paul, 32, 33t, 338n
Talent. *See* Insurance of player talent
Tampa Bay Buccaneers, 27t, 28t
Tampa Bay Devil Rays
  broadcast revenues, payrolls 2001, 22t
  capital appreciation of, 34t

history of, 59–60, 60t
posting system use by, 398t, 398
Tampa Bay Lightning, 31t
Tampa Bay Rays, 30t, 324t
Taylor, Fred, 457
Team quality
competitive balance in, 25 (*See also* Competitive balance)
insurance of (*See* Insurance of player talent)
selecting, 25–26
Tedford, Jeff, 390t
Teixeira, Mark, 339t
Tennessee Titans
attendance, performance 2010, 27t
franchise value 2010, 28t
practice facility naming rights, 124
repeat offenders policy, 248t, 248–254, 253n, 254n
Tennis. *See also* Association of Tennis Professionals (ATP); Women's Tennis Association (WTA)
age limits in, 479
gender discrimination in, 497–498, 498t
racial discrimination in, 492
Tennis Anti-Doping Program, 272
Tennis Australia, 237
Texas Rangers
bidding for Zito by, 386
broadcast revenues, payrolls 2001, 22t
capital appreciation of, 34t
franchise value 2010, 30t
history of, 60t
payrolls in, 7t
stadium financing in, 324t
Thomas, Hallis, 269–270
Thomas, Marcus, 244–246
Thompson, Alexis, 479–480
Thurman, Odell, 248t, 248–253
Ticket scalping, 110f, 110–113, 113n
Title IX (gender equality)
impacts on coaches, 502–503, 503t
interest accommodation test, 501
NCAA compliance, 499–500
overview, 14, 498–504
program expansion test, 501
proportionality test, 500
Tomlinson, LaDamian, 459
Toronto Blue Jays
broadcast revenues, payrolls 2001, 22t
capital appreciation of, 34t
franchise value 2010, 30t
history of, 59–60, 60t
stadium financing in, 324t
Toronto Maple Leafs, 6t, 31t
Toronto Raptors, 29t
Torre, Joe, 228
Trachsel, Steve, 168
Track and field
age limits in, 478t, 480
steroid policies, 271–272, 279
Tracking chips, 225
Trademarks, 23, 183
Tressel, Jim, 390t, 391
Tseng, Yani, 496t
Turning pro early
age limits, 477–480, 478t
athletic development, 468–469
benefits, 470–471
changed market conditions, 471
costs, 468–470, 469t
decision process, 468–471, 469t
economic model of, 473–476
educational development, 469
enjoyment of college life, 470
injuries, 470–471
leaving high school, 480–481
maturity, 469–470, 480–481
NFL draft results, 471–473, 473t
overview, 14, 467n, 467–468, 468n, 481
personal performance reduction, 471
poor team performance, 471
professional earnings, 470
Turtle Bay Resort, 96t
Two-part pricing, 104t, 106f, 107
Tyler, Jeremy, 480–481

U-grooves, 192–193
Uncertainty
bidding and, 146–147
expected utility model calculations, 4–5 (*See also* Expected utility model)
in multiyear contracts, 408–410
overview, 4–5
in turning pro early, 476
Unions. *See* Collective bargaining; Players' unions
United States Football League v. NFL, 189–190, 190n
United States Golf Association (USGA), 192–193
United States v. Socony-Vacuum Oil Co, 178n, 374n
United State Tennis Association (USTA), 191–192
University of Alabama, 410, 458
University of Southern California, 371–372
Upshaw, Gene, 338n, 435
U.S. Open Tennis Championship, 146–147
USA Network, 146–147
USFL (United States Football League), 9
Utah Jazz, 29t

Valverde, Jose, 428t
Vancouver Canucks, 31t
Van Pelt, Bo, 496t
Verdasco, Fernando, 498t

Vick, Michael, 129–130, 248t, 248–256, 253n, 256n, 456
VIP Connection, 210
Von Neumann-Morgenstern utility function, 161–163, 162f

Wachovia, 126
Wade, Dwayne, 456t
Wagner, Billy, 411–412
Walker, Todd, 426–427, 427t
Walk-on players antitrust litigation, 376–377, 377n
Waltrip, Michael, 230
Wang, Chien-Ming, 427t, 428t
Warner, Kurt, 167
Warrior Sports, 193
Washington, Kermit, 248, 249t
Washington Capitals, 31t
Washington Nationals. *See also* Montreal Expos
  capital appreciation of, 33–35, 34t
  franchise value 2010, 30t
  history of, 61t
  Nationals Park financing, 325–326
  stadium financing in, 325t
Washington Redskins
  attendance, performance 2010, 27t
  franchise values, 6t, 28t
  multiyear contracts with, 405
Washington Senators, 59–60
Washington Wizards, 29t, 472
Watson, Bubba, 496t
Weapons charges, 254–255, 255n
Weinke, Chris, 467, 467n
Weir, Mike, 205–206
Weis, Charlie, 395
Welfare triangle, 178
Welki, A. M., 93–95
West, Delonte, 249t
White v. NCAA, 377
Wie, Michelle, 469–470, 479–480, 496t
Wilfork, Vince, 251
Williams, Roy, 248t, 248–252
Williams, Serena, 498t
Williams, Venus, 226, 498t
Williams and Bullocks L.L.C., 456
Winner's curse, 145–146, 146f, 147f, 295–296
Wolfers, Justin, 234–235
Women's Tennis Association (WTA)
  age limits in, 478t, 479
  commissioner's salaries, 52
  gender discrimination in, 497–498, 498t
Wong, Mary Roy, 456
Woods, Tiger, 205–206, 227, 273, 456t
World Anti-Doping Agency (WADA), 263–264, 265
World Cup Skateboarding, 480
World Football League, 189
Wozniacki, Caroline, 498t
Wrestling, 502

Yang, Amy, 496t
Yao Ming, 339t
Youzhny, Mikhail, 498t

Zambrano, Carlos, 393, 418–419
Zito, Barry, 383, 385, 386, 387t, 413, 453
Zlatoper, T. J., 93–95
Zvonareva, Vera, 498t

Author Index

Adams, W., 196
Alexander, D. L., 44, 115
Allen, W. D., 262
Andersen, T.N., 507
Araujo, I. C., 337, 356
Areeda, P., 436, 450
Ashman, T. D., 381, 430
Asinof, E., 234

Baade, R. A., 290, 303, 314, 316, 319, 336, 356
Baimbridge, M., 156
Balfour, A., 84
Balsdon, E., 240
Banaian, K., 430
Barget, E., 303
Baumann, R., 316, 319
Becker, G. S., 219, 240, 262, 507
Bellemore, F. A., 507
Bergmann, T. J., 450
Berri, D. J., 21, 45, 84, 85, 95, 116, 381, 404
Birren, G. F. E., 186, 196
Blair, R. D., 25, 26, 44, 48, 63, 102, 115, 128, 150, 152, 156, 175, 196, 350, 361, 366, 381, 439, 450
Bodvarsson, O. B., 430, 507
Bollinger, C. R., 174
Borick, C. P., 337, 356
Bradbury, J. C., 15, 64, 84, 196, 286, 303, 404
Brastow, R. T., 507
Brock, J. W., 196
Brook, S. L., 84, 381, 404
Brown, L. J., 190
Brown, R. W., 368, 381, 507
Burgess, P. L., 427, 430
Bursik, P. B., 337, 356

Cain, L. P., 84
Cameron, S., 156
Carlino, G., 319
Chang, Y-M., 84
Choi, J. P., 63,
Ciecka, J., 84
Clapp, C. M., 303
Coase, R. H., 152, 156
Coates, D., 95, 303, 319, 450
Cochran, J. J., 319
Conlin, M., 404, 507
Coulombe, S., 508
Coulson, N. E., 319
Crompton, J. L., 319
Crooker, J. R., 84
Curry, J., 240
Cymrot, D. J., 507

Dawson, P., 156, 304, 319
DeGennaro, R. P., 45
DePasquale, C., 25, 26, 44
Depken, C. A., II., 45, 84, 303, 507
DeSchriver, T. D., 136
Digler, A., 286
Dinardo, J. E., 286
Dixit, A., 391, 404
Dobson, S., 84
Dohrman, G., 466,
Dorman, G., 351
Drape, J., 240
Duggan, M., 235, 240
Duqette, G. H., 466
Durrance, C. P., 25, 26, 44
Dworkin, J. B., 450
Dye, R. F., 319

Easton, S. T., 450
Eber, N., 286
Eckard, E. W., 84, 381
El-Hodiri, M., 64
Emerson, P. M., 507

Fainaru-Wada, M., 282, 286
Falconieri, S., 156
Farmer, A., 404, 419, 427, 430

Faurot, D. J., 404, 430
Fehr, S. A., 196
Fenn, A. J., 84, 85
Ferguson, D. G., 116
Fielding, L. W., 466
Findlay, D. W., 507
Fizel, J., 313, 430
Fleisher, A. A., III., 45, 361, 366, 381
Fong, L., 240
Ford, J. M., 507
Forrest, D., 156, 217
Fort, R. D., 15, 45, 64, 67, 68, 70, 73, 84, 85, 86, 116, 197, 304, 319, 337, 356, 450, 507
Freitas, R. E., 196
Frick, B., 84, 286
Funk. J. P., 508

Gabriel, P. E., 507
Gandar, J. M., 157
Gerrard, B., 136
Gill, A., 507
Glazer, A., 231, 240
Goddard, J., 84
Goff, B. L., 45, 361, 366, 381
Goldfein, S., 196
Gouguet, J., 303
Gould, J., 420, 430
Greenberg, M. J., 303
Grenier, G., 508
Groothuis, P. A., 304, 450, 484, 507
Gustafson, E., 84, 313, 430
Gwartney, J., 507

Haddock, D. D., 84,
Hadley, L., 84, 85, 313, 430
Hakes, J. K., 303
Hanssen, F. A., 507
Harris, C. B., 337, 356
Harrison, C. C., 363, 381
Harrison, J. L., 350, 361, 363, 381
Harrison, T., 450
Haugen, K. K., 286
Haupert, M., 45
Haworth, C., 507
Haynes, J. S., 128, 450
Heckelman, J. C, 240
Herndon, J., 186, 196
Hill, J. R., 450, 484, 507
Hinshaw, C. E., 157
Hirshleifer, D., 231, 240
Hirshleifer, J., 231, 240
Horowitz, I., 84, 15
Hotchkiss, J. L., 174
Hovenkamp, H., 175, 196, 436, 450
Hudson, I., 319
Humphreys, B. R., 70, 84, 95, 262, 303, 319, 507
Hylton, K. N., 175, 196

Jacobson, J., 351
Jensen, P. E., 136
Jewell, R. T., 507
Johnson, A. T., 304
Johnson, B. K., 304
Johnson, C., 507
Jones, G. A., 507
Jones, J. C. H, 116, 508

Kahane, L. H., 84
Kahn, L. M., 64, 361, 381, 417, 450, 508
Kanazawa, M. T, 508
Kaplan, D., 327, 336, 356
Kaserman, D. L., 48, 63, 102, 115, 150, 152, 156, 175, 196, 366, 381, 439, 450
Kendall, T. D., 262
Kepner, T., 240
Kern, W., 44
Kesenne, S., 45, 64, 84, 116
Knowles, G., 45
Koning, R. H., 85
Krattenmaker, T. G., 181, 196
Krautmann, A. C., 21, 45, 84, 85, 95, 116, 352, 430

La Croix, S. J., 507
Laband, D. N., 319
Lambrinos, J., 381, 430
Lande, R. H., 181, 196
Landes, W. M., 420, 430
Larsen, A., 85
Lavoie, M., 319, 508
Le Dressay, A., 116
Lee, Y. H., 64, 84, 85
Leeds, E. M., 127, 128, 136
Leeds, M. A., 127, 128, 136, 150, 156
Lehn, K., 174, 196
Lentz, B. F., 319
Leonard, W. M., II., 507
Leonard, J., 382
Lerner, A., 350
Lertwachara, K., 319
Levitt, S. D., 235, 240
Lewis, M., 508
Long, J. G., 337, 356
Longley, N., 508
Longo, A., 304, 319
Lopatka, J. E., 186, 191, 196

Maennig, W., 286
Marburger, D. R., 404, 427, 430, 431
Mason, D. S., 466
Matheson, V. A., 314, 316, 319, 336, 356
Maxcy, J., 64, 85, 417
McAfee, P. R., 384, 404
McAllister, S., 430
McCann, M. A., 484
McClain, D. L., 240
McCluskey, J. J., 262

Meehan, J. W., Jr., 45, 85
Meggyesy, D., 466
Miles, S. E., 507
Miller, L. K., 466
Miller, P. A., 45, 85, 336, 356, 431
Molitor, C. J., 484
Mondello, M. J., 85, 304
Morgenstern, O., 160, 174
Mulligan, J. G., 116

Nadeau, S., 508
Nash, J. F., Jr., 392, 404
Neale, W. C., 45
Nelson, R. A., 45, 85
Noll, R. G., 15, 64, 67, 95, 116, 156, 196, 290, 292, 304, 319, 337, 356, 450

Owen, J. G., 304, 337, 356

Palomino, F., 156
Parent, M. M., 136
Parkin, M., 15, 18, 45, 307, 466
Partridge, M. D., 507
Pauwels, W., 116
Pecorino, P., 404, 419, 427, 430
Pedace, R., 508
Peel, D. A., 45
Perloff, J. M., 132, 457, 466
Perri, T. J., 484
Petersen, J. E., 337, 356
Philips, L., 384, 404
Pickard, J. L., 337, 356
Pistolet, I., 127, 128, 136
Pitts, B. G., 466
Porter, P. K., 84, 116, 297, 304, 313
Preston, I., 240
Prinzinger, J., 382

Quinn, K. G., 337, 356
Quirk, J., 15, 45, 64, 67, 68, 70, 73, 84, 85, 197, 304, 319, 337, 356, 450

Raethz, L., 337, 356
Reid, C. E., 507
Richardson, T. V., 45, 85
Roberts, G. R., 197, 466
Robinson, J., 345
Rockerbie, D. W., 397, 450
Rodriguez. G., 319
Romano, R. E., 361, 381, 439, 450
Rosen, J. S., 484
Ross, S. F., 197
Rottenberg, S., 45, 70, 85
Ruseski, J. E., 262

Sakovics, J., 156
Salop, S. C., 181, 196
Sanders, S., 84, 85
Sanderson, A. R., 85, 290, 303
Sanghoo, B., 63
Sauer, R. D., 201
Sappington, D. E. M., 466
Schmalensee, R., 152
Schmidt, M. B., 45, 85, 381, 404
Schmitt, R. L., 507
Scoggins, J., 427, 430
Scoville, J., 450
Scully, G. W., 45, 64, 67, 73, 85, 351, 431, 508
Sherony, K., 45
Shmanske, S., 116, 496, 508
Shubnell, L. D., 337, 356
Siegfried, J. J., 157, 319
Simmons, R., 156, 217
Skeath, S., 391, 404
Slack, T., 136
Sloane, A. A., 450
Smith, D. R., 136, 507
Soebbing, B. P., 45
Sommers, P. M., 431
Spenner, E. L., 85
Spurr, S. J., 484
Stango, V., 404, 419, 427, 430
Stanton, T. J., 507
Steinberg, L., 466
Stewart, K. G., 116
Stigler, G. J., 230, 240, 345
Surdam, D. G., 85, 156, 404
Sutter, D., 86
Sykuta, M., 196
Szymanski, S., 15, 45, 64, 156, 157, 197, 240, 337, 356

Tainsky, S., 45, 286, 508
Thayer, M. A., 240
Thomas, C. R., 297, 304
Thomas, D. A., 45
Tollison, R. D., 45, 187, 197, 361, 366, 381
Tolone, W. L., 507
Tolsdorf, F., 286
Tygiel, J., 508

Utt, J., 86

Varian, H., 384, 404
Vicente-Mayoral, R., 84
von Allmen, P., 150, 156
von Neumann, J., 160, 174

Walsh, W. D., 508
Walton, H., 304, 319
Welki, A. M., 95
Whitehead, J. C., 304
Whitney, J. D., 86
Williams, L., 282, 286
Williamson, O., 152, 157
Willig, R., 152
Wilson, D. P., 45, 84

Winfree, J. A., 45, 197, 262, 286, 484, 508
Winkler, S., 86
Wolfers, J., 217

Yates, A. J., 240
Yost, M., 64

Zimbalist, A. S., 15, 45, 86, 157, 197, 290, 292, 304, 313, 319, 326, 337, 356, 382, 397, 450, 508
Zirin, D., 15
Zlatoper, T. J., 95
Zuber, R. A., 157